FOREIGN TRADE, INVESTMENT, AND THE LAW IN THE
PEOPLE'S REPUBLIC OF CHINA

EDITOR

Michael J. Moser

CONTRIBUTORS

Jesse T.H. Chang   Franklin D. Chu   Jerome Alan Cohen
Charles J. Conroy   Timothy A. Gelatt   David Y.W. Ho
Jamie P. Horsley   Stanley B. Lubman   John F. McKenzie
Michael J. Moser   Thomas Peele   Richard D. Pomp
Elson Pow   Clark T. Randt, Jr.   Mitchell A. Silk
Preston M. Torbert   Winston K. Zee   Zheng Zhaohuang, 鄭兆璜

⟨ **W9-DGW-532**

HONG KONG   OXFORD   NEW YORK
OXFORD UNIVERSITY PRESS
1987

Oxford University Press

Oxford   New York   Toronto
Petaling Jaya   Singapore   Hong Kong   Tokyo
Delhi   Bombay   Calcutta   Madras   Karachi
Nairobi   Dar es Salaam   Cape Town
Melbourne   Auckland

and associated companies in
Beirut   Berlin   Ibadan   Nicosia

© *Oxford University Press 1987*

First edition 1984
Second edition 1987
Published in the United States
by Oxford University Press Inc., New York

Library of Congress Cataloging-in-Publication Data

Foreign trade, investment, and the law in the People's
Republic of China.
Includes bibliographies and indexes.
1. Investments, Foreign—Law and legislation—China.
2. Taxation—Law and legislation—China.   I. Moser,
Michael J.   II. Chang, Jesse T. H.
LAW   343.51'087   87-11272
ISBN 0-19-584058-5   345.10387

British Library Cataloguing in Publication Data

Foreign trade, investment, and the law in
the People's Republic of China.
1. Investments, Foreign—Law and
legislation—China   2. Tariff—China
3. Commercial law—China
I. Moser, Michael J.   II. Chang, Jesse T.H.
345.106'7   [LAW]
ISBN 0-19-584058-5

Printed in Hong Kong by Liang Yu Printing Factory Ltd.
Published by Oxford University Press, Warwick House, Hong Kong

Acknowledgements

A volume of collected essays by different authors is by its very nature not the work of one person. None the less, it is the task of the editor to forge at least a semblance of unity of theme, style, and focus from disparate perspectives and personalities. In endeavouring to accomplish this task, my path has been made easier by the goodwill which has prevailed among the contributors throughout the project. I am grateful to each of them for agreeing initially to contribute to the volume and for their understanding and co-operation in dealing with the demands which a work of this kind requires.

In addition to the contributors, I am grateful to many others who have helped to bring this second edition to press. In particular I would like to express my thanks to Jozef ten Berge for assistance in compiling the table of legislation and the index; David Ben Kay and Stephen M. Nelson for help with proofreading the galleys; Dorothy Tang for assistance with typing, finding things when they were missing, and general organizational responsibility; and others at Baker & McKenzie, for generously providing logistical and other support to the project. As with the first edition, this volume benefited enormously from the guidance and determination of the staff of Oxford University Press, and I would like to express my gratitude to each of them here. I would also like to thank Yvonne, Yeone, and Anna-Sieglinde, for whom all my writing is done, for their patience and support.

Finally, I would like to acknowledge once again the very special contribution of my late father, Joseph G. Moser, who first suggested the idea of this book.

MICHAEL J. MOSER
Beijing
January 1987

Contents

Contributors

JESSE T.H. CHANG is a graduate in law of the Australian National University and the Columbia University School of Law. He is the Chief Representative for China and Legal Counsel for Credit Agricole, a leading international bank

FRANKLIN D. CHU who was born in China and received a JD degree from Yale Law School specializes in advising clients doing business in China. He is currently the Hong Kong resident partner of a major American law firm

JEROME ALAN COHEN, formerly Professor of Law and Director of East Asian Legal Studies at the Harvard Law School, is the author and editor of many books and articles on China and Chinese legal topics. He is a member of an international law firm and resides in Hong Kong and New York

CHARLES J. CONROY, a graduate of Yale University and the Columbia University School of Law, advises foreign clients doing business in China. He is a partner in an international law firm, and divides his time between Hong Kong, Beijing, and New York

TIMOTHY A. GELATT, a graduate of the Harvard Law School, currently practises law in New York City. He has written books and articles on Chinese taxation and other legal topics, and has acted as Lecturer on Chinese business law at Harvard Law School and the University of Paris

DAVID Y.W. HO is a graduate of Birmingham University and London University. He is a solicitor with an international law firm, and resides in Beijing

JAMIE P. HORSLEY is a graduate of the Harvard Law School and resided for over two years in Beijing, advising foreign companies doing business in China. She is a partner in an international law firm, resident in Hong Kong

STANLEY B. LUBMAN is a graduate of the Columbia University School of Law who practises law with a San Francisco law firm. He is a long-time specialist on China who has taught on Chinese law at the University of California (Berkeley), Yale, and Harvard. He writes frequently on Chinese legal topics

JOHN F. MCKENZIE, a graduate of Harvard University, specializes in international trade law and practises with an international law firm in San Francisco

MICHAEL J. MOSER, who holds a Ph.D. degree from Columbia University and a JD degree from the Harvard Law School, is the author of numerous books and articles on Chinese law. A practising attorney with an international law firm, he has worked for a number of years in Beijing and now resides in Hong Kong

THOMAS PEELE is a graduate of the Harvard Law School. He advises clients doing business in China, and has represented Chinese organizations in litigation in the United States. He practises law in the Washington, DC, office of an international law firm

RICHARD D. POMP, a graduate of the University of Michigan and Harvard Law School, is Professor of Law at the University of Connecticut, and serves as a consultant on tax policy to cities, states, the United States Congress, international organizations, and foreign countries

ELSON POW, a graduate in law and accounting from the University of New South Wales, is a member of an international law firm, and is based in Sydney. He specializes in advice on Chinese commercial law and practice

CLARK T. RANDT, JR., a graduate of Yale College and the University of Michigan Law School, practises law in Hong Kong as a member of an American law firm, and was formerly First Secretary and Commercial Attaché to the United States Embassy in Beijing

MITCHELL A. SILK is a graduate of Georgetown University and the University of Maryland School of Law, works for an international law firm, and currently holds a fellowship, researching and teaching at Beijing University

PRESTON M. TORBERT holds a doctorate in Chinese history from the University of Chicago and a JD degree from the Harvard Law School. He is a practising attorney with an international law firm, and is a frequent visitor to China

WINSTON K. ZEE, a graduate of the Georgetown University Law Center, is a practising attorney with an international law firm and divides his time between Hong Kong and Beijing

ZHENG ZHAOHUANG, 郑兆璜 , a graduate of the former Yenching University, Peking, holds a master's degree from Yale University and a doctorate from the University of Paris. He is Professor of International Law at the East China Institute of Politics and Law in Shanghai and Adviser to the Chinese Society of International Law. He is also attached to the Shanghai No.4 Law Office as an Attorney at Law

Introduction

MICHAEL J. MOSER

THE essays contained in this volume provide an introduction to the legal framework governing the conduct of business transactions with the People's Republic of China. Each chapter treats separately a specific topic relating to the legal aspects of trade, investment, and other commercial activities in China, surveys the relevant legislation in the field, and discusses some of the problems encountered in connection with their implementation. Unless otherwise noted, the essays address the status of legal developments as of January 1987.

This volume, like its predecessor first edition,[1] stems from a perceived need on the part of foreign business people, government policy-makers, and others with an interest in Chinese affairs for a greater knowledge of Chinese legal matters, particularly at a time when the People's Republic has begun dramatically to increase its economic contacts with the rest of the world. For the most part, the contributors to the volume are lawyers actively engaged in advising clients with commercial dealings in China. Despite this, their intention has not been to formulate a 'handbook' of China trade or to assemble a book of recipes for business success. Rather, the aim has been to provide an overview of the legal framework now being developed for the regulation of business activities involving Chinese and foreign companies and to shed some light on how this framework affects the conduct of business affairs in practice.

Before turning to the essays themselves, it will be useful to look briefly at the development of China's current legal system and the types of laws and regulations which affect business transactions with foreigners.

The emergence in China of a substantial body of laws and regulations applicable to business transactions with foreigners is a development which has occurred only very recently. Indeed, for much of the period since the establishment of the People's Republic in 1949, law and formal legal institutions have played a relatively minor role both domestically and in China's international economic relationships.[2]

Following the 'liberation' of the Chinese mainland in 1949, the Chinese Communist Party abolished the laws and judicial system established by the former Nationalist regime and proceeded to create a new legal system modelled generally on that of the Soviet Union. During the period up to 1957, a substantial number of laws were enacted, new judicial institutions were put into place, the legal profession was strengthened, and legal scholarship began to flourish. These promising developments ended, however, in the wake of the Party's anti-rightist campaign which followed the period of political liberalism encouraged by the 'Hundred Flowers' policy of 1957. Thereafter, the legal institutions earlier put into place began to atrophy and new legislative efforts were virtually halted as the Party exerted near total control over the legal system and promoted the subservience of law to politics.

The downward spiral in China's legal development reached its nadir with the launching in 1966 of the 'Great Proletarian Cultural Revolution'. During the following decade China's radical leaders exhorted the Red Guards to 'smash the procuracies and the courts', mete out 'revolutionary justice' to 'counter-revolutionaries', and 'put politics in command'. As a consequence, during this period China's legal system and formal legal institutions were practically destroyed and the nation's economic contacts with the outside world came to a halt.

Following the death of Mao Zedong in 1976 and the purge of the infamous 'Gang of Four', the nightmare of the Cultural Revolution ended. China's new leadership proclaimed the goal of a thorough remaking of the People's Republic through the realization of the 'Four Modernizations': modern industry, agriculture, science and technology, and defence. At the same time, interest in law and legality was revived. As from 1979, new policies were implemented to restore the 'socialist legal system'. These policies marked the beginning of the restoration and strengthening of formal judicial institutions and the legal profession, and the promulgation of a large number of new laws, developments which have continued to the present.

An important aspect of the Four Modernizations programme has been the inauguration of an 'open-door' economic policy which since 1978 has led to a dramatic increase in foreign trade and other economic contacts. China's new economic policies have transformed the character and dimensions of its economic relationships with foreign countries. In particular, the permissible forms of business transactions have been expanded and have become more complex, encompassing not only simple commodity sales and purchases but also technology licensing, co-operative production arrangements, and direct equity investments in the form of Chinese-foreign joint ventures and the establishment of wholly-owned companies. With the aim of regulating the scope and content of China's increasing economic contacts with the outside world, literally hundreds of laws and regulations have been promulgated or reinstituted since 1979 and scores of others are now being drafted.

As most of the essays in this volume are concerned with Chinese legal rules, it will be useful to consider briefly the types of rules used by China to regulate foreign business activities and their sources. In general, these fall into two different categories: published legislation, and internal (neibu) or restricted regulations.

Published legislation is issued in a variety of forms by Chinese legislative bodies and administrative agencies.[3] Under China's Constitution,[4] the power to enact and amend basic statutes (falu) in the civil area is granted to the National People's Congress (NPC). The NPC's Standing Committee may enact statutes in certain areas not specifically reserved to the NPC itself and may issue decrees (faling), decisions (jueyi), orders (mingling), and instructions (zhishi) based on existing laws when the NPC is not in session. In addition, China's State Council, designated by the Constitution as 'the highest organ of state administration',[5] as well as administrative organs directly responsible to the State Council, are authorized to issue administrative regulations (*guiding*) and measures (*banfa*) to implement existing legislation. Finally, local organs of state power such as local people's congresses and their standing committees at the provincial, municipal, and autonomous region levels are empowered to enact local laws and administrative regulations subject to the approval of the central government.

Access to published Chinese legislation has often proved to be a problem for foreigners. There is no officially published gazette or other compilation of Chinese laws and regulations that is updated on a regular basis. As a result, the student of Chinese law has had to rely on newspapers, magazines, and other publications which often print the texts of newly enacted legislation. These sources have not always proved to be entirely satisfactory, however. In many cases, legislation has not been made public until well after the date of promulgation even though the law has already been put into effect. Moreover, although 'unofficial' translations are sometimes circulated, all published laws are officially promulgated in Chinese. To meet the demands of foreigners for access to published rules and regulations, a number of commercial compilations of China's economic laws have recently begun to appear in English. However, the accuracy of the translations has varied and none of the compilations is entirely complete.[6] Moreover, there is a lack of uniformity among the various translations not only with respect to the substantive content of the statutes but also as regards the names of the laws. To relieve the reader of the burden of familiarizing himself with the various forms of citation for the same law, I have asked the contributors to this volume to conform to a uniform system of citation at least as regards the formal name of the law, leaving the abbreviated citation form to each author's preference. The complete citation form for the most important and most commonly cited laws is set forth in the Appendix, together with the original title in Chinese characters (see pp. 581–99).

Published rules and regulations, even when they are accessible to foreigners, form only a part of the legal framework governing business transactions in China. In addition, Chinese units and officials are guided in their dealings with foreigners by internal rules, the content of which in most cases may not be directly revealed. Most of these internal rules consist of directives which must be followed by Chinese negotiators in interpreting and implementing statutory law. Some herald the introduction of new policies which may in time find their way into published law. Others are simply a formalization of practices which have developed as a product of experience gained in similar or related transactions. Whatever their source, internal rules complicate the elucidation and definition of China's legal system and as such pose constant pitfalls in the way of attempts to understand the nature and operation of the rules regulating commercial transactions.

The legal framework established by China for the conduct of business transactions is still in its infancy. As a result, it is hardly surprising that

significant problems—such as lack of uniformity in the implementation
of existing laws, inconsistency of interpretation, and legislative lacunae—
remain to be resolved. In this regard, it is important to remind ourselves
that China's current law-making efforts cannot be viewed as an isolated
phenomenon, but are only one aspect of a much more complex and in-
finitely more difficult task aimed at the transformation of an economically
backward but culturally rich society. Seen from this perspective, the
essays in this volume should be viewed as portraying the beginning rather
than the end, and only a part rather than the whole, of a dynamic and
evolutionary process.

Notes

1. M. Moser (ed.), *Foreign Trade, Investment and the Law in the People's
Republic of China* (Hong Kong, Oxford University Press, 1984).
2. For a summary description of China's legal development, see S. Lubman,
'Emerging Functions of Formal Legal Institutions in China's Modernization', in
*China Under the Four Modernizations, Part 2: Selected Papers Submitted to the
Joint Economic Committee, Congress of the United States* (Washington, DC,
United States Government Printing Office, 1982), p. 285. Also see T. T. Hsia and
C. A. Johnson, *Law Making in the People's Republic of China: Terms, Proce-
dures, Hierarchy and Interpretation* (Washington, DC, United States Library of
Congress, 1986).
3. See F. H. Foster, 'Codification in Post Mao China', *American Journal of
Comparative Law*, Vol. 30, 1982.
4. Promulgated on 4 December 1982.
5. Constitution of the People's Republic of China, Art. 85.
6. Among the most widely circulated compilations are: *China's Foreign Economic Legislation* (Beijing, Foreign Languages Press, 1982); P. Chan, *China:
Modernization and its Economic Laws* (Hong Kong, The Economic Newspaper,
1982); *Laws and Regulations of the People's Republic of China*, Vols. I, II, and III
(Hong Kong, Kingsway International Publications, Inc., 1982, 1983, and 1985);
F. Chu, M. Moser, and O. Nee (eds.), *Commercial, Business and Trade Laws:
People's Republic of China* (Dobbs Ferry, Oceana Publications, Inc., 1982). The
most ambitious compilation is *China Laws for Foreign Business*, Vols. I, II, III,
and IV (Sydney, CCH Australia Limited, 1985), a bilingual collection of laws and
regulations periodically updated for subscribers.

1. The Regulation of China's Foreign Trade

JAMIE P. HORSLEY

I. Introduction

China's system for regulating foreign trade, traditionally highly centralized in view of the importance of controlling exports and imports in a
planned economy, is in a state of nearly constant flux. As part of its current drive towards rapid modernization, the Chinese government has
abandoned its insistence on self-reliance and has called for an unpreced-
ented expansion of foreign trade, to obtain from abroad necessary raw
materials, commodities, equipment, and technology, and to help pay for
these foreign imports with increased export earnings. In order to realize
this goal, China is seeking to stimulate and streamline foreign trade activity, in part by dispersing much direct trading authority to local governments and individual enterprises, rather than leaving it all in the hands of
the national foreign trade corporations.

This decentralization of direct foreign trade control is being accompanied by a legislative effort to establish commercial laws and administrative rules to regulate the newly sanctioned foreign trade activity more
indirectly, through such means as import and export licensing and inspection requirements and the imposition of, or exemption from, import
and export tariffs and taxes. China's administrative goal in this area is to
develop a system that efficiently balances increased local trading autonomy with overall central direction and control.

Since the adoption in late 1978 of an 'open-door policy' to welcome
foreign investment in and trade with China, China's foreign trade has
grown rapidly.[1] To date, the People's Republic of China has established
trade relations with over 176 countries and regions and has signed trade
agreements or protocols with some 94 countries.[2] Moreover, in addition
to becoming increasingly active in international trade matters under the
auspices of various United Nations bodies, China established relations
with the General Agreement on Tariffs and Trade (GATT) in 1980, began
to send official observers to GATT meetings in 1982, joined the GATT
arrangement regarding international textile trade in late 1983, was granted
formal observer status by GATT in late 1984, and formally applied to join
the GATT in July 1986.

China's open-door foreign trade policy is closely interrelated with
widespread political and economic reform that is intended to spur local
enterprise and individual initiative, and increase and improve production
through the easing of central administrative controls and greater reliance
on 'market forces'. Just as economic decision-making and profit account-

ability in certain sectors are devolving to lower administrative and enterprise levels, so in the area of foreign trade the authority to negotiate, sign, and implement contracts is becoming more diversified.

The actual process of decentralizing the foreign trade system began in 1979,[3] when authorities at the provincial, municipal, and autonomous regional level were first authorized gradually to take over control of the export of locally produced commodities and the import of locally required goods. These local authorities are now held accountable for their own foreign trade profits and losses, and are permitted to retain all or a portion of their foreign exchange trade earnings and pay taxes thereon, rather than turn all profits over to the central government as was previously required. Since 1979, certain provinces, especially Guangdong and Fujian, and the special municipalities of Beijing, Tianjin, and Shanghai, as well as other large coastal and inland cities, have been granted broad economic and trade autonomy,[4] and the Chinese ministries have been encouraged to set up their own specialized trading corporations to export the products under their respective jurisdictions and to import the commodities and technology that they need. Moreover, selected key enterprises have been permitted to engage directly in import and export trade within a specified scope. Nearly 15 per cent of China's total imports in 1984 were made by local enterprises in the provinces, rather than by or through central government units.[5]

The decentralization of trading authority has been accompanied by the adoption of certain 'flexible' forms of trade, such as processing and assembly of imported materials and parts, compensation trade, the seeking of foreign trade financing, leasing, the expansion of overseas channels for trade, and the export of Chinese labour and engineering for construction projects abroad.

The revitalization of foreign trade as a significant factor in the development of China's planned economy has been neither a smooth nor a straightforward process. The lack of an efficient foreign trade infrastructure and a comprehensive set of regulations or guidelines for trading activity, combined with local inexperience with respect to foreign trade matters, gave rise initially to unforeseen consequences. In the words of one Chinese official:

[Following the structural reform of China's foreign trade] more departments and enterprises began to engage in foreign trade. This in turn stimulated the central departments, local authorities and enterprises to create additional channels to do business abroad. However, some problems cropped up, such as indiscriminate importation of consumer goods, which had an adverse impact on the domestic market and production. Left unchecked, this would have impaired the development of China's industry and inflicted losses on the national economy. Expansion of some exports which were in short supply domestically also upset the state plan, and at that point enterprises even began to compete with each other to sell goods at lower prices on the world market. This was detrimental to the normal development of China's export trade, affected economic results and had a negative impact on normal profits earned by foreign firms handling Chinese goods regularly.[6]

The year 1980 witnessed the ascension of Premier Zhao Ziyang and a general movement to tighten central management of the economy, including foreign trade. This harnessing of the decentralization process did not represent a policy reversal, since an increasing number of provinces, municipalities, departments, and enterprises continued to be given expanded foreign trade autonomy. Rather, it signalled a realization that decentralization should evolve in a more planned and co-ordinated manner.

Since 1980, policy regarding foreign trade management has fluctuated between decentralization and recentralization. As of late 1984, the Ministry of Foreign Economic Relations and Trade (MOFERT) adopted a policy of separating government administration from decentralizing enterprise management and centralizing administrative control over import and export activity.[7]

In the administrative area, export and import licensing regulations have been issued and revised to improve control over the types, quantity, and prices of commodities being traded, as well as to ensure that only authorized Chinese units engage directly in foreign trade business. The watchdog Customs Administration has been separated from the foreign trade ministry and directly subordinated to the State Council, presumably to make it a more independent check on foreign trade activity, and the commodity inspection apparatus has been reorganized and strengthened to increase quality control over both exports and imports. In an exercise of more indirect control, import duties on over 100 commodities were adjusted upward or downward in late 1982 and export duties were imposed on more than 30 goods to inhibit trading in certain strategic items. Duty rates continue to be adjusted, and new regulations on import and export duties were promulgated by the State Council in March 1985.[8] As of 1986, the licensing system is in the process of being streamlined and extended, and the customs laws updated.

II. China's Foreign Trade Apparatus

In recent times, China's foreign trade management structure has been undergoing virtually continual readjustment. The basic decentralization of trading authority has been accompanied by occasional drives to recentralize a certain amount of administrative control and to define more clearly the division of authority and work between the central and local trade levels, and between governmental trade bodies and local enterprises, within the general framework of a unified plan and policy.

The more recent institutional developments in China's search for a foreign trade system under which the necessary control and co-ordination can be exercised without unduly dampening local trading initiative are (a) the establishment of special trade commissioner offices directly under MOFERT, and (b) reform of the national foreign trade corporation system.

In February 1983 MOFERT announced that chief trade commissioners and deputy trade commissioners had been dispatched to the four major port cities of Shanghai, Tianjin, Dalian, and Guangzhou.[9] Although the precise role of these special trade offices is not yet entirely clear, the chief trade commissioners are reported to have the equivalent of vice-ministerial status and are responsible for (a) supervising and co-ordinating foreign trade activities around the port cities where they are located, under a unified policy and plan determined by the central authorities; (b) strengthening administrative control over the export and import licensing system and issuing some export and import licences within a scope approved by MOFERT; (c) assisting the head offices of the national import and export corporations gradually to reach unified management over major export commodities; (d) convening trade-related joint conferences between economic and trade departments in the ports and inland areas; (e) setting up joint enterprises around the ports, specializing in different lines of trade; and (f) generally advising MOFERT on trade policy and reform of the foreign economic and trade structure.[10] Although the State Council is reported to have approved relevant provisional regulations governing these commissioners and their offices, no such regulations have been made public.[11]

The establishment of the special trade commissioner offices appears to be a move to reconcentrate below the centre some of the administrative authority that had been exercised by the local foreign trade departments and bureaux in the wake of decentralization. Each trade office has been assigned the task of strengthening 'traditional economic relations' between the port cities and China's hinterland by co-ordinating trade activities within designated parts of China. Shanghai is to supervise the East and South-west, including trade in Fujian province and its special economic zone at Xiamen; Tianjin, the North and North-west; Dalian, the North-east; and Guangzhou, the Central–South region, including Guangdong province and the three special economic zones there.[12] It remains to be seen what the role of the special trade offices will be with respect to areas such as Fujian and Guangdong provinces and their special economic zones, which have been given a great deal of independence in connection with economic and trade matters.

The second major institutional reform, that of changing the traditional role of the national foreign trade corporations, is discussed below in the context of describing the major foreign trade institutions.

The major institutions involved in China's foreign trade system are MOFERT, the national foreign trade corporations directly under MOFERT and their local branches, other import and export corporations specializing in particular commodities established by the State Council or ministries other than MOFERT, and the local foreign trade departments or bureaux and corporations administered by the provinces, special municipalities, other large cities, and autonomous regions, as well as official Chinese commercial offices located abroad.[13] Apart from the institutional participants, an increasing number of individual enterprises are being granted the authority to engage directly in export and import trade.

A. MOFERT

China's foreign trade apparatus is headed by MOFERT, which was established in March 1982 as an amalgamation of two former ministries and two commissions: the Ministry of Foreign Trade, the Ministry of Foreign Economic Relations, the Foreign Investment Commission, and the State Import-Export Commission. MOFERT is responsible for helping to formulate the national foreign trade plans in consultation with the State Planning Commission, managing the foreign trade system, approving export quotas and import and export licences, authorizing enterprises to conduct foreign trade, supervising technology transfers to Chinese enterprises, negotiating international trade agreements, and participating in relevant international trade organizations. In addition, MOFERT supervises the local foreign trade bureaux in each province, major city, and autonomous region, and some 15 specialized national foreign trade corporations that are primarily responsible for conducting foreign trade on behalf of China. MOFERT also controls several trade-related service companies, including the China Resources Company, the Foreign Trade Consultancy and Technical Services Corporation (CONSULTECH), and the Foreign Trade Science and Technology Service Corporation. The Customs Administration and the commodity inspection apparatus work closely on foreign trade management with MOFERT, but they are constituted as specialized agencies directly under the leadership of the State Council.

MOFERT is organized into 7 administrative and 13 functional or regional departments, including departments for general planning, foreign trade administration, treaties and law, import-export administration, and technology transfers.[14]

B. The National Foreign Trade Corporations

As part of the movement towards the decentralization of trade management and contracting authority, the monopolistic role played by the national foreign trade corporations (NFTCs) under MOFERT, headquartered in Beijing, and their local branches is gradually being reduced. Once primarily responsible for negotiating and conducting a major portion of China's foreign trade for their own account, they are now to operate independently from their administrative organs as agents on a commission basis.[15]

The NFTCs are constituted as independent legal entities, like subsidiaries of MOFERT. Each NFTC handles a separate category of trade commodities or services, such as chemicals, metals and minerals, textiles, arts and crafts, cereals, oil and foodstuffs, light industrial products, native produce and animal by-products, packing materials, the purchase of whole plants, and the licensing of technology.[16] The NFTCs have local branches in various cities that are supervised by the local authorities, with respect to administrative matters, as well as by the head office in Beijing,[17] and that are establishing specialized trading subsidiaries of their own.[18]

NFTC head offices apparently will act more and more as administrative centres, leaving the actual import and export business to their branches and subsidiaries, which may further specialize in exclusively handling certain commodities or handling export commodities that are locally produced.

Under the recent reform of the trade system, approved by the State Council in September 1984,[19] the NFTCs and other ministerial import-export corporations are to become independent of their administrative superior organizations and operate as independent accounting units responsible for their own profits and losses. These specialized corporations act as agents for the actual exporters or importers on a commission basis. With the exception of imports relating to turnkey projects and a few key commodities, which will still be handled by one of the NFTCs or other national specialized corporations,[20] Chinese importers and exporters will be free to select their own agents or, when so authorized, to trade directly.

Traditionally, the NFTCs also acted as trading middlemen for Chinese end-users or manufacturers. Although such Chinese entities might participate in trade negotiations,[21] the final contract was generally signed, and commercial aspects such as price and delivery terms concluded, by the relevant NFTC. Complaints over this system were frequently heard from both the Chinese end-user and the foreign seller, since the NFTC was typically more concerned with price and contract terms than the quality or appropriateness of the product involved. This division between enterprise decision-making and administrative authority is one of the defects that the current reforms are trying to address.

Because of the proliferation of new local and ministerial trading corporations and individual enterprises with trading authority that compete with the NFTCs, this traditional middleman function has been somewhat circumscribed, and the NFTCs will continue to face increasing competition in the future. The director of MOFERT's Foreign Trade Administration Department, Shen Jueren, estimates that, as of the end of 1982, nearly 1,000 enterprises had the authority to engage in foreign trade,[22] and by late 1984 some 600 import and export corporations had been established under central departments and the provinces.[23] However, the NFTCs apparently continue to be responsible for handling foreign trade on behalf of entities not authorized to trade directly and with respect to commodities beyond the authorized trading scope of various entities, as well as for the export and import of major and staple commodities[24] and other state-monopolized commodities such as cigarettes, alcoholic beverages, and pearls.[25]

The NFTCs normally implement China's bilateral trade agreements by negotiating and signing the individual contracts under those agreements, or else by arranging for some other entity to conclude the contracts under their supervision.

In the past, unless otherwise directed by the State Council, the NFTCs were also responsible for negotiating and contracting with foreign firms with respect to commission sales, imports for sales at exhibitions, maintenance services in China, and imports for various state departments as designated by the State Council, and handled jointly with the unit concerned the import of commodities that are highly monopolized in the international market.[26] It is not clear whether they will continue to fulfil these roles after the new reforms are completed.

In addition to trading, the NFTCs conduct foreign market research on the production and sales of various commodities,[27] and often act as distribution agents in China for foreign sellers.[28]

C. The Foreign Trade Bureaux and Local Foreign Trading Corporations

At the local level, the foreign trade bureaux, located in each province, special municipality, and autonomous region, are subject to the dual leadership of MOFERT and the local government.[29] These administrative bureaux are charged with the task of supervising local foreign trade enterprises and implementing their respective plans, conducting relevant market research and developing local sources for import and export commodity trade, and issuing some import and export licences for their localities.

Certain political subdivisions have been authorized to establish their own foreign trading corporations, which are responsible for exercising unified control over import and export trade (including a measure of authority over the local branches of the NFTCs), transportation, ship chartering, export commodity packaging and advertising, as well as other foreign trade matters relating to their locality.[30]

D. Independent Enterprises

To complicate further the trade management structure outlined above, designated state enterprises may also be given the authority to deal directly with foreign traders and conclude foreign trade contracts, at least up to a specified value or within the scope of an approved plan. In particular, large industrial enterprises located in coastal and other major cities may be authorized to export their own products directly, bypassing the NFTCs, provincial import-export corporations, and other authorized trading agents.[31]

E. Establishing a Foreign Trade Company

In order to stem and control the flood of new trading companies that were formed in the wake of foreign trade decentralization, early in 1984 MOFERT formulated provisions on establishing foreign trade companies.[32] In principle newly approved companies should not compete with existing companies but rather should open new markets. Such companies are to be independent economic and accounting entities that must pay taxes and be responsible for their own profits and losses, although they must also bear any import or export responsibilities allocated to them by the state. They must have stable sources of goods for export and export markets or have definite import customers and channels. Moreover, new companies must also show that they have the necessary operating capital and adequate professional foreign trade personnel.

All ministries, provinces, autonomous regions, special municipalities, and cities having the same economic powers as provinces, as well as productive enterprises, that wish to form a trading company must apply to MOFERT or its authorized agencies for approval and demonstrate that they meet the above qualifications. They must then register with the industrial and commercial authorities to obtain a business licence before they can commence operations.

F. Ascertaining Trade Authority

Given the continuing reorganization of the foreign trade structure and the many units now involved in foreign trade, the lines of trading authority are often unclear. Jurisdiction to make or approve a given foreign trade contract may depend upon the Chinese entity, the commodity, or the value of the contract involved, or a combination of these three factors. MOFERT has announced that it will publish lists of authorized export-oriented companies, indicating their respective scopes of authority.[33] In the meantime, foreign partners will generally have to rely upon the assurances of their Chinese counterparts or advice of the Treaty and Law Department of MOFERT, the China Council for the Promotion of International Trade (CCPIT), a Chinese law firm, or some other qualified Chinese consulting body that their contracts have been properly approved, are signed by the appropriate legal entity, and will be enforceable as written. Certain national law offices, such as those sponsored by the CCPIT's Legal Department and China International Economic Consultants, Inc., a subsidiary of the China International Trust and Investment Corporation (CITIC) located in Beijing, can issue legal opinions to this effect. Notarization of foreign trade contracts pursuant to the 1982 Provisional Regulations of the People's Republic of China on Notarization should also provide assurance that the trade contract is legal and binding on the parties.

In addition to the above procedures, foreign traders are well advised to request to see the business licence and charter or articles of incorporation of any state enterprise with which they deal directly in order to ascertain that such enterprise is in fact properly authorized to import or export directly. Enterprises that are to engage in foreign trade must submit their articles of association at the time they register to do business and should be willing to produce them for verification.

G. Specialized Agencies

Apart from the primary trading organizations, many specialized agencies render trade-related services. Some of these agencies, such as the China National Foreign Trade Transportation Corporation, which organizes the transport of China's imports and exports, are directly under the supervision of MOFERT. Others are independent entities. For example, the Bank of China handles trade financing and, together with the State Administration for Exchange Control, controls the use and disposal of foreign exchange; the People's Insurance Company of China provides relevant insurance coverage; and the China Ocean Shipping Company, the China Ocean Shipping Agency, and the China Ocean Shipping Tally Company are responsible for maritime matters. The Customs Administration and commodity inspection apparatus are discussed below.

No description of China's foreign trade structure would be complete without mention of the role of the CCPIT. Established in 1952 as a non-governmental 'people-to-people' organization, the CCPIT promotes economic and trade relations between China and foreign countries, organizes trade exhibitions in China and abroad, arranges technical exchanges, oversees the Foreign Economic and Trade Arbitration Commission and the Maritime Arbitration Commission, issues and certifies trade and marine transport documentation upon request, and offers legal counselling services in connection with trade negotiations, problems, or disputes.[34]

The CCPIT, headquartered in Beijing, is an autonomous body under the general sponsorship of MOFERT and other trade and economic organizations, which provide a portion of its finances. The CCPIT's board of directors is comprised of some 20 officials from MOFERT, the Bank of China, the People's Insurance Company of China, and other economic and trade departments.[35]

H. Methods of Foreign Trade

China's foreign trade is generally conducted either pursuant to bilateral exchange agreements with foreign governments and trade associations or in accordance with individual trade contracts, comprising what the Chinese refer to as 'payment' trade.

The great majority of trade agreements are intergovernmental and provide binding or non-binding exchange quotas of listed commodities.[36] Such trade is essentially barter trade in nature and does not usually involve actual foreign exchange payments. These trade agreements are normally supplemented by payments agreements specifying the currency that will serve as the unit of account and settlement, as well as of payment, should a trade deficit occur under the agreement. The relevant NFTCs, on behalf of the Chinese government, negotiate and sign the individual contracts implementing these trade agreements that contain the basic terms such as price and delivery.

Non-agreement or 'payment' trade accounts for the lion's share of China's import and export activity. As described above, the Chinese trading partner may be an NFTC or local branch thereof, a local foreign trading corporation, a ministerial import or export corporation, or an enterprise authorized to conduct foreign trade business directly. Business is conducted by correspondence, or by direct negotiations in China or abroad, at the semi-annual Guangzhou (Canton) Export Commodities Fair, or at various mini-fairs and exhibitions for specific commodities sponsored by Chinese or foreign organizations.

The Guangzhou trade fair has been held nearly every spring and autumn since 1957, with foreign attendance by invitation only. The fair has been scaled down somewhat and has become a less important way of meeting potential Chinese partners and doing business in the wake of the decentralization of foreign trade authority. However, it continues to provide a useful channel for making trade contacts in China.

In addition to pure import and export activities, foreign firms may contract for the processing of raw or semi-finished materials supplied by them, or for the assembly of supplied parts and components in China, or they may enter into compensation trade deals, providing for payment in commodities rather than in cash.[37] Some sales may also be made through exhibitions held in China with the assistance of the CCPIT.

III. Import and Export Controls

China's foreign trade is an integral part of the planned economy. MOFERT develops the national foreign trade plans, which must be approved ultimately by the National People's Congress as part of the overall national economic plan, in close co-ordination with other economic sectors. China exports goods basically in order to be able to earn the foreign exchange with which to purchase imported goods, technology, and services necessary for realizing its targeted socialist modernization.

China, like most countries, restricts imports and exports in a variety of ways, ranging from absolute bans on trading in certain commodities[38] to more limited restrictions achieved by means of centrally imposed quotas, issued by the State Planning Commission and MOFERT, and 'standards' requirements. China's import and export licensing system, resurrected in 1980 and recently revised, helps directly to implement national import and export plans, current trade policies, and quota restrictions, while the commodity inspection apparatus enforces the requirement that imports and exports meet applicable domestic or international standards. China also indirectly influences the nature and volume of two-way trade through the selective imposition of, or exemption from, customs duties.

A. Export Licensing

In 1980, the Chinese government provisionally put into effect a revised export licensing system, to be administered by MOFERT.[39] The Interim Procedures Concerning the System of Export Licensing (hereafter cited as the Export Licensing Procedures), effective from 3 June 1980, characterize export licensing as a necessary measure to strengthen control over export commodities and to co-ordinate the export trade activities of the various localities and departments concerned.[40] In general, the NFTCs and their branches, and other corporations approved by the state to engage in export business, are deemed to have obtained permission to export the commodities within the approved scope of their business and need not apply specifically for export licences covering those commodities.[41] These 'general' licences will not, however, apply in the case of (a) goods subject to a quota imposed by the country of import; (b) export commodities that MOFERT has restricted in order to prevent flooding of the international market; (c) commodities subject to a minimum export price imposed by MOFERT; (d) export commodities restricted or banned by the State Council; and (e) commodities subject to export controls imposed by MOFERT in order to meet conditions in the world market or due to foreign policy constraints. The latter condition, for example, would apply to the ban on all trade with South Korea, South Africa, and Israel, including re-exports of Chinese goods via Hong Kong or third countries.[42]

As of 15 February 1986, some 235 commodities reportedly had been placed under the special export licensing system, applicable to all Chinese exporters, 83 of which commodities required quota and export licence approval only when destined for Hong Kong and Macau.[43] Before February 1982, the list of controlled commodities covered only some 32 miscellaneous goods, including herbal medicines such as ginseng, pilous antler, and Chinese caterpillar fungus, red dates, freshwater pearls, leather work gloves intended for West Germany and Hong Kong, hempsole shoes destined for France, peppermint oil, Arab robes, resin, and reed matting. As of 2 February 1982, 48 additional commodities organized into 11 categories were also made subject to special export licensing. These additional commodities include crude and heavy oil and refined oil products; coal; rolled steel; pig iron, coke, ferro-alloys, and chromite ore; plate glass; cement; timber and timber products; non-ferrous metals; natural rubber; soda ash, caustic soda, polyethylene, polyprophylene phosphorous, sulphurous iron ore, sulphur, benzoic anhydride, and liquid hydrocarbons; and agricultural products such as rice, corn, soybeans, sugar, cotton, resin, tung oil, and tobacco.[44] As of 1 August 1982, drawn-work goods, including embroidered and hand-worked goods, were made subject to the export licensing system;[45] and as of 15 April 1983, when a total of over 90 commodities had been subjected to the system, silk garments, hand tools, l-cystine, ascorbic acid, tetracycline, sodium sulphate, and inner combustion engines and units also required a special export licence.[46]

Then, from 10 April 1984, 30 more commodities[47] were added, including grey cotton yarn, grey cotton fabrics (excluding cotton prints and dyed cloth), grey polyester cotton yarn, and grey polyester cotton fabrics (excluding polyester cotton prints and dyed cloth);[48] *cloisonné* or enamel (including *cloisonné* jewellery ornaments, furnishings, and articles for daily use); traditional Chinese stationery (that is, Xuan paper, ink-sticks, Chinese writing-brushes, and inkslabs); reed; carpets and rugs (including handmade and machine-made carpets and rugs, tapestries, velvet carpets and rugs, but excluding straw and gunny carpets, gunny tapestries, and silk carpets and rugs, with the exception of the export of carpets and rugs to the United States); peanuts (including peanut kernels and peanuts with shells, excluding cooked and preserved peanuts), sesame (that is, raw sesame, excluding cooked and preserved sesame), garlic (that is, fresh garlic and Huosuan garlic, excluding dried garlic pieces), tinned water-chestnuts, frozen suckling pigs, and eel fry; silk (including tussah cocoon, raw silk, processed silk yarn, dupion silk, spun silk, silk lustres, silk floss, filament, refuse silk, and cocoon and silk/blend fabric yarn consisting of the above materials); fire-fighting devices (that is, small fire extinguishers with decorative pottery or porcelain cases and glass cases filled with fire-extinguishing chemicals); civilian explosives and blasting materials (including various kinds of explosives, detonators, detonating fuses, non-electric blasting systems, detonating powder, and explosive chemicals); and Chinese medicines, including the rhizome of large-headed atracty-lodes, root of herbaceous peony, tuber of dwarf lilyturf, silver flower (including honeysuckle and honey silver flower), root of *bidentate achy-rathes, corydalis yanhusuo,* bark of tree peony, capsule of weeping forsythia, bark of official magnolia, fruit of medicinal cornel, tuber of elevated gastrodia, bezor, and root of baloonflower.

In late 1985, the following commodities were put on the export licence list, bringing the total to 151: leather work gloves, silk and satin, pottery and porcelain, frozen prawns, chestnuts, Hami melons, Wulong tea, bristle brushes, bean dregs, soybean cakes, cassia bark, cassia oil, ramie, ramie products, flax-weaving products, linseed-weaving products, hemp-weaving products, jute, bluish dogbane, sacks, toilet paper, Pian-zhanhuang, chloramphenicol, Tianjin pears, and Shatian pomelo.[49]

Most recently, the list of controlled commodities was increased to 235, although 83 of these commodities (mostly consisting of fresh, live, and frozen foods, cotton yarns, and other consumer goods) require licences only when shipped to the Hong Kong and Macau regions, where competition among too many Chinese sellers has depressed prices.[50]

Other reasons for controlling exports have included the desire to ensure adequate domestic supplies of critical commodities like crude oil, steel and steel products, non-ferrous metals, rubber, cereals, and sugar, and preventing Chinese exporters from violating exclusive distribution agreements with foreign customers.[51]

In addition to the special licences required of all Chinese exporting units for controlled commodities, special export licences are also necessary for (a) goods being exported by entities and individuals not authorized to engage in export business; (b) goods exported for foreign sales and exhibition; (c) goods exported directly, rather than through an NFTC or other authorized agent, by factories and enterprises that produce the goods under a processing or compensation trade contract with a foreign party; (d) goods being shipped out of China by diplomatic missions, representatives of foreign enterprises, foreign nationals, and tourists; and (e) goods exceeding a reasonable amount for personal use taken out of China by foreign nationals and tourists.[52]

The Export Licensing Procedures provide that MOFERT may at any time reduce, suspend, or terminate exports of any commodity to any country or region when the export (a) does not conform to Chinese policies with respect to the place of destination; (b) does not conform to the content and spirit of any relevant bilateral trade or payments agreement, such as the textile agreements that China has signed with the European Economic Community, the United States, and Canada; (c) must be postponed or curtailed due to an imbalance in China's foreign exchange situation; or (d) does not meet the standards set by the state or the relevant export contract, as determined by the commodity inspection authorities.[53]

Export licence applications must be filed with the Foreign Trade Administration Department of MOFERT in the case of (a) controlled commodities that MOFERT subjects to the special export licensing system;[54] (b) exports of commodities that must be handled jointly with the specialized NFTCs; (c) exports by ministries other than MOFERT and the departments and enterprises directly under them, if not otherwise authorized by MOFERT; and (d) cargo shipped out of China by foreign embassies in China.[55] The local foreign trade bureaux have been authorized by MOFERT to handle licence applications with respect to (a) commodities handled by the local export corporations and not coordinated by the NFTCs or by other specialized corporations; (b) cargo shipped out of China by foreign consulates in China; and (c) certain goods exported by local departments and enterprises.[56] As mentioned above, the special trade commissioner offices are also responsible for issuing some export licences.[57]

The term of each licence, which may not exceed six months, is determined on a case-by-case basis, except for general export licences, which reportedly are good for six-month periods.[58] Special licences will be granted separately on the basis of an application that describes the commodity and its specifications, destination, quantity, unit price, total price, delivery date, and method of payment.[59] The applicant retains one copy of the licence and presents two copies to the Customs authorities for inspection at the time of export. The Customs in turn forward one copy, stamped by Customs, to the local branch of the Bank of China for verification that the foreign exchange proceeds are properly collected.[60]

The foreign trade system has undergone extensive reform since the Export Licensing Procedures were formulated. A revised regulation can be expected in the not too distant future.

B. Import Licensing

The Chinese import licensing system, also administered by MOFERT, is designed to help implement the state import plans and to control the goods that the provincial and ministerial import corporations and authorized enterprises may buy and the foreign exchange expenditures therefor. In 1980, the Chinese implemented, but never made officially public, a provisional import licence system and rules concerning imports by localities.[61] These rules were replaced on 10 January 1984 by the Provisional Regulations of the People's Republic of China on the System of Import Licensing (hereafter cited as the Import Licensing Regulations)[62] and the implementing rules thereunder (hereafter cited as the Import Licensing Rules).[63]

The Chinese government periodically issues import guidelines for domestic units in accordance with its foreign exchange reserves situation and development needs. China has recently stressed the import of advanced technology and equipment in order to renovate existing enterprises, in a shift away from the import of complete plants and sets of equipment.[64] China generally adheres to the following import guidelines: (a) China will not import goods that are harmful to the people's health; (b) if China-made products fall short of demand in terms of quantity, quality, or variety, a limited amount of such goods may be imported; (c) imports of important raw materials and semi-finished materials that China cannot produce are encouraged; (d) priority is given to sophisticated technology and equipment that can advance China's modernization effort; and (e) China will permit imports of materials that are to be processed or assembled for export.[65]

Through the licensing system, China has severely curtailed imports of consumer or luxury goods, as well as production and assembly lines, in order to protect domestic industry and conserve valuable foreign exchange for more pressing needs.[66] From October 1982, special import licences were required for commodities such as vehicles (including bicycles), certain electronic equipment and household appliances, some business equipment, consumer goods, and chemical fibres and fabrics.[67] As of May 1984, watches, cameras, cotton cloth, garments, knitted chemical fibre shirts and trousers, skirts, hosiery and mosquito nets, rubber, sulphuric acid, 16 kinds of traditional medicines, demolition equipment for civil use, and timber were added to the controlled import list.[68] Additional items requiring import licences as of late 1985 include air-conditioners, hydraulic truck lifts, electronic microscopes, electronic colour scanners, X-ray fault detectors (CT), and open-end spinning machines.[69] As of March 1986, rubber, steel, and fertilizer had been added to the list, and some 45 major commodities required special import licences.[70]

As of mid-June 1985, the import of seven types of production and assembly lines (for colour and black-and-white televisions, radio recorders, household refrigerators and washing machines, room air-conditioners and light mini-vehicles) were apparently prohibited; some 43 items of equipment and technology were put on a list requiring joint import approval of MOFERT and the relevant ministry and the imposition of an import regulatory tax of not less than 10 per cent of FOB (free on board) prices; and 24 additional electrical and mechanical products will be subject to annual import plans drafted by the State Economic Commission and approved by the State Council, and most of those items will require import licences as of 1 November 1985.[71]

As of August 1985, MOFERT has instituted measures to inspect applications for the import of certain key commodities such as vehicles, televisions, and calculators to ensure that the necessary foreign exchange is available through the proper channels and that the price agreed in the import contract is reasonable.[72]

Pursuant to Article 4 of the Import Licensing Regulations, the NFTCs and authorized import corporations under the ministries and provincial governments are deemed to have a general licence with respect to commodities that they are authorized to handle, excepting only designated controlled imports and imports of prohibited goods.[73] In addition, uncontrolled goods imported within the scope of approved contracts with foreigners for processing, assembly, compensation trade, and construction projects, as well as articles for maintenance and consignment sale that are imported under contracts for the maintenance of foreign products and sales on consignment approved by MOFERT or other competent governmental authorities, do not require an import licence, except for any material, spare parts, and the finished products thereof under processing and assembly projects that are actually sold on the domestic Chinese market, rather than exported as originally planned.[74]

Other imports of uncontrolled goods that are exempt from the import licensing requirements include: (a) samples imported by or given to Chinese entities authorized to engage in import business in the course of their normal import and export activities or samples and articles for advertisement presented as gifts by foreign businessmen; (b) urgently needed work-related articles purchased abroad with government approval, at a price of US$5,000 or less per batch, by scientific research, cultural, athletic, medical, and health departments; (c) urgently needed parts and accessories for machines, meters, and instruments purchased abroad with government approval, at a total price of US$5,000 or less per batch, by factories, mines, and enterprises; and (d) commodities imported with special State Council or MOFERT approval.[75]

Chinese-foreign equity joint ventures do not need to apply for an import licence for any uncontrolled machinery, equipment, spare parts, and raw or other materials contributed as part of the foreign party's investment or, when such items cannot be purchased in China, otherwise needed for the venture's production within the scope of the approved joint venture contract.[76] Controlled commodities and imports beyond the approved business scope of a joint venture, however, will require a special import licence.

In sum, special licences will be required for all imports not falling within the categories listed above, that is, for all controlled goods regardless of the importing unit and for uncontrolled goods imported by entities not authorized to engage in the import business or by NFTCs and other authorized entities beyond the approved scope or monetary limit of their import authority.

Import licences will be denied or may be revoked when: (a) the state decides to suspend or cease the import of certain goods; (b) the import of goods would violate China's foreign policy; (c) the import would violate bilateral trade or payments agreements; (d) the import goods do not meet the state's hygienic or quarantine standards; (e) the import would be harmful to the state's interests; or (f) the import goods are procured by illegal means.[77]

Imports from South Korea, South Africa, and Israel are banned,[78] and imports from Taiwan, entitled for a time to special exemptions from licensing and payment of customs duties, have been made subject to the import licensing system and 'adjustment taxes', rather than duties, reportedly in order to discourage the excessive import of consumer goods from the island.[79]

Special provisions govern imports by special economic zone or Hainan Island enterprises, basically providing that Customs clearance will be required if such imports are subsequently sent to other parts of China.[80]

MOFERT, the provincial foreign trade bureaux and, as recently authorized, the four special trade commissioner offices may issue required import licences.[81] The division of responsibility in this respect is prescribed from time to time by MOFERT.

Licence applications must state the kind of commodities, quantity, specifications, price, usage, country of export, source of foreign currency, and the name of the foreign exporter.[82] Licences are to be valid for one year from the date of issue and may be extended upon application.[83] In the case of special applications, licences may be obtained in as little as two to three days.[84]

Although foreign traders are often told that the licensing system is an internal matter and the sole concern of the Chinese side, foreigners have a substantial interest in knowing that the licensing procedures have been duly complied with. In at least one reported case, the responsible Chinese ministry refused to approve a licence application for a provincial export contract ready to be signed, unless the negotiated price was raised by 15 per cent.[85] Moreover, orders are not to be placed by Chinese importers prior to obtaining any necessary import licences.[86] Thus, foreigners are advised to request proof or assurances that any necessary licences have been obtained or are forthcoming before expending time and money in negotiating a trade contract.[87] Even in the case of goods and Chinese units covered by a long-term general licence, one should ascertain that the particular order conforms to any price, quantity, and delivery terms applicable to the general licence.

C. Commodity Inspection

The Chinese commodity inspection network is designed to ensure that import and export goods meet national standards and any specifications contained in relevant contracts or trade agreements. All import and export goods are to undergo inspection at some stage.[88] Certain 'important' import and export commodities are required by Chinese law to go through inspection by the commodity inspection authorities and will not be cleared by Customs without certification that they have passed such inspection:

The Chinese Import and Export Commodity Inspection Bureau was established under the former Ministry of Foreign Trade pursuant to regulations approved in 1953,[89] which charged the Bureau with the task of controlling the quality of import and export commodities through inspection, survey, technical appraisal, and certification. The Bureau was reorganized into the General Administration of Import and Export Commodity Inspection and placed under the direct supervision of the State Council in February 1980,[90] and its name was changed to the State Administration of Import and Export Commodity Inspection (SACI) in 1982. The 1953 inspection regulations were replaced in 1984 with the Regulations of the People's Republic of China on the Inspection of Import and Export Commodities.[91] Despite these changes, the SACI's duties remain basically the same. Local commodity inspection bureaux under the direct supervision of the head office in Beijing have been established in all provinces (except Taiwan), autonomous regions, and special municipalities.

The SACI is responsible for certifying all major commodities designated in a list prepared by MOFERT (the Legal Inspection List), other commodities requiring inspection pursuant to the terms of export or import contracts, animals and plants and products thereof subject to quarantine, foodstuffs subject to sanitary inspection, and containers and ships' holds for shipping goods.[92] In addition, the SACI is authorized to conduct 'interventional' inspection of commodities not included on the Legal Inspection List, such as any goods suspected of being contaminated.[93] The SACI may also investigate cases of alleged import or export fraud and impose fines.[94]

In addition to the SACI, a number of other agencies have been charged with specialized quality assurance responsibilities. These include: (a) the Animal and Plant Quarantine Centre, responsible for the quarantine of plant imports and exports and for the quarantine of imported and exported animals and animal products other than wild animal products and animal by-products, which are under the jurisdiction of the SACI; (b) the Ship Inspection Bureau, responsible for the inspection of imported ships and major ship equipment; (c) the Medical and Sanitary Quarantine Centres under the Ministry of Public Health, responsible for the inspection of imported foodstuffs and drugs;[95] and (d) the National Bureau of Weights and Measures, responsible for inspecting imported weighing and measuring equipment.[96]

As of the end of 1985, over 250 export commodities and 15 import commodities were designated as legally requiring inspection. These commodities generally include those imported or exported in large volume in terms of quantity or value, traditional exports, exports of high revenue-earning potential, and commodities of fluctuating quality that may affect the health of humans or animals.[97] For example, in order to avoid the dumping on to the Chinese market of outdated or defective goods, regulations issued jointly by MOFERT, the Ministry of Commerce, and the SACI in September 1985 require that as of 1 October 1985 all imported electrical household appliances must undergo inspection by the commodities inspection authorities before being offered for sale.[98] In addition, commodities not legally or contractually required to undergo inspection are still subject to inspection by other authorized departments, and possibly by the SACI, to make certain that they comply generally with state laws, standards, and policies.[99]

Commodities are inspected for quality, conformance to relevant specifications, and packaging. Inspection is carried out in accordance with any applicable contractual provisions or else pursuant to standards set by the state or the departments concerned.[100] Inspection certificates must be presented to obtain customs clearance and are often used as settlement documents in the case of a dispute. China's standard export and import contracts previously provided that certificates issued by the SACI were to be used as conclusive evidence in the event of any dispute over quality, quantity, or other product specification. However, the Chinese recently have permitted foreign buyers to use the results of their own re-inspection as a basis for bringing claims.[101]

The China National Import-Export Commodities Inspection Corporation (CCIC) was set up in 1980, under the leadership of the SACI, specifically to deal with inspection work entrusted by foreign traders or Chinese units with respect to commodities not on the Legal Inspection List. The CCIC is authorized to issue certificates that are also legally effective for the purposes of customs clearance, calculating customs duties, and settling claims.[102] The CCIC will conduct inspection in accordance with any requirements set forth in the relevant contract or letter of credit. If inspection standards are not clearly defined by the contract, the CCIC will apply, in the case of imports, the prevailing standard of the country of origin or those that are internationally recognized and, in the case of exports, relevant Chinese standards.[103]

The CCIC has branches in Shanghai, Guangzhou, Tianjin, Dalian, Qingdao, Wuhan, and Nanjing.[104] In the summer of 1982, the CCIC established a Hong Kong subsidiary, China Inspection Company Limited (CICL), to act as the CCIC's inspection agent in Hong Kong and to provide inspection services to Hong Kong enterprises. Certificates issued by the CICL for goods imported by China via Hong Kong are recognized by the SACI for the purposes of accepting the goods and settling accounts.[105]

IV. Customs Regulations

The General Administration of Customs of the People's Republic of China, reorganized and placed directly under the State Council in February 1980 to replace the Customs Bureau of the former Ministry of Foreign Trade, is responsible for the overall management of customs work throughout China. The major responsibilities of the Customs Administration are to enforce China's foreign trade regulations through the supervision and control of goods, currency, means of conveyance, passenger baggage, and postal articles that enter or leave Chinese territory, the collection of customs duties and other taxes and fees that are to be collected by Customs, and the prevention of smuggling.[106] The Customs Administration has established some 40 offices and 27 sub-offices at ports, railway stations, airports, and international parcel post and mail exchange bureaux that are open for foreign trade, as well as at border areas open for passenger, parcel, and conveyance traffic. In addition, a branch office of the Customs Administration was set up in Guangzhou in 1980 to supervise the especially heavy customs traffic in Guangdong province.[107]

China announced in August 1983 that it had joined the 95-member Customs Co-operation Council (CCC), a Brussels-based international governmental customs organization. The CCC was formed to promote co-operation between the customs administrations of member states, to improve customs regulations and techniques, to exchange data about customs procedures, and to co-operate with other international organizations.[108] This move would seem to reflect China's concern with updating its customs system and further integrating itself into the international commercial community. Indeed, on the domestic front, MOFERT reports that the 1951 Customs Law is undergoing extensive revision to update its provisions and make the system more efficient. However, the exact content of the proposed new customs law, and its expected date of enactment, are not yet known.

A. Customs Formalities

All cargo and international means of conveyance must pass through Customs upon entry into or exit from Chinese territory. Cargo is released after verification of any required import or export licence or other official document of approval, as well as of inspection certificates in the case of goods subject to commodity inspection, animal or plant quarantine, medical tests, or other state restrictions.

All imports and exports, except those specially exempted, must be cleared through Customs by the cargo owner or his agent. Customs officials are responsible for checking that shipping marks, the number of packages, weight specifications, and country of origin or destination correspond with the terms of the relevant licence or trade document, and that the shipment does not violate any foreign trade regulations. In addition, Customs must ascertain whether there has been any damage to, or loss of, cargo and whether the quality and packaging satisfy applicable requirements.[109] After examination and approval, cargo will be released with the relevant shipping documents signed and verified by the Customs authorities.

As a rule, cargo is examined at the wharf, warehouse, or open yard at the place of entry into or exit from Chinese territory, but examination may take place elsewhere upon prior written request,[110] as in the case of goods packed in containers for import or export.[111] In addition, certain bulk cargo and dangerous or perishable goods may be cleared during loading or unloading so as to expedite their transport, prevent loss, and minimize operating costs.

Transit cargo from abroad destined for another foreign country is subject to Customs supervision and control while it is in China. In general, such goods may be inspected without unpacking or may be exempted from examination when the cargo is legal and appears to be above suspicion.[112] The transhipment of weapons and ammunition requires a special licence.[113]

Commodities imported for exhibition in China are subject to special procedures promulgated in 1975.[114] The Chinese organization hosting the exhibition must submit approval documents to the Customs office at the place of the exhibition prior to importation, and the exhibitor or his agent must also submit to that Customs office a list of exhibition goods and their specifications and value. Exhibition goods that are re-exported from China within three months from the end of the exhibition are exempt from import duties. However, products and exhibits sold or disposed of in China will be handled retroactively in accordance with normal licensing and duty regulations.

Gifts and commodity samples without commercial value that are accepted by Chinese government entities or Chinese enterprises may be cleared duty-free and without a licence, upon declaration to the Customs authorities by the recipient.[115]

Special rules[116] covering bonded goods, such as stored commodities needed to service international aircraft, and the warehouses in which they are kept, were issued in 1981. They exempt bonded goods from customs duty and normal licensing procedures. In addition, customs rules exempting raw materials, components, spare parts, fittings, and accessories imported by Customs-supervised 'bonded factories' and actually used to process goods for export were promulgated in 1983.[117]

All inward- and outward-bound vessels, trains, civil aircraft, and motor vehicles, as well as their cargo, are also subject to Customs supervision and must be covered by a declaration form and undergo inspection upon entering or leaving China.[118] Only after inspection and approval of the means of conveyance can unloading of the cargo, under Customs supervision, take place.

Incoming and outgoing personal baggage and goods brought into China through the mail (except by diplomatic personnel) are all subject to Customs supervision. Baggage and goods accompanying tourists and foreign residents in China are limited to reasonable amounts necessary for personal use. On entering or leaving China, non-diplomatic passengers must fill out baggage declaration forms. Specified items, such as foreign currency, wrist-watches, calculators, cameras, and jewellery, must be declared upon entering China and taken out again, or else the passenger will be subject to a potentially stiff fine. The import of arms, ammunition, or explosives of any kind, radio transmitter-receivers and parts, unauthorized *renminbi*, material detrimental to Chinese political, economic, cultural, and moral interests, illegal drugs, infected plant and animal matter, unsanitary foodstuffs, and other articles proscribed by regulations is forbidden.[119]

The export of arms, ammunition and explosives, radio transmitters and parts, *renminbi* and *renminbi*-denominated securities, unauthorized foreign currency and securities, materials containing state secrets or otherwise prohibited for export, rare animal and plant matter, precious metals and jewellery made therefrom in excess of permitted amounts,[120] and valuable cultural relics and rare books relating to China's revolution, history, and culture is also prohibited.[121] Cultural relics permitted for export, jewellery, precious stones and metals, and jade and ivory articles will be cleared by Customs only against verification of the relevant sales receipts issued by state-run friendship stores or cultural relic shops, plus a foreign exchange memorandum issued by the Bank of China showing that the purchase price thereof was paid with *renminbi* obtained by exchanging foreign currency.[122]

Most personal goods can be brought in duty-free, but the import of certain consumer goods such as wrist-watches, bicycles, cameras, radios, videos, sewing machines, foodstuffs, smoking materials, and liquor are restricted, and duty must be paid on amounts in excess of prescribed limits.[123] As in the case of unaccompanied imports, trade samples, gifts, advertising material, and the like brought into China by passengers for business purposes must be declared and will be cleared only after the Chinese recipient submits proper certification.[124]

B. Customs Duty

China pursues a protective tariff policy in order to safeguard its domestic economy from disruptive or undesirable imports and exports. Conversely, through duty exemptions or low rates of duty, China seeks to encourage the import of strategic commodities and materials to be processed or assembled for export, and the export of all commodities that are not in short supply domestically. In order to strengthen control in this respect, the Customs Administration announced in late 1981 that henceforth Chinese entities could no longer sign trade contracts that contained provisions purporting to exempt the contract commodity from duty without authorization.[125]

Regulations issued in March 1985 on the imposition of import and export duties[126] divide import and export commodities into 21 general categories containing some 99 groups and further specific classifications based on the natural properties, composition, and use of the commodities that basically follow the classification system adopted by the multinational Customs Co-operation Council. To encourage exports, the Chinese government does not levy customs duties on most export commodities. However, as of March 1985, 35 export commodities are subject to duties ranging from 10 per cent to 60 per cent. Export duties are generally levied on the basis of the FOB value as determined by the Customs authorities, less export duty.[127] Dutiable export commodities include coal, tungsten ores and concentrates, lignite, peat, iron alloys, pig and cast iron, several non-ferrous metals, camel and rabbit hair, goat skins, pearls, sugar, raw lacquer, some freshwater and seafood products, spices, and traditional Chinese medicinal goods. Many of these dutiable export goods also require a special export licence. One motive behind the imposition of the duties appears to be to restrain local trade units from exporting scarce strategic commodities that may be sold abroad at prices higher than those paid by the Chinese government or determined by the state price-control authorities.[128]

On the import side, two of the most extensive duty adjustments since the tariff system was instituted in 1951 took effect in January 1982, when the import duties on 149 commodities were adjusted upward or downward,[129] and in 1985, when a new tariff schedule, published as part of the 1985 Duty Regulations, reduced import rates on average by approximately 10 per cent.[130]

Commodities that were subject in 1982 to reduced rates, so as to encourage imports, fell into three general categories: (a) natural raw materials for industry and primary products such as rubber, timber, leather, and paper, which are in chronic short supply in China; (b) commodities temporarily in short domestic supply, such as crude oil, fuel oil, coal, cement, some chemicals, raw materials, and certain equipment for light and textile industries; and (c) components and spare parts for machines and instruments.[131] At the same time, import duties on most power, farming, mining, metallurgical, petroleum-exploiting, and universal machinery, machine tools, electric motors, automobiles, ships, and civil electrical appliances were raised to protect domestic manufacture.[132]

The import duty reductions in 1985 fell into roughly three categories also: (a) technology, materials, and equipment relating to the development of new technology; (b) raw materials, especially those vulnerable to natural conditions and that cannot be produced domestically in adequate quantities for the short term; and (c) food products and certain consumer goods that are needed to develop China's tourist industry and improve the people's livelihood.[133] The rates on over 55 per cent of goods listed on the tariff schedule were reduced and the minimum rate was lowered from 5 per cent to 3 per cent. Import duties were raised only on a small number of commodities that China can produce in sufficient quantities, in order to protect the development of her domestic production. However, an additional 'regulatory duty' of between 20 and 80 per cent, on top of the otherwise applicable duty, was imposed on imports of cars, motorcycles, minibuses, and off-road vehicles, video cassette recorders, large-screen colour television projection sets, minicomputers, digital automatic data-processing equipment and peripheral equipment, processed polyester yarn, synthetic chemical fabric, and unspecified 'other' commodities. This regulatory duty, which was effective from 15 July 1985, was allegedly applied because 'some localities and units had imported in a blind way commodities with big price differentials', causing 'an unfavorable impact on domestic economic development'.[134]

The customs duty rate schedule prescribes a general rate and a 'minimum' or preferential rate applicable to imports from countries that have signed trade agreements or treaties with China providing for lower tariff treatment. The general rates range from 8 to 180 per cent, while preferential rates range from 3 to 150 per cent.

Rates are set and adjusted on the basis of China's need for the commodities and the gap between their production costs in China and prices abroad.[135] Top-priority imports such as rice, wheat and maize, cooking oil, seeds, agricultural and animal goods, some special medicines, most printed matter, metal ores, gold, silver and platinum, crude oil, and astronomical and nautical instruments are exempt from import duty, while low duty rates of 3 to 20 per cent are imposed on other needed commodities such as non-exempt cereal grains, spices, beans, chemical fertilizers, pesticides, rubber, timber, paper pulp, certain rolled steel, industrial and farm machines, aircraft, rolling-stock, and trucks. Less crucial commodities and imports that can be produced in China are charged at higher rates, while the highest rates of all, currently 180 per cent general[136] and 150 per cent preferential, are applied to luxury items such as liquor, cosmetics, tobacco products, and edible delicacies.

In general, import duties are assessed on the basis of the CIF (cost, insurance, and freight) value. The Chinese Customs authorities calculate this amount on the basis of the wholesale price at the place the commodity was purchased, foreign export duties, and all packing, transport, insurance, and service expenses incurred before discharge at the port of importation.[137] If the foreign purchase price cannot be determined, the Customs office at the place of import is to assess the duty on the basis of the local wholesale price of similar goods (less import charges, taxes, and business expenses) or otherwise determine the dutiable value.[138]

Import duties are also levied at preferential rates on certain personal articles brought into China by passengers or through the mail. Rules issued in 1978[139] exempt printed matter and educational visual materials, contraceptives, gold, and silver, and tax 12 categories of foodstuffs, clothing, pharmaceuticals, electronic equipment, fabrics, and other items for daily use at rates ranging from 20 to 200 per cent. Most personal imports are also taxed on their CIF value. In September 1981, however, the Customs Administration announced that television sets, radio-recorders, and electronic computers brought in by individuals for private use will be taxed on the basis of the higher Chinese domestic retail prices in order to protect domestic production.[140]

Export duties are imposed on articles in excess of prescribed reasonable amounts taken out of China by overseas Chinese, foreigners residing in China, and Chinese nationals going abroad to visit relatives.[141]

China also levies tonnage dues on foreign vessels, Chinese vessels under foreign charter, and vessels owned or chartered by Chinese-foreign enterprises that call at Chinese ports.[142] Vessels under the flag of a country that has signed an agreement with China calling for most-favoured-nation treatment are subject to preferential rates. Tonnage dues, levied from the date of application for entry, may be paid for a period of three months or 30 days, at the option of the applicant. Those electing to pay on a monthly basis are charged at half the prescribed rates. Vessels used by diplomatic missions, vessels entering Chinese waters for 24 hours or less solely for purposes of repair or shelter and not unloading any cargo or passengers, and vessels requisitioned by, or under charter to, the central or local people's governments are exempt from tonnage dues.

C. Exemptions: Special Provisions for Foreign Investment, Assembly, and Compensation Trade

The 1951 Customs Law exempts or reduces otherwise payable import duties on the amount of goods lost or damaged during transport or during storage prior to Customs clearance, and on goods to be re-exported from China within six months.[143]

Advertising matter and trade samples without commercial value to be presented to Chinese units as gifts are also exempt from duty,[144] as well as from licensing requirements.

In addition, the Customs Administration has ruled that raw materials, spare parts, and necessary equipment imported by foreigners for processing, assembly, and small or medium-sized compensation trade transactions,[145] as well as machinery and equipment, spare parts, and raw materials brought in by foreigners as part of their investment in Chinese-foreign equity joint ventures or purchased with invested funds in accordance with their relevant contracts, may be exempted from import duty, as well as the Consolidated Commercial and Industrial Tax (hereafter cited as the Consolidated Tax), which is imposed on imports together with the customs duty.[146] Moreover, a Chinese-foreign joint venture may apply to the Ministry of Finance and the Customs Administration for exemption from the import duty and Consolidated Tax applicable to raw and other materials, spare parts, components, accessories, and packaging materials imported specifically to produce export commodities.[147] However, if any portion of such joint venture products made for export is for any reason instead sold on the domestic Chinese market, it will be subject retroactively to import duty (and the Consolidated Tax) on the raw materials, parts, and other items originally exempted.[148] Export commodities produced in connection with processing, assembly, and compensation trade, and by Chinese-foreign joint ventures may also be exempted from any otherwise applicable export duty.[149]

In 1979 the Chinese government issued special procedures, which apparently were implemented on a trial basis, for handling goods imported and exported in connection with processing and assembly for foreign customers.[150] These have been superseded in part by similar Customs rules concerning factories engaged in processing only, effective from 1 January 1984.[151] Pursuant to the more detailed 1979 Processing Procedures, the Chinese enterprise or NFTC concerned should file the appropriate certificate of approval of the transaction, a copy of the contract, and any required licence with the local Customs office within five days of signing the contract.[152] The Chinese party should then fill out a schedule of the commodities to be imported and the finished goods to be exported, and the Customs office will issue a registration booklet reflecting that information. This registration booklet, together with the normal customs declaration forms and other documentation, such as invoices or bills of lading, will be used as the basis for clearing the items without duty upon import and export. After full performance of the contract, the booklet must be handed in for cancellation. Under both sets of provisions all finished goods, as well as left-over materials and parts, must in principle be exported. Except in special circumstances, they may not be sold domestically or turned over to the foreign customer in China. The 1984 Processing Provisions also require registration of the materials imported and cancellation of such registration once the finished goods are exported. If they are in fact disposed of domestically, the normal import duty and licensing requirements will apply retroactively.[153]

Article 118 of the Customs Law also permits applications for exemption from customs duty in unspecified circumstances other than those described above. For example, imports of advanced technology and machinery samples approved by the state and of equipment, tools, and materials for developing China's special economic zones may under current regulations be exempted from the Consolidated Tax.[154] Since the import duty is generally collected by the Customs authorities together with the Consolidated Tax on imports at the point of entry of the goods, it is reasonable to assume that the above commodities may also be exempted, upon application, from the import duty. Similarly, certain goods and materials imported by a Chinese-foreign co-operative venture (as opposed to an equity joint venture) as part of the foreign partner's initial or additional investment may be exempted from import duties and the Consolidated Tax.[155]

In addition, special Customs rules applicable to representative offices of foreign enterprises and all resident foreign business staff in China (other than in the special economic zones) were promulgated in 1984.[156] Resident foreign staff are allowed to bring into China one shipment of personal effects (in reasonable quantities) after obtaining a residence permit. Imports of restricted goods, such as electrical appliances, in excess of allowable quantities will be permitted provided that applicable import duties are paid on the excess. The shipment of personal articles must be imported within six months of approval by the Customs. Office articles can be imported, without obtaining any otherwise required import licence but subject to the payment of customs duty, if they are imported in reasonable quantities and are intended to be used solely by the registered office concerned.

Finally, import duty on materials and equipment imported into China using funds provided by a medium- to low-interest foreign government loan or a mixed loan including an export credit may be exempted pursuant to the unpublished Supplementary Notification of the General Administration of Customs and MOFERT Concerning the Question of the Levy of and Exemption from Tax in the Utilization of Foreign Government Loans for the Import of Goods, even if the goods produced using such imported materials and equipment are not exported.[157]

D. Special Customs Provisions with Respect to the Co-operative Chinese-Foreign Exploitation of Offshore Oil in China

The Customs Administration and the Ministry of Finance have jointly issued special rules exempting from customs duties most imports of machinery, equipment, spare parts, components, and materials for direct use in the exploration for and co-operative Chinese-foreign development and exploitation of offshore oil, as well as machinery and other engineering equipment temporarily imported for exploration and guaranteed by the foreign petroleum contractors to be re-exported.[158] Crude oil received and exported by the foreign contractors is exempted from export duty, although crude oil is subject to payment of a 5 per cent Consolidated Tax and to export licensing procedures.

The Customs Administration has also exempted from customs duties the personal luggage and all household articles brought into China in one shipment by foreign personnel hired by foreign oil companies to work in China for more than one year.[159] Each employee is permitted to bring in one private car, subject to customs duty, and postal articles and personal baggage taken in or out of China during his residence in China will be handled in accordance with normal customs regulations, described above. The baggage and articles brought in by foreign employees working in China for less than one year are also to be handled in accordance with customs procedures regarding passengers coming to China for a short visit.

V. Conclusion

At this stage in the reform and decentralization of China's foreign trade system, although many new regulations have recently been promulgated, much confusion and uncertainty is evident. Some of the present rules for regulating foreign trade activity are incomplete or outdated or, like the 1951 Customs Law, are in the process of being revised; and many are not always implemented in a consistent manner.

The confusion exists for both Chinese and foreign parties. On the Chinese side, the rapid growth of foreign trade and dispersal of trading authority in recent years have brought many inexperienced Chinese personnel on to the scene, and some uncertainty on the part of all Chinese participants concerning the proper procedures and lines of authority seems inevitable during this period of structural and legislative reform. On the foreign side, the decentralization of foreign trade activity seems to afford greater opportunities for finding a variety of Chinese trade partners and bypassing the traditionally centralized and slow negotiation and approval process for concluding trade contracts. On the other hand, the increasing number of potential partners may make it more difficult or time consuming to locate appropriate Chinese parties, and the inexperience of the Chinese personnel involved may lead to some initial delays or errors due to lack of understanding of the complex trade procedures and restrictions.

The Chinese government is well aware of the present confusion and is striving to streamline the cumbersome system, train sufficient numbers of competent personnel, formulate or revise the necessary legislation, and strike the right balance between central direction and local initiative. The

Chinese are reported to be drafting a comprehensive foreign trade law but have not yet determined precisely what its scope and content will be.

In the reform process, China must also seek to balance domestic protectionism against its desire for free access to foreign markets. All nations, to one extent or another, employ some restrictive trade devices, such as tariff barriers, import quotas, licensing procedures, product standards and testing requirements, complex customs procedures, and direct or indirect subsidies to protect and control their domestic economies. As China's foreign trade activity has increased, China itself has encountered some difficulties in dealing with trade barriers imposed by other nations and has demonstrated its willingness to work toward mutual limitation of disruptive trade practices through entering into bilateral trade agreements and participating in various international trade forums, including its recent entry into the GATT textile arrangement and participation in the multinational Customs Co-operation Council.

China's current quest to achieve a dynamic but manageable foreign trade system is not unusual in international experience. All nations continually reorganize their trade institutions and their operative policies and rules to adapt to the ever-changing domestic and international economic situation. What may distinguish China in this regard is that it has only recently abandoned its commitment to self-reliance and truly 'opened the door' to foreign trade and investment. With China's decision to make expanded foreign trade a cornerstone of its economic development plan, the foreign trade system established in the 1950s to handle a relatively small amount of import and export activity needs a basic renovation. This process is certain to require several years and the acquisition of considerable practical experience.

Notes

1. The Ministry of Foreign Economic Relations and Trade reported that total exports and imports in 1985 amounted to a record US$59.21 billion, some 19 per cent up from the 1984 figure of US$49.97 billion. *China Daily*, 23 January 1986, p. 1. According to the PRC State Statistical Bureau, total two-way trade was even higher, about US$69.62 billion, or a jump of 30 per cent over 1984. *Xinhua News Bulletin* (Beijing), 1 March 1986, p. 21. During the period of the Sixth Five-Year Plan (1981–5), total foreign trade was targeted to reach US$57.4 billion, and China's former Minister of Foreign Economic Relations and Trade, Chen Muhua, has announced China's ambitious goal to quadruple its import and export volume by the year 2000, to reach some US$160 billion. *Xinhua News Bulletin* (Beijing), 20 September 1982, p. 22.

2. Editorial Board of the Almanac of China's Foreign Economic Relations and Trade, *1985 Almanac of China's Foreign Economic Relations and Trade* (Hong Kong, China Resources Trade Consultancy Co., 1985), notes to sketch map before table of contents (hereafter cited as the *1985 Trade Almanac*).

3. See A. Lee, 'Foreign Trade Decentralization: Its Origin and Future', *China Trader*, Vol. 4, June 1981, p. 66.

4. Guangdong province imported approximately US$1.1 billion, and Fujian province US$240 million, worth of foreign goods in 1984, while Beijing imported

US$256 million, Tianjin US$233 million, and Shanghai a total of US$800 million worth of foreign goods. *Business China*, 7 November 1985, pp. 166–7.

5. *Business China*, 7 November 1985, p. 164.

6. J.R. Shen, 'China's Import and Export Licensing System', *China's Foreign Trade*, No. 4, 1983, p. 6.

7. See D.C. Wang, 'Reforming the Foreign Trade Structure', *Beijing Review*, No. 43, 22 October 1984, p. 4; R. Delfs, 'Reverse for Full Ahead', *Far Eastern Economic Review*, 11 October 1984, p. 84; and extracts from MOFERT 'Report on Reform of the Foreign Trade System' of 14 August 1984, in *1985 Trade Almanac*, p. 388, note 2 above.

8. Regulations on Import and Export Duties of the People's Republic of China, in General Office of the Customs General Administration of the People's Republic of China, *The Official Chinese Customs Guide 1985/86* (London, Longman Group Ltd., 1985), p. 34 (hereafter cited as the *Customs Guide*).

9. *Renmin ribao* (*People's Daily*) (Beijing), 23 February 1983, p. 1.

10. *China's Foreign Trade*, No. 1, 1983, p. 11; and *China Market*, No. 4, April 1983, p. 11.

11. *Ta kung pao* (Hong Kong), 3 August 1982, p. 2.

12. *Shijie jingji daobao* (*World Economic Herald*) (Shanghai), 21 February 1983, p. 1 (hereafter cited as the *World Economic Herald*); and *Ta kung pao* (Hong Kong), 2 August 1982, p. 4.

13. The establishment of local import and export commissions directly responsible to the province, special municipality, or autonomous region that set them up to oversee all trade activity within their respective jurisdictions was first reported during 1980. Although they apparently still exist, the official literature on China's trade system does not specifically describe them or differentiate them from local foreign trade departments or bureaux, and they do not engage in actual trade transactions themselves. See, for example, T.A. Gelatt, 'Delegation Report from Chengdu', *Amcham* (Journal of the American Chamber of Commerce in Hong Kong), Vol. 19, October 1982, p. 14.

14. N. Ludlow, 'China's New Foreign Trade Structure', *China Business Review*, May–June 1982, p. 31.

15. 'Major Reform of Foreign Trade System', *China's Foreign Trade*, No. 2, 1985, p. 6.

16. A complete list of the NFTCs as constituted in 1982 can be found in China Council for the Promotion of International Trade, *China's Foreign Trade Corporations and Organizations* (Beijing, China Council for the Promotion of International Trade, 1983 edition). A more recent list can be found in Policy Research Department, Ministry of Foreign Economic Relations and Trade (ed.), *Guide to China's Foreign Economic Relations and Trade: Import-Export Special* (Hong Kong, Economic Information and Agency, 1984), p. 389 (hereafter cited as the *Import-Export Guide*).

17. National Council for US–China Trade, *China Business Manual* (Washington, DC, National Council for US–China Trade, 1981), p. 73 (hereafter cited as the *China Business Manual*). A highly placed foreign trade official privately informed the author that the head offices and branches of the NFTCs must register to obtain business licences with the State Administration for Industry and Commerce and may also have to register with the local tax authorities, although at present they appear to be exempt from taxation. *Xinhua News Bulletin*, 27 April 1983, p. 58.

18. China National Technology Import Corporation (TECHIMPORT), for example, has organized three companies of its own: the International Tendering Company (TECHTENDER), the Spare Parts and Components Company, and the Technology Trading Consultancy Company, descriptions of which appear in *Business China*, 24 January 1985, p. 13.

19. *China Daily* (Beijing), 20 September 1984, p. 1; extracts from the

MOFERT Report on Reform of the Foreign Trade System and the State Council approval thereof are given in *1985 Trade Almanac*, p. 388, note 2 above.

20. The State Council has organized several specialized national corporations to handle production and trade in certain industries. For example, the China Non-ferrous Metals Industry Corporation, a conglomerate directly under the State Council, through its subsidiary, the China Non-ferrous Metals Import and Export Corporation, is responsible for the import and export of non-ferrous and rare metals (China International Economic Consultants, Inc., *The China Investment Guide 1984/85* (London, Longman Group Ltd., 1984), p. 281 (hereafter cited as the *Investment Guide*); and the China National Tobacco Corporation is responsible for the centralized import and export of tobacco and tobacco products, equipment, and technology. *Investment Guide*, p. 294.

21. Article 28 of the 1983 Interim Regulations on State-owned Industrial Enterprises specifies that enterprises have the right to apply to export their products, to participate in trade talks together with the Chinese foreign trade agencies and to sign contracts with foreign firms, and to retain a share of the foreign exchange so earned. W.W.S. Lo, A.H.M. Wong, L.W.H. Wong, and W.H. Ming (eds.), *Commercial Laws & Business Regulations of the People's Republic of China* (Hong Kong, Tai Dao Publishing Ltd., 1984), Vol. II, pp. 35–6 (hereafter cited as *Commercial Laws, Vol. II*).

22. *World Economic Herald*, 13 December 1982, pp. 1–2, note 12 above. Another Chinese newspaper put the figure at more than 740 enterprises and departments, including some 480 engaged in export trade. *Guoji jingji xiaoxi (International Economic News)* (Beijing), 6 January 1983, p. 1.

23. Wang, note 7 above.

24. Speech by Jia Shi, a vice-minister of MOFERT, portions of which are reproduced in Ta kung pao, *China Handbook* (Hong Kong, Ta kung pao, 1982 edition), p. 539 (hereafter cited as the *China Handbook*).

25. Provisional Procedures for the Control of Imports by Localities in Foreign Trade, described in *China Economic News*, 13 October 1980, p. 2; and *China Economic News*, 14 October 1985, p. 6 (centralization of export of pearls in China National Arts and Crafts Import and Export Corporation).

26. Provisional Procedures for the Control of Imports in Foreign Trade, described in *China Economic News*, 13 October 1980, p. 2; and in Xinhua Publishing House, *The China Directory of Industry and Commerce and Economic Annual* (Beijing, Xinhua Publishing House, and Boston, Science Books International, Inc., 1982–3), p. EA-25 (hereafter cited as the *China Directory*).

27. China's Foreign Trade, Editorial Department, *China Trade Guide* (1980), p. 14 (hereafter cited as the *China Trade Guide*).

28. L. Edinger, 'Who Needs an FTC?', *Amcham*, Vol. 19, June 1982, p. 34.

29. *China Trade Guide*, p. 15, note 27 above. Some bureaux are called 'departments' and others 'commissions', but they all appear to function in the same manner.

30. *China Trade Guide*, p. 15, note 27 above.

31. V.K. Fung, 'China's Decentralization of Foreign Trade', *Asian Wall Street Journal*, 24 November 1982, p. 6; and *Wen wei po* (Hong Kong), 7 November 1982, p. 1. According to some reports, eliminating the need to go through the national foreign trade corporations may nearly halve the time required to fulfil an export contract. See, for example, *People's Daily*, 18 April 1983, p. 2 (article on the Beijing Silk Flower Factory). See, also, 'State gives firms new trade rights', *China Daily* (Beijing), 18 January 1986, p. 2 (about 130 state industrial enterprises being given the authority to handle trade independently).

32. *Ta kung pao* (Hong Kong), 19 April 1985, p. 2; see, also, a discussion of the role of enterprises in the reformed foreign trade system in MOFERT 'Report on Reform of the Foreign Trade System', *1985 Trade Almanac*, p. 390, note 2 above.

33. 'Export firms list out soon', *South China Morning Post, Business News*, 22 April 1986, p. 5.

34. *China Trade Guide*, p. 87, note 27 above.

35. *China Business Manual*, p. 68, note 17 above.

36. For more details, see *China Trade Guide*, p. 93, note 27 above; and C.J. Liu and L.S. Wang, *China's Foreign Trade: Its Policy and Practice* (San Francisco, CTPS-USA (S.F.) Inc., 1980), pp. 29–32.

37. Liu and Wang, pp. 37–9, note 36 above; and *China Handbook*, pp. 556–8, note 24 above.

38. A list of prohibited imports and exports may be found in *Customs Guide*, p. 237, note 8 above.

39. Interim Procedures of the State Import-Export Commission and the Ministry of Foreign Trade of the People's Republic of China Concerning the System of Export Licensing (hereafter cited as the Export Licensing Procedures), promulgated on 3 June 1980, and translated in Foreign Languages Press, *China's Foreign Economic Legislation* (Beijing, Foreign Languages Press, 1982), Vol. I, p. 182. These procedures reportedly are currently under revision to make the licensing process simpler and more efficient. Provisional Regulations for the Control of Foreign Trade, promulgated soon after Liberation on 8 December 1950, had required all organizations and individuals engaged in foreign trade to obtain import and export licences for designated goods. The 1950 Provisional Regulations and interim implementing rules on licensing were replaced in 1957 with the Procedures for Issuing Licences for Import and Export Goods, in Falu chubanshe (Legal Publishing House), *Zhonghua renmin gongheguo fagui huibian (Compilation of Legislation of the People's Republic of China)* (January–June 1957), Vol. 5, p. 168 (Beijing, Falu chubanshe (Legal Publishing House), 1981 edition). These procedures also required that the specialized foreign trade corporations, then established under the Ministry of Foreign Trade, and all other Chinese units, private merchants, and foreign businessmen obtain export and import licences for listed commodities. However, with the consolidation of the foreign trade apparatus in 1956, under which the foreign trade corporations achieved a virtual monopoly on foreign trade, the foreign trade corporations were deemed to have obtained the required licences, and the licensing system apparently fell into disuse until it was revived in 1980 in order to regulate the activities of the growing number of other authorized trading units.

40. Art. 1.

41. Art. 3. These entities file their business licences, which specify their authorized scope of business activity, with the Customs Administration, which enforces the licensing system.

42. *Asian Wall Street Journal*, 1 September 1982, p. 3.

43. *Guoji shangbao (International Commercial Journal)*, 17 February 1986, p. 2 (hereafter cited as the *International Commercial Journal*). Of these 235 commodities, MOFERT controls licensing for 32, the special trade commissioners handle licences for 42, and the provincial, autonomous regional, and special municipal trade bureaux are authorized to issue licences for the remaining 161.

44. Lists with translations of these 48 commodities were carried in several publications. See, for example, *China Business Report*, April 1982, p. 9; and *China Market*, No. 8, August 1982, p. 74.

45. *Zhongguo caimaobao (China's Finance and Trade Journal)*, 3 August 1982, p. 1.

46. *Xinhua News Bulletin*, 15 April 1983, pp. 18–19.

47. *China Economic News*, 2 April 1984, p. 2.

48. Licences for these four commodities are needed only for exports to the Hong Kong and Macau regions and Japan. *China Economic News*, 2 April 1984, p. 2.

49. *China Economic News*, 7 October 1985, p. 3.

50. 'Licenses ensure orderly exports', *China Daily*, 12 March 1986, p. 2; see, also, note 43 above.

51. See, for example, *Hong Kong Business Standard*, 19 June 1982, p. 1; and *China Market Intelligence*, June 1983, p. 1.

52. Export Licensing Procedures, Art. 4, note 39 above.

53. Export Licensing Procedures, Art. 5, note 39 above.

54. Such commodities currently include maize, canned mushrooms, mushrooms in salt water, cotton yarn, grey cotton fabrics, grey polyester cotton fabrics, polyester cotton yarn, cotton, angora, cashmere, crude oil and oil products, tungsten and tungsten products, coal, internal combustion machines and other machines for farm use, silk, leather work gloves, and satin. *China Economic News*, 29 April 1985, p. 6; and *International Commercial Journal*, 7 October 1985, p. 2, note 43 above.

55. *China Economic News*, 11 October 1982, p. 2.

56. *China Economic News*, 11 October 1982, p. 2; and *International Commercial Journal*, 7 October 1985, p. 2, note 43 above.

57. See *China Economic News*, 29 April 1985, p. 6; and *International Commercial Journal*, 7 October 1985, p. 2, note 43 above.

58. *Ta kung pao* (Hong Kong), 28 February 1982, p. 3.

59. Export Licensing Procedures, Art. 6, note 39 above.

60. Export Licensing Procedures, Art. 7, note 39 above.

61. *China Directory*, p. EA-24, note 26 above. See, for example, *Waimao zhishi shouce (Foreign Trade Handbook)* (Tianjin, Tianjin Science and Technology Publishing House, second edition, 1981), pp. 515–16 (hereafter cited as the *Foreign Trade Handbook*), which states that the Import Procedures were issued on 26 August 1980, together with the procedures governing imports by localities. See note 25 above.

62. *Commercial Laws, Vol. II*, p. 191, note 21 above.

63. *Commercial Laws, Vol. II*, p. 194, note 21 above.

64. *Xinhua News Bulletin*, 11 October 1982, p. 33.

65. Interview with Sun Chun, *China Economic News*, 12 October 1981, p. 2.

66. *China Daily* (Beijing), 12 October 1982, p. 2; *World Economic Herald*, 13 December 1982, p. 2, note 12 above; and *Business China*, 10 October 1985, p. 145.

67. *Foreign Trade Handbook*, p. 516, note 61 above. The commodities requiring a special import licence include: cars, tourist buses, tool trucks, jeeps, small tonnage passenger-cargo vehicles, motorcycles and bicycles; television sets, television-picture tubes, radio sets, radio recorders, complete sets of video-recording equipment and video recorders; household refrigerators, sewing machines, and washing machines; cameras, photographs, and electric fans; copying machines, electronic computers and calculators, recording and video tape duplication equipment; and certain chemical fibres and fabrics. *China Economic News*, 11 October 1982, p. 2.

68. *Commercial Laws, Vol. II*, pp. 198–9, note 21 above.

69. *Business China*, 10 October 1985, p. 147.

70. *China Daily Business Weekly* (New York), 5 March 1986, p. 3.

71. *Business China*, 10 October 1985, pp. 145–7.

72. *Wen wei po* (Hong Kong), 13 August 1985, p. 8.

73. A list of designated controlled goods is to be published annually by the State Planning Commission, and imports of controlled goods will require the approval of the said Commission. Import Licensing Rules, Art. 6, note 63 above.

74. Import Licensing Regulations, Art. 5, note 62 above; and Import Licensing Rules, Arts. 5 and 17, note 63 above.

75. Import Licensing Regulations, Art. 7, note 62 above; and Import Licensing Rules, Arts. 7 and 16, note 63 above.

76. Import Licensing Regulations, Art. 9, note 62 above; and the Implementing Act for the Law of the People's Republic of China on Joint Ventures Using

Chinese and Foreign Investment (hereafter cited as the JV Regulations), Art. 63, in *China Economic News*, Supplement No. 4, 3 October 1983.

77. Import Licensing Regulations, Art. 10, note 62 above.

78. *China Economic News*, 12 October 1981, p. 2; and V.K. Fung, 'China Reasserts its Ban on Trade with 3 Nations', *Asian Wall Street Journal*, 1 September 1982, p. 3.

79. 'Statement by Spokesman of the Customs Administration Concerning Customs Procedures and Taxation of Commerce between the Mainland and Taiwan', *Zhonghua renmin gongheguo guowuyuan gongbao (State Council Gazette)*, 28 May 1980, p. 120 (hereafter cited as the *State Council Gazette*); V.K. Fung, 'China Curbs Imports of Taiwan Products', *Asian Wall Street Journal*, 24 February 1982, p. 1; and V.K. Fung, 'China Begins Imposing Tax on All Imports from Taiwan', *Asian Wall Street Journal*, 30 March 1983, p. 1.

80. Import Licensing Rules, Art. 14, note 63 above.

81. Import Licensing Regulations, Art. 3, note 62 above; and Import Licensing Rules, Art. 3, note 63 above.

82. Import Licensing Regulations, Art. 11, note 62 above.

83. Import Licensing Regulations, Art. 12, note 62 above; and Import Licensing Rules, Art. 12, note 63 above.

84. Interview with Shen Jueren, *World Economic Herald*, 13 December 1982, p. 2, note 12 above.

85. *China Business Report*, April 1982, p. 9.

86. Import Licensing Rules, Art. 2, note 63 above.

87. See, also, J.R. Shen, 'China's Import and Export Licensing System', *China's Foreign Trade*, No. 4, 1983, p. 7. Mr Shen, who is the Director of the Foreign Trade Administration Department of MOFERT, also states: 'If a Chinese enterprise fails to obtain a licence for unjustifiable reasons, it will be held responsible for all consequences arising therefrom'.

88. Regulations of the People's Republic of China on the Inspection of Import and Export Commodities, Art. 2, note 91 below.

89. Provisional Regulations on the Inspection and Testing of Import and Export Commodities, effective from 3 January 1954, in *China Trade Guide*, p. 101, note 27 above.

90. General Administration of Import and Export Commodity Inspection, *Import and Export Commodity Inspection in China* (Beijing, General Administration of Import and Export Commodity Inspection, 1981), pp. 1–2; and Notice of the State Administration for Import and Export Commodities of the People's Republic of China, 28 January 1983 (on file with the author).

91. Promulgated by the State Council on 28 January 1984 (hereafter cited as the Inspection Regulations); see, also, the Detailed Rules for the Implementation of the Regulations on the Inspection of Import and Export Commodities (hereafter cited as the Inspection Rules), promulgated by the SACI on 1 June 1984. English translations of these documents can be found in *China Economic News*, 27 February 1984, p. 8, and 17 December 1984, p. 5, respectively.

92. See, for example, Regulations of the People's Republic of China on the Quarantine of Animal and Plant Imports and Exports, promulgated by the State Council on 4 June 1982, in *State Council Gazette*, 25 July 1982, p. 503, note 79 above, and a list of objects subject to plant and animal quarantine in *China Economic News*, 31 December 1984, p. 7; the Measures of the People's Republic of China for the Hygienic Control of Foodstuffs for Export, promulgated by the SACI on 16 July 1984, an English language description of which appears in *China Economic News*, 11 February 1985; the Measures for Inspection of Ships' Holds Carrying Cereals, Oils, Foodstuffs and Frozen Products for Export in *China Economic News*, 2 July 1984, p. 1, effective from 1 July 1984; and Measures for the Inspection of Containers for Shipment, in *China Daily*, 7 July 1984, p. 2, also effective from 1 July 1984.

93. Inspection Regulations, Art. 20, note 91 above.

94. Inspection Regulations, Art. 23, note 91 above; and Inspection Rules, Art. 40, note 91 above.

95. See, also, Food Hygiene Law of the People's Republic of China (For Trial Implementation), approved on 19 November 1982, Art. 28 (concerning the inspection of imported food, additives, containers, packaging materials and tools and equipment used for food handling), in *East Asian Executive Reports*, Vol. 5, January 1983, Section A; and the Pharmaceutical Control Law of the People's Republic of China, approved on 20 September 1984, Art. 28 (concerning the inspection of imported pharmaceuticals) (text of the law and translation thereof on file with the author).

96. See Inspection Rules, Art. 7, note 91 above.

97. A recently published list can be found in *Import-Export Guide*, p. 524, note 16 above.

98. *Xinhua News Bulletin*, 28 September 1985, p. 58; and *Jingji cankao (Economic Reference)*, 30 September 1985, p. 7.

99. *Foreign Trade Handbook*, p. 517, note 61 above.

100. See, for further details, *China Trade Guide*, pp. 101–3, note 27 above; and Liu and Wang, pp. 108–12, note 36 above.

101. Liu and Wang, p. 112, note 36 above.

102. *China Market*, No. 8, August 1982, p. 37.

103. *China Market*, No. 8, August 1982, p. 37.

104. For the addresses of these offices, see *China Trade Guide*, pp. 114–16, note 27 above.

105. *China Market*, No. 8, August 1982, p. 39.

106. Provisional Customs Law of the People's Republic of China (hereafter cited as the Customs Law) promulgated on 18 April 1951, Art. 2, in *Customs Guide*, p. 11, note 8 above.

107. Zhonghua renmin gongheguo haiguan zongshu (General Administration of Customs of the People's Republic of China), *Zhongguo haiguan fagui shouce (Handbook of China's Customs Regulations)* (Hong Kong, Wen wei po, 1982), pp. 13–14 (chart), (hereafter cited as the *Customs Handbook*); and Charts 1.1 (Organization and Structure of the Chinese Customs) and 1.2 (List of Customs Houses), in *Customs Guide*, pp. 3–5, note 8 above.

108. 'China Joins Customs Co-operation Council', *Xinhua News Bulletin*, 3 August 1983, p. 8.

109. *China Trade Guide*, p. 119, note 27 above; and Liu and Wang, p. 132, note 36 above.

110. *China Trade Guide*, p. 120, note 27 above; and Liu and Wang, p. 133, note 36 above.

111. Provisional Procedures for the Supervision and Control of Import and Export Containers and their Contents, issued by the Customs Administration on 29 June 1981, effective from 1 August 1981, in *Customs Guide*, p. 208, note 8 above.

112. Liu and Wang, p. 134, note 36 above.

113. Liu and Wang, p. 134, note 36 above.

114. Procedures for the Supervision and Control by Customs of Goods Imported for Exhibition, promulgated by the Ministry of Foreign Trade, and effective from 3 November 1975, an English translation of which can be found in *Customs Guide*, p. 214, note 8 above. See, also, Procedures for Holding Exhibitions in China, in *Import-Export Guide*, p. 604, note 16 above.

115. Liu and Wang, p. 133, note 36 above; and *China Trade Guide*, p. 120, note 27 above. See, also, Regulations Governing the Supervision and Control over, and Duty Collection on, Inward and Outward Samples and Advertising Products, effective from 1 July 1982, in *Customs Guide*, p. 209, note 8 above.

116. Provisional Procedures of the Customs of the People's Republic of China

for the Supervision and Control of Bonded Cargo and Bonded Warehouses, issued by the General Administration of Customs on 10 February 1981, and effective from 1 March 1981, in *Customs Guide*, p. 211, note 8 above.

117. See Rules of the Customs of the People's Republic of China Governing Supervision and Control over Bonded Factories for Inward Processing of Imported Parts and Materials, effective from 1 January 1984, in *Customs Guide*, p. 212, note 8 above. See, also, the description of the 1979 Procedures for Developing Processing, Assembly and Small and Medium-scale Compensation Trade with Foreign Interests, in *Wen wei po* (Hong Kong), 8 October 1982, p. 4.

118. See the following rules of the Chinese Customs, issued by the former Ministry of Foreign Trade, the English texts of which appear in *Customs Guide*, note 8 above: (a) Procedures for the Supervision and Control of Vessels Engaged in International Navigation and Cargo Carried thereon (31 December 1958); (b) Procedures for the Supervision and Control of Railway Trains Leaving and Entering Chinese Territory and the Cargo, Passenger Baggage and Parcels Carried thereon (5 November 1958), co-issued with the Ministry of Railways; (c) Provisional Procedures for the Supervision and Control of Motor Vehicles Entering and Leaving Chinese Territory and Cargo Carried thereon (29 August 1963); (d) Procedures for the Supervision and Control of International Civil Aircraft (1 October 1974); and (e) Procedures for the Supervision and Control of Small-scale Vessels Coming from or Going to Hong Kong and Macau (10 July 1958).

119. Customs Guide for Passengers Entering and Leaving the People's Republic of China, in *China Trade Guide*, pp. 137–9, note 27 above. See, also, the following customs regulations in *Customs Guide*: (a) Regulations Governing the Import and Export of Articles by Foreign Diplomatic Missions in China and their Officers (1 January 1977); (b) Regulations Governing the Declaration of Articles Imported and Exported by Foreign Diplomatic Missions in China and their Officers (1 January 1977); (c) Regulations Concerning the Import and Export of Articles by Resident Offices and their Staff of Foreign Enterprises and Press in China (20 April 1984); (d) Provisions for the Supervision of Luggage and Articles Carried into and out of China by Overseas Chinese who Return Home to Visit their Relatives (28 November 1983); (e) Regulations for Control over Baggage of Passengers Coming from or Going to Hong Kong and Macau (1 July 1979), promulgated by the former Ministry of Foreign Trade; (f) Regulations Governing Supervision and Control over Inward and Outward Postal Articles (Revised) (25 September 1984); (g) Regulations Governing Supervision and Control over Personal Postal Articles Sent to or from Hong Kong and Macau (Revised) (25 September 1984); (h) Regulations Governing Control over Inward and Outward Articles Brought in or Posted by Overseas Chinese Students and Students from Hong Kong and Macau Studying on China's Mainland (20 August 1984); and (i) Customs Notice to Foreign Tourists (24 February 1982).

120. *China Trade Guide*, p. 138, note 27 above; see, also, Regulations of the General Administration of Customs and the People's Bank of China for Carrying Gold or Silver into or out of China (effective from 15 February 1984), in *Customs Guide*, p. 229, note 8 above.

121. *China Trade Guide*, p. 138, note 27 above; see, also, Customs Regulations Governing Control over Outward Cultural Relics Carried or Shipped by Passengers and Posted by Individuals (15 February 1985), in *Customs Guide*, p. 230, note 8 above.

122. *China Trade Guide*, p. 139, note 27 above.

123. Procedures of the People's Republic of China Concerning the Levy of Import Duty on Articles in Passengers' Baggage and Personal Postal Articles, approved by the State Council on 16 June 1978, and put into force by the former Ministry of Foreign Trade on 1 August 1978, in *China Trade Guide*, pp. 132–3,

note 27 above; see, also, Customs Regulations Governing Supervision and Control over Inward and Outward Postal Articles (25 September 1984), in *Customs Guide*, p. 225, note 8 above.

124. *China Trade Guide*, p. 120, note 27 above; and Liu and Wang, p. 135, note 36 above.

125. *China Daily* (Beijing), 1 January 1982, p. 1.

126. The Regulations on Import and Export Duties of the People's Republic of China, in *Customs Guide*, p. 34, note 8 above (hereafter cited as the Duty Regulations). The Duty Regulations and attached Customs Import and Export Tariff Rate Schedule (hereafter cited as the Tariff Rate Schedule) replace the Import and Export Duty Rates of the Customs of the People's Republic of China, effective from 16 May 1951, in *Customs Handbook*, pp. 49–129, note 107 above; and the Provisional Implementing Regulations of the Customs of the People's Republic of China Concerning Import and Export Duties, approved on 4 May 1951, English text in China International Economic Consultants, Inc., and Economic Information & Consultancy Co. (eds.), *Guide to Investment in China* (Hong Kong, Economic Information and Agency, 1982), pp. 152–6.

127. Customs Law, Art. 116, note 106 above; and Duty Regulations, Art. 14, note 126 above.

128. *Business China*, 16 June 1982, p. 86.

129. *China Daily* (Beijing), 1 January 1982, p. 1.

130. *Xinhua News Bulletin* (Beijing), 7 March 1985, p. 2.

131. Z. Li, 'Adjustment of China's Policy on the Customs', *China's Foreign Trade*, No. 6, 1982, p. 5. Adjusted rates are set forth in the Tariff Rate Schedule, note 126 above.

132. Li, p. 5, note 131 above.

133. *Jingji ribao (Economic Daily)*, 7 March 1985, pp. 3–4. For example, the preferential rate on steel was reduced from 35 per cent to 15 per cent, paper from 7.5 per cent to 3 per cent, and telex machinery from 12.5 to 9 per cent.

134. *Journal of Commerce*, 16 July 1985, p. 2; and *China Daily Business Weekly* (New York), 31 July 1985, p. 2.

135. H. Xue, 'Inside China's Tariff System', *China Business Review*, September–October 1981, p. 52. Pursuant to Article 3 of the Duty Regulations, note 126 above, a Tariff Commission comprised of the General Administration of Customs, MOFERT, the Ministry of Finance, the State Planning Commission, the State Economic Commission, and other relevant departments is to set and adjust import and export duties.

136. This top rate was reduced in 1985 from the previous rate of 250 per cent.

137. Customs Law, Art. 115, note 106 above; and Duty Regulations, Art. 9, note 126 above.

138. Duty Regulations, Art. 10, note 126 above.

139. Procedures of the People's Republic of China Concerning the Levy of Import Duties on Articles in Passengers' Baggage and Personal Postal Articles, effective from 1 August 1978, in *China Trade Guide*, pp. 132–3, note 27 above.

140. *Xinhua News Bulletin*, 26 September 1981, p. 22.

141. Provisional Rules of the Customs of the People's Republic of China for the Supervision and Control of Articles in Baggage of Incoming and Outgoing Overseas Chinese and other Passengers, effective from 5 April 1978, in *China Trade Guide*, pp. 134–6, note 27 above.

142. Provisional Procedures of the Customs of the People's Republic of China for Levying Tonnage Dues on Vessels, effective from 19 September 1952, in *China Trade Guide*, pp. 122–4, note 27 above.

143. Customs Law, Arts. 120–3, note 106 above.

144. Customs Law, Art. 121, note 106 above.

145. *Customs Handbook*, p. 149, note 107 above; see, also, Rules of Customs

Governing Supervision and Control over Bonded Factories that Process Imported Materials (hereafter cited as the 1984 Processing Provisions), effective from 1 January 1984, in *Customs Guide*, p. 212, note 8 above.

146. JV Regulations, Art. 71, note 76 above. MOFERT officials have also stated publicly and in writing that foreign investors that establish wholly foreign-owned enterprises in China may enjoy the same preferential treatment in respect of imports and exports that is accorded to equity joint ventures. See, for example, *China Economic News*, 17 September 1984, p. 1. See, also, Regulations of the General Administration of Customs, the Ministry of Finance and MOFERT Concerning the Supervision and Control over, and the Levying and Exemption of Duties on Imports and Exports of Chinese-Foreign Joint Ventures, effective from 1 May 1984, in *Customs Guide*, p. 183, note 8 above.

147. JV Regulations, Art. 71, note 76 above.

148. JV Regulations, Art. 71, note 76 above; see, also, *Customs Handbook*, p. 149, note 107 above; and Procedures for the Development of Processing, Assembly and Medium and Small-scale Compensation Trade (hereafter cited as the 1979 Processing Procedures), issued by the State Council on 3 September 1979 and reportedly being implemented in Shenzhen, Guangzhou, and Dongbei, described in *Wen wei po* (Hong Kong), 8 October 1982, p. 4; and (Trial) Customs Rules Relating to the Supervision and Control of and Levy of and Exemption from Customs Duty and Tax on Imports and Exports for Processing, Assembly and Medium and Small-scale Compensation Trade (undated) (hereafter cited as the Customs Processing Rules), in Zhao Chengbi (ed.), *Waimao shiwu shouce (Handbook of Practical Foreign Trade Work)* (Shenyang, Liaoning renmin chubanshe (Liaoning People's Publishing House), 1982), pp. 553–5.

149. JV Regulations, Art. 72, note 76 above; 1979 Processing Procedures, para. 3, note 148 above; and Customs Processing Rules, Art. 3, note 148 above.

150. See note 148 above.

151. 1984 Processing Provisions, note 145 above.

152. 1979 Processing Procedures, para. 2, note 148 above; and *Customs Handbook*, p. 149, note 107 above. Except for those import and export commodities that MOFERT has designated as requiring a special licence and export commodities subject to a quota in the country of destination, materials, parts and equipment brought in for processing, assembly, or compensation trade, and the finished export products or compensation commodities, do not require a licence. *Customs Handbook*, p. 147, note 107 above; and the 1979 Processing Procedures, para. 3, note 148 above.

153. 1979 Processing Procedures, para. 5, note 148 above; 1984 Processing Provisions, Art. 3, note 145 above; and Customs Processing Rules, Art. 6, note 148 above.

154. Provisions of the Ministry of Finance Concerning the Levy of and Exemption from Industrial and Commercial Tax on Import and Export Commodities, approved by the State Council on 30 December 1980, effective from 1 January 1981, *State Council Gazette*, 1 March 1981, p. 15, note 79 above.

155. Provisions of the General Administration of Customs, the Ministry of Finance and MOFERT Concerning the Supervision of and Imposition of or Exemption from Tax on Imports and Exports by Chinese-Foreign Co-operative Ventures, effective from 1 February 1984, in *Commercial Laws, Vol. II.*, p. 252, note 21 above.

156. Regulations Concerning the Import and Export of Articles by Resident Offices and their Staff of Foreign Enterprises and Press in China, effective from 1 May 1984, in *Customs Guide*, p. 220, note 8 above.

157. Issued in June 1984. Information based on interviews with officials in MOFERT and the General Administration of Customs in December 1985.

158. Rules for the Levy and Exemption of Customs Duties and the Consolidated Industrial and Commercial Tax on Imports and Exports in Connection with the Chinese-Foreign Co-operative Exploitation of Offshore Petroleum,

approved by the State Council and promulgated on 1 April 1982 in General Office, Customs Administration of the People's Republic of China, *A Compilation of Regulations of Customs Control on Chinese-Foreign Co-operative Exploitation of Offshore Petroleum* (Beijing, General Office of the Customs Administration of the People's Republic of China, 1984), p. 49 (hereafter cited as the *Offshore Petroleum Guide*).

159. Customs Notice Concerning the Import of Personal Baggage and Articles by Staff of Foreign Oil Companies in Connection with the Chinese-Foreign Co-operative Exploitation of Offshore Petroleum, issued on 1 April 1982 (copy on file with the author), and Rules Governing Control over Inward and Outgoing Vessels and Goods for the Purpose of Chinese-Foreign Co-operative Exploitation of Offshore Petroleum and Personal Effects Belonging to Foreign Personnel Working in China, effective from 1 June 1984, in *Offshore Petroleum Guide*, p. 41, note 158 above.

2. China's Tax System: An Overview and Transactional Analysis

TIMOTHY A. GELATT AND RICHARD D. POMP

I. Introduction

As recently as 1979, the People's Republic of China had no systematic way of taxing foreign business. During the summer of that year, the Chinese invited several American tax professors to help initiate a group of China's tax officials into the arcane world of source rules, foreign tax credits, and tax treaties. Because the Chinese had, for so many years, been largely divorced from the Western legal, financial, and accounting professions, much of that summer was spent in bridging this gap. Today, however, Chinese officials converse fluently with foreigners about the merits of per-country limits versus overall limits on the foreign tax credit, the differences between the United Nations and the OECD model tax treaties, the attribution of income and expenses of foreign companies, and other complex tax issues. The sophistication with which foreign tax concepts are being absorbed and put to use in developing China's tax system represents a significant achievement by China's Ministry of Finance and provides a record of accomplishment for other Chinese organizations to emulate as they work to create a legal infrastructure for foreign business.

Since 1979, China, which has an extensive and complex domestic tax structure,[1] has adopted three major taxes affecting foreign business activity: the Individual Income Tax,[2] the Joint Venture Income Tax,[3] and the Foreign Enterprise Income Tax.[4] In addition, tax regimes have begun to be designed to cover investment in the Special Economic Zones (SEZs), and numerous other cities and areas in China designated as points of attraction for foreign investment. The major pieces of the Chinese tax system are now in place. The resulting structure comports well with generally accepted international practice and concepts, reflecting what Ministry of Finance officials had often told foreigners—that wherever possible, China would opt for membership in the mainstream of the international tax community.

A foreigner doing business in China now faces a situation similar to that encountered elsewhere: a variety of available business and investment vehicles, each with different tax consequences, creating opportunities for tax planning. The tax consequences of various activities, however, are not always obvious from a reading of the statutes or regulations. Initially, when China's new tax laws for foreign business had just been issued, foreigners had no choice but to speculate on the tax treatment of specific transactions with only the general and imprecise language of the statutes

as a guide. Foreigners quickly learned that the Chinese would not necessarily interpret their tax laws in the same manner as a Western-trained
lawyer. Rigorous statutory construction, no matter how logically im-
peccable or internally consistent, was not always persuasive in dealings
with tax officials, nor was it necessarily probative in predicting a transaction's treatment.

More recently, this state of uncertainty has given way to a body of
accumulated experience, as the tax authorities' administrative posture on
key issues has slowly emerged. Unfortunately, this administrative posture
is still often set forth in documents not available publicly and must be
gleaned from discussions with ranking officials and the collective experience of foreigners. None the less, while some fundamental questions remain unanswered, the tax consequences of common transactions can now
be described with a degree of accuracy not previously possible.

Tax planning for doing business in China is not only feasible but also
essential. Foreigners, however, should not necessarily pursue the opportunities that exist to minimize or eliminate their Chinese taxes. Whenever
the Chinese tax is fully creditable against its home country tax, a foreign
company should consider such potential benefits as the goodwill and increased business opportunities that might accrue from contributing to the
Chinese fisc. As the experience of certain multinationals in other countries demonstrates, a history of paying little or no tax, even if completely
legal, can stigmatize a company and ultimately prove detrimental to its
interests.

This chapter presents an overview of the tax structure generally applicable to foreign business. Part II analyses the individual income tax, the
industrial and commercial tax, the joint venture income tax, and the foreign enterprise income tax. Part III traces the effect of the major taxes
discussed in Part II on common forms of doing business in China, distill-
ing the interpretations and administrative practices of the tax authorities
in the context of common types of transactions, including representative
offices, compensation trade, co-operative ventures, and equity joint ventures. Part III thus applies on a transactional basis the analysis presented
in Part II.

II. An Overview of the Tax Structure for Foreign Business

A. The Individual Income Tax Law

i. Taxpayers
China's Individual Income Tax Law (IITL), passed on 10 September
1980,[5] follows the pattern used throughout the world by providing different tax treatment for non-residents and residents. Further, the treatment
of a resident varies depending on the length of his residency.
a. Residents for Less than One Year   An individual not residing in
China or an individual residing in China for less than one year is subject
to taxation on income gained within China.[6] The regulations provide a

favourable exception to this rule for an individual who is resident for not more than ninety *consecutive* days[7] during the taxable year. Such a person is exempt from taxation on any compensation paid by an employer outside China for services performed within China.[8]

A Notice issued in June 1981 by the Ministry of Finance[9] interpreting the ninety-day exemption rule clarified what foreign taxpayers had already discovered in their dealings with local tax bureaux—that the word 'consecutive' is not to be interpreted literally and that 'residency' is interpreted as the right to remain in China, as evidenced by a taxpayer's visa. More specifically, the Notice provides that a foreigner entering China with a visa valid for more than ninety days is presumptively a resident for more than ninety days and is therefore subject to tax on all income gained within China starting from the date on which he entered the country. Absences from China are disregarded for the purpose of the ninety-day exemption provided the taxpayer returns at any time during the effective period of his visa.[10] Consequently, a businessman who repeatedly visits China on a multiple-entry visa valid for more than ninety days may find himself ineligible for the ninety-day exemption even if he is in China for less than a total of ninety days. Recently, however, the Ministry of Finance has provided a special exception for foreigners temporarily in China on visas valid for more than ninety days who leave and re-enter China several times during the period covered by their visa. A foreigner who stays in China for fewer than one-third of the days covered by his visa, including any extensions granted in China, is exempt from the IITL. If the number of days spent in China exceeds one-third of the visa period, the foreigner is taxable from the date of his first entry into China until the date of his final departure.[11]

Although not found in either the Notice or any other document, a special interpretation of the ninety-day exemption is applied to foreigners entering China on short-term visas, typically valid for between thirty and sixty days. Foreigners who obtain a succession of short-term visas will have their periods of stay in China aggregated for the purpose of determining their eligibility for the ninety-day exemption, even if these periods straddle more than one tax year.[12] Absences from China of over thirty days, however, trigger an entirely fresh count. For example, a businessman who: (a) obtains a short-term visa and remains in China for thirty days; (b) leaves China for less than thirty days and then returns on a new visa and remains for another thirty days; and (c) leaves China for more than thirty days; and (d) returns to China under a new visa and stays for thirty-one days, remains eligible for the ninety-day exemption. His absence from China for more than thirty days erases, for the purposes of the exemption, the sixty days that were already spent in China. By comparison, if the same businessman had, after his second visit, left for less than thirty days and had then returned again for thirty-one days, he would have become taxable on his income gained within China starting from his initial date of entry.

A foreigner whose visa is valid for 'less than ninety days'[13] need not register with the tax authorities. If it could be 'determined in advance', however, that his visa would be extended beyond ninety days, he must register from the beginning of his stay. If the extension could not have been determined in advance, the foreigner may wait until the end of the ninety days and then register.[14] At this time, he must pay taxes owed for the prior three months.[15] Chinese tax authorities have been unclear about how they will determine whether an extension could have been 'determined in advance'. Also uncertain is whether a foreigner whose extension could have been 'determined in advance' but who does not pay tax from the outset of his stay in China will be subject to the IITL's penalty provisions.[16]

b. Residents for One Year or More   Under the IITL, an individual residing in China for a full 365 days within a taxable year—defined as a calendar year—[17] is taxable on income 'gained within or outside' China.[18] The regulations provide an exception to this rule in the case of an individual who resides in China for one year or more but not for more than five years. While this individual is taxable on his income gained within China, he is taxable on income gained outside China only if it is remitted to China.[19] An individual residing in China for more than five years is, under the regulations, taxable on his world-wide income regardless of whether income gained outside China is remitted to China.[20] However, in a 1983 document, the Ministry of Finance reversed its policy on non-China-source income. Under this document, such income will *not* be taxable regardless of whether it is remitted to China. This exemption applies whether the residency is for one year or more, or for more than five years, provided that the foreigner's presence is attributable to his employment by a joint venture, co-operative venture, or foreign enterprise in China and not to a general intention to take up long-term residency in China.[21]

The regulations state that 'temporary absences' from China during the tax year are not counted for purposes of the one-year or more residency provision.[22] Consistent with this regulation, the 1981 Notice clearly indicates that foreigners with one-year residence permits or visas who leave China and return during the effective period of their permits or visas (including extensions approved after entry) are considered residents of China for one full year regardless of the amount of time actually spent abroad.[23]

ii. Source Rules
Under the regulations, the following items of income are considered as gained or sourced within China:[24] income from work and compensation for services performed within China; dividends and bonuses gained within China; remuneration for staff members sent to work abroad by any Chinese government office; fees for the use of proprietary rights within China; rent for the lease of property within China; and interest from within China. These items of income are considered as gained within China regardless of where the income is actually paid.[25]

Notwithstanding these regulations, Chinese tax officials have adopted a rather startling view regarding the source of wage and salary income of foreigners, deeming all wage and salary income earned by an over-ninety-day resident of China (as defined in the MOF Notice) during his period of residency as gained or sourced in China and thus taxable. No distinction is made, in other words, between the concept of *residency*, which subjects a foreigner to tax, and that of *source*, which determines the income upon which he is taxed. The holder of a six-month visa who, for example, spends four of those months working in China and two months working in the United States could be taxable in China on all of the wage and salary income earned during the entire six months, despite the regulation's indication that only compensation for services performed 'within China' is China-source income. Recently, the Ministry of Finance has indicated some flexibility on this question. If a foreign employee spends part of his time serving as a resident representative of a foreign company in China, and some of his time as a representative of the company in another location, and if the company pays the employee a separate salary for his work in China or can provide proof of the portion of his overall salary attributable to his work in China, the employee will be taxed only on his salary attributable to work in China.[26]

iii. Tax Base

The individual income tax is levied on wages and salaries,[27] compensation for personal services,[28] fees for the use of proprietary rights,[29] interest,[30] dividends,[31] bonuses,[32] and rental income.[33] The Ministry of Finance may classify other items of income as taxable.[34]

Per diem or fixed periodic allowances paid by foreign companies to their employees in China are taxable as wages or salaries. Not taxable, however, are advances or reimbursements by foreign companies to their employees for specific 'company expenses'—including lodging, transportation, postage, telephone and telegraph, office expenses, advertisement, and business-related entertainment expenses, provided that the employer submits 'proof' that is verified by the local tax authorities. This 'proof' must establish that the payments were for 'company expenses' and not for food, laundry, or other personal expenses of the employee, and were not part of the employee's salary.[35] Reimbursement or payment of an employee's Chinese income tax by a foreign company gives rise to taxable income for the employee.[36]

In calculating taxable income, certain statutory allowances are provided against specific categories of income. In the case of wages and salaries, for instance, a monthly deduction of RMB800 is allowed.[37] These statutory deductions are automatically allowed regardless of whether actual expenses are greater than or less than the stipulated amount. No other deductions are allowed under the IITL.[38]

iv. Rates

Wages and salaries are taxed monthly under a seven-bracket progressive rate schedule. The standard RMB800 deduction is built into the rate schedule through a zero bracket for monthly income under RMB800. Monthly income between RMB801 and RMB1,500 is taxed at 5 per cent; monthly income between RMB1,501 and RMB3,000 is taxed at 10 per cent. After RMB3,000, the marginal tax rate increases by ten percentage points until it reaches 40 per cent on income between RMB9,001 and RMB12,000. Income above RMB12,000 is taxed at 45 per cent.[39] Compensation for personal services, royalties, interest, dividends, bonuses, rents, and 'all other kinds of income' are taxed at a flat rate of 20 per cent.[40]

B. The Industrial and Commercial Tax

The industrial and commercial tax,[41] which generates a substantial portion of China's tax revenue,[42] can be generally described as a broad-based turnover tax or as a combination of cascading sales and excise taxes. Unlike the sales taxes that are used in the United States, which generally apply only at the retail level, the industrial and commercial tax is imposed at each stage of production when taxable goods or services are transferred from entity to entity. The tax is also levied at the retail level when the goods or services are sold to the ultimate consumer.[43] Unlike a value added tax, no credit is provided for any tax previously paid. The Chinese recognize the detrimental economic effects of the industrial and commercial tax's pyramiding structure and are converting it into a value added tax.[44]

i. Taxpayers and Taxable Activities

The Consolidated Industrial and Commercial Tax Act (CICTA) and its regulations,[45] both adopted in 1958, form the basic structure of the industrial and commercial tax system. The CICTA applies to enterprises in China engaged in the production of industrial products, the import of foreign goods, commercial retailing, communications, transportation, or the rendering of services.[46] The tax is paid only with respect to business conducted by establishments within China.[47]

The tax is usually imposed on the gross amount of proceeds received from the sale of goods and services. Taxpayers engaged in the purchase of agricultural products or the import of foreign goods, however, pay the tax on the amount of their purchases.[48] In the case of imported industrial goods, the tax is computed on the basis of the sum of the cost-insurance-freight (CIF) price of the goods and the customs duty divided by 1 minus the industrial and commercial tax rate.[49] In the case of imported agricultural products, the tax is computed only on the basis of the CIF price.[50]

ii. Taxable Items and Rates

Over 100 categories of taxable industrial and agricultural products are listed in the CICTA's tables, some of which are divided further into subcategories. Rates range from 1.5 per cent (for cotton grey cloth) to 69 per cent (for Grade A cigarettes), with over forty different rates within this range.[51] A 5 per cent catch-all rate applies to any industrial product that is not listed specifically in the categories of taxable items; no similar catch-all rate applies to unlisted agricultural products. Taxable items under the categories of services and commercial retailing are subject to tax rates ranging from 3 per cent to 7 per cent.[52] A surtax of 1 per cent may be levied by local governments.[53]

In general, the industrial and commercial tax rates are set low on those goods and services which the state is seeking to encourage. Industrial goods tend to be taxed at lower rates than are consumer goods. Among consumer goods, necessities tend to be taxed lower than luxuries. Possibly as a way of reducing the pyramiding problem, the rates seem generally to be set low on goods that are likely to be inputs into the chain of production and distribution rather than final products.

The industrial and commercial tax, like any turnover tax, provides an advantage for a firm that is vertically integrated. In order to reduce this advantage, the industrial and commercial tax is applied to certain items produced by an enterprise and used by the same enterprise in further production, to certain products manufactured by an industrial enterprise and used by the enterprise in capital construction, and to products that are transferred from the production to the retail department of an enterprise that retails its own products.[54]

C. The Joint Venture Income Tax Law

i. Taxpayers

Under the Joint Venture Law of July 1979, an equity joint venture with Chinese and foreign investment must be organized as a limited liability company incorporated in China.[55] This Chinese joint venture corporation and its branches within or without China are taxable under the JVITL.[56]

The JVITL applies to all joint ventures for which contracts were approved on or after 10 September 1980.[57] Joint venture contracts approved before 10 September 1980 which contain tax rates or incentives different from those in the JVITL are subject to special transitional rules. These joint ventures are allowed to enjoy the benefits of any tax rates and incentives that were agreed upon for the initial period of the venture.[58] Subsequent extensions of these joint ventures, however, are subject to the JVITL's rates and other provisions.[59]

ii. Tax Base

The income tax is imposed on a joint venture's world-wide income derived from 'production, business, and other sources'.[60] 'Income from other sources' includes dividends, bonuses, interest, royalties, rental income, 'and other income'.[61] The law contains no capital gains concept; income or loss from the sale of fixed assets enters into the year's accounts at its full amount.[62]

Taxable income is defined as 'net income' after deduction of costs, expenses, and losses, and is computed on a calendar-year basis under accrual accounting.[63] Losses may be carried forward for five years.[64]

Detailed rules are provided for the depreciation of fixed assets and for the amortization of intangible assets.[65] These rules follow generally accepted accounting practices.[66] Assets worth less than RMB500 that have a 'short' useful life may be expensed rather than depreciated.[67] In general, fixed assets are depreciated on the basis of their 'original price' (cost) less residual value using the straight-line method of depreciation.[68]

A minimum useful life is prescribed for three broad classes of fixed assets: twenty years for houses and buildings, ten years for trains, ships, machines, equipment and other facilities used for production, and five years for electronic equipment and transportation equipment other than trains and ships.[69] The regulations do not specify what useful life applies for assets not covered by these three classes.

The regulations provide for the amortization of intangible assets, which include know-how, patents, trade marks, the right to use a site, and copyrights.[70] Goodwill is not mentioned. Intangible assets are amortized over the term provided for their use, or, if no term is provided, over a ten-year period.[71] Expenses incurred in starting up a joint venture are amortized once the venture begins operating. The amount of amortization cannot exceed 20 per cent per year.[72]

A detailed list of allowable costs, expenses, or losses is not set forth in either the law or the regulations. However, the regulations list various items that are not allowable in computing taxable income.[73] This list includes the JVITL tax and surtax (other taxes, such as the industrial and commercial tax, are deductible),[74] fines and penalties, and expenditures that must be capitalized. Business-related entertainment expenses are limited to 0.3 per cent of total sales income or 1 per cent of total operational income.[75] In addition, a deduction for 'interest on capital' is denied.[76]

The regulations provide a set of rules for computing the taxable income of a service joint venture, a commercial joint venture, and an industrial joint venture.[77] Although these rules are complicated, the calculation of taxable income appears to be consistent with Western practices and concepts.

Under the regulations, inventory is computed at cost.[78] The regulations specifically list three computational methods—first-in first-out (FIFO), shifting average, and weighted average—but leave open the possibility of using other methods.[79]

The Joint Venture Law provides that the net profit of a joint venture can be distributed after the joint venture income tax is paid and after payments are made into the venture's reserve funds, workers' bonus and welfare funds, and expansion funds.[80] Chinese sources have confirmed that payments made *into* these funds are not currently deductible,[81] a position that is consistent with the practice of the United States and other countries.

The Ministry of Finance's position with respect to payments made out of the three funds, though not reflected in any public document, is that withdrawals from the reserve and expansion funds are deductible for tax purposes, either currently if used for a current expense or over time through depreciation if used for the purchase of capital assets. Withdrawals made from the workers' bonus and welfare funds, however, are not deductible.[82]

iii. Rates

The JVITL provides for a basic 30 per cent tax rate.[83] In addition, a local surtax of 10 per cent of the tax paid is levied for use by the local treasuries, bringing the total tax rate, assuming no reductions, to 33 per cent.[84] 'On account of special circumstances', the surtax can be eliminated or reduced by the government of the province, municipality, or autonomous region in which the joint venture is located.[85]

A tax of 10 per cent is normally levied on a foreign participant that remits its share of profits out of China, though exemption from this tax has been granted to certain favoured joint ventures under State Council regulations to encourage foreign investment, promulgated in October 1986.[86] The imposition of this 10 per cent tax is similar to the practice of many countries, including the United States,[87] which levy a tax on the payment of dividends to foreign shareholders. One significant distinction, however, is that the Chinese 10 per cent tax applies only to profits remitted out of China. Accordingly, a dividend that is reinvested within China without first being remitted outside China will be free of the 10 per cent tax.[88]

The JVITL provides for a number of possible rate reductions or exemptions. Implementing an incentive referred to in the Joint Venture Law,[89] the JVITL allows a newly established joint venture that is scheduled to operate for a period of ten years or more to apply for a full exemption from tax in its first profit-making year and a 50 per cent reduction in the following two years.[90] These periods have subsequently been extended to two years of exemption and three subsequent years of 50 per cent reduction and further periods of tax reduction have recently been made available to certain types of ventures.[91] The first profit-making year is defined as the year in which a joint venture begins to make a profit after taking into account any loss carry-overs.[92] Under the Joint Venture Law, these exemptions and reductions are limited to a joint venture 'equipped with up-to-date technology by world standards'.[93] This requirement is not found in the JVITL, but it is unclear whether its absence signals any change in policy. In any event, most if not all of the joint ventures operating in China today appear to be enjoying a tax exemption and reduction scheme.

The JVITL implements another tax incentive referred to in the Joint Venture Law[94] by allowing a participant that reinvests in China[95] for at least five consecutive years its share of profits from a joint venture to obtain, upon approval by the tax authorities, a refund of 40 per cent of the income tax paid on the reinvested funds.[96] The refund is apparently granted upon the taxpayer's stated intent to reinvest for the five-year period; if the funds are withdrawn before the end of the period the taxpayer must pay back the refunded tax.[97] The tax refund, which is paid to the reinvesting participant and not to the joint venture, does not include the local surtax.[98]

As the final step in the calculation of its tax liability, a joint venture may take a credit for income taxes paid abroad on income earned outside China. The credit cannot exceed the Chinese tax payable on the income earned abroad.[99]

D. The Foreign Enterprise Income Tax Law

The Foreign Enterprise Income Tax Law (FEITL), effective as of 1 January 1982,[100] filled a major gap in the Chinese tax structure. Before the FEITL's adoption, the only tax law of apparent applicability to foreign investment was the 1980 JVITL. The JVITL, however, covers only equity joint ventures, which constitute a relatively small part of business activity in China. A greater proportion of foreign investment activity has so far taken the form of non-equity or 'contractual' joint ventures, sometimes known as co-operative production ventures. The JVITL does not apply to this mode of investment, which is not conducted through a joint venture corporation.[101] Until the FEITL was adopted, the tax consequences of non-equity joint ventures had been unclear.

The FEITL divides taxpayers into two basic categories: foreign companies, enterprises, and other economic organizations that have 'establishments'[102] in China, and those which do not. Taxpayers that have establishments are generally taxed on their net income at progressive rates. Taxpayers that do not have establishments are taxed on certain categories of China-source income—for example, interest, rent, and fees for the use of proprietary rights—[103] at a flat rate of 20 per cent which is levied on the gross amount of the income and is withheld by the payor.[104] In broad outline, this approach is similar to that adopted by many other countries.

i. Definition of Establishment

The significant difference in tax treatment between a progressive tax on net income and a 20 per cent flat tax on gross income makes it critical for a foreign company to determine whether it has an 'establishment'. The FEITL and its regulations provide that 'establishments' refer to organizations, sites, or business agents engaging in production or business operations either independently or in co-operative production or joint business operations with Chinese enterprises. 'Organizations' include management organizations, branches, and representative offices. 'Sites' include factories, sites where natural resources are being exploited, and sites where construction, installation, assembly, exploration, and other projects are undertaken.[105]

The tax administration's current administrative posture suggests that 'establishment' will not be interpreted as broadly as the statute and regulations might seem to allow, but rather will be interpreted in a manner akin to the concept of a 'permanent establishment' commonly embodied in tax treaties. In other words, the Chinese will require a high order of presence or activity in China before concluding that an 'establishment' exists. For example, representative offices that are characterized as engaged in information-gathering or liaison activities for their head offices,[106] or independent agents[107] are unlikely to be regarded as 'establishments', a position in accord with that of many tax treaties, including those which China has signed with the United States, the United Kingdom, and other countries.

ii. Tax Base

Taxpayers with establishments in China are taxed on their income from 'production, business operations, and other sources'.[108] The definitions of these types of income basically parallel those in the JVITL.[109]

Although the law and regulations clearly intend to reach a broad range of income, they fail to answer a critical question: will foreign companies with establishments be taxable on their world-wide income or just on their China-source income? Chinese tax officials have indicated that only China-source income is taxable under the FEITL,[110] a position that in principle is consistent with international practice. The FEITL is silent, however, on the source rules applicable to significant categories of income. While source rules are included for dividends, interest, rentals, and technology fees earned by companies without establishments in China,[111] no rules are provided for such major categories as sales or manufacturing income of companies with Chinese establishments.[112]

Provisions in the FEITL governing the definition and calculation of taxable income generally follow the JVITL. The list of non-deductible expenditures[113] substantially overlaps that in the JVITL.[114] Particularly noteworthy is the FEITL's incorporation of the JVITL's denial of a deduction for 'interest on capital'.[115] The FEITL Regulations provide at least some limitation on the interpretation of this highly controversial provision by allowing the deduction of 'reasonable' interest on loans deemed by the local tax authorities to be 'normal loans'.[116] While no definitive interpretations of 'reasonable' and 'normal' yet exist, the regulations suggest, at the least, that 'interest on capital' will not be read to deny a deduction for all interest paid.[117]

The FEITL prohibits a deduction of fees paid by a foreign company to its head office for the use of proprietary rights.[118] This prohibition is presumably intended to prevent foreign companies from avoiding tax in China by reducing their income through transactions that may lack economic substance. The effect of this provision is tempered, however, by the allowance of deductions for payments to the head office for overhead and administrative expenses attributable to the Chinese establishment and for payments for services performed by the head office for the establishment provided these payments are properly documented and approved by the local tax authorities.[119] Little experience exists to determine the degree of vigilance the Chinese will exert in monitoring these fees, which in many cases could be substituted for the above-mentioned prohibited payments as a means of reducing taxable income in China.

The depreciation and amortization provisions of the FEITL are generally similar to those of the JVITL.[120] Special rules are provided for companies in offshore petroleum and coal projects—most notably, a provision that fixed assets involved in the development and subsequent stages of these projects may be depreciated in a 'composite' manner over at least six years.[121]

A provision in the FEITL not found in the JVITL involves taxpayers who cannot provide acceptable documentation of their costs and expenses. In these situations, the local tax authorities may assess taxes by imputing a 'normal' rate of profit based on that of other similar businesses. For companies engaged in trade, the imputed profit rate is applied to net sales; for other companies, it is applied to gross business income.[122] At present, it is unclear how the Chinese will determine which businesses are similar enough to the taxpayer's to serve as a norm.[123]

iii. Rates

The tax rates for foreign companies with establishments in China range from 20 per cent on the portion of annual income up to RMB250,000 to 40 per cent on income over RMB1 million.[124] In addition, the localities levy a tax of 10 per cent, not on the amount of the national income tax paid, as under the JVITL, but rather on the amount of taxable income.[125] Consequently, the total tax rates range from 30 per cent to 50 per cent, though a reduction in or exemption from the local tax may be available for certain enterprises.[126]

The FEITL's provisions on tax exemptions and reductions are generally more restrictive than those of the JVITL. Under the JVITL, equity joint ventures are entitled to apply for exemptions and reductions provided only that they are scheduled to operate for at least ten years. By comparison, the FEITL not only incorporates the ten-year rule, but also requires that a foreign company seeking an exemption for the first profit-making year and a reduction for the following two years[127] be engaged in certain types of 'low-profit' operations.[128] Whereas most equity joint ventures have received tax holidays and rate reductions, few foreign companies are likely to engage in the types of 'low-profit' operations that qualify for tax preferences under the FEITL.[129]

iv. Taxpayers without Establishments

Foreign companies without establishments in China are taxable only on their China-source dividends, interest, rentals, fees for the use of proprietary rights, and 'other' income as determined by the Ministry of Finance.[130] These categories of income are taxed under the FEITL at a flat 20 per cent rate and no deductions or credits are allowed for any expenses incurred in the generation of the income.[131]

a. Dividends   Dividends are from Chinese sources if they are obtained from or represent profits shared with enterprises in China.[132] Although this definition could be read to cover dividends paid by joint venture corporations and perhaps dividends paid by non-Chinese corporations with China-source income, officials have indicated that neither of these situations is subject to the FEITL.[133] In the first case, dividends paid by joint venture corporations are not subject to the FEITL, presumably because their taxation is governed exclusively by the JVITL.[134] In the second case, involving, for example, a dividend paid by a United States corporation with a Chinese establishment, administrative considerations weigh heavily toward excluding the income from the FEITL.[135] Dividends paid to foreign companies by their wholly owned subsidiaries in China will presumably be subject to the 20 per cent tax.

b. Interest   The withholding tax also applies to interest 'gained from China' from deposits, loans, and securities, as well as other interest 'such as that from payments made for others and deferred payments'.[136] Exemptions are available to foreign banks lending to China's various state banks and to certain of China's 'trust and investment corporations'[137] at a 'preferential rate'.[138] Although the term 'preferential rate' is defined in the FEITL Regulations only to mean a rate at least 10 per cent below the prevailing international financial market rate,[139] subsequent Ministry of Finance regulations[140] have provided for a number of other situations in which foreign banks may, upon the approval of the local tax organs, be exempted from the withholding tax. These include loans made to China's state banks or trust and investment companies at the 'international interbank rate for call funds', a term that includes the LIBOR rate or similar interbank rate. An exemption, however, may also be available for loans at up to 0.5 per cent above the interbank rate, depending on the term of the loan.[141] Loans to the China National Offshore Oil Corporation, the body responsible for the co-operative offshore oil exploration and development projects with foreign oil companies, may also, under certain circumstances, be exempted from the withholding tax.[142]

In response to the negative impact that the FEITL's 20 per cent withholding tax was apparently having on lending to China, the rate has been reduced to 10 per cent for loan contracts signed between 1983 and 1990.[143] Contracts signed and approved before 1 January 1983, the effective date of the regulation reducing the rate, remain subject to the then effective tax provisions for the life of the contract.[144]

c. Rentals   Also subject to the FEITL withholding tax is income derived from the rental of property for use in China.[145] Chinese entities are becoming increasingly interested in leasing foreign capital equipment, which among other advantages may enable them to avoid some of the foreign exchange and import licence regulations that hamper their outright purchase of this type of equipment.[146] While rental payments are generally taxable to the foreign lessor at 20 per cent under the FEITL withholding tax,[147] special tax treatment applies to 'lease-sale' or 'hire-purchase' transactions. In these transactions, a leasing company rents a piece of equipment to the Chinese with ownership ultimately passing to the Chinese. Hence, in contrast to an actual 'rental' transaction, the payments made by the Chinese in a 'lease-sale' arrangement contain a portion attributable to the 'principal', or purchase price, of the equipment. These payments also include a component that may be characterized by the parties as a 'lease' fee but is actually interest, usually imposed at a rate that represents the leasing company's cost of funds it borrowed to obtain the equipment in question. Finally, payments made to the leasing company also include a service charge or spread imposed by the leasing company over its own cost of funds, that is, over the interest component mentioned above.

Under a 1983 tax regulation, the portion of the payments attributable to the purchase price is exempt from tax.[148] In addition, the regulation reduces the tax on the interest component in these lease-sale transactions to 10 per cent for transactions made between 1983 and 1990, and provides for total exemption of tax for interest in lease-sales under certain circumstances.[149] The service charge or spread imposed by the leasing company is taxable, but at a reduced rate of 10 per cent.[150]

d. Fees for the Use of Proprietary Rights   Perhaps the most significant targets of the FEITL withholding tax are what the Chinese term 'fees for the use in China of proprietary rights', a concept encompassing royalties or licence fees for the use in China of patents or other proprietary technology, trade marks, and copyrights.[151] In addition, fees for technical training,[152] technical services, and technical documentation provided by a foreign company to an entity in China are considered to fall within this category of income.[153] Income from computer software—whether 'sold' or 'licensed'—may also be taxed under this rubric.[154]

Fees received by foreign companies for such services as consultation with Chinese enterprises on management methods and assistance in performing feasibility studies, fees for technical seminars, and fees for the design of construction sites and equipment are not taxable to the extent that they do not involve the transfer of the right to the use of proprietary technology.[155] In addition, fees paid under equipment sale contracts in respect of designs for the installation and use of the equipment and diagrams for equipment manufacture and maintenance are not taxable.[156]

Partly in response to significant foreign pressure, especially from companies whose home countries allow no foreign tax credit, the Ministry of Finance has provided for the possibility, with the approval of the tax authorities,[157] of a reduction in the withholding tax to 10 per cent for certain technology-related fees, and of a total exemption from the tax if the technology is 'advanced' and offered on 'preferential' terms.[158] The categories eligible for this special tax treatment include nuclear technology, certain types of computer technology, and technology used in agriculture, energy exploration, and conservation.[159]

III. The Tax Consequences of Various Forms of Business Activity

A foreign company contemplating business with China can choose from a variety of approaches not dissimilar from those existing in other countries. At one end of the spectrum, a foreign company can simply export its goods or technology to China, either through an outright sale, or through a licensing or leasing arrangement. In conjunction with these activities, some technical training or ancillary support services might be provided to the Chinese customer. At the other end of the spectrum, a company seeking a more substantial involvement can enter into a compensation trade agreement, a co-operative equity joint venture, or even establish a wholly owned enterprise.

A company may decide that in order to explore and pursue business opportunities in China, it needs a permanent presence in the country. Having made this decision, a company can choose several approaches— retaining one of the many trading or consulting firms with offices in Beijing and other major Chinese cities to represent its interests, appointing an exclusive agent, or establishing a representative office in China.

Numerous factors will influence how a foreign company will structure its business activities in China. Many of these factors will involve internal company policy with respect to doing business abroad and the degree of commitment and involvement the company seeks with China. In addition, China's expanding system of laws and regulations governing foreign business must be considered, with taxation becoming an increasingly prominent factor.

As China's tax structure for foreign business becomes more complex, the tax ramifications of different forms of business become more significant. For instance, under the current Chinese approach, mere intermittent sales to China will not subject a foreign company's income to taxation. If, however, the foreign company also provides installation, training, or other services at the end-user's site over a period of time, the company may be creating an 'establishment', subjecting its service income to the progressive foreign enterprise income tax.[160] If its activities are not sufficient to create an establishment, the withholding tax may instead apply on some of the technical service income.[161] The various forms of joint Chinese-foreign business associations also result in different treatment under China's income and other tax laws. In addition, although a discussion of the bilateral tax treaties which China has signed with various countries is beyond the scope of this chapter, investors from countries covered by these treaties will need to consider their terms, as well as Chinese tax law, in structuring their activities.

The following sections explore on a transactional basis the tax consequences of several common forms of business activity in China. Specifically discussed are representative offices and business agents, consignment sales and service centres, compensation trade, co-operative ventures, contracted projects, equity joint ventures, and wholly foreign-owned enterprises.[162] In all of these cases, the special tax incentives that may be available in the SEZs and other localities need to be considered by investors. See Chapter 5.

A. Representative Offices and Business Agents

The most common form of independent foreign business presence in China at present is the 'representative office' (*daibiao jigou*), authorized under a 1980 regulation.[163]

'Representative offices' are included within the FEITL's definition of 'establishment'.[164] Until 1985, however, the treatment of these offices was unclear. The rules for the registration of representative offices provide that 'representative offices of foreign enterprises shall be representative offices that engage in activities that are not direct business operations'.[165] Chinese tax authorities stated informally on various occasions that offices that remained within this guideline and performed merely liaison activity would not be taxed. It soon became evident, however, that some offices were conducting more than just liaison activity and were engaging in actual business. The need for tax rules to deal with these different types of representative office was obvious.

In May 1985, new provisions on the taxation of foreign representative offices (the Representative Office Tax Provisions) were promulgated to respond to this need.[166] The Representative Office Tax Provisions apply not only to representative offices registered in accordance with the 1980 regulations but also to offices of foreign enterprises that have not registered under those rules.[167] A representative office of a foreign industrial or manufacturing company that confines its activities to liaison, research, and consulting services for its 'head office'—defined as the corporate entity that actually established the office—should continue to be exempted from taxation, provided it receives no payments for these services.[168] In addition, income received by representative offices that act as agents primarily outside China for enterprises located within China is exempt from taxation.[169]

Under the new rules, the offices of foreign service companies—consultants, accountants, trading companies, banks, lawyers, and other representative offices that act as more than non-profit, information-gathering, support arms for their head offices by providing services to third parties on a compensated basis—are taxed on their income attributable to services rendered in China, regardless of where the income is received.[170] If some of the services giving rise to taxation under the Representative Office Tax Provisions are performed inside China by the office and some outside China by the head office, the foreign company may submit explanatory documentation to the local tax authorities who will determine the amount subject to tax in China.[171]

Income generated by representative offices taxable under the Representative Office Tax Provisions is subject to the FEITL at the normal progressive rates. These rates are applied to net income, as described in Part II D of this chapter. However, companies with representative offices in China that cannot provide accurate evidence of the offices' costs and expenses are taxed on the deemed profit basis;[172] 10 per cent of the gross income generated by the office is subject to the FEITL rates.[173]

All representative offices are subject to the CICTA on the import of office equipment and other items.[174] In addition, the gross revenues generated by representative offices taxable under the Representative Office Tax Provisions are taxed at the CICTA rate of 5 per cent,[175] even if the type of service rendered by the representative office is not expressly listed in the table of taxable items and tax rates of the CICTA.[176] The local tax authorities may assess an additional surtax of 1 per cent on the amount of CICTA payable, bringing the total CICTA rate to 5.05 per cent.[177]

Actual branch operations of foreign companies, as opposed to representative offices, do not yet exist except in the case of foreign banks, which are allowed to have branches in certain areas of China. These branches are considered 'operating establishments' and are taxed on their net income at the progressive rates. They are also subject to the CICTA.[178]

Some companies do business in China not through their own representative offices but through one of the many foreign trading companies or consulting firms that have set up representative offices in China's major cities. As discussed above, these trading or consulting firms are taxable on the commissions and other fees generated by their representative offices. More uncertainty exists regarding the clients of these firms. Under a possible interpretation of the FEITL, any foreign company transacting business through another firm operating in China could be deemed to have 'set up a business agent in China',[179] thereby having an establishment that is taxable on its China-source income. Chinese tax officials, however, have expressed their intention to incorporate into the FEITL the common distinction between independent and dependent agents.[180] If this distinction is adopted, a foreign company's use of a trading or other firm that also acts for other companies will not create an establishment for the purposes of the FEITL. The appointment, on the other hand, of an agent that acts exclusively for the foreign company may create an establishment and subject the foreign company to taxation on its Chinese net income. This issue awaits more practical experience before any conclusions can be drawn.

B. Consignment Sales and Service Centres

Foreign companies that sign agreements with Chinese corporations under which the latter sell the foreign company's products on a consignment or agency basis, or under which the Chinese set up a service centre to service and sell parts for the foreign company's machinery in China, may be subject to tax under the FEITL, the CICTA, or under both. A Ministry of Finance tax notice[181] provides that in cases where an independent place of business is established by a Chinese entity with its sole or primary function being the sale of a foreign company's products, or the maintenance or sale of parts for a foreign company's machinery, the foreign company will be subject to the FEITL establishment tax on any 'profit' it earns from the service centre[182] and subject to the CICTA on its 'business income'.[183]

If, on the other hand, no place of business is specially established but a Chinese corporation simply sells a foreign company's goods on a consignment or agency basis, the latter will not be subject to the FEITL. Depending on the nature of the consignment or agency arrangement, the foreign company may be subject to the CICTA. If the Chinese party does not actually purchase the goods but simply takes delivery and sells them at a price set by the foreign company, or at a mutually agreed price—the parties sharing the sales proceeds according to an agreed ratio—the foreign company will be subject to the CICTA on its share of the sales proceeds.[184] If, however, the Chinese first import the goods from the foreign company and resell them at their own price, the foreign company will be exempt from the CICTA.[185]

C. Compensation Trade

In a typical compensation trade, or counter-trade, project, a foreign company provides machinery, equipment, or technology to a Chinese entity and receives payment in kind. The payment in kind can consist of goods produced with the transferred assets, other goods, or some combination of the two. The foreign company usually resells these goods on the international market or in its home market.

Compensation trade can be broadly characterized in two ways. The Chinese sometimes describe compensation trade as a loan transaction: the foreign company 'lends' the machinery or equipment to the Chinese unit and the loan is repaid in kind. Under this interpretation, the value of the repayment in kind represents both principal and interest. Alternatively, compensation trade can be viewed as an instalment sale of the machinery or equipment, or what the Chinese term a 'deferred payment' arrangement.[186] Under this interpretation, each payment in kind represents a partial payment of the purchase price and an interest component.[187] The foreign company may also provide some training or technical services together with the equipment. In this case, a portion of the payment in kind would be payment for these services. Also, the portion of the product payment attributable to any technology transferred may be viewed as a licence fee, or, in the Chinese terminology, a 'fee for the use of proprietary rights'.[188]

The tax consequences of compensation trade depend upon which interpretation is adopted, upon whether the foreign company is deemed to have an establishment in China, and upon the applicable source rules. For example, if the instalment sale characterization were adopted, and if the foreign company were deemed to have an establishment in China, then, at the least, the interest component inherent in the payment in kind would presumably be taxable on a net basis at progressive rates, as would any technology fees. Moreover, if the sale of the machinery and equipment generated China-source income—an unknown question at present because the relevant source rules have not been formulated—any gain on the sale would also be taxable.[189] If the foreign company were not deemed to have an establishment, only the interest component and any technology or service fees would be taxable on a withholding basis. The gain on the sale, even if it were China-source income, would not be taxable under the FEITL's withholding tax because it would not be one of the categories of income subject to that tax.[190]

If the loan characterization were adopted, and if the foreigner were deemed to have an establishment in China, the interest component inherent in the in-kind payment would again be taxable on a net basis at progressive rates, as would any technology fees. If the foreigner were actually to receive back the equipment or machinery at the end of the loan, no further tax consequences would result. Usually, however, the foreign company does not receive back the actual assets that were lent; instead, it receives back the value of such assets in kind. If the lent assets themselves are not returned, the putative loan is similar to an instalment sale. The loan of an asset that is repaid in kind would appear to constitute a realization under generally accepted principles of taxation. If the gain realized were treated as China-source income, it could be taxed on a net basis at the FEITL's progressive rates. If the loan characterization were adopted but the foreigner were not deemed to have an establishment in China, the interest component and technology or service fees would be taxable on a gross withholding basis.

A critical element in the tax treatment of compensation trade is whether the foreign company is deemed to have an establishment. Although the FEITL does not refer explicitly to compensation trade arrangements, these projects could fall within the 'site' category of the definition of 'establishment'.[191] The Chinese, however, have stated that they do not view compensation trade arrangements as creating an establishment.[192] Therefore, until recently, foreign companies were taxed on the part of the payments in kind that represented payments of interest, technology, or service fees under the 20 per cent gross withholding tax. The amount of this tax was withheld in kind.[193]

Subsequently, however, both for administrative reasons and to encourage this type of business, the Chinese have decided to allow a provisional exemption from the FEITL withholding tax, with the approval of the tax authorities, for both interest and leasing fees paid in kind.[194] However, this exemption only applies if both the principal and interest in a compensation trade arrangement are paid in kind. If the interest is paid in kind but the principal is paid with foreign exchange, the interest remains subject to the withholding tax.[195] This latter situation is not common in compensation trade transactions.

No explicit exemption has been provided from the FEITL withholding tax for technology service fees paid in kind, although the 1983 regulations reducing or eliminating the taxation of technology and related service fees in certain circumstances will benefit many companies engaged in compensation trade.[196] Thus, at least for the present, foreign companies engaging in compensation trade and related projects will in most cases be exempt from Chinese income taxation.

The products received by the foreign party in a compensation trade transaction or the income from their resale could conceivably be subject to the CICTA. However, the CICTA has not been applied to these cases. The tax authorities apparently consider that compensation trade is not, as regards the foreign participant, 'business conducted by an establishment within China'.[197]

D. Co-operative Ventures

In co-operative ventures, also known as non-equity or 'contractual' joint ventures or co-production projects, the Chinese and foreign parties contribute resources or technology and share profits according to a contractual formula. In some cases, the profits are paid in kind with the goods produced by the venture. In a 'classic' co-operative venture, the Chinese and foreign parties calculate and pay tax separately,[198] the Chinese under relevant domestic tax legislation, the foreign party under the FEITL and other relevant tax laws. As a matter of practice, in some co-operative ventures, the venture is treated as a unit for the purpose of calculating taxable income, and the Chinese and foreign parties then pay tax separately on their respective shares of the venture's net income.[199]

In any event, in the classic scenario, foreign companies engaging in co-operative ventures have an establishment in China and are taxable under the FEITL on their China-source net income at progressive rates.[200] Foreign companies receiving their profits in kind calculate their gross income 'based on the sales price to a third party or by reference to the prevailing market price of the goods in question'.[201] The 'market price' refers to the current sales price in China of the goods, but this price will be used only if no actual third-party sale takes place.[202]

The foreign participant in a co-operative venture that imports items in connection with its participation is generally subject to the CICTA. Exemptions from both the CICTA and customs duties are allowed for certain items imported by foreign companies participating in co-operative petroleum projects, for 'advanced' equipment unobtainable in China imported as part of the investment in co-operative ventures in a wide range of fields including energy, transport, agriculture, and scientific research, and for materials and parts imported for the purpose of processing for export.[203] A reduction or exemption may also be available for various imports in connection with co-operative hotel construction projects.[204] To the extent that items imported tax-free are sold in the interior of China, the CICTA and duties must be paid at that time.[205]

The CICTA is imposed on the sale of products produced by co-operative ventures under the normal rules. If the foreign party receives its profits from the venture in kind, the consolidated tax is applied to the sales proceeds if the products are sold from or within China. If the foreign company takes its in-kind share out of China for later resale in its home market or on the international market, it is unclear whether the Chinese will assess the consolidated tax in kind or use a 'prevailing market price' theory such as that used for the purposes of the FEITL and collect the tax in cash.[206]

Many export sales by co-operative ventures will benefit from a complete exemption from the CICTA granted by recent investment encouragement regulations. The exemption applies to all products except crude oil, finished oil products, and other products that may be stipulated by the state.[207] Foreign companies that do pay the industrial and commercial tax on sales or service income may deduct that amount in computing their taxable income for the purposes of the FEITL.[208]

E. Contracted Projects

A foreign company whose business activity consists of what the Chinese call a 'contracted project', such as a construction, installation, assembly, or other service project, is deemed to have an 'establishment' in China by virtue of the project 'site', and is therefore taxable under the FEITL on its China-source net income at progressive rates.[209]

The definition of an installation or site could encompass three situations that are common in China. The first includes the case of a foreign company that sells equipment to a Chinese entity and then sends employees to the customer's site for a period of time to provide ancillary installation, construction, training, or related services. The second situation involves a foreign company that contracts with a Chinese entity for a construction project, seismic survey, or other service project, with perhaps the incidental sale of some machinery or equipment. This situation includes the foreign companies hired to perform exploration and other work for China's offshore oil development projects. The third situation covers a foreign company that provides on-site installation, training, or other technical services in conjunction with a transfer of technology.

The first situation has been explicitly exempted from establishment tax treatment until 1990.[210] In this situation, even if establishment treatment were applied after 1990, only the service income and not the sales income would be taxable, since income from the sale of goods or equipment to China by a foreign company is not regarded as China-source income.[211] Also exempted from establishment tax treatment until 1990 is the on-site provision of technical instruction, consultation, and other technical services to Chinese enterprises for the reform of their existing technology.[212] In the case of a foreign company's on-site installation and the provision of technical services in connection with a transfer of new technology, the third situation described above, the Chinese seem not to be applying establishment treatment at present.[213]

The only situation described above to which establishment tax treatment has so far been widely applied is the second one—that of foreign companies contracting for a service project in China. Companies in this situation may pay tax on the basis of their actual net income, calculated in accordance with the normal FEITL rules.[214] However, for companies engaging in contracted projects that are unable adequately to substantiate their costs and expenses, the Chinese have provided for a system of taxation under which the FEITL rates are applied to a deemed profit of 10 per cent of total receipts from a project.[215]

The Chinese have not set a minimum period within which a contracted project can be completed without creating an establishment for tax purposes. The FEITL Regulations provide only that foreign enterprises that have operated in China for less than one year are taxable on the income earned during the actual period of operation.[216] In addition, the deemed profit tax system mentioned above is said to be particularly intended to meet the needs of companies involved in 'relatively short' projects,[217] suggesting that no minimum period is contemplated for tax purposes. Minimum periods within which certain types of projects can be completed without creating an establishment are being incorporated into the tax treaties China has been negotiating and signing with various countries.[218]

Service income earned by foreign companies from contracted projects in China is subject to the CICTA. The Chinese have provided the same exemptions under the CICTA, valid until 1990, as those granted under the FEITL for service income earned in connection with equipment sales and in connection with technology reform projects for Chinese enterprises.[219] Companies such as the petroleum service subcontractors, taxable on the establishment basis under the FEITL, pay the CICTA and may deduct the latter tax in calculating taxable income under the FEITL.[220] Although the CICTA is normally imposed on gross receipts,[221] the deduction of certain expenses by companies engaged in contracted projects, for CICTA as well as FEITL purposes, is allowed.[222] These expenses include payments to a Chinese or foreign subcontractor,[223] payments for the purchase of equipment outside China for purposes of the project, and payments for data analysis and processing done outside China.[224]

F. Equity Joint Ventures

As discussed in Part II, equity joint ventures are taxed on their income under the JVITL and are also subject to the CICTA.[225]

Various exemptions from the industrial and commercial tax for imports are available to equity joint ventures.[226] Machinery, equipment, parts, and other materials imported under a joint venture contract as part of the foreign party's capital contribution to the venture are exempt from the industrial and commercial tax, as well as from customs duties.[227] A joint venture that imports equipment or machinery, parts, or other materials using funds that do not exceed the total amount of investment of the venture is exempt from the industrial and commercial tax and customs duties,[228] as is a venture that, with the authorization of the same authorities that approved the joint venture, imports with additional capital machinery, equipment, parts, and other materials whose production and supply cannot be guaranteed in China.[229] Also free from the industrial and commercial tax and customs duties are raw materials, auxiliary materials, parts, components, and packaging materials imported by a joint venture for the production of export products.[230] To the extent that any items imported tax-free are diverted for sale in China or incorporated into products for sale in China, taxes will be imposed as appropriate.[231]

Export sales are treated like any other 'sale' for the purpose of the industrial and commercial tax.[232] Consequently, a joint venture that exports its products is in principle subject to the tax. However, equity joint ventures have been exempted from the tax on exports, with the exception of crude oil, finished oil products, and other products stipulated by the state.[233] In addition, joint ventures that 'have difficulty' at the beginning of their operations paying tax on products produced for domestic sale may apply for a reduction in or exemption from the industrial and commercial tax for a fixed period.[234]

Equity joint ventures may be subject to the real estate tax,[235] which is imposed on the beneficial owners of buildings located in cities, townships, and mining areas.[236] If the Chinese participant in a joint venture contributes a building as part of its capital contribution to the venture, or the venture otherwise acquires a building, the joint venture is the taxpayer for purposes of the real estate tax. If, on the other hand, the joint venture rents buildings from the local government, the lessor will remain the taxpayer.[237] The tax is imposed on owner-occupied buildings at the annual rate of 1.2 per cent of the original value of the building reduced by a 'residual' of 10 to 30 per cent determined by the local authorities, which is presumably intended to reflect economic depreciation.[238]

G. Wholly Foreign-owned Enterprises

No specific tax law yet exists for wholly foreign-owned enterprises. The law governing wholly foreign-owned enterprises, promulgated in April 1986,[239] provides simply that these enterprises will be taxed under 'the relevant tax regulations of the state'.[240] PRC officials have made it clear that wholly foreign-owned enterprises are at present taxed under the FEITL,[241] although a new tax law may ultimately be developed for these enterprises.[242] The law on wholly foreign-owned enterprises also contemplates 'preferential treatment' in the form of tax reductions and exemptions and reinvestment incentives, though no specific provisions are provided.[243] In addition to the FEITL, wholly foreign-owned enterprises are also subject in relevant circumstances to the CICTA and the real estate tax.[244] The various regulations designed to encourage foreign investment that have been promulgated on a central and local level include wholly foreign-owned enterprises within the scope of the tax and other preferences that they provide.[245]

IV. Conclusion

Now that the major elements of the tax structure for foreign business are in place, Chinese officials can turn their attention to resolving ambiguities, filling lacunae, and responding to the myriad of situations and complexities unanticipated when the statutory framework was being constructed—tasks faced by tax administrators everywhere. These further developments will occur against a backdrop of the highly significant changes unfolding on China's domestic tax front. These changes include the imposition of a corporate income tax on state enterprises that had previously turned all their profits over to the state,[246] and the trial use of a value added tax to correct defects in the industrial and commercial tax.[247]

These domestic experiments seem designed to further a major goal— the use of taxation as an 'economic lever' that will assure the state treasury an appropriate share of an enterprise's income while encouraging both initiative and productivity. To a large extent, the evolution of the tax system for foreign business reflects this same philosophy. The Chinese have attempted to balance their right as a sovereign nation to participate in the gains accruing to foreign companies with the need to encourage foreigners to provide capital and technology. The result thus far is a generally conventional tax system.

Foreign businessmen are of course heartened by these developments, but Third World countries might be disappointed. Unlike many other developing countries, China is in a position to innovate and formulate alternative approaches to the traditional patterns of international taxation—patterns that have evolved in the context of the developed countries and should not be imported indiscriminately by a developing country.[248]

But neither the international business community nor the Third World should pass final judgment on China's tax structure. The adoption of a generally orthodox approach probably results more from inexperience than from a decision not to innovate. As tax officials gain more experience and confidence, they are likely to develop techniques and approaches that deviate from the mainstream and fulfil the expectations of many Third World leaders that China will emerge as an intellectual leader in tax issues. In every area of its contemporary legal development, China stresses the importance of 'walking on two legs' and 'letting foreign things serve China'. Taxation should prove to be no exception.

Notes

The authors are grateful for the assistance of Ms Susan Baldwin in the updating and revision of the notes and text of this chapter.

1. For detailed descriptions of the Chinese tax system, see R. Pomp, T. Gelatt, and S. Surrey, 'The Evolving Tax System of the People's Republic of China', *Texas International Law Journal*, Vol. 16, No. 11, 1981, pp. 12–40, and sources cited therein, in note 7, p. 13. This system is now undergoing significant reforms. See notes 246, 247, and accompanying text.

2. The Individual Income Tax Law of the People's Republic of China, passed by the Third Session of the Fifth National People's Congress on 10 September 1980 (hereafter cited as the IITL); and Detailed Rules and Regulations for the Implementation of the Individual Income Tax Law of the People's Republic of China, approved by the State Council on 10 December 1980 and promulgated by the Ministry of Finance on 14 December 1980 (hereafter cited as the IITL Regulations).

3. The Income Tax Law of the People's Republic of China Concerning Joint Ventures Using Chinese and Foreign Investment, passed by the Third Session of the Fifth National People's Congress on 10 September 1980 (hereafter cited as the JVITL); and Detailed Rules and Regulations for the Implementation of the Income Tax Law of the People's Republic of China Concerning Joint Ventures Using Chinese and Foreign Investment, approved by the State Council on 10 December 1980 and promulgated by the Ministry of Finance on 14 December 1980 (hereafter cited as the JVITL Regulations).

4. The Income Tax Law of the People's Republic of China Concerning Foreign Enterprises, passed by the Fourth Session of the Fifth National People's Congress on 13 December 1981 (hereafter cited as the FEITL); and Detailed Rules and Regulations for the Implementation of the Income Tax Law of the People's Republic of China Concerning Foreign Enterprises, approved by the State Council on 17 February 1982 and promulgated by the Ministry of Finance on 21 February 1982 (hereafter cited as the FEITL Regulations).

5. A Notice issued by the State Council provides that in the case of contractual provisions, signed and approved by the 'state organs in charge' before the promulgation of the IITL, 'granting preferential treatment as regards the tax burden on the income of individuals, the matter is to be carried out in accordance with the originally fixed provisions of the contract'. This treatment will only be valid for the initial term of the contract in question; subsequent extensions of the contract will be subject to the IITL without exception. Notice of the State Council Regarding Questions of the Levy of Taxation on Chinese-Foreign Joint Venture and Co-operative Projects, 21 September 1982, Art. 3 (hereafter cited as the State Council Notice), in Zhonghua renmin gongheguo guowuyuan gongbao (People's Republic of China State Council Gazette), 1982, pp. 695 and 696 (hereafter cited as the State Council Gazette). See also [Document] Regarding the Question of Levy and Exemption of Taxation on Wages and Salaries of Technical Personnel Sent to China to Work by Foreign Businesses in Order to Perform Contracts Signed Before the Promulgation of the [Individual Income] Tax Law, 20 November 1980 (hereafter cited as the Wage and Salary Document), in Zhonghua renmin gongheguo caizheng bu shuiwu zongju (People's Republic of China Ministry of Finance General Bureau of Taxation), Zhongguo duiwai shuiwu shouce (Handbook of China's Foreign Taxation), Vol. I (Beijing, China Finance and Economy Press, 1983), pp. 70–2 (hereafter cited as the Handbook, Vol. I). All documents in the Handbook, Vol. I, and the Handbook, Vol. II, note 35 below, are official documents of the Ministry of Finance. Under the State Council Notice, contractual provisions stipulating that the Chinese party agrees to pay any Chinese taxes, including individual income taxes, imposed on the foreign party as a result of the contract, remain valid for the initial term of the contract.

6. IITL, Art. 1, para. 2, note 2 above.

7. IITL Regulations, Art. 5(1), note 2 above. Our italics.

8. IITL Regulations, Art. 5(1), note 2 above. The term 'employer outside China' refers to an entity that is not taxed in China on its net income and therefore cannot deduct the wages in question from its gross income. T. Gelatt, discussion with Ministry of Finance tax official, 23 February 1983. See, also, Reply to Questions Concerning the Individual Income Taxes Payable by Employees of Companies Engaged in Offshore Petroleum Exploitation and Contracting Operations, 18 November 1983 (on file with the authors). This Notice serves to clarify the concept of 'employer outside China' as meaning an employer that does not have a taxable establishment in China.

9. Notice of the Ministry of Finance Regarding Several Questions of Individual Income Tax, 2 June 1981, in Zhongguo jingji nianjian (Almanac of China's Economy) (Beijing, Economic Management Magazine Press, 1982), p. III-57 (hereafter cited as the Almanac). This Notice (hereafter cited as the MOF Notice) formed the basis for a Notice of 30 June 1981 issued to foreign taxpayers and reissued in 1985 by the Beijing Municipal Tax Bureau Foreign Tax Collection Office (FTCO).

10. MOF Notice, Art. 6, note 9 above. The MOF Notice states that the localities may 'leniently' interpret this principle under 'exceptional circumstances'. See the new Ministry of Finance Policy discussed in the text accompanying note 11 below.

11. Notice of the General Bureau of Taxation of the Ministry of Finance Regarding Various Policy and Operational Questions on Individual Income Tax, 18 February 1986, Zhongguo shuiwu (China Tax), No. 4, 1986, p. 38, Art. 1, hereafter cited as the 1986 IITL Notice. Presumably, the exemption for foreigners who are actually in China for one-third or less of their visa period would not apply to a foreigner holding a visa valid for over 270 days who was actually in China for more than ninety days. See text below. Most multiple-entry visas, however, do not exceed 180 days.

A businessman whose visa is valid for ninety days or more must register with the tax authorities. A foreigner who leaves China without intending to return must cancel his tax registration.

12. See MOF Notice, Art. 6, note 9 above.

13. MOF Notice, Art. 6, note 9 above. It is unclear why the Notice uses the formulation 'less than ninety days' rather than 'ninety days or less'. See IITL Regulations, Art. 5(1), note 2 above; and text accompanying note 7 above.

14. MOF Notice, Art. 6, note 9 above.

15. T. Gelatt, discussion with the FTCO, 8 October 1981.

16. See IITL, Arts. 11 and 12, note 2 above; and IITL Regulations, Arts. 21 and 22, note 2 above.

17. IITL Regulations, Art. 2, para. 2, note 2 above.

18. IITL, Art. 1, para. 1, note 2 above; and IITL Regulations, Art. 2, para. 1, note 2 above. It is unclear how literally this rule will be interpreted if the 365 days straddle two taxable years. For example, if a foreigner enters China on 2 January of year 1, when will he be considered as having resided for a full 365 days within a taxable year—on 2 January of year 2, or on 1 January of year 3, the latter being the result under a literal interpretation of the rule? The authors understand that the law is not being interpreted literally and periods that straddle two taxable years are aggregated.

19. IITL Regulations, Art. 3, note 2 above.

20. IITL Regulations, Art. 3, note 2 above.

21. Notice [of the Ministry of Finance] Regarding the Exemption from Tax Reporting and Payment of Individual Income Tax for Income Gained Outside China by Personnel of Foreign Nationality Working in China, 7 March 1983. In effect, the benefit to foreigners of this liberalization will primarily result in the areas of non-wage and salary income, because of the PRC's peculiar interpretation of China-source wages and salaries. See text following note 25 below. Foreigners residing in China and working for Chinese organizations apparently will not benefit from this rule on foreign-source income.

22. IITL Regulations, Art. 2, para. 1, note 2 above.

23. MOF Notice, Art. 7, note 9 above. The emphasis of these rules is understandably on when a foreigner obtains or severs his residency; eventually, rules will have to be developed regarding the circumstances under which a Chinese citizen can sever his residency for tax purposes.

24. IITL Regulations, Art. 5, note 2 above.

25. IITL Regulations, Art. 5, note 2 above.

26. 1986 IITL Notice, Art. 2, note 11 above. This ruling will affect many foreign companies who rotate their employees periodically between, for instance, their China and Hong Kong offices. It remains to be seen what kind of 'proof' the Chinese tax authorities will require for the allocation approach described in the text.

27. IITL, Art. 2(1), note 2 above. Wages and salaries include incentive bonuses (*jiangjin*) and 'year-end extras'. IITL Regulations, Art. 4(1), note 2 above.

The Chinese regard that portion of technical service fees paid by the Chinese party in technology transfer or equipment sale contracts which represents wages and salaries paid by the foreign party to its personnel performing services in China in connection with the contract as wage and salary income taxable under the IITL to the personnel in question, assuming the personnel do not fall within the ninety-day exemption, see text accompanying notes 7–11 above. Wage and Salary Document, note 5 above; and [Document] On the Question of Levy of Taxation on the Income of Foreign Personnel Sent to China by Foreign Companies to Provide Services, *Handbook*, Vol. I, pp. 73–4, note 5 above. In cases where the foreign company is taxed on its gross income, that portion of the technical service fee which is taxable as wage and salary income to foreign individuals may also be taxable to the foreign company under the FEITL because there will be no offsetting deduction. See text accompanying notes 153, 155, and 157–9 below.

28. IITL, Art. 2(2), note 2 above. Compensation for personal services includes earnings from such personal services as design, installation, drafting, medical treatment, law practice, and accounting. IITL Regulations, Art. 4(2), note 2 above. A glossary of IITL terminology specifies that compensation for personal services is limited to fees for the above services paid on a case-by-case basis and does not cover, for instance, the income of lawyers or accountants who are paid on a salary basis. 'Explanation of Terms in the Two Income Tax Laws', *Renmin ribao (People's Daily)*, 4 September 1980, p. 4. Presumably, the differentiation is similar to that drawn under United States law between independent contractors and employees.

29. IITL, Art. 2(3), note 2 above. These fees include income from the provision and transfer of patent rights, copyrights, proprietary technology, and 'other rights'. IITL Regulations, Art. 4(3), note 2 above.

30. IITL, Art. 2(4), note 2 above. Interest includes interest received from deposits, loans, and securities. IITL Regulations, Art. 4(4), note 2 above. Some types of interest, such as that on savings deposits in China's state banks, are exempt from taxation. IITL, Art. 4(2), note 2 above.

31. IITL, Art. 2(4), note 2 above. 'Dividends' refers to dividends 'from investment'. IITL Regulations, Art. 4(4), note 2 above.

32. IITL, Art. 2(4), note 2 above. 'Bonuses' (*hongli*) refers to bonuses 'from investment', IITL Regulations, Art. 4(4), note 2 above, and seems to cover a distribution to investors that is not based on shares of stock, such as a distribution to members of a collective.

33. IITL, Art. 2(5), note 2 above. Rental income includes income from the rental of houses, warehouses, machinery and equipment, motor vehicles and boats, and other kinds of property. IITL Regulations, Art. 4(5), note 2 above.

34. IITL Regulations, Art. 4(6), note 2 above. Income from the sale of property is not mentioned in either the IITL or the IITL Regulations and it is unclear whether the Ministry of Finance will classify this income as taxable should it become significant in the future.

35. MOF Notice, Art. 1, note 9 above. See also Notice of the Ministry of Finance Regarding Questions of Individual Income Tax Payment of Foreign Work Personnel in China, 24 October 1980, Art. 5, in *Almanac*, p. III-50, note 9 above; and Ministry of Finance Supplementary Explanation 2, 7 July 1981, *Handbook*, Vol. I, p. 77, note 5 above. Subsidies received by foreign personnel resident in China during brief trips out of China are considered China-source income and are taxable with that month's wages and salary. [Document] Regarding the Question of Levy of Taxation on Subsidies Earned by Foreign Taxpayers on Short Trips out of China, 7 July 1981, in *Handbook*, Vol. I, p. 74, note 5 above. See text accompanying and following note 26 above. Presumably, such subsidies that represent 'company expenses' will not be taxable if adequate proof is available. See accompanying text. Per diem allowances paid by foreign companies to their employees travelling on business within China are 'provisionally' exempt from taxation under a 1982 ruling. [Document] Regarding the Question of Levy of Individual Income Tax on Subsidies Earned by Long-term Representatives of Foreign Businesses Travelling on Business within China, 18 May 1982, in Zhonghua renmin gongheguo caizheng bu shuiwu zongju (People's Republic of China Ministry of Finance General Bureau of Taxation), *Zhongguo duiwai shuiwu shouce (Handbook of China's Foreign Taxation)*, Vol. II (Beijing, China Finance and Economy Press, 1984), p. 17 (hereafter cited as the *Handbook*, Vol. II).

Originally, food consumed in a non-business setting was considered to be a personal expense of the employee, and payments for such food by a foreigner's employee were taxable. A recent notice of the Ministry of Finance appears to liberalize the treatment of payments by foreign companies for the food expenses of their employees in China. Such payments will not be taxable provided that they reimburse the employee for the cost of food and that sufficient documentation exists. Apparently, it is irrelevant whether these expenses are of a business or personal nature. Fixed per diem or monthly food subsidies, however, will continue to be taxable as part of wages or salary. Notice of the General Tax Bureau of the Ministry of Finance on the Question of Whether or Not Food Subsidies to Taxpayers Should Be Included in Wage and Salary Income and Taxed, 18 January 1984, *Caizheng (Finance)*, No. 5, 1984, p. 43.

Various other exemptions from taxation are provided, for instance, for prizes and awards for scientific, technological, or cultural achievements, and the Ministry of Finance has the power to exempt income other than that specifically listed in the IITL and IITL Regulations. See IITL, Art. 4, note 2 above; and IITL Regulations, Arts. 8–10, note 2 above.

36. The 1986 IITL Notice, Art. 5, note 11 above, provides a formula for calculating the individual income tax payable by an employee whose tax is paid by his employer.

37. IITL, Art. 5(1), note 2 above. As of 1 December 1986, US$1 equals RMB3.7.

38. Despite this general position under the IITL, in at least one published case the Ministry of Finance has allowed a resident foreign businessman to deduct alimony payments from his taxable income in China, in addition to his standard RMB800 deduction. The reasoning behind this decision was that the RMB800 deduction was intended to cover 'normal living expenses' and not extraordinary expenses such as alimony payments. [Document] Regarding the Question of Whether the American [. . .] May Deduct from his Income Alimony Payments to his Former Wife, *Handbook*, Vol. I, p. 83, note 5 above. The Ministry should expect that it will be called upon to refine its reasoning as taxpayers attempt in the future to deduct a whole range of expenses they claim to be 'extraordinary'.

Another exception to the IITL rules on deductions has recently been made for overseas Chinese not resident in China who obtain income from the leasing of houses in China. Under the IITL, non-residents are not entitled to any deduction, including the standard deduction, from rental or other types of China-source income. IITL Regulations, Art. 11, note 2 above. In order to encourage overseas Chinese to build houses in China, however, they will now be permitted to deduct from their rental income any Chinese real estate tax paid on the rented houses, as well as repair expenses. Deductible repair expenses are limited to RMB800 for each tax period. 1986 IITL Notice, Art. 4, note 11 above.

39. IITL, Art. 3(1), note 2 above, and Schedule of Individual Income Tax Rates. Because wages and salaries are taxed monthly under a progressive rate schedule, the MOF Notice provides a special 'income-averaging rule' for taxpayers receiving several months' incentive bonuses in one month. If the bonus income results in the recipient's being taxed at a higher marginal tax rate than otherwise, a special calculation is provided. First, the bonus income attributable to services performed in the month in question (rather than the total amount of bonuses received that month) is added to that month's wages or salary. The marginal tax rate applicable to the resulting amount serves as a ceiling on the marginal rate applicable to all of the bonus income received that month, plus that month's wages or salary. In other words, while all of the bonus income and wages or salary is taxed in the month received, the marginal tax rate is determined as if only that month's bonus had been received. MOF Notice, Art. 2, note 9 above.

40. IITL, Art. 3(2), note 2 above.

For a discussion of the administrative and enforcement procedures under the IITL, see Pomp, Gelatt, and Surrey, pp. 49–51, note 1 above.

41. Consistent with Chinese practice, the term 'industrial and commercial tax' is used in this chapter to refer generically to the turnover tax applied under the Consolidated Industrial and Commercial Tax Act (CICTA), see note 45 below and accompanying text, as well as under other domestic Chinese tax legislation.

42. See Guojia shuishou jiaocai bianxie zu (National Taxation Teaching Materials Editorial Group), *Guojia shuishou* (*National Taxation*) (Beijing, China Finance and Economy Press, 1983), pp. 31–2 (hereafter cited as *National Taxation*).

43. The tax had not in the past been imposed on wholesalers. See *National Taxation*, p. 40, note 42 above. More recently, the scope of the tax was expanded to include wholesalers. Regulations of the Ministry of Finance Regarding the Levy of the Industrial and Commercial Tax on Wholesale Business Income from Goods, undated, *State Council Gazette*, 1983, p. 1051, note 5 above; and Report of the Ministry of Finance Regarding the Levy of the Industrial and Commercial Tax on Wholesale Business Income from Goods, 16 October 1983, *State Council Gazette*, 1983, p. 1049, note 5 above. See also Supplementary Regulations of the Ministry of Finance Regarding the Levy of the Industrial and Commercial Tax on Wholesale Business Income from Goods, 14 January 1984, *Caizheng*, No. 4, 1984, p. 45.

44. Several different forms of value added tax are being employed. See, for example, Li Xinjian, 'How Did the City of Wuhan Implement the Value Added Tax on a Trial Basis for Textile Products?', *Zhongguo shuiwu*, No. 9, 1985, p. 23; and Notice of the Ministry of Finance Regarding the Levy of and Exemption from Product Tax, Value Added Tax and Business Tax for Enterprises and Farmers in Villages and Towns, 25 January 1985, *Zhongguo shuiwu*, No. 4, 1985, p. 45. In addition to these experiments with a value added tax, experiments began in the autumn of 1984 to convert the existing industrial and commercial tax into several separate taxes, similar to the situation existing before the CICTA. See 'Explanation of the Implementation of the Change from Profits Turnover to Taxation for State Enterprises and Reform of the Industrial and Commercial Tax System', *State Council Gazette*, 1984, p. 791, note 5 above; see, also, Pomp, Gelatt, and Surrey, pp. 16–18, note 1 above.

45. Consolidated Industrial and Commercial Tax Act of the People's Republic of China (Draft) (cited elsewhere in this volume as the Consolidated Industrial and Commercial Tax Regulations of the People's Republic of China), passed in principle by the One Hundred and First Meeting of the Standing Committee of the National People's Congress on 11 September 1958 and promulgated for trial implementation by the State Council on 13 September 1958 (hereafter cited as the CICTA); and Detailed Rules and Regulations for the Implementation of the Consolidated Industrial and Commercial Tax Act of the People's Republic of China (Draft), promulgated for trial implementation by the Ministry of Finance on 13 September 1958 (hereafter cited as the CICTA Regulations).

46. CICTA, Art. 2, note 45 above.

47. CICTA Regulations, Art. 2, note 45 above.

48. CICTA, Arts. 5 and 6, note 45 above.

49. CICTA, Art. 6, note 45 above; and CICTA Regulations, Art. 11, note 45 above. See *National Taxation*, p. 45, note 42 above. As an example, if the CIF price = RMB12,000, the customs duty = RMB2,400, and the industrial and commercial tax rate is 10 per cent, the industrial and commercial tax is levied on (12,000 + 2,400) ÷ (1 − 10 per cent), or RMB16,000.

50. CICTA Regulations, Art. 11, note 45 above.

For a discussion of the collection and enforcement procedures for the industrial and commercial tax, see Pomp, Gelatt, and Surrey, pp. 26–8, note 1 above.

51. CICTA, note 45 above, and Schedule of Taxable Items and Rates. Various adjustments of the industrial and commercial tax rates have taken place over the years, including a major adjustment in July 1982. Notice of the Ministry of Finance Regarding the Adjustment of the Industrial and Commercial Tax Rates on Certain Products and the Expansion of Taxation Items (hereafter cited as the Industrial and Commercial Tax Notice), *State Council Gazette*, 1982, p. 552, note 5 above.

52. CICTA, note 45 above, and Schedule of Taxable Items and Rates.

53. The surtax is levied under an internal Ministry of Finance Notice of 1961. The authors know of the existence of this Notice but have not seen the actual text.

54. CICTA, Art. 4, note 45 above; and CICTA Regulations, Arts. 6 and 12, note 45 above.

55. The Law of the People's Republic of China Concerning Joint Ventures Using Chinese and Foreign Investment, passed by the Second Session of the Fifth National People's Congress on 1 July 1979 (hereafter cited as the Joint Venture Law), Art. 1 and Art. 4, para. 1; and Implementing Act for the Law of the People's Republic of China Concerning Joint Ventures Using Chinese and Foreign Investment, promulgated by the State Council on 20 September 1983 (hereafter cited as the Joint Venture Implementing Act), Art. 19.

56. See JVITL, Art. 1, note 3 above. Any tax due on a branch's income is paid in China by the head office. JVITL, Art. 1, para. 2, note 3 above. The legal definition of the term translated as 'branch' is unclear. The Chinese term, *fenzhi jigou*, might also include subsidiaries, so that income earned by a subsidiary of a Chinese joint venture would be subject to the JVITL.

57. Notice of the Ministry of Finance, *Ta kung pao*, 10 November 1980, p. 1 (hereafter cited as the Notice of the Ministry of Finance). For explanations in English, see *China Economic News*, 17 November 1980, p. 3; and *Business China*, 25 November 1980, p. 175.

58. Notice of the Ministry of Finance, note 57 above. See, also, State Council Notice, Art. 1, note 5 above. In the relatively few cases where a joint venture contract had provided for a higher rate than that imposed by JVITL, the latter will apply.

59. Notice of the Ministry of Finance, note 57 above; and State Council Notice, note 5 above.

60. JVITL, Art. 1, para. 1, note 3 above. A non-exclusive list of examples of 'production and business income' is provided in JVITL Regulations, Art. 2, para. 1, note 3 above.

61. JVITL Regulations, Art. 2, para. 2, note 3 above.

62. JVITL Regulations, Art. 15, note 3 above.

63. JVITL, Art. 2, note 3 above; and JVITL Regulations, Arts. 7 and 23, note 3 above.

64. JVITL, Art. 7, note 3 above. There is no provision for the carry-back of losses.

65. JVITL Regulations, Arts. 10, 13, 16, and 17, note 3 above.

66. See Accounting Regulations of the People's Republic of China for Joint Ventures Using Chinese and Foreign Investment, promulgated by the Ministry of Finance on 4 March 1985. For an English translation, see *East Asian Executive Reports*, August 1985, pp. 22–31.

67. JVITL Regulations, Art. 10, note 3 above. 'Short' is interpreted as less than one year. Explanation Regarding the Scope of Fixed Assets, 1 December 1981, *Handbook*, Vol. I, p. 13, note 5 above.

68. JVITL Regulations, Art. 12, note 3 above. Under 'special circumstances' a joint venture may be granted permission by the tax authorities to use accelerated depreciation. JVITL Regulations, Art. 13, para. 2, note 3 above. For the rules on the determination of original price and residual value in various circumstances, see JVITL Regulations, Art. 12, note 3 above.

69. JVITL Regulations, Art. 13, para. 1, note 3 above. A Notice of the Ministry of Finance provides for certain situations in which shorter lives than the minimum prescribed in the regulations may be used:
(a) where a joint venture's term is shorter than the minimum useful life prescribed in the regulations and the Chinese will own the asset after the term of the joint venture;
(b) where equipment of an acidic or alkaline nature prone to excessive corrosion is used, or where factories and buildings are subject to continuous vibration; and

(c) where machines or equipment that are perennially operated on a continuous basis to increase their productivity are used.

Notice of the Ministry of Finance Regarding Several Questions on the Joint Venture Income Tax, 8 June 1981, Art. 6 (hereafter cited as the Joint Venture Tax Notice), in *Almanac*, p. III-60, note 9 above.

70. JVITL Regulations, Art. 16, para. 1, note 3 above.

71. JVITL Regulations, Art. 16, para. 2, note 3 above.

72. JVITL Regulations, Art. 17, note 3 above.

73. See JVITL Regulations, Art. 9, note 3 above.

74. See JVITL Regulations, Art. 8, note 3 above.

75. JVITL Regulations, Art. 9(9), note 3 above. Presumably, joint ventures that do not engage in sales use the 1 per cent test. In no event can a joint venture deduct entertainment expenses that are not 'relevant to production and operations'. JVITL Regulations, Art. 9(9), note 3 above.

76. JVITL Regulations, Art. 9(3), note 3 above. This provision is intended to deny a deduction by the joint venture of interest on loans incurred by a joint venture partner to obtain its capital contribution to the joint venture. However, interest on loans later incurred by the joint venture company for business purposes is deductible. If the loan was used to purchase a capital asset, the interest must be capitalized and added to the cost of the asset. T. Gelatt and colleagues, discussions with Ministry of Finance tax officials, 1983 and 1985. Apparently, the provision is also intended to prohibit the deduction of what are actually dividends or distributions of profits. See Wang Xuanhui, 'Clarify the Procedures for Computation of Losses and Gains, Reasonably Stipulate the Scope of Deduction of Expenditures', *Caizheng*, No. 8, 1982, p. 35.

77. See JVITL Regulations, Art. 8, note 3 above. For an analysis of these rules in the context of standard Western accounting rules, see T. Gelatt and R. Pomp, 'Tax Aspects of Doing Business with the People's Republic of China', *Columbia Journal of Transnational Law*, Vol. 22, No. 3, 1984, p. 453, note 149.

78. JVITL Regulations, Art. 18, note 3 above.

79. JVITL Regulations, Art. 18, note 3 above. Chinese officials have apparently stated that the last-in first-out (LIFO) method is also acceptable. D. Foster and J. Horsley, 'Business Operations in the People's Republic of China', *Tax Management Portfolio*, No. 443, 1983, p. A-20. The permission of the local tax authority must be obtained to change accounting methods. JVITL Regulations, Art. 18, note 3 above.

80. Joint Venture Law, Art. 7, para. 1, note 55 above.

81. Yu Dongzhou, 'A Critique of the Law on Joint Ventures Using Chinese and Foreign Investment from the Viewpoint of Legislative Technique', *Shehui kexue zhanxian (Social Science Battlefront)*, No. 2, 1980, p. 123; and T. Gelatt, discussion with Ministry of Finance tax official, 22 November 1982.

82. T. Gelatt, discussion with Ministry of Finance officials, 1984. See, also, Notice of General Tax Bureau of the Ministry of Finance on the Question of How Joint Ventures Should Account for Advance Expenses or Reserve Funds in Calculating Taxable Income, 18 January 1984, *Caizheng*, No. 5, 1984, p. 44. Payments made out of the workers' bonus and welfare funds are apparently viewed as a form of profit-sharing akin to a non-deductible dividend. This view is inconsistent, however, with allowing a deduction for workers' bonuses paid out of general joint venture funds.

In addition to payments into the three funds discussed in the text, a joint venture is required to pay a sum equal to 2 per cent of the total actual wages of staff and workers of the venture into a trade union fund. One source states that payments into the trade union fund must be made out of after-tax profits, like payments made into the three other funds. Shanghai shehui kexue yuan (Shanghai Academy of Social Sciences), *Zhongwai hezi jingying qiye (Chinese-Foreign Joint Ventures)* (Shanghai, Shanghai Academy of Social Sciences Press, 1984), p. 250. Tax officials in Beijing, on the other hand, have indicated that payments made into the trade union fund are deductible in calculating taxable income. T. Gelatt colleague, discussion with Beijing tax officials, 1985. This issue remains to be resolved by the Ministry of Finance.

83. JVITL, Art. 3, note 3 above.

84. JVITL, Art. 3, para. 1, note 3 above; and JVITL Regulations, Art. 3, para. 1, note 3 above. The local tax is collected together with the national tax and later distributed to the local authorities.

85. JVITL Regulations, Art. 3, para. 2, note 3 above.

Numerous local regulations for the encouragement of foreign investment issued in 1986 afford reductions of and exemptions from the local income surtax under the JVITL as well as the local tax applicable to foreign investors in projects other than equity joint ventures, under the FEITL, see note 125 below and accompanying text. For instance, under Article 2 of Certain Provisions of Shanghai Municipality for the Encouragement of Foreign Investment, implemented as of 1 November 1986, all equity, co-operative and wholly foreign-owned enterprises that qualify as 'export enterprises' (EEs) or technologically advanced enterprises (TAEs) will be exempt from local tax or surtax for the period during which exemption from national tax applies under relevant provisions of law (see note 91 below and accompanying text) and for three further years thereafter. For the next three years, these enterprises will pay local tax or surtax at half the normal rate.

86. The 10 per cent tax is provided for in JVITL, Art. 4, note 3 above; and JVITL Regulations, Art. 4, note 3 above.

The Provisions of the State Council of the People's Republic of China for the Encouragement of Foreign Investment, promulgated by the State Council on 11 October 1986 (hereafter cited as the State Council Provisions), exempt foreign investors in EEs and TAEs, see note 85 above, from tax on remitted profits. State Council Provisions, Art. 7, above. Since the State Council Provisions apply to wholly foreign-owned enterprises as well as to equity and co-operative ventures, this exemption might have been presumed to apply to the 20 per cent tax on dividends that may be imposed under the FEITL on the foreign investor in a wholly foreign-owned enterprise, see text following note 135 below, as well as to the 10 per cent tax under the JVITL. Implementing rules under the State Council Provisions published by the Ministry of Finance, however, indicate that the rule will only apply to equity ventures. Implementing Measures of the Ministry of Finance to Implement the Tax Preference Articles of the Provisions of the State Council for the Encouragement of Foreign Investment (hereafter cited as Tax Preference Measures), promulgated on 31 January 1987, Art. 1.

87. See United States Internal Revenue Code (hereafter cited as the IRC), §§ 871(a)(1)(A) and 881(a)(1).

88. See JVITL Regulations, Art. 4, note 3 above; and Wang Xuanhui, 'A Discussion of the Income Tax Burden on Chinese-Foreign Joint Ventures', Caizheng, No. 6, 1982, p. 21. It is unclear how the Chinese will treat a situation in which the dividend is initially deposited in a bank account within China and subsequently remitted outside China. Presumably, the 10 per cent tax applies when the dividend is withdrawn and remitted abroad, but rules will have to be developed to identify what part of the withdrawal from the deposit represents the dividend, and what part represents interest or principal.

To implement the 10 per cent tax, the Chinese will also need to develop rules defining the term 'profits'. The term cannot be synonymous with taxable income because certain outlays, such as the payment of the joint venture tax, reduce the amount of profits available for distribution even if they are not deductible for the purposes of calculating taxable income. Unless the calculation of profits takes into account such outlays, the 10 per cent tax might be levied on a distribution that actually constitutes a return of a shareholder's capital, rather than a distribution of profits. For the United States rules on what constitutes a distribution of profits, see IRC, §§ 301, 312, and 316, note 87 above.

89. Joint Venture Law, Art. 7, para. 2, note 55 above.

90. JVITL, Art. 5, para. 1, note 3 above. As the Chinese text makes clear, the following two years refer to the two years immediately subsequent to the first profit-making year and not, as has been understood by some foreigners, to the second and third profit-making years.

If a joint venture starts in mid-tax year, and makes a profit that tax year, that tax year is considered to be its first profit-making year for the purpose of the above provision of the JVITL. However, this rule may be modified in 'special circumstances' upon application to and consideration by the local tax authorities. [Document] Regarding the Question of the Periods of Tax Reduction and Exemption for Newly Opened Joint Ventures, 8 June 1981, *Handbook*, Vol. I, p. 12, note 5 above.

Certain types of enterprises are entitled to further tax reductions. Joint ventures in 'low-profit' operations such as farming or forestry, or ventures located in remote, undeveloped, outlying areas may apply for a 15–30 per cent reduction in income tax for an additional ten-year period. JVITL, Art. 5, para. 2, note 3 above. The local tax authorities are empowered to approve the initial years of exemption and reduction, but the Ministry of Finance must approve the additional ten-year reduction. JVITL, Art. 5, note 3 above.

91. Decision Regarding Amendment of the Joint Venture Income Tax Law of the People's Republic of China, passed by the Second Session of the Standing Committee of the Sixth National People's Congress, 2 September 1983 (hereafter cited as the JVITL Amendment Decision), Art. 1. It is unclear from the JVITL Amendment Decision whether these extended holidays and reductions apply to pre-existing joint ventures. A subsequent Ministry of Finance Notice provides that the extended holidays and reductions will apply to pre-existing ventures which have not yet earned profits or whose tax exemption and/or reduction periods have not expired. Notice of the Ministry of Finance Regarding the Earnest Implementation of the Decision of the Standing Committee of the National People's Congress Regarding Amendment of the Joint Venture Income Tax Law of the People's Republic of China, 12 October 1983 (hereafter cited as the Joint Venture Implementation Notice), Art. 1.

Under the State Council Provisions, note 86 above, EEs and TAEs, see note 85 above, qualify for additional periods of tax reduction, as well as those already provided for by law. EEs will enjoy a 50 per cent reduction of the normal tax rate for any year in which the 'production value' of exported products reaches or exceeds 70 per cent of the total production value of the relevant enterprise's products for such year. State Council Provisions, Art. 8, note 86 above. TAEs will continue for an additional three years to pay tax at half rate. State Council Provisions, Art. 9, note 86 above. While these 'additional' periods of tax reduction clearly apply to equity joint ventures, the State Council Provisions left it unclear whether and in what manner they would apply to co-operative ventures and wholly foreign-owned enterprises which, outside the special economic zones and other areas with special tax regimes, do not normally enjoy any tax holiday periods under the FEITL. See text accompanying notes 127 to 129, below. The Tax Preference Measures, note 86 above, clarify that these preferences will indeed apply to co-operative ventures and wholly foreign-owned enterprises, and set forth detailed rules for the application of the tax reduction scheme to such projects. Tax Preference Measures, Arts. II and III, note 86 above.

A question not specifically covered by the JVITL is whether the various tax holidays and reductions include the local surtax. However, Ministry of Finance officials have said that the local surtax is included in the holidays and reductions. Speech by Liu Zhicheng, Director of the General Bureau of Taxation, Ministry of Finance, in Los Angeles on 8 June 1981. Because the local surtax is based on a percentage of the national tax *paid*, see text accompanying note 84 above, the Ministry's position avoids the administrative complication of requiring a taxpayer entitled to a national tax holiday or reduction to calculate its national tax that would otherwise have been paid for the sole purpose of calculating the local surtax.

92. JVITL Regulations, Art. 5, note 3 above. This approach favours investors since it means that an initial period of start-up losses will not count against the joint venture's period of eligibility for tax exemption or reduction.

93. Joint Venture Law, Art. 7, para. 2, note 55 above.

94. Joint Venture Law, Art. 7, para. 3, note 55 above.

95. The JVITL Regulations specify that the profits must be reinvested in the same or another Chinese joint venture. JVITL Regulations, Art. 6, note 3 above. See, also, Joint Venture Tax Notice, Art. 1(1), note 69 above, stating that to qualify for the refund of tax the profits may be invested in the same joint venture or another existing joint venture in China, or used to form a new joint venture with a Chinese entity.

Under Article 10 of the State Council Provisions, note 86 above, a foreign investor in an equity or co-operative joint venture or a wholly foreign-owned enterprise that reinvests its profits to establish or expand an EE or a TAE, note 85 above, for a period of at least five years, will receive a refund of all the tax previously paid on the reinvested amount. Since an EE or TAE may be an equity or co-operative venture, or a wholly foreign-owned enterprise, the State Council Provisions considerably expand the scope of the reinvestment incentive under the JVITL as interpreted above. This expanded reinvestment incentive will apply only to profits earned for 1986 and later years that are reinvested. Tax Preference Measures, Art. III, note 86 above. The Chinese will need to develop accounting rules to determine whether 1986 or earlier profits are being used for reinvestment.

96. JVITL, Art. 6, note 3 above; and JVITL Regulations, Art. 6, note 3 above. Although these articles could be read as requiring that all of a participant's after-tax profit must be reinvested to obtain a refund, China's finance minister, Wang Bingqian, in discussions in September 1980 with American lawyers in Washington, DC, indicated that any part of the profit reinvested would entitle the investor to a proportional refund. Thus, if a participant reinvested 50 per cent of its after-tax profit, it would receive a refund of 40 per cent of 50 per cent of the tax paid on the pre-tax profit. Presumably, a participant will be deemed to have paid a portion of the JVITL tax equal to the percentage of its equity participation in the venture.

97. JVITL, Art. 6, note 3 above. It is unclear whether during the five-year period reinvested funds can be withdrawn from one joint venture in China and reinvested in another joint venture in China without triggering the payback requirement. It is also unclear what approach, for example FIFO or LIFO, will be used in determining the 'age' of any withdrawn funds for purposes of the five-year rule.

98. Joint Venture Tax Notice, Art. 1(4), note 69 above. A foreign participant which repatriates its tax refund is not subject to the 10 per cent tax on remitted profits. See notes 86–8 above and accompanying text. Joint Venture Tax Notice, Art. 1(5), note 69 above. Presumably, the Chinese felt that the tax incentive to reinvest would be undercut if the refund were subject to the 10 per cent tax on remitted profits.

99. JVITL, Art. 16, para. 1, note 3 above; and JVITL Regulations, Art. 32, note 3 above. A per-country limitation is used for the joint venture tax credit. Joint Venture Tax Notice, Art. 4, note 69 above.

For a full discussion of the JVITL's administrative and enforcement provisions, see Pomp, Gelatt, and Surrey, pp. 61–3, note 1 above.

100. FEITL, note 4 above; and FEITL Regulations, note 4 above. Under the State Council Notice, Art. 1, note 5 above, 'preferential provisions' regarding enterprise income tax burdens in contracts signed and approved before the FEITL remain valid for the life of the contract, but will not apply to any extensions. The preferential provisions referred to include provisions, common in investment, technology transfer, and other contracts signed before the FEITL, under which

the Chinese party is to pay all taxes arising in China under the contract. These provisions are prohibited in contracts signed after the FEITL. See [Document] Regarding Questions Relating to Taxation of Such Contracts as Introduction of Technology Contracts, Loan Contracts and Leasing Contracts Approved before the Promulgation of the Tax Law, 29 March 1982, *Handbook*, Vol. I, p. 37, note 5 above.

101. See Chapter 3.

102. The Chinese term is *jigou*.

103. FEITL, Art. 11, para. 1, note 4 above. The Chinese term, *texuquan shiyongfei*, is translated as 'royalties' in the Chinese unofficial translation of the FEITL, see *China Daily*, 17 December 1982, p. 2. The term 'royalties' is too narrow and fails to capture the intended scope of *texuquan shiyongfei*. The precise Chinse term for 'royalties' in the Western sense of that term is *ticheng fei*.

104. This approach is widely known as a 'withholding tax'. Technically, withholding is a means of collecting a tax and should not be used to refer to the imposition of a tax. None the less, because the term 'withholding tax' has been commonly adopted throughout the world, it is used in this chapter.

105. FEITL, Art. 1, para. 2, note 4 above; and FEITL Regulations, Art. 2, note 4 above.

106. See p. 57 of the text.

107. See p. 58 of the text.

108. FEITL, Art. 1, para. 1, note 4 above.

109. See FEITL Regulations, Art. 4, note 4 above.

110. The language of the FEITL, Art. 1, para. 1, note 4 above, stating that 'in the *People's Republic of China*, the income of foreign enterprises [with establishments in China] from production, business operations and other sources will all be taxed according to the provisions of this law' (our italics), is ambiguous, but could be read to mean that only income from China is taxable. See also Wang Xuanhui, 'Reasonably Explain the Source of Taxable Income, Encourage Low Interest Loans and Deposits', *Caizheng*, No. 10, 1982, p. 43.

111. FEITL, Art. 11, para. 1, note 4 above; and FEITL Regulations, Art. 27, note 4 above.

112. To the extent that Chinese subsidiaries of foreign companies are taxed under the FEITL, see note 105 above, the Chinese will presumably tax their worldwide income, as in the case of joint ventures, see text accompanying note 60 above, to avoid the use of China as a tax haven for shell companies having no China income.

113. FEITL Regulations, Art. 10, note 4 above.

114. The FEITL Regulations provide a more complex scheme regarding business entertainment expenses than the JVITL. See FEITL Regulations, Art. 13, note 4 above. The FEITL Regulations also prohibit deductions for all 'other expenditures not related to production or operations', FEITL Regulations, Art. 10(10), note 4 above, a prohibition presumably intended to be implicit in the JVITL. Examples of such expenditures given by an official commentary are moving expenses, staff retirement funds, educational expenses for staff's children, and extraordinary losses from natural disasters. 'Explanation of Terms in the [FEITL Regulations]', *Handbook*, Vol. I, p. 133, note 5 above.

115. FEITL Regulations, Art. 10(3), note 4 above.

116. FEITL Regulations, Art. 12(3), note 4 above.

117. Interest on a bank loan incurred by a participant in a co-operative venture for its contribution to the venture has in the past been deductible by that participant, provided it meets the 'reasonable' and 'normal' tests. T. Gelatt, discussion with Ministry of Finance tax official, 23 February 1983. However, in recent negotiations, some investors in co-operative venture projects have been told that a percentage—generally about 30 per cent—of loan funds used by the foreign party as its contribution to a co-operative venture will be treated as a foreign party's

'own funds', and interest on that amount will not be deductible for FEITL purposes.

In addition, a Ministry of Finance document provides that interest on a loan taken out for investment in a project in China may only be deducted currently as an expense after the project enters the production or operating phase. Until that time, the interest must be capitalized and depreciated or amortized as part of the cost of the property that the loan was used to acquire. [Document] Regarding the Question of Listing Interest on Loans of a Foreign Enterprise as an Expense, 7 May 1982 (hereafter cited as the Interest Document), in *Handbook*, Vol. I, pp. 41–2, note 5 above. Similarly, interest on loans taken out after a project begins operating to acquire new capital equipment may only be charged currently as an expense after the equipment goes into use; before that time, it must be capitalized. Interest Document, pp. 41–2.

A Chinese official has said that 'reasonable' interest means interest 'not above the general interest rate on commercial loans'. Wang, p. 36, note 76 above. See also Interest Document, above, p. 41; and 'Explanation of Terms in the [FEITL Regulations]', *Handbook*, Vol. I, p. 134, note 5 above, stating that a 'normal loan' is one incurred by an enterprise that actually needs funds because its production or operating capital is insufficient or because the enterprise's own capital cannot satisfy the investment requirement of a particular project, or is incurred for expansion of the scale of production or operations. 'Any [such] loan on which the interest rate is not higher than the commercial lending rate at the location where the loan is obtained, and for which a loan contract has been signed, may be considered a "normal loan".'

118. FEITL Regulations, Art. 10(9), note 4 above. See note 103 above. No definition of head office is provided. If the Chinese adopt the narrow definition of head office that they are adopting in the context of representative offices, see note 168 below and accompanying text, the thrust of the provision will be avoidable through the use of related corporations.

For example, consider a US corporation with a Chinese establishment. Royalties for the use of proprietary rights paid by the establishment to the corporation in the US would presumably not be deductible because they would constitute fees paid to the head office. Suppose, however, that the US corporation transferred the proprietary rights to a subsidiary. Unless the subsidiary were considered to be the establishment's head office, royalties paid to it would now be deductible.

119. FEITL Regulations, Art. 11, para. 1, note 4 above.

120. See FEITL Regulations, Arts. 14, 15, 16, 17, 18, 19, 21, and 22, note 4 above.

121. FEITL Regulations, Art. 18, para. 3, note 4 above. See Wang Xuanhui, 'Distinguish Capital Expenditures and Expenses, Establish the System of Depreciation and Amortization of Property', *Caizheng*, No. 9, 1982, p. 40. A detailed discussion of offshore oil tax issues may be found in Chapter 6.

122. FEITL Regulations, Art. 24, para. 1, note 4 above.

123. Apparently the Chinese will look to domestic businesses or other foreign businesses in China. An official commentary has warned of the need to be sensitive to differences among enterprises, such as differing scales of operation, which may invalidate their comparison for tax purposes. Wang Xuanhui, 'Adopt Reasonable Substitutional Methods to Calculate the Amount of Taxable Income', *Caizheng*, No. 12, 1982, p. 36. Taxpayers subject to this imputed profit system must still supply their accounting records, vouchers, and so on, to the tax authorities. Wang, p. 36, above.

124. FEITL, Art. 3, note 4 above.

125. FEITL, Art. 4, para. 1, note 4 above. See FEITL Regulations, Art. 5, note 4 above.

126. Enterprises with an annual profit of RMB1 million or less qualify for a potential reduction or exemption upon the approval of the provincial-level people's governments. FEITL, Art. 4, para. 2, note 4 above; and FEITL Regulations,

Art. 6, note 4 above. Some enterprises are entitled to reductions in or exemptions from the local tax under local investment encouragement rules. See note 85 above.

For the administrative rules governing foreign companies with establishments, see Provisional Regulations of the General Bureau of Taxation of the Ministry of Finance of the People's Republic of China Regarding Tax Registration of Foreign Enterprises for the Commencement and Termination of Operations, promulgated by the General Bureau of Taxation of the Ministry of Finance of the People's Republic of China on 15 April 1982; FEITL, Arts. 7, 8, 10, 14, 15, and 16, note 4 above; and FEITL Regulations, Arts. 33, 35, and 43–7, note 4 above.

127. See note 90 above. The JVITL definition of the first profit-making year as the first profit-making year after exhausting the five-year loss carry-over, see note 92 above and accompanying text, is not repeated in the FEITL, which contains the same loss carry-over as the JVITL. See FEITL, Art. 6, note 4 above. The same definition will apparently be applied in practice. National Council for United States–China Trade meeting with the Beijing Municipal Tax Bureau, FTCO, 19 March 1982.

The FEITL does not state whether the possible holidays or reductions apply to the local 10 per cent tax. Administratively, there is no reason why these holidays or reductions should necessarily apply, since unlike in the case of the JVITL, see text accompanying note 84 above, the FEITL's local tax is not a function of the national tax. See note 91 above. However, a Chinese tax official has indicated that the local tax is included in the holidays and reductions under the FEITL. 'Interview with Liu Zhicheng, Director, General Bureau of Taxation, Ministry of Finance', *Zhongguo caimaobao* (*China Finance and Trade Journal*), 17 December 1981, p. 1. At least with respect to certain favoured enterprises, this position is made clear in some local regulations. See, for example, the Shanghai rule cited in note 85 above.

128. FEITL, Art. 5, note 4 above; and FEITL Regulations, Art. 7, note 4 above. Examples of low-profit operations mentioned in the FEITL and its regulations are farming, forestry, animal husbandry, and those low-profit enterprises engaged in exploiting coal resources in deep wells. Under the JVITL, the low-profit requirement has to be satisfied only in order to qualify for the ten-year, 15–30 per cent rate reduction (after the initial exemption and reduction). See note 90 above. Neither the JVITL nor the FEITL defines 'low profit' in this context.

129. See note 128 above.

130. FEITL, Art. 11, para. 1, note 4 above; and FEITL Regulations, Art. 27, note 4 above. Under the State Council Notice, Art. 2, note 5 above, preferential tax treatment of foreign or Hong Kong businesses receiving fees for the use of proprietary rights provided in contracts signed and approved before the promulgation of the FEITL continues to be valid for the initial life of the contract.

131. FEITL Regulations, Art. 28, note 4 above. This article indicates that 'separate stipulations' may alter this gross withholding treatment.

132. FEITL Regulations, Art. 27, para. 2, note 4 above.

133. See Foreign Taxation Section, General Bureau of Taxation, Ministry of Finance 'Questions and Answers on Foreign Taxation (2)', *Caizheng*, No. 7, 1982, p. 39; and T. Gelatt, discussion with Ministry of Finance tax official, 22 November 1982.

134. See text accompanying notes 86–8 above.

135. A withholding tax on distributions by foreign corporations with China-source income to their foreign shareholders *was* included in a 1981 draft of the FEITL circulated for comment but was later dropped. Comment of Carl Nordberg at Practising Law Institute Conference on 'Legal Aspects of Doing Business with China', New York, 27 January 1983.

136. FEITL Regulations, Art. 27, para. 3, note 4 above. Included within the scope of this provision is interest paid by foreign companies with establishments in China such as co-operative ventures, see text accompanying note 200 below, on

loans related to that establishment. A Ministry of Finance document suggests, however, that only interest that is allowed to be currently deducted as an expense by such companies is subject to the withholding tax. Interest Document, p. 42, note 117 above. See note 117 above. Implementation of the withholding tax in these situations may be difficult since the interest will usually be paid by the foreign company outside China.

137. Chinese corporations that have reportedly been granted approval to grant tax exemptions under this provision include the China International Trust and Investment Corporation, the Shanghai International Trust and Investment Corporation, and the Tianjin International Trust and Investment Corporation. These corporations, in addition to acting as intermediaries between foreign investors and potential Chinese partners, may under their charters accept loans from abroad for investment projects.

138. FEITL, Art. 11, para. 3, note 4 above; and FEITL Regulations, Art. 30, note 4 above.

139. FEITL Regulations, Art. 29, para. 2, note 4 above.

140. Provisional Regulations of the Ministry of Finance of the People's Republic of China Regarding the Reduction and Exemption of Income Tax Relating to Interest Earned by Foreign Businesses from China, 7 January 1983 (hereafter cited as the Interest Regulations).

141. Interest Regulations, Art. 2(1), note 140 above; and T. Gelatt, discussion with Ministry of Finance tax official, 9 March 1983. Under current practice, a margin of 0.5 per cent above LIBOR is acceptable only for loans of three or more years. For loans of one and two years, only spreads of 0.25 per cent and 0.375 per cent, respectively, are acceptable for the purpose of the withholding tax exemptions. T. Gelatt colleague, discussion with Ministry of Finance tax official, 11 November 1986.

When the state bank of the country of a foreign seller provides a seller's credit for the purchase of equipment by a Chinese buyer, the interest paid by the Chinese buyer will be exempt from tax if the rate does not exceed that charged for a buyer's credit by the state bank in the seller's country. Interest Regulations, Art. 2(3), note 140 above.

142. Interest Regulations, Art. 2(2), note 140 above. Under this provision, the interest rate must be no higher than the interbank interest rate for call funds. See note 141 above, and accompanying text.

143. Interest Regulations, Art. 1, note 140 above. The provision of the Interest Regulations only reduces the withholding tax for contracts signed between 1983 and 1985; the deadline has since been extended for five years. Notice of the Ministry of Finance Concerning Extension of the Term of Reduction of Income Tax on Interest and Leasing Fees Derived from China by Foreign Businesses, 6 January 1986, *Zhongguo shuiwu*, No. 2, 1986, p. 33.

144. Interest Regulations, Art. 6, note 140 above.

145. FEITL, Art. 11, para. 1, note 4 above; and FEITL Regulations, Art. 27, para. 4, note 4 above. The Ministry of Finance has provided that income earned by foreign companies from the rental of ships to Chinese shipping agencies which are used in international transport will be exempt from the withholding tax. Income from the rental of ships that are used in China's coastal waters or inland rivers will be subject to the tax. Notice of the Ministry of Finance Regarding the Permission for Provisional Exemption of Income Tax for Rental Payment Made for the Rental of Foreign Ships for Use in International Transport, 27 January 1984, *Caizheng*, No. 4, 1984, p. 47.

146. See T. Moore and R. MacNeil, 'Leasing in China Comes of Age', *East Asian Executive Reports*, January 1986, p. 9.

147. FEITL, Art. 11, para. 1, note 4 above.

148. Interest Regulations, Art. 3, para. 1, note 140 above.

149. Interest Regulations, Art. 3, paras. 1 and 2, note 140 above. To be exempt from taxation, interest in a lease-sale transaction must meet the criteria of the

Interest Regulations regarding interest in the seller's credit situation. Interest Regulations, Art. 3, para. 2, note 140 above; see note 141 above.

150. Interest Regulations, Art. 3, para. 2, note 140 above. This spread is referred to in the cited provision as the 'amount remaining after deduction of the interest'.

151. FEITL Regulations, Art. 27, para. 5, note 4 above. See note 103 above.

152. Fees for training conducted in China or abroad are normally taxable provided they relate to technology to be used in China. See Notice of the General Taxation Bureau of the Ministry of Finance Regarding Several Provisions Concerning Questions on the Levying of Income Tax on Chinese-Foreign Joint Ventures, Co-operative Production Ventures and Wholly Foreign-owned Enterprises, 21 April 1986, Art. 3, *Zhongguo shuiwu*, No. 6, 1986, p. 38.

153. See [Document] Regarding the Calculation and Levy of Income Tax on Fees for the Use of Proprietary Technology (hereafter cited as Technology Document), 14 October 1982, *Handbook*, Vol. II, p. 10, note 35 above; and Provisional Regulations of the Ministry of Finance of the People's Republic of China Regarding the Reduction of and Exemption from Income Tax on Fees for the Use of Proprietary Technology, 13 December 1982 (hereafter cited as the Technology Regulations), Art. 1.

154. There are two possible situations involving computer software. In the first, a foreign company merely sells computer programmes to the Chinese, with or without computer equipment, and the Chinese use the programmes as desired. The technology that would enable the Chinese to write and develop programmes of their own is not transferred. This situation is regarded by the Ministry of Finance as the simple sale of a good, and the resulting income is not taxable. In the second, technology for creating computer programmes is transferred to the Chinese, and the resulting income is treated as fees for the use of proprietary technology, taxable under the FEITL withholding tax if the company has no establishment in China. T. Gelatt, discussion with Ministry of Finance tax official, 9 March 1983.

155. Technology Regulations, Art. 2, note 153 above.

156. Technology Document, Art. 2, note 153 above.

157. See Technology Regulations, Art. 3, note 153 above. This provision makes it clear that without the approval of the tax authorities, the units introducing the technology may not grant tax reductions or tax exemptions.

158. Technology Regulations, Art. 1, note 153 above. In determining whether technology is 'advanced' for the purpose of the Technology Regulations' tax exemption, the importing Chinese entity must evaluate which of the available technologies will be most effective, and transmit its findings to the tax authorities for a decision. T. Gelatt, discussion with Ministry of Finance tax officials, 9 March 1983, and experience in negotiations, 1984 and 1985. In determining whether the technology is offered on 'preferential terms', the tax authorities will consider such factors as whether the cost is low relative to comparable technology, whether free training is included, whether payment may be made in kind rather than in cash (see text accompanying note 196 below) and whether the Chinese transferee may continue to use the technology free of charge after the termination of the contract. T. Gelatt, discussion with Ministry of Finance tax official, 9 March 1983.

159. Technology Regulations, Art. 1, note 153 above.

160. See p. 53 of the text.

161. See p. 53 of the text.

162. The tax treatment of wholly foreign-owned enterprises is discussed briefly since the Chinese have yet to publish specific tax rules or incentives for such enterprises. See text accompanying notes 239–45 below.

163. See Provisional Regulations of the State Council of the People's Republic of China Concerning the Control of Resident Representative Offices of Foreign Enterprises, promulgated by the State Council on 30 October 1980 (hereafter

cited as the Office Regulations); and Measures of the State Administration of Industry and Commerce of the People's Republic of China Regarding the Control of Registration of Resident Representative Offices of Foreign Enterprises, approved by the State Council on 5 March 1983, and promulgated by the State Administration of Industry and Commerce and effective on 15 March 1983 (hereafter cited as the Office Registration Measures).

164. FEITL, Art. 1, para. 2, note 4 above; and FEITL Regulations, Art. 2, para. 1, note 4 above.

165. Office Registration Measures, Art. 3, note 163 above.

166. Interim Provisions of the Ministry of Finance of the People's Republic of China Concerning the Levy of the Industrial and Commercial Consolidated Tax on Resident Representative Offices of Foreign Enterprises, approved by the State Council on 11 April 1985, and promulgated by the Ministry of Finance on 14 May 1985, Art. 1 (hereafter cited as the Representative Office Tax Provisions).

167. T. Gelatt colleague, conversation with Ministry of Finance tax official, 25 May 1985; and Provisions of the Foreign Tax Sub-Bureau of the Beijing Municipal Tax Bureau Concerning Some Specific Questions on the Interim Provisions Concerning the Levy of the Industrial and Commercial Consolidated Tax and Enterprise Income Tax on Resident Representative Offices of Foreign Enterprises, issued on 30 June 1985, Art. 10 (hereafter cited as the Beijing Tax Bureau Provisions).

168. Representative Office Tax Provisions, Art. 1, para. 1, note 166 above; and Supplementary Provisions Concerning the Question of the Levy of the Industrial and Commercial Consolidated Tax and Enterprise Income Tax on Resident Representative Offices of Foreign Enterprises, issued on 14 October 1985, Art. 4. The narrow definition of the 'head office' means that companies whose representative offices perform services for affiliated members of the same corporate group, as is commonly the case, may become taxable under the Representative Office Tax Provisions.

169. Representative Office Tax Provisions, Art. 1, para. 2, note 166 above.

170. Representative Office Tax Provisions, Art. 2, note 166 above. Beijing Tax Bureau Tax Provisions, Art. 6, note 167 above.

171. Representative Office Tax Provisions, Art. 3, note 166 above. The office must submit the relevant agency contract or other 'equivalent documentary evidence' in support of its argument for an allocation of income between the China office and the head office. If this evidence is sufficient, the local tax offices have been authorized by the Ministry of Finance to allocate 50 per cent of income under the contract in question as taxable income in China, or, in special cases, to determine the appropriate percentage on the basis of the actual circumstances. Notice of the General Tax Bureau of the Ministry of Finance Concerning the Question of the Calculation and Levy of Tax on the Determined Amount of Income of Resident Representative Offices of Foreign Enterprises, 19 September 1985, Art. 2.

172. See text accompanying notes 122 and 123.

173. Representative Office Tax Provisions, Art. 4, note 166 above, provides for a 15 per cent deemed profit rate. This rate was reduced to 10 per cent in October 1986. Notice of the Ministry of Finance Concerning the Issue of the Levy of Tax on a Reduced Rate of Deemed Profit for Resident Representative Offices of Foreign Enterprises, 6 October 1986, *Zhongguo shuiwu*, No. 12, 1986, p. 22.

The Beijing Tax Bureau has been experimenting with yet another formula for assessing tax of some offices, based on the offices' outlays and expenditures. See Supplementary Provisions of the Foreign Tax Sub-Bureau of the Beijing Municipal Tax Bureau Concerning the Method of Computing the Levy of Industrial and Commercial Consolidated Tax and Foreign Enterprise Income Tax on Resident Representative Offices of Foreign Enterprises, 15 November 1985. This approach is being applied to major multinational companies whose China representative offices work on behalf of one or more entities within the corporate group other than the entity that actually established the office. Other cities in China are also using this approach in certain cases.

174. See text accompanying note 48 above; and Office Regulations, Art. 10, para. 1, note 163 above.

175. Representative Office Tax Provisions, Art. 4, note 166 above.

176. Beijing Tax Bureau Provisions, Art. 8, note 167 above.

177. See text accompanying note 53 above. The levy of the industrial and commercial consolidated tax on resident representative offices of foreign enterprises was implemented from 1 June 1985; the foreign enterprise income tax was calculated and levied retroactively to the beginning of 1985. Beijing Tax Bureau Provisions, Art. 9, note 167 above.

178. The rate applicable to foreign bank branches is not specified in the CICTA. See CICTA, Schedule of Taxable Items and Rates, note 45 above.

179. See FEITL Regulations, Art. 2, para. 1, note 4 above.

180. Comments of PRC tax officials at Hong Kong seminar on 'PRC Taxation and Accounting Practices', 15 June 1982. This distinction is generally incorporated in the various tax treaties that China has signed or is negotiating with other countries.

181. Notice of the General Tax Bureau of the Ministry of Finance Regarding Questions of the Levy of Tax on the Agency or Consignment Sale of Goods or the Establishment of Maintenance Service Centres and the Agency Sale of Spare Parts and Fittings by Chinese Corporations and Enterprises Entrusted by Foreign Businesses, 6 October 1983 (hereafter cited as the Consignment Notice).

182. Consignment Notice, Art. 1, note 181 above. The term 'profit' presumably corresponds to the concept of net income under the FEITL.

183. Consignment Notice, Art. 1, note 181 above.

184. Consignment Notice, Art. 2, note 181 above. An exception exists for chemical products and instruments and equipment for use by Chinese and foreign ocean-going freighters sold by Chinese enterprises on behalf of foreign businesses. These may be exempted from the CICTA regardless of how the prices are determined, on the assumption that they will be provided directly from bonded warehouses to the freighters. Consignment Notice, Art. 4, note 181 above.

185. Consignment Notice, Art. 3, note 181 above. Under a possible reading of the Consignment Notice, a foreign company would be exempt from the FEITL, as well as the CICTA, even if an independent place of business existed for the sale of its products, so long as the pricing were handled as described in the text. See Consignment Notice, Arts. 1 and 3, note 181 above.

186. See text accompanying note 136 above.

187. Related to this characterization is a lease sale or hire purchase, where each payment in kind includes a 'lease fee' consisting of interest and a partial payment of the purchase price of the equipment.

188. See note 103 above and accompanying text.

189. Although no written source rules exist, such a sale is currently *not* considered as generating China-source income. See text accompanying note 211 below.

190. See text accompanying note 130 above; and T. Gelatt, discussion with Ministry of Finance tax official, 23 February 1983. See [Document] on the Question of the Levy of Income Tax on Revenue from Patent Rights and Proprietary Technology, 8 May 1982 (hereafter cited as the Patent and Technology Document), *Handbook*, Vol. II, p. 6, note 35 above.

191. See text accompanying note 105 above.

192. T. Gelatt, discussion with Ministry of Finance tax official, 9 March 1983.

193. The FEITL Regulations, Art. 32, note 4 above, appear to contemplate such an application of the withholding tax, stating that income on which the withholding tax is to be applied may include payments made in kind. The Chinese

payor in this type of situation apparently withheld products equal in value to 20 per cent of the total payback and converted these into cash for payment to the tax authorities.

194. Interest Regulations, Arts. 2(5) and 3, para. 3, note 140 above. On the lease-sale aspect of compensation trade, see note 187 above. The Interest Regulations also cover arrangements, akin to compensation trade, whereby the foreigner provides equipment or technology with which a Chinese unit processes or assembles materials or parts into finished goods for the foreigner. Like compensation trade, these projects can be characterized as loans or instalment sales. The Chinese entity in these cases often discounts the processing or assembly fees payable to the Chinese entity by the foreigner. The discount is in lieu of the payment by the Chinese of principal and interest for the equipment. Under the Interest Regulations, this discount will not result in withholding tax. Interest Regulations, Art. 2(5), note 140 above.

195. Reply of the Ministry of Finance Regarding the Question of Exemption from Income Tax in Cases of the Use of Products to Repay the Price and Interest for Equipment and Fees for the Use of Proprietary Technology, 9 March 1983 (hereafter cited as the Interest Reply), *Caizheng*, No. 5, 1983, p. 45.

196. See note 158 above and accompanying text. Because in-kind payments save foreign exchange for China, their use will be a positive factor in determining whether technology is being offered on 'preferential terms'. If the 'advanced' test is also satisfied, the technology may be eligible for the withholding tax exemption under the Technology Regulations, note 153 above.

The title of the Interest Reply, note 195 above, makes reference to 'fees for the use of proprietary technology'. However, neither the Technology Regulations, note 153 above, nor the Interest Regulations, note 140 above, provide any blanket exemption for technology fees paid in kind, so the import of the above reference is unclear.

197. See text accompanying note 47 above. This analysis parallels the Chinese view that compensation trade does not create an 'establishment' for the purposes of the FEITL. See text accompanying note 192 above. Compare the situation with regard to co-operative ventures.

198. FEITL Regulations, Art. 3, note 4 above. A Chinese tax official analogizes co-operative ventures to partnerships in the Western sense for tax purposes. Wang Xuanhui, 'Concretely Explain the Scope of Taxpayers, Give Lenient Consideration to the Tax Burden of Medium and Small Enterprises', *Caizheng*, No. 7, 1982, p. 42. This separate tax payment for participants in co-operative ventures is applicable in the absence of special stipulations. FEITL Regulations, Art. 3, note 4 above. A tax official has suggested that in the case of small-scale co-operative projects where it is not 'convenient' to calculate and pay tax separately, such special stipulations may be made. Wang, p. 42, above.

The Chinese have sometimes in the past referred to a 'Type A' contractual joint venture that, despite the name, is treated for most purposes like an equity joint venture and taxed under the JVITL. See *Zhongguo touzi zhinan (Guide to Investment in China)* (Beijing, Economic Daily, 1982), a book sponsored by the Ministry of Foreign Economic Relations and Trade (MOFERT) (hereafter cited as the MOFERT Guide), pp. 46–7 (all page references cited refer to the Chinese text). See, however, note 199 below and accompanying text.

199. This approach is somewhat akin to the United States treatment of partnerships. Interestingly, early drafts of a law on co-operative ventures imply that a co-operative venture is a tax-paying unit, as do the State Council Provisions, note 86 above.

200. FEITL, Arts. 1–3, note 4 above; and FEITL Regulations, Arts. 2 and 4, note 4 above. In some cases a deemed profit system may be applicable to foreign companies in contractual joint ventures. See note 215 below and accompanying text.

201. FEITL Regulations, Art. 26, para. 1, note 4 above.

202. See FEITL Regulations, Art. 26, para. 1, note 4 above; and Wang Xuanhui, 'Determine Prices, Reasonably Calculate the Amount of Income from Division of Products', *Caizheng*, No. 1, 1983, p. 35. Wang suggests that since the CICTA will also be levied on the foreigner's share of products, see text accompanying note 206 below, 'leniency' should be applied in determining the relevant price for application of the FEITL Regulations, Art. 26, para. 1, note 4 above. He further suggests that in the case of agricultural and related products, the price may be determined by reference to the commercial purchase price for state enterprises; for industrial products, the ex-factory price may be used or, if there is no ex-factory price, the commercial wholesale price for state enterprises may be used as a reference. Wang, p. 36, above.

203. See Regulations Concerning the Levy and Exemption of Customs Duties and the Consolidated Industrial and Commercial Tax on Imports and Exports of Goods for Chinese-Foreign Co-operative Exploitation of Offshore Petroleum, approved by the State Council on 28 February 1982 and promulgated by the General Administration of Customs and the Ministry of Finance on 1 April 1982; and Regulations Concerning the Supervision and Control of and the Levy and Exemption of Tax on Goods Imported and Exported by Chinese-Foreign Co-operative Ventures, promulgated on 31 January 1984 by the General Administration of Customs, the Ministry of Finance, and the Ministry of Foreign Economic Relations and Trade (hereafter cited as the Co-operative Venture Tax Regulations), Arts. 4(1) and (2), and 6.

204. Co-operative Venture Tax Regulations, Art. 4(3), note 203 above. Article 4(3) refers to 'Regulations Regarding the Levy and Exemption of Tax on Materials Imported for the Construction of Tourist Hotels by Absorbing Overseas Chinese Capital and Foreign Capital'. These regulations were apparently formulated in 1979 but have never been made public.

205. Co-operative Venture Tax Regulations, Arts. 6 and 9, note 203 above.

206. Wang, p. 36, note 202 above, suggests that the latter may be the Chinese intention. In at least one case, however, that of co-operative offshore petroleum projects, the Chinese have provided for the consolidated tax to be levied in kind. Regulations Regarding the Use of Crude Oil for the Payment of the Industrial and Commercial Consolidated Tax and the Mining Area Use Fee in the Chinese-Foreign Co-operative Development of Oil, 3 April 1982. To the extent that the co-operative venture sells products as an independent unit, the CICTA may be imposed on the venture rather than on the individual parties. See note 199 above and accompanying text.

207. State Council Provisions, Art. 11, note 86 above. The Co-operative Venture Tax Regulations, note 203 above, provide that customs duties must be paid on co-operative venture products to which export duties apply. Co-operative Venture Tax Regulations, Art. 8, note 203 above. Although the State Council Provisions make no mention of customs duties, it is likely that duties will not be imposed to the extent that an exemption from the CICTA is granted. In any event, export duties currently apply to a very small number of products, such as traditional Chinese medicines, and will rarely be relevant to foreign investment projects.

The exemption granted by the above-cited article of the State Council Provisions also applies to equity ventures and wholly foreign-owned enterprises.

208. FEITL Regulations, Art. 9, note 4 above.

209. FEITL, Arts. 1–3, note 4 above; and FEITL Regulations, Arts. 2 and 4, note 4 above.

210. Provisional Regulations of the Ministry of Finance Regarding the Levy of the Industrial and Commercial Consolidated Tax and Enterprise Income Tax on Foreign Businesses Contracting for Project Work and Providing Labour Services, 5 July 1983 (hereafter cited as the Project and Labour Regulations), Art. 2(1). See, also, Patent and Technology Document, note 190 above.

211. T. Gelatt, discussion with Ministry of Finance tax official, 9 March 1983.

See also Chen Zelin and Cui Tinglan, 'Several Problems Worthy of Note in Concluding Economic Contracts with Foreigners', *Zhongguo shuiwu*, No. 11, 1986, p. 26.

212. Project and Labour Regulations, Art. 2(2), note 210 above.

213. To the extent that service or related income received under any of the situations discussed in the text accompanying notes 210–13 is deemed to involve fees for the use of proprietary technology, it will be taxable under the FEITL withholding tax. See Project and Labour Regulations, Art. 2, note 210 above; and see text accompanying notes 151–5 above. This question may be affected by the terms of tax treaties China has signed or is negotiating with various countries.

214. The rules for the calculation of net income for a service company under the FEITL correspond to those under the JVITL. See note 77 above.

215. This system was initially available only to subcontractors in the petroleum development projects. FEITL Regulations, Art. 24, para. 2, note 4 above; and [Document] Regarding the Question of Calculation of the Income of Enterprises Contracting for the Exploration and Development of Offshore Petroleum Resources, 6 April 1982, in *Handbook*, Vol. I, p. 40, note 5 above. Although the wording of the regulations could be interpreted to mean that the deemed rate is mandatory for petroleum subcontractors, and one commentator, Wang, p. 36, note 123 above, so states, in the past officials have said that while subcontractors are likely in most cases to prefer the deemed profit system, they may also elect to substantiate their actual costs and calculate their taxable income according to the FEITL's usual rules. T. Gelatt, discussion with Ministry of Finance tax official, 22 November 1982. The Chinese have since developed new rules for oil subcontractors with respect to the deemed profit system. Under these rules, applied by the Offshore Oil Tax Bureau, but not formally published, drilling subcontractors are required to pay tax on their net income and may not use the deemed profits approach. All other subcontractors in the offshore oil business must generally use the deemed profits system, but can apply to the local tax authorities for net income tax treatment.

Net income tax treatment will be approved only if evidence satisfactory to the tax authorities is provided by the taxpayer showing that it: (a) has an account in China with the Bank of China; (b) is able to determine the profits and losses of its Chinese operations independently of its other operations; (c) is able to maintain independent accounting records and books that apply exclusively to its Chinese operations; and (d) is able to provide 'lawful' vouchers for all expenses (that is, vouchers that will be acceptable to the Chinese tax authorities). In addition, the taxpayer must provide evidence, certified by a foreign accounting firm that maintains a registered representative office in China, of the original purchase price of any rig, vessel, or other capital item directly used in performing operations under the subcontract in order that the tax authorities can verify depreciation deductions. If the application of the taxpayer is approved, but the taxpayer is subsequently unable to meet any of the requirements set forth above, the local tax authorities may impose fines and other penalties on the taxpayer and may change the basis of taxation.

In 1983, the Chinese extended the 10 per cent deemed profit system to all foreign businesses contracting for projects and providing labour services in China. Project and Labour Regulations, Art. 3, note 210 above. Under this provision, a foreign company may, with the confirmation of the local tax office, use the deemed profit system in a case where the period of work or provision of services is relatively short and accurate evidence of costs and expenses cannot be provided.

Neither the FEITL Regulations nor the Project and Labour Regulations would appear to limit the use of the deemed profit system to foreign companies contracting independently for projects in China. Thus, this system would appear to be applicable to a foreign company participating in a contractual joint venture (see pp. 60–1 of the text) for the performance of a construction project, exploration services, and so on.

216. FEITL Regulations, Art. 34, note 4 above. A commentary points out that the intent of this provision is to tax foreign enterprises operating for less than one year at the FEITL rate applicable to the actual income earned, rather than basing the tax rate on the annualized amount of income. Wang Xuanhui, 'Facilitate Tax Payment Procedures on the Basis of a Strict and Impartial Tax System', *Caizheng*, No. 2, 1983, p. 32.

217. Project and Labour Regulations, Art. 3, note 210 above.

218. See, for example, Agreement between the Government of the United States of America and the Government of the People's Republic of China for the Avoidance of Double Taxation and the Prevention of Tax Evasion with Respect to Taxes on Income, 10 August 1984, Art. 5, para. 3, *Taxation and Accounting*, No. 88, 1984, p. J-1. The Project and Labour Regulations, Art. 6, note 210 above, make it clear that where tax treaties exist they will prevail over the Project and Labour Regulations.

219. Project and Labour Regulations, Art. 2, note 210 above. See text accompanying notes 210–12 above.

220. FEITL Regulations, Art. 9, note 4 above.

221. See text following note 47 above.

222. Project and Labour Regulations, Art. 1, note 210 above.

223. Project and Labour Regulations, Art. 1(1), note 210 above. A foreign company engaged in project work in China which subcontracts part of the project to another foreign company is responsible for withholding the CICTA from its payments to the latter. If the deemed profit rate has been adopted for the latter, the foreign contractor must also withhold the FEITL. Project and Labour Regulations, Art. 4, note 210 above.

224. Project and Labour Regulations, Arts. 1(2) and (3), note 210 above. Like the deemed profit system, the tax treatment described in notes 222–4 and accompanying text would appear to apply to the foreign company in a co-operative venture as well as a foreign company performing a contracted project independently in China. See note 215 above.

225. In 1972, a draft Industrial and Commercial Tax Act was promulgated, simplifying the language of the CICTA and adjusting the taxable items and rates, but not otherwise altering the basic structure of the industrial and commercial tax as set out in the CICTA. Industrial and Commercial Tax Act of the People's Republic of China (Draft), approved and transmitted by the State Council on 30 March 1972 (hereafter cited as the 1972 Act). For the text of the 1972 Act, see Guowuyuan jingji fagui yanjiu zhongxin bangongshi, Zhongguo shehui kexue yuan faxue yanjiu suo minfa, jingjifa yanjiu shi (State Council Economic Law Research Centre Office and Chinese Academy of Social Sciences Civil Law and Economic Law Research Sections), *Chengzhen feinongye geti jingji fagui xuanbian* (*Compendium of Laws and Regulations on the Non-agricultural Individual Economy in Cities and Towns*) (Beijing, Workers' Press, 1982), pp. 32–41. Until recently, in cases where the CICTA rates were lower than those of the 1972 Act, which had replaced the CICTA for Chinese domestic enterprises, equity joint ventures were allowed to enjoy the CICTA rates, and vice versa. [Document] Regarding the Question of the Levy of the Consolidated Industrial and Commercial Tax on Chinese-Foreign Joint Ventures, Co-operative Ventures and Enterprises Wholly Owned by Foreign Investors (hereafter cited as the CICTA Document), 2 June 1983, *Handbook*, Vol. II, p. 20, note 35 above.

Now that the 1972 Act has been superseded for Chinese enterprises by further reforms of the industrial and commercial tax system, see note 44 above and accompanying text, the Ministry of Finance has provided in a 1985 Notice that Chinese-foreign joint ventures, co-operative ventures, and wholly foreign-owned enterprises shall pay the consolidated industrial and commercial tax at the tax rates prescribed in the CICTA. However, the situation of enterprises that, prior to the new Notice, were paying tax at lower rates in accordance with the CICTA Document may 'temporarily' not be changed. Notice of the Ministry of Finance

Regarding the Question of the Levy of the Consolidated Industrial and Commercial Tax on Chinese-Foreign Joint Ventures, Co-operative Ventures and Enterprises Wholly Owned by Foreign Investors, 29 April 1985, *Zhongguo shuiwu*, No. 7, 1985, p. 36.

226. See Regulations Regarding the Supervision and Control of the Levy of and Exemption from Tax on Goods Imported and Exported by Chinese-Foreign Joint Ventures, promulgated by the General Administration of Customs, the Ministry of Finance, and the Ministry of Foreign Economic Relations and Trade on 30 April 1984 (hereafter cited as the Joint Venture Goods Regulations), *State Council Gazette*, 1983, p. 365, note 5 above.

227. Joint Venture Goods Regulations, Art. 4(1), note 226 above. Joint Venture Implementing Act, Art. 71(1), note 55 above. 'Other materials' are defined for the purpose of this provision and those cited in notes 228–9 below as referring to materials required for a joint venture's construction of the factory or site and for installation and reinforcement of machinery. Joint Venture Implementing Act, Art. 7(1), note 55 above.

228. Joint Venture Goods Regulations, Art. 4(2), note 226 above. Joint Venture Implementing Act, Art. 71(2), note 55 above. The 'total amount of investment' of a joint venture is defined as the total of the basic construction funds and the production circulating funds (working capital) needed to be invested in accordance with the scale of production stipulated in the joint venture contract and charter. Joint Venture Implementing Act, Art. 20, note 55 above.

229. Joint Venture Goods Regulations, Art. 6, note 226 above. Joint Venture Implementing Act, Art. 71(3), note 55 above.

230. Joint Venture Goods Regulations, Art. 6, note 226 above. Joint Venture Implementing Act, Art. 71(4), note 55 above.

Equity and co-operative joint ventures and wholly foreign-owned enterprises importing materials which they are to process into finished products for export will benefit from newly established procedures under which such materials are treated as bonded goods and exempted from the industrial and commercial tax and customs duties unless the materials are sold in China. See Procedures of the Customs of the People's Republic of China for the Administration of Materials and Parts that Enterprises with Foreign Investment Need to Import in order to carry out Product Export Contracts, promulgated by the General Administration of Customs on 24 November 1986 (hereafter cited as 1986 Customs Provisions). Under emerging national and local investment rules, customs and CICTA exemption may also in some circumstances be available for the import of materials by a joint venture or other foreign investment enterprise even if the end-product is not exported, provided the items are sold in China as import substitutes. See, for example, 1986 Customs Provisions, Art. 5, above; and Certain Provisions of the Beijing Municipal People's Government Concerning the Implementation of the Provisions of the State Council for the Encouragement of Foreign Investment, issued on 11 October 1986 (hereafter cited as Beijing Provisions), Art. 13.

231. Joint Venture Goods Regulations, Art. 6, note 226 above. Joint Venture Implementing Act, Art. 71, para. 2, note 55 above.

232. T. Gelatt, discussion with Ministry of Finance tax official, 22 November 1982.

233. State Council Provisions, Art. 11, note 86 above. The exemption also presumably applies to customs duties. See note 207 above.

234. Joint Venture Implementing Act, Art. 72, para. 2, note 55 above. Local investment rules issued by various cities and provinces in 1986 make similar provisions. See, for example, Beijing Provisions, Art. 23, note 230 above. Any industrial and commercial tax paid on sales income is deductible in computing taxable income under the JVITL. JVITL Regulations, Art. 8, note 3 above.

235. A new real estate tax law has recently been issued. Provisional Real Estate Tax Act of the People's Republic of China, issued by the State Council on 15 September 1986 (hereafter cited as the PRETA). Although it does not explicitly

88   FOREIGN TRADE, INVESTMENT, AND THE LAW

state, the PRETA appears to supersede the Provisional Urban Real Estate Tax Act
of 1951, see Gelatt and Pomp, p. 438, note 77 above. The 1951 Act had applied to
both land and buildings; the PRETA applies only to buildings. Joint ventures had,
in any event, been exempted from land tax under an internal 1980 document. T.
Gelatt, discussion with PRC legal official, 30 June 1983.
    236. PRETA, Art. 1, note 235 above.
    237. PRETA, Arts. 2 and 3, note 235 above.
    238. PRETA, Arts. 3 and 4, note 235 above. In the case of buildings contrib-
uted to a joint venture by the Chinese party, the 'original value' will presumably
be the value assigned to the building for purposes of capital contribution. If the
original value cannot be determined, the local tax authorities may assign a value
by reference to similar buildings. PRETA, Art. 3, note 235 above.
    239. The Law of the People's Republic of China on Wholly Foreign-owned
Enterprises, approved by the Fourth Session of the Sixth National People's Congress on 12 April 1986 (hereafter cited as the Foreign-owned Enterprise Law).
    240. Foreign-owned Enterprise Law, Art. 17, note 239 above.
    241. See (Minister of Foreign Economic Relations and Trade) Zheng Tuobin,
'Explanation of the "Law of the People's Republic of China on Wholly Foreign-
owned Enterprises"', Jingji cankao (Economic Reference), 18 April 1986, p. 7.
    242. T. Gelatt, conversation with PRC legal official, 18 April 1986. The
FEITL, which applies by its terms to 'foreign enterprises', is not well suited
for taxing wholly foreign-owned enterprises, if the latter are regarded as subsidiaries of their foreign owner, incorporated in China with independent legal
status. Unfortunately, the Foreign-owned Enterprise Law does not explicitly
define these enterprises as independent subsidiaries, stating only that they are not
branches. Foreign-owned Enterprise Law, Art. 2, note 239 above.
    243. Foreign-owned Enterprise Law, Art. 17, note 239 above.
    244. See text accompanying notes 235–8 above.
    245. See notes 85, 86, 91, 95, and 126; see also note 207 and accompanying text.
    246. Under these experiments, state enterprises are paying income tax at a rate
of 55 per cent with the balance of their profits divided between the government
and the enterprise. Gradually, profit turnovers to the state are being phased out
and taxation will be used exclusively to determine the state's share of an enterprise's profit. Small-scale state enterprises are using an eight-rate progressive income tax system with no further turnover of profits to the state. In addition to the
income tax on state enterprises, various other taxes, such as a fixed assets tax, or
'fee', and an 'adjustment tax' used to compensate for income differentials among
enterprises attributable to exogenous factors, are being employed on an experimental basis. See A. Bennett, 'China Slowly Levies New Taxes Designed to
Spur Development', Asian Wall Street Journal, 18 March 1983, p. 1; 'Changing
from Profits Turnover to Taxation is the Direction', Jingji ribao (Economic Daily), 1 March 1983, p. 1; 'Why Are the Eight-Scale Progressive Tax Rates Applied
to Small-Scale Enterprises?', Jingji ribao, 1 March 1983, p. 2; Chai Wen, 'The
Direction of Changing from Profits Turnover to Payment of Taxes Should be
Confirmed', Caizheng, No. 2, 1983, p. 23; 'Actively Support Enterprises Carry-
ing Out the Change from Profits Turnover to Payment of Taxes', Renmin ribao,
30 March 1983, p. 1; Provisional Regulations of the Ministry of Finance Regard-
ing the Levy of Income Tax on State Enterprises, 29 April 1983, in W. W. S. Lo,
A. H. M. Wong, L. W. H. Wong, and W. H. Ming (eds.) Commercial Laws &
Business Regulations of the People's Republic of China (Volume II) (Hong Kong,
Tai Dao Publishing Ltd., 1984), p. 127; Wang Chuanlun, 'Some Notes on Tax
Reform in China', The China Quarterly, March 1984, p. 53; Wang Bingqian,
'Explanation Regarding the Implementation of Changing from Profits Turnover
to Payment of Taxes for State Enterprises and Reforms of the Industrial and
Commercial Tax System', State Council Gazette, 1984, p. 791, note 5 above; Yuan
Zhenyu, 'The Superiority of Changing from Profits Turnover to Payment of
Taxes for State Enterprises', Zhongguo shuiwu, No. 10, 1985, p. 28; and 'Opin-

ions of the General Bureau of Taxation of the Ministry of Finance Regarding Strengthening the Management of Levy of Income Tax on State Enterprises', *Zhongguo shuiwu*, No. 2, 1986, p. 34.

247. See note 44 above and accompanying text.

248. The need to re-examine these traditional patterns is graphically illustrated by the United Nations' work on a model tax treaty for use between the developed and developing countries. The United Nations' involvement was in response to the OECD's model tax treaty, which has been widely accepted by the developed countries in their bilateral agreements, and has been used to some extent as a model for the tax treaties China has been concluding with various countries, but is considered by many developing countries as unresponsive to their special circumstances and needs.

3. Foreign Investment in China: The Legal Framework

MICHAEL J. MOSER

FOREIGN investment in the People's Republic of China is a phenomenon that has emerged only very recently. For nearly thirty years following the Communist 'liberation' in 1949, China eschewed direct participation by foreign capitalist entities in the nation's economy. As a result, when China embarked on its open-door policy in the late 1970s the nation's planners and economic managers lacked experience in how to absorb and regulate foreign investments, and the country had no body of law capable of providing a viable framework for foreign investment activity. Viewed against this background, China's success in recent years in attracting foreign investment and in developing a legal infrastructure for the regulation of foreign economic activity has been remarkable. According to Chinese sources, during the period 1979–85 China attracted direct foreign investments from companies in 28 countries amounting to more than US$16 billion.[1] During the same period China promulgated more than fifty laws relating specifically to foreign investment; and more than three times as many laws and regulations touching on matters dealing with investments by foreigners have been put into effect.

This chapter will provide a description of the basic legal framework governing foreign investment in China today. The main focus of the chapter will be on national legislation relating to four different forms of foreign investment in China, namely (a) compensation trade; (b) 'cooperative' business arrangements; (c) equity joint ventures; and (d) wholly foreign-owned enterprises. Local rules applicable to investments in the special economic zones (SEZs) and the fourteen open coastal port cities are discussed in Chapter 5.

I. The Approval of Foreign Investment Projects

Before turning to discuss the legal aspects of different types of investment in China, it will be useful to examine briefly current Chinese rules and practices relating to the approval of foreign investment projects.

Despite China's current policies encouraging foreign investment and recent experiments with the market mechanism in some economic sectors, the People's Republic remains committed to the basic principles of a planned socialist economy. As a result, the approval of foreign investment projects is closely linked to China's state planning mechanism.

State planning is mandated by the Chinese Constitution, which vests in the State Council the authority to draw up and implement the national economic plan with the aim of ensuring 'the proportionate ordinated growth of the national economy'.[2] Precisely how such p formulated is not well understood. What is known, however, is general all proposed projects utilizing foreign capital or technolog are to be undertaken directly by Chinese ministries and bureaux at the state level or by administrations and bureaux at the provincial or munici-pal levels, as well as such projects as are undertaken indirectly through subordinate corporations or other business units of such entities, must first be submitted to the relevant state or provincial economic planning commission for examination. Upon approval, the projects will then be included in the commissions' annual plans which are sent to the State Council for ratification.[3]

Viewed within the context of China's economic planning system, the foreign investment approval process is principally a policing mechanism instituted for the purpose of ensuring that only those projects that are 'in the plan' are allowed to be implemented. As a matter of law, a project must first have been approved and included in the annual plan before the Chinese corporation, factory, or other business unit is authorized to con-duct negotiations with a foreign party.[4] To prevent the implementation of unauthorized investment projects, and to confirm that authorized pro-jects will be carried out within the scope originally set by the state plan, all projects must be approved by the relevant government authorities be-fore the contracts and agreements entered into between the foreign inves-tor and its Chinese counterpart may be considered legally binding. As a matter of practice, this approval process often begins during the initial stages of discussion between the parties with the preparation of feasibility studies and the signing of non-binding letters of intent which are sub-mitted by the Chinese side to its higher authorities for review. The final step in this process is the issue of formal approval of the signed contract by what the Chinese refer to as 'the examination and approval author-ity' (shenpi jigou).

Precisely what level of approval—local or central—is required for different types of project has been the source of much confusion for for-eign investors. The reason for this uncertainty lies in the fact that there is as yet no national legislation which comprehensively spells out the approval procedures for investment projects. The only existing national legislation that addresses the issue squarely is the Joint Venture Law which requires that equity joint ventures be approved by the Foreign Investment Com-mission, now a part of the Ministry of Foreign Economic Relations and Trade (MOFERT), functioning under the new name of the Foreign Investment Bureau.[5] This provision has, however, since been amended, in effect, by the Joint Venture Law's Implementing Act, promulgated in 1983.[6] This law provides that the MOFERT may in certain circumstance entrust its approval powers to other authorities, but the Act itself does not specify who these entrusted authorities may be. Nor does the Act address approval matters relating to forms of investment other than equi-ty joint ventures.

In the absence of clear statutory guidance regarding the appropriate approvals required for different types of investment project, foreign investors and their legal counsel have had to rely on evidence gleaned from Chinese practice and the advice of their Chinese counterparts for information concerning the current status of Chinese policy regarding for-´ eign investment approvals. According to these sources, the following rules were being applied at the beginning of 1987.[7]

The basic criteria that are considered in determining the identity of the appropriate approval authority are the total amount of Chinese and foreign investment involved in the project and its location. As a general rule, any project with a total investment of US$5 million or less need only be approved by the ministry under whose authority the project is being undertaken or by the government of the province, municipality, or autonomous region where the project is located. All projects with a total investment in excess of this ceiling must be approved directly by MOFERT.

Exceptions to this general rule exist. For example, the municipal authorities of Beijing, Guangzhou, and Dalian, and the governments of Guangdong, Fujian, and Liaoning provinces may approve projects with a total investment not exceeding US$10 million, and the municipal governments of Shanghai and Tianjin have been authorized to approve investment projects up to a ceiling of US$30 million. In addition, special rules exist with respect to the approval of foreign investment projects located in the SEZs established in Guangdong and Fujian provinces. With respect to light industrial projects with an investment of under RMB30 million and heavy industrial projects with an investment of up to RMB50 million, the SEZ authorities possess independent approval authority. However, the products produced by such projects must be 'primarily' for export. Where the above conditions are not met, the project must be approved by the State Council.

It should be kept in mind that the criteria mentioned above for determining the proper approval authority for an investment project are not in all cases rigid. For example, a project involving a total investment below a specific ceiling may be deemed to be of particular national importance, with the result that central rather than local government approval will be required. Similarly, an investment project which may be negotiated and entered into by a ministry or one of its subordinate business units may only be coincidentally located in an SEZ. In such cases, the amount of the investment and the location of the project are given less weight in determining the proper approval authority. Rather, the decisive factors appear to be the nature of the project and the relative importance of the Chinese unit that sponsors or participates directly in its implementation. It should also be noted that local authorities will generally be permitted to exercise their approval powers only when the project does not require an allocation of raw materials by the state and the nation-wide balance of fuel and power distribution, transportation capacity, and export quotas is not affected.

Finally, several additional special rules should be mentioned. First, the approval limits mentioned above apply only to what are classified as 'productive projects' (*shengchanxing xiangmu*) or those investment projects which are engaged in production activities. Projects which are classified as non-productive, such as those in the services sector, are not subject to any approval limits and are generally within the jurisdiction of local authorities. A second point worth noting concerns the approval of projects for the establishment of joint venture leasing companies, joint venture investment companies, and wholly foreign-owned enterprises. Under current policy rules, all of the above projects must be approved by the MOFERT, regardless of the amount of the investment.

One concomitant of the decentralization of approval authority in recent years has been the development at the local level of rules regarding the approval procedures for investment projects. Many of these are classified as *neibu*, or 'internal', for use only by Chinese organizations, while others have been made public. An example of the latter is a set of regulations issued by the Shanghai Municipal People's Government in 1984.[8]

Under these regulations, which apply to all equity and co-operative joint ventures as well as wholly foreign-owned enterprises established in Shanghai, projects with a total investment not exceeding US$2 million may be approved by the local district government of the municipality, and projects with an investment of more than US$2 million but not more than US$5 million may be approved by the bureau within the municipal government which is in charge of the project. The grant of approval authority may only be exercised where the project does not involve the construction of new plants and where the parties themselves are able to arrange for the supply of energy and raw materials, product sales, and foreign exchange balance. Moreover, the exercise of approval authority in such cases seems to be in the nature of a recommendation, as the regulations require that the final approval certificate be issued by the Municipal Commission of Foreign Economic Relations and Trade (the Municipal Commission). Projects with an investment of more than US$5 million but less than US$30 million may be approved directly by the Municipal Commission provided that the products manufactured by the project are 'badly needed by the state' and the parties are able to arrange for themselves such matters as the supply of energy and raw materials and foreign exchange balance. Projects exceeding the scope specified in the regulations are to be referred to Beijing for approval by the MOFERT.

As the Shanghai regulations and our earlier discussion regarding approval authority make clear, the scope of authority granted to local entities for the independent approval of investment projects has widened considerably in recent years. At the same time, however, many of the criteria which must be satisfied before such authority may be exercised are fuzzy. Consequently, there is still a good deal of scope in the system for the central government to intervene in and, if it desires, to override the decisions of local authorities. The possibility of such intervention is particularly great in the case of equity joint ventures. Under the Implementing Act, contracts approved by local agencies pursuant to a valid exercise of authority must still be sent to the MOFERT in Beijing 'for the record' (*bei an*).[9] Although this procedure would seem to entail a simple administrative filing with the central authorities for record-keeping purposes, it has in practice often been used by the MOFERT as the basis for a thorough re-review of the contract and the project. Such experiences suggest that investors would do well to keep in mind that what the state gives to local authorities by way of approval powers, it may also take away.

II. Compensation Trade

Compensation trade (*buchang maoyi*) is perhaps the simplest form of foreign investment in China. Broadly defined as any transaction involving the purchase by a Chinese entity of foreign capital equipment and technology with repayment being made in kind from the production of such equipment and technology, compensation trade has been aptly described as essentially 'an intermediary step between traditional foreign trade and conventional capital investment'.[10]

Compensation trade first began to develop in the mid-1970s but was largely restricted in the initial stage to arrangements between Hong Kong firms and Chinese enterprises in Guangdong and Fujian provinces. Since then, however, this form of investment has extended throughout China. According to official Chinese statistics, more than 1,100 compensation trade transactions were consummated between 1979 and mid-1984 involving investments of approximately US$800 million.[11]

Compensation trade in its pure form is essentially a loan transaction.[12] The loan principal, which consists of the agreed purchase price of the equipment, is repaid in fixed instalments of products which are produced directly with the equipment purchased; in addition, there is an interest factor which is usually built in and which is also paid in kind. Variations on this pure form of compensation trade also exist. One such variation is a type of combined processing and compensation trade arrangement. Under this arrangement, the Chinese party processes materials supplied by the foreign side on consignment, using equipment provided by the foreign side. The Chinese party earns a fee for its processing services, from which are deducted instalment payments attributable to the purchase of the processing equipment. A similar type of hybrid arrangement exists with respect to assembly operations combined with the purchase of equipment by Chinese enterprises. Other variations on the pure compensation trade model also exist. For example, in some cases repayment for technology and equipment provided by the foreign party may be made with products other than those manufactured using such equipment and technology.

At the time of writing, there is no national Chinese legislation that deals specifically with compensation trade.[13] None the less, a number of laws do affect the conduct of compensation trade transactions. For example, the Foreign Exchange Control Regulations and the Detailed Rules issued thereunder govern the handling of foreign exchange earned by the Chinese party in hybrid arrangements involving processing and assembly operations.[14] In addition, China's normal commodity inspection rules relating to the export of goods[15] and Chinese customs and tax laws also apply to compensation trade transactions. With respect to customs and tax treatment, however, specific provisions exist which provide special benefits to both Chinese and foreign parties in a compensation trade arrangement. An exemption from the Consolidated Industrial and Commercial Tax, normally levied on importers of capital equipment,[16] may be granted. Moreover, foreign parties may be exempted from Chinese income tax with respect to payments received by them pursuant to compensation trade arrangements.[17]

Compensation trade arrangements have not been without their problems. The most important of the problems encountered by foreign investors has been the lack of adequate quality control, resulting in frequent disputes over claims for defective goods. For many investors, however, the risk that such problems will occur is outweighed by the numerous advantages of the compensation trade format over other forms of investment in China. Among these advantages are, firstly, the fact that the risks involved are relatively low. The term of most compensation trade agreements is three to five years and investments are typically less than US$1 million. In addition, many investors have been able to arrange guarantees from the Bank of China to secure payment for products. Secondly, as noted above, income earned by foreign parties pursuant to compensation trade arrangements generally has not, to date at least, been subject to Chinese taxation. Finally, compensation trade arrangements are particularly flexible and do not require joint management or any similar organization for their execution. As a result the foreign party need not become directly involved in the day-to-day operations of the Chinese partner.

III. Co-operative Business Arrangements

The term 'co-operative business (*hezuo jingying*)' refers to a wide variety of arrangements whereby Chinese and foreign entities agree to co-operate for a specified period of time for the purpose of jointly producing certain items or rendering certain services or for any other specified task. Co-operative business arrangements are notable for their broad scope and flexibility and have proved to be an extremely popular form of foreign investment in China.

Co-operative business arrangements may in general be divided into two major categories: joint development arrangements and co-operative joint ventures. The main characteristics of these forms are described below.

A. Joint Development

Joint development (*hezuo kaicai*) arrangements have to date been limited to Chinese-foreign activities with respect to the exploration and development of oil and gas reserves. Under this type of arrangement, foreign investors agree to conduct exploration programmes at their own financial risk. Once petroleum is discovered, both parties make investments to develop the finds jointly. Income from commercial production is distributed to the parties in accordance with a fixed formula that takes into account exploration costs, development expenses, and allocable profits. At the end of 1985, China had approved 35 joint development contracts in the offshore oil sector involving investments of more than US$1.6 billion.[18]

Since 1981, when China began its offshore oil development programme in earnest, the Chinese government has made strenuous efforts to put into place a regulatory regime governing joint petroleum development activities. These efforts have included the promulgation of the national Petroleum Regulations, the formulation of a Model Petroleum Contract, and the enactment of special customs and tax rules, registration regulations, and other rules. These laws and other legal aspects of joint petroleum development are discussed in detail in Chapter 6 of this volume.

B. Co-operative Joint Ventures

Co-operative joint ventures—sometimes also referred to as 'co-operative business enterprises' (*hezuo jingying qiye*) and 'contractual' joint ventures—are the most common form of co-operative business arrangement. As of November 1985, more than 3,000 co-operative joint ventures had been approved by the Chinese government with a total pledged investment of over US$5.5 billion.[19]

While differing considerably from true equity joint ventures, co-operative joint ventures are formed for many of the same purposes. For example, co-operative joint ventures have been established for the joint construction and management of hotels, to provide services in the offshore oil industry, and for the production of manufactured goods. In addition, this investment format has been used as a vehicle for joint Chinese-foreign tenders in projects supported by the World Bank and, more recently, for the joint development of coal and other mineral resources. Many co-operative joint ventures are formed as short-term 'trial co-operation agreements' which contemplate the formation of full equity joint ventures at a later stage. Others, however, are established on a long-term basis in the belief that the advantages of the contractual format outweigh those provided by the statutory equity joint venture.

Unlike joint development activities and equity joint ventures, co-operative joint ventures are not as yet governed by any specific set of promulgated regulations. It is known that a Co-operative Joint Venture Law has been drafted and is expected to be formally promulgated in 1987. In the interim, certain 'internal' (*neibu*) rules—not generally available to foreigners and based largely on the provisions contained in the draft law—are being applied by Chinese negotiators. For the most part, however, these rules only consist of broad guidelines for the formation of contractual joint ventures. As a result, at present the establishment and operations of co-operative joint ventures are based principally on the provisions contained in the contract—and these are largely a matter for negotiation in each individual case.[20]

i. Forms
Co-operative joint ventures may take one of two different forms. In the 'true' or pure form, no company or other legal entity separate and distinct from the contracting parties is established. In the absence of a separate corporate body, each party is responsible for making its own contributions to the venture, paying its own taxes on profits distributed to it and bearing its own liability for risks and losses. In true contractual joint ventures of this type, there exists a clear separation of the liabilities, rights, and obligations of the parties, all of which must be specified in the underlying contract.

The second type of co-operative joint venture is actually a hybrid form of investment vehicle which takes on some of the characteristics of both true co-operative joint ventures and pure equity joint ventures. In this format, a 'business entity' which has the status of a legal person is established. Under the draft law, such entities may elect to constitute themselves with limited liability. In such cases, the draft law requires that the liability of each party extend to the value of its respective contributions to the enterprise.

ii. Capital Contributions and Profit Distribution
Capital contributions by the parties in both types of co-operative joint venture may take any of the forms specified in the Joint Venture Law. These include industrial property rights and know-how, buildings, plant and equipment, land-use rights, trade marks, and cash. In addition, the parties to a co-operative joint venture may also contribute natural resource rights, labour, and utilities, none of which is permitted under the equity joint venture format.

The treatment of capital contributions in co-operative joint ventures and equity joint ventures may differ considerably. In a true contractual joint venture such contributions are not treated as part of the 'equity' or 'registered capital', as they would be in an equity joint venture. Rather, they are viewed as separate contributions made by the parties to the project or undertaking. As a result, the parties to true contractual joint ventures are able to avoid many of the protracted debates regarding the valuation of contributions in kind to the registered capital of the company, which often plague equity joint venture negotiations. By contrast, capital contributions to hybrid co-operative joint ventures are treated in very much the same way as capital contributions to equity joint ventures. In co-operative joint ventures, however, the registered capital of the enterprise may be smaller than the combined contributions of the parties.[21] Moreover, the parties' contributions or 'investment' may be 'recovered' by means of fixed asset depreciation or any other approved investment recovery method prior to the distribution of taxable profits.[22]

The distribution of profits in contractual joint ventures is an area where there are significant differences from the practices employed by equity joint ventures. Under the co-operative joint venture format, the ratio agreed by the parties for the sharing of profits of the venture may be different from the ratio of the parties' capital contributions. The method employed by equity joint ventures, as prescribed by the Joint Venture Law, takes a different approach. Under this system, the joint venture partners are required to share the profits in accordance with the ratio of their capital contributions. Consequently, contractual joint ventures are considerably more flexible than equity joint ventures, permitting various schemes whereby the profit share owing to the parties is not tied to the value of their contributions but may increase or decrease over the life of the contract.

iii. Management and Operation
In equity joint ventures, the foreign party is generally able to exercise a certain degree of control over the management and operations of the venture. In accordance with the Joint Venture Law's Implementing Act, the Board of Directors is the 'highest organ of authority' of the venture and seats on the board are allocated to the parties on the basis of their respective equity holdings. Although by law the chairman of the board of an equity joint venture must be appointed by the Chinese side, in practice the general manager is usually appointed by the foreign party, a fact which generally ensures that the foreign investor has a voice in the day-to-day operation of the joint venture.

Hybrid co-operative joint ventures typically adopt a management system that closely resembles that of equity joint ventures. In the case of true contractual joint ventures, however, the management structure is a good deal more flexible. Most ventures of this type are governed by a joint management committee or similar organization consisting of representatives of each of the parties. Because no independent corporate entity exists, there is no executive officer as such, although a 'legal representative' of the venture is usually appointed.

A major practical problem confronted by the parties to a true contractual joint venture relates to the absence of a legal entity that is capable of contracting on behalf of both parties jointly. Under China's domestic Economic Contract Law,[23] only Chinese legal persons have the capacity to enter into binding contracts with other Chinese entities for the lease of land, the procurement of supplies, and other purposes. As a result of these strictures, the Chinese partner is usually named as the contracting party in such cases, with powers of attorney granted by the foreign side authorizing the Chinese partner to act on its behalf in the interests of both parties pursuant to the joint venture contract.

In most of its day-to-day operations, a co-operative joint venture is subject to the same types of regulations and restrictions regarding insurance, the purchase of raw materials, marketing, and labour management as are applicable to equity joint ventures. These rules are discussed in detail in Part IV of this chapter.

iv. Taxes and Customs Duties
Under the draft Co-operative Joint Venture Law each party to the joint venture is required to pay its own taxes on profits earned from the dis-

tributions of the joint venture. For the foreign party this means that net income is taxed under the Foreign Enterprise Income Tax Law at progressive rates ranging from 30 per cent to 50 per cent, including a local surtax.[24] As a matter of practice, however, some hybrid-type co-operative joint ventures have applied for and received tax treatment under the provisions of the Joint Venture Income Tax Law and the Detailed Rules issued thereunder.[25] Due to the generous tax holidays provided under the Joint Venture Income Tax Law, treatment for tax purposes as an equity joint venture may in certain cases be more favourable to foreign investors.[26]

In addition to the enterprise income tax, co-operative joint ventures are also subject to China's other tax laws. For example, individual income tax is imposed on the income of personnel stationed in China in connection with the joint venture.[27] In addition, the Consolidated Industrial and Commercial Tax is also levied on the import of items and on the sale of products of the co-operative joint venture.[28] Finally, customs duties also apply to the importation of certain items and the export of products. It should be noted that in early 1984 new regulations were issued liberalizing the tax treatment of co-operative joint ventures, providing exemptions from the Consolidated Industrial and Commercial Tax and customs duties in certain cases.[29]

Finally, a brief word should be said about the tax treatment of co-operative joint ventures in China's SEZs and in the fourteen open coastal cities. Under regulations in force in these areas, the income of co-operative joint ventures may in certain circumstances be taxed at the preferential rate of 15 per cent. In addition, a number of exemptions from taxes and customs duties and other tax incentives are available to co-operative joint ventures. For a detailed discussion of taxation in these areas, see Chapter 5 of this volume.

v. Foreign Exchange Controls
In general, co-operative joint ventures are subject to the same foreign exchange rules that apply to equity joint ventures.[30]

vi. Registration
Upon approval by the relevant foreign investment authorities, co-operative joint ventures are required to register with the local bureau of the State Administration for Industry and Commerce (SAIC) before commencing business operations. In the case of hybrid ventures, it is the business entity itself that is registered and issued with a business licence. By contrast, true contractual joint ventures register as a 'project' in the names of both parties. The registration regulation, which was formulated to govern equity joint ventures but which is applied by analogy to contractual joint ventures, provides for the payment of fees upon registration in accordance with the amount of registered capital of the joint venture.[31] As not all contractual joint ventures have an equity capital, the registration authorities generally look to the amount of total investment in the project as the basis for the computation of fees. In many instances, the value of such interests is difficult to compute, with the result that, in

practice, registration fees for contractual joint ventures may be levied at the maximum statutory rate of RMB30,000.

IV. Equity Joint Ventures

Of the various forms of investment in China, equity joint ventures have attracted the most attention from both foreign investors and the Chinese authorities. The possibility that foreign companies would be permitted to engage in direct equity investments in Chinese companies was first rumoured in the Western press in 1978. These rumours, which were greeted with a good deal of excitement by foreign investors, became a reality in 1979 when China enacted the Joint Venture Law. Since then, literally thousands of foreign firms have gone to China to discuss the establishment of equity joint ventures. Their initial enthusiasm was shared and encouraged by the Chinese government, which saw in the equity joint venture format a means by which Chinese companies could absorb advanced technology and Western managerial skills and become major foreign exchange earners in the world's leading markets.

Despite these high expectations, during the initial phase of China's open-door policy, equity joint ventures have proved to be something of a disappointment. As of September 1983, only 112 equity joint ventures had been formally established in China, involving a total foreign investment of approximately US$260 million.[32] Most of these investments have been in small- and medium-scale projects, largely concentrated in the tourist and service industries and in the production of consumer goods. As a result, foreign investments on a project basis have tended to be comparatively small, averaging US$2–3 million.[33]

The reasons for the failure of equity joint ventures to live up to early Chinese and foreign expectations are numerous. First, the general downturn in the world economy in the early part of the 1980s led to a reduction in foreign investment generally. Moreover, this downturn coincided with the introduction of economic 'readjustment' policies by the Chinese government during 1980–1, as a consequence of which a number of proposed projects were shelved. Secondly, many foreign investors have been sceptical of the benefits of direct equity investments in China, particularly when compared with the more generous terms granted to foreign investors by neighbouring Asian states.[34] Finally, extraordinary difficulties have been encountered by foreign investors in attempting to establish joint ventures in China. Negotiations have often proved to be lengthy and complicated, being burdened by the bureaucratic style of Chinese decision-making. In addition, because of China's lack of experience in establishing and operating equity joint ventures, many fundamental issues have had to be hammered out and resolved on a case-by-case basis. As a result of these difficulties, many foreign investors who were initially enthusiastic about the establishment of equity joint ventures in China abandoned their original investment plans in favour of more flexible business arrangements such as compensation trade and contractual joint ventures.

In an effort to recapture some of the initial excitement generated by equity joint ventures, the Chinese government began in 1983 to institute a number of reforms aimed at making the equity joint venture format more attractive to foreign investors. Partly as a consequence of these reforms, investment in joint ventures thereafter began to accelerate. In 1985 alone, 1,300 equity joint ventures were approved, bringing the total number of equity joint ventures to more than 2,300.[35] Foreign investment in these projects totals more than US$1.5 billion. According to the MOFERT, more than 90 per cent of the joint ventures which have commenced commercial operations are earning a profit. Only four equity joint ventures have failed and less than ten are said by the MOFERT to experience 'serious' management or financial problems.[36]

Of all the forms of investment in China, only the equity joint venture is governed by a substantial body of published law. However, the statutory framework governing equity joint ventures has not been built up in one stroke but has tended to evolve in a piecemeal fashion. The Joint Venture Law of 1 July 1979, while in many ways a path-breaking piece of legislation, consists of a mere 15 articles and states little more than the general principles to be adhered to in establishing and operating equity joint ventures. This law has been followed by a number of detailed regulations addressing specific issues such as the registration of joint ventures, labour management, taxation, customs treatment, foreign exchange, and borrowing by joint ventures from the Bank of China. In 1983, China issued the long-awaited detailed rules under the Joint Venture Law in the form of an Implementing Act. This law consists of 118 articles that attempt to pull together a number of earlier statutory threads and spell out the main features of equity joint ventures. Further regulations issued in 1986–7 encourage investment in equity joint ventures.

At present, therefore, the various laws and regulations applicable to equity joint ventures, when viewed as a whole, provide for a fairly systematic regulatory regime. None the less, a number of gaps remain in this system which continue to pose problems for foreign investors. The following pages provide an outline of the main provisions of this statutory framework and discuss a number of the problem areas encountered by investors in establishing and operating equity joint ventures.

A. Nature and Legal Status

Both the Joint Venture Law and the Implementing Act provide that equity joint ventures shall take the form of a 'limited liability company' (*youxian zeren gongsi*) incorporated and registered in the People's Republic of China.[37] In addition, the Implementing Act states that equity joint ventures are 'Chinese legal persons' (*zhongguo faren*).[38] As such, equity joint ventures are, according to the Act, 'subject to the jurisdiction and receive the protection of Chinese law'.[39] Each of these statements raises significant legal questions for foreign investors which existing Chinese law can only partly answer.

The first question relates to the definition of 'limited liability company'. At present China has no national company law, although local rules regarding companies have been put into effect in the SEZs. According to Chinese officials, matters relating to the organization, powers, and responsibilities of joint venture companies will be dealt with in the national legislation which is now being drafted. However, it is not expected to be formally promulgated for some time. In the interim, investors must rely on the provisions set forth in existing joint venture legislation to provide guidance as to the legal dimensions of the prescribed limited liability company form. In this regard, the Joint Venture Law and the Implementing Act themselves provide the basic outline of a general company law, with provisions relating to the capital contributions, the registered capital, the transfer of interests, the management structure, and the dissolution of the company. With respect to the issue of 'limited liability', however, the legislation goes no further than to state that the liability of the parties shall be 'limited to the amount of the capital contribution subscribed by each'[40] and that the parties 'shall share the profits, risks and losses in proportion to their respective contributions to the registered capital'.[41]

While the concept of 'legal person' was not defined at the time the Joint Venture Law was promulgated, recent legislative developments have now shed some light on this issue. According to the General Principles of the Civil Law, promulgated on 12 April 1986, the basic components of the definition of 'legal person' include the right to own, use, and dispose of property; the right to carry out management and production activities independently; and the capacity to sue and be sued in a court of law.[42] However, as the Civil Law is still new, many questions remain as to how these statutory principles will be interpreted and applied to equity joint ventures. Moreover, their application to joint ventures established prior to the effective date of the Civil Law is unclear.

Few foreign investors would dispute the fact that a joint venture company incorporated in China should be subject to the jurisdiction of Chinese laws. None the less this requirement has proved troublesome for many investors. On the one hand, problems frequently arise in connection with various administrative documents and rulings which, although not officially promulgated by any legislative body, are often claimed by Chinese negotiators to have the same legal effect as 'laws'. The problem is complicated by the fact that many of these regulations are classified as 'internal' (neibu) and may not be revealed to foreigners. Hence, investors often find themselves in the position of being bound by rules which are unpublished and whose authority is uncertain.[43]

Uncertainty also exists with respect to the impact of subsequently enacted legislation on the provisions contained in joint venture contracts. At a time when China is actively engaged in the task of building a comprehensive legal framework, investors are justifiably concerned that their rights spelled out in contracts entered into today may be unfairly impaired by future legislative enactments. In the past, Chinese officials took the view that, in general, newly created laws should take precedence over previously executed contracts. For example, a statement issued by the MOFERT in 1981 provides that:

In accordance with generally accepted international practice, a contract signed before a new law is enacted should be bound by the new law. Nevertheless, execution of some provisions in the contract may continue even though these provisions run counter to the newly promulgated laws or regulations.[44]

Subsequently, however, an apparently different view has been adopted. Under the Foreign Economic Contract Law, which came into effect on 1 July 1985, 'equity joint venture contracts...may continue to be valid when new laws are enacted'.[45]

In the light of this statement and continuing uncertainties surrounding the issue, many foreign investors have attempted to insert protective provisions in joint venture contracts. In general, explicit language to the effect that the contract shall prevail over subsequent legislation is not accepted by the Chinese authorities. However, 'renegotiation clauses' and similar provisions have been successfully negotiated in some cases. These generally provided that in the event that a new law is enacted which adversely affects the economic benefit of the contract to the foreign investor the new law shall be observed by the parties but the contract shall be renegotiated or other action shall be taken on the Chinese side to ensure that the foreign investor's interest is not harmed.

In at least one area, taxation, developing Chinese practice indicates that the provisions contained in joint venture contracts will be permitted to prevail over subsequent legislation. One of the earliest joint venture agreements, approved before the enactment of the Joint Venture Income Tax Law, provided for an income tax rate of 31.5 per cent. When the tax law was put into effect a year later, the Chinese authorities agreed to abide by the contract rather than enforce the higher statutory rate.[46] More recently, new tax laws have extended preferential provisions to existing contracts, providing that the new benefits will apply only to the original contract period but not to any period of extension. To what extent this approach will be followed in other areas is, however, unclear.

B. Establishment

The Joint Venture Law, the Implementing Act, and related regulations contain a number of provisions regarding the establishment of equity joint ventures. The major topics addressed by the laws include documentation, capitalization, external financing, approval procedures, and registration.

i. Documentation

The Implementing Act contains specific rules regarding the documentation that must be produced by the parties during different stages of the negotiations for the establishment of a joint venture.[47] The Act provides that during the initial stage the Chinese party must submit to its superior unit a 'project proposal' and a 'preliminary feasibility study report' relating to the project. Once these documents have been agreed to and approved by the relevant approval authority, the Chinese party may then commence work with its foreign counterpart on the preparation of a formal feasibility study. Upon completion of the study, the parties are directed to negotiate and execute a joint venture agreement, the joint venture contract, and the corporate charter or articles of association.

To a large extent, the documentation requirements contained in the Act are a reflection of practices that have developed for the purpose of implementing internal Chinese approval procedures. These procedures involve the monitoring of business discussions between Chinese units and foreign companies with the aim of ensuring that only those projects that are included in the state plan are actually concluded and implemented. In addition, the documentation requirements serve the added function of allowing the Chinese authorities to assess at an early stage the various proposals of competitors. In general, only the most promising proposals will be permitted to proceed from the stage of the preliminary feasibility report to actual contract negotiations.

The most important documents that are drawn up in connection with the negotiation and establishment of a joint venture are (a) the letter of intent, (b) the joint venture agreement, (c) the feasibility study, and (d) the joint venture contract and articles of association.

a. The Letter of Intent   The 'letter of intent' (*yixiang shu*) is usually the first document signed by the parties to a proposed joint venture. In most cases this document, also sometimes called a 'memorandum of agreement' (*beiwang lu*), contains little more than a brief summary of the parties' negotiations to date, a statement of their intention to pursue the establishment of a joint venture, and a listing of the main items of agreement, such as location, purpose, investment, registered capital, sales channels, and other items. Other letters of intent are considerably more detailed and may themselves be short-form contracts. In any case, such documents are generally viewed as being not legally binding. None the less, it is advisable for the document to contain language to the effect that the letter reflects only the preliminary views of the parties and that the final agreement of the parties is subject to the completion of the feasibility study and the execution of a binding joint venture contract.

b. The Joint Venture Agreement   The joint venture agreement (*xie yi*) is, under Chinese law, quite distinct from the joint venture contract (*he tong*), as only the latter represents the final agreement of the parties. Hence, the 'agreement' is often thought of as a kind of intermediary step between the letter of intent and the contract. Many agreements take the form of a draft contract or a summary of the contract. Under the Implementing Act, the parties may dispense with the signing of a joint venture agreement if they choose.[48]

c. The Feasibility Study   The feasibility study is an extremely important document, especially from the Chinese perspective. For the Chinese joint venture partner, the study is a 'justification' for the project and is used primarily to 'sell' the joint venture to Chinese approval authorities.

Without an acceptable feasibility study, the negotiation and completion of a joint venture may not proceed.

As a result of the importance of the feasibility study, it is advisable for potential joint venture parties to spend considerable efforts to produce an accurate and meaningful study. Such a study should address at least the points set forth in the outline attached as Appendix 3A to this chapter.

d. The Joint Venture Contract and Articles of Association In general, Chinese law views the contract as the fundamental document which provides for the establishment of the venture by the parties and the articles of association or 'charter' as the company's code of governance, similar to the memorandum and articles of an English company. The Act contains detailed provisions regarding the topics that must be addressed in these documents and provides that in the event of conflict between the two, the provisions contained in the contract are to govern.[49] The Act also requires that both the joint venture contract and the charter must be written in Chinese.[50] However, a foreign language version of the documents may also be prepared, if the parties agree, in which event both language versions are to have 'equal validity'.[51]

Prior to the promulgation of the Implementing Act, two issues which were often the focus of contentious debate in the negotiation of joint venture contracts were the governing law and the provisions for dispute settlement. With respect to the first issue, the foreign party typically argued that, as Chinese law was incomplete in many respects, the governing law of the contract should be the law of his home country or some other third country. These debates have now stopped, as the Implementing Act explicitly requires that 'the conclusion, validity, interpretation, and implementation of joint venture contracts and the resolution of disputes thereunder shall all be governed by Chinese law'.[52] In practice, however, the Chinese authorities have in some instances conceded ground on this issue and have permitted the inclusion of provisions allowing foreign arbitrators to supplement Chinese law with 'commonly accepted international commercial practices' where no existing Chinese rule addresses a particular issue.[53]

With respect to dispute settlement, foreign investors have, in general, preferred third-country arbitration, while the Chinese have argued strongly for 'friendly discussions' and mediation, failing which the disputes should be referred to arbitration in China. The Implementing Act has now cast into law what had, during the three years prior to its promulgation, developed as the typical compromise on this issue.[54] Under the Implementing Act, friendly discussions and mediation are required as an initial step in attempting to resolve the dispute. If such efforts fail, however, the dispute may be submitted to arbitration in China, in the country of the defendant, or in a third country, depending on the agreement of the parties.[55] Interestingly, the Act also provides that in the absence of a written arbitration agreement, either party may bring suit in the Chinese courts.[56]

Although joint venture documentation differs from project to project, the basic items which should be addressed in the contract and the kinds of provisions acceptable to the Chinese approval authorities have become increasingly standardized. Moreover, the MOFERT has itself published a 'model' joint venture contract and articles of association which are set forth in Appendices 3B and 3C to this chapter. Although foreign investors and their legal advisers may find these 'models' inadequate, they do provide a useful indication of Chinese views as to the form and contents of joint venture documentation.

ii. Capitalization
The central concept employed by Chinese law in discussing the capitalization of equity joint ventures is 'registered capital' (zhuce ziben). According to the Implementing Act, registered capital refers to the total amount of the capital contribution subscribed by the parties to the joint venture which is registered with the Chinese registration authorities at the time the venture is formally established.[57] Therefore, registered capital is essentially the parties' equity in the venture and is to be distinguished from the concept of 'total investment' (touzi zonge) which includes external borrowings of the venture itself.[58]

The Provisional Regulations of the SAIC Concerning the Ratio between the Registered Capital and the Total Amount of Investment of Joint Ventures Using Chinese and Foreign Investment were promulgated on 1 March 1987, replacing internal MOFERT rules issued in 1985.[59] Under these regulations, joint ventures with a total investment of up to US$3 million must have capital of 70 per cent of the total investment. For joint ventures with a total investment of US$3–10 million, registered capital must be at least half of the investment amount. At least 40 per cent of the total investment must be provided as equity in joint ventures with a total investment of US$10–30 million. In projects where the total investment exceeds US$30 million, a minimum registered capital of one-third of the total investment is required.

The Joint Venture Law requires that the foreign party hold not less than 25 per cent of the registered capital of the joint venture.[60] No maximum is specified, leaving open at least the possibility that the foreign party may hold up to 99 per cent. In practice, however, the distribution of registered capital in most joint ventures established to date has been either 50:50 or 49:51, the majority position in the latter case usually being held by the Chinese side. In general, registered capital is to be expressed in renminbi, although foreign currency may be used if both parties agree.[61] Evidence of each party's ownership of its share of the company's registered capital is provided by the issue of 'certificates of capital contribution'. The certificates are issued by the company in accordance with a prescribed form after verification by a Chinese accountant that the contributions of both sides have been fully paid up.[62]

The Implementing Act contains a number of restrictions pertaining to the registered capital of a joint venture. For example, joint ventures are not permitted to reduce the amount of their registered capital during the term of the contract.[63] The registered capital may be increased but only if the board of directors has passed a formal resolution to this effect and the action is then approved by the original approval-granting authority.[64] A more significant restriction relates to transfer and assignment. The Act provides that a transfer or assignment of all or part of the registered capital owned by one party is not valid without the consent of the other party and the approval of the original approval-granting authority.[65] Moreover, if one party wishes to effect any such transfer or assignment, the other party is granted 'a pre-emptive right' to purchase the interest offered to the third party.[66] Finally, the Act provides that no assignment to a third party may be made on terms more preferential than the conditions for assignment to the other joint venture party.[67]

As noted earlier, the capital contributions of the parties that make up the registered capital of the joint venture may take a variety of forms, including cash, contributions in kind (such as machinery and equipment), and intangible property (such as proprietary technology, trade marks, and other industrial property rights). In addition, the Chinese side is permitted to contribute rights to the use of a site as part of its capital contribution.

The Implementing Act imposes a number of restrictions on contributions in kind made by foreign joint venture partners. For example, machinery, equipment, and other materials must meet all of the following criteria before they may be used as capital contributions: (a) they must be 'indispensable' to the production of the joint venture; (b) they must be items that China itself is not able to produce, or is able to produce but only at 'overly high' prices or under circumstances where supply and quality cannot be guaranteed; and (c) the foreign party's valuation of the items must not be higher than the international price for similar items.[68] Similar restrictions apply to industrial property rights or proprietary technology contributed by the foreign party as capital contributions in kind. These must (a) enable the joint venture to produce products that China 'urgently needs' or that are suitable for export; (b) permit the joint venture to improve the quality and function of existing products and raise productivity; and (c) contribute to the conservation of energy and raw materials.[69]

One of the most vexing problems in negotiating the capital structure of joint ventures has been the valuation of contributions in kind made by the parties. In general, Chinese negotiators have tended to adopt the strategy of first eliciting from the foreign side the proposed valuation of its contributions in kind and then matching that amount by assigning an equal, and usually highly inflated, value to its contributions of factory buildings and land-use rights. On the basis of the principle of 'equality and mutual benefit', the Chinese negotiators will then demand reductions in the valuation proposed by the foreign side before they will accept a reduction in the value of their own contributions.

Under the Implementing Act, the foreign party is required to supply evidence of the basis for its valuation of intangible property provided as its capital contribution.[70] Such evidence includes patent and trade-mark registration certificates, documents indicating the state of validity, the technical characteristics, and the practical value of the property, and other information. In the event of a dispute regarding the valuation of intangibles and contributions in kind, a third party agreed upon by the Chinese and foreign sides may be retained to make a binding assessment.[71] However, this procedure may not be applied in the case of the valuation of land provided by the Chinese side as part of its capital contribution.[72] Finally it should be noted that any valuation ultimately agreed to by the parties is subject to the approval of the Chinese party's 'higher authorities' and the formal approval-granting organ.[73]

iii. External Financing

Chinese law permits joint ventures to borrow funds from either the Bank of China or foreign banks to satisfy the financing requirements of the venture over and above the funds provided by way of the parties' capital contributions.[74] Borrowings by joint ventures from the Bank of China are governed by a specific set of rules contained in the Provisional Measures for Providing Loans to Joint Ventures Using Chinese and Foreign Investment by the Bank of China (hereafter cited as the Loan Measures).[75] The Loan Measures authorize the Bank of China to provide three different types of loan to joint ventures: working capital loans, loans for the settlement of accounts, and loans for the purchase of fixed assets.[76] Such loans may be extended in either *renminbi* or a foreign currency and must be repaid by the borrower in the same currency in which they were advanced.[77]

The Loan Measures specify a number of requirements that must be fulfilled by a prospective borrower before its loan application can be approved.[78] For example, the joint venture must be approved and registered; it must abide by Chinese laws; it must have opened a bank account with the Bank of China; and it must be 'creditworthy and well managed'. The most important requirement relates to security. Under the Loan Measures, the joint venture must provide either a pledge of collateral as security for the loan or a guarantee acceptable to the Bank of China. As China has no nation-wide system of mortgages applicable to property owned by joint ventures, the most common security device has been the guarantee. In general, the Bank of China has preferred either an unconditional and irrevocable letter of guarantee from the parent companies or a bank guarantee arranged by the parent companies in accordance with the ratio of capital contributions to the joint venture.

The procedures to be followed in applying for a loan include submission to the Bank of China of a formal application specifying the purpose for which the loan is to be used, together with a resolution of the board of directors of the joint venture ratifying the loan application, copies of the joint venture contract, and other relevant documents.[79] Upon approval of the application, the parties are then to negotiate and sign the loan agreement and security documentation.

Interest on *renminbi* loans from the Bank of China is fixed in accordance with the rate set by the People's Republic of China.[80] In general, this rate is slightly higher than the rate normally charged to Chinese state-owned enterprises. The Loan Measures provide that the interest rate on foreign currency loans 'shall be set by the Bank of China'.[81] In practice, this rate has tended to follow closely the LIBOR rate. Interest penalties on overdue payments of principal and interest on Bank of China loans are calculated at a rate equal to the original interest rate plus 20 to 50 per cent of such a rate.[82]

iv. Approval Procedures

The Implementing Act provides that joint ventures must be approved by the MOFERT.[83] However, as noted in Part I of this chapter, local authorities may in some instances be authorized by the MOFERT to exercise approval powers on its behalf. When applying for the approval of a joint venture, the Chinese party is required to submit the following documents to the approval authority: (a) a formal application for approval; (b) a copy of the feasibility study; (c) executed copies of the joint venture agreement, the joint venture contract, and the company charter; (d) a list of the names of the persons appointed to the board of directors of the joint venture; and (e) signed opinions regarding the establishment of the joint venture from the superior unit of the Chinese joint venture partner.[84] Within three months from the date of receipt of these documents, the approval authority must notify the parties of its disposition towards the application.[85] The approval authority is empowered to reject any application that contains 'improper points' and may demand that amendments be made to any of the documents, failing which an approval will not be granted.[86]

It should be noted that in cases where local approval authorities are empowered to approve joint ventures, the Implementing Act requires that a report be made by such an authority to the MOFERT and that the actual certificate of approval be issued by the MOFERT. In June 1986, however, this provision was in effect amended by the announcement that the MOFERT had delegated its authority to issue certificates of approval to the local approval-granting authorities.[87]

v. Registration

Under the Implementing Act, a joint venture is required to register with the local bureau of the State Administration for Industry and Commerce (SAIC) in the place where its head office is located, within one month of the issue of the formal certificate of approval.[88] The procedures for effecting registration are set forth in the Measures for the Registration of Joint Ventures Using Chinese and Foreign Investment (hereafter cited as the Registration Measures), promulgated by the State Council on 26 July 1980.[89]

When applying for registration, a joint venture is required by the Registration Measures to provide the following documents to the registration organ: (a) a completed application form, containing such information as the name of the joint venture, its scope of operations, the registered capital of the joint venture, a list of the names of the members of the board of directors and management personnel, and the total number of employees; (b) a copy of the certificate of approval; (c) three copies each of the

Chinese and foreign-language texts of the joint venture agreement, the joint venture contract, and the company charter; and (d) a copy of the foreign party's business licence or other similar document issued by the authorities of its home country.[90] Upon approval of the application, and the payment of a fee, the joint venture will then be issued with a formal business licence.

Fees for the registration of joint ventures are levied in accordance with the Registration Fee Regulations.[91] Under these regulations, joint ventures with a registered capital of RMB10,000,000 or less are required to pay a fee equal to 0.1 per cent of the registered capital; if the registered capital of the venture is in excess of this amount, the portion above RMB10,000,000 is assessed at the rate of 0.05 per cent.[92]

The Registration Measures require that changes to previously registered items be notified to the registration organ and appropriate amendments be made to the registration records.[93] A fee of RMB100 is imposed for each such change.[94] Moreover, if a joint venture increases its registered capital, a surcharge fee must be paid on the increased amount in accordance with the rates set forth in the preceding paragraph.[95]

C. Management Structure

The Joint Venture Law and the Implementing Act provide for a two-tiered system of management for joint ventures. At the first level is the board of directors, which constitutes 'the highest organ of authority of a joint venture' and 'decides all major questions'.[96] The second level consists of the joint venture's managerial staff, who are 'responsible for daily operational and managerial work'.[97]

Members of the board of directors are appointed by the parties to the joint venture and hold office for a term of four years.[98] According to the Implementing Act, the composition of the board of directors is to be determined 'by discussion' between the parties. The board must contain at least three members, but no maximum is specified by the law. The distribution of seats on the board is to be fixed 'by reference' to the ratio of capital contributions, leaving open at least the theoretical possibility that a foreign party holding a majority of the registered capital of a joint venture could control the board. However, the Act requires that the position of chairman be held by a Chinese appointee and provides that the vice-chairman may be appointed by the foreign side.

Joint ventures are required to convene meetings of the board of directors at least once a year.[99] The Act states that meetings are to be called by the Chinese chairman. However, many joint ventures stipulate in their charters that board meetings may also be convened upon the request of the foreign side's directors. The Act requires that a quorum of two-thirds of the directors present is required before a meeting of the board of directors may be convened. Directors unable to attend a meeting may issue a proxy authorizing a representative to act on their behalf.

Decision-making by the board of directors of joint ventures has tended to be a source of frustration for foreign investors. Under the Implementing Act, unanimity is required for certain fundamental decisions regarding the joint venture such as charter amendments, termination, changes in the registered capital of the joint venture, and mergers.[100] All other decisions, however, may be made in the manner specified in the joint venture's charter.[101] The mechanism usually adopted is majority voting, but this has not generally proved to be workable. In practice, Chinese negotiators will usually insist that seats on the board be allocated equally between the parties. As a consequence, each side's appointees tend to vote as a block, requiring, in effect, that all decisions made by the board be unanimous.

Decision-making at the managerial level has been no less problematic. Although the Joint Venture Law is silent on the matter, the Implementing Act mandates the use of the deputy system whereby the various management positions of the joint venture each have a deputy.[102] What has evolved in practice is that in most joint ventures the foreign side appoints the top management personnel, such as the general manager, and the Chinese side appoints the corresponding deputies, such as the deputy general manager. As a result of this bifurcated structure, managerial decisions must generally be based on agreement between the expatriate manager and his deputy. Therefore the scope for independent decision-making by foreign managerial personnel is usually quite limited.

In general, directors of a joint venture receive no fixed remuneration but are compensated by the joint venture for their travel costs, accommodation, and other expenses incurred while attending board meetings. Under the Implementing Act, the wage treatment of 'high-level' managerial personnel is to be decided upon by the board of directors.[103] The experience of most joint ventures has been that in determining wage levels for the company's managers the Chinese side will argue forcefully for the adoption of a policy of 'equal treatment' for both Chinese and expatriate personnel. Few foreign parties to joint ventures have been successful in overcoming Chinese insistence on this point, at least as regards acceptance of the principle. As a result, most efforts have been focused on attempting to limit its application to only the top rung of the venture's personnel or devising some other compromise solution. One such solution commonly employed is to provide for a comparable 'basic wage' for both Chinese and foreign managers, the latter receiving additional compensation in the form of generous hardship allowances, home leaves, living allowances, and other expatriate subsidies.

D. Labour Management

Matters relating to staff and workers employed by joint ventures are governed by the Regulations on Labour Management in Joint Ventures Using Chinese and Foreign Investment (hereafter cited as the Labour Regulations), promulgated by the State Council on 26 July 1980.[104]

The Labour Regulations prescribe the use of a contract system for the employment of joint venture personnel.[105] The contract is required to contain provisions regarding employment terms, dismissal and resignation, wages, working hours, labour insurance, discipline, and other matters, and must be approved by the labour management department of the local people's government where the joint venture is established. In general, the labour contract is to be signed between the joint venture and the labour union organization established by the staff and workers of the joint venture. In small-scale joint ventures, however, the contract may be signed between the venture and workers and staff members individually.

A major concern of foreign investors has been the extent to which joint ventures are permitted to exercise control over the appointment and dismissal of staff and workers. Under the Labour Regulations, a joint venture may either employ workers recommended by the local labour department or, with the consent of the labour department, recruit workers on its own.[106] In either case, the regulations provide that tests may be administered in the course of selecting personnel.[107] Despite these provisions, in practice most joint ventures have been staffed by personnel seconded by the Chinese side from its own unit. Although some joint ventures have been successful in implementing screening and other procedures to ensure that only qualified personnel are assigned by the Chinese side, most ventures have been under pressure to accept the recommendations of the Chinese partner without instituting formal selection procedures.

With respect to the dismissal of joint venture personnel, the law provides that workers and staff members 'who have become redundant because of changes in production and technical conditions' and personnel who 'fail to meet the requirements of the enterprise after training and are not suitable for transfer to other types of work' may be released from employment.[108] In such cases compensation is to be paid to the dismissed workers and alternative employment is to be arranged for them by the local labour bureau.[109] Although these provisions seem encouraging, their practical effect is muted by other stipulations contained in the Labour Regulations. These require that dismissals be reported to the local labour bureau for approval[110] and authorize the venture's labour union organization to lodge an objection to the dismissal with the board of directors.[111] If the matter cannot be resolved there through consultations, the aggrieved employee may request arbitration before the labour bureau.[112] If either party objects to the arbitration ruling, he may initiate a suit in a Chinese court.[113] As a result of these provisions, foreign investors have found that the dismissal of a joint venture employee is extremely difficult to enforce without the agreement of the Chinese partner.

The Labour Regulations provide that the wage levels for workers and staff members of a joint venture shall be set at '120 per cent to 150 per cent of the real wages received by workers and staff members of state-owned enterprises of the same trade in the same locality'.[114] In addition, joint ventures are required to pay for labour insurance, medical expenses, and other subsidies provided to workers in state-owned enterprises.[115] As a result of these subsidies and other payments, the total remuneration paid to Chinese workers in a joint venture is often two to three times the amount of the worker's basic wage.

As noted earlier, the Labour Regulations contemplate the formation of a labour union organization consisting of the Chinese employees of joint ventures that operate on a relatively large scale. The Implementing Act provides that joint venture employees 'have the right' to establish labour unions and to 'develop labour union activities' in accordance with Chinese labour laws.[116] Once established, the labour union is empowered to 'represent the interests' of staff and workers and is charged with, among other tasks, supervising the implementation of labour contracts, organizing political, scientific, and technical studies, and educating workers to observe labour discipline.[117] Under the Act, labour union representatives are granted the right to attend meetings of the board of directors of the joint venture and to voice their opinions with respect to production and operational activities, issues relating to wages and benefits provided to workers, and labour discipline.[118] Although union representatives are not permitted to vote at such meetings, the Act directs the board of directors to 'heed the opinions of the labour union' and obtain its co-operation.[119]

Joint ventures are required by the Act to 'actively support' the labour union formed by their employees.[120] Such support includes providing an office for the union and facilitating cultural and athletic activities. Joint ventures are also required to allocate, on a monthly basis, 2 per cent of the total amount of wages paid to staff and workers for payment into a labour union fund. The use of such funds is left to the discretion of the labour union, subject to regulations formulated by the All-China Federation of Labour Unions.

On 19 January 1984 China promulgated additional rules regarding labour matters in the form of Provisions for the Implementation of the Regulations on Labour Management in Joint Ventures Using Chinese and Foreign Investment. This law spells out in greater detail a number of provisions contained in the Labour Regulations, including remuneration and welfare schemes for joint venture personnel, labour protection, training, and labour discipline. Among the provisions of the 1984 law that go beyond clarification to impose new requirements on joint ventures are those that relate to the recruitment and dismissal of joint venture workers and staff members. Under the 1984 law, joint ventures must formulate a 'labour plan' for approval by the Chinese labour authorities and inclusion in 'the state labour plan'. The apparent aim of this requirement is to ensure that Chinese labour is allocated to joint ventures in a co-ordinated way, and that emphasis is placed on satisfying the labour needs of joint ventures locally. The 1984 law states that joint ventures must recruit workers within the localities stipulated by the labour authorities. Where qualified personnel are not available locally, the joint venture must obtain the consent of the local labour authority before it may recruit workers from outside the locality. In addition to restricting the freedom of joint ventures with respect to recruitment, the 1984 law limits the circumstances under which joint venture personnel may be dismissed. For example, the law prohibits dismissal where workers and staff members are undergoing medical treatment due to a work-related ailment, or are in hospital.

Dismissal is also not permitted in the case of women workers and staff members 'who are six months pregnant or more or are on maternity leave'.

E. Operational Matters

The Implementing Act authorizes joint ventures to conduct their operational activities 'autonomously', subject to Chinese laws.[121] Among the most important Chinese legal stipulations that affect the operations of joint ventures are provisions dealing with the leasing of land, insurance and bank accounts, the purchase of raw materials, marketing, and the licensing of technology by joint ventures.

i. Land Use

As mentioned previously, the Chinese party to a joint venture may supply the land needed by a joint venture for its plant and office facilities as part of its capital contribution. Alternatively, the joint venture may lease a site from the local department in charge of land in the place where the joint venture conducts its operations. In either case, the joint venture obtains only a leasehold interest in the site and not ownership, and assignment of this interest to third parties is not permitted.[122]

If the site is leased by the joint venture directly, the Implementing Act requires that the venture enter into a lease contract with the local department in charge.[123] The standards for lease payments are to be determined in accordance with such factors as the proposed use of the site, its geographical and environmental conditions, whether or not expenses are incurred by the local government in requisitioning the site, and other factors.[124] In certain types of project, such as those involving agriculture or animal husbandry, the joint venture may be permitted to pay land-use fees calculated as a percentage of the venture's income.[125] Special preferential treatment with respect to lease payments may also be granted to joint ventures that are established in economically underdeveloped areas.[126]

The Implementing Act requires that lease payments be made annually during the lease contract period.[127] During the first five years of the contract, lease charges are fixed.[128] Thereafter, the fees may be adjusted once every three years to take into account changes in the local economy, general geographic and environmental conditions, and factors relating to local supply and demand.[129]

ii. Insurance and Bank Accounts

Joint ventures are required to maintain appropriate insurance cover on their assets by securing policies with the People's Insurance Company of China.[130] Foreign insurance companies may only participate on the basis of reinsurance schemes entered into with the People's Insurance Company.

After having obtained a formal business licence, joint ventures are required to open foreign exchange deposit accounts and *renminbi* deposit accounts with the Bank of China.[131] Foreign exchange deposit accounts may also be opened with banks abroad or in Hong Kong and Macau upon the approval of the State General Administration of Exchange Control.[132]

iii. Purchasing

The Implementing Act grants freedom to joint ventures to purchase such items as machinery, equipment, raw materials, fuel, spare parts, office supplies, and vehicles, either in China or from sources abroad, provided that where conditions are equal priority is given to Chinese sources of supply.[133] With respect to the purchase of items in the Chinese domestic market, joint ventures are required to follow the procedures established for purchasing by Chinese state-owned enterprises; these limit the sources of supply to designated Chinese units.[134] Items to be purchased from abroad must fall within the scope of the joint venture's operations as specified in the joint venture contract. In the event that current Chinese regulations require an import licence for such items, the joint venture is required to prepare an annual import plan for approval by the relevant authorities and apply for the necessary licences on a six-monthly basis.[135]

The Implementing Act contains a number of stipulations regarding the pricing of necessary materials and services procured on the Chinese market.[136] Gold, silver, platinum, petroleum, coal, and timber used in the production of export products are priced in accordance with prevailing international prices for such commodities, as determined by the State General Administration of Exchange Control or the relevant foreign trade department, as appropriate. Payments for such items may be made in either foreign exchange or *renminbi*. With respect to purchases of export or import commodities handled by Chinese foreign trade corporations, the prices are to be fixed by reference to international market prices and payment must be made in foreign exchange. Finally, joint ventures are granted equal treatment with Chinese state-owned enterprises with respect to the purchase price of coal used for fuel, oil for vehicles, and other items which are used for the production of goods to be sold in the Chinese domestic market, and for fees charged for water, electricity, gas, heating, goods transport, and certain services provided to joint ventures by Chinese enterprises.[137]

Under the Act, purchases by joint ventures from Chinese enterprises should be conducted in accordance with China's domestic Economic Contracts Law.[138] This law spells out the procedures for forming, implementing, and enforcing contracts between Chinese legal persons and specifies the rights and responsibilities of the parties in the event of breach of contract. Contracts between joint ventures and foreign suppliers are generally governed by the Foreign Economic Contract Law.

iv. Marketing

Joint ventures are 'encouraged' by the Chinese government to export their products, largely with the aim of earning foreign exchange and opening up international markets to Chinese goods. As a result, most joint ventures established to date have been obliged to gear their marketing efforts primarily towards foreign rather than domestic sales. The only circumstances under which Chinese law permits joint ventures to sell

their products 'mainly' on the Chinese market are when the goods produced are items that China 'urgently needs' or when they serve a function
as import-substitutes.[139]

The Implementing Act authorizes joint ventures to handle the export
of their products in the manner decided by the parties.[140] Prices may be
set by the joint venture itself, subject only to the requirement that such
prices be reported to the Chinese price control authorities for the
record.[141] By contrast, domestic sales must be carried out in accordance
with the rules applicable to sales by Chinese state-owned enterprises.[142]
These rules require that certain types of products that are subject to
planned distribution be sold to designated Chinese units for resale to
end-users. In other cases, however, joint ventures may distribute their
products directly. Prices for goods sold domestically must generally
be fixed at levels determined by the state price control authorities. In
some instances, however, international market prices may be adopted,
provided that prior approval has been obtained from the price control
department.

v. Technology Transfer

Most joint ventures involve the transfer of technology, either from the
foreign joint venture party as part of its capital contribution or by means
of a separate licensing agreement, or from a third party. The Implementing Act requires that all such agreements be approved by the relevant
approval authority and conform to a specific set of stipulations.[143] These
stipulations require that royalties generally be adopted as the form
of payment, and that the royalty rate be 'fair and reasonable' and 'not
higher than the common international level'. Unless otherwise agreed by
the parties, the technology transfer agreement should not impose geographical, quantity, or price restrictions on the marketing of the licensed
product, and the joint venture is to have the right to purchase equipment,
parts, and raw materials from sources of its own choice. Of most importance, perhaps, are the stipulations requiring that the technology transfer
agreement must generally not last for more than ten years and that upon
expiry of the agreement the joint venture must be given the right to continue to use the technology. For foreign parties who license technology to
joint ventures with a term longer than ten years these stipulations are
particularly disadvantageous, as they constitute, in effect, a requirement
that the foreign party contribute the technology free of charge during the
later years of the venture's existence.

In 1985, China promulgated two additional sets of regulations which
apply to transfers of technology by foreign companies to joint ventures.
These regulations are the Regulations of the People's Republic of China
on the Control of Technology Import Contracts, promulgated on 24 May
1985, and the Procedures for Examination and Approval of Technology
Import Contracts, put into force in September 1985.

Under these regulations central government control of technology
transfer contracts has been strengthened. For example, the new rules
will require that each contract be approved by the MOFERT or its desig-

nate. In addition, the regulations specify the types of clauses which, at a minimum, must be contained in technology transfer contracts. These include:

(a) the names, nationalities, main offices, or residences of the parties to the contract;

(b) the date and place of the signing of the contract;

(c) a reference to the type of contract and the classification and scope of the objects of the contract;

(d) the technical conditions, quality, standards, specifications, and quantity of the objects of the contract; the contents, scope, and necessary description of the technology to be imported, including an attached list of any patents and trade marks involved; the technical objectives that are expected to be reached and the period and measures for the realization of each of the various objectives;

(e) the duration, place, and method of performance;

(f) price conditions, the amount of payment, the mode of payment, and various supplementary costs; the remuneration, the composition of remuneration, and the method of payment: the price and payment method in the contract should be reasonable;

(g) a provision stating whether the contract can be assigned or conditions for the assignment of the contract;

(h) compensation for breach of contract and other liabilities;

(i) the method of settlement when disputes arise from the contract: the method of resolving disputes arising from the transfer of property rights should be clearly and reasonably provided for;

(j) the language(s) used in the contract and its (their) effectiveness.

Finally, the regulations also set forth a list of the types of clauses which may *not* be included in technology transfer contracts. These include clauses granting tax benefits to the foreign party without the prior approval of the tax authorities. In addition, provisions which impose 'unreasonable restrictions' on the joint venture or the Chinese party (the 'receiving party') are also prohibited. Such 'unreasonable restrictions' include:

(a) requiring the receiving party to accept attached conditions which are unrelated to the technology to be imported, including the purchase of unnecessary techniques, technical services, raw materials, equipment, or products;

(b) restricting the receiving party from purchasing raw materials, spare parts, component parts, or equipment freely from different sources;

(c) restricting the receiving party from developing and improving the technology to be imported;

(d) restricting the receiving party from acquiring from other sources similar technology or technology of the same kind which is in competition with the technology acquired;

(e) imposing on the parties unequal conditions for the exchange of information relating to improvements of the technology;

(f) restricting the quantity, variety, and sales price of products manufactured by the receiving party using the technology to be imported;

(g) unreasonably restricting the sales channels and export markets of the receiving party;

(h) prohibiting the receiving party from continuing to use the technology to be imported after the contract expires; and

(i) requiring the receiving party to pay remuneration or assume obligations with regard to patents which are not in use or have become invalid.

When a foreign company provides technology to a joint venture pursuant to a separate contract and receives royalties or other payment for such technology the company will be subject to tax on the income received. In general, under Article 11 of the Foreign Enterprises Income Tax Law, a withholding tax of 20 per cent of the gross amount of 'royalties' will be imposed. Such fees are deemed to include all 'fees for the use of proprietary technology', such as fees for blueprints and documentation, fees for technical services, and fees for personnel training, as well as royalties and other payments.

Under the Provisional Regulations of the Ministry of Finance Regarding the Reduction and Exemption of Income Tax on Fees for the Use of Proprietary Technology, issued on 13 December 1982, tax reductions and exemptions are available in certain circumstances. For example, tax will be levied at a reduced rate of 10 per cent where the fees fall within one of the following categories.

(a) Fees received for the use of proprietary technology provided for the development of agricultural, forestry, fishery, and animal husbandry production, in such areas as the following: the improvement of soil or grasslands, the exploitation of barren hills, and the full use of natural conditions; new varieties of animals and plants; the production of agricultural pesticides with high effectiveness and low toxicity; conducting scientific production management in agriculture, forestry, fishery, and animal husbandry, maintaining the ecological balance, and strengthening ability to resist natural disasters.

(b) Fees received for the use of proprietary technology provided to the Chinese side in the conducting of scientific research or scientific experiments for China's academies of science, institutes of higher learning, and other scientific research units, or the conducting of scientific research in co-operation with China's scientific research units.

(c) Fees received for the use of proprietary technology provided for China's key construction projects in the fields of exploiting energy and developing communications and transport.

(d) Fees received for the use of proprietary technology provided in the areas of energy conservation and the prevention and cure of environmental pollution.

(e) Fees for the following proprietary technology provided for China's development of important technical spheres:
   (i) technology for the production of major advanced electronic equipment;
   (ii) nuclear technology;
   (iii) technology for the production of large-scale integrated circuits;

(iv) technology for the production of optical-integration microwave semiconductors and microwave integrated circuits; and
technology for the manufacture of microwave electron tubes;

(v) technology for the manufacture of ultra-high-speed computers
and microprocessing machines;

(vi) technology for fibre-optics communications;

(vii) technology for long-distance, super-high-pressure, direct-
current electricity transmission;

(viii) technology for the liquefaction, gasification, or multiple use of
coal.

Exemptions from tax are also available where the technology is 'specially advanced' and the terms are 'preferential'. Tax reductions may be
granted by the local tax bureau while tax exemptions must be approved
by the Ministry of Finance.[144]

F. Foreign Exchange Controls

China's Foreign Exchange Control Regulations impose a number of
stringent restrictions on joint ventures.[145] The most important of these is
the requirement that all foreign exchange deposits and disbursements of a
joint venture flow through the venture's bank account with the Bank of
China or a bank approved by the Bank of China. Because the Chinese
currency, *renminbi*, is not convertible into foreign exchange, the effect of
these provisions is to require joint ventures to generate all of the foreign
exchange necessary for the remittance of foreign exchange dividends, for
other distributions to the foreign joint venture party, and for the payment
of all foreign exchange expenses incurred by the venture in the course of
its operations.

The strictures imposed by this system have posed significant problems
for investors who look upon joint ventures primarily as a vehicle for
entry into the Chinese domestic market, and they are one of the major
reasons why most joint ventures established to date have felt compelled to
export a sufficient quantity of their products to satisfy their foreign
exchange requirements. As part of the Chinese government's efforts to
enhance the attractiveness of joint ventures, these restrictions were liberal-
ized to a certain extent with the promulgation on 1 August 1983 of the
Detailed Rules for the Implementation of Foreign Exchange Control
Regulations Relating to Overseas Chinese Enterprises, Foreign Enterprises and Chinese-Foreign Joint Ventures.[146] These rules dovetail with
related rules contained in the Joint Venture Law's Implementing Act,
both of which held out the promise that joint ventures would be granted
greater access to the Chinese domestic market.

Under the 1983 foreign exchange rules, foreign exchange may be used
as the currency of settlement between Chinese domestic enterprises and
joint ventures where the products sold by a joint venture are import-
substitutes and the buyer is a Chinese unit engaged in foreign trade business; where the products constitute items required for the production of
import or export goods handled by Chinese units engaged in foreign

trade business; in construction contracts; and in other cases approved by the State General Administration of Exchange Control.[147] Article 75 of the Implementing Act gives further assurances to foreign investors by providing that where an approved contract permits a joint venture to sell its products 'mainly' on the domestic market, problems encountered by joint ventures in maintaining a foreign exchange balance may be resolved by way of a foreign exchange subsidy from the local government in charge of the product or the State Planning Commission.[148]

Despite the promise of the 1983 regulations, few joint ventures have in fact been permitted to take advantage of the provisions set forth therein. As dissatisfaction among foreign investors has grown, many potential projects have been halted and others already established have begun to encounter severe problems in maintaining a foreign exchange balance.[149]

In response to these pressures, on 15 January 1986 the Chinese government issued Regulations Concerning the Question of Balance of Foreign Exchange Receipts and Expenditures for Joint Ventures Using Chinese and Foreign Investment (cited hereafter as the Foreign Exchange Balance Regulations).[150] The Foreign Exchange Balance Regulations reaffirm the general principle that joint ventures should export to generate sufficient foreign exchange to maintain a balance of foreign exchange receipts and expenditures, but their significance lies in the exceptions to this principle that they allow. The Foreign Exchange Balance Regulations provide basically five ways in which a joint venture may achieve a foreign exchange balance. These are as follows.

i. Exports

As noted above, the Foreign Exchange Balance Regulations restate the general principle that joint ventures should export their own products in order to generate foreign exchange. More importantly, the new regulations underline the importance of any commitment made by a joint venture in its joint venture contract (including the joint feasibility study) as to the proportion of its production which will be exported. Article 7 of the Foreign Exchange Balance Regulations states that in cases in which the joint venture does not fulfil its export commitment as stated in the joint venture contract, the Chinese authorities will not assume any responsibility for resolving the foreign exchange imbalance of the joint venture. Thus, while the main thrust of the Foreign Exchange Balance Regulations is to provide ways by which a joint venture may achieve a foreign exchange balance other than through exports of its own products, the regulations would appear to prohibit the use of these methods by a joint venture which has not fulfilled its export commitment.

ii. Domestic Sales

The Foreign Exchange Balance Regulations contain three stipulations regarding domestic sales. The first of these, Article 4, is similar to the rule set forth in Article 75 of the Implementing Act, but it is considerably less ambiguous and more detailed. It states that domestic sales may be made if the following conditions are satisfied: (a) the products are urgently needed in China; (b) the products are highly sophisticated ones made with advanced technology and key technology, or are products of superior quality that are competitive in international markets; (c) the products have been determined to qualify by the appropriate authorities; (d) the domestic sales have been approved by the proper authorities; and (e) the provisions for domestic sales are contained in contracts between the joint venture and its customers. The Foreign Exchange Balance Regulations do not make clear whether the purchasers will pay foreign exchange for domestic sales approved pursuant to Article 4 or whether the joint venture will be provided with foreign exchange by the foreign exchange authorities to the value of such domestic sales. The regulations state merely that a proposal for foreign exchange balance through domestic sales under Article 4, which has been approved, will be entered into the long-term or annual plan for the use of foreign exchange.

The second means of domestic sales is through import-substitution, as provided in Article 5 of the Foreign Exchange Balance Regulations. The conditions of sale of the joint venture's products on the domestic market in the form of import-substitutes are similar to those stated in Article 4 of the regulations, as noted above. The criteria for qualifying as an import-substitute are somewhat different, however, and the foreign exchange is allocated from a different part of the foreign exchange plan.

To qualify as an import-substitute, the products produced by the joint venture must meet the following conditions: (a) they are products that would otherwise have to be imported into China for a long period, or that China urgently needs to import; (b) the project is approved by the proper authorities; and (c) the prices are international prices. Where products meet these criteria, the approved plan for domestic sales is reported to the state planning authorities or the local planning committees for inclusion in the long-term or yearly plan for the use of foreign exchange for imports.

The third way in which a joint venture may make domestic sales of its products is under Article 8 of the Foreign Exchange Balance Regulations. In this case, the sales are made to domestic enterprises that have the ability to pay in foreign exchange. This rule, which is similar to, but broader than, the prior rule, requires that the domestic customers must be located outside the special economic zones and the technical development zones of the open coastal cities, and that approval for such domestic sales must be obtained from the state foreign exchange authorities.

iii. Exports of Others' Products
The Foreign Exchange Balance Regulations, in accord with recent policy, also allow joint ventures to obtain foreign exchange through the export of others' products. According to Article 6 of the regulations, the exported products may be 'domestic products', that is, not necessarily those of the joint venture itself, but products of other Chinese entities. A joint venture may export such products only under the following conditions: (a) it has obtained the approval of the MOFERT; (b) if the products are man-

aged by the state on a unified basis and are subject to an export quota and an export licence, special approval must be obtained from the MOFERT; and (c) the export sales must be made through the marketing relationships of the foreign joint venture party. This last condition seems to indicate that products which would be eligible for purchase and export by a joint venture would only be products which the producing entity or its related foreign trade corporation was not able to sell abroad. It is unclear whether the purchase and resale of products abroad would be subject to other restrictions not mentioned in the Foreign Exchange Balance Regulations, such as the prior requirement that the joint venture process or otherwise add value to the products before exports would be permitted.

iv. The Transfer of Foreign Exchange between Joint Ventures
A new means of resolving a foreign exchange imbalance that is permitted by the Foreign Exchange Balance Regulations is to adjust the excess foreign exchange earnings of one joint venture with the foreign exchange deficit of another. The joint venture with excess foreign exchange could, in effect, transfer its excess foreign exchange to the other joint venture. Approval for adjusting foreign exchange income and expenditures in this manner is subject to approval by the state foreign exchange authorities and, in addition, to approval by both parties to the joint venture. In practice, it is likely to prove difficult to obtain the approval of the Chinese party to a joint venture which has excess foreign exchange. Also, it is unclear whether this approval of the joint venture parties could take the form of a provision in the joint venture contract, or whether such approval would have to come at a later time.

v. The Reinvestment of Local Currency in Other Joint Ventures
Another new alternative proposed by the Foreign Exchange Balance Regulations to resolve a foreign exchange imbalance is to allow the foreign investor to reinvest its earnings in local currency from that joint venture in another joint venture that would generate foreign exchange. In such a case, the foreign exchange earnings of the second joint venture would enable dividends and other amounts to be remitted in foreign exchange. This solution to an imbalance, like the transfer of foreign exchange between joint ventures, will only be available to foreign parties engaged in two or more joint ventures in China and will, therefore, probably not be practicable for most foreign investors for the time being.

G. Taxation

Equity joint ventures are subject to a variety of taxes, including an income tax, the Consolidated Industrial and Commercial Tax, the Real Estate Tax, and the Vehicle and Vessel Licence Tax, customs duties, and import taxes. In addition, expatriate personnel assigned to work in a joint venture are required to pay individual income tax on their wages and salaries earned in China.

The most important tax legislation applicable to joint ventures is the

Joint Venture Income Tax Law and the Detailed Implementing Rules issued thereunder.[151] The Joint Venture Income Tax Law taxes the net income of joint ventures at a flat rate of 33 per cent, and comprises a national tax of 30 per cent and a local surtax of 10 per cent of the amount of tax paid. In addition, the law imposes a 10 per cent withholding tax on dividends which the joint venture remits out of China to the foreign party. Various forms of tax incentive and preferential treatment are provided to certain types of joint venture engaged in relatively low-profit operations involving farming and forestry projects, and tax rebates may be obtained in certain circumstances by foreign parties to a joint venture who reinvest their profits in the venture. Among the most important incentives provided by the law are tax holidays. Pursuant to an amendment of the tax law in September 1983, joint ventures scheduled to operate for a period of at least ten years are eligible for an exemption from taxation during the first two profit-making years and may be taxed at only one-half of the normal rate during the three subsequent years.

The Consolidated Industrial and Commercial Tax, a type of turnover tax, is imposed on imports by joint ventures and on their gross receipts from sales and service transactions.[152] Specific rates vary from item to item and range from 2.5 per cent to 69 per cent. Consolidated tax payments attributable to sales or service income may be deducted by the joint venture when computing taxable income under the Joint Venture Income Tax Law. In addition to the Consolidated Tax, customs duties are also levied on imports by joint ventures.

In mid-1983, the Chinese government issued new regulations providing for exemptions from the Consolidated Tax and customs duties with respect to certain items.[153] Under these regulations, exemptions may now be granted for imported machinery, equipment, spare parts, and other materials related to the production activities of the joint venture that are provided by way of capital contributions in kind or are purchased with funds provided as part of the registered capital of the venture. In addition, items of the same type for which production or supply in China cannot be guaranteed may be imported free of the Consolidated Tax and customs duties when purchased with a joint venture's other funds. Finally, the regulations also provide tax exemptions for imported raw materials, auxiliary materials, components, spare parts, and packaging materials used in connection with products produced by joint ventures for export. It should be noted that these exemptions do not apply to imported vehicles for office use, which continue to be subject to the levy of the Consolidated Tax and customs duties at ordinary rates.

The Real Estate Tax is imposed on factories or other buildings that have been provided by the Chinese side as part of its capital contribution to a joint venture.[154] The tax rate is 1.2 per cent per year and is levied on the value assigned to the property by a local appraisal committee. Where a joint venture leases a building the tax is usually paid by the Chinese lessor.

Finally, the Vehicle and Vessel Licence Tax is imposed on joint ventures which own and operate motorized vehicles or vessels. The tax is imposed at the discretion of local authorities and the tax rates are generally nominal.

H. Accounting and Profit Distribution

The Joint Venture Income Tax Law contains a number of provisions setting forth the accounting rules to be followed when calculating the taxable income of joint ventures. These provisions have been supplemented by various stipulations contained in the Implementing Act and the Accounting Regulations of the People's Republic of China for Joint Ventures Using Chinese and Foreign Investment, promulgated by the Ministry of Finance on 4 March 1985.

The accounting rules enunciated in these laws require that joint ventures formulate an accounting system in accordance with Chinese regulations and 'the circumstances of the joint venture'. Once formulated, the accounting system adopted by the joint venture must be reported, for the record, to the finance department of the joint venture's unit-in-charge and the tax bureau in the locality where the joint venture is located.

In general, the accounts of a joint venture must be kept on an accrual basis, and the debit and credit method of keeping accounts must be used. Moreover, all of the vouchers, account books, and statements prepared by the joint venture must be in the Chinese language and must be submitted to the local tax authorities before being put into use. If the parties of the joint venture agree to use bilingual documentation, this may also be approved.

Joint ventures are required 'in principle' to adopt the *renminbi* as the standard currency for the keeping of accounts. However, a foreign currency may be used when agreed by both parties. This is typically the case when the majority of the revenues of the joint venture are in a foreign currency. However, where a foreign currency is used as the unit of account, separate accounting books in *renminbi* must also be maintained by the joint venture.

Under the applicable laws, the Gregorian calendar year from 1 January to 31 December must be used as the fiscal year for all joint ventures.

Finally, in the case of a conflict between the accounting method devised by a joint venture and the provisions stipulated in the Joint Venture Income Tax Law, tax liability is to be computed according to the provisions of the tax law.

In most joint ventures, the accountant is appointed by the Chinese side and a deputy or assistant accountant is appointed by the foreign party. The accountants are responsible for preparing quarterly and annual accounting statements for distribution to the joint venture parties, the local tax office, and other authorities, including the original approval-granting organ. Such statements must be audited by a Chinese registered accountant before they may be deemed valid.[155] In some joint ventures, the foreign party has been given the right to conduct at its own expense a separate audit of the joint venture's accounts, but such audits are not binding for the purposes of Chinese law unless they are conducted by a qualified Chinese accountant.

The system for distributing the profits of a joint venture is fixed by the Joint Venture Law, as supplemented by provisions contained in the Implementing Act.[156] This system is based on the computation of the after-tax net profit of the joint venture, from which are deducted amounts allocated to the joint venture's reserve fund, an incentive and welfare fund for the venture's employees, and an enterprise expansion fund. The actual amounts allocated to such funds may be decided by the board of directors and are usually calculated as a fixed percentage of the after-tax net profit. Amounts remaining after such deductions may be distributed to the joint venture parties in accordance with the ratio of their capital contributions. However distributions are not mandatory and current profits may be retained for distribution in later years.

I. Term and Termination

Chinese law does not specify any fixed term for joint ventures. The Implementing Act provides only that 'in principle' the average term should be between ten and thirty years, although longer terms may be permitted.[157] Under an amendment made to the Implementing Act on 15 January 1984, the maximum term may now be extended to fifty years or more in certain circumstances.[158] Moreover, the Act permits joint ventures to extend their life beyond the scheduled term, subject to the agreement of the parties and government approval. As a result, the duration of the venture is left to negotiation between the parties, taking into account the nature of the project, the wishes of the parties, and the attitude of the Chinese government. Joint ventures approved in 1984 had an average duration of approximately twelve years.

For most foreign investors, the scheduled duration of the venture is of less concern than the issue of what their rights and obligations will be upon termination and under what circumstances they will be permitted to end their participation in the joint venture prior to the expiration of its term. The Implementing Act permits the early dissolution of a joint venture in the event of a breach of contract by one of the parties, where the enterprise suffers heavy losses or is unable to attain its stated business goals, or upon the occurrence of other events stipulated in the joint venture contract.[159] In the event that the reason for the termination is a breach of contract which makes the joint venture unable to continue its operations, the breaching party is liable to compensate the venture for the losses incurred thereby.[160]

Upon the termination of the joint venture, the board of directors is required to establish a liquidation committee consisting of board members appointed by the parties.[161] This committee is entrusted with the tasks of compiling an inventory of the joint venture's assets and liabilities and formulating a plan for liquidation, which must be ratified by the board of directors and implemented under the supervision of the Chinese department in charge of the joint venture. After the clearance of the joint venture's debts, the remaining property may be distributed to the parties in accordance with the ratio of their capital contributions or some other method agreed to by the parties. In the event that the value of the remaining assets exceeds the amount of the joint venture's registered capital, the excess will be regarded as profit and will be subject to tax.[162] In addition, that portion of the distribution owing to the foreign party and remitted abroad which exceeds its original capital contribution will be subject to a 10 per cent withholding tax.[163]

Although the Implementing Act contemplates that joint ventures will be able to make distributions to the parties upon liquidation, a major fear of foreign investors has been that the Chinese side will prevent them from doing so. The fear is grounded in the belief that the Chinese members of the liquidation committee will insist on a low valuation of the company's assets and then arrange for their sale to a related Chinese entity, thereby permitting the Chinese side to continue the operations of the joint venture in a modified form. To diminish the likelihood that this will occur, many foreign investors have attempted to negotiate contract language that would require that the valuation of the joint venture's assets be performed by a foreign broker or at least that the assets be sold at auction in the international market. In other instances, language has been proposed that would permit the Chinese side to exercise a right of first refusal to purchase the foreign party's interest in the venture (the value of this interest being calculated on the basis of the proportional value of the company's assets when viewed as part of a going concern, with the addition of a value to reflect the future profitability of the enterprise). These and similar attempts to ensure that liquidation will be conducted in a fair manner have met with varied success, although the Chinese willingness to accept such proposals has tended to increase over time.

V. Wholly Foreign-owned Enterprises

On 12 April 1986 the National People's Congress promulgated the Law of the People's Republic of China on Wholly Foreign-owned Enterprises.[164] The enactment of this legislation marks a new phase in China's open-door policy and presents new opportunities for foreign companies contemplating investments in China.

Prior to 1986, the establishment of wholly foreign-owned enterprises in China was restricted for the most part to the SEZs in Guangdong and Fujian provinces. The legal basis for such ventures was to be found in Article 1 of the Regulations on Special Economic Zones in Guangdong Province (the SEZ Regulations) which permits foreign investors 'to open up factories with their own investment' as well as to form joint ventures with Chinese enterprises.[165] The same rules permitting wholly foreign-owned investments were applied in the Fujian SEZ. In addition, in 1984 Shanghai published its own regulations providing for the establishment of wholly foreign-owned ventures.[166] Hence, even before the promulgation of the Wholly Foreign-owned Enterprises Law a number of ventures were established in the SEZs and in Shanghai. According to the MOFERT, between 1979 and the end of 1985 more than 120 wholly foreign-owned ventures were approved involving investments of more than US$300.[167]

The purpose of the new law is to provide the formal legal groundwork for the establishment of wholly foreign-owned enterprises in China, as well as the framework for regulating the activities of such enterprises on a nation-wide basis. Consisting of 24 articles, the law itself falls short of this goal and establishes little more than the basic principles of this framework. However, detailed implementing rules are now being drafted and these are expected to be promulgated before the end of 1987.

Under the law, wholly foreign-owned enterprises (*duzi qiye*) are defined as 'enterprises established within the territory of China...the entire capital of which is invested by foreign investors'. Branch offices and 'other economic entities' established by foreign enterprises in China are specifically excluded from the definition.[168]

The precise legal status of wholly foreign-owned enterprises in China is not addressed by the law, and in the absence of a company law other Chinese regulations shed little light on the issue. The law itself says only that wholly foreign-owned enterprises which 'meet the requirements of Chinese law' shall obtain the status of 'Chinese legal persons'.[169]

As is customary with Chinese investment legislation, the new law provides assurances to foreign investors that their 'lawful rights and interests' will be protected by the laws of China.[170] The law also states specifically that the state 'will not nationalize or expropriate wholly foreign-owned enterprises'.[171] However, this commitment is qualified by a further provision which permits expropriation under 'special circumstances'.[172] In such a case, the law promises that 'legal procedures' will be followed and 'appropriate compensation' will be given.[173] No further elaboration is given in the law.

Under the law, wholly foreign-owned enterprises are established by application to the MOFERT or other authorities designated by China's State Council.[174] After receipt of the application, the relevant approval authority must approve or reject the application within ninety days. If approval is granted the foreign investor is required, within thirty days from the date of the approval certificate, to apply for registration with the local bureau of the State Administration for Industry and Commerce and obtain a business licence. The date of issuance of the business licence is deemed to be the date of establishment of the enterprise.

The law contains no detailed provisions regarding the procedures to be followed in submitting an application for the establishment of a wholly foreign-owned enterprise. It must be assumed that these matters will be addressed in the detailed regulations now being drafted. In the interim, the MOFERT has indicated that investors should conduct application procedures by reference to the Shanghai Regulations.

Under the Shanghai Regulations, the first step in the establishment of a wholly foreign-owned enterprise in Shanghai is the appointment of a local unit to assist with the application process. The appointment is to be made by means of a written power of attorney or other agreement. The responsibility of the unit is to help the foreign investor in settling problems such as the use of land, the arrangement of the labour force, the supply of raw materials and marketing, the supply of water and electricity, insurance, transportation, and environmental protection. In addition, the unit is responsible jointly with the department in charge of the industry concerned and, in accordance with the requirements of the entrustment granted by the foreign investor, for submitting a project proposal in triplicate to the Shanghai Municipal Commission of Foreign Economic Relations and Trade (the SMERT). Copies of the project proposal are also to be forwarded to the Shanghai Municipal Planning Commission (SMPC) and relevant commissions and offices. Upon receipt of the project proposal, the SMERT is required to conduct a study jointly with the SMPC. Within one month of receipt of the project proposal, the SMERT must give the unit an official written reply, which is to be passed on to the foreign investor.

Upon receiving a favourable reply on the proposal from the SMERT, the foreign investor, with the assistance of the unit, must then prepare and submit to the SMERT ten copies of the following documents: (a) an application for the establishment of the foreign enterprise; (b) the feasibility study for the project; (c) the articles of association of the enterprise; (d) various relevant agreements initialled with the Chinese units concerned for the use of land, the supply of water and electricity, and so on; (e) a list of candidates for directorships and senior positions; and (f) the power of attorney or other entrustment given to the unit. For the purposes of examination and approval, the above-mentioned documents must be submitted in the Chinese language. Texts in a foreign language may also be submitted for reference use.

The MOFERT has indicated that the letter of application, mentioned above, should include the following information: (a) the name, nationality, and legal address or residence of the foreign investor; (b) the name, nationality, and job title of the investor or his legal representative(s); (c) the name of the wholly foreign-owned enterprise; (d) the total land area and floor space required for the enterprise, and the location and area of the construction site; (e) the total amount of the investment or the registered capital; (f) the name, types, specifications, applications, and main properties of the product(s) to be manufactured, the scale of production, and the development plans; (g) the volume of the product(s) to be sold in the Chinese market and on the international market; (h) the planned foreign currency income and expenses; (i) the investment implementation plan; (j) the number of workers and staff required, their remuneration, labour protection and welfare, and so on; (k) the sources of raw materials; (l) the proposed duration of the operation; (m) the credit references of the applicant; and (n) other information that the applicant deems necessary.

When transferring the other documents mentioned above to the SMERT, the unit must enclose written opinions relating to the establishment of the enterprise signed by both that unit and the department in charge of the industry concerned.

Under the law, applications for the establishment of wholly foreign-owned enterprises are restricted to projects which are 'beneficial to the development of China's national economy' and which either adopt 'advanced technology and equipment' or 'export all or most of their products'.[175] Project proposals which involve activities which are 'forbidden' or 'restricted by the state' will be rejected.[176] Although no list of proscribed or restricted projects has yet been published, it is clear from the law that emphasis is to be placed on productive ventures with export potential rather than projects in the service industry or those which primarily involve sales on the domestic market.

The law provides that wholly foreign-owned enterprises shall enjoy autonomy in their operational and management activities and prohibits interference by other organizations in the enterprise's affairs.[177] However, like joint ventures, wholly foreign-owned enterprises are subject to supervision by the local 'department in charge' and all operating and production plans must be submitted to this authority 'for the record'.[178]

With respect to matters of employment, the law requires wholly foreign-owned ventures to adopt a labour contract system similar to that which applies to joint ventures.[179] In addition, the staff and workers of wholly foreign-owned enterprises are permitted by the law to establish a trade union organization and the enterprise is obliged to provide the 'necessary facilities' for the activities of the union.[180] The law contains no provisions regarding the employment, dismissal, or remuneration of Chinese employees. It is assumed that such matters are to be handled in accordance with local labour rules.

Wholly foreign-owned enterprises are required to establish and maintain an accounting system in China and to submit audited financial statements to and accept supervision by the local finance and tax departments. Although the law does not specifically address the issue, it is assumed that wholly foreign-owned enterprises will be subject to a tax on their net profits under the Foreign Enterprise Income Tax. In addition, various other taxes, such as the Consolidated Industrial and Commercial Tax, the Vehicle and Vessel Licence Tax, the Real Estate Tax, customs duties, and import taxes will apply to the operations of wholly foreign-owned enterprises. Under the law, wholly foreign-owned enterprises will be eligible to enjoy preferential treatment in tax reductions and exemptions but these are not specified.[181] The law does, however, provide for a tax refund for wholly foreign-owned enterprises which reinvest their profits within China. Although the manner in which this tax refund provision will be implemented is not spelled out in the law, Ministry of Finance officials have indicated that the tax refund rules applicable to equity joint ventures will be applied to wholly foreign-owned enterprises 'by reference'.[182]

Wholly foreign-owned enterprises are subject to China's Foreign Exchange Control Regulations in the same way as joint ventures.[183] Although the 'lawful profits and other lawful income' of investors may be remitted abroad under the law, the remittability of such profits will depend in practice on the extent to which the enterprise generates foreign exchange income.[184] Under the law, wholly foreign-owned enterprises are required to maintain a balance between foreign exchange receipts and expenditures and to resolve any foreign exchange problems without assistance from the state.[185] However, where an enterprise which sells its products on the Chinese domestic market experiences problems of foreign exchange imbalance, the authorities which approved such sales are to be responsible for resolving the problem.[186]

The law does not specify any minimum or maximum term for wholly foreign-owned enterprises. However, most enterprises approved to date have had a maximum term of ten years. Under the law, investors are permitted to apply for an extension of the term of the enterprise within 180 days prior to the expiration of the scheduled term.

Upon termination, wholly foreign-owned enterprises are required by the law to liquidate 'in accordance with legal procedures' and go through the procedures for cancellation of their business licence.[187] Until the law's detailed implementing rules have been published it is not possible to say how such liquidation will be conducted, although it is assumed that such matters would be addressed in the articles of association of the enterprise.

VI. Further Rules for the Encouragement of Foreign Investment

On 11 October 1986 the State Council promulgated Provisions for the Encouragement of Foreign Investment.[188] The Provisions were intended as a response by the Chinese government to growing dissatisfaction among foreign companies with the Chinese investment climate in 1986, including high local costs, lack of foreign exchange, and excessive bureaucracy.[189] The Provisions attempt to address these problems by providing for specific remedial measures as well as a number of additional incentives to investment in equity and co-operative joint ventures and wholly foreign-owned enterprises.

The Provisions draw a distinction between 'export enterprises' and 'technologically advanced enterprises' on the one hand and all other enterprises with foreign investment on the other. Export enterprises are defined as joint ventures and wholly foreign-owned enterprises engaged in production whose products are mainly for export and which enjoy a foreign exchange surplus.[190] Technologically advanced enterprises are production enterprises which employ 'advanced technology' and which are engaged in developing new products or in upgrading or replacing products in order to increase foreign exchange through increased exports or for import substitution.[191] Decisions on how a particular project is to be classified are made by local representatives of the MOFERT.

Under the Provisions, the most important investment incentives and benefits are granted to export enterprises and technologically advanced enterprises. These include the following.

(a) Exemption from payment of all subsidies to Chinese staff and workers, except for labour insurance, welfare, and housing subsidies.

(b) Reduction in land-use fees. In general, such fees should not exceed

RMB5–20 per square metre per annum where the development fee and land-use fee are computed and charged together; where the development fee is computed and charged on a one-time basis the land-use fee should not exceed RMB3 per square metre per annum.

(c) Priority in obtaining water, electricity, transportation services, and communication facilities, with fees to be calculated and charged in accordance with the standards for state-owned enterprises.

(d) Priority in obtaining loans from the Bank of China.

(e) Exemption from tax on the remittance by the foreign investor of its profits abroad.

(f) For export enterprises, a further 50 per cent reduction in enterprise income tax beyond the statutory holiday period where exports are 70 per cent or more of total production during the year in which the tax reduction is to be taken. Where an export enterprise located in one of the SEZs or in one of the open coastal cities already enjoys a tax rate of 15 per cent, the reduced tax rate for qualifying enterprises will be 10 per cent.

(g) For technologically advanced enterprises, a further 50 per cent reduction in enterprise income tax for three years beyond the statutory tax holiday period.

(h) A tax refund for foreign investors who reinvest their profits in export and technologically advanced enterprises for not less than five years.

The Provisions extend a number of investment incentives and benefits to all joint ventures and wholly foreign-owned enterprises, including those already approved and established as of the date of promulgation of the law.[192] These include the following.

(a) Exemption from the Consolidated Industrial and Commercial Tax for most products manufactured and exported by enterprises.

(b) The right to export products directly or through agents.

(c) Simplified export licensing procedures.

(d) Simplified import licensing and customs procedures.

(e) The right to 'adjust' foreign exchange surpluses and deficiencies among other enterprises with foreign investment under the supervision of the foreign exchange control departments.

(f) The right to autonomy in managing and operating the enterprise, including the right of the enterprise to determine its own organizational structure and personnel system, to employ and dismiss senior managerial personnel, to increase the number of workers, or to dismiss workers.

(g) The right to refuse to pay 'unreasonable charges'.

Since the promulgation of the Provisions, a number of additional measures have been taken by the Chinese government to implement the new rules. For example, in December 1986, regulations were issued by the Customs to liberalize procedures applicable to the importation of materials and parts needed by enterprises with foreign investment for the production of export goods.[193] At the same time, rules were passed by the Ministry of Labour and Personnel containing stipulations regarding the rights of enterprises with foreign investment independently to hire and

rs, and matters relating to the wages, insurance, and welfare
hinese employees.[194] In addition, foreign exchange trading
een opened in Shanghai, Guangzhou, and Shenzhen per-
rises with foreign investment to exchange *renminbi* for
cies.[195] According to Chinese officials, further liberalizing
measures will be taken in various other supplementary regulations to be
issued pursuant to the Provisions.[196]

VII. Conclusion

For a society that remains committed to Communist ideals, China has
demonstrated an extraordinary degree of flexibility in permitting a variety
of forms of foreign investment. Moreover, the efforts that have been made
to date to establish a legal framework for the regulation of investment
activities are admirable. None the less, it is important to bear in mind the
fact that foreign investment is still relatively new to China; thus its
future is to a large degree unpredictable. As a result, the ultimate test of
China's commitment to foreign investment lies in how liberally it chooses
to interpret and implement its newly established legal framework rather
than in the strict letter of the laws themselves.

Notes

1. Statistics provided by the Ministry of Foreign Economic Relations and
Trade quoted in the *China Daily*, 30 January 1986, p. 2.
2. The Constitution of the People's Republic of China, promulgated on
4 December 1982, Arts. 15 and 89.
3. The foregoing description of the foreign investment planning process is
based on a speech entitled 'China Investment Needs Mutual Understanding',
delivered by Gu Xiancheng, former Vice-President of China International Economic Consultants, Inc. The speech was delivered in Tokyo and Hong Kong at the
China Update Conference sponsored by the Institute for International Research,
14–18 November 1983.
4. Gu speech, note 3 above.
5. See The Law of the People's Republic of China on Joint Ventures Using
Chinese and Foreign Investment, adopted at the Second Session of the Fifth
National People's Congress on 1 July 1979 and promulgated on 8 July 1979, Art.
3 (hereafter cited as the Joint Venture Law). For an English translation of the Joint
Venture Law, see F. Chu, M. Moser, and O. Nee (eds.), *Commercial, Business
and Trade Laws: People's Republic of China* (Dobbs Ferry, Oceana Publications
Inc., 1982), Part 9, p. 3.
6. See The Implementing Act for the Law of the People's Republic of China on
Joint Ventures Using Chinese and Foreign Investment, promulgated by the State
Council on 20 September 1983, Art. 8 (hereafter cited as the Implementing Act).
All references to the Implementing Act are to an English translation on file with
the author.
7. The information contained in the following paragraphs is also drawn in part
from State Council Document *Guo fa* No. 138, issued in 1984. This document
contains a summary of current foreign investment approval procedures and poli-

cies, and was prepared for the exclusive use of Chinese foreign investment officials. The text of the document is internal (*neibu*) and only a description of its
contents has been available to the author.

8. See Regulations of Shanghai Municipality on the Conduct of Talks and the
Procedures of Examination and Approval Regarding the Establishment of
Chinese-Foreign Joint Ventures and the Acceptance of Self-run Enterprises Being
Invested in and Established by Foreign Businesses, promulgated for trial im-
plementation on 1 July 1984 (hereafter cited as the Shanghai Regulations).

9. See Implementing Act, Art. 8, note 6 above.

10. See P. Torbert, 'China's Joint Venture Law: A Preliminary Analysis',
Vanderbilt Journal of Transnational Law, No. 4, Fall 1979, p. 822.

11. Figures reported in *Wen wei po*, 20 September 1984, p. 1.

12. The following discussion is based largely on *China: A Business Guide*
(Tokyo, Japan External Trade Organization, 1979), pp. 155–6; J. Cohen and O.
Nee, 'All About Compensation Trade, Part I', *Asian Wall Street Journal*, 3 July
1979, p. 4 and 'Part II', *Asian Wall Street Journal*, 4 July 1979, p. 4; and Torbert,
pp. 822–7, note 10 above. See, also, M. Moser, *Business Strategies for the People's
Republic of China* (Hong Kong, Longman China Intelligence Publications, 1986),
pp. 10–20.

13. Provisions regarding compensation trade are contained in the Regulations
of the Shenzhen Special Economic Zone on Foreign Economic Contracts, promulgated on 7 February 1984. However, these provisions do little more than
define compensation trade arrangements and set out the kinds of provision which
must be included in compensation trade contracts entered into between entities in
the Shenzhen SEZ. General provisions regarding contracts are also contained in
the Foreign Economic Contract Law of the People's Republic of China, adopted
at the Tenth Session of the Standing Committee of the Sixth National People's
Congress on 21 March 1985 and put into force on 1 July 1985 (hereafter cited as
the Foreign Economic Contract Law).

14. Provisional Regulations on Foreign Exchange Control of the People's Republic of China (hereafter cited as the Foreign Exchange Control Regulations),
promulgated by the State Council on 18 December 1980, and Detailed Rules for
Foreign Exchange Control for Enterprises with Overseas Chinese Capital, Enterprises with Foreign Capital and Chinese-Foreign Joint Venture Enterprises
(hereafter cited as the Detailed Rules for Foreign Exchange Control), approved by
the State Council on 19 July 1983 and promulgated by the State Administration of
Foreign Exchange Control on 1 August 1983. All subsequent references to these
two laws are to English translations on file with the author.

15. For a discussion of commodity inspection procedures, see Chapter 1 of this
volume.

16. A detailed discussion of the Consolidated Industrial and Commercial Tax
is set forth in Chapter 2 of this volume.

17. See Chapter 2 of this volume.

18. See *South China Morning Post, Business News*, 2 October 1985, p. 1.

19. Figures reported in *China Economic News*, 4 November 1985, p. 1.

20. Early drafts of the Co-operative Joint Venture Law which this author has
seen contained a clause providing for retroactive application of the law to all
co-operative joint ventures existing at the time of promulgation. Such a provision
would seem to be in conflict with Article 40 of the Foreign Economic Contract
Law which provides that provisions contained in approved co-operative joint
venture contracts will remain in effect when new laws are enacted.

21. Under current regulations, however, co-operative joint ventures must still
meet the same equity/total investment ratios as are applicable to equity joint ventures. See note 59 and the accompanying text below.

22. See 'China's MOFERT Legal Experts on Contractual JV's', *China Economic News*, 4 November 1985, p. 3.

23. Economic Contract Law of the People's Republic of China, promulgated

on 13 December 1981, Art. 2. An English translation of this law appears in Chu, Moser, and Nee, Part 5, note 5 above.

24. The Income Tax Law of the People's Republic of China Concerning Foreign Enterprises (hereafter cited as the Foreign Enterprise Income Tax Law), promulgated on 13 December 1981. The Foreign Enterprise Income Tax Law has been supplemented by the Detailed Rules and Regulations for the Implementation of the Income Tax Law of the People's Republic of China Concerning Foreign Enterprises (hereafter cited as the Foreign Enterprise Income Tax Detailed Rules), promulgated by the Ministry of Finance on 21 February 1982. English translations of the Foreign Enterprise Income Tax Law and the Foreign Enterprise Income Tax Detailed Rules are in Chu, Moser, and Nee, Part 13, note 5 above.

25. The Income Tax Law of the People's Republic of China Concerning Joint Ventures Using Chinese and Foreign Investment (hereafter cited as the Joint Venture Income Tax Law), promulgated on 10 September 1980, and the Detailed Rules and Regulations for the Implementation of the Income Tax Law of the People's Republic of China Concerning Joint Ventures Using Chinese and Foreign Investment (hereafter cited as the Joint Venture Income Tax Detailed Rules), promulgated by the Ministry of Finance on 14 December 1980. English translations of both the Joint Venture Income Tax Law and the Joint Venture Income Tax Detailed Rules appear in Chu, Moser, and Nee, Part 13, note 5 above.

26. For a discussion of the operation of the Foreign Enterprise Income Tax and the Joint Venture Income Tax see Chapter 2 of this volume.

27. Chapter 2 of this volume discusses China's individual income tax.

28. See note 16 above.

29. See Regulations Regarding the Supervision and Control of and Levy and Exemption of Tax on Goods Imported and Exported by Chinese-Foreign Cooperative Ventures, promulgated on 31 January 1984 and put into effect on 1 February 1984. The original Chinese text and an English translation of this law are on file with the author.

30. See Part IV of this chapter.

31. See the Provisional Regulations on Standards for the Payment of Registration Fees by Joint Ventures (hereafter cited as the Registration Fee Regulations) issued in March 1982 by the General Administration for Industry and Commerce of the People's Republic of China, subsequently renamed the State Administration for Industry and Commerce of the People's Republic of China. The provisions referring to contractual joint ventures are set forth in Arts. 1 and 4.

32. See 'Creating a More Favourable Investment Environment for Foreign Investors', text of a speech prepared by Liu Yimin, Director, Department of Foreign Investment of the Ministry of Foreign Economic Relations and Trade and delivered at a seminar in Hong Kong on China's New Joint Venture Legislation, sponsored by Economic Information and Agency, on 11 November 1983.

33. Liu speech, note 32 above.

34. See 'Problems that Can Arise from Investment in China', text of a speech delivered by Kazuo Tomabechi, Managing Director of the Industrial Bank of Japan, at the China Update Conference held in Tokyo under the sponsorship of the Institute for International Research, 14–15 November 1983. According to Mr Tomabechi, the investment environment in Taiwan, Korea, Indonesia, Malaysia, and Singapore is far more attractive than that in the People's Republic.

35. See *International Trade* (Beijing), January 1986, p. 12.

36. The information in this and the preceding sentences was reported in *China Daily*, 30 January 1986, p. 2.

37. Joint Venture Law, Art. 4, note 5 above; and Implementing Act, Art. 19, note 6 above.

38. Implementing Act, Art. 2, note 6 above.

39. Implementing Act, Art. 2, note 6 above.

40. Implementing Act, Art. 19, note 6 above.

41. Joint Venture Law, Art. 4, note 5 above.

42. General Principles of Civil Law of the People's Republic of China, adopted at the Fourth Session of the Sixth National People's Congress on 12 April 1986.

43. See the Introduction to this volume.

44. Quoted in 'Questions and Answers Concerning Foreign Investment in China', *China Economic News* (Supplement 3), 12 May 1983, p. 5.

45. Foreign Economic Contract Law, Art. 40, note 13 above.

46. The case referred to is the Schindler Elevator Joint Venture. See J. Cohen (ed.), *Legal Aspects of Doing Business in China 1983* (New York, Practising Law Institute, 1983), p. 82.

47. Implementing Act, Art. 9(1), note 6 above.

48. Implementing Act, Art. 13, note 6 above.

49. Implementing Act, Arts. 13, 14, and 16, note 6 above.

50. Implementing Act, Art. 9, note 6 above.

51. Implementing Act, Art. 9, note 6 above.

52. Implementing Act, Art. 15, note 6 above.

53. In general, however, the Chinese will require that these 'commonly accepted' practices also be acceptable to the Chinese party. A formulation that has been widely adopted in the petroleum area provides that: 'The validity, interpretation and implementation of the Contract shall be governed by the law of the People's Republic of China. Failing the relevant provisions of the law of the People's Republic of China for its implementation or interpretation of the Contract, the principles of the applicable laws widely used in petroleum resources countries acceptable to the CNOOC and the Contractor shall be applicable.'

54. Implementing Act, Arts. 109 and 110, note 6 above.

55. Arbitration in China is discussed in Chapter 16 of this volume.

56. Implementing Act, Art. 111, note 6 above.

57. Implementing Act, Art. 21, note 6 above.

58. Implementing Act, Art. 20, note 6 above.

59. See 'China's Move Hits Joint Venture Plans', *Asian Wall Street Journal*, 10 January 1986, p. 1.

60. Joint Venture Law, Art. 4, note 5 above.

61. Implementing Act, Art. 21, note 6 above.

62. Implementing Act, Art. 32, note 6 above.

63. Implementing Act, Art. 22, note 6 above.

64. Implementing Act, Art. 24, note 6 above.

65. Implementing Act, Art. 23, note 6 above.

66. Implementing Act, Art. 23, note 6 above.

67. Implementing Act, Art. 23, note 6 above.

68. Implementing Act, Art. 27, note 6 above.

69. Implementing Act, Art. 28, note 6 above.

70. Implementing Act, Art. 29, note 6 above.

71. Implementing Act, Art. 25, note 6 above.

72. Implementing Act, Art. 5, note 6 above.

73. Implementing Act, Art. 30, note 6 above.

74. Implementing Act, Art. 78, note 6 above.

75. Approved by the State Council and promulgated by the Bank of China on 13 March 1981. For an English translation of the Loan Measures, see Chu, Moser, and Nee, Part 9, note 5 above.

76. Loan Measures, Art. 2, note 75 above.

77. Loan Measures, Art. 3, note 75 above.

78. Loan Measures, Art. 4, note 75 above.

79. Loan Measures, Art. 7, note 75 above.

80. Loan Measures, Art. 6, note 75 above.

81. Loan Measures, Art. 6, note 75 above.

82. Loan Measures, Art. 8, note 75 above.

83. Implementing Act, Art. 8, note 6 above.

84. Implementing Act, Art. 9, note 6 above.

85. Implementing Act, Art. 10, note 6 above.
86. Implementing Act, Art. 10, note 6 above.
87. Implementing Act, Art. 8, note 6 above. See *China Economic News*, 16 June 1986, p. 1.
88. Implementing Act, Art. 11, note 6 above.
89. An English translation of the Registration Measures is included in Chu, Moser, and Nee, Part 9, note 5 above.
90. Registration Measures, Art. 3, note 89 above.
91. See note 31 above.
92. Registration Fee Regulations, Art. 1, note 31 above.
93. Registration Measures, Art. 7, note 89 above.
94. Registration Fee Regulations, Art. 2, note 31 above.
95. Registration Fee Regulations, Art. 1, note 31 above.
96. Implementing Act, Art. 33, note 6 above.
97. Implementing Act, Art. 38, note 6 above.
98. This requirement, and the others referred to in this paragraph, are all contained in the Implementing Act, Art. 34, note 6 above.
99. The provisions referred to in this paragraph are contained in the Implementing Act, Art. 35, note 6 above.
100. Implementing Act, Art. 36, note 6 above.
101. Implementing Act, Art. 36, note 6 above.
102. Implementing Act, Art. 38, note 6 above.
103. Implementing Act, Art. 94, note 6 above.
104. An English translation of the Labour Regulations appears in Chu, Moser, and Nee, Part 9, note 5 above.
105. Labour Regulations, Art. 2, note 104 above.
106. Labour Regulations, Art. 3, note 104 above.
107. Labour Regulations, Art. 3, note 104 above.
108. Labour Regulations, Art. 4, note 104 above.
109. Labour Regulations, Art. 4, note 104 above.
110. Labour Regulations, Art. 5, note 104 above.
111. Labour Regulations, Art. 6, note 104 above.
112. Labour Regulations, Art. 14, note 104 above.
113. Labour Regulations, Art. 14, note 104 above.
114. Labour Regulations, Art. 8, note 104 above.
115. Labour Regulations, Art. 11, note 104 above.
116. Implementing Act, Art. 95, note 6 above.
117. Implementing Act, Arts. 96 and 97, note 6 above.
118. Implementing Act, Art. 98, note 6 above.
119. Implementing Act, Art. 98, note 6 above.
120. Implementing Act, Art. 98, note 6 above.
121. Implementing Act, Art. 7, note 6 above.
122. Implementing Act, Art. 53, note 6 above.
123. Implementing Act, Art. 47, note 6 above.
124. Implementing Act, Art. 49, note 6 above. According to an internal Chinese regulation issued by the State Council, land-use fees should be fixed within the range of RMB5–300 per square metre per annum. See Provisional Regulations Concerning the Use of Land for Construction by Joint Ventures Using Chinese and Foreign Investment, issued on 26 July 1980.
125. Implementing Act, Art. 50, note 6 above.
126. Implementing Act, Art. 50, note 6 above.
127. Implementing Act, Art. 52, note 6 above.
128. Implementing Act, Art. 51, note 6 above.
129. Implementing Act, Art. 51, note 6 above.
130. Joint Venture Law, Art. 8, note 5 above.
131. Joint Venture Law, Art. 8, note 5 above; and Implementing Act, Art. 74, note 6 above.

132. Implementing Act, Art. 76, note 6 above.
133. Implementing Act, Art. 57, note 6 above.
134. Implementing Act, Art. 58, note 6 above.
135. Implementing Act, Art. 63, note 6 above.
136. Implementing Act, Art. 65, note 6 above.
137. Joint Venture Law, Art. 65(3), note 5 above.
138. Implementing Act, Art. 67, note 6 above.
139. Implementing Act, Art. 61, note 6 above.
140. Implementing Act, Art. 62, note 6 above.
141. Implementing Act, Art. 66, note 6 above.
142. Implementing Act, Art. 66, note 6 above.
143. Implementing Act, Art. 46, note 6 above.
144. For further discussion regarding the taxation of technology transfer transactions, see Chapter 2 in this volume.
145. See note 14 above.
146. See note 14 above.
147. Detailed Rules for Foreign Exchange Control, Art. 12, note 14 above.
148. Implementing Act, Art. 75, note 6 above.
149. See 'Sleepy Beijing Jeep Plant Irks AMC', *International Herald Tribune*, 21 April 1986, p. 7.
150. Promulgated by the State Council on 15 January 1986 and put into effect on 1 February 1986. The contribution of my colleague, Preston M. Torbert, to the following paragraphs is gratefully acknowledged.
151. See note 25 above. For a detailed discussion of the taxation of joint ventures see Chapter 2 of this volume.
152. See note 16 above.
153. Regulations for the Control of and Payment and Exemption of Taxes on Items Imported by Chinese-Foreign Joint Ventures, issued pursuant to the Document of the General Customs Office, the Ministry of Finance, and the Ministry of Foreign Economic Relations and Trade, (83) *Shu shui*, No. 377 (undated).
154. The Real Estate Tax is discussed in Chapter 2 of this volume.
155. Implementing Act, Art. 90, note 6 above.
156. Joint Venture Law, Art. 7, note 5 above; and Implementing Act, Arts. 57 and 58, note 6 above.
157. Implementing Act, Art. 100, note 6 above.
158. The 'special circumstances' include those where the project involves a large investment, a long construction period, and a low return on invested capital; where the project involves advanced technology or key technology for producing sophisticated products; or where the project involves the production of products which are internationally competitive. See Amendment to Article 100 of the Implementing Act, adopted by the State Council on 15 January 1986.
159. Implementing Act, Art. 102, note 6 above.
160. Implementing Act, Art. 102, note 6 above.
161. Implementing Act, Arts. 103 and 104, note 6 above.
162. Implementing Act, Art. 106, note 6 above.
163. Implementing Act, Art. 106, note 6 above.
164. Hereafter cited as the WFOE Law. The law was adopted at the Fourth Session of the Sixth National People's Congress on 12 April 1986 and put into effect on the same date.
165. Promulgated on 26 August 1980 by the Standing Committee of the National People's Congress. For an English translation of the regulations, see Chu, Moser, and Nee, Part 14, note 5 above.
166. See the Shanghai Regulations, note 8 above.
167. Statistics provided by the MOFERT.
168. WFOE Law, Art. 2, note 164 above.
169. WFOE Law, Art. 8, note 164 above.
170. WFOE Law, Art. 4, note 164 above.

171. WFOE Law, Art. 5, note 164 above.
172. WFOE Law, Art. 5, note 164 above.
173. WFOE Law, Art. 5, note 164 above.
174. WFOE Law, Arts. 6 and 7, note 164 above.
175. WFOE Law, Art. 3, note 164 above.
176. WFOE Law, Art. 3, note 164 above.
177. WFOE Law, Art. 11, note 164 above.
178. WFOE Law, Art. 11, note 164 above.
179. WFOE Law, Art. 13, note 164 above.
180. WFOE Law, Art. 13, note 164 above.
181. WFOE Law, Art. 17, note 164 above.
182. WFOE Law, Art. 17, note 164 above; personal discussion with Ministry of Finance officials.
183. WFOE Law, Art. 18, note 164 above.
184. WFOE Law, Art. 19, note 164 above.
185. WFOE Law, Art. 18, note 164 above.
186. WFOE Law, Art. 18, note 164 above.
187. WFOE Law, Art. 21, note 164 above.
188. The Provisions of the State Council of the People's Republic of China for the Encouragement of Foreign Investment, hereafter cited as the Provisions. The Provisions were put into effect on the date of their promulgation.
189. See L. do Rosario, 'Foreign Investment: A Small Step Forward', *China Trade Report*, Vol. XXIV, December 1986, p. 1.
190. The Provisions, Art. 2, note 188 above.
191. The Provisions, Art. 2, note 188 above.
192. The Provisions, Art. 19, note 188 above.
193. See Procedures of the Customs of the People's Republic of China for the Administration of Materials and Parts which Enterprises with Foreign Investment Need to Import in Order to Perform Product Export Contracts, promulgated and put into effect on 1 December 1986.
194. See Provisions of the Ministry of Labour and Personnel of the People's Republic of China on the Right of Autonomy of Enterprises with Foreign Investment in the Hiring of Personnel and on Wages, Insurance and Welfare Expenses of Staff and Workers, promulgated and put into effect on 1 December 1986.
195. See 'Currency Exchange Makes Debut in Shanghai', *China Daily*, 7 November 1986, p. 2.
196. See L. do Rosario, note 189 above. In addition to those already mentioned, the following additional regulations were issued in early 1987 pursuant to the Provisions: Implementing Measures of the Ministry of Foreign Economic Relations and Trade on the Confirmation and Examination of Export Enterprises and Technologically Advanced Enterprises with Foreign Investment, promulgated 20 January 1987 (stipulating procedures for qualifying as an 'export' or 'technologically advanced' enterprise); Implementing Measures of the Ministry of Finance for Preferential Tax Provisions of the Regulations of the State Council for the Encouragement of Foreign Investment, promulgated on 30 January 1987 (clarifying tax preferences granted in the Provisions); Measures of the Ministry of Foreign Economic Relations and Trade on Balancing the Foreign Exchange Receipts and Expenditures of Enterprises with Foreign Investment by Purchasing Chinese-made Products for Export, promulgated on 20 January 1987 (permitting, under limited circumstances, the purchase of local products for resale abroad to overcome 'temporary' foreign exchange problems); Rules for Foreign Investment Enterprises Applying for Import and Export Licences, promulgated on 24 January 1987 (further simplifying licensing procedures); and Provisional Measures Concerning the Mortgage of Foreign Exchange for *Renminbi* Loans, promulgated on 12 December 1986 (providing for interest-free *renminbi* loans to foreign investment enterprises against security of foreign exchange deposits).

Appendix 3A. Outline of a Feasibility Study for a Chinese-foreign Joint Venture

I. General Introduction
 1. Description
  A. Project title
  B. Partners to the joint venture
  C. Investment and duration of the joint venture
  D. Site of the joint venture
  E. Projected date of completion of the feasibility study
  F. Parties responsible for the feasibility study
 2. Foreign partner in the joint venture
  A. Name of the firm
  B. Content of the technology transfer
  C. Business of the foreign partner
  D. Objective of the joint venture
 3. Principal stages in the feasibility study
  A. Exchange of technical information
   (a) Details of past meetings
   (b) Plans for future meetings
 4. Principal problems affecting the project
II. Market Requirements
 1. Requirements of the Chinese market
  A. Name of product, trade mark, and use of trade mark
  B. Imports of the products into China
   (a) Quantity of imports over the last five years
  C. Potential markets for the products in China
   (a) [list]
   (b) [list]
  D. Development of use of the products in China
   (a) Testing
   (b) Advertising
 2. World markets for the products
  A. Estimated long-term demand for the products
  B. Competitiveness of the products
 3. Sales plan of the products
  A. Sales network for the products in domestic and foreign markets
   (a) Network in China
   (b) Network in foreign countries
  B. Selling price of the products in foreign and domestic markets
III. Production Programme for the Joint Venture
 1. Building and space requirements for the joint venture
  A. Office and factory buildings
  B. Factory buildings for utilities and auxiliary production facilities

    C. Finished-product warehouse
    D. Raw material and auxiliary materials storage
    E. Waste-treatment area
  2. Product production at home and abroad
    A. Production and scientific research conditions in China
    B. Production conditions abroad
  3. Products and production capacity
    A. Names and specifications of products
      (a) [list]
      (b) [list]
      (c) [list]
    B. Production capacity
      (a) [list]
      (b) [list]
      (c) [list]
  4. Outline of technology in production
    A. Raw materials
    B. Technology
    C. Process flow and description
      (a) Consumption of raw materials
      (b) Finishing and packing
      (c) Selection of equipment
        (i)   Material for equipment
        (ii) Types of equipment
        (iii) List of equipment
      (d) Stage A
      (e) Stage B
      (f) Stage C
      (g) Stage D
IV. Supply of Main Materials
  1. Raw materials and auxiliary materials
    A. Name, specification, annual and start-up consumption, and source of supply of raw materials
    B. Name, specification, annual and start-up consumption, and source of supply of auxiliary materials
  2. Power supply
    A. Industrial water
    B. Clean water
 V. Conditions of Plant Area
  1. General conditions of the proposed plant
  2. Site conditions for the joint venture plant
    A. Attached drawing of the plant area
    B. Attached list of conditions on plant construction area
VI. Technical Engineering
  1. Utilities
    A. Water supply and sewerage
    B. Power supply
    C. Steam supply

2. Auxiliary services
   A. Refrigeration station
   B. Cooling-water unit
3. Provision of service and welfare
   A. Principles of design of service facilities
   B. Principles of design of welfare facilities
4. Civil engineering
5. General plan
   A. Layout plan
   B. Transportation
VII. Waste Treatment
   1. Environment of the proposed plant
   2. Pollutants from the joint venture plant
   3. Treatment of pollutants
   4. Existing problems and suggestions
VIII. Labour Organization and Personnel Requirements
   1. Organization structure and personnel requirements
   2. Qualification and record of service of staff members
   3. Training programme for personnel
   4. Working system
      A. Annual operating hours
      B. Working times for personnel
IX. Execution Plan of the Project
   1. Arrangement for execution plan of the project
      A. Letter of intent
      B. Feasibility study
      C. Chinese government approval
      D. Signing of contract and articles of association
      E. Joint venture implemented
   2. Construction schedule of the project
X. Economic Benefit Analysis for the Venture
   1. Principles and basis for financial evaluation
      A. Total investment
      B. Stock
      C. Loans
      D. Types, specification, and pricing of the products
      E. Price of imported raw materials
      F. Rate of profit
      G. Exchange rate
      H. Royalty payments
      I. Foreign exchange balance

Appendix 3B. Sample Contract for Joint Ventures Using Chinese and Foreign Investment*

Chapter 1 General Provisions

In accordance with the 'Law of the People's Republic of China on Joint Ventures Using Chinese and Foreign Investment' and other relevant Chinese laws and regulations, _____ Company and _____ Company, adhering to the principle of equality and mutual benefit and through friendly consultations, agree to jointly invest to set up a joint venture enterprise in _____ the People's Republic of China.

Chapter 2 Parties of the Joint Venture

Article 1

Parties to this contract are as follows: _____ Company (hereinafter referred to as Party A), registered with _____ in China, and its legal address is at _____ (street) _____ (district) _____ (city) _____ China.

Legal representative: Name:
                     Position:
                     Nationality:
_____ Company (hereinafter referred to as Party B), registered with _____. Its legal address at _____.

Legal representative: Name:
                     Position:
                     Nationality:
(Note: In case there are more than two investors, they will be called Party C, D . . . in proper order.)

Chapter 3 Establishment of the Joint Venture Company

Article 2

In accordance with the 'Law of the People's Republic of China on Joint

_____
*Drafted by the Department of Treaties and Law, Ministry of Foreign Economic Relations and Trade.

Ventures Using Chinese and Foreign Investment' and other relevant Chinese laws and regulations, both parties of the joint venture agree to set up ＿＿＿＿＿ joint venture limited liability company (hereinafter referred to as the joint venture company).

Article 3

The name of the joint venture company is ＿＿＿＿＿ Limited Liability Company.
   The name in foreign language is ＿＿＿＿＿.
   The legal address of the joint venture company is at ＿＿＿＿＿ street ＿＿＿＿＿ (city) ＿＿＿＿＿ province.

Article 4

All activities of the joint venture company shall be governed by the laws, decrees and pertinent rules and regulations of the People's Republic of China.

Article 5

The organization form of the joint venture company is a limited liability company. Each party to the joint venture company is liable to the joint venture company within the limit of the capital subscribed by it. The profits, risks and losses of the joint venture company shall be shared by the parties in proportion to their contributions to the registered capital.

Chapter 4   The Purpose, Scope and Scale of Production and Business

Article 6

The goals of the parties to the joint venture are to enhance economic co-operation technical exchanges, to improve the product quality, develop new products, and gain a competitive position in the world market in quality and price by adopting advanced and appropriate technology and scientific management methods, so as to raise economic results and ensure satisfactory economic benefits for each investor.
   (Note: This article shall be written according to the specific situations in the contract.)

Article 7

The productive and business scope of the joint venture company is to produce ＿＿＿＿＿ products; provide maintenance service after the sale of the products; study and develop new products.
   (Note: It shall be written in the contract according to the specific conditions.)

Article 8

The production scale of the joint venture company is as follows:
1. The production capacity after the joint venture is put into operation
   is _____.
2. The production scale may be increased up to _____ with the
   development of the production and operation. The product varieties
   may be developed into _____.
   (Note: It shall be written according to the specific situation.)

Chapter 5   Total Amount of Investment and the Registered Capital

Article 9

The total amount of investment of the joint venture company is RMB
_____ (or a foreign currency agreed upon by both parties).

Article 10

Investment contributed by the parties is Renminbi _____, which
will be the registered capital of the joint venture company.
   Of which: Party A shall pay _____ Yuan, accounts for _____
%; Party B shall pay _____ Yuan, accounts for _____ %.

Article 11

Both Party A and Party B will contribute the following as their invest-
ment:
Party A: cash _____ Yuan
         machines and equipment _____ Yuan
         premises _____ Yuan
         the right to the use of the site _____ Yuan
         industrial property _____ Yuan
         others _____ Yuan, _____ Yuan in all.
Party B: cash _____ Yuan
         machines and equipment _____ Yuan
         industrial property _____ Yuan
         others _____ Yuan, _____ Yuan in all.
   (Note: When contributing capital goods or industrial property as investment, Party A and Party B shall conclude a separate contract to be a
part of this main contract.)

Article 12

The registered capital of the joint venture company shall be paid in
_____ installments by Party A and Party B according to their respective proportion of their investment.

Each installment shall be as follows:
(Note: it shall be written according to the concrete conditions.)
Article 13

In case any party to the joint venture intends to assign all or part of his investment subscribed to a third party, consent shall be obtained from the other party to the joint venture, and approval from the examination and approval authority is required.

When one party to the joint venture assigns all or part of his investment, the other party has preemptive right.

Chapter 6   Responsibilities of Each Party to the Joint Venture

Article 14

Party A and Party B shall be respectively responsible for the following matters:

Responsibilities of Party A:
Handling of applications for approval, registration, business license and other matters concerning the establishment of the joint venture company from relevant departments in charge of China;

Processing the application for the right to the use of a site to the authority in charge of the land;

Organizing the design and construction of the premises and other engineering facilities of the joint venture company;

Providing cash, machinery and equipment and premises...in accordance with the stipulations in Article 11;

Assisting Party B to process import customs declaration for the machinery and equipment contributed by Party B as investment and arranging the transportation within the Chinese territory;

Assisting the joint venture company in purchasing or leasing equipment, materials, raw materials, articles for office use, means of transportation and communication facilities etc.;

Assisting the joint venture company in contacting and settling the fundamental facilities such as water, electricity, transportation etc.;

Assisting the joint venture in recruiting Chinese management personnel, technical personnel, workers and other personnel needed;

Assisting foreign workers and staff in applying for the entry visa, work license and processing their travelling matters;

Responsible for handling other matters entrusted by the joint venture company.

Responsibilities of Party B:
Providing cash, machinery and equipment, industrial property...in accordance with the stipulations in Article 11, and responsible for shipping capital goods such as machinery and equipment etc. contributed as investment to a Chinese port;

Handling the matters entrusted by the joint venture company, such as selecting and purchasing machinery and equipment outside China, etc.;

Providing needed technical personnel for installing, testing and trial production of the equipment as well as the technical personnel for production and inspecting;

Training the technical personnel and workers of the joint venture company;

In case Party B is the licensor, it shall be responsible for the stable production of qualified products of the joint venture company in the light of design capacity within the stipulated period;

Responsible for other matters entrusted by the joint venture company. (Note: It shall be written according to the specific situation.)

Chapter 7   Transfer of Technology

Article 15

Both Party A and Party B agree that a technology transfer agreement shall be signed between the joint venture company and the party B (or a third party) so as to obtain advanced production technology needed for realizing the production and operation purpose and the production scale stipulated in Chapter 4 in the contract, including products designing, technology of manufacturing, means of testing, materials prescription, standard of quality and the training of personnel etc.

(Note: It shall be written in the contract according to the concrete conditions.)

Article 16

Party B offers the following guarantees on the transfer of technology:

(Note: article applies only when Party B is responsible for transferring technology to the joint venture company.)

1. Party B guarantees that the overall technology such as the designing, technology of manufacturing, technological process, tests and inspection of products (Note: The name of the products shall be written) provided to the joint venture company must be integrated, precise and reliable. It is to meet the requirement of the joint venture's operation purpose, and be able to obtain the standard of production quality and production capacity stipulated in the contract;

2. Party B guarantees that the technology stipulated in this contract and the technology transfer agreement shall be fully transferred to the joint venture company, and pledges that the provided technology should be truly advanced among the same type of technology of Party B, the model, specification and quality of the equipment are excellent and it is to meet the requirement of technological operation and practical usage;

3. Party B shall work out a detailed list of the provided technology and technological service at various stages as stipulated in the technology

transfer agreement to be an appendix to the contract, and guarantee its performance;

4. The drawings, technological conditions and other detailed information are part of the transferred technology and shall be offered on time;

5. Within the validity period of the technology transfer agreement, Party B shall provide the joint venture company with the improvement of the technology and the improved information and technological materials in time, and shall not charge separate fees;

6. Party B shall guarantee that the technical personnel and the workers in the joint venture company can master all the technology transferred within the period stipulated in the technology transfer agreement.

Article 17

In case Party B fails to provide equipment and technology in accordance with the stipulations in this contract and in the technology transfer agreement or in case any deceiving or concealing actions are found, Party B shall be responsible for compensating the direct losses to the joint venture company.

Article 18

The technology transfer fee shall be paid in royalties. The royalty rate shall be _____ % of the net sales value of the products.

The term of the royalty payment is the same as the term for the technology transfer agreement stipulated in Article 19 of this contract.

Article 19

The term for the technology transfer agreement signed by the joint venture company and Party B is _____ years. After the expiration of the technology transfer agreement, the joint venture company shall have the right to use, research and develop the imported technology continuously.

(Note: The term for a technology transfer agreement is generally no longer than 10 years, and it shall be approved by the Ministry of Foreign Economic Relations and Trade or other examination and approval authorities entrusted by the Ministry of Foreign Economic Relations and Trade.)

Chapter 8   Selling of Products

Article 20

The products of joint venture company will be sold both on the Chinese market and on the overseas market, the export part accounts for _____ %, _____ % for domestic market.

(Note: An annual percentage and amount for outside and inside selling will be written out according to practical situations, in normal conditions, the amount for export shall at least meet the needs of foreign exchange expenses of the joint venture company.)

Article 21

Products may be sold on overseas markets through the following channels:

The joint venture company may directly sell its products on the international market, which accounts for _____ %.

The joint venture company may sign sales contracts with Chinese foreign trade companies, entrusting them to be the sales agencies or exclusive sales agencies, which accounts for _____ %.

The joint venture company may entrust Party B to sell its products, which accounts for _____ %.

Article 22

The joint venture's products to be sold in China may be handled by the Chinese materials and commercial departments by means of agency or exclusive sales, or may be sold by the joint venture company directly.

Article 23

In order to provide maintenance service to the products sold both in China or abroad, the joint venture company may set up sales branches for maintenance service both in China or abroad subject to the approval of the relevant Chinese department.

Article 24

The trade mark of the joint venture's products is _____ .

Chapter 9   The Board of Directors

Article 25

The date of registration of the joint venture company shall be the date of the establishment of the board of directors of the joint venture company.

Article 26

The board of directors are composed of _____ directors, of which _____ shall be appointed by Party A, _____ by Party B. The chairman of the board shall be appointed by Party A, and its vice-chairman by Party B. The term of office for the directors, chairman and vice-chairman is four years, their term of office may be renewed if continuously appointed by the relevant party.

Article 27

The highest authority of the joint venture company shall be its board of directors. It shall decide all major issues (Note: The main contents shall be listed in the light of the Article 36 of the Regulations for the Implementation of the Joint Venture Law) concerning the joint venture company. Unanimous approval shall be required before any decisions are made concerning major issues. As for other matters, approval by majority or a simple majority shall be required.

(Note: It shall be explicitly stipulated in the contract.)

Article 28

The chairman of the board is the legal representative of the joint venture company. Should the chairman be unable to exercise his responsibilities for some reason, he shall authorize the vice-chairman or any other directors to represent the joint venture company temporarily.

Article 29

The board of directors shall convene at least one meeting every year. The meeting shall be called and presided over by the chairman of the board. The chairman may convene an interim meeting based on a proposal made by more than one third of the total number of directors. Minutes of the meetings shall be placed on file.

Chapter 10   Business Management Office

Article 30

The joint venture company shall establish a management office which shall be responsible for its daily management. The management office shall have a general manager, appointed by party _____, _____ deputy general managers, _____ by party _____; _____ by party _____. The general manager and deputy general managers whose terms of office are _____ years shall be appointed by the board of directors.

Article 31

The responsibility of the general manager is to carry out the decisions of the board and organize and conduct the daily management of the joint venture company. The deputy general managers shall assist the general manager in his work.

Several department managers may be appointed by the management office, they shall be responsible for the work in various departments respectively, handle the matters handed over by the general manager and deputy general managers and shall be responsible to them.

Article 32

In case of graft or serious dereliction of duty on the part of the general manager and deputy general managers, the board of directors shall have the power to dismiss them at any time.

Chapter 11   Purchase of Equipment

Article 33

In its purchase of required raw materials, fuel, parts, means of transportation and articles for office use, etc., the joint venture company shall give first priority to purchase in China where conditions are the same.

Article 34

In case the joint venture company entrusts Party B to purchase equipment on the overseas market, persons appointed by Party A shall be invited to take part in the purchasing.

Chapter 12   Preparation and Construction

Article 35

During the period of preparation and construction, a preparation and construction office shall be set up under the board of directors. The preparation and construction office shall consist of _____ persons, among which _____ persons will be from Party A, _____ persons from Party B. The preparation and construction office shall have one manager recommended by Party _____, and one deputy manager by Party _____. The manager and deputy manager shall be appointed by the board of directors.

Article 36

The preparation and construction office is responsible for the following concrete works: examining the designs of the project, signing the project construction contract, organizing the purchasing and inspecting of relative equipment etc., working out the general schedule of project construction, compiling the expenditure plans, controlling project financial payments and final accounts of the project, drawing up managerial methods and keeping and filing documents, drawings, files and materials, etc., during the construction period of the project.

Article 37

A technical group with several technical personnel appointed by Party A and Party B shall be organized. The group, under the leadership of the preparation and construction office, is in charge of the examination, supervision, inspection, testing, checking and accepting, and performance checking for the project design, the quality of the project, the equipment and materials and the imported technology.

Article 38

After approval by both parties, the establishment, remuneration and the expenses of the staff of the preparation and construction office shall be covered in the project budget.

Article 39

After having completed the project and finished the turning over procedures, the preparation and construction office shall be dissolved upon the approval of the board of directors.

Chapter 13   Labor Management

Article 40

Labor contract covering the recruitment, employment, dismissal and resignation, wages, labor insurance, welfare, rewards, penalties and other matters concerning the staff and workers of the joint venture company shall be drawn up between the joint venture company and the Trade Union of the joint venture company as a whole, or the individual employees in the joint venture company as a whole or individual employees in accordance with the 'Regulations of the People's Republic of China on Labor Management in Joint Ventures Using Chinese and Foreign Investment and its Implementation Rules'.

Article 41

The appointment of high-ranking administrative personnel recommended by both parties, their salaries, social insurance, welfare and the standard of travelling expenses etc. shall be decided by the meeting of the board of directors.

Chapter 14   Taxes, Finance and Audit

Article 42

The joint venture company shall pay taxes in accordance with the stipulations of Chinese laws and other relative regulations.

Article 43

Staff members and workers of the joint venture company shall pay individual income tax according to the 'Individual Income Tax Law of the People's Republic of China'.

Article 44

Allocations for reserve funds, expansion funds of the joint venture company and welfare funds and bonuses for staff and workers shall be set aside in accordance with the stipulations in the 'Law of the People's Republic of China on Joint Ventures Using Chinese and Foreign Investment'. The annual proportion of allocations shall be decided by the board of directors according to the business situation of the joint venture company.

Article 45

The fiscal year of the joint venture company shall be from January 1 to December 31. All vouchers, receipts, statistic statement and reports shall be written in Chinese.

(Note: A foreign language can be used concurrently with mutual consent.)

Article 46

Financial checking and examination of the joint venture company shall be conducted by an auditor registered in China and reports shall be submitted to the board of directors and the general manager.

In case Party B considers it necessary to employ a foreign auditor registered in another country to undertake annual financial checking and examination, Party A shall give its consent. All the expenses thereof shall be borne by Party B.

Article 47

In the first three months of each fiscal year, the manager shall prepare previous year's balance sheet, profit and loss statement and proposals regarding the disposal of profits, and submit them to the board of directors for examination and approval.

Chapter 15   Duration of the Joint Venture

Article 48

The duration of the joint venture company is _____ years. The establishment of the joint venture company shall start from the date on which the business license of the joint venture company is issued.

An application for the extension of the duration, proposed by one party and unanimously approved by the board of directors, shall be submitted to the Ministry of Foreign Economic Relations and Trade (or the examination and approval authority entrusted by it) six months prior to the expiry date of the joint venture.

Chapter 16 The Disposal of Assets after the Expiration of the Duration

Article 49

Upon the expiration of the duration, or termination before the date of expiration of the joint venture, liquidation shall be carried out according to the relevant laws. The liquidated assets shall be distributed in accordance with the proportion of investment contributed by Party A and Party B.

Chapter 17 Insurance

Article 50

Insurance policies of the joint venture company on various kinds of risks shall be underwritten with the People's Republic of China. Types, value and duration of insurance shall be decided by the board of directors in accordance with the stipulations of the People's Insurance Company of China.

Chapter 18 The Amendment, Alteration and Termination of the Contract

Article 51

The amendment of the contract or other appendices shall come into force only after a written agreement has been signed by Party A and Party B and approved by the original examination and approval authority.

Article 52

In case of inability to fulfil the contract or to continue operation due to heavy losses in successive years as a result of force majeure, the duration of the joint venture and the contract shall be terminated before the time of expiration after unanimously agreed upon by the board of directors and approved by the original examination and approval authority.

Article 53

Should the joint venture company be unable to continue its operation or achieve its business purpose due to the fact that one of the contracting parties fails to fulfil the obligations prescribed by the contract and articles of association, or seriously violates the stipulations of the contract and articles of association, that party shall be deemed to have unilaterally terminated the contract. The other party shall have the right to terminate the contract in accordance with the provisions of the contract after approval by the original examination and approval authority, and to claim damages. In case Party A and Party B of the joint venture company agree to continue the operation, the party who fails to fulfil its obligations shall be liable to the economic losses thus caused to the joint venture company.

Chapter 19   Liabilities for Breach of Contract

Article 54

Should either Party A or Party B fail to pay on schedule the contributions in accordance with the provisions defined in Chapter 5 of this contract, the breaching party shall pay to the other party _____ % of the contribution starting from the first month after exceeding the time limit. Should the breaching party fail to pay after 3 months, _____ % of the contribution shall be paid to the other party, who shall have the right to terminate the contract and to claim damages to the breaching party in accordance with the stipulations in Article 53 of the contract.

Article 55

Should all or part of the contract and its appendices be unable to be fulfilled owing to the fault of one party, the breaching party shall bear the responsibilities thus caused. Should it be the fault of both parties, they shall bear their respective responsibilities according to actual situations.

Article 56

In order to guarantee the performance of the contract and its appendices, both Party A and Party B shall provide each other the bank guarantees for the performance of the contract.

Chapter 20   Force Majeure

Article 57

Should either of the parties to the contract be prevented from executing the contract by force majeure, such as earthquake, typhoon, flood, fire, war and other unforeseen events, and their happenings and consequences are unpreventable and unavoidable, the prevented party shall notify the other party by cable without any delay, and within 15 days thereafter provide the detailed information of the events and a valid document for evidence issued by the relevant public notary organization for explaining the reason of its inability to execute or delay the execution of all or part of the contract. Both parties shall, through consultations, decide whether to terminate the contract or to exempt the part of obligations for implementation of the contract or whether to delay the execution of the con-

tract according to the effects of the events on the performance of the
contract.

Chapter 21   Applicable Law

Article 58

The formation of this contract, its validity, interpretation, execution and
settlement of disputes shall be governed by the relevant laws of the
People's Republic of China.

Chapter 22   Settlement of Disputes

Article 59

Any disputes arising from the execution of, or in connection with the
contract shall be settled through friendly consultations between both
parties. In case no settlement can be reached through consultations, the
disputes shall be submitted to the Foreign Economic and Trade Arbitration Commission of the China Council for the Promotion of International Trade for arbitration in accordance with its rules of procedure. The
arbitral award is final and binding upon both parties.
Or
Any disputes arising from the execution of, or in connection with the
contract shall be settled through friendly consultations between both
parties. In case no settlement can be reached through consultations, the
disputes shall be submitted to _____ Arbitration Organization in
_____ for arbitration in accordance with its rules of procedure. The
arbitral award is final and binding upon both parties.
Or
Any disputes arising from the execution of, or in connection with the
contract shall be settled through friendly consultations between both
parties. In case no settlement can be settled through consultations, the
disputes shall be submitted for arbitration.
Arbitration shall take place in the defendant's country.
If in China, arbitration shall be conducted by the Foreign Economic
and Trade Arbitration Commission of the China Council for the Promotion of International Trade in accordance with its rules of procedure.
If in _____ the arbitration shall be conducted by _____ in
accordance with its rules of procedure.
The arbitral award is final and binding upon both parties.
(Note: When formulating contracts, only one of the above-mentioned
provisions can be used.)

Article 60

During the arbitration, the contract shall be observed and enforced by
both parties except for matters in dispute.

Chapter 23   Language

Article 61

The contract shall be written in a Chinese version and in a _____ version. Both language versions are equally authentic. In the event of any discrepancy between the two aforementioned versions, the Chinese version shall prevail.

Chapter 24   Effectiveness of the Contract and Miscellaneous

Article 62

The appendices drawn up in accordance with the principles of this contract are integral parts of this contract, including: the project agreement, the technology transfer agreement, the sales agreement. . .

Article 63

The contract and its appendices shall come into force beginning from the date of approval of the Ministry of Foreign Economic Relations and Trade of the People's Republic of China (or its entrusted examination and approval authority).

Article 64

Should notices in connection with any party's rights and obligations be sent by either Party A or Party B by telegram or telex, etc., the written letter notices shall be also required afterwards. The legal addresses of Party A and Party B listed in this contract shall be the posting addresses.

Article 65

The contract is signed in _____, China by the authorized representatives of both parties on _____, 19____.

For Party A   For Party B
(Signature)   (Signature)

Appendix 3C. Sample Set of Articles of Association for Joint Ventures Using Chinese and Foreign Investment*

Chapter 1 General Provisions

Article 1

In accordance with the 'Law of the People's Republic of China on Joint Ventures Using Chinese and Foreign Investment' and the contract signed by _____ company (hereinafter referred to Party A) and _____ company (hereinafter referred to Party B), these articles of association are hereby formulated.

Article 2

The name of the joint venture company shall be _____ Limited Liability Company.
Its name in foreign language is _____.
The legal address of the joint venture company is at _____.

Article 3

The names and legal addresses of the parties to the joint venture are:
Party A: _____ Company at _____.
Party B: _____ Company at _____.

Article 4

The joint venture company is a limited liability company.

Article 5

The joint venture company has the status of a legal person and is subject to the jurisdiction and protection of China's laws concerned. All of its activities shall be governed by Chinese laws, decrees and other pertinent rules and regulations.

Chapter 2 Purpose and Scope of Business

Article 6

The purpose of the joint venture company is to produce and sell _____ products and to reach _____ level to obtain satisfactory economic benefits for the parties to the joint venture company.

---

*Drafted by the Department of Treaties and Law, Ministry of Foreign Economic Relations and Trade.

(Note: Each joint venture company complete according to its own conditons.)

Article 7

The business scope of the joint venture company is to design, manufacture and sell _____ products and provide after-sale services.

Article 8

The scale of production of the joint venture company is as follows:
_____ year _____ (unit of quantity)
_____ year _____
_____ year _____

Article 9

The joint venture company may sell its products on the Chinese domestic market and on the international market, its selling proportion is as follows:
_____ (year): _____ % for export; _____ % for the domestic market.
_____ (year): _____ % for export; _____ % for the domestic market.
(Note: The means of marketing, method and obligations will be stipulated according to concrete conditions.)

Chapter 3   The Total Amount of Investment and the Registered Capital

Article 10

The total amount of investment of the joint venture company is RMB _____. Its registered capital is RMB _____.

Article 11

The investment contributed by each party is as follows:
Party A: Investment subscribed is RMB _____, accounts for _____ % of the registered capital, among which,
Cash _____,
Machinery and equipment _____,
Premises _____,
Land use right _____,
Industrial property _____,
Others _____.
Party B: Investment subscribed is RMB _____, accounts for _____ % of the registered capital, among which,
Cash _____,

Machinery and equipment _____,
Industrial property _____,
Others _____.

Article 12

The parties to the joint venture shall pay in all the investment subscribed according to the time limit stipulated in the contract.

Article 13

After the investment is paid by the parties to the joint venture, a Chinese registered accountant invited by the joint venture company shall verify it and provide a certificate of verification. According to this certificate, the joint venture shall issue an investment certificate which includes the following items: name of the joint venture; date of the establishment of the joint venture; names of the parties and the investment contributed; date of the contribution of the investment, and the date of issuance of the investment certificate.

Article 14

Within the term of the joint venture, the joint venture company shall not reduce its registered capital.

Article 15

Should one party assign all or part of its investment subscribed, consent shall be obtained from the other party or the joint venture. When one party assigns its investment, the other party has preemptive right.

Article 16

Any increase or assignment of the registered capital of the joint venture company shall be approved by the board of directors and submitted to the original examination and approval authority for approval. The registration procedures for changes shall be dealt with at the original registration and administration office.

Chapter 4   The Board of Directors

Article 17

The joint venture shall establish the board of directors which is the highest authority of the joint venture company.

Article 18

The board of directors shall decide all major issues concerning the joint venture company. Its functions and powers are as follows:

— deciding and approving the important reports submitted by the general manager (for instance: production plan, annual business report, funds, loans, etc.);
— approving annual financial reports, budgets of receipts and expenditures, distribution plan of annual profits;
— adopting major rules and regulations of the company;
— deciding to set up branches;
— amending the articles of association of the company;
— discussing and deciding the termination of production, termination of the company or merging with another economic organization;
— deciding the engagement of high-rank officials such as the general manager, chief engineer, treasurer, auditor etc.;
— being in charge of expiration of the company and the liquidation matters upon the expiration of the joint venture company;
— other major issues which shall be decided by the board of directors.

Article 19

The board of directors shall consist of _____ directors, of which _____ shall be appointed by Party A and _____ by Party B. The term of office for the directors is four years and may be renewed.

Article 20

Chairman of the board shall be appointed by Party A and vice chairman of the board by Party B.

Article 21

When appointing and replacing directors, a written notice shall be submitted to the board.

Article 22

The board of directors shall convene _____ meeting(s) every year. An interim meeting of the board of directors may be held based on a proposal made by more than one third of the total number of directors.

Article 23

The board meeting will be held in principle at the location of the company.

Article 24

The board meeting shall be called and presided over by the chairman. Should the chairman be absent, the vice chairman shall call and preside the board meeting.

Article 25

The chairman shall give each director a written notice 30 days before the date of the board meeting. The notice shall cover the agenda, time and place of the meeting.

Article 26

Should a director be unable to attend the board meeting, he may present a proxy in written form to the board. In case the director neither attends nor entrusts others to attend the meeting, he will be regarded as having abstained.

Article 27

The board meeting requires a quorum of over two thirds of the total number of directors. When the quorum is less than two thirds, the decisions adopted by the board meeting are invalid.

Article 28

Detailed written records shall be made for each board meeting and be signed by all the directors in attendance or by the attended proxy. The record shall be made in Chinese and _____, and shall be filed with the company.

Article 29

The following issues shall be unanimously agreed upon by the board of directors:
    (Note: It should be stipulated according to each company's concrete situations.)

Article 30

The following issues shall be passed by over two thirds of the total number of directors or by over half of the total number.
    (Note: It should be stipulated according to each company's concrete situations.)

Chapter 5   Business Management Organization

Article 31

The joint venture company shall establish a management organization. It consists of production, technology, marketing, finance and administration offices etc.
    (Note: It should be stipulated according to each company's concrete situations.)

Article 32

The joint venture company shall have one general manager and _____ deputy general manager(s) who are engaged by the board of directors. The first general manager shall be recommended by party _____, deputy general manager(s) by party _____.

Article 33

The general manager is directly responsible to the board of directors. He shall carry out the decisions of the board of directors, organize and conduct the daily production, technology and operation and management of the joint venture company. The deputy general managers shall assist the general manager in his work and act as the agents of the general manager during his absence and exercise the functions of the general manager.

Article 34

Decisions on the major issues concerning the daily work of the joint venture company shall be signed jointly by the general manager and deputy general managers, after which they shall come into effect. Issues which need co-signatures shall be specifically stipulated by the board of directors.

Article 35

The term of office for the general manager and deputy general managers shall be _____ years, and may be renewed at the invitation of the board of directors.

Article 36

At the invitation of the board of directors, the chairman, vice-chairman or directors of the board may concurrently be the general manager, deputy general managers or other high-ranking personnel of the joint venture company.

Article 37

The general manager or deputy general managers shall not hold posts concurrently as general manager or deputy general managers of other economic organizations in commercial competition with their own joint venture company.

Article 38

The joint venture company shall have one chief engineer, one treasurer and one auditor engaged by the board of directors.

Article 39

The general engineer, treasurer and auditor shall be under the leadership of the general manager.

The treasurer shall exercise leadership in financial and accounting affairs, organise the joint venture company to carry out overall business accounting and implement the economic responsibility system.

The auditor shall be in charge of the auditing work of the joint venture company, examine and check the financial receipts and expenditure and the accounts, and submit written reports to the general manager and the board of directors.

Article 40

The general manager, deputy general manager, chief engineer, treasurer, auditor and other high-ranking personnel who ask for resignation shall submit their written reports to the board of directors in advance.

In case any one of the above-mentioned persons is guilty of graft or serious dereliction of duty, he may be dismissed at any time upon the decision of the board. Those who violate the criminal law shall be under criminal sanction.

Chapter 6   Finance and Accounting

Article 41

The finance and accounting of the joint venture company shall be handled in accordance with 'The Accounting System for Joint Ventures Using Chinese and Foreign Investment' formulated by the Ministry of Finance of the People's Republic of China.

Article 42

The fiscal year of the joint venture company shall coincide with the calendar year, i.e. from January 1 to December 31 on the Gregorian calendar.

Article 43

All vouchers, account books, statistic statements and reports of the joint venture company shall be written in Chinese.

Article 44

The joint venture company adopts RMB as its accounts keeping unit. The conversion of RMB into another currency shall be in accordance with the exchange rate of the converting day published by the State Administration of Exchange Control of the People's Republic of China.

Article 45

The joint venture company shall open accounts in RMB and foreign currency with the Bank of China or other banks agreed by the Bank of China.

Article 46

The accounting of the joint venture company shall adopt the internationally used accrual basis and debit and credit accounting system in their work.

Article 47

Following items shall be covered in the financial accounts books:
1. The amount of overall cash receipts and expenses of the joint venture company;
2. All material purchasing and selling of the joint venture company;
3. The registered capital and debts situation of the joint venture company;
4. The time of payment, increase and assignment of the registered capital of the joint venture company.

Article 48

The joint venture company shall work out the statement of assets and liabilities and losses and gains accounts of the past year in the first three months of each fiscal year, and submit them to the board meeting for approval after being examined and signed by the auditor.

Article 49

Parties to the joint venture have the right to invite an auditor to undertake annual financial check and examination at their own expense. The joint venture company shall provide convenience for the checking and examination.

Article 50

The depreciation period for the fixed assets of the joint venture company shall be decided by the board of directors in accordance with the 'Rules for the Implementation of the Income Tax Law of the People's Republic of China Concerning Joint Ventures with Chinese and Foreign Investment'.

Article 51

All matters concerning foreign exchange shall be handled in accordance with the 'Provisional Regulations for Exchange Control of the People's Republic of China', and other applicable regulations as well as stipulations of the joint venture contract.

Chapter 7   Profit Sharing

Article 52

The joint venture company shall draw reserve funds, expansion funds and bonuses welfare funds for staff and workers after payment of taxes. The proportion of allocation is decided by the board of directors.

Article 53

After paying the taxes in accordance with law and drawing the various funds, the remaining profits will be distributed according to the proportion of each party's investment in the registered capital.

Article 54

The joint venture company shall distribute its profits. The profit distribution plan and the amount of profit distributed to each party shall be published within the first three months of each fiscal year.

Article 55

The joint venture company shall not distribute profits unless the losses of previous fiscal years have been made up. Remaining profits from previous years can be distributed together with that of the current year.

Chapter 8   Staff and Workers

Article 56

The employment, recruitment, dismissal and resignation of the staff and workers of the joint venture company and their salaries, welfare benefits, labor insurance, labor protection, labor discipline and other matters shall be handled according to the 'Regulations of the People's Republic of China on Labor Management in Joint Ventures Using Chinese and Foreign Investment' and its implementation rules.

Article 57

The required staff and workers to be recruited by the joint venture company will be recommended by the local labor department or the joint venture will do so through public selection examinations and employ those who are qualified with the consent of the labor department.

Article 58

The joint venture company has the right to take disciplinary actions, record a demerit and reduce salary against those staff and workers who violate the rules and regulations of the joint venture company and labor disciplines. Those involved in serious cases may be dismissed. Discharging of workers shall be filed with the labor and personnel department in the locality.

Article 59

The salary treatment of the staff and workers shall be set by the board of directors according to the specific situation of the joint venture, with reference to pertaining stipulations of China, and shall be specified in detail in the labor contract.

The salary of the staff and workers shall be increased correspondingly with the development of production and the improvement in the ability and technical skills of the staff and workers.

Article 60

Matters concerning the welfare funds, bonuses, labor protection and labor insurance etc. shall be stipulated respectively in various rules by the joint venture company, to ensure that the staff and workers can engage in production and work under normal conditions.

Chapter 9   The Trade Union Organization

Article 61

The staff and workers of the joint venture company have the right to establish trade union organizations and carry out activities in accordance with the stipulations of the 'Trade Union Law'.

Article 62

The trade union in the joint venture company is the representative of the interests of the staff and workers. The tasks of the trade union are: to protect the democratic rights and material interests of the staff and workers pursuant to the law; to assist the joint venture company to arrange and make rational use of welfare funds and bonuses; to organize political, professional, scientific and technical studies, carry out literary, artistic and sports activities; and to educate staff and workers to observe labor disciplines and strive to fulfil the economic tasks of the joint venture company.

Article 63

The trade union of the joint venture company will sign labor contracts with the joint venture company on behalf of the staff and workers, and supervise the implementation of the contracts.

Article 64

Persons in charge of the trade union of the joint venture company have the right to attend as nonvoting members and to report the opinions and demands of staff and workers to meetings of the board of directors held to discuss issues such as development plans, production and operational activities of the joint venture.

Article 65

The trade union shall take part in the mediation of disputes arising between the staff and workers and the joint venture company.

Article 66

The joint venture company shall allot an amount of money totalling 2% of all salaries of the staff and workers of the joint venture company as trade union's funds, which shall be used by the trade union in accordance with the 'Managerial Rules for the Trade Union Funds' formulated by the All China Federation of Trade Unions.

Chapter 10   Duration, Termination and Liquidation

Article 67

The duration of the joint venture company shall be _____ years, beginning from the day when the business license is issued.

Article 68

An application for the extension of duration shall, proposed by both parties and approved at the board meeting, be submitted to the original examination and approval authority six months prior to the expiry date of the joint venture. Only upon the approval may the duration be extended, and the joint venture company shall go through registration formalities for the alteration at the original registration office.

Article 69

The joint venture may be terminated before its expiration in case the parties to the joint venture agree unanimously that the termination of the joint venture is for the best interests of the parties.

Termination of the joint venture before the term expires shall be decided by the board of directors through a plenary meeting, and it shall be submitted to the original examination and approval authority for approval.

Article 70

Either party shall have the right to terminate the joint venture in case one of the following situations occurs:

(Note: It shall be stipulated according to each joint venture company's concrete situation.)

Article 71

Upon the expiration or termination of the joint venture before its term ends, the board of directors shall work out procedures and principles for the liquidation, nominate candidates for the liquidation committee, and set up the liquidation committee for liquidating the joint venture company's assets.

Article 72

The tasks of the liquidation committee are: to conduct a thorough check of the property of the joint venture company, its claims and indebtedness; to formulate a liquidation plan. All these shall be carried out upon the approval of the board of directors.

Article 73

During the process of liquidation, the liquidation committee shall represent the company to sue and be sued.

Article 74

The liquidation expenses and remuneration to the members of the liquidation committee shall be paid in priority from the existing assets of the joint venture company.

Article 75

The remaining property after the clearance of debts of the joint venture company shall be distributed among the parties to the joint venture according to the proportion of each party's investment in the registered capital.

Article 76

On completion of the liquidation, the joint venture company shall submit a liquidation report to the original examination and approval authority, go through the formalities for nullifying its registration in the original registration office and hand in its business license, at the same time, make an announcement to the public.

Article 77

After winding up of the joint venture company, its account books shall be left in the care of the Chinese participant.

Chapter 11   Rules and Regulations

Article 78

Following are the rules and regulations formulated by the board of directors of the joint venture company.

1. Management regulations, including the powers and functions of the managerial branches and their working rules and procedures;
2. Rules for the staff and workers;
3. System of labor and salary;
4. System of work attendance record, promotion and awards and penalty for the staff and workers;
5. Detailed rules for staff and workers' welfare;
6. Financial system;
7. Liquidation procedures upon the dissolution of the joint venture company;
8. Other necessary rules and regulations.

Chapter 12   Supplementary Articles

Article 79

The amendments to the Articles of Association shall be unanimously agreed and decided by the board of directors and submitted to the original examination and approval authority for approval.

Article 80

The Articles of Association is written in the Chinese language and the _____ language. Both language versions shall be equally authentic. In the event of any discrepancy between the two above-mentioned versions, the Chinese version shall prevail.

Article 81

The Articles of Association shall come into effect upon the approval by the Ministry of Foreign Economic Relations and Trade of the People's Republic of China (or its entrusted examination and approval authority). The same applies in the event of amendments.

Article 82

The Article of Association is signed in _____ of China by the authorized representatives of both parties on _____, 19____.

For Party A   For Party B
(Signature)   (Signature)

4. Technology Transfer to China: Policies, Law, and Practice

STANLEY B. LUBMAN*

I. Introduction

This chapter discusses the negotiation of agreements for the transfer of technology to the People's Republic of China (PRC) against a background of changing policies, evolving legal rules, and long-standing practice. Such transfers are possible in a variety of contexts other than the pure licence, such as counter-trade and equity joint ventures. Although this chapter does not directly discuss such other transactions, its subject-matter is common to them.

The chapter first considers the changes in Chinese policies on technology transfer and then examines the new legal framework which is emerging as the Chinese leadership comes to appreciate the need to establish rules for transactions which were formerly not expressly subject to promulgated laws. Finally there is a discussion of common contract clauses and the problems encountered in negotiating technology transfers.

II. Changes in Chinese Policies towards Technology Transfer

A. The Movement away from Whole-plant Imports

Chinese imports of technology since 1949 have been characterized by four peaks.[1] During the first, throughout the 1950s, technology transfer was effected largely through the importation by China of large, complete sets of equipment, mostly from the Soviet Union and Eastern Europe. Speaking of the period 1952–60, one expert observer has said:

It was largely that experience which shaped Chinese attitudes toward technology. In that 7-year period, China was the recipient of what was undoubtedly the most comprehensive technology transfer in modern industrial history . . . The Soviet contribution encompassed much more than their production technology. It ran the gamut from scientific and technical education to project design, and from production engineering to creating a modern industrial organization, complete with planning, budgeting, and management systems.[2]

This major infusion of technology under Soviet tutelage was to cause

---

* The author is grateful for the assistance of Gregory C. Wajnowski, associate at Heller, Ehrman, White & McAuliffe.

technology transfer to be conceptually linked to large projects; and in the eyes of some Chinese leaders the Soviet experience also tied technology transfer to dependence on imports. After the Sino-Soviet break in 1960, China engaged in a long and costly experiment with 'self-reliance' throughout the 1960s and well into the following decade, which hampered the modernization of her industry.

A second wave of importation of complete plants took place from 1973 to 1977. Also, for the first time since the PRC was established in 1949, the imports included contracts with American firms, notably Pullman-Kellogg, from whom the Chinese purchased eight large ammonia plants worth US$215 million in 1972. As one Chinese commentator later stated, the transactions of this period emphasized 'large sets, large series, high speed, high efficiency, automatic control and the highly integrated use of thermal energy'.[3] Once again, as in the late 1950s, imported technology was principally embodied in large plants.

Some of the problems which Chinese commentators have perceived in projects associated with this stage have influenced current Chinese thinking on technology imports. Of particular interest is the view that because the technology that was imported was incorporated into large plants, it has been difficult to absorb it and learn from it. The difficulties have included construction delays in many projects; in others, the plants have operated below capacity because of shortages of raw materials and energy. Chinese critics have stated that the returns on the investment in some of these projects have been low. Chemical fertilizer plants, in particular, encountered considerable shortages of raw materials, oil, and gas, and the rise in the price of oil affected the profitability of a number of other plants.

One of the projects that has encountered major difficulties is at Wuhan, where iron and steel manufacturing facilities were imported from Germany and Japan. There, not only did power shortages greatly impede testing, but also facilities were constructed and made ready at differing and uneven rates. It was discovered that the entire province in which the plant is located lacks the power needed for the new plant. In addition, it proved difficult to integrate the old and new sections of the plant. Moreover, some of the imported technology and equipment was found to be too advanced for Chinese needs, so that the plant now produces steel sheets that are too thin to be used in old Chinese casting equipment, and some types of steel for which there is little demand from Chinese end-users.[4]

The third wave of buying, a short-lived spree in 1978–9, again included large projects, such as the Baoshan Iron and Steel Complex in Shanghai which was allocated approximately one-third of the total amount of funds committed during this brief period.[5] Most of the 22 projects contracted for were metallurgical and petrochemical projects which consumed a high amount of energy and caused other extensive economic dislocations. They have required the import of raw materials such as iron ore and other materials such as refractory materials and chemicals. These imports caused other distortions such as shipping and storage problems. Moreover, the planning for these projects was poor, and some projects were authorized without prior feasibility studies and were carried out without strict adherence to orderly construction procedures. A thorough assessment of needs, and of the relationships between the imported projects and the rest of the Chinese economy was also lacking.

'Readjustment', the reaction to the errors summarized above, began in 1979 and caused the suspension or cancellation of some of the largest projects and a reappraisal of import policies. In the last few years, a noticeable new orientation towards technology transfer has developed, a delayed but probably desirable response to the perceived errors of the three previous waves of imports. Now, in a fourth wave, fewer whole plants are likely to be contracted for, and greater conservatism has been shown in making commitments for large expenditures of foreign exchange. Emphasis has been placed on rehabilitating and improving existing factories. Of particular interest has been the move away from importing technology that is incorporated into equipment and towards the importation of technology and know-how, a shift which Chinese commentators have variously characterized as a move from 'hardware' to 'software', or from 'eggs' to 'hens'.

The lessons of the great buying spree of 1978 have also caused commentators to urge better planning and feasibility studies, with a view to planning for the integration of domestically manufactured equipment with that purchased from abroad. A warning has been given that it is not necessary to purchase the most advanced 'state of the art' technology, but that it is preferable to consider the appropriateness of the technology and the Chinese capacity to absorb it. Other criteria which have been emphasized include reducing energy consumption, promoting import substitution, and, at the same time, increasing the Chinese capacity to export and thereby earn foreign exchange to repay the transferors of technology. Some of these aims may be mutually inconsistent but the fact that they have been articulated represents the outcome of considerable reflection on, and criticism of, blind adherence to earlier Soviet models, although the latter continue to dominate the institutions encountered by foreign transferors of technology.

B. The Transfer of Technology within China

Greater emphasis on absorbing technology has also resulted in an increased interest in the more efficient use of Chinese domestic resources for developing and transmitting technology. In recent years, Chinese leaders have become acutely aware of the weaknesses in their science and technology and research and development systems.[6] These shortcomings are particularly evident in four crucial areas: (a) the difficulty in incorporating scientific research results into large-scale production; (b) limited management capabilities, especially in such areas as operations research and systems management; (c) the backwardness of key technical prerequisites, particularly with regard to precision instruments; and (d) the shortage of qualified scientific and technical personnel.

Chinese leaders have attacked these problems in earnest since the late 1970s, by means of such policies as sending thousands of students and scholars abroad, developing domestic postgraduate education, and improving living and working conditions for intellectuals generally. Many of the constraints mentioned above can only be eased gradually, however, and remedial measures will require time. Consequently, a solution to these problems must be a long-term goal.

Potential licensers must be aware of these important influences on the Chinese capacity to absorb technology. They should not underestimate Chinese resources, which include the 'capacity to mobilize large amounts of technical, financial and personnel resources to accomplish a particular task',[7] experience in handling 'engineering-related problem-solving tasks',[8] and strong official encouragement favouring technology transfer. At the same time, however, the Chinese suffer from severe technical constraints. They have a history of 'poor performance in translating research results into the serial production process',[9] which stems in part from a lack of adequate testing and measurement instrumentation, a lack of numerically controlled machine tools, and an excessively vertical integration which reduces technical specialization. As a result, standardization in quality-control instrumentation and precision-testing equipment is low. Perhaps even greater constraints on the capacity to absorb foreign technology are imposed by poor management and inadequate planning. Chinese 'bureaucratism', the primacy of economic output quotas, and the verticality and cellularity of the Chinese industrial and research and development systems impede innovation and the flow of information. These problems have compelled the attention of Chinese and foreign observers alike, and their observations are instructive to foreign partners in technology transfer transactions.

C. Continuing Policy Debates

Among the noteworthy discussions of Chinese policy is a study by the former director of the Technology Import and Export Department of the Ministry of Foreign Economic Relations and Trade (MOFERT), who has referred to the existence of a 'planless, chaotic situation despite the supposed inclusion of technology imports in national and local plans'.[10] The author states that, because 'everyone wants to have a system of his own',[11] irrationalities arise, such as the importation of the same technology by two different bureaux under the same commission,[12] and decisions by local departments to import technology in violation of the guidelines issued by the State Council.[13]

The same author cites the irrationalities of basing decisions on technology on administrative orders rather than on economic considerations, which lead to an inability to manage the process of technology transfer and to the importation of technology that cannot be effectively integrated into the Chinese economy.[14] 'Market feedback' should be the source of technological innovation, urges the author, but China's planning system impedes such innovation. Despite some economic reforms, Chinese enterprises lack both contact with their markets and power to control the use of their funds.[15]

In the concluding portion of his article[16] the author stresses the lack of a large-scale perspective on the implications of technology imports. He also urges analytical feasibility studies instead of the 'simple and crude' ones which are at present too common,[17] and the rationalization of various means for promoting technology imports, such as foreign investment, foreign exchange control, taxation, and the technological transformation of existing enterprises.[18] The function of government organizations should be limited to conducting disciplined quantitative analysis of the economic benefits and costs of particular projects.[19]

Unless and until far-reaching economic reforms reduce the grip of rigid planning on the Chinese economy, the defects stressed above will continue to plague foreigners and Chinese alike. The practical consequences of these problems are extensive. Foreign transferors of technology are likely to continue to find that their Chinese counterparts fail to take infrastructural weaknesses into account and fail to plan for sales and pricing of the products manufactured with the imported technology.[20]

D. The Reorganization of the Chinese Foreign Trade Apparatus

Another influence on the Chinese importation of technology has been the repeated reorganization of the Chinese foreign trade bureaucracy. In 1978 it was decided to reduce the rigidities in the highly centralized, Soviet-style foreign trade apparatus which had existed in China since 1949. This led to the introduction of massive decentralization.[21] For technology transfer, a direct consequence of this decentralization was that whilst formerly only a few agencies, notably the China National Technical Import Corporation (Techimport), had the authority to enter into contracts with foreign companies for the importation of technology, new organizations now appeared on the scene ready to contract for technology imports.

The problems ensuing from decentralization—considerable lack of co-ordination and planning, duplication and confusion, and the signing of contracts which departed from economic plans—prompted the Chinese leadership to move towards partial recentralization.[22] Attempts have been made to co-ordinate and monitor the activities of entities which are permitted to engage in trade transactions in addition to the traditional foreign trade corporations. However, the proliferation of organizations permitted to engage in foreign trade transactions has meant that technology transfer is no longer the province of a very small number of organizations. Nor is it limited to Beijing; for the special economic zones (SEZs) and a number of cities (such as Shanghai, Dalian, and Tianjin) and provinces are now able to enter into trade transactions.[23]

Organizational flux and the resulting confusion have also created problems, some of the practical implications of which are discussed below. Although many of these problems may be transitional, foreign business men and their advisers must be prepared to encounter a considerable overlapping of jurisdictions, bureaucratic rivalries, and delays in their dealings with Chinese partners. The Chinese leadership, well aware of the difficulties caused by these problems, have addressed them in a series of laws and regulations.

III. The Emerging Legal Framework

A. The Shenzhen Regulations

The first legislation specifically devoted to rules applicable to the non-tax aspects of technology transfer was the Provisional Regulations of the Shenzhen Special Economic Zone on the Introduction of Technology, promulgated by the Guangdong Provincial People's Congress in February 1984 (hereafter cited as the Shenzhen Provisional Technology Regulations). The Regulations of the Shenzhen Special Economic Zone on Foreign Economic Contracts (hereafter cited as the Shenzhen Foreign Economic Contract Regulations) were also promulgated in February 1984. These contain rules applicable to all contracts involving foreign and Chinese enterprises in the Shenzhen SEZ.[24]

B. The Technology Import Contract Regulations

The most important rules governing technology transfer elsewhere in China are the Regulations of the PRC for the Administration of Technology Import Contracts (hereafter cited as the Technology Regulations), promulgated by the State Council on 24 May 1985.[25] The most noteworthy advance of the Technology Regulations was their recognition that proprietary know-how and trade secrets and not merely patented know-how could be transferred and protected.[26] The Technology Regulations further stipulate certain essential requirements of technology import contracts, such as a description of the scope of the subject technology, the means of compensating the foreign supplier, the duration, the technical objectives, and the measures necessary to attain such objectives.

The Technology Regulations also establish certain requirements for imported technology which are expressed only in a general manner and have not yet been rigorously enforced in practice. Article 9 states that the foreign seller may not, without the permission of the approving authority, 'force the purchaser to accept unreasonable restrictive requirements', such as: (a) requiring the purchaser to purchase unnecessary technology or technical services, raw materials, products, or equipment unrelated to the transferred technology; (b) restricting the purchaser from buying from other parties; (c) preventing the purchaser from developing or improving the imported technology; or (d) preventing the purchaser from obtaining similar or competitive technology from other sources.

The Technology Regulations also seek to limit the kinds of technology for which approval will be granted, although the requirements are stated in very general terms. To receive approval the technology must be 'advanced', be 'appropriate', and meet at least one of the following criteria:

(a) be able to develop or produce new products;
(b) be able to improve product quality and performance, reduce production costs, and conserve energy or materials;
(c) be conducive to the full exploitation of local resources;
(d) be able to expand product exports and increase foreign exchange earnings;
(e) be conducive to environmental protection;
(f) be conducive to safety in production;
(g) be conducive to improving business management;
(h) help to raise the level of science and technology.[27]

These desiderata are not ranked in order of importance, and no promulgated guidelines exist to determine relative priorities. It is obvious that not all of the goals expressed can be simultaneously pursued. Administrative practice and policies will perhaps provide clues as to priorities.

Further and exigent requirements are established in a general section of the regulations on warranties. Echoing the terms of the Techimport standard contracts, the Technology Regulations require the supplier to 'guarantee' not only that it lawfully owns the technology involved, but also that the technology is 'complete, without error, and able to attain the objectives' stated in the contract.[28] The transferor of technology must provide an adequate definition of the technology to be transferred and the goals to be guaranteed, so that the expectations of the parties will be clear.

In practice, the Technology Regulations establish an outline which is subject to considerable variation by both negotiators and approving officials. Although the enumeration of the advantages which such contracts are required to bring to China and the list of unacceptable restrictions reflect an understandable Chinese concern, their broad phrasing creates considerable scope for discretion. Nevertheless, the situation is better than it was before the Technology Regulations were promulgated, when governing principles existed but were 'for internal use' only and not permitted to be shown to foreigners.

C. The Foreign Economic Contracts Law

It is important to emphasize that the Technology Regulations must be read in conjunction with the Law of the People's Republic of China on Economic Contracts Involving Foreign Interests (hereafter cited as the Foreign Economic Contracts Law), which came into force on 1 July 1985. The Foreign Economic Contracts Law provides a framework for all contracts between Chinese and foreign parties, with the exception of contracts for joint ventures, which are governed by different legislation. It establishes general rules which will apply to all contracts between foreigners and Chinese, including those involving technology transfer. Thus it contains rules relating to content, as well as liability and damages for breach.[29]

D. Regulations on the Approval of Technology Import Contracts

Legislation has also appeared purporting to define and regulate the process of approval of technology transfer agreements. Even before such legislation was promulgated, it was apparent to foreign observers that internal regulations required intending Chinese importers of technology to submit to their superior authorities a project proposal which compared various alternatives and justified a preference for a particular technology over others.[30] The proposal must contain the details of the technology and the transferor involved, the enterprise to which the technology will be imported, the products to be manufactured, requirements for raw materials and other resources including electricity, an estimate of the amount of local currency and foreign exchange likely to be involved in the transfer, the proposed mode of repayment, and schedules for further negotiations, foreign trips, and a feasibility study.

The Procedures for Examination and Approval of Technology Import Contracts (hereafter cited as the Approval Procedures), approved by the State Council on 26 August 1985,[31] suggest that there are three levels of authority involved in approvals of project proposals and feasibility studies. Piecing together what is known about internal regulations, and adding this to the Approval Procedures, observers believe that approval by the State Planning Commission is required for projects which will cost more than US$50 million; ministries or other authorities directly under the control of the State Council are required to approve projects costing between US$5 and US$50 million; and local governments, municipalities, special economic zones, and coastal cities and cities which are directly under the central government may approve projects costing under US$5 million. Certain areas, such as Shanghai, may also have special authority to approve projects valued at up to US$30 million.

After approval has been received a feasibility study must be conducted to analyse the marketing, price, and distribution of products to be manufactured using the imported technology, the details of production, such as the site, equipment, production technology, source of raw materials and energy, methods of transportation, and production co-ordination, and the environmental considerations. In theory, fairly detailed information is required, such as long-term import statistics for any items which must be imported in large quantities in order to carry out the technology transfer, specifications of export and domestic markets, some consideration of alternative technologies, and the technical and economic details of the technology transfer itself. In recent years increasing importance has been placed on economic analysis, covering return on investment, cash flow, and the net current value of the investment. Moreover, the feasibility study must include the opinions of the State Administration of Exchange Control and the Ministry of Finance regarding the availability of foreign exchange and domestic currency, respectively, as well as appraisals by the State Science and Technology Commission of the technology itself and of the equipment required by machine-building organizations. Despite the detailed information in theory required, it seems that it has been both permissible and possible to present the necessary data and the conclusions drawn from them with greater brevity than the applicable regulations require.

The Technology Regulations provide that after a contract is signed it must be submitted to the approving agency, which is stated to be MOFERT or any agency designated by MOFERT. The Technology Regulations further state that a decision must be made within sixty days after the contract has been submitted to the approving agency, and that if no decision has been made within that period the contract shall take effect 'automatically'.[32] This last provision is probably intended to spur a sluggish bureaucracy to prompt action, but it is doubtful that such a legalism will be allowed to outweigh concern for supervising outlays of foreign exchange and imports of foreign technology.

Regardless of the approving agency, certain provisions of the contract may have to be approved by yet another agency in a different administrative hierarchy. The most important issue which may be involved is taxation: certain Chinese regulations discussed below provide for preferential tax treatment for certain transactions involving technology transfer, but the parties cannot know whether they are entitled to such treatment and, if so, to what extent. Some local tax bureaux and the Ministry of Finance, although they are unwilling to give written opinions, are increasingly willing to provide informal advice prior to the signing of contracts if they are given the opportunity to review the complete contracts, with the attached appendices, after the parties have initialled them.

E. Comment

To foreigners who are often baffled by the size of Chinese negotiating teams, the discussion above may indicate why the Chinese side must include, for sizeable projects, representatives of the importer (for example, the foreign trade organization which is the formal Chinese party to the contract), the enterprise at which the technology is to be introduced, and the organizations responsible for manufacturing necessary equipment.

The foregoing survey of the principal legislation applicable to agreements for the transfer of technology is necessarily only a general guide. It is difficult to gauge the precise degree of impact which such rules may have on any particular transaction. Moreover, existing rules are likely to be supplemented by additional legislation. Nevertheless, the amount of legislation promulgated in the brief period during which the policy of 'opening to the West' has been in effect suggests the importance placed by the Chinese leadership on creating a regulatory framework for agreements that were formerly concluded in a legal vacuum. The vacuum is far from filled, however, and it is in the course of negotiating individual transactions that practice will be created and spread.

IV. Negotiating Technology Licences in China

The discussion that follows reviews terms and practice in agreements to license technology, and is followed by some brief concluding observations. It is based principally on experience in negotiations with Techimport and, in recent years, with other Chinese organizations.

A. *The Coverage of the Licence*

The licenser (whom Chinese organizations insist on calling the 'Seller') can expect the Chinese side (the 'Buyer') to attempt to define as broadly as possible the scope of the contract and the technical documentation which the licenser is expected to deliver. For example, a standard Techimport clause provides for the Seller to grant the Buyer the right to design and manufacture the product in China, and to provide 'all relevant technical documentation including design, calculations and research reports, quality control, product drawings, manufacturing technology, inspection, installation, operation and maintenance' of the product, as defined in an appendix.[33] The terminology employed in contracts with other organizations may not be so detailed, and often the shortened form employed obligates the Seller to transfer documentation 'identical' with that which it uses. References to 'assembly drawings', 'process instructions', 'equipment operation instructions', 'tool drawings', and 'parts and material specifications' are also common.

Problems have sometimes been encountered in the past in obtaining agreement on a satisfactory formulation of the technical documentation. Chinese end-users may be particularly demanding. They and the organization handling the commercial negotiations may want to list types of documents which a licenser does not ordinarily supply to licensees, such as engineers' notebooks. Perhaps influenced by the rigid and highly bureaucratic, Soviet-style system that they adopted in the past, Chinese engineers seem to assume that foreign companies are more orderly in keeping track of their research than they may be in practice. In some negotiations, Buyers have agreed to accept clauses which require Sellers to supply only the documentation that is readily available.

Similar problems may also arise in defining the extent of the improvements to which the Chinese should be entitled under the agreement. As in many developing countries, both end-users and commercial negotiators are concerned about licensers selling technology for products which may soon be replaced. Given the suspiciousness of potential Chinese licensees, and their need to justify their transactions to their superiors and to other organizations which must approve the transactions, licensers are well advised to be sensitive to this problem. Licensers may find that, if they are unwilling to agree to include improvements throughout the term of the licence without charging any additional technology fee, the Chinese licensee may insist that the royalty rate decline after the expiry of the period during which improvements will be transferred. On the other hand, problems have sometimes been encountered in dealing with improvements by the *Chinese* licensee; the Chinese side will want to own them, and may expect a fee for the use of them from the licenser after the licence has expired.

Throughout the course of discussions of the contents of the technology which is to be transferred, the foreign side should attempt to ascertain the sophistication of the prospective licensee and the structure of the enterprise to which the technology will be transferred. One study of the experience of an American company in transferring technology in the context of a joint venture is apposite here.[34] The author notes that when the Chinese selected the transferor-partner's technology, the choice was made by engineers whose information was 'almost purely technical' and who lacked information on the 'appropriateness, cost effectiveness, maturity and field feasibility of the technologies they read about'.[35] He also remarks that it may be necessary to pay considerable attention to the existing manufacturing organization of the transferee, and to the cooperation among various departments of the enterprise which may be required to effect the transfer.

At the same time, the transferor should be careful to anticipate the burdens which may be involved in effecting the transfer. Transferors, especially if they are inexperienced, often underestimate the cost of assembling and verifying the drawings and other documents that may be involved.

B. *Price, Payment, and Valuation Conditions*

A standard Techimport form provides for the payment of a lump-sum contract price in instalments. The first instalment is payable after the signing of the contract and receipt of an export licence, the second instalment within thirty days after receipt of the technical document has been certified, and the third within thirty days after successful completion of the acceptance test has been certified. The percentages of the instalments are left blank in the contract form, and are obviously negotiable.

An alternative method of payment that has been acceptable to Techimport is a small down payment and a royalty computed either according to an agreed number of planned units or according to the number actually produced. A lump-sum royalty is also possible. In some cases Techimport may require the Seller to provide detailed information on how it has calculated its proposed royalty, after which Techimport may provide its own calculation of a per-unit royalty (a figure which the Seller may expect to be low).

Licensers may expect considerable differences of opinion on the valuation of their technology. The Chinese inevitably and understandably prefer low fees and low royalty rates. They express considerable antipathy towards even considering the cost of the licenser's research and development efforts. Reflecting Chinese concern about the overvaluation of technology, the Shenzhen Provisional Technology Regulations provide that when technology is capitalized as part of the establishment of a joint venture, the value of the technology may not exceed 20 per cent of the registered capital of the enterprise, and the foreign side must also supply an equivalent amount of 'cash or materials as investment capital'.[36]

After the parties have agreed on the value of the technology, other difficulties with respect to pricing can be anticipated. If the licenser expects royalties, he may find that the Chinese side ordinarily prefers to key them to its net profits or actual sales, while the licenser may be more interested in establishing a minimum, regardless of the value of Chinese production or sales.

C. The Buying Back and Export of Products

The Chinese frequently attempt to require the licenser to buy back from the Chinese licensee a quantity of the licensed product. The differences between the parties on this matter may be fundamental: the licenser may not want the product at all, but even if he wishes to accept some shipments he may be doubtful of the Chinese capacity to sell to him competitively. The parties may also find it difficult to agree on the price, especially since the Chinese may prefer a fixed price while the licenser will normally want a provision for adjustments to be made to reflect changes in world market prices.

Merely to mention these issues is to suggest the difficulty they pose and the additional time and trouble they may add to a negotiation. It has been possible for parties to compromise by agreeing on the buy-back of some parts and components, although any licenser who contemplates obtaining such parts and components from a Chinese enterprise other than the one where the licensed technology will be used is likely to be disappointed; the current organization of the Chinese economic system makes such flexibility virtually impossible.

Chinese licensees commonly insist on obtaining rights to export products manufactured with the licensed technology. This reflects policy emphases on the need for the transaction to earn foreign exchange and the desire to enlarge China's export capacity. Indeed, the Shenzhen Provisional Technology Regulations provide:

Products using the manufactured technology should have lawful and reasonable international markets. If the sale of the products is affected due to reasons caused by the supplier [of the technology], the supplier must pay for the loss.[37]

It appears that internal regulations make it mandatory or nearly mandatory for Chinese licensees to exact *some* export rights, and it is not uncommon for the parties to agree to exports to markets with which the licenser may not be greatly concerned, but often only after considerable negotiation on the subject.

D. Duration

Negotiations on this clause have been marked by the reluctance of Chinese licensees to sign agreements that obligate them to make payments over long periods of time, or to be dependent on licensers for components or raw materials. A period of five years has been common, in this author's experience, although longer periods are possible. The Shenzhen Provisional Technology Regulations provide that 'the term of the contract must, in general, not exceed five years, except in a case where technology is regarded as investment capital [although the term may be extended with the approval of the Shenzhen government]'.[38] The Technology Regulations provide that the duration of a licence shall not exceed ten years without special approval.[39]

E. Training and Technical Assistance

The foreign licenser will find the Chinese side eager to receive training and technical assistance, but reluctant to pay more than a limited per diem fee for such assistance. It is rare for this fee to exceed several hundred US dollars per day. Chinese licensees commonly request that such charges be included in the technology fee and that they should not be separately identified in the contract. Standard Chinese documentation on training requires the insertion of the details on the person/days to be spent in either country by the personnel of the other side. Responsibility for international travel and for living expenses is negotiable, although it is both common and reasonable to provide cost of living adjustments to foreign personnel in China.

Quite apart from the inclusion in the contract of appropriate language on financial responsibility for such costs, it is essential to include language on the living and working conditions of foreign personnel in China. This is especially important because the precise conditions under which foreign personnel (and, in some cases, their dependants) will live are often not studied carefully by the Chinese side or discussed in detail by the two sides at the time the contract is negotiated.

F. Acceptance Tests

Some of the most potentially vexing problems in negotiating licensing transactions arise from the clause on acceptance tests. Chinese licensees frequently seem to regard these transactions as sales of bundles of documents which are intended to ensure that the licensee, after using the instructions contained in the documents, will produce a product which meets the contract specifications. Techimport's standard contract clause does not contain language which requires the Buyer to follow the licenser's instructions strictly, although Chinese negotiators will agree to insert such a requirement if the licenser insists.

Another aspect of Chinese attitudes that colours these transactions is the assumption that the two parties are contracting to enter into a relationship in which the Seller will have a long-standing and continuous duty to assist the Buyer. So paramount is this relationship, and the obligation to assist the licensee, that the licensee's failure to follow correctly the licenser's technical specifications may be regarded as almost irrelevant. The Chinese side will first of all assume that the procedure for establishing fault, if the product fails to pass the acceptance test, should be strictly bilateral, by consultation between the parties. In addition, it will want the contract to reflect the agreement that, by nature of the relationship between the parties, the two will together work out and resolve any difficulties that may arise, without looking to any third-party dispute settlement.

Clauses on acceptance tests, whether in Techimport standard-form contracts or in others which are known to this author, are similar in their organization and language. Such clauses commonly provide that the tests shall be conducted in China in the presence of the Seller's technicians, with test methods and other technical aspects to be provided in detail in an appendix. If the acceptance test demonstrates that the product conforms to the specifications agreed on in advance, then the parties are required to sign an acceptance certificate.

If, however, the product fails to pass the acceptance test, the clause requires both parties to consult together, analyse the causes, conduct another acceptance test, and, as one Techimport clause has it, 'clarify the responsibility'. The clause may also require that, in such event, the period for which the Seller is required to keep his technicians in China may be extended for an agreed number of weeks.

The clause further provides that if responsibility for the failure is determined by the parties to lie with the Buyer, then the parties shall sign a certificate of acceptance test 'termination', but standard Techimport language still requires the Seller to 'assist the Buyer in taking means to eliminate the defects'. If responsibility lies with the Seller, Techimport contracts require the Seller to 'correct his mistakes as soon as possible', supply the Buyer with the correct documentation, and assist the Buyer in taking measures to eliminate the defects. If the defect cannot be remedied within an extended time period agreed by the parties, then the Seller must pay a penalty under the penalty clause in the contract, to which the clause on acceptance tests cross-refers, and which is normally expressed in terms of a percentage of the contract price. Since the penalty clause is in its terms directly addressed to the problems of incompleteness, incorrectness, and unreliability of the documentation, the cross-reference is very awkward.

This awkward Techimport language has remained unchanged for years, probably because it is invoked very rarely. In the Chinese view, the parties have entered into a complex relationship which does not amount merely to the sale of a commodity, and they are expected to work out their problems in the context of that relationship. This outlook may express a cultural attitude towards the nature of the relationship created by the contract, as well as the dependence of the Buyers on knowledgeable and expert licensers. Whatever the reason, licensers should expect their Chinese counterparts to think in terms of a continuing relationship that extends beyond the end of the licenser's formal obligations under the agreement.

Both parties must agree at the outset on a precise definition of the test methods that will be used, and on the standards that will be used to measure the conformity of the tested sample or prototype to contract specifications. The Chinese side may have high expectations for the finished product.[40] If the end-user representatives are technically competent, it should not be too difficult to reach agreement with them on these matters, which are normally the subject of a detailed appendix.

G. *The Guarantee and the Penalty*

The lengthy guarantee clause in the standard Techimport contract requires the Seller to guarantee that the documentation 'shall be the latest technical achievement possessed by the Seller' at the effective date or while the contract is in effect. The documentation must also be 'complete, correct, reliable, legible and dispatched in time'. Definitions of these terms are then supplied, of which the most notable is that of 'correct', which requires that the documentation shall be 'without mistake' and that the 'parts and components to be manufactured by skilled and experienced people strictly in accordance with the documentation shall be [products that are deemed to meet contract standards]'. Thus the performance of the product is made a function of the 'correctness' of the documentation.

If the Buyer discovers that the documentation does not comply with the foregoing stipulations, the Seller must dispatch the missing documentation. A penalty is provided for delay, in terms of a percentage of the contract price which increases with the length of the delay. The same penalties are theoretically applicable to 'incorrect' or 'unreliable' documentation.

The standard contract provides for a ceiling on all the above-mentioned penalties of 5 per cent of the contract price. Since the penalties stated are cross-referred to in the clause on acceptance tests, this ceiling presumably applies when the Chinese-manufactured sample product does not pass the acceptance test.

Licensers are understandably concerned about the extent of their guarantees of performance after equipment prototypes or manufacturing facilities, as the case may be, are completed and tested. The quality of materials and equipment used by the Chinese side, the technical level of the personnel on both sides, and the test methods may influence the performance of the tested product. Chinese negotiators emphasize the importance of co-operation to assure a satisfactory outcome; both sides must test the equipment together, after agreeing on the tests and the specifications.

In practice, Techimport appears to be most reluctant to invoke penalty clauses, preferring first to investigate and decide on the nature of the defect and the method of its elimination, and then to concentrate on bringing the quality of the product up to contract specifications. Negotiations suggest that this view of the transaction is so strong that it may be possible to bargain hard to limit or even eliminate the penalty, although the Chinese are much less flexible with regard to the guarantee of quality.

The selection of locally sourced products is likely to vex any transferor of a complicated industrial product. Thus, as one American engineer has written of his experiences:

the lack of an identical locally-produced equivalent material or component, a frequent occurrence, requires that either a substitute be selected, which may necessitate re-engineering if the material or component differs significantly from the original, or results in pressures to import the component.[41]

If the transferor purchases from outside vendors a significant portion of such materials or components, it may be necessary to import or reverse-engineer them.[42]

H. The Licence Agreement and Third Parties: Patent Infringement, Restrictions on Use, and Confidentiality

i. Patent Infringement

Chinese contractual language on this issue, if it exists at all, is at best skeletal. The standard Techimport clause on patent infringement is very general, requiring the Seller to bear the full 'relevant legal and economic responsibilities' arising out of any alleged patent infringement. Techimport has recently insisted on more specific language, requiring the licenser to assist the licensee and to defend at its expense any claim against the licensee for patent infringement. The Shenzhen Provisional Technology Regulations provide:

if the patent rights are invalidated halfway through the process or if the applications for patent rights are refused, the recipient will have the right to revise or terminate the contract.[43]

Licensees have been known to insist on contract clauses that would give them the same rights.

ii. Confidentiality and Unauthorized Use

The problem of protecting proprietary information in China is a legitimate concern for any company considering a transaction involving technology transfer. A confidentiality clause frequently used by Techimport provides that 'within the validity time of the contract, the Buyer shall not disclose or publish in any form to any third party *outside* China the contents of the know-how supplied by the Seller to the Buyer' (my italics). It may be rather more difficult to persuade Techimport to accept non-disclosure to entities *inside* China.

It is a curious fact that, when foreign negotiators have tried to limit disclosure within China to the end-user with whom negotiations have been carried out, some Techimport negotiators have been willing to state (in private) that any Chinese organization other than Techimport or the end-user would constitute a 'third party' to whom disclosure would be unauthorized. Yet some of these same Techimport negotiators have also been unwilling to express this interpretation in the contract. In one negotiation known to this author, the Techimport representative agreed to add language preventing disclosure by the Buyer 'to any person without connection with the present contract', language that is still not completely satisfactory. Fortunately, however, other importing organizations and end-users in China seem to be increasingly willing to limit disclosure or use of the licensed know-how to a named manufacturing facility. This is an encouraging sign that the need for more explicit protection is gaining wider recognition in the PRC.

Yet, despite the likelihood that protection against improper disclosure may be possible, a company must none the less ask what remedies are available if it suspects or discovers that its technology has been improperly disclosed.

China's new Patent Law, discussed below, provides for damages for infringement. Nevertheless, it is still important to rely on the contract, which Chinese legal specialists consistently assure foreigners will always be honoured. Foreign companies should obtain a clear contractual expression of the obligations of the Chinese partner not to disclose or duplicate licensed technology or other proprietary information without the licenser's consent. It is also necessary to insist that licensees agree to require key employees to sign agreements obligating them not to disclose or transfer the protected technology. In licensing and other trade or investment agreements a satisfactory clause on dispute settlement should also be included.

The need for stronger guarantees has led some to ask whether Chinese courts can enforce contractual stipulations prohibiting technology transfer. In practice, although the role of courts in Chinese society has expanded recently, and although the courts are intended to resolve disputes with foreigners,[44] foreigners would be well advised to look initially to extrajudicial remedies. They should first contact the Chinese party to the contract whom they suspect is breaching the confidentiality of the technology concerned. Restrained, tactful, but nevertheless unambiguous expressions of concern that duplication of the company's technology would violate a prior agreement should convey the company's message convincingly. If such discussions do not succeed, the company should bring the violation to the attention of a high-level agency, such as a ministry, whose authority runs *vertically* down to the organization that has violated the contract or is duplicating the technology. Another course would be to seek out other organizations with equal or greater political clout that can approach the bureaucratic hierarchy *horizontally*. These choices are not mutually exclusive. For example, if a licenser believes that a provincial chemical enterprise is wrongfully duplicating its technology, the licenser should complain not only to the enterprise's superiors (the vertical route), but also to the local government (the horizontal route), and to MOFERT.

Regardless of how much progress is made towards regularizing Chinese law, the settlement of disputes involving foreigners is more likely to be through negotiation than through any form of third-party adjudication. Foreigners who encounter problems arising out of alleged contract violations should realize that the system is highly incomplete and try to gain access to, and seek the assistance of, non-judicial Chinese agencies that have a large stake in China's commercial credibility abroad.

iii. Other Third-party Problems
The problems discussed so far have in common the fact that they involve third parties to the contract. Other potentially serious third-party problems deserve attention, such as the need to ascertain the authority of a particular prospective partner.

As noted above, the number of Chinese agencies authorized to negotiate technology transfer agreements has increased dramatically in the last five years. Given the blurred lines of authority that exist, a foreign firm may have to discount the assurances of Chinese organizations that claim to possess the authority not only to enter into technology transfer agreements, but also to protect the foreign firm in certain necessary ways. Consider, for example, a promise made to a United States firm by a provincial bureau of the chemical industry that factories in other provinces will not export to the United States. Does the provincial bureau really have the means to prevent its parent body, the Ministry of Chemical Industry, from transferring the necessary know-how to subordinate plants in other provinces or to prevent their provincial bureaux from negotiating with competing licensers? The United States company would do well to be sceptical. Suppose, too, that the bureau cautions the foreigner not to go elsewhere, such as higher authorities in Beijing, for assurances. If the foreign company is confronted with a choice between accepting a local organization's assurances at face value, or appearing to be impolite or mistrustful, it seems desirable to try to obtain fuller assurances and support at the central level, and to tell the local Chinese organization that such action is being taken. It behoves the foreigner to risk embarrassment in order to avoid future legal problems.

I. Dispute Settlement

i. Practice

It has long been standard for Techimport to agree to third-country arbitration, reflecting a compromise between foreigners' unwillingness to agree to arbitration by the Foreign Economic and Trade Arbitration Commission of the China Council for the Promotion of International Trade (CCPIT) and Chinese unwillingness to litigate in a foreign court. The standard Techimport arbitration clause calls for arbitration in Stockholm, according to the rules of the Stockholm Chamber of Commerce or of the United Nations Commission on International Trade Law (UNCITRAL).

ii. Choice of Applicable Law

A major problem in dispute settlement clauses, likely to become more difficult to resolve in a manner satisfactory to foreign licensers, is the choice of the applicable law, which standard Chinese contracts conspicuously omit. The general trend, however, is changing. In a relatively small number of transactions, particularly loan transactions involving the Bank of China, Chinese parties have agreed to the applicability of foreign law. More often, though, in the few cases in which they are willing to agree to reference to foreign law, Chinese parties to transactions would prefer to allow the arbitrators to choose the applicable law, a solution which obviously injects even further uncertainty into the dispute. Recently, in a variety of transactions which reflect both an earlier and lingering distaste for submission to foreign law and the later development of Chinese laws and regulations applicable to foreign trade transactions, Chinese negotiators have insisted that Chinese law must apply.

iii. The Impact of Legislation

The Shenzhen Foreign Economic Contract Regulations provide that in arbitration arising out of contracts performed in the Guangdong SEZs, co-operative activities, contracts relating to natural resources, and other contracts which have a 'close relationship to Chinese sovereignty', Chinese law must be applied.[45] The same provision of the law provides that arbitration of disputes arising out of these contracts shall be arbitrated by the arbitration organs in the SEZs, but that the parties 'may choose other arbitral organs'. There is no reference to any right of the parties to choose to apply a law other than Chinese law, which suggests an intent to require that disputes arising out of all contracts in the SEZs with foreigners, involving technology transfer and otherwise, must be decided according to Chinese law.

The Foreign Economic Contracts Law deals with certain issues related to dispute settlement in a manner that should reassure foreign traders. The parties are allowed to choose the law that will govern their contract and, if they fail to choose the law, the arbitrators or courts which settle disputes arising out of such a contract are directed to apply the law of the place with the closest connection to the contract, thereby adopting a well-established principle of international law.[46] Although contracts will be subject to certain provisions of Chinese law in any event, such as those related to approvals by administrative agencies, the drafters of the Foreign Economic Contracts Law took a pragmatic view of Chinese law itself, and provided that, even when contracts are governed by Chinese law, if Chinese law lacks 'relevant stipulations' the arbitrators or courts may apply 'international practice'.[47] With regard to the forum for dispute settlement, the parties may choose to arbitrate in China or abroad, although the possibility of bringing suit in foreign courts is implicitly excluded.

iv. The Likely Lasting Impact of Chinese Practice

Although the Foreign Economic Contracts Law represents a welcome step forward, it is not likely to replace quickly almost forty years of customary practice, particularly in transactions conducted by the foreign trade corporations under the authority of MOFERT. Many matters not directly and explicitly addressed by the Foreign Economic Contracts Law are likely to be determined by past Chinese practice.

Thus, despite references to the applicable law and to fora for dispute settlement, there is no reason to foresee that Chinese negotiators will abandon their long-standing aversion to choosing a foreign law to apply to their contractual disputes. Moreover, mention of the possibility of arbitration in a third country is hardly the equivalent of willingness to arbitrate there. Many thousands of Chinese contracts have been signed over the years containing clauses which specified that arbitration could be conducted in Stockholm, but at the time of writing (November 1986), no arbitration of a dispute arising out of a Chinese contract has yet been held in Stockholm. Disputes involving contracts with such clauses have presumably been settled by the process of negotiation and compromise that the Chinese have historically preferred to use in foreign trade disputes. At the same time it is of more than passing interest that Chinese arbitration officials have stated in conversation to this author and others that the number of arbitrations in China involving foreigners has grown in recent years. Litigation involving foreigners in Chinese courts has also occurred, although cases are apparently still rare.

Experience suggests that in general, quite apart from clauses on arbitration, Chinese negotiators remain inclined to begin with the form contracts to which they are accustomed. At the same time, however, the Foreign Economic Contracts Law provides a standard against which Chinese contracts, form or otherwise, can be measured.

Limitations of space make it impossible to discuss at length the implications of the conclusions reached here. Suffice it to say that the insistence that Chinese law should apply to disputes involving investment in China, because China is the host country, is consistent with the view of many other developing nations. At the same time, the newness and irregularity of the application of Chinese laws on foreign trade and investment detract considerably from the uniformity and certainty of the promulgated Chinese rules as they are carried out in practice. The problem of ascertaining Chinese law will not be solved merely by the publication of these rules; here, too, as in technology transfer, the infrastructure does not yet match Chinese expectations. Furthermore, Chinese legal officials seem likely to continue to advocate compromise and conciliation as the most desirable methods of settling disputes.[48]

V. Taxation

Income earned in China by foreign companies is subject to taxation at either a progressive rate of up to 40 per cent if the foreign company has an 'establishment' in China, or at a 20 per cent withholding rate on interest, royalties, and other passive income, if such company does not have an 'establishment' in China.[49] Consequently, foreign transferors of technology or proprietary knowledge will be taxed on royalties paid pursuant to technology transfer agreements. Tax treaties signed by the PRC with a number of other nations, such as the United States,[50] reduce the withholding tax on royalties, in most cases to 10 per cent.

Notwithstanding China's tax laws, a transferor without an establishment in China may avoid, be exempt from, or pay a reduced withholding tax on royalties. In some transactions, especially those which took place immediately following the promulgation of the Foreign Enterprise Income Tax Law (cited hereafter as the FEITL), foreign transferors and Chinese transferees agreed that the Chinese would pay any and all taxes levied. This practice met with the disapproval of the Ministry of Finance.[51] The Chinese may also sometimes offer to reimburse the foreign side for taxes withheld from royalty payments; however, Ministry of Finance officials have stated that this too violates its policy.

In order to promote the import of advanced technology, in January 1983 the Ministry of Finance adopted regulations which generally reduced to 10 per cent the tax rate on royalties from the transfer of technology.[52] In addition, 'where the technology is advanced and the terms preferential', royalties could be wholly exempted from the withholding tax. The regulations also eliminated the withholding tax on income from various consulting fees, technology and construction fees, and technical assistance and technical service fees, provided that no transfer of technology was involved and the transferor had no establishment in China. Once the Tax Treaty becomes effective, these regulations will lose some of their significance. However, they will continue to be important for transferors who desire a total exemption from taxation on royalties, as well as for transferors from countries with which China has not entered into a similar tax treaty.

As might be expected, obtaining a reduction or exemption from the withholding tax on royalty payments requires a separate approval process, involving either the Ministry of Finance or local tax bureaus; tax reductions will be decided locally whereas tax exemptions will be decided by the Ministry of Finance. Chinese authorities charged with approving transactions must also liaise with tax authorities to determine the tax treatment of a particular transaction. The timing of the notification of the tax treatment of a particular transaction is of obvious importance to the transferor, and may affect both price and payment terms. Although the situation is improving and Chinese tax officials have recently on occasion been willing to approve tax reductions prior to the approval of a particular transaction, foreign transferors desiring tax reductions or exemptions must still rely on informal interpretations or suggestions from local tax bureaux or from the Ministry of Finance prior to the approval of the contract.

Another method of avoiding the withholding tax on royalty payments is to characterize the payments by the transferee to the transferor as something other than 'royalties', thus avoiding characterization of the payments as the type of income to which the withholding tax applies. The Ministry of Finance has confirmed, for example, that where a foreigner is repaid for his technology and know-how in products, such payments are not taxable under the FEITL.[53] A considerable tax incentive therefore exists to fold technology transfer into co-production or counter-trade transactions rather than to enter into pure technology licensing agreements. Also, where technical assistance, training, or documentation is related to the sale of equipment to China, corresponding payments are specifically exempt from the withholding tax.[54] Thus, where a foreigner sells equipment to China and at the same time transfers technology related to the equipment in the form of technical training, technical assistance, or design documentation, it is possible to avoid being subject to Chinese tax, provided that the payments are properly characterized. Foreigners must be sensitive to this nuance, as it may result in substantial tax savings.

It is perhaps of even greater significance to foreign sellers that services related to the sale of machinery and equipment or provided to transform China's existing technology are exempt from the FEITL and the Consolidated Industrial and Commercial Tax.[55] Where a clear distinction cannot be drawn between services that are connected with a transfer of technology and services that are connected with a sale of hardware, all income related to such services will be subject to the withholding tax.[56] The treatment of income related to home office engineering services is not yet uniform, and in some instances known to the author tax has been withheld. Also fees specifically related to documentation may be taxable if the Chinese tax authorities decide they are related to the transfer of technology rather than to the sale of hardware.[57]

VI. Chinese Patent Law

China's new Patent Law now extends legal protection of industrial property rights beyond the protection afforded by contract, which previously was all that was available to a foreign party. Changes in the strictly domestic sphere have preceded the consideration of protection of foreign patents. New regulations on the reward and certification of inventions were issued in late 1978. A State Patent Bureau was established in late 1979, and interest in international patent protection has grown. In February 1980, China sent a delegation to the World Intellectual Property Organization (WIPO) meeting in Geneva to discuss revision of the Paris Convention, and the PRC has been a member of WIPO since then. Finally, after many years, marked first by neglect of patent matters and then by slow and patient study of foreign patent legislation and administration, the Patent Law of the People's Republic of China was passed on 12 March 1984 by the Standing Committee of the National People's Congress. For a discussion of the salient features of the new law, the reader is referred to Chapter 13 of this volume.

VII. Future Laws

The legal background for contracts will certainly grow in complexity as Chinese law-drafters continue to pursue their work energetically. For example, the General Principles of Civil Law, promulgated in April 1986, contain skeletal principles of tort liability, yet plant the kernel for a product liability law by providing that a person injured by 'defective' goods may hold responsible both the seller and the manufacturer.[58] The General Principles also state a general rule which could be of great interest to foreigners: if a contract must be violated because the intervention of a higher-level authority makes performance impossible, the party violating the contract must first pay damages before seeking redress from the higher-level authority.[59]

Moreover, Chinese negotiating teams, which increasingly include persons who have legal training, are growing in sophistication about Western law and trade practices. Thus, some years ago, Techimport negotiators began to insist that foreign transferors of technology agree to be liable not only for physical injuries or property damage directly caused by defects in products correctly manufactured with foreign technology, but also for loss of profits caused thereby. They have also begun to oppose strongly a tactic employed by foreign sellers of whole plants and technology, who have long been accustomed to limiting their liability for injurious consequences of the use or misuse of technology and equipment transferred under the contract to the total contract price. It may be that practice will be overtaken by the development of doctrine: although such clauses continue to be employed, the time is likely to come soon when an injured third party will sue the foreign party to the contract, and claim, as he could in the United States or Western Europe, that such a contract clause could not impede his right to recovery.

VIII. Conclusion

The foregoing discussion has only touched on some of the problems that may arise in the course of negotiations. Other forces may shape transactions or their outcomes. For example, the influence of United States export controls on technology transfer to the PRC has not been considered here. The ability of the United States Department of Defense to hamper or delay the issuing of export licences despite attempts by successive United States Presidential Administrations to relax stringent limitations is legendary; bureaucratic inertia does not exist only on the Chinese side of the Pacific.

This chapter began with a survey of changing Chinese policies, which will no doubt continue to show variations that will affect transactions of the type discussed here. Moreover, if any current Chinese policy is likely to be implemented on a long-term basis, it is the commitment to import technology. It would be difficult for China's leaders to contemplate carrying out a genuine effort to modernize Chinese industry without carrying on with such a commitment. If this perception is accurate, China will continue to import considerable quantities of technology in the foreseeable future, and the legal framework for transactions giving expression to the policy should therefore continue to develop and increase in definition.

Yet even if policy remains consistent and new laws add greater certainty to the expectations of parties to technology transfer transactions, some problems in the relations between foreign transferors and Chinese transferees of technology are likely to remain. For example, it has been common for Chinese negotiators to want to include broad expressions of licensers' obligations in contracts, and to disdain detailed documentation, especially if it is legalistic. In this regard, foreign licensers would be well advised to render some of their favourite legalisms into plain English; at the same time, they should insist on documentation that adequately covers the contingencies which most concern them.

The foregoing advice seems especially appropriate in light of the fact that the Chinese side, viewing the contract as a document that creates a strong relationship between the parties, may view that relationship as the basis for requesting favours or other actions by the licenser which the licenser views as additional impositions and sometimes as costly burdens. If the contract is sufficiently detailed, unwelcome elasticity in interpreting the agreement may be more easily resisted. Also, elementary as it may seem, unwritten commitments by either side should be avoided as much as possible. This is particularly true in view of the fact that the Chinese side may have difficulties in performing obligations which involve the co-operation of another Chinese organization which was not consulted when the contract was drafted.

Perhaps the greatest source of problems between licensers and licensees in China is the frequent gap between high Chinese expectations and the inability of the Chinese infrastructure to aid realization of such expectations. This is reflected in many aspects of transactions involving transfers of technology, ranging from Chinese hopes about the speed and effectiveness with which the technology can be transferred, learned, and applied, to such mundane but important details as the availability and adequacy of Chinese goods and services and living quarters for expatriate employees.

At the same time, responsibility for misunderstandings which may arise because of the gap between Chinese hopes and the limited resources of the Chinese economy and Chinese society cannot be laid exclusively on the Chinese side. Foreign business men are frequently inexcusably ignorant about the realities of the Chinese economy simply because they have not taken the trouble to inform themselves adequately. Perhaps because China is so distant and is assumed to be unknowable, Western business men often take less trouble to inform themselves about China than they would take to inform themselves about a Western nation with which they might discuss a similar transaction. Given the amount of literature now available, not only in English but also in other Western languages,[60] failure to learn about recent developments in China has become even more unwarranted than it was before.

This chapter has focused on three disparate elements of the business environment in which the foreigner finds himself in China. Policy has been changeable, the legal framework is new and uncertain, and practice is difficult to follow closely. However, new regularities have begun to appear, albeit slowly, which have stabilized the expectations of the parties to the transactions discussed here. In the foreseeable future, each side will have to continue its efforts to understand the other. Foreigners should not demand Chinese adherence to exaggerated ideals. At the same time, it is hoped that Chinese agencies will sustain their efforts to fashion fair, uniform, and ascertainable rules and practice.

Notes

1. The discussion in this section is based on Chen Weiqin, 'The Direction of Introducing Technology Should Be Changed', *Jingji guanli* (*Economic Management*), No. 4, April 1981, pp. 22–5, translated in 'Joint Publications Research Service China Report' (hereafter cited as the JPRS), 29 June 1981, *Economic*

Affairs, No. 146, pp. 27–32; Lin Senmu, 'Lessons Drawn from the Importation of 22 Complete Sets of Equipment', *Jingji guanli*, No. 6, June 1981, in JPRS, No. 78743, 13 August 1981, *Economic Affairs*, No. 160, pp. 13–18; Rao Bin, 'Provide Technical Equipment for Different Departments of the National Economy to Raise Economic Results', *Jingji guanli*, No. 4, April 1982, in JPRS, No. 81087, 21 June 1982, *Economic Affairs*, No. 240, pp. 25–33; Zhu Yuening, 'Give Weight to the Importation of Technology and Machinery', *Renmin ribao (People's Daily)*, 9 August 1982, in *Foreign Broadcast Information Service, Daily Report, China* (hereafter cited as the FBIS), 13 August 1983, pp. K12–K15; Xinhua News Agency, 'Technology Import Official on Trade Policies', in FBIS, 25 October 1982, pp. K17–K18; Huang Bingwen, 'Technological Transformation is a Strategic Measure in Revitalizing Industry', *Fujian ribao (Fujian Daily)*, 26 November 1982, in JPRS, No. 82986, 2 March 1983, *Economic Affairs*, No. 317, pp. 22–5; Commentator, 'Boldly Import Technology in Transforming Small and Medium-sized Enterprises', *Renmin ribao*, 14 January 1983, in FBIS, 18 January 1983, pp. K1–K2; Chen Lianzhen, 'A Breakthrough is Necessary in Importing Advanced Technology', *Fujian ribao*, 23 January 1983, in JPRS, No. 83440, 10 May 1983, *Economic Affairs*, No. 337, pp. 76–9; Wang Dekuan, 'Knowledge is Strength and Wealth', *Nanfang ribao (Southern Daily)*, 31 January 1983, in JPRS, No. 93367, 29 April 1983, *Economic Affairs*, No. 333, pp. 43–4; Zi Yu and Gao Xiaoxiao, 'Through Importing Advanced Equipment from Foreign Countries and Supporting Improvement in Industrial Technology, the Shanghai Foreign Trade Department Vigorously Promotes Production of Export Commodities and has Improved Industrial Technology in 323 Items, Resulting in an Annual Increased Output of 11.4 Billion Yuan', *Jiefang ribao (Liberation Daily)*, 19 February 1983, in JPRS, No. 83440, 10 May 1983, *Economic Affairs*, No. 337, pp. 74–5; Commentator, 'Do a Good Job in Digesting Imported Technology', *Renmin ribao*, 27 March 1983, in FBIS, 14 April 1983, pp. K6–K8; and Denis Fred Simon, 'China's Capacity to Assimilate Foreign Technology: An Assessment', in *China Under the Four Modernizations—Selected Papers Submitted to the Joint Economic Committee, US Congress* (Washington, Government Printing Office, 1982), Vol. 1, pp. 514–52 (cited hereafter as *China Under the Four Modernizations*). See, also, Liu Jingtong, *On Introducing Technology to China* (New York, China-International Business Series, East Asian Institute, School of International and Business Affairs, Graduate School of Business, Columbia University, 1983); and R. Conroy, 'Technological Innovation in China's Recent Industrialization', *China Quarterly*, No. 97, March 1984, pp. 1–23.

2. Hans Heymann, Jr., 'Acquisition and Diffusion of Technology in China', in *China, A Reassessment of the Economy, Compendium of Papers Submitted to the Joint Economic Committee, Congress of the United States* (Washington, Government Printing Office, 1975), p. 686.

3. Chen, 'The Direction of Introducing Technology . . .', p. 28, note 1 above.

4. Simon, pp. 543–4, note 1 above.

5. On the vicissitudes of the Baoshan Iron and Steel Complex, see Martin Weil, 'The Baoshan Steel Mill: A Symbol of Change in China's Industrial Development Strategy', in *China Under the Four Modernizations*, Vol. I, p. 365, note 1 above.

6. This paragraph and the two following are based on Simon, pp. 514–52, note 1 above.

7. Simon, p. 537, note 1 above.

8. Simon, p. 538, note 1 above.

9. Simon, p. 540, note 1 above.

10. Cao Jiarui, 'The Present Condition of, and Problems in China's Technological Imports (Part 1)', *Liaowang Overseas Edition*, No. 18, 5 May 1986, translated in FBIS, 16 May 1986, pp. K5 and K6, cited hereafter as Cao, Part 1.

11. Cao, Part 1, p. K7, note 10 above.

12. Cao, Part 1, p. K7, note 10 above.

13. Cao, Part 1, p. K8, note 10 above.

14. Cao Jiarui, 'The Present Condition of, and Problems in China's Technological Imports (Part 2)', *Liaowang Overseas Edition*, No. 19, 12 May 1986, translated in FBIS, 22 May 1986, pp. K10 and K11, cited hereafter as Cao, Part 2.

15. Cao, Part 2, p. K12, note 14 above.

16. Cao Jiarui, 'The Present Condition of, and Problems in China's Technological Imports (Part 3)', *Liaowang Overseas Edition*, No. 20, 19 May 1986, translated in FBIS, 30 May 1986, p. K13, cited hereafter as Cao, Part 3.

17. Cao, Part 3, p. K16, note 16 above.

18. Writing about his experience in a joint venture to which considerable technology was transferred, one American engineer has noted that on the one hand the Chinese often wanted large-scale grandiose plant, but in a setting of 'marginal, small, old buildings'. Steven Hendryx, 'Implementing a Technology Transfer Agreement in China', text of a speech made in Hong Kong, September 1985, p. 7.

19. For similar views, see also Chen Qingdao and Yin Zisheng, 'Problems of Technology Imports to China', *Tianjin kexuexue yu kexue jishu guanli (Science of Science and Management of Science and Technology)*, translated in JPRS-CGT-86-025, 1 July 1986, p. 14; 'China Has Been Importing Redundant Technology', *Financial Times*, 19 August 1985 (quoting a MOFERT statement). The conclusions drawn by an American observer are strikingly parallel to those quoted above, namely that 'Chinese state enterprises are simply not equipped to undertake the complex, interlocking tasks of a modern, market driven, financially independent corporation' (Hendryx, p. 9, note 18 above). He adds: 'in the centrally planned economy, enterprise does not market, so there is no feedback from the market; there is a chronic shortage of industrial goods and there is no competition, so customers take what they can get; and, as noted, there is low motivation. It should be no surprise that quality suffers. Past attempts to regulate quality have of course failed' (p. 10).

20. For an excellent analysis of current problems in the transfer and adoption of foreign technology based on the author's experience on a number of projects, see Joseph Y. Battat, 'Transfer of Computer and Data Processing Technologies: First-Hand Experience of a Foreign Consultant', in *China's Economy Looks Toward the Year 2000*, Vol. 2, *Economic Experiences in Modernizing China, Selected Papers Submitted to the Joint Economic Committee, US Congress* (Washington, Government Printing Office, 1986), pp. 233–53. The author notes the impact of Marxist economic philosophy which influences planners to emphasize productive forces but disregard managerial and technical know-how; he stresses the 'counter-productive' economic environment (see p. 245). He also stresses the non-existence or weakness of the concepts of opportunity cost, marginal analysis, and investment analysis, and the effect of certain systemic factors, such as scarcity, 'system inertia', a lack of accountability, differences between the goals of local and external organizations, and differences between the goals of foreign trade corporations and end-users. See, also, Denis Fred Simon, 'The Evolving Role of Technology Transfer in China's Modernization', in *China's Economy Looks Toward the Year 2000*, pp. 254–86, who, while noting the problems discussed here, also predicts 'the emergence of a limited number of so-called "pockets of excellence" in the Chinese economy over the next several years—created through a combination of foreign technology and indigenous efforts' (p. 281).

21. A Chinese planner has explained the reasoning behind such a shift: 'Since liberation, the system of foreign trade has basically been the one China learned from the Soviet Union in the 1950s. It has emphasized monopoly, control and high concentration. Consequently, all import and export trading is centralized and dealt with by the state-run foreign trade corporations. Lacking authority to decide for themselves in operational and financial matters, these corporations have grown accustomed to acting in accordance with administrative orders and requesting instruction from high levels, thus introducing red tape into their operations.

In managing and supervising business, they care little about loss, wastage and the turnover and application of funds, nor do they pay any attention to economic accounting and efficiency. Since the head office is far away in Beijing, how can it completely understand the situation in other parts of the country? As a result, what should have been interfered with has been left alone and what should have been left alone has been interfered with. The fact is that the head office is incapable of supervising the branch office. . .

In reforming the foreign trade system, we should encourage local initiative . . .'. Zhang Chongwen, 'The System of Foreign Trade Must Be Reformed', *Jingji guanli*, No. 12, December 1979, translated in JPRS, No. 75345, *Economic Affairs*, No. 49, 21 March 1980, pp. 60–1.

The decentralization was described as follows: 'The head offices of a number of national import and export corporations under the Ministry of Foreign Trade now deal with only a few, important commodities. Most of the national import and export business is done by coastal or local trading corporations, or by newly-established corporations under other ministries and departments. The new corporations set up by ministries and the Chinese Academy of Sciences will also engage in joint ventures, co-publication, compensatory trade, processing and assembly work.

Foreign trade corporations have been set up in the municipalities of Beijing, Tianjin and Shanghai, the provinces of Guangdong, Fujian, Liaoning and Hebei, and the Guangxi Zhuang Autonomous Region. These corporations handle their own import-export business as well as foreign trade transportation, chartering, warehousing, packaging and advertising.' See 'Reform of Foreign Trade Structure Described', in FBIS, 31 December 1980, pp. L41–L42.

22. See, for example, Stanley B. Lubman, 'Trade Contracts and Technology Licensing', in J.A. Cohen (ed.), *Legal Aspects of Doing Business in China 1983* (New York, Practising Law Institute, 1983), pp. 12–27.

23. A further partial recentralization of foreign trade was announced in March 1984. A spokesman for the Ministry of Foreign Economic Relations and Trade stated on 15 March 1984 that 'the [Ministry] would exercise overall administrative power over foreign trade and reinstitute the system of unified leadership and management. All major export and import goods will be put under the unified management of national foreign trade corporations . . .'; see 'Centralized Control of Foreign Trade Announced', in FBIS, 15 March 1984, pp. K3–K4. See, also, 'Trade Ministry Official Interviewed on Protection of Rights of Foreign Licensers', *China Economic News*, 23 January 1984, p. 3: 'After the expansion of the department and local authority, the organ to examine and approve technology transfer controls and to supervise the fulfillment of the contract obligations by the technology licensed enterprise is still the Ministry of Foreign Economic Relations and Trade, or some other organ authorized . . . in the light of actual needs.'

24. The Shenzhen Provisional Technology Regulations and the Shenzhen Foreign Economic Contract Regulations were approved by the Standing Committee of the Guangdong Provincial People's Congress on 11 January 1984, and promulgated by the Guangdong Provincial People's Congress on 7 February 1984. They were published in *Nanfang ribao*, 8 February 1984. An English translation of these regulations may be found in *China Laws for Foreign Business* (Sydney, CCH Australia Limited, November 1985).

25. An English translation of these regulations appeared in *East Asian Executive Reports*, July 1985, p. 28.

26. Technology Regulations, Art. 2, note 25 above.

27. Technology Regulations, Art. 3, note 25 above.

28. Technology Regulations, Art. 6, note 25 above.

29. The Foreign Economic Contracts Law has been published in English in *China Business Review*, July–August 1985, pp. 54–5 and in *East Asian Executive Reports*, May 1985, pp. 27–9. For discussions of the Law soon after it appeared see, for example, J. Cohen, 'The New Foreign Economic Contract Law', *China Business Review*, July–August 1985, p. 52; S. Lubman and C. Randt, 'Another

Legal Milestone', *China Trade Report*, May 1985, Vol. XXIII, p. 12; T. Gelatt and R. Kraiem, 'The Foreign Economic Contract Law: More Autonomy for Contracting Parties', *East Asian Executive Reports*, May 1985, p. 9.

30. In practice, as the discussion cited earlier suggests, the appraisal is not normally conducted in terms of the choice facing the PRC or even the particular industry involved on a nation-wide basis. Cao, Part 1, p. K7, note 10 above.

31. Measures for the Examination and Approval of Technology Import Contracts, *East Asian Executive Reports*, 15 November 1986, p. 26.

32. Technology Regulations, Art. 5, note 25 above.

33. Standard Techimport contract in the author's files.

34. Steven Hendryx, p. 3, note 18 above.

35. Hendryx, p. 36, note 18 above.

36. Shenzhen Provisional Technology Regulations, Art. 23, note 24 above.

37. Shenzhen Provisional Technology Regulations, Art. 12, note 24 above.

38. Shenzhen Provisional Technology Regulations, Art. 19, note 24 above.

39. Technology Regulations, Art. 8, note 25 above.

40. Summarizing common complaints of Japanese transferors of technology, one author lists the following: 'The Chinese seek guarantees in terms of finished products, which are difficult or impossible to make; Japanese corporations concerned are asked to achieve quality standards even higher than those adopted in Japan...'. M. Yabuuchi, 'Technology Transfer and Technological Reform of Existing Enterprises In China', *JETRO China Newsletter*, No. 64, September–October 1986, p. 9.

41. Hendryx, p. 5, note 18 above.

42. Hendryx, p. 5, note 18 above.

43. Shenzhen Provisional Technology Regulations, Art. 12, note 24 above.

44. The Foreign Economic Contracts Law (Art. 38) provides for settlement of disputes by Chinese or 'other arbitration bodies' or, if the contract in question lacked an arbitration clause and the parties do not agree to arbitrate, in a Chinese court.

45. Shenzhen Foreign Economic Contract Regulations, Art. 35, note 24 above.

46. Foreign Economic Contracts Law, Art. 5, note 29 above.

47. Foreign Economic Contracts Law, Art. 5, note 29 above.

48. A characteristic expression of current Chinese views on this subject is Shao Xunyi, 'Conciliation Is a Good Method for Settling International Economic and Trade Disputes—An Introduction to China's Practice of Conciliation', paper presented to the Seventh International Arbitration Congress, Hamburg, West Germany, 7–11 June 1982.

49. The Foreign Enterprise Income Tax Law of the PRC. An English translation may be found in *China Laws For Foreign Business*, para. 32-500(y), note 24 above. See, also, Chapter 2 of this volume.

50. Agreement Between the Government of the United States of America and the Government of the People's Republic of China for the Avoidance of Double Taxation and the Prevention of Tax Evasion with Respect to Taxes or Income, in *International Legal Materials*, Vol. XXIII, No. 4, July 1984.

51. Document Regarding Questions Related to Taxation of Such Contracts as Introduction of Technology Contracts..., Ministry of Finance Document No. 102, p. 2, 29 March 1982, cited in Chapter 2 of this volume: see p. 66, n. 5 and pp. 75–6, n. 100.

52. Provisional Regulations of the Ministry of Finance of the People's Republic of China Regarding the Reduction and Exemption of Income Tax on Fees for the Use of Proprietary Technology, *China Laws for Foreign Business*, para. 39-600(1), note 24 above.

53. 'Finance Ministry Spokesman on Income Tax Reduction and Exemption for Foreign Companies', *China Economic News*, No. 11, 21 March 1983, pp. 3 and 4.

54. Interim Provisions of the Ministry of Finance Concerning the Levy of the

Consolidated Industrial and Commercial Tax and the Enterprise Income Tax on Foreign Businesses that Contract for Projects and Operations and Provide Labor Services, Document 83, *Cai shuizi*, No. 149, 5 July 1983.

55. See Interim Provisions of the Ministry of Finance, note 54 above.

56. Issues Concerning Calculating Income Tax Levied on Royalties for Know-how, Ministry of Finance, General Tax Bureau Document No. 143, Art. 3, 14 October 1982.

57. Issues Concerning Calculating Income Tax, Art. 2, note 56 above.

58. General Principles of Civil Law, Art. 122.

59. General Principles of Civil Law, Art. 116.

60. See, for example, *Schweiz-China*, published quarterly by the Swiss-China Chamber of Commerce in Zurich; *Economie et Commerce*, published by Comité France-Chine in Paris; and *Chinas Recht*, translations of Chinese laws, circulated by Franz Muenzel of the Max Planck Institut für Internationales Privatrecht in Hamburg.

5. Law and Investment in China's Special Investment Areas

ELSON POW AND MICHAEL J. MOSER

ONE of the most widely publicized aspects of China's post-Mao economic modernization programme has been the gradual establishment of defined areas throughout China which offer special incentives to foreign investors and various types of preferential treatment for enterprises located in those areas. The establishment of special investment areas began in 1979 with the creation of three *jingji tequ* or 'special economic zones' (SEZs) in the municipalities of Shenzhen, Zhuhai, and Shantou in Guangdong province. Xiamen in Fujian province became the fourth SEZ in 1980. In 1983, Hainan Island in southern China was granted the status of a special administrative zone under the jurisdiction of the Guangdong Provincial People's Government with many of the powers of an SEZ. Within the same policy framework, the State Council then announced the opening of the fourteen coastal cities in May 1984, and gave conception to three special delta economic zones in January 1985.[1]

These special investment areas have been established on the basis of two broad principles. Firstly, foreign investors and enterprises located in the special areas are to enjoy preferential treatment in the form of lower tax rates and easier entry and exit procedures. Secondly, the local government authorities are to have greater decision-making power than was previously available to them in China. It is to be noted that this does not confer on any of the special investment areas any autonomy of a political nature. These special areas are to be contrasted with the position of Hong Kong after 1997, at which time Hong Kong will become a special administrative region with a degree of not only economic but also political independence.[2]

Of all the special areas established to date, the four SEZs and the four major coastal cities, Dalian, Guangzhou, Shanghai, and Tianjin, are most advanced in their development. That development includes the formulation of a legal framework for investment in these areas that differs in many important respects from that which is applicable in China generally. In this legislative process it is noteworthy that, apart from the Interim Regulations on the Control of Environment in the Open Economic Areas which were promulgated by the Bureau of Environmental Protection on 17 March 1986, there is as yet no other published law or regulation which treats the various special investment areas distinctly from the rest of China.

This chapter will describe the regulatory regime that has been established to govern investment and other economic activity in the SEZs, the 14 coastal cities, Hainan Island, and the delta economic zones. Part I concentrates on the SEZs, with Section A providing a background discussion focusing on the origins of the SEZs, government policy goals, and investment patterns in the zones to date; Sections B and C examine the relevant laws and regulations affecting the conduct of business in the SEZs and discuss the major types of preferential treatment granted to SEZ enterprises; and Section D examines the special investment rules applicable to the Shekou industrial zone, a part of the Shenzhen SEZ, within the context of the general SEZ legislation. Part II is devoted to the fourteen coastal cities, with Section A providing background material, Section B describing the investment incentives available in these cities, and Section C discussing the legal framework that is being formulated. Part III examines Hainan Island and the three delta economic zones and their scheme of development.

I. The Special Economic Zones

A. Background

Although the roots of the 'special zone' concept can be traced back to the 1960s,[3] the present-day SEZs did not formally come into being until 1980. Searching for means to enhance the attractiveness of investment in China, the Chinese government in early 1979 dispatched a number of teams of economists and planners abroad to conduct research on 'export' or 'free trade' zones.[4] Subsequently, in July of that year, the State Council issued a directive granting Guangdong province wide-ranging powers to devise and implement flexible economic policies aimed at promoting tourism, foreign trade, and investment.[5] One month later, in August 1979, Shantou municipality in Guangdong announced that it had set up a 'trade and investment zone', and in September the bordering municipalities of Shenzhen and Zhuhai declared themselves 'special export zones'.[6] Finally, in August 1980, the Shantou, Shenzhen, and Zhuhai zones were renamed 'special economic zones' and put under the unified management of the newly created Administrative Committee of the Special Economic Zones of Guangdong Province.[7] The designation of an area in Xiamen, Fujian province, as the Xiamen SEZ took place in October 1980.[8]

China's decision to establish SEZs can be seen to have been motivated by a number of policy goals.[9] First, and perhaps foremost, is the aim to realize significant economic benefits from the zones. Like other developing countries which have set up 'free trade zones', 'special industrial estates', and similar zones on their borders, China has viewed the establishment of the SEZs as a useful means of accelerating the development of export-oriented enterprises while simultaneously increasing local employment and foreign exchange earnings.[10] In addition, the SEZs have been seen to be of value in serving more long-term goals. Unlike their counterparts in other developing countries, China's SEZs have not limited foreign investment to small-scale assembly and processing operations but have encouraged investment in major infrastructure projects such as the construction of roads, waterworks, airports, and harbours.[11]

A second goal pursued by Chinese planners in establishing the SEZs has been to use the zones as a bridge for the introduction of foreign technology, know-how, and management techniques to other parts of China.[12] Seen from this perspective, the promotion of regional economic development is only one aspect of government policy; in addition, the zones play a role in the national development plan, thereby serving China's overall socialist modernization drive.

A third, and somewhat related, function of the SEZs is to serve as centres for education and experimentation.[13] Isolated geographically, the SEZs are viewed as hothouses of economic development in which China is able, within a controlled environment, to gain experience in dealing with capitalist economies and to experiment with economic reforms which may be adopted elsewhere in China. Chinese publications have frequently elaborated on this theme, describing the SEZs as 'pilot projects' which, in the words of one writer, provide 'a testing ground for integrated economic development that co-ordinates development in infrastructure, regulation and law, industrial projects, construction, tourism and foreign investment'.[14] It should be observed, however, that the SEZs are not the exclusive domain for economic experimentation in China. From time to time other cities or provinces in China have become the testing ground for specific reformist ideas, among them the trial implementation of bankruptcy rules in Chongqing, Shenyang, Taiyuan, and Wuhan; and the establishment of a financial network consisting of Changzhou, Chongqing, Guangzhou, Shenyang, and Wuhan which will permit state enterprises in those cities to issue stocks and bonds and which will enable the cities themselves to borrow from each other and to experiment with various financing concepts.[15]

In choosing Guangdong and Fujian as the locations for China's SEZs, the nation's planners were prompted by a number of special considerations which tend to complement and support its policy goals.[16] Among the most important of these are geographical factors. Firstly, being situated along the coast, the zones are ideally located to facilitate the importation of raw materials and the exportation of finished products to the international market. Secondly, Guangdong province and Fujian province together constitute the ancestral home for most overseas Chinese and therefore hold a special attraction for these investors. In particular, many of the Chinese in Taiwan have their origins in Fujian. For many wealthy overseas Chinese the opportunity to assist in the development of the motherland and simultaneously obtain a return on their investments holds both a sentimental and a practical appeal. Finally the proximity of the SEZs to Hong Kong provides investors with easy access to the zones, and permits the SEZs to tap the infrastructural resources of one of the world's most important financial centres.

In addition, there is reason to believe that China's choice of Guangdong province as the location for three of the SEZs was also influenced by political considerations. The New Territories of Hong Kong, which border the Shenzhen SEZ, are scheduled to be returned to Chinese sovereignty when Britain's lease on the area expires in 1997.[17] Some commentators have suggested that, by seeking to accelerate the pace of economic development on the Chinese side of the border and promote economic integration between Hong Kong and Guangdong, China has the ultimate goal of developing a formula for reunification by which Hong Kong might retain its present economic system within the framework of a 'super SEZ' or at least of erasing the economic boundary between the two areas and thereby facilitating the reunification process.[18]

The Shenzhen Special Economic Zone, located directly across the border from Hong Kong, is the largest of the SEZs. Having an area of 327.5 square kilometres, the zone occupies approximately one-sixth of the total area of Shenzhen municipality.[19]

Shenzhen's general development plan divides the zone into five districts.[20] At the western end of the zone, on the east coast of the Zhujiang (Pearl River) estuary, is the Shekou industrial zone.[21] During the period 1979–85, RMB313 million (US$85 million) was invested in the district on infrastructure construction.[22] As a result, Shekou enjoys a comparatively well-developed infrastructure featuring such facilities as a 600-metre dock capable of handling vessels of between 3,000 and 5,000 d.w.t.[23] and a microwave communications exchange which provides direct-dial telephone and automatic telex links between the district and Hong Kong.[24] The district has also initiated a daily hydrofoil service to Hong Kong and has made extensive improvements to the highway connecting the district to central Shenzhen city.[25] As of the end of 1985, the district had attracted HK$1.4 billion (US$180 million) in foreign investment.[26] The projects include container manufacturing, flour-milling, steel-rolling, screw manufacturing, and others.[27] The district does not welcome simple assembly and processing operations and hopes in the long term to concentrate on high-technology enterprises.[28] In addition, because of the strategic location of the district, district planners expect to play an important role in China's offshore oil development programme.[29] The Chiwan Bay area adjacent to the district is under development by the Ministry of Petroleum Industry as a rear supply base to support oil exploration activities in the South China Sea.[30]

The other districts in the Shenzhen SEZ include the Shangbu district and the Luohu commercial area, which are both located in the middle section of the zone, a tourist district in the eastern sector, and a residential district near the Shenzhen Reservoir. The Shangbu district is being developed as an industrial area focusing on electronics, textiles, and other light industries and is the location of the American Pepsi Cola bottling plant, as well as numerous small assembly and processing operations.[31] The Luohu commercial area is being planned as the business centre for the zone.[32] Property development projects in the eastern sector are being geared mainly to the overseas Chinese and Hong Kong and Macau Chinese markets and consist largely of residential construction.[33] Tourist development projects range from co-operative ventures with Hong Kong tourist agencies for transport and package tours to the zone's scenic areas to larger projects, such as the proposed development by a Swiss company of a large tourist complex and the construction of a Holiday Inn.[34]

Shenzhen recently has concentrated more of its efforts on industrial projects, signing contracts with foreign investors for such major works as an aluminium manufacturing plant and a lubricant factory.[35] It has also sought to solve some of its energy needs by contracting for the construction of a coal-fired power plant at Shajiao.[36]

The Zhuhai Special Economic Zone, located across the border from the Portuguese enclave of Macau, currently occupies a total of 15.16 square kilometres.[37] The zone has been divided by planners into six sectors:

(a) Gongbei, for administration, culture, finance, and commerce;
(b) Xiawan, for the production of materials for the building industry;
(c) Beiling, for light industries including textiles and electronics;
(d) Shihuashan, as a distribution centre and one of the bases for oil exploration in Nanhai;
(e) Jida, for tourism and commerce;
(f) Yinkeng (Silver Valley), a tourist and recreational centre with superior residential quarters.[38]

After concentrating initially on the development of tourism, Zhuhai in recent years has sought to focus investment on industrial projects.[39] Foreign investment in the zone between 1981 and October 1984 totalled US$190 million. Almost half of the projects were in the industrial sector, with the remainder being tourism, commercial, and real estate projects. The zone has one heliport which can accommodate thirty helicopters, a multi-purpose deep-water port at Jiuzhou, and an adjoining oil-supply base to service the nearby offshore oil exploration.[40] The Zhuhai zone is the smallest of all the SEZs though there is talk of expanding it when all the available land has been utilized.[41]

The Shantou Special Economic Zone is the least developed of the SEZs.[42] Located along the north-east coast of Guangdong province, the zone suffers from a poor road system and the absence of a rail link with other parts of China.[43] In 1985, the Chinese government decided to expand the zone from its original 1.6 square kilometres to the current 52.6 square kilometres. Under this expansion plan, Shantou was divided into two major areas, the Longhu area with 22.6 square kilometres, and the Guangao peninsula area of thirty square kilometres. The latter is the location for a large oil refinery with an annual capacity of ten million tons of crude oil, as well as a supply base for oil exploration in the South China Sea.[44]

The fourth SEZ, Xiamen, is located on the coast in Fujian province. It began with an area of 2.5 square kilometres situated in the Huli district of Xiamen municipality, but in March 1984 the Xiamen SEZ was extended to the whole of Xiamen Island.[45] The island has an area of 124 square kilometres, making the Xiamen zone the largest SEZ after Shenzhen.[46]

The Jiangtou district, in the eastern part of the island, supplements the Huli district as an area for industrial development. High-rise buildings and living quarters are planned for Yuandang New Town, which is near Yuandang Harbour. There are also plans for four tourist resorts.[47]

Xiamen has developed at a steady pace, although without much of the fanfare associated with Shenzhen. Apart from attracting substantial investments from several major multinational corporations, Xiamen boasts the first regional aviation company and the first China-based joint venture bank with Chinese and foreign investors. Between 1980 and 1985, 296 investment contracts were signed in Xiamen, bringing in direct foreign investment of US$660 million. The area offers international air links, four 50,000 d.w.t. berths at Dongdu pier, good but overburdened rail connections, and international direct dialling to the United States, Japan, and Hong Kong. There is, however, a lack of well-constructed roads for transporting goods inland. Up to now most of the infrastructure development has taken place in the Huli district. It will be some time before the whole of Xiamen Island can offer equally good facilities to investors.[48]

Since the establishment of the SEZs investment has proceeded at a rapid pace. From 1980 to the end of 1985, the zones have used US$1.28 billion of foreign capital in their development, an amount which accounts for about 20 per cent of the total foreign investment in China.[49]

One of the major characteristics of foreign investment in China has been the predominance of investments from Hong Kong and Macau, which account for 80 per cent of total direct investment.[50] This phenomenon is particularly evident in the SEZs, leading some observers to remark that economic activity in the zones has become to a large extent a 'family affair'.[51]

Largely because of its size, its comparatively well-developed infrastructure, and its proximity to Hong Kong, Shenzhen has succeeded in capturing the lion's share of investment in the SEZs so far. By the end of 1984, more than 3,000 agreements had been signed with foreign investors committing HK$15 billion (US$1.9 billion). In contrast to earlier years, when more than half of the total investment projects involved light industrial and small-scale processing and assembly operations, the zone is now attracting more and more larger-scale industrial investments.[52]

While the other zones are beginning to intensify their attempts to attract investment, Shenzhen has unveiled a detailed long-range development plan which calls for exports to reach US$5.2 billion per annum by 1990,[53] and annual industrial output to reach US$7.1 billion by the year 2000.[54] The draft plan, announced in September 1982, outlines a number of development projects in the areas of light industry, agriculture, tourism, and transportation, and anticipates that before the end of the century foreign investment in these projects will exceed US$7.2 billion.[55] Under the plan, it is expected that by the year 2000 there will be 1,500 enterprises employing more than 200,000 workers, but at the end of 1985 Shenzhen's population had already reached 400,000 and the zone had more than 750 industrial enterprises.[56]

B. The 1980 Guangdong SEZ Regulations

The basic regulatory framework for investment and other economic activity in the Guangdong SEZs is established by the Regulations on Special Economic Zones in Guangdong Province (hereafter cited as the SEZ Regulations).[57] Adopted by the Fifteenth Session of the Standing Committee of the Fifth National People's Congress on 26 August 1980,[58] the SEZ Regulations are the first piece of legislation promulgated specifically to govern business in the special zones. Consisting of only 26 brief articles, the law is none the less ambitious in scope. Apart from providing for the creation of the Guangdong SEZs, it establishes the administrative structure for managing and co-ordinating economic activity in the zones and sets forth the basic preferential terms offered to investors there.

A similar but less detailed set of measures has been adopted for the Xiamen SEZ,[59] though the formulation of the legal framework for this zone only really began in July 1984 when the Eighth Session of the Standing Committee of the Sixth People's Congress of Fujian Province adopted five regulations for the zone governing the registration of enterprises, land use, labour management, the import of technology, and association with inland parts of China.[60] These regulations are discussed in detail in Section C of Part I of this chapter.

At the outset it is important to note that neither the SEZ Regulations nor the Xiamen measures purport to establish a legal regime for the special zones which is separate and distinct from China's national legal system. The SEZ Regulations state that '[e]nterprises and individuals in the Special Zones must abide by the laws, decrees and relevant regulations of the People's Republic of China'.[61] The same article goes on to state that '[w]here specific stipulations are provided herein, such specific stipulations shall be implemented in accordance with these Regulations'.[62] Based on these provisions, national laws remain applicable in the zones at least to the extent that they have not been superseded, in whole or in part, by specific provisions contained in the SEZ Regulations.

i. Administrative Organization

The SEZ Regulations provide for the establishment of three different organizations, each of which plays a role in administering the zones. The most important of these is the Administrative Committee of the Special Economic Zones of Guangdong Province (referred to hereafter as the ADCOM). The basic function of the ADCOM is 'to carry out unified management of the special zones on behalf of the Guangdong Provincial People's Government'.[63] To this end, the SEZ Regulations grant to the ADCOM a wide range of responsibilities and powers. These include the drawing up and implementation of development plans for the SEZs; the approval of investment projects in the zones; control over matters relating to the registration of business enterprises and the allocation of land in the zones; the co-ordination of relations among taxation, customs, post and telecommunications, banking, and other organizations in the SEZs; the supply of workers and staff members needed by enterprises established in the zones; the operation of educational, cultural, health, and other public welfare facilities; and the maintenance of 'law and order' in the zones.[64] In addition to the foregoing, the ADCOM is responsible for the development of the local infrastructure, including land-levelling projects and the provision of public utilities.[65] The SEZ Regulations provide that 'when necessary' the ADCOM may utilize foreign investment to 'participate' in the development of such projects.[66]

In addition to the ADCOM, the SEZ Regulations provide for the establishment of a separate organization charged with developing and co-ordinating local investment activity. This organization, the Development Company for the Special Economic Zones in Guangdong Province (referred to hereafter as the Development Company), provides business facilitation services for foreign investors and is empowered to raise funds, engage in trust and investment activities, set up enterprises either independently or in co-operation with foreign investors, and act as agent on behalf of foreign investors in connection with the purchase of commodities from or the sale of commodities to Chinese entities outside the zones.[67]

Finally, the SEZ Regulations also provide for the establishment in each of the zones of a local advisory committee comprised of 'experts in China and abroad and concerned individuals who are enthusiastic about China's modernization programme'.[68] These committees serve as consultative bodies to the ADCOM and the Development Company but have no administrative powers themselves.[69]

The administrative organization established by the SEZ Regulations has been generally well received by investors in the zones, who reportedly encounter fewer bureaucratic entanglements than do investors engaged in projects elsewhere in China.[70] None the less, there are indications that administrative authority has become increasingly diffused as the number of local administrative agencies has grown. As a result, investors in the zones are often unsure of where the final administrative authority in a number of crucial areas actually rests. The problem has its genesis in the various supplementary regulations adopted subsequent to the SEZ Regulations which delegate to local agencies certain responsibilities which the SEZ Regulations had entrusted to the ADCOM. For example, under the SEZ Business Registration Regulations, registration is to be handled by the local administrative bureaux of industry and commerce.[71] The Shenzhen Land Regulations provide that municipal authorities shall issue land-use certificates and allot land within the zone to investors there.[72] Finally, the SEZ Labour and Wage Regulations grant to municipal labour bureaux in each of the zones responsibility over labour issues.[73] In each of these cases an apparent conflict exists with the provisions contained in the SEZ Regulations.[74] However, no attempts have yet been made to clarify whether the local agencies named in the supplementary regulations are to act in conjunction with, under the supervision of, or independent of the ADCOM.

Another related issue which investors will wish to see clarified concerns the question of what approval is required for SEZ investment projects. Under the SEZ Regulations, the ADCOM is vested with the power to 'examine and approve' investment projects in the zones.[75] Although this provision was intended to streamline approval procedures by providing for a single approval-granting agency, it appears that, at least in practice, the ADCOM's approval powers are not exclusive. For example, the SEZ Business Registration Regulations imply that the municipal government in each of the zones, in addition to the ADCOM, has the power to give approval.[76] Moreover, press reports indicate that the State Council's Office of SEZ Affairs in Beijing also has approval power over projects in the zones.[77] Although SEZ officials indicate that 'in most cases' only ADCOM approval is necessary,[78] questions remain as to when municipal-level approval is by itself sufficient and when central government approval is mandatory.

ii. The Scope and Forms of Investment

The SEZ Regulations encourage investment in the zones by 'foreign citizens, overseas Chinese, compatriots in Hong Kong and Macao and their companies and enterprises'.[79] There is special encouragement for overseas Chinese to invest in the SEZs. In particular, the Shenzhen authorities have prescribed measures which confer special preferential treatment on investment in the zone's 'overseas Chinese city'.[80] The preferential treatments are more favourable than those applicable to foreign investors generally in the SEZs. Areas affected include import and export taxes, income taxes, land-use fees, management, domestic sales, and entry and exit formalities. The State Council also enacted measures in 1983 to confer special preferential treatment on compatriots from Taiwan who invest in the SEZs.[81] The preferential treatments include (a) an income tax holiday for the first four profit-making years and a 50 per cent reduction in income taxes in the ensuing five years, where the investment is for a term of ten years or more; (b) the right to sell on the domestic market 30 per cent of the products of the enterprise; and (c) exemption from land-use fees for the first five years. The measures also apply to investments on Hainan Island.

The SEZ Regulations provide a wide scope for investment, including 'industry, agriculture, animal husbandry, fish breeding and poultry farming, tourism, housing and construction, research and manufacture involving high technologies and techniques', as well as 'other trades of common interest to investors and the Chinese side'.[82]

Regarding the permissible forms of investment in the zones, the SEZ Regulations provide that projects may be undertaken by foreign investors 'with their own investment'[83] or 'by means of joint ventures with Chinese investment'.[84] The latter category is intended to include both equity and 'co-operative' or 'contractual' joint ventures.[85] In the case of equity joint ventures the law contains no provisions regarding minimum investment shares. Under China's national Joint Venture Law,[86] the share of foreign participants in equity joint ventures should 'in general not be less than twenty-five (25) per cent' of the total equity of the venture.[87] In the absence of specific language regarding this issue in the SEZ Regulations, the same rule presumably applies to equity joint ventures established in the zones. The law's provision that investors may 'open factories with their own investment'[88] and 'independently operate their own enterprises'[89] has been particularly attractive to foreign business interests.[90] Until mid-1984, the sole proprietorship investment pattern had not been permitted outside the SEZs.[91]

iii. Enterprise Operations
The SEZ Regulations contain several brief provisions regarding the operations of zone enterprises. Investors 'wishing to open factories or set up various economic enterprises' in the SEZs are required to register and obtain a land-use certificate.[92] Bank accounts are to be opened with the Bank of China branch in the SEZs or with 'other banks set up with China's approval' in the zones.[93] A similar provision relating to insurance for SEZ enterprises is also included.[94] Finally, upon termination of operations, an SEZ enterprise is required to 'report the reasons for termination' to the ADCOM and thereafter 'go through the procedures for termination and clear all debts'.[95] After these procedures have been completed, 'the assets of the enterprise may be transferred and its funds may be remitted out of China'.[96] Many of these provisions are dealt with in greater detail in subsequent SEZ legislation and regulatory policies described in Section C of Part I of this chapter.

iv. Foreign Exchange
The SEZ Regulations provide that the 'lawful profits' of investors, as well as the wages and other 'legitimate income' of non-Chinese SEZ personnel, after payment of income tax, may be remitted out of China 'in accordance with the stipulations of the foreign exchange control measures of the Special Zones'.[97] At the time of writing, comprehensive foreign exchange rules formulated specifically for the SEZs have yet to be announced. In the interim, the national foreign exchange control regulations are being applied in the zones.[98]

On 16 November 1985, the Shenzhen government promulgated the Provisional Measures of the Shenzhen Special Economic Zone on Foreign Exchange Adjustment. The objective of these measures is to facilitate currency conversion of *renminbi* and foreign currency funds held by enterprises in the zone in accordance with a floating rate of exchange, and in the process to curb the black market in currency transactions.[99] The concept would obviously be welcomed by many foreign investors who have or expect to have excess *renminbi* funds from their projects in China. A foreign exchange adjustment centre is being established to implement the measures on a trial basis.

The only other loosening in the national foreign exchange regulations which has occurred to date pertains to restrictions imposed on the possession of foreign exchange by Chinese residents in the SEZs. Workers in some SEZ enterprises are being permitted to receive a certain percentage of their wages in Hong Kong dollars or foreign exchange certificates.[100] In addition, under rules issued by the Bank of China, bank branches in Shenzhen and Zhuhai may accept Hong Kong dollar deposits from residents in the zones.[101] Funds may be withdrawn from such accounts in *renminbi*, foreign exchange certificates, or Hong Kong dollars.[102]

Debate has raged over the last few years on whether or not the SEZs should have their own currency.[103] At present in Shenzhen there are three currencies in circulation: *renminbi*, foreign exchange certificates, and Hong Kong dollars. Prices of goods and services vary in accordance with the type of currency offered for payment. The currency most in demand is Hong Kong dollars. Customers who are willing to make payment in this currency receive the best price. Proponents of the SEZ currency argue that these three currencies can be replaced by the one SEZ currency and thus eliminate the rampant trading in currencies. In April 1986, Qian Jiaju, a member of the Standing Committee of the China Political Consultative Conference, put paid to these rumours by announcing that the government has decided for the time being not to issue an SEZ currency.[104] There is a fear that the appearance of another currency will simply exacerbate the existing disorder in Shenzhen, including the buying and selling of currencies on the black market. Since the SEZ currency is intended to be one that is freely convertible into foreign exchange, some of these problems can be expected to remain if the currency is introduced. However, Qian did not deny that such a currency could come into use when the SEZs become a foreign exchange earner for the country.[105]

v. Production, Marketing, and Customs
The SEZ Regulations provide special encouragement for the use of Chinese 'machinery and equipment, raw and other materials and other goods' in production activities in the zones.[106] Under the regulations, enterprises that purchase production inputs made in China will be granted 'preferential' prices based on the rates that are charged for similar commodities bound for export from China, provided that settlement for such purchases is made in foreign exchange.[107] Since Chinese export prices are highly subsidized, SEZ enterprises will benefit from lower-cost production inputs by purchasing required items from Chinese suppliers.

In the event that SEZ investors choose to import production inputs, rather than purchase them domestically, the SEZ Regulations provide for favourable customs treatment upon entry. The law provides that imported 'machinery, equipment, spare parts, fittings, raw and other materials, transport vehicles and other materials required for production' shall be exempt from 'import taxes' provided they are 'necessary'.[108] Similar preferential treatment may also be granted to 'necessary' consumer goods imported for use by the personnel of SEZ enterprises.[109] Under Article 13, 'articles for daily use' may be exempt from import taxes, or subject to full or reduced duties, 'depending on the particular circumstances of the case'.

According to Chinese sources, 'import taxes' in this context has been interpreted to include both import duties and the Consolidated Industrial and Commercial Tax, a cascading excise tax imposed at various stages of production which is also applicable to the import of goods.[110] Whether an exemption from import duties and the consolidated tax is granted will presumably be left to the discretion of the Customs authorities. Under informal policy guidelines announced in August 1981, all imports into the zones must be approved in accordance with China's import licence regulations so that, theoretically at least, the preferential treatment provided under the SEZ Regulations could be denied.[111] In practice, however, this has not yet proved to be a problem with respect to production inputs, although a number of investors have continued to voice complaints about delays in obtaining customs clearance, especially in Shenzhen.

The basic philosophy which underlies the provisions granting preferential customs treatment to imports is that enterprises in the zones should be primarily export-oriented. Article 9 of the SEZ Regulations provides that the products of SEZ enterprises 'shall be sold in the international market' and permits domestic sales only after an approval has been obtained from the ADCOM.[112] According to one source, such approval must be applied for at the same time as the investment contract is submitted for approval.[113] The granting of the application is largely dependent on whether the SEZ authorities view the product as constituting a valuable import substitute. In the event that domestic sales are permitted, the SEZ Regulations provide that a 'supplementary payment' of customs duties and the consolidated tax must be made with respect to production inputs which had previously been allowed into the zones tax free.[114] Such a payment, of course, largely erases the customs benefits provided to investors in the SEZs.

Some of the rules relating to customs discussed above have been either modified or clarified by a set of rules promulgated by the Customs General Administration of China in March 1986. A discussion of these rules is contained in Section C of Part I of this chapter.

vi. Taxation

The SEZ Regulations also contain provisions relating to the tax treatment of enterprises established in the zones. Such treatment is considerably more favourable than that which is provided for under tax rules applicable in China generally.

Under China's national legislation, equity joint ventures are subject to a 30 per cent income tax on net profits.[115] In addition, such ventures must also pay a local income tax equal to 10 per cent of the amount of national income tax assessed.[116] In the case of 'co-operative' and 'co-production ventures' the net profits of the foreign party are subject to taxation at progressive rates, ranging from 20 to 40 per cent, under the Foreign Enterprise Income Tax Law (FEITL).[117] The FEITL also provides for the payment of a local income tax of 10 per cent, calculated on the basis of taxable income.[118] Under Article 14 of the SEZ Regulations, the tax rate for 'enterprises' in the SEZs is set at 15 per cent. According to SEZ officials, the term 'enterprises' includes not only equity joint ventures but also wholly owned foreign ventures and 'co-operative' or 'co-production' ventures.[119] No local income tax is levied in the zones, although such tax is levied elsewhere in China.[120]

In addition to offering a comparatively low rate of taxation, the SEZ

Regulations promise investors a number of other tax incentives. For example, under Article 16 of the SEZ Regulations, enterprises that reinvest their profits in the zones for five years or more may be eligible for a reduction of or exemption from income tax on such reinvested profits. Article 14 of the law promises 'special preferential treatment' to enterprises that have been set up within two years of the date of promulgation of the SEZ Regulations, enterprises with an investment of US$5 million or more, and enterprises involving 'higher technologies' or 'a longer financing cycle'.[121]

The SEZ Regulations fail to address specifically a number of important issues related to the taxation of enterprises and individuals in the zones. For example, the law is silent as to the method for computation of taxable income, as well as payment deadlines and procedures. At the moment, such matters are apparently being handled in accordance with the provisions in China's national tax legislation. However, other tax issues raised by the SEZ Regulations have been clarified by regulations promulgated by the State Council in November 1984, and are discussed in Section C of Part I of this chapter.

vii. Labour Management

The SEZ Regulations also contain special provisions relating to labour management in the zones. The law provides that local employees of SEZ enterprises may be recruited 'through the introduction of local labour service companies' established in each of the zones or by investors themselves.[122] If investors recruit workers independently they must obtain the prior consent of the ADCOM.[123] Regardless of the method of recruitment, workers may be 'tested and selected by the enterprise'.[124] The terms of employment—including wage levels, bonuses, labour insurance, and other matters—are to be stipulated in labour contracts entered into between the enterprise and the individual worker 'in accordance with regulations' set by the ADCOM.[125] Workers may be dismissed or may resign of their own accord 'in accordance with the provisions contained in the labour contract'.[126]

viii. Other Incentives

Finally, other types of preferential treatment for investors in the zones are also promised in the SEZ Regulations. For example, 'simplified entry and exit procedures' are promised 'for the convenience of foreign personnel, overseas Chinese and Hong Kong and Macao compatriots going in and out of the Special Zones'.[127] Land in the zones is provided to investors 'in accordance with actual needs' and 'specific measures' are promised to address such matters as the period of land use, fees and payment procedures, and other 'preferential treatment'.[128]

C. Subsequent Legislative and Regulatory Developments
   in the SEZs

The SEZ Regulations are not intended by themselves to provide a comprehensive legal regime for the Guangdong special zones. As in much of

China's other investment legislation, in a number of areas the law provides little more than a statement of general principles and leaves the details to be filled in by supplementary regulations and implementing rules. Since the passage of the SEZ Regulations in 1980, there have been significant legislative and regulatory developments affecting all four SEZs. The most important of these developments have concerned eight issues: (a) access to and from the SEZs; (b) business registration; (c) labour management and wages for SEZ workers; (d) land use, construction, and real estate transactions; (e) taxation; (f) banking and finance; (g) accounting; and (h) contracts and technology transfers.

i. Entry and Exit

A common complaint of foreign investors in China generally has concerned the nation's cumbersome and time-consuming visa regulations. As an incentive to investors, the SEZ Regulations promised 'simplified' procedures for business men travelling to and from the SEZs. Apparently intended to fulfil this promise, the Provisional Regulations of the Special Economic Zones in Guangdong Province Governing the Entry and Exit of Personnel (hereafter cited as the Entry and Exit Regulations)[129] were adopted on 17 November 1981 at the Thirteenth Session of the Standing Committee of the Fifth People's Congress of Guangdong Province. The Entry and Exit Regulations came into force on 1 January 1982.

Consisting of only twelve articles, the Entry and Exit Regulations apply only to 'foreigners, overseas Chinese, Hong Kong and Macao compatriots and Taiwan compatriots';[130] they are expressly made inapplicable to 'Chinese cadres, staff members, workers and other personnel working in the Special Zones' who are required to follow the 'existing regulations'.[131] In Shenzhen, these 'existing regulations' were published in March 1986 in the form of Regulations for the Control of Personnel Coming and Going Between the Shenzhen Special Zone and Inland Areas (hereafter cited as the Inland Personnel Regulations).[132] The regulations came into force on 1 April 1986,[133] the date on which the Shenzhen Special Economic Zone Control Line formally came into being. This line, generally referred to as the 'second line', formally separates the Shenzhen SEZ from the rest of China. The 'first line' comprises the existing boundary between Shenzhen and Hong Kong.[134]

The purpose of introducing the 'second line' is to define more clearly the Shenzhen 'special' zone and to ensure that the zone focuses its economic development more in relation to international markets than the local Chinese market. By setting up properly enforced control points along the 'second line', the authorities hope to regulate the flow of both people and goods into and out of the zone and to clamp down on such undesirable practices as smuggling and black market activities. Once the zone is properly segregated, the authorities in Shenzhen can give full vent to the special conditions and preferential measures designed to attract foreign investors.[135]

The Inland Personnel Regulations apply to travel through the 'second line'. Their provisions call for the establishment of control points on roads,[136] walkways,[137] wharfs,[138] and railway stations.[139] Every person travelling between the Shenzhen SEZ and inland China must pass through one of these control points and must possess the requisite certificate or other 'valid documents'.[140] Persons working or residing in the zone will be issued with special certificates to permit travel into and out of the zone. Persons who originate from the inland areas will gain admittance to the zone if they have entry and exit permits. Foreigners, overseas Chinese, and compatriots of China can pass through the 'second line' by relying on their normal visas or 'home visit permits' (*hui xiang zheng*) issued by the Chinese authorities.[141] For them, the 'second line' simply imposes an additional entry-exit formality. The Customs authorities will also be present at the control points to enable people to make customs clearances.[142]

Travel through the 'first line', that is, from outside China directly to the SEZ or from the SEZ directly to foreign countries, is still governed by the Entry and Exit Regulations. Under these regulations, foreign passport holders are required to obtain visas prior to entry into the SEZs. However, foreigners and overseas Chinese who 'have set up factories or various other kinds of business' or who 'have bought residences in or live in the Special Zones' and who need to enter and leave 'on a regular basis' may apply for multiple entry and exit visas on the strength of a 'letter of proof' from the SEZ Development Company.[143] The regulations provide for a simplification of the existing entry procedures for residents of Hong Kong and Macau who travel to China holding 'home visit permits'.[144]

The Entry and Exit Regulations also provide for the issue of group visas for individuals joining tour groups from Hong Kong or Macau to the SEZs.[145] In addition, the regulations permit transport vehicles to travel between the zones and Hong Kong or Macau after obtaining approval from the relevant municipal people's government and a pass from the local public security bureau.[146] Finally, the regulations hold out the promise of a liberalization of customs procedures for personnel entering and leaving the SEZs. The regulations provide that such matters shall be handled in accordance with the 'customs regulations for the Special Zones' as opposed to the customs rules generally applicable in China.[147]

With one exception, the Entry and Exit Regulations generally have proved to be a disappointment to investors who had hoped for the promulgation of a more liberal entry/exit regime. In fact, in practical terms the regulations offer investors in the zones no greater benefits than those available to businesses in other parts of China. For example, as a result of a nation-wide liberalization of visa procedures, most business men who travel frequently to China are now eligible for multiple-entry visas, the major concession provided by the regulations. The one exception applies in relation to the visa procedures for persons travelling to Shenzhen from Hong Kong. Applicants can now obtain visas in Hong Kong on the strength of an invitation from the Chinese host organization without having the invitation first approved by the organization's supervising authority and the Shenzhen government.[148]

Another area where the Entry and Exit Regulations have not matched investors' expectations concerns the movement of transport vehicles between the zones and Hong Kong. Although Article 10 of the regulations specifically provides for such travel, the implementation of this provision has been restrictive. Under trial rules developed by the Hong Kong government in co-operation with the SEZ authorities and announced in May 1982, cross-border vehicular permits have been limited to larger enterprises with active interests in the zones as opposed to property owners and small businesses.[149] Moreover, enterprises are restricted to obtaining only one permit applicable to one specific vehicle and one specific driver.[150] If the vehicle breaks down or the driver falls ill, the enterprise can be denied access to the zone.

Finally, although the Entry and Exit Regulations promised a liberalization of customs procedures at the SEZ border, to date investors have experienced little improvement.[151] The introduction of the 'second line' and its strict control may, in time, lead to a relaxation of the controls exercised at the 'first line'.

ii. Business Registration

The SEZ Regulations impose a registration requirement on enterprises operating in the zones and specify certain procedures which are to be followed upon the termination of operations. The Provisional Regulations of the Special Economic Zones of Guangdong Province Governing the Registration of Business Enterprises (hereafter cited as the Business Registration Regulations),[152] which were adopted by the Thirteenth Session of the Standing Committee of the Fifth People's Congress of Guangdong Province on 17 November 1981 and which came into force on 1 January 1982, amplify and in some respects amend these provisions. A largely similar set of regulations was approved by the Eighth Session of the Standing Committee of the Sixth People's Congress of Fujian Province for the Xiamen SEZ on 14 July 1984.[153] In Shenzhen, the Detailed Implementing Rules of the Shenzhen Special Economic Zone Governing the Registration of Business Enterprises (hereafter cited as the Shenzhen Business Registration Rules),[154] promulgated in February 1984, provide further detailed input with respect to enterprises in that zone.

Under the Business Registration Regulations, all foreign-owned enterprises, joint ventures, and co-operative enterprises in the SEZs must register with the SEZ's 'administrative organization for industry and commerce' and obtain a 'registration certificate' or 'business licence' prior to commencing operations.[155] When applying for registration, such enterprises are required to complete a detailed application form and submit copies of (a) the 'approval documents' issued by the municipal government or the SEZ administrative committee; (b) the 'agreement, contract and articles of association signed by the parties to the enterprise, together with a list of the names of the members of the board of directors'; and (c) the certificate of registration pertaining to the investor issued by the authorities in his home country, together with evidence of the investor's creditworthiness.[156] The Business Registration Regulations also require enterprises setting up resident representative offices in the SEZs to register with the SEZ authorities, and they specify the procedures that must be followed to effect registration.[157] In Shenzhen, enterprises carrying out construction or renovation work are required by the Shenzhen Business Registration Rules to apply for the appropriate registration certificate.[158] The rules in Shenzhen also prescribe additional documents to be tendered by applicants for any of the registrations described above.[159] These rules also set out fees for registration.[160]

SEZ enterprises and representative offices are deemed to be established on the date of issue of the registration certificate.[161] Registration is normally effective for one year but may be renewed.[162] Once registered, enterprises and representative offices are required to open bank accounts with the Bank of China (or another approved bank) and register with the local tax authorities.[163]

When a registered enterprise changes any of the items appearing on the register—for example, when it changes its address, or extends the contract term or the amount of its registered capital—the enterprise must obtain approval from the municipal or SEZ administrative authorities and go through 'change of registration procedures' with the SEZ administrative organization for industry and commerce and the tax authorities.[164] Article 7 of the Shenzhen Business Registration Rules provides that when a Chinese-foreign joint venture seeks to register a change, there must be an agreement in writing signed by the joint venture parties. To effect deregistration, an enterprise must cancel its original registration with the relevant authorities and return the registration certificate or business licence.[165]

The Business Registration Regulations authorize the SEZ administrative organization for industry and commerce to 'supervise and inspect' SEZ enterprises.[166] Violators of the regulations may be 'warned, fined or ordered to shut down operations', depending on the seriousness of the offence.[167] In Shenzhen, the fines can be as high as RMB20,000.[168]

Article 2 of the Business Registration Regulations provides that the registration procedures for foreign banks will be specified in 'separate regulations'. The relevant regulations for setting up representative offices are the Provisional Regulations for the Establishment of Representative Offices in China by Overseas Chinese and Foreign Financial Institutions, issued by the People's Bank of China on 1 February 1983.[169] Under this law, foreign banks which set up 'representative offices' in the SEZs are limited to 'non-profit' activities such as liaison, consulting, and other services.[170] Regulations allowing the establishment of branch banking in the zones by foreign banks were promulgated on 2 April 1985. A discussion of these regulations is set out in subsection vi below.

iii. Labour and Wages
The SEZ Regulations contain four provisions which outline the labour management system in the zones. The Provisional Regulations of the Special Economic Zones of Guangdong Province Governing Labour and Wages for Business Enterprises (hereafter cited as the SEZ Labour and

Wage Regulations),[171] which came into effect on 1 January 1982, expand upon these provisions and treat in detail many issues which the SEZ Regulations had addressed only indirectly.

Although the scope of the SEZ Labour and Wage Regulations includes foreign-owned enterprises and co-operative enterprises as well as equity joint ventures in the SEZs,[172] it is useful to consider the law's provisions alongside those contained in China's national legislation on labour management for joint ventures.[173] By comparison with the national labour rules, the SEZ Labour and Wage Regulations appear to provide for more favourable and flexible treatment of labour issues.

Under both the national joint venture labour rules and the SEZ Labour and Wage Regulations, the basic terms for the employment of workers are to be specified in and governed by 'labour contracts'.[174] The national rules provide that, except in the case of small-scale ventures, the contract is to be signed between the enterprise and the labour union organization comprising all Chinese workers employed by the enterprise.[175] The position in the Guangdong SEZs is a little unclear. The SEZ Labour and Wage Regulations provide that labour contracts shall be entered into between the enterprise and each individual staff member and worker.[176] If this were the case, enterprises in the SEZs would have greater flexibility in determining the terms of employment for different workers as well as more direct control over individual employees. Yet the Regulations of the Special Economic Zones in Guangdong Province on Labour Unions in Enterprises (hereafter cited as the SEZ Union Regulations)[177] provide that labour unions in enterprises are to assist workers in signing individual labour contracts with the enterprises or are to sign collective labour contracts with the enterprises on behalf of workers.[178] The implication is that workers can either individually sign contracts with the enterprise or collectively sign one contract with the enterprise.

Differences also appear in the provisions relating to the hiring of workers. While both the national rules and the SEZ Labour and Wage Regulations provide that workers may be hired either upon the recommendation of local labour departments or by the enterprise itself,[179] the SEZ rules appear to provide investors with greater flexibility with respect to workers provided by Chinese units. Under the SEZ Labour and Wage Regulations, such workers may be hired on a probationary basis of from three to six months, thereby enabling enterprises to test their skills before a final employment decision is made.[180] In addition, the SEZ Labour and Wage Regulations contain a specific provision permitting the employment of non-Chinese citizens by SEZ enterprises.[181] The terms and conditions of employment of such personnel are to be determined by the enterprise itself.

Another difference between the national and the SEZ labour rules relates to the provisions for the payment of wages and other benefits for workers. Under the national regulations, wage levels for workers in joint venture enterprises are to be set at 120–150 per cent of the wages paid to workers in state-owned enterprises engaged in the same type of business and in the same locality as the joint venture.[182] In addition, the regulations require that labour insurance, medical expenses, and other kinds of government subsidies for workers shall be paid by the joint venture 'in accordance with the standards prevailing in state-owned enterprises'.[183] By contrast, the SEZ Labour and Wage Regulations appear to provide greater flexibility to investors. According to Article 7, labour service fees in the zones are not tied to the wage levels prevailing in state-owned enterprises and are presumably subject to negotiations; the actual amounts are to be determined 'at the time the labour contract is signed according to the type of enterprise and the kind of work'.[184] In addition, the enterprise is free to choose the form of wages—hourly, weekly, or piece-work—as well as the system to be adopted regarding bonuses and employee subsidies.[185]

Unlike the national labour rules the SEZ Labour and Wage Regulations contain specific rules for the allocation of labour service fees and related matters. Under the regulations, 70 per cent of the total amount of labour service fees is to be paid directly to the employee as wages; 5 per cent is to be retained by the enterprise for the cost of employee benefits; and 25 per cent is to be paid to the state for social labour insurance and employee subsidies.[186] The SEZ Labour and Wage Regulations also address the issue of wage increases in zone enterprises and provide that wages are to be increased on an annual basis by 5–15 per cent, the actual amount of the increase depending on 'the degree of technical and work proficiency' of the employee.[187] Finally, the SEZ rules also contain stipulations regarding the work schedule for enterprise employees. In general, SEZ enterprises are to operate on the basis of a six-day working week and an eight-hour day, with additional pay for overtime work.[188] In addition, the rules provide that SEZ enterprises are required to follow the system of legal holidays and leave stipulated by the Chinese state.[189]

The SEZ Labour and Wage Regulations also contain specific provisions dealing with two areas of special concern to investors—the resignation and discharge of enterprise employees. Like the national labour rules, the SEZ Labour and Wage Regulations provide that workers shall have the right to resign from an enterprise.[190] The SEZ rules go further than the national legislation, however, by addressing a matter which was left unresolved in the national labour rules, namely that of how to deal with the problem of workers who have been assigned to a venture merely to acquire free training and who, at the termination of their training period, resign from the enterprise to return—fully trained—to their original units. Under the SEZ Labour and Wage Regulations, if a worker has benefited from training of more than three months he may not ordinarily resign until the expiration of one year from the date of the completion of the training programme.[191] Otherwise, the worker is obliged to compensate the enterprise for the cost of his training.[192]

On the matter of dismissal of enterprise workers, the SEZ rules follow closely the language found in the national labour legislation. Under the SEZ Labour and Wage Regulations, enterprises enjoy the right to dismiss employees 'who have become redundant as a result of changes in production and technical conditions, [or] who fail to meet the requirements of the enterprises'.[193]

However, dismissal is only permitted if the affected worker, after training, cannot be transferred within the enterprise to other types of work.[194] Unlike the national labour rules, the SEZ Labour and Wage Regulations require SEZ enterprises to provide severance pay to dismissed employees, with the amount of each payment being determined on the basis of the length of employment.[195] With respect to disciplinary measures, the SEZ rules grant enterprises the right to impose warnings, wage reduction, and other measures, in addition to the discharge of workers.[196] Workers who have been disciplined or dismissed by enterprises may appeal to the local labour bureau or institute a suit in the people's court.[197]

Notwithstanding the apparent flexibility granted by the SEZ Labour and Wage Regulations to SEZ enterprises in labour and management matters, the rights of SEZ enterprises in these matters are also subject to control by the SEZ Union Regulations. Thus, dismissal of a union member from the enterprise requires the consent of the superior labour union organization.[198] In Zhuhai, for instance, a worker who is a member of the labour union in an enterprise cannot be dismissed from that enterprise unless the Labour Union Federation of Zhuhai city has given its consent.[199]

According to Article 4 of the SEZ Union Regulations, staff and workers of any enterprise in which there is capital contribution from a foreigner or an overseas Chinese compatriot have the right to establish a labour union for that enterprise. All staff and workers of an enterprise, including foreign and overseas Chinese staff, can join the union.[200] Apart from protecting the legitimate interests of staff and workers and supervising the observance by the enterprise of relevant labour laws and regulations, the union's responsibilities include assisting with staff training and educating the staff on matters of discipline.[201]

In enterprises that have a large number of workers, the union can appoint full-time officials who should then be released from production duties. These officials will receive their wages from the labour union fund, but their other working benefits are to be the same as those of other workers and should be provided by the enterprise.[202] Representatives of unions are also permitted to attend meetings of boards of directors of enterprises held to discuss labour issues and important matters such as the development plans and production and operational activities of enterprises. Such representatives are not entitled to vote at such meetings.[203]

In Xiamen, the Xiamen Labour Management Regulations[204] contain some innovative provisions and generally impose a stricter system for labour and wage management than regulations in other SEZs. Overtime work is limited to twelve hours a week. Overtime pay is not to be less than 150 per cent of normal wages. The minimum overtime pay for work performed on holidays is increased to 200 per cent of wages.[205] The regulations also specify the rates for sick leave pay.[206] An SEZ enterprise may dismiss its workers in accordance with its labour contracts, but in the case of dismissals, the dismissed worker is to be paid compensation based on his period of service with the enterprise.[207] This requirement to pay compensation applies even when the worker is discharged upon the expiration of the labour contract.[208] Such a measure imposes an additional burden on the enterprise, since the enterprise is already required each month to pay 25 per cent of its total monthly wages to a social labour insurance fund to be used for such purposes as providing pensions for retired or dismissed employees.[209] A trained employee who works for less than two years with the enterprise may be asked to repay some of his training expenses.[210]

Despite the relatively detailed regulations on labour and wages in the SEZs, one critical issue relates to the manner in which the local SEZ labour bureaux will administer and interpret the rules. Under the regulations, these organizations must approve all labour contracts entered into between enterprises and workers and are required to give their consent if an enterprise chooses to hire workers on its own.[211] In addition, local labour bureaux must also approve the wage levels for workers and are empowered to 'examine' decisions taken by enterprises to dismiss employees or impose other disciplinary measures.[212] As a result of the wide-ranging powers granted to the local labour bureaux, the attitudes and policies adopted by these units will in large measure determine whether or not investors actually receive the benefits provided by the regulations.[213]

Although the SEZ labour rules are relatively new, it appears that investors have on the whole been generally satisfied with their implementation thus far. However, conditions in the zones have tended to dampen the practical effect of some of the more attractive provisions contained in the rules. For example, although many enterprises would like to recruit their own workers the task has proved to be a difficult one, largely because there is no readily available pool of workers in the zones from which to choose.[214] Given the difficulties imposed by China's household registration system in bringing in workers from outside the zones, most investors have had little alternative but to accept workers supplied to them by the labour bureaux. In addition, enterprises which have attempted to dismiss workers have encountered resistance from SEZ authorities.[215] Even in circumstances where a labour bureau has agreed that dismissal may be justified, it has little incentive to approve the dismissal as the bureau must then fix alternative employment for the worker and continue to pay the worker's wages until such employment is found.[216]

iv. Land Use, Urban Construction, and Real Estate Transactions
The SEZ regulations provide that land in the zones will be supplied to investors 'in accordance with actual needs' and promise that 'separate stipulations' will be formulated to provide 'preferential treatment' to investors with respect to the period of land use, land-use fees, and payment methods. As of June 1986 only the Shenzhen and Xiamen SEZs have issued regulations intended to fulfil this promise. The other two zones— Shantou and Zhuhai—are expected to issue their own regulations in the

future.[217] However, until such rules are announced, it is likely that these zones will follow the general outlines of land-use policy established by the other two SEZs.

Shenzhen has the most detailed regulations on land use. Under the Provisional Regulations Governing Land in the Shenzhen Special Economic Zone (hereafter cited as the Shenzhen Land Regulations),[218] land rights granted to investors are rights of usage only and not of ownership, and all forms of land sales are strictly prohibited.[219] Investors requiring the use of land in the zone must submit an application to the municipal planning department.[220] Once the application has been approved, the investor is required to make arrangements for payment of the land-use fee, after which the land area will be demarcated and a 'Land-use Certificate' will be issued.[221] Within six months from the date of the certificate, the investor must submit the 'overall design drawing' and 'construction and production plans' relating to the project to the municipal authorities; within nine months from such date ground-breaking must occur.[222] In the event that these deadlines are not met, the regulations provide that the Land-use Certificate may be revoked and any fees paid prior to such date will not be refunded.[223] Delays in the production schedule of the project occurring after ground-breaking may also result in revocation of the Land-use Certificate, unless the delay can be justified to the municipal authorities and they agree to an extension of the term for project completion.[224] Finally, upon completion, the project must be inspected and approved by 'the responsible authorities' before operations may commence.[225]

The Shenzhen Land Regulations provide that the duration of land leases will differ depending on the nature of the project and 'actual needs'.[226] Nevertheless, the law does contain specific provisions that specify the maximum permissible duration for land leases. For example, land leases for industrial and tourist enterprises may be granted for up to thirty years; for agriculture-related and commercial enterprises (including restaurants) the limit is twenty years; and for marketable housing projects and educational, scientific, or medical enterprises the limit is fifty years.[227]

The regulations also spell out the standards that will be applied in calculating land-use fees, and permit adjustments to be made once every three years from the date of promulgation of the regulations. Increases are not to exceed 30 per cent of the then-prevailing rates.[228] Fees may be paid in one lump-sum payment or on an instalment basis.[229] If they are paid by instalment, interest will be charged at a rate of 8 per cent per annum unless the entire amount is paid within two years in which case no interest will be charged.[230]

Since the enactment of the Shenzhen Land Regulations in 1981, two supplementary regulations have been promulgated governing land-use fees. Pursuant to the Measures of the Shenzhen Special Economic Zone Concerning the Adjustment of Land Use Fees and Preferential Treatment for the Reduction of and Exemption From Land Use Fees (hereafter cited as the Shenzhen Land Use Fee Adjustment Measures),[231] land-use fee rates prescribed in the Shenzhen Land Regulations were replaced by a new regime of fees. Land in the Shenzhen SEZ was divided into three categories, with a range of fees set for each type of land use in each category of districts. The highest range of fees applies to land in Category I, which includes the Luohu, Shangbu, and Shatoujiao Districts. Next follows land in Category II, which includes the Shekou and Shahe Industrial Districts. Category III comprises all areas outside the Category I and Category II districts, and enjoys the lowest range of land-use fees.[232]

In each category of districts, land use is divided into seven possible types: (a) industrial use and warehouses, (b) commercial use, guest-houses, and restaurants, (c) commercial residential use and hostels, (d) tourism, (e) open-air amusement areas, (f) open-air dumps, parking lots, and quarries, and (g) horticultural use, animal husbandry, and aquatic breeding.[233] Land use of types (e), (f), and (g) attracts the lowest rates of land-use fees. Type (b) land use is subject to the highest rates, being RMB49–100 per square metre per year for land in Category I districts.[234] Type (a) land use in Category I districts is charged a fee of RMB5–12 per square metre per year.[235]

On 22 November 1985, the Shenzhen Special Economic Zone Land Use Fee Implementing Measures (hereafter cited as the Shenzhen Land Use Fee Implementing Measures)[236] were promulgated. These measures confirmed that land-use fees were to be set in accordance with the natural conditions of the relevant district and the type of use of land by the relevant project.[237] The measures also prescribed the types of land-use fees to be paid in connection with various specific activities, such as banking, insurance, commercial servicing, and post and telecommunications.[238] According to the Shenzhen Land Use Fee Implementing Measures, the tax authorities are charged with the responsibility of collecting land-use fees,[239] approving reduction of or exemption from land-use fees,[240] and checking on tax payment and land use by persons paying land-use fees.[241] Fees must be paid with foreign exchange certificates. If an enterprise has difficulty in doing so, it can apply for approval to pay in *renminbi*.[242] A penalty of 0.5 per cent is payable for each day that any fee is overdue in payment.[243]

Reduction of or exemption from land-use fees is available in any one of ten circumstances described in Article 10 of the Shenzhen Land Use Fee Implementing Measures. Qualifying circumstances include use of land for development, use of land for basic construction, use of land reclaimed from the sea, use of land for projects with relatively more advanced technology, use of land by enterprises which export at least 50 per cent of their production, and difficulty in paying fees due to *force majeure* or other special circumstances.

The situations in which reductions of or exemptions from land-use fees can be obtained are given in far greater detail and scope in the Shenzhen Land Use Fee Implementing Measures than in the preceding regulations and measures promulgated by the Shenzhen authorities, so they must be taken to have prevailing force. Unfortunately, it is not clear whether this prevailing force is to apply in all respects. In Article 8 of the Shenzhen Land Use Fee Implementing Measures, for instance, it is stated that land-use fees can be paid in one lump sum or seasonally, but there is no mention of whether interest is payable when fees are paid by instalments, as is provided in the Shenzhen Land Regulations.[244]

The Xiamen regulations on land use differ from the Guangdong regulations in some respects.[245] Xiamen offers a use period of forty years for land used for industrial projects.[246] This is ten years more than the period prescribed for the Shenzhen SEZ.[247] During the approved project construction period, a discount of 50 per cent of the land-use fee is granted.[248] Unspecified preferential terms are available if land-use fees for three years are paid in advance in one lump sum.[249] Investors who wish to reserve land for future development may do so by paying 50 per cent of the prescribed land-use fee. The maximum reservation period is two years. If investors then proceed to use the land before the reservation period expires, payment of the first year's land-use fee is exempted.[250]

Investors attracted to the SEZs by promises of 'cheap land' should proceed cautiously. Certainly, the basic land fees in the SEZs are cheaper than prevailing rates in Hong Kong.[251] Moreover, they compare favourably with rates charged in similar 'special' zones in other parts of the world. For example, basic 'under roof' rates for factory space in Jamaica, Barbados, Columbia, and the Dominican Republic range from US$2.50 to US$3.50 per square foot.[252] In reality, however, the apparent benefits of 'low' SEZ rates are partially offset by hidden costs.[253] For instance, Article 21 of the SEZ Regulations requires investors to pay the costs of linking up their power supply, water supply, sewer system, and telecommunications lines within their land-use area to main lines outside. With these extra charges added on to the basic land-use fee, total land costs in the SEZs end up being comparable to costs incurred by investors in other parts of China.

The Shenzhen Land Regulations contain a number of provisions dealing with matters related to construction in the zone. The law states that all 'units and individuals' must abide by the zone's 'overall construction plan'[254] and empowers the Shenzhen municipal government to 'requisition, appropriate or nationalize' land within the zone 'based on construction needs'.[255] In the event that land is 'requisitioned' or 'houses or other structures' are demolished 'due to construction requirements', compensation is to be paid.[256] Moreover, the regulations provide that investors must carry out construction in accordance with the municipal government's stipulations regarding 'space allocation ratios and greenery ratios'[257] and comply with 'Chinese building standards and fire prevention and safety requirements'.[258]

These and a number of other provisions relating to construction in the Shenzhen SEZ are further elaborated on in the Provisional Measures of Shenzhen Municipality Governing Urban Construction (hereafter cited as the Construction Measures), adopted on 1 July 1982 by the Shenzhen Municipal People's Government.[259] Consisting of sixty detailed articles, the Construction Measures address five different areas concerning construction activity in the zone.

The first topic dealt with by the measures is the management of land used for construction purposes. This section of the law sets forth the procedures for the requisitioning of land in the zone for construction projects, including the procedures to be followed by foreign investors who wish to obtain Land-use Certificates. In most important respects the provisions dealing with foreign investors follow those found in the Shenzhen Land Regulations. However the Construction Measures do contain several new provisions regarding land use which will be of concern to investors.

The first of the new provisions contained in the Construction Measures provides that land that has been approved for construction may be 'readjusted' or 'withdrawn' at any time and without notice owing to 'urban construction requirements'.[260] Although the provision goes on to provide that 'reasonable compensation' will be paid in such cases, the law provides no indication of the kinds of circumstances under which 'readjustment' or 'withdrawal' may occur. The second provision states that where the urban plan calls for the development of 'complementary projects'— such as 'cultural, educational and public health facilities'—near a construction site, the investment for such projects shall be borne 'jointly' by the 'units located at the site'.[261] In this context 'units' presumably includes foreign investors and joint and co-operative ventures. How various units in the vicinity of a site are to bear the costs for complementary projects, and to what extent, is not specified by the law.

Among the other topics addressed by the Construction Measures are rules for construction work management, including the procedures to be followed to obtain building permits, and rules regarding the size, spacing, and siting of buildings;[262] rules for the management of municipal projects, including road construction, the laying of telecommunication and electricity cables and pipelines, and related projects;[263] and rules for the management of survey and design work and the regulation of construction firms operating in the zones.[264] Regarding the latter topic, the law provides that wholly owned foreign enterprises in the zone may entrust design work to foreign firms, but co-operative or joint venture enterprises must first obtain the approval of the Shenzhen SEZ's Office of the Chief Engineer before the services of foreign design or architectural firms may be retained for projects in the zone.[265] With respect to the performance of actual construction work, the Construction Measures specify that such work may only be undertaken by enterprises registered in the zone.[266] In the case of foreign construction companies, a performance guarantee must be provided before such registration is permitted.[267]

Commercial and residential property development projects in the Shenzhen SEZ have spawned an active market in local real estate transactions. In order to strengthen the legal basis for such transactions, the Guangdong Provincial People's Congress passed, on 15 November 1983, the Regulations of the Shenzhen Special Economic Zone on the Control of Commercial Real Estate (hereafter cited as the Real Estate Regulations).[268] The law contains provisions regarding the purchase, sale, and other forms of transfer of property rights and sets forth a number of rules pertaining to the leasing of buildings in the zone. In addition, the law established a system for the registration of real property and the mortgage of real estate in the SEZ.[269] Although the provisions contained in the law are brief and relatively unsophisticated, the Real Estate Regulations constitute an important first step toward the establishment of a comprehensive regulatory system for real estate transactions.

v. Enterprise and Individual Income Tax
Until November 1984, the SEZ authorities had been implementing a number of unpublished rules relating to the taxation of the income of SEZ enterprises and personnel.[270] On 15 November 1984, the Provisional Regulations of the State Council of the People's Republic of China Regarding the Reduction of and Exemption from Enterprise Income Tax and Industrial and Commercial Consolidated Tax in the Special Economic Zones and the Fourteen Coastal Port Cities (hereafter cited as the Incentive Regulations) were promulgated,[271] thereby formally establishing the tax regime for the SEZs.

The Incentive Regulations firstly confirm that tax is to be levied at the reduced rate of 15 per cent on income earned by Chinese-foreign equity joint ventures, Chinese-foreign contractual joint ventures, and wholly owned foreign enterprises which are established in the SEZs.[272] For businesses engaged in production, a two-year tax holiday is, upon application, available from the first profit-making year, followed by a 50 per cent reduction in taxes in the ensuing three years.[273] However, businesses engaged in service trades qualify for lesser tax relief and only where the foreign investment exceeds US$5 million or the term of the venture is ten years or more.[274] This tax treatment thus differs from that obtainable under the national tax legislation. On the one hand the Incentive Regulations are less favourable to investors than the Joint Venture Income Tax Law, under which any joint venture with a term of ten years or more qualifies for a tax holiday in the first two profit-making years and a 50 per cent reduction in taxes in the ensuing three years.[275] On the other hand, the Incentive Regulations provide a more generous treatment for investors who would otherwise be subject to the Foreign Enterprise Income Tax Law, which requires an enterprise not only to satisfy the ten-year rule but also to be engaged in certain types of low-profit operation.[276] Moreover, tax relief under the Foreign Enterprise Income Tax Law endures for a shorter duration.[277]

The Incentive Regulations confer power on the local SEZ authorities to decide whether or not to levy the local income tax.[278] More importantly, the regulations finally confirm that no withholding tax is to be imposed when foreign parties to joint ventures remit their share of profits from the SEZs.[279] Income received by foreign enterprises which have no establishments in China is subject to tax at 10 per cent,[280] reduced from the rate of 20 per cent applicable under the Foreign Enterprise Income Tax Law.[281] Application can be made for further relief from tax where the conditions for providing funds and equipment are preferential or where the technology transferred is advanced.[282]

Liability for Industrial and Commercial Consolidated Tax and for customs tariff is governed by the Incentive Regulations and the subsequently promulgated Regulations of the Customs General Administration of the People's Republic of China Governing Goods, Means of Conveyance, Luggage Articles and Postal Articles Entering and Leaving the Special Economic Zones (hereafter cited as the Goods Control Regulations).[283] In both cases the general scheme is that machinery, equipment, raw materials, spare parts, and means of transport which are imported for production purposes or for an enterprise's own use are exempt from both the tax and the tariff. Without state approval, goods imported into SEZs cannot be transhipped to other parts of China.[284] Other goods which are imported within the government-approved quota enjoy a 50 per cent reduction in tax and tariff.[285] Goods produced by SEZ enterprises and exported are free from export taxes and duties.[286] If, instead, the goods are shipped to inland China with the approval of the authorities, it will be necessary to make up for the previously exempted tax and tariff.[287] Sales within the SEZ are taxed in accordance with the rules for the taxation of imports.[288] Articles imported by foreign personnel for personal use are also exempt from the tax and tariff.[289]

Local SEZ tax authorities have also begun to provide favourable treatment with respect to individual income taxation of foreign personnel resident or working in the zones. Under the national Individual Income Tax Law,[290] monthly wages and salaries in excess of RMB800 are taxed at progressive rates ranging from 5 to 45 per cent.[291] In the SEZs, however, tax officials have been applying a lower rate scale of from 3 to 30 per cent on the same monthly amounts.[292] Another area where the tax authorities have provided more favourable treatment than that which is provided for under the national tax law concerns foreign-source income. Whereas the detailed regulations for the implementation of the Individual Income Tax Law require that foreigners resident in China for a period of five years or more pay tax on their world-wide income,[293] the SEZ authorities have indicated that non-China-source earnings will be exempt from taxation in the zones regardless of the length of residence.[294]

vi. Banking and Finance
The SEZs are also being used as a testing ground for the development of China's financial system. Even though four foreign banks have been permitted to maintain their branch operations in Shanghai for the last forty years,[295] the scope of activity for foreign banks in China has only recently been expanded to a more traditional branch banking level with the promulgation of regulations permitting the establishment of foreign bank branches in the SEZs. With these regulations, together with those governing the activities of state-owned non-banking financial institutions, and the granting of loans secured by property mortgages, the SEZs, particularly Shenzhen and Xiamen, are gradually formulating the framework for a financial centre.

The most significant piece of legislation to date is the Regulations Governing Foreign Banks and Joint Chinese-Foreign Banks in the Special

Economic Zones of the People's Republic of China (hereafter cited as the Banking Regulations) released by the State Council on 2 April 1985.[296] The regulations permit foreign banks to apply for a licence to carry on business as a branch in the SEZs or to set up a branch in partnership with a Chinese enterprise. A number of banks which had already established representative offices in Shenzhen have succeeded in obtaining licences to upgrade their operations to a branch.[297] In Xiamen, a Hong Kong-based company joined with three Chinese entities in forming the first China-based joint venture bank.[298]

The stated purpose of the Banking Regulations is to expand international, economic, and financial co-operation so as to facilitate the import of foreign capital and technology.[299] Underlying this is the recognition that China's modernization programme needs the development in parallel of a modern financial system. It is also acknowledged that such a financial system should not consist only of traditional commercial banks. Non-bank financial institutions in Shenzhen now number about fifteen, and include a Chinese-foreign joint venture leasing company, trust and investment corporations, insurance companies, and finance companies.[300] Moreover, those non-bank financial institutions which are state owned are now subject to the Provisional Measures of Shenzhen Special Economic Zone for the Control of Non-bank State-owned Financial Institutions.[301]

The authorities in Shenzhen are also experimenting with a system enabling loans to be made on the security of a range of properties. The Interim Measures of Shenzhen Special Economic Zone on Bank Mortgage Loans[302] apply to all loans made by banks and other financial institutions in Shenzhen to enterprises in Shenzhen with foreign capital. Article 5 of the measures lists the following properties as being capable of being the subject of security: real estate, goods and materials, value bonds, payment certificates, and other rights including share rights in Chinese-foreign equity joint ventures and rights to profit and property in Chinese-foreign contractual joint ventures.

Whilst the three pieces of legislation will need to be refined as the authorities gain experience in the financial field, they indicate that the government has a clear policy to promote the development of the financial system within the SEZs.[303] Moreover, this development is not to be limited to traditional banking but is to include trust, investment, insurance, and securities trading activities.[304] Tax incentives are also being offered to encourage finance activities.[305] Foreign banks which have set up in the Shenzhen SEZ will not be subject to the consolidated industrial and commercial tax at least until 1995.[306] Until 1995, the interest received by foreigners and Hong Kong or Macau Chinese on their deposits in Shenzhen will be free of tax.[307] Interest earned by foreign, Hong Kong, and Macau banks on their loans to foreign banks in Shenzhen at international interbank interest rates is also exempt from withholding tax,[308] as is the interest paid at such rates by Shenzhen branches to their foreign head offices.[309]

vii. Accounting

Following the promulgation of the Accounting Law of the People's Republic of China[310] and the Accounting System for Joint Ventures with Chinese and Foreign Investment of the People's Republic of China,[311] the Guangdong government released on 14 February 1986 the Regulations Governing Accounting for Foreign Enterprises in the Special Economic Zones of Guangdong Province (hereafter cited as the SEZ Accounting Regulations).[312] These regulations apply to so-called foreign enterprises, which are equity joint ventures, contractual joint ventures, foreign enterprises, and—a new form of entity—Chinese-foreign companies limited by shares.[313] They set out the general principles on accounting for these foreign enterprises, resorting to the national Accounting System for Joint Ventures for detailed rules on accounting procedures.[314]

The accounting matters of these foreign enterprises in the Guangdong SEZs are under the control of the municipal bureaux of finance of the various zones.[315] Each enterprise is to have a chief accountant[316] and an internal auditor,[317] though small enterprises are exempted from the requirement to have an internal auditor.[318] The chief accountant's duty is to assist the general manager of the enterprise in managing financial accounting affairs.[319] The responsibility for accounting work rests, however, with the general manager.[320] All accounting vouchers, books, and reports must be kept within the zone in which the enterprise is located.[321] The annual accounting statements and accounts must be audited by a certified accountant who is registered in China.[322] In equity joint ventures and contractual joint ventures, each party is also permitted to inspect the enterprise's accounts at its own cost.[323] Finally, there are sanctions against conduct such as forging, altering, or deliberately destroying accounting vouchers and books, acting on original records which are known to be false or illegal, and failing to comply with the revenue/expenditure rules set out in the accounting system for the enterprise or the Chinese state.[324] In some cases, if the general manager or the board of directors insist on acting in contravention of the rules, they will assume liability in place of the enterprise's accounting personnel.[325] The seriousness with which the authorities view accounting responsibilities is demonstrated by the sanctions, which range from fines of RMB1,000 and RMB10,000, to an order to cease carrying on business, to action under criminal law.[326]

viii. Economic Contracts and Technology Transfers

In early 1984 the People's Government of Guangdong Province issued two sets of regulations which are likely to have a far-reaching impact on business and investment activity in the SEZs. These are the Regulations of the Shenzhen Special Economic Zone on Foreign Economic Contracts (hereafter cited as the Shenzhen Contracts Regulations), promulgated on 7 February 1984, and the Provisional Regulations of the Shenzhen Special Economic Zone on the Introduction of Technology (hereafter cited as the Shenzhen Technology Regulations), promulgated on 8 February 1984.[327]

The Shenzhen Contracts Regulations, consisting of 41 articles divided into seven chapters, establish the general principles governing the conclusion, performance, amendment, and termination of economic contracts. The regulations apply to contracts entered into among the various organizations and enterprises operating in the Shenzhen SEZ, including joint ventures, wholly owned foreign enterprises, and Chinese companies and governmental organizations, so long as such contracts are to be performed within the Shenzhen SEZ.[328] However, several provisions in the regulations differ significantly from the national Foreign Economic Contracts Law which came into force on 1 July 1985,[329] so foreign parties need to be aware of these differences and, in some instances, must determine which provisions will prevail in the event of any inconsistency between the law and the regulations.

To begin with, the Shenzhen Contracts Regulations describe various kinds of contract and list the types of clauses to be included. The list covers contracts for joint ventures, co-operation projects, compensation trade, and assembly and processing transactions.[330] By contrast, Article 12 of the Foreign Economic Contracts Law simply lists the clauses to be included generally in any contract. Under the law, contracts which by law or administrative regulations require state approval have no effect until such approval is obtained.[331] Material changes to such contracts also necessitate approval.[332] In Shenzhen, all contracts must be approved by the Shenzhen government or its delegated authority in order to be valid.[333] Any change to the contract requires similar approval.[334] Once the approval is issued, the contract needs to be registered with both the Shenzhen Administration for Industry and Commerce and the Shenzhen Tax Bureau.[335] Article 29 of the Shenzhen Contracts Regulations contains a requirement which may sometimes be hard to comply with. If the duration of a contract is to be extended, approval for the extension must be sought at least six months before the expiration date. Parties who have expended considerable effort to reach written agreement in Shenzhen may be perturbed by Article 25, which implies that contract provisions in conflict with Chinese laws and regulations are invalid. There is no protection available in the contract, as there is under the Foreign Economic Contracts Law, against subsequently enacted legislation.[336] Among other provisions in the Shenzhen Contracts Regulations which deserve study are Articles 35 and 40. It is possible to construe Article 35 as meaning that the arbitration of contracts for joint ventures, co-operative projects, and the development of natural resources, and other contracts which have a close relationship with China's sovereignty, can only be conducted in China, though not necessarily in Shenzhen. Under Article 40, where a contract is in a foreign language as well as the Chinese language, the Chinese version prevails. Nevertheless, if the contract is written only in a foreign language (with no Chinese counterpart), that contract should govern.

The Shenzhen Technology Regulations provide the statutory framework for the transfer of technology between foreign enterprises and Chinese enterprises in the Shenzhen SEZ. Consisting of 25 articles, the regulations contain provisions outlining the various clauses that must be included in a technology-transfer contract and the procedures that are to be followed in applying for and obtaining approval for the transaction from the Shenzhen Municipal People's Government.[337] Under the regulations, the technology transfer may take place in the context of a variety of transactions, including compensation trade, licensing trade, co-operative arrangements, consultation services arrangements, and equity joint ventures.[338] In the case of equity joint ventures, however, technology may be provided as part of the capital contribution up to a limit of 20 per cent of the total registered capital of the venture.[339] This requirement and a number of others are not found in the Regulations of the People's Republic of China for the Control of Technology Import Contracts promulgated by the State Council on 24 May 1985 (hereafter cited as the National Technology Regulations).[340]

A provision in the Shenzhen Technology Regulations that is likely to prove troublesome to potential investors is the requirement that the products produced with the introduced technology have access to the international market. In the event that the Chinese side incurs losses due to 'influence' on its product sales caused by the foreign party, the Chinese side may demand compensation.[341] There are several other differences between the Shenzhen Technology Regulations and the national legislation. Except where the technology forms part of the investment contribution, technology import contracts in Shenzhen are generally not to exceed five years.[342] The national regulations confer a more generous period of ten years.[343] The Shenzhen Technology Regulations require the foreign transferor of technology to 'guarantee' that the Chinese party will master the entire technology and method of operation,[344] and to 'guarantee the legal effectiveness of the anticipated results of the introduced technology'.[345] It is open to argument whether Article 6 of the National Technology Regulations is more or less restrictive. It provides that the transferor should 'guarantee that it is the lawful owner of the technology to be provided' and that 'the technology to be provided is complete, without error, effective and able to reach the objectives as provided for in the contract'.

According to the Shenzhen Technology Regulations, the technology to be imported must be applicable advanced technology, having clear economic results,[346] and the relevant contract for the transfer of technology should not contain any unreasonable restrictions or unfair provisions.[347] The National Technology Regulations have expanded on these concepts. Article 3 lists the criteria of which at least one must be satisfied by the technology to be imported, these criteria being those which are important to China's modernization programme. Article 9 sets out nine clauses which are deemed restrictive and which are prohibited from contracts. Foreign parties transferring technology to Shenzhen will thus find it necessary to refer to the national legislation (including the accompanying Measures for Examination and Approval of Technology Import Contracts)[348] in addition to the Shenzhen regulations when negotiating technology-transfer transactions in this SEZ.

The regulations governing the import of technology into Xiamen are less stringent than the regulations applicable to Shenzhen.[349] In Xiamen, there is no prescribed maximum duration for technology-transfer contracts, nor any limit on the amount of technology that can be contributed as capital to any equity joint venture. There is also no enforced guarantee of access to international markets or of the effectiveness of the anticipated results of the imported technology. What may be of concern to licensers who are sub-licensing technology to the Chinese is that the Chinese may request a copy of the head licensing contract.[350] The relevant department of the Xiamen government is to monitor and control the application and effects of imported technology. Where the technology causes environmental damage or is unable to attain the expected technical and economic targets, the department can request the Xiamen government to suspend the preferential terms for the imported technology and take appropriate action.[351] Article 7 is interesting because it formalizes the already established practice for Chinese licensees to seek approval first from the delegated authority of the Xiamen municipal government of the letter of intent and feasibility study for technology to be acquired. The technology-transfer contract, when signed, is to be approved by higher authorities.

D. Investment Rules for the Shekou Industrial Zone

The Shekou district of Shenzhen municipality was designated as a separate special zone prior to the promulgation of the SEZ Regulations. In 1979 the China Merchants' Steam Navigation Company Ltd. (CMSN), a Hong Kong company under the control of the Ministry of Communications, received direct authorization from the State Council to develop the Shekou district as an 'industrial zone'.[352] Since then, the CMSN has invested large amounts of its own funds to develop the district and has played the key role in managing investment activity there. Although Shekou technically became a part of the Shenzhen SEZ after the passage of the SEZ Regulations in 1980, it has retained its independence to a large degree and has even issued its own rules to govern investment in the district.

The Shekou rules are contained in an 'investor's handbook' published by the CMSN which, among other things, sets forth the 'particulars of making investment' in the SEZ. The handbook was originally issued in January 1980[353] but was revised after the promulgation of the SEZ Regulations and republished in September 1981.[354] The legal status of the rules is clouded. They have apparently never been formally enacted by a Chinese legislative body although they are being applied in practice within the zone.[355]

Covering such matters as tax rates, land costs, and labour management, the Shekou rules deal with many of the same topics that are addressed in the SEZ Regulations and related legislation. However, the treatment given to such issues by the Shekou handbook is far less detailed than that found in the SEZ laws. Moreover, disparities exist between the Shekou rules and the other SEZ laws regarding a number of issues. According to Shekou officials, the SEZ Regulations and related laws will be followed 'in principle' in the zone, but the Shekou rules will take precedence over those laws where the rules contain specific provisions at variance with provisions found in the general SEZ legislation.[356]

Like the SEZ Regulations, the Shekou rules provide a wide scope for foreign investors. Generally, 'all trades that have positive significance in international economic co-operation and technical exchanges' are welcome in the zone but particular emphasis is placed on 'trades that are rapidly developing or involve high technologies and techniques or are still non-existent in China at the present stage'.[357] However, certain types of projects may not be established in the zone. These include compensation trade and assembly or processing projects as well as projects that cause pollution, employ outmoded equipment, or produce products that are subject to Chinese export quotas.[358]

The rules permit foreign investors to establish either wholly owned enterprises or joint ventures in the zone.[359] Wholly owned foreign enterprises are required to pay an annual 'management fee' to the CMSN, based on a certain percentage of the 'total turnover' of the enterprise.[360] The fee represents an additional cost of doing business in Shekou, as the SEZ Regulations do not require such payments from wholly owned foreign enterprises in the other zones. Joint ventures are to be established between foreign investors and the CMSN; the rules do not contemplate joint ventures between foreigners and other Chinese organizations, although in practice minority equity participation by such organizations is permitted.[361] In general, a party's investment shall be not less than 25 per cent of the total.[362] The parties are free to determine the management structure of the venture, but the chairman of the board of directors is to be appointed by the CMSN.[363] The rules provide that the duration of the contract period for enterprises in the zone is to be determined according to 'the particular line of business of the enterprise'.[364] However, the rules stipulate an 'average term' of 25 years and provide for extensions of the scheduled term.[365]

The rules also address certain matters of a legal nature not dealt with by the SEZ Regulations or related legislation. The rules provide that in preparing the 'memorandum and articles of association' for enterprises in the zone 'reference' may be made to both Hong Kong and international practices.[366] The rules also provide for arbitration in the event of disputes between the parties. Arbitration may be conducted by an arbitral body in China or by another arbitral body 'agreed upon by the parties'.[367]

Enterprises requiring land in the zone are to apply to the Real Estate Company of the Shekou Industrial Zone, a subsidiary of the CMSN.[368] Land-use fees are charged at rates of from HK$2 to HK$4 per square foot per year, somewhat lower than the average rates in Shenzhen generally.[369] Power consumption in Shekou is charged at the same rates as are charged in Hong Kong for electricity used for industrial purposes.[370] Water charges are collected at rates that are 20 per cent lower than the prevailing rates in Hong Kong.[371]

Like the SEZ Regulations, the Shekou rules promise that 'entry and exit formalities will be simplified'.[372] The only significant benefit granted to foreign passport holders under the rules that is not found in the Entry and Exit Regulations relates to simplification of visa procedures. Under the Shekou rules, travellers to the zone by land may obtain visas within two days by presenting their passports to the CMSN directly.[373] Travellers by sea may obtain visas at the Shekou wharf prior to entry.[374]

With respect to import and export duties, the Shekou rules contain provisions which follow policies outlined in the SEZ Regulations. Imported means of production which are 'necessary' are exempt from import duties but may only be used inside the zone.[375] Similar provisions apply to consumer goods with the exception of cigarettes and liquor which are subject to 50 per cent of normal import duties.[376] Products of Shekou enterprises are exempt from export duties unless they are sold on the domestic market.[377]

The first issue of the CMSN's 'handbook' for investment in Shekou, issued prior to the promulgation of the SEZ Regulations, provided for a 'corporation profit tax' of 10 per cent.[378] The revised edition of the handbook, however, provides for a tax rate of 15 per cent, thus bringing Shekou into line with the tax rate applicable in the SEZs generally.[379] The revised rules also provide that agreements signed prior to the promulgation of the SEZ Regulations when the 10 per cent rate was in effect continue to benefit from the earlier, lower rate.[380]

As regards tax holidays, the Shekou rules provide for a three- to five-year holiday for 'all enterprises'.[381] In addition, the rules provide 'special preferential treatment' for enterprises with an investment of US$5 million or more, those that employ 'higher technologies' or have a longer capital turnover cycle, and enterprises that have not yet been established in China.[382] Although this language echoes that found in the SEZ Regulations, Shekou officials maintain that the criteria for eligibility for larger tax holidays will be interpreted more flexibly in the district than elsewhere in the SEZs.

Regarding labour management, the Shekou rules appear to be less liberal than the labour and wage regulations applicable in the SEZs generally. The rules provide that all enterprises must hire workers and other personnel from the Shekou Labour Services Company;[383] unlike the SEZ Labour and Wage Regulations, the rules do not provide for independent recruitment by enterprises themselves. Moreover, under the Shekou rules, labour contracts are signed between the enterprise and the Labour Services Company.[384] The alternative of having labour contracts signed between the enterprise and the individual worker, as provided by the SEZ Regulations is not available. Although enterprises in Shekou have the right 'to scrutinize' candidates for employment, and may dismiss employees who 'seriously violate' labour rules,[385] such rights are likely to prove to be of little practical importance so long as the local Labour Services Company maintains a monopoly over labour supply.

With respect to the wage system in the zones, the rules provide that all enterprises shall pay wages to employees in Hong Kong dollars.[386] Average monthly wages are to be higher than wages paid by Chinese enterprises but lower than those paid in Hong Kong for the same type of enterprise.[387] The rules provide that a certain percentage of the total amount of wages may be drawn by the Labour Services Company and 'set aside' for employee welfare funds and medical benefits. Salaries and benefits for technicians or managerial personnel from Hong Kong and abroad are to be 'fixed separately'.[388]

The Shekou rules also contain several brief provisions regarding foreign exchange control. The rules provide that foreign currency shall be used for accounting and bookkeeping purposes by all enterprises in the zone and require that quarterly balance sheets be submitted to the Shekou Industrial Zone Administration.[389] The rules also state that foreign exchange may be 'freely remitted both inwards and outwards' provided that such transactions are conducted through banks in the zone.[390] What this means in practice is unclear. Shekou officials indicate that the procedures stipulated in China's national foreign exchange law must still be followed although the law itself will be interpreted 'more flexibly'.[391]

II. The Fourteen Coastal Cities

A. Background

The decision to 'open' the fourteen coastal cities and Hainan Island was announced by Premier Zhao Ziyang on 15 May 1984 following a special visit made by Deng Xiaoping to the three special economic zones of Shenzhen, Zhuhai, and Xiamen earlier that year, during the course of which he expressed satisfaction with the achievements of those zones. The decision called for certain special policies designed for the SEZs to be applied to the coastal cities of Dalian, Qinhuangdao, Tianjin, Yantai, Qingdao, Lianyungang, Nantong, Shanghai, Ningbo, Wenzhou, Fuzhou, Guangzhou, Zhanjiang, and Beihai, as well as Hainan Island. The special policies involve mainly two aspects, more preferential tax treatment and access to the domestic market for foreign investors, and extension of the decision-making power of local authorities in economic and technical co-operation projects with foreigners. Together with the four SEZs, the fourteen coastal cities are to form a line along China's coast that would serve as China's front to the outside world.[392]

The opening of the fourteen coastal cities gives foreign investors a far wider choice of places in which to locate their projects. The cities had a combined industrial output in 1983 of RMB142.5 billion, equal to 23 per cent of the nation's total. Their ports handled more than 250 million tonnes of cargo in that year, which is 97 per cent of the nation's total.[393] The cities are clearly more economically developed than other areas in China. The cities have better services in communication, industrial quality, and level of technology and management, and more developed scientific, educational, and cultural establishments. In addition, the cities have had more experience in developing foreign economic and trade relations and possess the network for promoting economic and technical co-operation with the rest of China.[394]

The opening of the fourteen coastal cities is designed to attract more foreign investment and technology to China.[395] The SEZs have so far attracted only a limited range of industries which are suited to the environment of a new, developing, industrial and commercial centre.[396] China's leaders recognize that many of the nation's existing enterprises are located in the main industrial cities and need economic and technical rejuvenation. Foreign investment and technology must be attracted to these places in order that reform may be carried out. The other reason advanced for opening the cities is the slow pace at which foreign technology is being transferred from the SEZs to the rest of China. Owing to the experimental nature of the SEZs, they have been more or less isolated from the remaining parts of the country. There is a 'second line' between the largest SEZ, Shenzhen, and its surrounding area which inhibits physical entry and exit. The other SEZs also control access to their zones. In addition, all the SEZs are located in a pocket in the south of China, away from some of the traditional major industrial centres situated around the Changjiang (Yangtze) Delta and Bohai.[397]

The solution for increasing the tempo of China's economic modernization is to develop each of the coastal cities in two fashions. Firstly, each city is to establish an economic and technical development zone (ETDZ) in which investors and enterprises can enjoy much of the preferential treatment available to enterprises in the SEZs. Industries which are best suited to a city will be encouraged for development in that city's ETDZ. This contrasts with the SEZs, which are able to engage not only in industrial projects but also in a variety of other commercial activities including tourism. Another difference between the SEZs and the ETDZs is that each ETDZ is still under the control of the local government whereas the SEZs are administratively independent. Finally, the ETDZs are not expected to have control lines similar to those set up in Shenzhen.[398]

As of August 1986, ETDZ sites have been designated in twelve of the fourteen coastal cities. Beihai and Wenzhou have not commenced work on their ETDZs, mainly because of inadequate transportation facilities in these cities. Of the twelve cities, Shanghai plans to continue to develop two districts which have previously been earmarked for special attention but which have now gained the status of ETDZs.[399] In the other eleven cities, the local authorities have typically located their ETDZs on the outskirts of the existing city area. The zones range in size from an area of 4.62 square kilometres for Nantong to an area of 58 square kilometres for Guangzhou.[400] In general, the development of the zones has been mapped out in stages. Infrastructure facilities are being planned or constructed. At the same time the authorities in each zone are earnestly wooing foreign investors to set up operations in their zone and drawing up a list of the types of economic and technical projects which they wish to undertake with foreign capital.[401]

The second part of the development plan for the coastal cities concerns the existing part of each of the cities, referred to as Old Urban Areas. In these places the authorities are seeking mainly to renovate existing enterprises.[402] Preferential treatment for investors in these Old Urban

Areas are not as favourable as those available in the ETDZs.[403] Notwithstanding this, the greater proportion of investments in the coastal cities to date has occurred in the Old Urban Areas. Even in the larger cities such as Dalian, Guangzhou, and Tianjin, the ETDZs are only now completing the work on infrastructure facilities. During this initial development phase of the ETDZs, there seems to be a 'wait and see' attitude on the part of foreign investors, who are comparing the ETDZs not only in terms of the preferential treatment being offered but also in terms of what other investors are locating their businesses there. Naturally some of the investments in the Old Urban Areas predate the decision to 'open' the fourteen coastal cities for special development, but Chinese enterprises and foreign investors alike are bound to find from time to time that it is more economical and more convenient to modernize an existing plant than to set up afresh in a new area where transport and communication facilities are still inadequate.[404]

Clearly there are and will continue to be differences in the way in which the cities develop,[405] in the same way that there are discrepancies in the current growth rate of the SEZs. Some of the cities already possess a very solid industrial base. The total value of industrial output in Shanghai and Tianjin in 1983 was RMB67.8 billion and RMB22.9 billion respectively. On the other hand the industrial output produced in each of Qingdao and Beihai in 1983 was less than RMB150 million.[406] The authorities recognize the differences between the cities, granting to Shanghai and Tianjin the authority to approve projects with a total investment value of up to US$30 million. The approval limit for Guangzhou and Dalian is US$10 million, while all other cities are limited to US$5 million.[407]

In the second half of 1985, there were reports that China's leaders were displeased with the progress being made by the SEZs and the fourteen coastal cities and proposed decelerating the development in ten of the cities. There has been no official discouragement of investments in the ten cities since, and by all accounts the Incentive Regulations continue to be implemented in each of the fourteen cities. However, the central government has withdrawn the authority of the ten cities to approve foreign venture projects and has placed such authority in the hands of the relevant provincial and autonomous governments. Senior Chinese officials have also expressed the view that the ten smaller cities are less advanced in their modernization programme and, not unexpectedly, efforts will be concentrated on promoting the industrial development in the other four cities—Dalian, Guangzhou, Shanghai, and Tianjin—which over time are to pass on their experience to the other 'open' cities.[408]

B. Investment Incentives

i. Uniform Incentives
In November 1984, the State Council issued the Incentive Regulations, granting incentives for investments and enterprises in the coastal cities.[409] In addition to these regulations, each city is now promulgating its own list of preferential treatment to supplement the national regulations.

The Incentive Regulations contain provisions governing the SEZs and Hainan Island as well as rules covering the coastal cities. So far as the coastal cities are concerned, the Incentive Regulations distinguish between investments in the ETDZs and those in the Old Urban Areas, offering more favourable treatment to investments in the ETDZs. The intent of the Incentive Regulations (as evidenced by several provisions) seems to be that they should supplement the range of preferential treatment already available to foreign investors under pre-existing laws and regulations.[410]

The incentives available under the Incentive Regulations can be summarized as follows:

a. *Enterprise Income Tax*   All productive equity joint ventures, contractual joint ventures, and wholly owned foreign ventures established in the ETDZs pay income tax at the rate of 15 per cent.[411] This compares with a rate of 30 per cent set by national legislation for equity joint ventures,[412] and a progressive rate of 20 to 40 per cent levied under the Foreign Enterprise Income Tax Law for other types of foreign ventures in China.[413] According to the Incentive Regulations, ventures with a term of at least ten years can, with approval, enjoy a tax holiday in the first two profit-making years and a 50 per cent reduction in taxes in the ensuing three years.[414] Previously, under national legislation, only equity joint ventures and other types of foreign ventures which were low-profit operations qualified for this type of tax concession.[415]

In the Old Urban Areas the 15 per cent tax rate will be available, with the approval of the Ministry of Finance, only if the project is technology intensive or know-how intensive, or if the amount of foreign investment is at least US$30 million and there is a long recoupment period for the investment, or if the project pertains to energy, transport, or port construction. A venture which fails to qualify for the 15 per cent tax rate could still obtain a 20 per cent reduction in its normal income tax if it falls within one of the industries specified in the Incentive Regulations.[416] There is no mention of tax concessions for ventures which have a term of at least ten years, but presumably equity joint ventures can still enjoy the right of a tax holiday in the first two years and a 50 per cent tax reduction in the ensuing three years under the national legislation.

b. *Withholding Tax*   The 10 per cent withholding tax on dividends is exempted for ventures established in the ETDZs.[417] The Incentive Regulations do not address the question in relation to ventures in the Old Urban Areas, so it may be supposed that the withholding tax still applies to dividends remitted by enterprises in these areas.

Investors who have no establishments in the fourteen coastal cities are subject to a 10 per cent withholding tax on income obtained from the cities, including dividends, interest, rentals, and royalties.[418]

c. *Consolidated Tax and Customs Duties*   Enterprises established in the ETDZs enjoy an exemption from the Consolidated Tax when they import construction materials, production equipment, raw materials, spare parts, components, means of transport, and office supplies for their own use. However, they must make up for the Consolidated Tax payable on imported raw materials, spare parts, and components if these are then used in products for sale in China.[419]

The Incentive Regulations provide slightly less favourable treatment to enterprises in the Old Urban Areas. Production equipment, operational equipment, construction materials, means of transport, and office supplies imported by these enterprises are exempt from the Consolidated Tax only if these items constitute part of the investment.[420] Raw materials, spare parts, components, packaging materials, and so on are exempt also if they are imported for use in producing export goods.[421]

The concessions for Consolidated Tax expressed above apply also to customs duties. At the Investment Symposium held in Hong Kong in 1984 to promote the opening of the fourteen coastal cities, Chinese officials stated that customs duties will also be exempted in accordance with the rules set out above.[422] Although the Incentive Regulations do not address the question of customs duties, regulations subsequently promulgated separately by each of the cities in respect of their ETDZs extend the concessions to include customs duties.[423]

All export products are exempt from the Consolidated Tax, unless they are of a kind that is subject to export restrictions.[424] Foreign workers in the fourteen coastal cities are also able to take in reasonable quantities of household goods and means of transport without incurring the Consolidated Tax.[425]

ii. Additional Incentives

Apart from the investment incentives set out in the Incentive Regulations, the authorities in each city are granting additional preferential terms to foreign investors. Some cities, such as Dalian, Ningbo, Tianjin, and Guangzhou, have promulgated regulations specifying the incentives available in their respective ETDZs.[426] Other cities have yet to formalize their lists of preferential treatment and have merely publicized the incentives that they intend to offer to investors.[427]

In those cities which have promulgated regulations embodying additional incentives, the approach towards granting incentives differs from city to city. Additional incentives granted by some cities are more extensive than those available in other cities. Also, in some cities, the terms of preferential treatment are clearly prescribed in regulations, whereas the regulations of other cities leave the precise treatment to be determined separately by the authorities. A case in point is land-use fees in Tianjin, which are not specified in any of Tianjin's regulations for its ETDZ. The land-use fees applicable in the ETDZs of Dalian and Guangzhou are set out in their respective regulations. In the ETDZs of both Dalian and Guangzhou, further concessions in income tax are obtainable if a venture is a low-profit operation or involves advanced technology.[428] In many of the cities, local income tax can be reduced or in some cases exempted.[429] The Consolidated Tax can be reduced or exempted if an enterprise encounters difficulty in making payment.[430] In Guangzhou the land-use fee[431] and in Dalian also the site-development fee[432] can be reduced.

The Guangzhou regulations contain two other interesting sets of incentives. Foreign investors who provide especially advanced technology or invest large sums in the Guangzhou ETDZ can apply to have their relatives relocated either to the municipality or to the ETDZ in Guangzhou.[433] This incentive was obviously drafted in order to attract investments from the large contingent of overseas Chinese people who have their origins in Guangdong province. The Guangzhou authorities are also making a special effort to attract investment from other areas of China. The Interim Regulations on Certain Questions Relating to Inland Associated Enterprises (Undertakings) in the Guangzhou Economic and Technical Development Zone encourage Chinese enterprises outside the ETDZ to form joint ventures in the ETDZ and offer them preferential treatment more favourable than that offered to foreign investors.[434]

The cities which have promulgated regulations for their ETDZs all provide special incentives to those foreign investors who establish their ventures during the early life of the ETDZs or who participate in the construction of infrastructure facilities.[435] At the same time, some of the cities are adjusting their incentive rules as they experiment with the new investment regime.[436] There is no doubt that the competition among the various cities will also prompt the authorities to review their incentive rules on a constant basis.

C. The Legal Framework

The legal framework for the opening of the fourteen coastal cities is found in the context of the Incentive Regulations only. There is no other published law or regulation which specifically governs the overall scheme of development for these cities, although all investors and enterprises in these locations must of course comply with the growing array of laws and regulations applicable generally to investors and enterprises throughout China.

Consistent with the government's stated policy of giving the authorities in the fourteen coastal cities a major say in their own development, the authorities in some of the cities have begun promulgating regulations to formalize the establishment of their respective ETDZs and to cover specific aspects of economic activity within their jurisdiction. With the exception of Shanghai,[437] most of this legislation has been directed at the ETDZs.[438] In this regard, the more established industrial cities have been most active in legislating for their ETDZs.[439] The remaining cities can be expected to follow suit in due course. In the meantime the regulations which are already in force should provide a fair guide to the kinds of rules that foreign investors will encounter in the coastal cities.

i. Administration

The governments in each of the coastal cities are forming administrative committees to administer the development of their ETDZs. Each committee is in essence an arm of the city's municipal government. In general, the committees have the power to formulate and implement the development plan for the zone, to co-ordinate the work of various departments of the municipal government who have offices in the zone, to examine and approve investment projects, to administer and supervise enterprises within the zone, to administer labour staff in the zone, to formulate and implement zonal regulations, and to attend to relations with foreigners.[440] Committees are also being empowered to establish entities to carry out business activities in the zones. In some cases, these entities are taking part in joint ventures which are being established in their respective zones.

The Administrative Committee does not in every case have exclusive control over the zone. In the Guangzhou ETDZ, the local administrative office for industry and commerce is responsible for the administration of contracts signed by an ETDZ enterprise or contractor,[441] and for ensuring that the parties observe their contractual rights and obligations. The office also has the authority to supervise and inspect ETDZ enterprises, and to act against any enterprise which violates the law.[442]

ii. Forms of Investment

Foreigners are permitted to invest in the zones by forming equity joint ventures or contractual joint ventures with Chinese parties, or by establishing wholly owned operations.[443] Prior to July 1984 wholly owned foreign ventures were permitted only in the SEZs. Other forms of investment should not be ruled out. The regulations for the Guangzhou ETDZ, for instance, permit foreign investors to set up leasing ventures and to deposit cash with or buy shares and bonds from Chinese financial institutions in the zone. Other forms of investment permissible under Chinese law are also possible.[444] The only overriding criterion in most cases is that the investment should carry advanced technology.[445]

iii. Registration Procedures

The Administrative Committee for the ETDZ is the sole approval authority for investment projects in the zone.[446] Once approval is obtained, the enterprise applies for a business licence or registration certificate from the administrative office for industry and commerce situated in the zone.[447] The prerequisites for registration, the procedure for changes in the registration particulars, and the procedure for terminating registration are all very similar to the regulations applicable in the SEZs.[448]

Upon the issue of its business licence or registration certificate, the enterprise is required to open an account with the Bank of China or another authorized bank. Other formalities to be fulfilled include registration with tax and customs authorities.[449]

iv. Land Use

Regulations governing land use in the ETDZs generally follow the tenor of the regulations covering land use in the Shenzhen SEZ. The procedure for obtaining the right to use land and for construction is the same throughout.[450] The one notable difference is that in the Guangzhou ETDZ, no time limit is prescribed in the regulations for drawing up blueprints or for breaking ground for construction. The matter is left to be decided by the Guangzhou ETDZ Planning Office.[451]

Land-use fees and site-development fees differ from city to city but a true comparison of the fees imposed by the various cities requires some effort. Some zones combine land-use fees and site-development fees into one single fee.[452] The site-development fee often encompasses charges for land requisition and public facilities.[453] The costs of installing and connecting electricity, water, drainage, and telecommunication lines can also be separately imposed.[454]

In the ETDZ of such cities as Dalian and Ningbo, fees are reduced according to a progressive scale for investors who establish their production enterprises in the ETDZ before 1988.[455] In the Guangzhou ETDZ, the land-use fee can be postponed or exempted for an enterprise which incurs gross economic losses as a result of *force majeure*, natural disasters, or 'other special circumstances'.[456]

The duration of land leases in the ETDZs again reflects the periods granted by the Shenzhen Land Regulations. A notable exception is the Dalian ETDZ, which has a maximum term of forty years for land for industrial use instead of the usual term of thirty years.[457]

Rules are also being formulated to control construction activities in the ETDZs. Thus the Qinhuangdao Municipal Government has promulgated the Provisional Measures for the Control of Construction and Development in the Qinhuangdao Municipality ETDZ (hereafter cited as the Qinhuangdao Construction Measures).[458] According to these measures, the Qinhuangdao Municipality Baitaling Construction and Development Corporation is responsible for organizing and structuring the zone's plan and its development.[459] It determines the site for projects in the zone.[460] If the design work is to be undertaken by an outside entity, the approval of the Corporation is required, together with a hefty fee.[461] Tenders for basic construction work are arranged by the Corporation.[462] The actual construction work needs to be carried out in co-operation with the Corporation.[463]

v. Labour and Wage Regulations
Like the SEZ regulations, the regulations in the ETDZs on labour and wages afford enterprises greater decision-making power on labour issues than does the national legislation.[464] Again, the regulations differ among the zones. Only the more salient differences are discussed here.

It seems that an enterprise may sign labour contracts with staff and workers either collectively or individually, though this is expressly stated in the regulations of only one of the ETDZs.[465] The probationary period of employment can be a period of up to six months' duration in Tianjin.[466] In Guangzhou the period is one to three months.[467] The Dalian regulations specify three to six months.[468]

By implication, the regulations permit the hiring of workers from outside China. In Tianjin, this right is expressly stated.[469] In several of the zones, the staff can resign from the enterprise by giving one month's notice, but if the worker has received at least three months' training, he is liable to compensate the enterprise for his training costs when he resigns within one year after the completion of training.[470] The Guangzhou ETDZ regulations introduce the concept of possible lifetime employment, prohibiting a worker from resigning where this is not permitted by the labour contract.[471]

In all cases, the wage standard is set by the enterprise in consultation with the workers.[472] The minimum wage standard is set either by the ETDZ Administrative Committee or by reference to the wage standard in state-owned enterprises in the locality.[473] Overtime work carries premium wage standards.[474] In one instance, the premium is set at twice the amount of the basic wage standard for work performed on an official holiday or festival.[475]

Some ETDZs also set minimum annual wage increments.[476] Others leave the matter to the discretion of the enterprise.[477] There is also no uniform standard for the allocation of wages to social security, labour insurance, and other worker welfare funds. The total formula needs to be carefully compiled in each case.[478]

A severance payment is required when workers are dismissed in some zones,[479] though in one zone the formula for compensation is to be determined by the zone authorities.[480] In all cases, however, the practical implementation of some of these regulations will of course face the same difficulties as those that are being encountered in the SEZs. Although the rules for employment are becoming liberal, elements of the overall labour system in China render it difficult to put the liberalization policies into full effect.[481]

vi. Economic Contracts

The Dalian Municipal Government has issued a set of measures regulating economic contracts which involve enterprises in the Dalian ETDZ.[482] Joint venture enterprises and wholly owned foreign enterprises in the zone need to observe the measures when they contract with each other or with local Chinese enterprises.[483] Since some joint ventures gain the status of legal persons in China, this means that the measures extend to contracts which are solely between entities with the status of a legal person in China. The scope of the Dalian measures is to be contrasted with the national regime for contract law, under which contractual arrangements with non-Chinese parties are governed by the Foreign Economic Contracts Law,[484] while those between Chinese legal persons fall within the ambit of the Economic Contracts Law.[485]

The Dalian measures to a large extent mirror the provisions of the national Foreign Economic Contracts Law, but a number of provisions peculiar to the Dalian measures are worth noting. Parties to a contract need to exercise care when corresponding with each other in connection with that contract. Article 16 provides that relevant correspondence and other written documents can be interpreted as amending or supplementing the contract. A party which tenders a deposit or bond under a contract is unable to reclaim it if he fails to perform under the contract. If the party accepting the deposit or bond is at fault, he is required to refund double the amount.[486] Article 27 introduces the concept of joint rights and liabilities where a party to the contract consists of two or more persons. Article 9 is a useful provision. It requires that persons who sign contracts on behalf of contracting parties must be properly authorized. This provision will assist a party to a contract who wishes to ask for evidence of the signing authority granted to the representative of the other party.

Article 25 states that, if a party fails to perform under a contract, the other party can suspend its performance and can also have a lien on property that it is holding from the defaulting party during the performance of the contract. According to the newly enacted General Principles of the Civil Code, the non-defaulting party should be able to dispose of the property and have a preferential right to the proceeds of such disposal in liquidating its claims under the contract.[487] For a party whose contractual rights have been infringed upon, any application for arbitration generally must be made within one year after he knows or should have known about such infringement. However, the one-year limitation does not apply where that party is 'willing to bear the liability'.[488] This provision should be contrasted with Article 39 of the Foreign Economic Contracts Law, which imposes a limitation period of four years for action on a contract for sale of goods.

Article 21 may give rise to difficulties in the implementation of contracts. Where laws are promulgated after the contract comes into effect and such laws are inconsistent with the provisions in the contract, Article 21 preserves the 'validity' of the contractual provisions, unless the new laws specifically provide otherwise. By saying that the 'validity' of contractual provisions will be preserved, it presumably means that the contractual provisions will still govern. Article 40 of the national Foreign Economic Contracts Law addresses a similar situation with less ambiguous language, stating that the contract may still be executed in accordance with its provisions.

vii. Technology Transfer

In promulgating the Provisional Regulations for Import of Technology in Guangzhou Economic and Technical Development Zone (hereafter cited as the Guangzhou ETDZ Technology Regulations),[489] the Guangzhou Municipal People's Government has sought to combine the provisions in three pieces of existing legislation: the National Technology Regulations,[490] the national Measures for Examination and Approval of Technology Import Contracts,[491] and the Shenzhen Technology Regulations.[492] The Guangzhou government has, however, introduced a few additional clauses. For example, it is a common requirement that the technology to be imported must be advanced, appropriate, and capable of producing tangible economic efficiency. The Guangzhou regulations define each of these terms for the first time. 'Advanced' technology means technology that is more advanced than technology of the same type in China, and is being used or developed in an industrially developed country, or will enable a certain business or product of China, Guangdong province, or Guangzhou municipality to attain advanced world standard.[493]

Technology is 'appropriate' when it can be used in production research in the ETDZ, can expedite the technical reformation of enterprises in Guangzhou, Guangdong province, and inland areas, and is suited to the nation's actual circumstances.[494] The criteria for capability to produce tangible economic efficiency are similar to those set out in the national regulations.[495]

Interestingly, the usual duration of technology import contracts is set at ten years.[496] The Shenzhen regulations offer only five years.[497] The Guangzhou authorities also expect to approve contracts more quickly—within forty days—[498] instead of three months in Shenzhen[499] and sixty days in the rest of the country.[500] The Guangzhou regulations, however, require that once the contract is approved, it must be registered with both the ETDZ tax authorities and the zone's administrative office for industry and commerce.[501]

Two other provisions special to Guangzhou bear mention. Firstly, according to Article 23, the supplier of technology is responsible for compensating for all economic losses incurred as a result of a third party's complaint of infringement of patent rights. The difficulty for some foreign suppliers is that the Chinese enterprise may sell products to a third country in which the licensed technology is patented or owned by a party unrelated to the supplier. When this practice is applied on a world-wide basis to include countries in which the foreign supplier otherwise has no commercial interest, the burden posed by Article 23 can be quite substantial. Secondly, Article 13 of the Guangzhou regulations lists a range of preferential treatments available to foreign suppliers. They include reductions in taxes and land-use fees, extension of the contract term, and priority for Chinese purchasers of the supplier's products. A certain number of the foreign supplier's relatives may even be given jobs, with one or more taking part in the management of the local enterprise as representatives of the supplier.

viii. Shanghai

Unlike many of the other coastal cities subject to the 'open' policy, Shanghai has been promulgating regulations to cover foreign economic activities in all parts of the city. Two areas in Shanghai, the Minhang zone in south-west Shanghai and the Hongqiao zone to the west of Shanghai, were earmarked for development in 1983, before the opening of the coastal cities.[502] The Shanghai authorities intend to continue with their pre-existing plans for the development of these zones without introducing any new special measures, although the State Council has agreed to confer on these two zones the status of ETDZs and therefore to enable them to enjoy the preferential treatment granted to ETDZs under the Incentive Regulations.[503]

The three major Shanghai regulations affecting foreign investors concern the procedure for the establishment of joint ventures and wholly owned ventures, labour management in joint ventures, and the supply, distribution, and pricing of materials and goods for joint ventures.[504]

The Regulations of Shanghai Municipality on Negotiations and Examination and Approval Procedures Relating to Establishment of Joint Ventures Using Chinese and Foreign Investment and Acceptance of Foreign Investment for Establishing Self-run Enterprises (Trial Implementation) were promulgated by the Shanghai Municipal People's Government on 1 July 1984 (hereafter cited as the Shanghai Enterprise Regulations).[505] Subsequently, in September 1984, measures implementing these regulations on a trial basis were issued.[506] However, these two pieces of provisional legislation appear to have been superseded somewhat by regulations promulgated in June 1986. The Regulations Regarding the Application for and Examination and Approval of Chinese-Foreign Equity Joint Ventures, Chinese-Foreign Co-operative Joint Ventures and Wholly Foreign-owned Enterprises in Shanghai (hereafter cited as the Shanghai Regulations 1986)[507] do not refer to either piece of pre-existing legislation but are presumed to have overriding force because they are not termed provisional. Nevertheless, the pre-existing legislation should retain some significance because it contains far more detail than the Shanghai Regulations 1986. That detail is in itself interesting because it reveals the actual procedure adopted by the Chinese for negotiating projects with foreigners and for obtaining the necessary approvals.

The Shanghai Enterprise Regulations divide negotiations into two stages, exploratory discussions and discussions of substance.[508] All district and county governments and all departments and units may, either on their own initiative or at the request of foreign business men, conduct exploratory talks with them concerning the establishment of joint ventures.[509] On the basis of these talks, the Chinese party is to submit a preliminary feasibility study and project proposal for approval, ultimately by the Shanghai Foreign Economic Relations and Trade Commission (SFERTC) in conjunction with the Shanghai Planning Commission and other relevant authorities. Substantive negotiations cannot begin until this approval has been granted.[510] According to Article 6 of the Shanghai Regulations 1986, documents of a binding nature also should not be signed before the project proposal is approved. Once granted, the approval remains valid for one year.[511]

During the second stage of negotiations, legal documents are drafted. Article 2 of the Shanghai Enterprise Implementing Measures requires the first draft to be rendered in the 'Chinese party's suggested version'. A formal feasibility study is also required to be prepared jointly by the Chinese and foreign parties. This study, together with the joint venture contract and other documents, is then submitted for final approval. Notwithstanding that contracts can be in both the Chinese language and a foreign language and that the Foreign Economic Contracts Law seems to enable both versions to have equal validity at law,[512] Article 2 deems the Chinese version to be the basis on which the project is to be examined and approved. This is consistent with the practice of the government authorities in Beijing.[513]

The Shanghai Regulations 1986 do not specify the approval limits of the various authorities. For guidance on this point, one must turn to the pre-existing legislation which divides the authority for examining and approving projects into four categories.[514] In summary, a project whose total investment does not exceed US$5 million, which does not need to build, extend, or restructure premises, which is capable of arranging sources of energy, supply of raw materials, and sale of products, and which can balance its foreign exchange earnings and expenditure, can be approved by a competent authority authorized by SFERTC once the Commission has approved the initial project proposal. A production project whose total investment is between US$5 million and US$30 million, and which cannot satisfy all the criteria listed above, must be jointly examined and approved by SFERTC, the Shanghai Planning Commission, and other competent commissions. The role of the Ministry of Foreign Economic Relations and Trade in Beijing in these procedures is unclear, as Article 5(2) of the Shanghai Enterprise Implementing Measures provides for the certificate of approval to be issued by SFERTC on behalf of the Ministry. This procedure also applies to a non-production project whose total investment is US$5 million or more and whose foreign exchange balance does not need assistance from the state. A production project with more than US$30 million in total investment requires ultimate approval from the Ministry of Foreign Economic Relations and Trade, the State Planning Commission, and other relevant ministries and commissions under the State Council.

Foreign investors who wish to establish their own enterprises in Shanghai need first to locate a local organization which is authorized to deal in foreign economic relations and trade to support their application.[515] The choice of this local supporter is critical, as it will assume the task of briefing the investor on local rules and conditions, introducing the investor to various relevant authorities, submitting for approval the project proposal on behalf of the investor, and assisting the investor in negotiations with local authorities on contracts governing such matters as land use, factory construction, employment of labour, channels of supply of materials and sale of products, transportation, insurance, and supply of utilities.[516] The application for approval of the project must be accompanied by an opinion from the local supporting organization.[517] Although Article III(3) of the Shanghai Enterprise Implementing Measures states that local approval may be sufficient for the establishment of some wholly owned businesses, Article 16 of the Shanghai Regulations 1986 clearly provides that approval of all wholly owned projects must be obtained from competent departments of the State Council.

The Shanghai legislation on labour management[518] is enacted pursuant to the national regulations on labour management in equity joint ventures, but contractual joint ventures in Shanghai are also required to refer to these regulations in their operations.[519] The Shanghai regulations confirm the now common practice of requiring joint ventures to seek employees first from among the existing employees of the Chinese parties.[520] They also adopt the practice of subjecting new employees to probationary periods of three to six months.[521] An important distinction is drawn between employees whose employment terminates because they have chosen to resign or because their employment contract expires, and employees who are dismissed before their contract expires.[522] All employees whose employment terminates for any reason whatsoever are entitled to a termination fee equal to one month's salary for each full year of employment with the joint venture. Where the period of employment exceeds ten years, the termination fee is at the rate of one and a half month's salary for each full year. If the employee is dismissed during the term of his employment contract, he becomes entitled to an additional severance fee equal to his salary for three to six months.[523]

Salaries for joint venture employees are to be increased gradually in accordance with improvements in the joint venture's production and management activities, employees' technical skills, and labour efficiency.[524] According to Article 11 of the regulations, salary levels can also be reduced if the joint venture experiences production and management difficulties and suffers losses. However, any reduction must be negotiated with the labour union.

The regulations also require joint ventures to pay to the authorities compensation for food and housing subsidies provided by the state to employees.[525] The housing subsidy can be reduced if the joint venture has built, purchased, or rented housing for employees.[526] Concern for the welfare of employees is most evident in Article 23 which stipulates that joint ventures should assign employees whose sole responsibility is to manage labour and industrial safety. According to this Article, joint ventures should also provide employees with accident-prevention gear and nutritional foods where this is warranted by the actual needs of production and work.

Under the regulations on the supply, distribution, and pricing of materials and goods, a joint venture must each year draft an import and export plan.[527] If a joint venture encounters difficulties in importing or exporting goods or materials or in conducting such importing or exporting in quantities sufficient to satisfy the joint venture's needs, it can apply to SFERTC for assistance.[528] These difficulties will be encountered with respect to goods or materials which require a licence for their import or export. In the case of exports, the Commission will seek to have foreign trade corporations in China buy the joint venture's products with foreign exchange. Article 9 of the regulations confirms the situation that has always existed under the national regulations. The prices of products sold by a joint venture in the domestic market shall be set in accordance with the national price control regulations and shall be paid for in *renminbi*, unless the State Price Control Department has approved their sale at international market prices.

The rather different types of legislation being formulated in Shanghai probably reflect the special position held by Shanghai in China's economy since the early part of this century.[529] Known for years as the 'Paris of the East', Shanghai today remains the largest industrial and commercial city in China. The value of its industrial output in 1983 constituted 11 per cent of the nation's total. Its exports accounted for 16.6 per cent of

China's total export volume in 1983 while 30 per cent of China's cargo is handled through Shanghai's harbour.[530] Yet the volume of foreign investment in this city to date pales beside the investments which have been attracted to southern China. Some of Shanghai's problems include overcrowding for residents and factories, a congested transport network, poor communications facilities, and a languid response to new business proposals. These problems have now been recognized by the central government, which has decided to allocate a higher percentage of funds to Shanghai for the reconstruction of its outdated and overburdened infrastructure facilities. There is also a plan to concentrate development on the service industries. Despite the difficulties, expectations for Shanghai have always been, and will remain, high.[531] The city exudes a confidence that it can overcome whatever problems there might be, especially when those problems also have a marked effect on the nation's economic drive.

III. The Delta Economic Zones and Hainan Island

In February 1985 the State Council designated three coastal areas to be 'opened' up for investment and development.[532] The three areas comprise the Changjiang Delta Open Economic Zone, the Zhujiang Delta Open Economic Zone, and the Southern Fujian Delta Open Economic Zone. At the same time, Chinese officials indicated that the Liaodong and Shandong peninsulas would also be opened to outside investment at an opportune time in the future so as to form a continuous belt of opened cities and areas along China's coast from Dalian in the north to Beihai in the south.[533] The three delta zones contain a number of cities and counties, and are to concentrate on trade, industry, and agriculture, focusing particularly on the processing of agricultural products and export industries.[534]

The Changjiang Delta Zone encompasses the cities of Suzhou, Wuxi, and Changzhou in Jiangsu province and Jiaxing and Huzhou in Zhejiang province. Industrial development is being concentrated on 64 satellite towns in the region. The region is one of the most richly endowed areas in the country. Set in an area of about 27,000 square kilometres, the region is recognized as having a well-developed industrial base and transportation network. In 1984, the five cities had a combined industrial and agricultural output of RMB46.92 billion. In every city except Huzhou, there is a significant textiles industry. Huzhou is a major supplier of freshwater fish.[535]

The Zhujiang Delta Zone comprises an area of about 25,000 square kilometres situated in the southern part of Guangdong province. The zone covers Fanyu and Zengcheng counties in Guangzhou municipality; Foshan city and its three counties of Nanhai, Gaoming, and Shunde; Jiangmen city and its five counties of Heshan, Xinhui, Kaiping, Enping, and Taishan; Bao'an county in Shenzhen city; Doumen county in Zhuhai city; and Dongguan county in Huiyang prefecture. Industrial development is being concentrated on 64 satellite towns in the region. The region is close to the South China Sea oilfields and has temperate climatic conditions and good transportation links with Macau, Hong Kong, and surrounding countries.[536] Although the zone's industrial and agricultural output in 1984 was, at RMB16.5 billion, far less than the output of the Changjiang Delta Zone,[537] it has attracted substantially more investment from foreigners and overseas Chinese. This can be attributed to the zone's proximity to Hong Kong and the fact that the zone represents the indigenous home of many Chinese abroad. Another influencing factor is that three of the fast-growing SEZs are situated within the zone.[538]

The Southern Fujian Delta Zone also has a favourable climate and easy access to Hong Kong and other nearby places outside China. Included in the zone are Xiamen city's Tong'an county, Zhangzhou city, Longhai county, Zhangpu county, and Dongshan county in Longxi prefecture; and Quanzhou city, Hui'an county, Nan'an county, Jinjiang county, Anxi county, and Yongchun county in Jinjiang prefecture. A major industry in the zone is textiles. The total industrial and agricultural output of the zone in 1984 was estimated to be RMB6.41 billion. Investment by foreigners and overseas Chinese is again small in comparison with the Zhujiang Delta Zone.[539]

The three delta economic zones contain within their boundaries the SEZs and some of the fourteen coastal cities. Although the development of the delta economic zones will proceed independently of the other special areas contained within the zones,[540] the delta zones are bound to be influenced significantly by these other areas.[541] The delta zones are, however, still in the planning stage so it is not yet clear exactly how the delta economic zones will coexist with the other special areas. Certainly the SEZs and ETDZs will retain the most preferential incentives ahead of other areas in the location, as evidenced by the range of preferential treatments recently announced by the Guangdong provincial government.[542] These preferential treatments are available as from 1 November 1985 to foreign investors who establish operations in the Zhujiang Delta Zone. The incentives announced are very similar to those set out in the Incentive Regulations for foreigners who invest in the Old Urban Areas of the fourteen coastal cities, with emphasis being placed on the renovation of existing enterprises. Enterprises in the Zhujiang Delta Zone can pay income tax at a rate 20 per cent less than the usual rate. This means a tax rate of 24 per cent for equity joint ventures, and a tax rate of between 16 and 32 per cent for foreign investors carrying on business in the form of other vehicles who are normally subject to tax under the Foreign Enterprise Income Tax Law. The local income tax can be reduced or exempted.

An income tax rate of 15 per cent can, with approval from the Ministry of Finance, apply where the investment is made directly in an energy, transportation, or port project, or involves intensive technology or know-how, or is a production project involving an investment of more than US$30 million and the period for investment recovery is long.

Profits earned from the investment are free from withholding tax when they are remitted abroad. The following items are exempt from customs duties and consolidated industrial and commercial tax: (a) equipment and construction materials which form part of the investment and are imported for the enterprise's production use and management; (b) raw materials, spare parts, components, and packaging materials which are imported to produce export goods; and (c) means of transport and office equipment for the enterprise's own use.[543]

The Zhujiang River Delta Zone will grow more quickly than the other delta economic zones, at least in the immediate future. Apart from the influence of the three SEZs in Guangdong province, the zone's proximity to Hong Kong will give it a continued impetus for modernization. The increase in the volume of people, goods, and money in the area is dramatic and has given rise to speculation that the zone, together with Hong Kong and Macau, will eventually form one huge financial and commercial centre.[544]

As discussed above, Hainan Island also enjoys the policies of a special economic zone. The island has administrative autonomy and has been earmarked by the State Council for rapid development.[545] Hainan Island has special significance for China because it has an abundance of natural resources and its location in the South China Sea is strategically important for China's national defence. In addition, it represents the largest discrete tropical area in China.[546] The authorities on Hainan Island have the power to approve foreign investment projects which have fixed assets valued at not more than US$5 million, so long as the projects do not affect the country's export quotas or the national or provincial conditions for balancing production and construction.[547] According to Article I(10) of the Incentive Regulations,[548] the tax concessions for foreign investors on Hainan Island are to be determined with reference to the concessions applicable in the SEZs. Thus the investment incentives offered by the island include an enterprise income tax rate of 15 per cent and exemption from customs duties on imports of construction materials, machinery, equipment, production raw materials, seeds, and animals for breeding. During the first three years after production has commenced, an enterprise which has difficulty paying the Consolidated Tax can seek an exemption or reduction.[549]

After the indiscriminate spending of state-allocated foreign exchange funds was halted in 1985, Hainan Island resumed the task of exploiting its rich natural resources.[550] Officials in charge of the Hainan Island Administrative Zone plan to focus development on industry (including the processing of agricultural products), mining, and tourism and to enhance the production of tropical crops, livestock, and seafood.[551] A consortium of Australian companies is currently engaged in exploring for petroleum on the island.[552] The resources possessed by Hainan Island are not in doubt. They need only to be harnessed properly in order to create a vital commercial and industrial centre in the most lush tropical environment in China.[553]

IV. Conclusion

In the last two years, the special investment areas in China have come under greater scrutiny by both the Chinese government and foreign investors and observers. Some of the praise for the initial growth rate of the SEZs has been replaced by scepticism about the type of development that has occurred and the undesirable peripheral practices that have sprung up. The SEZs, particularly Shenzhen, have not attracted the advanced technology for industry which is needed to lead China's technology modernization. Instead, Shenzhen has concentrated on trade, tourism, and property development.[554] Likewise the fourteen coastal cities have failed to live up to their promises of fast and sustained growth in the right industrial sectors,[555] though the squeeze on foreign exchange spending since the early part of 1985 has tempered development.

The investment environment in these special investment areas is still far from ideal. Energy, transportation, and communications require the most urgent attention. Shenzhen suffers from inadequate electricity supplies, while both Shenzhen and Zhuhai are still without an airport. In most of the fourteen coastal cities, transportation links with the ETDZ are still being developed. Skilled people are also in short supply. The special areas need to attract technocrats from both the hinterland and overseas to train the local population. Commercial and tourism developments have been the most prominent as they provide the fastest returns on investment, causing development in industry to lag behind. In any event, the investments in industry in the SEZs are generally limited to processing and assembly operations, as opposed to the manufacture of high-technology products. The balance of foreign exchange earnings and expenditure remains a problem for Chinese authorities and foreign investors alike. The primary cause is that, up to now, the emphasis has been on production as opposed to marketing functions, and the quality of goods has not been able to attain the standards necessary for sale on the international market. Finally, an enormous effort in improving financial management in the SEZs is required to solve problems such as the smuggling of goods and unlawful trading in currencies.[556]

Despite these difficulties, one cannot ignore the fact that the special investment areas, especially the SEZs, continue to attract substantial foreign investors. There are signs, too, that investments are gradually being shunted into the right industrial sectors. For instance, in 1985 Shenzhen is reported to have exported 43 per cent of its output. Industrial output in the four SEZs in 1985 stood at RMB4.84 billion, more than five times the value of output in 1979. Conditions for investment are also being improved. The SEZs now boast 60 square kilometres of developed area, covering industry, commerce, tourism, and residences. As of the end of 1985, there were 900 newly established factories in operation in the SEZs.[557] Connections between the SEZs and the inland areas of China are being given more attention, with 25 central government departments and 27 provinces, municipalities, and autonomous regions having signed industrial co-operation agreements with Shenzhen.[558]

Just as China's modernization programme calls for an enormous effort in order to succeed, the proper development and utilization of the various special investment areas likewise require concerted work by many people. Having achieved so much already, the authorities and workers in the special investment areas are not likely to yield to the difficulties that have arisen, but can be expected to strive to solve these problems in order to ensure that the various special rights conferred on the areas by the central government are preserved. The resolution of these difficulties will add to the attraction of the special investment areas for foreign investors.

The ever-changing investment scene in China also imposes extra tasks on foreigners who contemplate establishing businesses in the special investment areas. As China opens up more areas to foreign investors, municipal and provincial governments will compete even harder for investors' capital and technology by offering more favourable, or sometimes simply different, incentives. Whilst this enlarges the range of options open to foreigners, it also requires foreigners to make comparative studies of the incentives, laws, and other conditions applicable in the various areas. At this stage, it is difficult to carry out such a study thoroughly, because there is no easy access to the rules and regulations promulgated by the various authorities. Moreover, the authorities are continually revising their rules and regulations as they gain experience in economic and financial management. The difficulty that investors generally have in deciding where to locate their operations in a developing country are multiplied manifold in a country the size of China, but the potential of this market could well justify the effort required to determine the most suitable investment location.

Notes

1. See *China Investment Guide 1986* (Hong Kong, Longman Group Limited, 1986); *14 Coastal Cities of the PRC Handbook* (Hong Kong, Wah kwong Newspapers Ltd., 1985); 'NPC Bill on Hainan Jurisdiction Adopted', *China Daily*, 26 May 1984, p. 1; 'Development Plan Approved for Hainan Island', *China Daily*, 13 July 1983, p. 3; 'China Opens Three More Coast Areas', *China Daily*, 5 March 1985.
2. See White Paper, 26 September 1984, *Joint Declaration of the Government of the United Kingdom of Great Britain and Northern Ireland and the Government of the People's Republic of China on the Question of Hong Kong* (London, HMSO, 1984).
3. See J. Kamm, 'Importing Some of Hong Kong...Exporting Some of China', *China Business Review*, March–April 1980, p. 29.
4. China reportedly investigated 30 such zones in over 40 countries. See F. Chi, 'China's Newborn SEZs and their Strategic Significance', *Economic Reporter*, August 1981, p. 11.
5. Kamm, p. 28, note 3 above.
6. Kamm, p. 28, note 3 above.
7. See 'NPC Approved Regulations on Guangdong Special Economic Zones', *China Economic News*, 1 September 1980, p. 2.
8. See *Investment Guide to Xiamen Special Economic Zone* (Hong Kong,

Hongkong and Shanghai Banking Corporation in association with The Construction and Development Corporation of Xiamen Special Economic Zone, 1984).

9. For Chinese views of the role to be played by the SEZs in the nation's economic development see Chi, note 4 above; Stas, 'What's Going on in the SEZs', *Economic Reporter*, August 1981, p. 14; D. Xu, 'China's Special Economic Zones', *Beijing Review*, 14 December 1981, p. 14; and 'Leader of State Administrative Commission on Import and Export Affairs on Development and Administration of Special Economic Zones', *China Economic News*, 29 June 1981, p. 3. See also D. Chu, 'The Costs of the Four SEZs to China', *Economic Reporter*, June 1982, p. 18.

10. See Xu, p. 16, note 9 above.

11. See J. Stepanek, 'China's SEZs: Terms in the Special Economic Zones Compare Well With Those in Other Parts of the World', *China Business Review*, March–April 1982, p. 39. Hopewell Holdings, the Hong Kong conglomerate, has announced plans to invest more than US$300 million to develop the infrastructure in the Shenzhen area. One key Hopewell project is the planned construction of China's first modern highway from Hong Kong to Guangzhou via the Zhuhai and Shenzhen SEZs. See 'China's Enterprise Zones: Leaky Capitalist Enclaves', *The Economist*, 27 November 1982, p. 87; and 'Hopewell's HK$4.6 Billion Projects Marks Investment Trends in Key South China Special Economic Zone', *China Economic News*, 28 December 1981, p. 7.

12. See Xu, p. 15, note 9 above.

13. See Xu, p. 15, note 9 above.

14. Stas, p. 14, note 9 above.

15. See 'Bankruptcy Issue Heating Up in China', *Asian Wall Street Journal*, 13 August 1986, pp. 1 and 7; and 'New Bank Financing Set-up Tried in 5 Cities', *China Daily*, 8 April 1986, p. 1.

16. Stas, p. 14, note 9 above.

17. For both legal and historical analyses of this issue, see P. Wesley-Smith, *Unequal Treaty 1898–1997: China, Great Britain and Hong Kong's New Territories* (Hong Kong, Oxford University Press, revised edition, 1983).

18. See Ho Li, '*Xin Xianggang?—Shenzhen tequ neiwang*' (A New Hong Kong?—An Inside View of the Shenzhen Special Zone), *Qishi niandai* (*The Seventies*), March 1982, p. 16.

19. *Introduction to Shenzhen Special Economic Zone Investment Environment and Shenzhen SEZ Development Co.* (undated pamphlet published by Shenzhen Special Economic Zone Development Company), p. 16 (hereafter cited as the *Introduction to Shenzhen SEZ*).

20. Ho, p. 16, note 18 above.

21. For a discussion of the origins of the Shekou Industrial Zone, see Section D of Part I of this chapter.

22. 'Shekou Industries Point to Way Ahead', *China Daily*, 6 August 1986, p. 2.

23. T. Gorman, 'Deep Ditch and Snake Mouth: New Boom Towns in the Pearl River Delta', *Pacific*, 3 November 1982, p. 72.

24. 'Shekou SEZ Begins to Show its Advantages', *Economic Reporter*, December 1981, p. 23. See also Gorman, p. 72, note 23 above.

25. *Introduction to Shenzhen SEZ*, pp. 16–17, note 19 above.

26. 'Shekou Industries Point to Way Ahead', note 22 above.

27. Gorman, p. 72, note 23 above. See also L. Kraar, 'A Little Touch of Capitalism', *Fortune International*, 18 April 1983, p. 125.

28. See note 357 below and accompanying text.

29. Gorman, p. 72, note 23 above.

30. K. Woodward and R. Goodwin, 'Supplying Offshore Services', *China Business Review*, March–April 1982, p. 15.

31. See A. Li, 'Shenzhen Special Economic Zone', *Amcham*, October 1981, p. 21; F. Sum, 'Shenzhen SEZ: Hong Kong Money Moves North', *Pacific*, 3 November 1982, p. 68; F. Sum and S. Chapman, 'How to Move Your Money

North', *Pacific*, 3 November 1982, p. 76; and F. Ching, 'China's Shenzhen Gives Capitalism a Shot at Success', *Asian Wall Street Journal*, 13 August 1982, p. 1.

32. 'Shenzhen—China's First Special Economic Zone', *Beijing Review*, 14 December 1981, p. 18.

33. See Gorman, p. 71, note 23 above.

34. See S. Wong, 'Weekend Resorts; Shenzhen's Recreation Reservoirs', *Pacific*, 3 November 1982, p. 79.

35. See *Business China*, 28 July 1986, p. 111.

36. See *Business China*, 26 May 1986, p. 79.

37. The zone initially had an area of 6.8 square kilometres, but this was expanded to 15.16 square kilometres in 1983. See *Trade and Investment Guide to Guangdong* (Hong Kong, the Hong Kong and Shanghai Banking Corporation in association with the Guangdong Province Foreign Economic and Trade Commission, April 1985), p. 45.

38. *14 Coastal Cities of the PRC Handbook*, pp. 72–3, note 1 above.

39. See 'No more room left in Zhuhai', *China Trade Report*, March 1985, p. 1.

40. *Trade and Investment Guide to Guangdong*, pp. 45–6, note 37 above and 'Zhuhai's Development Blueprint Mapped Out', *Intertrade*, May 1986, pp. 64–5.

41. 'No more room left in Zhuhai', note 39 above.

42. See 'The "poor little son" races to catch up', *South China Morning Post*, 10 January 1986; and 'Updating the Zones: Progress and Problems in Xiamen, Shantou', *Business China*, 10 February 1986, pp. 18–19 (hereafter referred to as 'Updating the Zones').

43. See 'Updating the Zones', p. 19, note 42 above.

44. *Trade and Investment Guide to Guangdong*, pp. 49–50, note 37 above.

45. *14 Coastal Cities of the PRC Handbook*, pp. 76–7, note 1 above.

46. 'Changes in Xiamen Zone', *Business China*, 14 November 1984, p. 163.

47. *14 Coastal Cities of the PRC Handbook*, pp. 76–7, note 1 above.

48. See 'Changes in Xiamen Zone', note 46 above; 'Update on Xiamen', *Business China*, 29 August 1985, p. 127; 'Updating the Zones', note 42 above; and 'Xiamen Redresses "Unwarranted Fees"', *China Daily*, 22 July 1986, p. 2.

49. 'Zones Enter New Stage of Economic Development', *China Daily*, 17 February 1986, p. 1.

50. 'Foreign Loans Grow to $2.5 bn in First Half', *China Daily*, 31 July 1986, p. 1.

51. See Stepanek, p. 38, note 11 above.

52. See *Trade and Investment Guide to Guangdong*, pp. 38–40, note 37 above. According to this Guide, foreign industrial enterprises in Shenzhen accounted for more than one-third of the value of the zone's total industrial output in 1983.

53. 'China's Enterprise Zones: Leaky Capitalist Enclaves', p. 87, note 11 above.

54. Gorman, p. 71, note 23 above.

55. See C. Zheng, *'Erlinglinglingnian de Shenzhen'* (Shenzhen in the Year 2000), *Qishi niandai (The Seventies)*, March 1982, p. 26; and 'Shenzhen Zone Plan Wins Fresh Support', *China Daily*, 22 September 1982, p. 1.

56. 'China: Reorienting Outwards', *Far Eastern Economic Review*, 6 February 1986, pp. 34–5; and 'Zones Enter New Stage of Economic Development', note 49 above.

57. An English translation of the SEZ Regulations appears in F. Chu, M. Moser, and O. Nee (eds.), *Commercial, Business and Trade Laws: People's Republic of China* (Dobbs Ferry, Oceana Publications, Inc., 1982), Pt. 14.

58. The SEZ Regulations came into effect on the date of their promulgation.

59. See 'Regulations for Xiamen (Amoy) Special Economic Zone', *China Economic News*, 6 April 1981, pp. 2–3.

60. The five regulations are: Regulations of Xiamen Special Economic Zone on the Registration of Enterprises (hereafter cited as the Xiamen Enterprise Registration Regulations); Regulations of Xiamen Special Economic Zone on Land Use

(hereafter cited as the Xiamen Land Use Regulations); Regulations of Xiamen Special Economic Zone on Labour Management (hereafter cited as the Xiamen Labour Management Regulations); Regulations of Xiamen Special Economic Zone on the Import of Technology (hereafter cited as the Xiamen Technology Regulations); and Regulations of Xiamen Special Economic Zone on Economic Association with Inland Areas (hereafter cited as the Xiamen Inland Association Regulations). These regulations were promulgated on 24 February 1985 and became effective on that date. An English translation of these regulations appears in *China Economic News*, 25 March 1985, 15 April 1985, 25 March 1985, 22 April 1985, and 15 April 1985 respectively.

61. SEZ Regulations, Art. 2, note 57 above.
62. SEZ Regulations, Art. 2, note 57 above.
63. SEZ Regulations, Art. 3, note 57 above.
64. SEZ Regulations, Art. 23, note 57 above.
65. SEZ Regulations, Art. 5, note 57 above.
66. SEZ Regulations, Art. 5, note 57 above.
67. SEZ Regulations, Art. 25, note 57 above.
68. SEZ Regulations, Art. 5, note 57 above.
69. SEZ Regulations, Art. 5, note 57 above.
70. But see Kraar, p. 125, note 27 above, quoting a manager of the Continental Grain Co.: 'What in other countries can be resolved with a simple letter or phone call takes a lot of time and discussion with officials. This is still China.'
71. See note 155 below and accompanying text.
72. See note 220 below and accompanying text.
73. See notes 211, 212, and 213 below and accompanying text.
74. See note 64 above and accompanying text.
75. SEZ Regulations, Art. 23, note 57 above.
76. See note 156 below and accompanying text.
77. See 'Special Zones Get Watchdog Office', *South China Morning Post*, 26 June 1982, p. 12. According to this report, the Office of SEZ Affairs has been 'charged with the task of examining major, costly projects'.
78. Moser, conversation with ADCOM official.
79. SEZ Regulations, Art. 1, note 57 above.
80. 'Shenzhen Special Zone Overseas Chinese City: Current Measures of Preferential Treatment for Investments', *Wen wei po*, 25 February 1986, p. 12.
81. Measures of the State Council Concerning Special Preferential Treatment for Taiwan Compatriots Investing in Special Economic Zones, promulgated by the State Council on 5 April 1983.
82. SEZ Regulations, Art. 4, note 57 above.
83. SEZ Regulations, Art. 1, note 57 above.
84. SEZ Regulations, Art. 4, note 57 above.
85. Moser, conversation with ADCOM official. For a discussion of the distinctions between the types of joint ventures see Chapter 3 in this volume.
86. Law of the People's Republic of China On Joint Ventures Using Chinese and Foreign Investment, adopted by the Second Session of the Fifth National People's Congress on 1 July 1979 and promulgated on 8 July 1979 (hereafter cited as the Joint Venture Law). An English translation of the Joint Venture Law appears in Chu, Moser, and Nee, Pt. 9, note 57 above.
87. Joint Venture Law, Art. 4, note 86 above.
88. SEZ Regulations, Art. 1, note 57 above.
89. SEZ Regulations, Art. 10, note 57 above.
90. According to Chinese reports, as of June 1986, foreign investors had contracted to establish 130 wholly owned business in China. See 'China Moves to Help Foreign Enterprises', *South China Morning Post*, 6 August 1986, pp. 1 and 3.
91. There were reports in 1983 that the 3-M Corporation had received approval to establish a wholly owned plant in Shanghai, and Pow's conversation with an official from the Shanghai Foreign Economic Relations and Trade Commission

revealed that a Japanese company also received approval to set up a wholly owned enterprise at about the same time, but the first legislation permitting this form of investment was promulgated by the Shanghai municipal government on 1 July 1984. See note 515 below and accompanying text.

92. SEZ Regulations, Art. 7, note 57 above.

93. SEZ Regulations, Art. 8, note 57 above.

94. SEZ Regulations, Art. 8, note 57 above. Insurance may be obtained 'from the People's Insurance Company of China in the Special Zones or other insurance companies set up in the Special Zones with China's approval'.

95. SEZ Regulations, Art. 11, note 57 above.

96. SEZ Regulations, Art. 11, note 57 above.

97. SEZ Regulations, Art. 15, note 57 above.

98. The central piece of legislation is the Provisional Regulations of the People's Republic of China Governing Foreign Exchange Control, promulgated by the State Council on 18 December 1980. An English translation of the law is on file with the authors. For a discussion of this law and other foreign exchange legislation see Chapter 9 in this volume.

99. The full text of these measures has not been publicized, but their promulgation was reported in *Ta kung pao*, 18 November 1985, p. 1 and *China Economic News*, 16 December 1985, p. 6.

100. See Kraar, p. 127, note 27 above.

101. The rules have not been made publicly available but are reported in 'Shenzhen, Zhuhai Residents May Have Accounts in HK Dollars', *Ta kung pao*, 4 April 1982, p. 5. See, also, 'Shenzhen, Zhuhai Banks Offer Foreign Currency Accounts', *China Daily*, 11 April 1982, p. 2.

102. See note 101 above.

103. See 'Shumchum "money" needs careful study', *South China Morning Post*, 18 June 1983, p. 1; 'New Currency for Shenzhen', *Business China*, 9 May 1985, p. 70; and 'Shenzhen Seeks Forex Formula', *South China Morning Post*, 18 December 1985, p. 5.

104. See *'Tequ huobi jueding bufaxing'* (Decision Not to Issue Special Zone Currency), *Ta kung pao*, 1 April 1986, pp. 1 and 2.

105. See note 104 above.

106. SEZ Regulations, Art. 17, note 57 above.

107. SEZ Regulations, Art. 17, note 57 above.

108. SEZ Regulations, Art. 13, note 57 above.

109. SEZ Regulations, Art. 13, note 57 above.

110. Moser, discussion with Chinese tax official. See also T. Gelatt, 'China's Special Economic Zones', in J. Cohen (ed.), *Legal Aspects of Doing Business in China 1983* (New York, Practising Law Institute, 1983), p. 186. For a detailed description of the Consolidated Tax see Chapter 2 in this volume.

111. Gelatt, p. 161, note 110 above.

112. SEZ Regulations, Art. 9, note 57 above.

113. Gelatt, p. 160, note 110 above.

114. SEZ Regulations, Art. 9, note 57 above.

115. See The Income Tax Law of the People's Republic of China Concerning Joint Ventures Using Chinese and Foreign Investment, adopted by the Third Session of the Fifth National People's Congress on 10 September 1980, Art. 3 (hereafter cited as the JVITL). An English translation of the law appears in Chu, Moser, and Nee, Pt. 13, note 57 above.

116. JVITL, Art. 3, note 115 above.

117. The Income Tax Law of the People's Republic of China Concerning Foreign Enterprises, adopted by the Fourth Session of the Fifth National People's Congress on 13 December 1981, Art. 3 (hereafter cited as the FEITL). An English translation of the law appears in Chu, Moser, and Nee, Pt. 13, note 57 above.

118. FEITL, Art. 4, note 117 above.

119. Moser, conversation with tax official. However, it should also be noted

that the benefits of the lower SEZ tax rates are not available to an enterprise simply because such an enterprise has a presence in the zones; in addition, the income-producing activity of the enterprise must have a direct connection with the SEZs. Based on these principles, the Ministry of Finance has ruled that foreign oil companies that register offices in the SEZs but conduct exploration and production work, and thus derive their income from, outside the zones may not benefit from the 15 per cent profit tax provision. See V. Fung, 'China Clarifies Rules on Foreign Banks', *Asian Wall Street Journal*, 29 June 1983, p. 1.

120. See Incentive Regulations, Art. I(3), note 271 below and accompanying text.

121. SEZ Regulations, Art. 14, note 57 above.

122. SEZ Regulations, Art. 19, note 57 above.

123. SEZ Regulations, Art. 19, note 57 above.

124. SEZ Regulations, Art. 19, note 57 above.

125. SEZ Regulations, Art. 21, note 57 above.

126. SEZ Regulations, Art. 20, note 57 above.

127. SEZ Regulations, Art. 18, note 57 above.

128. SEZ Regulations, Art. 12, note 57 above.

129. An English translation of the Entry and Exit Regulations is on file with the authors. There is no corresponding legislation in the Xiamen SEZ.

130. Entry and Exit Regulations, Art. 2, note 129 above.

131. Entry and Exit Regulations, Art. 11, note 129 above.

132. The Inland Personnel Regulations were adopted by the Eighteenth Session of the Standing Committee of the Sixth People's Congress of Guangdong Province on 22 February 1986.

133. Inland Personnel Regulations, Art. 16, note 132 above.

134 See '*Shen zhen te qu "er xian" qi yong*' (Commencing Use of Shenzhen Special Zone 'Second Line'), *Ming pao*, 1 April 1986, p. 1. The scheme to isolate the SEZs from the rest of China is implicit in the Entry and Exit Regulations. In fact, Shenzhen for some time has had a barbed-wire fence erected along the border of the municipality with the rest of China (see Ho, p. 17, note 18 above). The Inland Personnel Regulations put this scheme formally into place.

135. See note 134 above. See also the Inland Personnel Regulations, Art. 1, note 132 above.

136. Inland Personnel Regulations, Art. 3, note 132 above.

137. Inland Personnel Regulations, Art. 4, note 132 above.

138. Inland Personnel Regulations, Art. 5, note 132 above.

139. Inland Personnel Regulations, Art. 6, note 132 above.

140. Inland Personnel Regulations, Art. 8, note 132 above.

141. Inland Personnel Regulations, Art. 8, note 132 above.

142. Inland Personnel Regulations, Art. 11, note 132 above.

143. Entry and Exit Regulations, Art. 3(1), note 129 above.

144. Entry and Exit Regulations, Art. 3(2), note 129 above.

145. Entry and Exit Regulations, Art. 5, note 129 above.

146. Entry and Exit Regulations, Art. 10, note 129 above.

147. Entry and Exit Regulations, Art. 7, note 129 above.

148. See '*Shenzhen jianhua qianzheng shouxu*' (Shenzhen Simplifies Visa Procedures), *Ta kung pao*, 19 November 1984, p. 2.

149. See 'Border Procedures for Private Cars in Shenzhen', *China Trader Weekly Bulletin*, 9–15 May 1982, p. 4.

150. 'Border Procedures for Private Cars in Shenzhen', note 149 above.

151. See, for example, Kraar, p. 126, note 27 above, quoting a Pepsico manager's complaints that the 19-mile trip from the company's Shenzhen plant to Hong Kong often takes four to five hours: 'It would take only an hour or two if not for the slow customs clearance at China's border.' However, a few flexible measures for entry and exit by motor vehicles were implemented in April 1985. See '*Xianggang qiche jinchu Shenzhen: liangge kouan, dou ke tongxing* (Hong

Kong Cars Entering and Leaving Shenzhen: Passage Possible through Two Ports), *Wen wei po*, 29 April 1985, p. 4. See also M. Moser, 'Guangdong's SEZs: Four New Regulations Fill Important Gaps', *China Business Review*, March–April 1982, p. 40.

152. An English translation of the Business Registration Regulations is on file with the authors.

153. Xiamen Enterprise Registration Regulations, note 60 above.

154. An English translation of these Rules appears in *China Economic News*, 29 October 1984, p. 1.

155. Business Registration Regulations, Art. 2, note 152 above. The 'administrative organisation for industry and commerce' refers to the local unit of the General Administration for Industry and Commerce (GAIC). See R. Lutz, 'The General Administration for the Control of Industry and Commerce: Its Mandate Spans the Spectrum of Regulatory Functions', *China Business Review*, March–April 1983, p. 25. In mid-1983 the GAIC changed its name to the State Administration for Industry and Commerce of the People's Republic of China and is now commonly referred to in English as the SAIC.

156. Business Registration Regulations, Art. 3, note 152 above.

157. Business Registration Regulations, Art. 5, note 152 above.

158. Shenzhen Business Registration Rules, Art. 2, note 154 above.

159. Shenzhen Business Registration Rules, Art. 2, note 154 above.

160. Shenzhen Business Registration Rules, Art. 11, note 154 above.

161. Business Registration Regulations, Art. 6, note 152 above.

162. Business Registration Regulations, Art. 9, note 152 above.

163. Business Registration Regulations, Art. 7, note 152 above.

164. Business Registration Regulations, Art. 8, note 152 above.

165. Business Registration Regulations, Art. 11, note 152 above.

166. Business Registration Regulations, Art. 12, note 152 above.

167. Business Registration Regulations, Art. 12, note 152 above.

168. Shenzhen Business Registration Rules, Art. 14(1), note 154 above, imposes a fine of up to RMB20,000 on representative offices of foreign companies which carry on business activities without registration or engage in direct profit-making activities. The sanction includes an order to cease such activities.

169. An English translation of the law appears in *China Economic News*, 21 February 1983, p. 1.

170. Provisional Regulations for the Establishment of Representative Offices in China by Overseas Chinese and Foreign Financial Institutions, Art. 8, note 169 above.

171. The SEZ Labour and Wage Regulations were adopted by the Thirteenth Session of the Standing Committee of the Fifth People's Congress of Guangdong Province on 17 November 1981. An English translation of the SEZ Labour and Wage Regulations is on file with the authors.

172. SEZ Labour and Wage Regulations, Art. 2, note 171 above.

173. Regulations on Labour Management in Joint Ventures Using Chinese and Foreign Investment, promulgated by the State Council on 26 July 1980 (hereafter cited as the JV Labour Regulations). An English translation of the JV Labour Regulations appears in Chu, Moser, and Nee, Pt. 9, note 57 above.

174. JV Labour Regulations, Art. 2, note 173 above; and SEZ Labour and Wage Regulations, Art. 2, note 171 above.

175. JV Labour Regulations, Art. 2, note 173 above.

176. SEZ Labour and Wage Regulations, Art. 2, note 171 above.

177. The SEZ Union Regulations were adopted by the Thirteenth Session of the Standing Committee of the Sixth People's Congress of Guangdong Province on 8 May 1985.

178. SEZ Union Regulations, Art. 7, note 177 above.

179. SEZ Labour and Wage Regulations, Art. 4, note 171 above; and JV Labour Regulations, Art. 3, note 173 above.

180. SEZ Labour and Wage Regulations, Art. 4, note 171 above.
181. SEZ Labour and Wage Regulations, Art. 19, note 171 above.
182. JV Labour Regulations, Art. 8, note 173 above.
183. JV Labour Regulations, Art. 11, note 173 above.
184. SEZ Labour and Wage Regulations, Art. 7, note 171 above.
185. SEZ Labour and Wage Regulations, Art. 9, note 171 above.
186. SEZ Labour and Wage Regulations, Art. 8, note 171 above.
187. SEZ Labour and Wage Regulations, Art. 7, note 171 above.
188. SEZ Labour and Wage Regulations, Art. 10, note 171 above.
189. SEZ Labour and Wage Regulations, Art. 11, note 171 above.
190. SEZ Labour and Wage Regulations, Arts. 15 and 16, note 171 above; and
JV Labour Regulations, Arts. 4 and 7, note 173 above.
191. SEZ Labour and Wage Regulations, Art. 29, note 171 above.
192. SEZ Labour and Wage Regulations, Art. 29, note 171 above.
193. SEZ Labour and Wage Regulations, Art. 16, note 171 above.
194. SEZ Labour and Wage Regulations, Art. 16, note 171 above.
195. SEZ Labour and Wage Regulations, Art. 16, note 171 above.
196. SEZ Labour and Wage Regulations, Art. 17, note 171 above.
197. SEZ Labour and Wage Regulations, Art. 18, note 171 above.
198. SEZ Union Regulations, Art. 18, note 177 above.
199. SEZ Union Regulations, Art. 5, note 177 above, state that the Labour
Union Federations of the cities of Shenzhen, Zhuhai, and Shantou shall exercise
unified leadership over labour unions in enterprises in their respective special
zones.
200. SEZ Union Regulations, Art. 23, note 177 above. Two of the precondi-
tions to a foreign or an overseas Chinese worker joining the union are that his
main source of income is in the form of wages and that he endorses the 'Constitution of the China Labour Union'.
201. SEZ Union Regulations, Arts. 6, 8, 9, and 10, note 177 above.
202. SEZ Union Regulations, Art. 16, note 177 above.
203. SEZ Union Regulations, Art. 12, note 177 above.
204. See note 60 above.
205. Xiamen Labour Management Regulations, Art. 11, note 60 above.
206. Xiamen Labour Management Regulations, Art. 12, note 60 above.
207. Xiamen Labour Management Regulations, Art. 14, note 60 above.
208. Xiamen Labour Management Regulations, Art. 14, note 60 above.
209. Xiamen Labour Management Regulations, Art. 8, note 60 above.
210. Xiamen Labour Management Regulations, Art. 15, note 60 above.
211. SEZ Labour and Wage Regulations, Art. 4, note 171 above.
212. SEZ Labour and Wage Regulations, Art. 17, note 171 above.
213. See Moser, p. 42, note 151 above. See also 'Hiring and Firing in Guangdong's Special Economic Zones', Business China, 20 January 1982, p. 9.
214. See 'Seminar Offers Insights into SEZs', China Trader, June 1982, p. 96.
215. 'Seminar Offers Insights into SEZs', note 214 above.
216. 'Seminar Offers Insights into SEZs', note 214 above.
217. See T. Gelatt, 'Land, Entry Laws in China's Economic Zones', Asian Wall
Street Journal, 11 February 1982, p. 8.
218. Adopted by the Thirteenth Session of the Standing Committee of the
Fifth People's Congress of Guangdong Province on 17 November 1981 and put
into effect on 1 January 1982 (hereafter cited as the Shenzhen Land Regulations).
An English translation of the Shenzhen Land Regulations is on file with the
authors.
219. Shenzhen Land Regulations, Art. 5, note 218 above.
220. Shenzhen Land Regulations, Art. 8, note 218 above.
221. Shenzhen Land Regulations, Art. 8, note 218 above.
222. Shenzhen Land Regulations, Art. 9, note 218 above.

223. Shenzhen Land Regulations, Art. 9, note 218 above.

224. Shenzhen Land Regulations, Art. 9, note 218 above.

225. Shenzhen Land Regulations, Art. 9, note 218 above.

226. Shenzhen Land Regulations, Art. 15, note 218 above.

227. Shenzhen Land Regulations, Art. 15, note 218 above.

228. Shenzhen Land Regulations, Art. 16, note 218 above.

229. Shenzhen Land Regulations, Art. 18, note 218 above.

230. Shenzhen Land Regulations, Art. 18, note 218 above.

231. The Shenzhen Land Use Fee Adjustment Measures were approved by the Guangdong provincial government on 2 June 1984; Article III prescribes 1 July 1984 as the day that the measures became effective.

232. Shenzhen Land Use Fee Adjustment Measures, Art. I, note 231 above.

233. Shenzhen Land Use Fee Adjustment Measures, Art. I, note 231 above.

234. Shenzhen Land Use Fee Adjustment Measures, Art. I(1), note 231 above.

235. Shenzhen Land Use Fee Adjustment Measures, Art. I(1), note 231 above.

236. The Shenzhen Land Use Fee Implementing Measures came into force on the date of promulgation.

237. Shenzhen Land Use Fee Implementing Measures, Art. 5, note 236 above.

238. Shenzhen Land Use Fee Implementing Measures, Art. 5, note 236 above.

239. Shenzhen Land Use Fee Implementing Measures, Art. 4, note 236 above.

240. Shenzhen Land Use Fee Implementing Measures, Art. 15, note 236 above.

241. Shenzhen Land Use Fee Implementing Measures, Art. 12, note 236 above.

242. Shenzhen Land Use Fee Implementing Measures, Art. 9, note 236 above.

243. Shenzhen Land Use Fee Implementing Measures, Art. 13, note 236 above.

244. See Shenzhen Land Regulations, Art. 18, note 218 above.

245. Xiamen Land Use Regulations, note 60 above.

246. Xiamen Land Use Regulations, Art. 6(1), note 60 above.

247. Shenzhen Land Regulations, Art. 15(1), note 218 above.

248. Xiamen Land Use Regulations, Art. 7, note 60 above.

249. Xiamen Land Use Regulations, Art. 8, note 60 above.

250. Xiamen Land Use Regulations, Art. 10, note 60 above.

251. See Moser, p. 44, note 151 above.

252. Stepanek, p. 38, note 11 above.

253. See 'Legal Framework for Investors to China's Special Economic Zones (SEZs)', *Economic Reporter*, February 1982, pp. 21 and 22.

254. Shenzhen Land Regulations, Art. 3, note 218 above.

255. Shenzhen Land Regulations, Art. 2, note 218 above.

256. Shenzhen Land Regulations, Art. 6, note 218 above.

257. Shenzhen Land Regulations, Art. 11, note 218 above.

258. Shenzhen Land Regulations, Art. 12, note 218 above.

259. The Chinese text of the law appears in *Shenzhen tequ bao* (*Shenzhen Special Zone News*), 12 July 1982, p. 2. An English-language translation of the text is on file with the authors.

260. Construction Measures, Art. 12, note 259 above.

261. Construction Measures, Art. 13, note 259 above.

262. Construction Measures, Arts. 19–25, note 259 above.

263. Construction Measures, Arts. 26–30, note 259 above.

264. Construction Measures, Arts. 31–49, note 259 above.

265. Construction Measures, Art. 33, note 259 above.

266. Construction Measures, Art. 42, note 259 above.

267. Construction Measures, Art. 43(5), note 259 above.

268. The original Chinese version and an English translation are on file with the authors.

269. The Regulations of Shenzhen Special Economic Zone Governing Mortgage Loans has since provided further rules on the mortgage of real estate. See Chapter 10 in this volume for details.

270. See M. J. Moser (ed.), *Foreign Trade, Investment and the Law in the People's Republic of China* (Hong Kong, Oxford University Press, first edition 1984), p. 163.

271. An English translation of the Incentive Regulations is on file with the authors.

272. Incentive Regulations, Art. I(1), note 271 above.

273. Incentive Regulations, Art. I(1), note 271 above.

274. Incentive Regulations, Art. I(1), note 271 above.

275. JVITL, Art. 5, note 115 above and Decision Regarding Amendment of the Joint Venture Income Tax Law of the People's Republic of China, adopted by the Second Session of the Standing Committee of the Sixth National People's Congress on 2 September 1983.

276. FEITL, Art. 5, note 117 above.

277. FEITL, Art. 5, note 117 above.

278. Incentive Regulations, Art. I(2), note 271 above.

279. Incentive Regulations, Art. I(3), note 271 above.

280. Incentive Regulations, Art. I(4), note 271 above.

281. FEITL, Art. 11, note 117 above.

282. Incentive Regulations, Art. I(4), note 271 above.

283. The Goods Control Regulations were promulgated by the Customs General Administration of China and came into effect on 1 April 1986. In Shenzhen, detailed implementing rules promulgated by the Kowloon Customs Administration also came into effect on 1 April 1986. The rules contain 29 provisions on customs control and the levy of customs duties.

284. See Incentive Regulations, Art. I(5), note 271 above and Goods Control Regulations, Arts. 9 and 11, note 283 above.

285. See Incentive Regulations, Art. I(5), note 271 above and Goods Control Regulations, Art. 9(c), note 283 above.

286. See Incentive Regulations, Art. I(6), note 271 above and Goods Control Regulations, Art. 10, note 283 above.

287. See Incentive Regulations, Art. I(8), note 271 above and Goods Control Regulations, Art. 12, note 283 above.

288. See Incentive Regulations, Art. I(7), note 271 above and Goods Control Regulations, Arts. 9 and 12, note 283 above.

289. See Incentive Regulations, Art. I(5), note 271 above and Goods Control Regulations, Art. 17, note 283 above.

290. Individual Income Tax Law of the People's Republic of China, adopted by the Third Session of the Fifth National People's Congress on 10 September 1980 and put into effect on the same date. An English translation of the law appears in Chu, Moser, and Nee, Pt. 13, note 57 above.

291. Individual Income Tax Law, Art. 3, note 290 above.

292. See Gelatt, p. 178, note 110 above.

293. See Detailed Rules and Regulations for the Implementation of the Individual Income Tax Law of the People's Republic of China, adopted by the State Council on 10 December 1980 and promulgated by the Ministry of Finance on 14 December 1980, Art. 3. For an English translation of the law see Chu, Moser, and Nee, Pt. 13, note 57 above.

294. See Gelatt, p. 179, note 110 above. It should be noted that the national tax rules regarding this issue have also recently been relaxed to some extent. Under a document issued by the Ministry of Finance, non-China-source income of a foreigner whose presence in China is due to employment there will not be taxable in China regardless of the length of residence and regardless of whether such income is remitted into China. See Notice Concerning the Exemption from Reporting and Payment of Individual Income Tax for Income Earned Outside China by Personnel of Foreign Nationality Working Within China (Document (83) *Cai shui* No. 62), issued by the Ministry of Finance on 7 March 1983. An English translation of this document is on file with the authors.

295. The four banks are Hongkong and Shanghai Banking Corporation, Stan-

dard Chartered Bank, Overseas Chinese Bank Ltd. of Singapore, and Bank of East Asia of Hong Kong.

296. An English translation of the Banking Regulations appears in *China Economic News*, 29 April 1985, pp. 2–4.

297. As of June 1986, 13 foreign banks have been granted licences to operate branches in Shenzhen and 6 banks have licences in Xiamen. Among them are Hongkong and Shanghai Banking Corporation, BCCI (Overseas) Ltd. (a subsidiary of Bank of Credit & Commerce International), Standard Chartered Bank, The Bank of Tokyo, Ltd., Hokkaido Takushoku Bank, Sanwa Bank Ltd., Banque Indosuez, Société Generale, Banque Nationale de Paris, United Overseas Banking Corporation of Singapore, and Chiyu Banking Corporation of Hong Kong. The Nanyang Commercial Bank, a Hong Kong-based bank which is part of the Bank of China group, also has branches in Shenzhen and Shekou.

298. Xiamen International Bank opened for business in Xiamen on 28 November 1985 with paid-in capital of HK$420 million. See 'Money Matters: JV Bank May Have Competitive Edge in Xiamen Zone', *Business China*, 27 January 1986, p. 9.

299. Banking Regulations, Art. 1, note 296 above.

300. See '*Shenzhen xingcheng jinrong tixi*' (Shenzhen forms financial system), *Wen wei po*, 2 February 1986, p. 3.

301. These measures were approved by the People's Bank of China before promulgation by the Guangdong Provincial People's Government. An English translation appears in *China Economic News*, 21 January 1985, pp. 1–3.

302. These measures were approved by the People's Bank of China before promulgation by the Guangdong Provincial People's Government. An English translation appears in *China Economic News*, 21 January 1985, pp. 3–4.

303. See 'The Chinese Conundrum', *Asiabanking*, June 1985, pp. 20–2.

304. See note 300 above. See also Provisional Measures of Shenzhen Special Economic Zone for the Control of Non-bank State-owned Financial Institutions, note 301 above.

305. See Supplementary Regulations of Shenzhen Special Economic Zone on the Question of Reduction and Exemption of Taxes for Enterprises (hereafter cited as the Shenzhen Supplementary Tax Regulations), which came into effect on 1 July 1986.

306. Shenzhen Supplementary Tax Regulations, Art. 4, note 305 above.

307. Shenzhen Supplementary Tax Regulations, Art. 5, note 305 above.

308. Shenzhen Supplementary Tax Regulations, Art. 6, note 305 above.

309. Shenzhen Supplementary Tax Regulations, Art. 7, note 305 above.

310. Adopted by the Ninth Session of the Standing Committee of the Sixth National People's Congress on 21 January 1985. An English translation of this law appears in *China Daily*, 17 May 1985, p. 2.

311. Promulgated by the Ministry of Finance on 4 March 1985. An English translation of these regulations appears in *China Daily*, 11–14 June 1985.

312. The SEZ Accounting Regulations came into effect on 1 March 1986.

313. The SEZ Accounting Regulations, Art. 2, note 312 above.

314. The SEZ Accounting Regulations, Art. 11, note 312 above.

315. The SEZ Accounting Regulations, Art. 12, note 312 above.

316. The SEZ Accounting Regulations, Art. 9, note 312 above.

317. The SEZ Accounting Regulations, Art. 10, note 312 above.

318. The SEZ Accounting Regulations, Art. 10, note 312 above.

319. The SEZ Accounting Regulations, Art. 9, note 312 above.

320. The SEZ Accounting Regulations, Art. 4, note 312 above.

321. The SEZ Accounting Regulations, Art. 7, note 312 above.

322. The SEZ Accounting Regulations, Art. 13, note 312 above.

323. The SEZ Accounting Regulations, Art. 12, note 312 above.

324. The SEZ Accounting Regulations, Arts. 14, 15, 16, and 17, note 312 above.

325. SEZ Accounting Regulations, Art. 17, note 312 above. Where the general

manager or board of directors of an enterprise insists on contravening the revenue/expenditure rules set out in the accounting system for the enterprise or the Chinese state, Article 14 renders the accounting personnel of the enterprise still liable if they fail to report the matter to the authorities.

326. See SEZ Accounting Regulations, Arts. 15, 16, 17, and 18, note 312 above.

327. Both laws came into effect on the date of promulgation. All references to the Shenzhen Contracts Regulations and the Shenzhen Technology Regulations are to English-language translations of the laws on file with the authors.

328. Shenzhen Contracts Regulations, Art. 2, note 327 above.

329. An English translation of the Foreign Economic Contracts Law is on file with the authors.

330. See Shenzhen Contracts Regulations, Arts. 15, 16, 17, and 18, note 327 above.

331. Foreign Economic Contracts Law, Art. 7, note 329 above.

332. Foreign Economic Contracts Law, Art. 33, note 329 above.

333. Shenzhen Contracts Regulations, Art. 5, note 327 above.

334. Shenzhen Contracts Regulations, Art. 27, note 327 above.

335. Shenzhen Contracts Regulations, Art. 31, note 327 above.

336. Article 40 of the Foreign Economic Contracts Law provides that joint venture contracts and contracts for exploration and development of natural resources which are to be performed in China may be executed in accordance with their terms even when there are new stipulations of law.

337. Shenzhen Technology Regulations, Arts. 15, 16, and 17, note 327 above.

338. Shenzhen Technology Regulations, Art. 4, note 327 above.

339. Shenzhen Technology Regulations, Art. 23, note 327 above.

340. An English translation of the National Technology Regulations is on file with the authors.

341. Shenzhen Technology Regulations, Art. 12, note 327 above.

342. Shenzhen Technology Regulations, Art. 19, note 327 above.

343. National Technology Regulations, Art. 8, note 340 above.

344. Shenzhen Technology Regulations, Art. 10, note 327 above.

345. Shenzhen Technology Regulations, Art. 11, note 327 above.

346. Shenzhen Technology Regulations, Art. 5, note 327 above.

347. Shenzhen Technology Regulations, Art. 18, note 327 above.

348. Promulgated by the Ministry of Foreign Economic Relations and Trade on 18 September 1985. An English translation of the measures is on file with the authors.

349. Xiamen Technology Regulations, note 60 above.

350. Xiamen Technology Regulations, Art. 12, note 60 above.

351. Xiamen Technology Regulations, Art. 15, note 60 above.

352. 'Shekou SEZ Begins to Show its Advantages', p. 22, note 24 above.

353. See *Investor's Handbook. The Shekou Industrial Zone in Shenzhen* (Hong Kong, China Merchants' Steam Navigation Co., Ltd., January 1980) (hereafter cited as the first Shekou Handbook).

354. See *Investor's Handbook. China Merchants' Shekou Industrial Zone in Shenzhen Special Economic Zone in Guangdong Province* (Hong Kong, China Merchants' Steam Navigation Co., Ltd., revised and enlarged edition, September 1981) (hereafter cited as the Shekou Handbook).

355. See 'Guangdong Zone Rules Cloud More Issues Than They Clarify', *Business China*, 24 September 1980, p. 137; and T. Gelatt, 'Laws for China's Economic Zones Are Unclear', *Asian Wall Street Journal*, 10 February 1982, p. 12.

356. Moser, conversation with CMSN official. See also Gelatt, p. 180, note 110 above.

357. Shekou Handbook, p. 22, note 354 above.

358. Shekou Handbook, p. 22, note 354 above.

359. Shekou Handbook, p. 21, note 354 above.

360. Shekou Handbook, p. 11, note 354 above.

361. Moser, conversation with CMSN official.

362. Shekou Handbook, p. 22, note 354 above.

363. Shekou Handbook, p. 22, note 354 above.

364. Shekou Handbook, p. 22, note 354 above.

365. Shekou Handbook, p. 22, note 354 above.

366. Shekou Handbook, p. 22, note 354 above.

367. Shekou Handbook, p. 24, note 354 above.

368. Shekou Handbook, p. 22, note 354 above.

369. Shekou Handbook, p. 22, note 354 above; and Gelatt, p. 181, note 110 above.

370. Shekou Handbook, p. 24, note 354 above.

371. Shekou Handbook, p. 24, note 354 above.

372. Shekou Handbook, p. 23, note 354 above.

373. Shekou Handbook, p. 23, note 354 above.

374. Shekou Handbook, p. 23, note 354 above.

375. Shekou Handbook, p. 23, note 354 above.

376. Shekou Handbook, p. 23, note 354 above.

377. Shekou Handbook, p. 23, note 354 above.

378. First Shekou Handbook, p. 13, note 353 above.

379. Shekou Handbook, p. 23, note 354 above.

380. Shekou Handbook, p. 23, note 354 above.

381. Shekou Handbook, p. 23, note 354 above.

382. Shekou Handbook, p. 23, note 354 above.

383. Shekou Handbook, p. 23, note 354 above.

384. Shekou Handbook, p. 23, note 354 above.

385. Shekou Handbook, p. 23, note 354 above.

386. Shekou Handbook, p. 23, note 354 above.

387. Shekou Handbook, p. 23, note 354 above.

388. Shekou Handbook, p. 24, note 354 above.

389. Shekou Handbook, p. 24, note 354 above.

390. Shekou Handbook, p. 24, note 354 above.

391. Moser, conversation with CMSN official.

392. 14 Coastal Cities of the PRC Handbook, pp. 26 and 29, note 1 above.

393. China Investment Guide 1985 (Hong Kong, Longman Group Limited, 1985), p. 81.

394. 14 Coastal Cities of the PRC Handbook, p. 30, note 1 above.

395. See 14 Coastal Cities of the PRC Handbook, pp. 29–31, note 1 above; speech of Wei Yuming, Vice Minister of the Ministry of Foreign Economic Relations and Trade, reported in Ta kung pao, 9 November 1984, p. 8; and answers by an official of the State Council to a series of questions, reported in Economic Daily, 16 July 1984, p. 2.

396. See 'Shenzhen SEZ to Introduce Industrial Projects', China Economic News, 2 September 1985, pp. 9–10; and 'List of Suitors Growing', China Trade Report, July 1984, p. 8.

397. 'Zhongguo yanhai kaifangchengshi yu tequ' (Open Coastal Cities and Special Zones of China), Wen wei po, 18 November 1984, p. 2.

398. 'Zhongguo yanhai kaifangchengshi yu tequ', note 397 above. See also interview with Gu Mu, State Councillor, reported in Wen wei po, 14 December 1984, p. 3.

399. See 14 Coastal Cities of the PRC Handbook, note 1 above, and note 503 below and accompanying text.

400. See 14 Coastal Cities of the PRC Handbook, pp. 251 and 379, note 1 above.

401. See China Investment Guide 1986, pp. 83–119, note 1 above; 14 Coastal Cities of the PRC Handbook, note 1 above; and 'Officials from 14 Cities Are Eager for Funds, Flexible in Deal-Making', Business China, 14 November 1984, pp. 161–2.

402. See *14 Coastal Cities of the PRC Handbook*, note 1 above.

403. See Incentive Regulations, Arts. II and III, note 271 above.

404. See 'A Coastful of Questions', *China Trade Report*, March 1985, pp. 1 and 4.

405. See 'What Individual Cities Are Planning: Update on 14-City Focus, Part 2', *Business China*, 29 August 1984, p. 127; and *'Shisi chengshi tiaojian butong'* (Conditions of 14 Cities Different), *Ta kung pao*, 10 November 1984.

406. See *China Investment Guide 1986*, note 1 above.

407. Speech of Wei Yuming, note 395 above; and *Trade and Investment Guide to Guangdong*, p. 55, note 37 above. The approval limit for Guangzhou was initially US$5 million but subsequently increased to US$10 million.

408. See *'Zhongguo yanhai kaifangchengshi you shisige jianzhi sige'* (Open Coastal Cities of China Reduced From 14 to 4), *Ming pao*, p. 4 and 'Special Powers for 10 Open Cities Curtailed', *Intertrade*, May 1986, p. 68.

409. See note 271 above.

410. One example is the statement in Article II(1) of the Incentive Regulations that an enterprise which has a term of ten years or more qualifies for a holiday from enterprise income tax in the first two years and a 50 per cent reduction in such tax in the ensuing three years. This is identical to the treatment available under the JVITL (see note 415 below and accompanying text). See also Guangzhou ETDZ Regulations, Art. 22, note 423 below, which states that ETDZ enterprises in Guangzhou can also enjoy preferential treatment available under national legislation.

411. Incentive Regulations, Art. I(1), note 271 above.

412. See note 275 above.

413. FEITL, Art. 3, note 117 above.

414. Incentive Regulations, Art. II(1), note 271 above.

415. See notes 275, 276, and 277 above and accompanying text.

416. Incentive Regulations, Art. III(1), note 271 above.

417. Incentive Regulations, Art. II(3), note 271 above.

418. Incentive Regulations, Arts. II(4) and III(3), note 271 above.

419. Incentive Regulations, Art. II(5), note 271 above.

420. Incentive Regulations, Art. III(4), note 271 above.

421. Incentive Regulations, Art. III(6), note 271 above.

422. Speech of Wei Yuming, note 395 above.

423. See, for example, Provisional Regulations of Guangzhou Economic and Technical Development Zone, promulgated by the Guangzhou Municipal People's Government on 9 April 1985 (hereafter cited as the Guangzhou ETDZ Regulations), Art. 16, and Regulations of Dalian Economic and Technical Development Zone on Several Preferential Treatment, promulgated by the Dalian Municipal People's Government on 15 October 1984 (hereafter cited as the Dalian ETDZ Regulations), Arts. 14 and 16.

424. Incentive Regulations, Arts. II(6) and III(5), note 271 above.

425. Incentive Regulations, Arts. II(7) and III(7), note 271 above.

426. See Dalian ETDZ Regulations, note 423 above; Regulations Governing Tianjin Economic and Technical Development Zone, passed by the Twenty-first Meeting of the Standing Committee of the Tenth People's Congress of Tianjin Municipality on 20 July 1985 (hereafter cited as the Tianjin ETDZ Regulations); Provisional Regulations of Economic and Technical Development Zone of Ningbo Municipality, passed by the Fourteenth Meeting of the Standing Committee of the Sixth People's Congress of Zhejiang Province on 15 June 1985 (hereafter cited as the Ningbo ETDZ Regulations); and Guangzhou ETDZ Regulations, note 423 above.

427. See, for example, Preferential Treatment Given to Joint Ventures Established in Qinhuangdao Municipality, an informal document dated 17 September 1984 and issued by Qinhuangdao authorities, and 'Qingdao, Yantai Offer

Preferential Treatments on Taxes, Credit Loans, Foreign Exchange, etc.', *China Economic News*, 23 July 1984, pp. 6–7.

428. Dalian ETDZ Regulations, Arts. 3 and 4, note 423 above, and Implementing (Provisional) Measures of Guangzhou Economic and Technical Development Zone on Industrial and Commercial Tax, promulgated by the Guangzhou Municipal People's Government on 9 April 1985 (hereafter cited as the Guangzhou ETDZ Tax Measures), Art. 10.

429. See, for example, Guangzhou ETDZ Tax Measures, Art. 8, note 428 above; Dalian ETDZ Regulations, Art. 12, note 423 above; Tianjin ETDZ Regulations, Art. 34, note 426 above.

430. See Guangzhou ETDZ Regulations, Art. 14, note 423 above; Guangzhou ETDZ Tax Measures, Art. 5(4), note 428 above; Dalian ETDZ Regulations, Art. 20, note 423 above; and Tianjin ETDZ Regulations, Art. 20, note 426 above.

431. Trial Measures of Guangzhou Economic and Technical Development Zone Governing Land Use, promulgated by the Guangzhou Municipal People's Government on 9 April 1985 (hereafter cited as the Guangzhou ETDZ Land Use Measures), Art. 14.

432. Dalian ETDZ Regulations, Art. 25, note 423 above.

433. Guangzhou ETDZ Regulations, Art. 21, note 423 above.

434. Arts. 7 and 8. Similar legislation has been promulgated for the Xiamen SEZ. See note 60 above.

435. See Dalian ETDZ Regulations, Arts. 25 and 26, note 423 above and Measures of Dalian Economic and Technical Development Zone Governing Land Use, promulgated by the Dalian Municipal People's Government on 15 October 1984 (hereafter cited as the Dalian ETDZ Land Use Measures), Art. 17; Guangzhou ETDZ Regulations, Art. 20, note 423 above; Tianjin ETDZ Regulations, Art. 34, note 426 above; and Implementing Measures of Ningbo Municipality Governing Land Use by Joint Ventures Using Chinese and Foreign Investment, adopted by the Fourteenth Session of the Standing Committee of the Sixth People's Congress of Zhejiang Province on 15 June 1985 (hereafter cited as the Ningbo Land Use Measures), Arts. 16 and 17.

436. Dalian ETDZ Land Use Measures, Arts. 15 and 16, note 435 above, specified the land-use fees and site-development fees payable by investors. By October 1985, the Dalian authorities had revised the amounts of these fees.

437. See notes 502 and 503 below and accompanying text.

438. See notes 426 and 435 above.

439. See note 426 above.

440. See, for example, Measures of Dalian Economic and Technical Development Zone Governing Enterprise Registration, promulgated by the Dalian Municipal People's Government on 15 October 1984 (hereafter cited as the Dalian ETDZ Registration Measures); Trial Measures of Guangzhou Economic and Technical Development Zone Governing Enterprise Registration, promulgated by the Guangzhou Municipal People's Government on 9 April 1985 (hereafter cited as the Guangzhou ETDZ Registration Measures); and Regulations of Tianjin Economic and Technical Development Zone Governing Enterprise Registration, adopted by the Twenty-first Session of the Standing Committee of the Tenth People's Congress of Tianjin Municipality on 20 July 1985 (hereafter cited as the Tianjin ETDZ Registration Regulations).

441. Guangzhou ETDZ Registration Measures, Art. 15, note 440 above.

442. Guangzhou ETDZ Registration Measures, Art. 16, note 440 above.

443. These forms of investment are specifically referred to in the Incentive Regulations and by implication are permitted in each of the 14 coastal cities. However, in some of the cities, the permissible forms of investment are specifically set out in the local laws. See Ningbo ETDZ Regulations, Art. 4, note 426 above and Guangzhou ETDZ Regulations, Art. 3, note 423 above.

444. Guangzhou ETDZ Regulations, Art. 3, note 423 above.

445. See Guangzhou ETDZ Regulations, Art. 20, note 423 above, and Tianjin ETDZ Regulations, Art. 6, note 426 above.

446. See Dalian ETDZ Registration Measures, Art. 2, note 440 above; Guangzhou ETDZ Registration Measures, Art. 2, note 440 above; and Tianjin ETDZ Regulations, Art. 12, note 426 above.

447. See Dalian ETDZ Registration Measures, Art. 2, note 440 above; Guangzhou ETDZ Registration Measures, Art. 2, note 440 above; and Tianjin ETDZ Regulations, Art. 12, note 426 above.

448. See Section C of Part I of this chapter.

449. See Dalian ETDZ Registration Measures, Art. 7, note 440 above; Guangzhou ETDZ Registration Measures, Art. 11, note 440 above; and Tianjin ETDZ Regulations, Arts. 13 and 14, note 426 above.

450. See Section C of Part I of this chapter.

451. Guangzhou ETDZ Land Use Measures, Art. 8, note 431 above.

452. See, for example, Ningbo Land Use Measures, Art. 11, note 435 above.

453. See Dalian ETDZ Land Use Measures, Art. 16, note 435 above and Ningbo Land Use Measures, Art. 13, note 435 above.

454. See Dalian ETDZ Land Use Measures, Art. 20, note 435 above; Guangzhou ETDZ Land Use Measures, Art. 23, note 431 above; and Regulations of Tianjin Economic and Technical Development Zone Governing Land, adopted by the Twenty-first Session of the Standing Committee of the Tenth People's Congress of Tianjin Municipality on 20 July 1985 (hereafter cited as the Tianjin Land Regulations), Art. 13.

455. Dalian ETDZ Land Use Measures, Art. 17, note 435 above and Ningbo Land Use Measures, Art. 17, note 435 above.

456. Guangzhou ETDZ Land Use Measures, Art. 20, note 431 above.

457. Dalian ETDZ Land Use Measures, Art. 13, note 435 above.

458. An English translation of these measures is on file with the authors.

459. Qinhuangdao Construction Measures, Art. 5, note 458 above.

460. Qinhuangdao Construction Measures, Art. 8, note 458 above.

461. Qinhuangdao Construction Measures, Art. 18, note 458 above.

462. Qinhuangdao Construction Measures, Art. 23, note 458 above.

463. Qinhuangdao Construction Measures, Arts. 26, 27, and 28, note 458 above.

464. See Section C of Part I of this chapter.

465. Regulations of Tianjin Economic and Technical Development Zone Governing Labour Management, adopted by the Twenty-first Session of the Standing Committee of the Tenth People's Congress of Tianjin Municipality on 20 July 1985 (hereafter cited as the Tianjin ETDZ Labour Regulations), Art. 9. The legislation in Dalian and Guangzhou simply states that enterprises shall sign labour contracts with staff and workers.

466. Tianjin ETDZ Labour Regulations, Art. 9, note 465 above.

467. Trial Measures of Guangzhou Economic and Technical Development Zone Governing Labour and Wages in Enterprises, promulgated by the Guangzhou Municipal People's Government on 9 April 1985 (hereafter cited as the Guangzhou ETDZ Labour Measures), Art. 5.

468. Measures of Dalian Economic and Technical Development Zone Governing Labour and Wages in Enterprises, promulgated by the Dalian Municipal People's Government on 15 October 1984 (hereafter cited as the Dalian ETDZ Labour Measures), Art. 4.

469. Tianjin ETDZ Labour Regulations, Art. 10, note 465 above. References to non-local workers in Dalian ETDZ Labour Measures, Art. 17, note 468 above and Guangzhou ETDZ Labour Measures, Art. 18, note 467 above, give rise to the implication that such workers may be employed.

470. Dalian ETDZ Labour Measures, Art. 12, note 468 above; Guangzhou ETDZ Labour Measures, Art. 8, note 467 above; and Tianjin ETDZ Labour Regulations, Art. 23, note 465 above.

471. Guangzhou ETDZ Labour Measures, Art. 8, note 467 above.

472. Dalian ETDZ Labour Measures, Arts. 5 and 7, note 468 above; Guangzhou ETDZ Labour Measures, Art. 11, note 467 above; and Tianjin ETDZ Labour Regulations, Arts. 12 and 15, note 465 above.

473. Guangzhou ETDZ Labour Measures, Art. 11, note 467 above and Tianjin ETDZ Labour Regulations, Art. 12, note 465 above. There is no provision prescribing a minimum wage standard in the Dalian legislation.

474. Dalian ETDZ Labour Measures, Art. 8, note 468 above; Guangzhou ETDZ Labour Measures, Art. 12, note 467 above; and Tianjin ETDZ Labour Regulations, Art. 16, note 465 above.

475. Tianjin ETDZ Labour Regulations, Art. 16, note 465 above.

476. Dalian ETDZ Labour Measures, Art. 5, note 468 above and Guangzhou ETDZ Labour Measures, Art. 11, note 467 above.

477. Tianjin ETDZ Labour Regulations, Art. 12, note 465 above. The percentage of annual wage increment is decided in consultation with the enterprise's labour union.

478. See Dalian ETDZ Labour Measures, Art. 6, note 468 above; Guangzhou ETDZ Labour Measures, Arts. 10 and 15, note 467 above; and Tianjin ETDZ Labour Regulations, Arts. 13 and 14, note 465 above.

479. Dalian ETDZ Labour Measures, Art. 12, note 468 above; Guangzhou ETDZ Labour Measures, Art. 7, note 467 above; and Tianjin ETDZ Regulations, Art. 22, note 465 above.

480. Tianjin ETDZ Labour Regulations, Art. 22, note 465 above.

481. See Section C(iii) of Part I of this chapter.

482. The Measures of Dalian Economic and Technical Development Zone Governing Foreign Economic Contracts were promulgated by the Dalian Municipal People's Government on 15 October 1984 (hereafter cited as the Dalian ETDZ Contracts Measures). An English translation of this legislation is on file with the authors.

483. Dalian ETDZ Contracts Measures, Art. 2, note 482 above.

484. See note 329 above.

485. Adopted by the Fourth Session of the Fifth National People's Congress on 13 December 1981.

486. Dalian ETDZ Contracts Measures, Art. 29, note 482 above.

487. See Art. 89 of the General Principles of the Civil Code, adopted by the Fourth Session of the Sixth National People's Congress on 12 April 1986 and implemented as of 1 January 1987. An English translation of this legislation is on file with the authors. Note that the wording of Art. 25 of the Dalian ETDZ Contracts Measures is very similar to that of Art. 23 of the Shenzhen Contracts Regulations.

488. Dalian ETDZ Contracts Measures, Art. 44, note 482 above. See, however, Chapter VII of the General Principles of the Civil Code, note 487 above.

489. The Guangzhou ETDZ Technology Regulations were promulgated by the Guangzhou Municipal People's Government on 9 April 1985. An English translation of this legislation appears in *China Economic News*, 17 June 1985, pp. 2–6.

490. See note 340 above.

491. See note 348 above.

492. See note 327 above.

493. Guangzhou ETDZ Technology Regulations, Art. 5, note 489 above.

494. Guangzhou ETDZ Technology Regulations, Art. 5, note 489 above.

495. See Guangzhou ETDZ Technology Regulations, Art. 5, note 489 above and National Technology Regulations, Art. 3, note 340 above.

496. Guangzhou ETDZ Technology Regulations, Art. 16, note 489 above.

497. Shenzhen Technology Regulations, Art. 19, note 327 above.

498. Guangzhou ETDZ Technology Regulations, Art. 28, note 489 above.

499. Shenzhen Technology Regulations, Art. 16, note 327 above.

500. National Technology Regulations, Art. 4, note 340 above.

501. Guangzhou ETDZ Technology Regulations, Art. 28, note 489 above.

502. *China Investment Guide 1986*, p. 100, note 1 above. See also P. Torbert, 'Shanghai Update: Further Opening to Foreign Investment', *East Asian Executive Reports*, September 1984, pp. 8–10.

503. Pow, conversation with official from Shanghai Foreign Economic Relations and Trade Commission, 1986, and '*Hu xin pi liang jing ji kai fa qu*' (Shanghai's new establishment of two technical development zones), *Wen wei po*, 9 August 1986, p. 12.

504. On 1 January 1986 a set of detailed regulations came into force governing foreign firms which contract to provide design or construction services in Shanghai.

505. An English translation of the regulations appears in Shanghai Foreign Economic Relations and Trade Commission (ed.), *Shanghai Overseas Investment Utilization Manual* (Shanghai, Shanghai Translation and Publishing Centre, Inc., 1986), pp. 220–8.

506. An English translation of the Measures of Shanghai Municipality on Implementation of 'Regulations of Shanghai Municipality on Negotiations and Examination and Approval Procedures Relating to Establishment of Joint Ventures Using Chinese and Foreign Investment and Acceptance of Foreign Investment for Establishing Self-Run Enterprises' (hereafter cited as the Shanghai Enterprise Implementing Measures) appears in *Shanghai Overseas Investment Utilization Manual*, pp. 228–41, note 505 above.

507. An English translation of the regulations is on file with the authors.

508. Shanghai Enterprise Regulations, Art. 3, note 505 above.

509. Shanghai Enterprise Regulations, Art. 3, note 505 above.

510. Shanghai Enterprise Regulations, Art. 3, note 505 above and Shanghai Enterprise Implementing Measures, Art. I(1), note 506 above.

511. Shanghai Regulations 1986, Art. 8, note 507 above.

512. This implication arises by virtue of Article 12(10) of the Foreign Economic Contracts Law which states that parties to a contract can stipulate the language(s) used in the contract and its (their) validity. Article 9 of the Implementing Regulations of the Joint Venture Law in fact states that where joint venture documents are written in two languages, both versions are to have equal validity.

513. Pow, conversation with officials from Ministry of Foreign Economic Relations and Trade.

514. Shanghai Enterprise Regulations, Art. 4, note 505 above and Shanghai Enterprise Implementing Measures, Art. II(5), note 506 above.

515. Shanghai Enterprise Regulations, Art. 6, note 505 above, and Shanghai Regulations 1986, Art. 14, note 507 above.

516. Shanghai Enterprise Regulations, Art. 6, note 505 above and Shanghai Enterprise Implementing Measures, Art. III(1), note 506 above.

517. Shanghai Enterprise Regulations, Art. 6, note 505 above.

518. The Measures of Shanghai Municipality on Labour Management in Joint Ventures Using Chinese and Foreign Investment (hereafter cited as the Shanghai Labour Measures) came into effect on 1 November 1984.

519. Shanghai Labour Measures, Art. 25, note 518 above.

520. Shanghai Labour Measures, Art. 6, note 518 above. However, Article 3 does permit a joint venture to recruit not only from suburban parts of Shanghai but also from other places in China after first having given priority to employees of the Chinese party and having found no suitable employees in Shanghai municipality.

521. Shanghai Labour Measures, Art. 7, note 518 above.

522. See Shanghai Labour Measures, Arts. 9 and 10, note 518 above.

523. Shanghai Labour Measures, Arts. 9 and 10, note 518 above.

524. Shanghai Labour Measures, Art. 11, note 518 above.

525. Shanghai Labour Measures, Art. 15, note 518 above.

526. Shanghai Labour Measures, Art. 16, note 518 above.

527. The Provisional Regulations of Shanghai Municipality on Supply and Distribution of Goods and Materials and the Control of Prices for Joint Ventures using Chinese and Foreign Investment (hereafter cited as the Shanghai Goods Regulations) came into effect on 20 December 1984.

528. Shanghai Goods Regulations, Arts. 3 and 4, note 527 above.

529. See 'The Error of its Ways', *Far Eastern Economic Review*, 28 November 1985, pp. 56–9.

530. *China Investment Guide 1985*, p. 100, note 393 above.

531. See 'The Error of its Ways', note 529 above.

532. 'China Opens Three More Coast Areas', note 1 above. See also 'China to Open Three More Coastal Areas', *Hong Kong Standard*, 4 March 1985, p. 1.

533. 'China Opens Three More Coast Areas', note 1 above.

534. *China Investment Guide 1986*, pp. 125–34, note 1 above.

535. *China Investment Guide 1986*, pp. 127–9, note 1 above.

536. *China Investment Guide 1986*, pp. 130–2, note 1 above, and 'Pearl River Delta Economic Zone Expands', *China Trader*, 7 July 1986.

537. *China Investment Guide 1986*, p. 132, note 1 above.

538. See *China Investment Guide 1986*, pp. 129 and 132, note 1 above and 'Makings of a Megalopolis', *Far Eastern Economic Review*, 10 April 1986, pp. 82–3.

539. *China Investment Guide 1986*, pp. 132–4, note 1 above.

540. See 'A Coastful of Questions', note 404 above. The different range of preferential treatments announced by the Guangdong Municipal People's Government for the Zhujiang Delta Economic Zone in October 1985 also indicates that the delta economic zones will be treated separately from the other special investment areas.

541. See 'Makings of a Megalopolis', note 538 above.

542. The range of preferential treatments was reported in *Wen wei po*, 14 October 1985, p. 2 and 30 October 1985, p. 3.

543. See reports in *Wen wei po*, note 542 above.

544. See 'Makings of a Megalopolis', note 538 above.

545. See Eight Rules of Chinese Central Government, State Council on Expanding Hainan's Decision-making Power in Foreign Economic and Trade Matters (hereafter cited as the Hainan Rules), promulgated in April 1983; 'NPC bill on Hainan jurisdiction adopted', *China Daily*, 26 May 1984, p. 1; and '*Dang zhongyang guowuyuan jueding jiakuai kaifa jianshe Hainandao*' (Party Central Committee, State Council decide to accelerate development and construction of Hainan Island), *Renmin ribao*, 12 July 1983, pp. 1 and 2.

546. See '*Dang zhongyang guowuyuan jueding jiakuai kaifa jianshe Hainandao*', note 545 above.

547. Hainan Rules, Paragraph (2), note 545 above.

548. See note 271 above.

549. See also Section C(v) of Part I of this chapter.

550. See 'Premier Paints Rosy Picture for Hainan's Future', *China Daily*, 20 February 1986, p. 1.

551. See *14 Coastal Cities of the PRC Handbook*, pp. 465–70, note 1 above.

552. See 'Hainan Permit Promising', *Australian Financial Review*, 6 June 1985.

553. See *14 Coastal Cities of the PRC Handbook*, pp. 465–70, note 1 above.

554. See 'China Wants Faster Development of SEZs', *Hong Kong Standard*, 3 March 1986, p. 1; and 'China: Reorienting Outwards', note 56 above.

555. See 'A Coastful of Questions', note 404 above.

556. See 'China Wants Faster Development of SEZs', note 554 above and 'China: Reorienting Outwards', note 56 above.

557. See 'SEZ Guidelines', *China Daily*, 15 March 1986, p. 4.

558. See 'Zones Enter New Stage of Economic Development', note 49 above.

6. Legal Aspects of Offshore Oil and Gas Exploration and Development in China

MICHAEL J. MOSER

THIS chapter is intended to provide an overview of the salient legal aspects of Chinese-foreign co-operative activities relating to the exploration and development of offshore oil and gas resources in China. Part I describes the background and current status of China's programme to enlist the co-operation of foreign enterprises in offshore oil projects. Parts II and III describe the regulatory regime developed for co-operative activities in the offshore oil sector, focusing on the Petroleum Regulations and the Model Contract respectively. Part IV examines the Chinese tax rules applicable to offshore oil and gas projects. Finally, Part V reviews several miscellaneous regulations affecting the operations of foreign companies involved in oil and gas activities, including registration rules, special import tax and customs provisions and environmental protection rules.

I. Background

With oil reserves estimated at between 30 billion and 100 billion barrels, China's continental shelf is believed to contain the largest untapped oil deposits remaining in the world today.[1] As onshore production levelled off in the late 1970s, China's leaders decided to embark on a programme to develop the nation's offshore reserves in co-operation with foreign oil companies.[2] By so doing, China not only hopes to bring its offshore production on stream within the shortest possible time, but also seeks to gain training, technology, and managerial experience from its foreign partners. It is anticipated that most of the production from China's offshore wells will be used to satisfy burgeoning domestic demand, although a portion of crude production may be exported to earn foreign exchange.[3]

The first phase in China's programme to involve foreign companies in the development of its offshore oil began in 1979, when foreign oil companies were invited to enter into geophysical survey agreements with the China National Oil and Gas Exploration and Development Corporation (CNOGEDC), opening up blocks in the South China Sea and the South Yellow Sea to initial exploration activity.[4] The costs of the surveys were borne by the foreign parties who were obliged, under the terms of their agreements with the CNOGEDC, to turn over all seismic information and interpretation. In exchange, participating foreign companies were given assurances that they would be granted bidding rights to selected blocks to be opened up for joint Chinese-foreign exploration and development in the near future.

Prior to the opening of competitive bidding, China moved forward in negotiations for exploration and development contracts with selected companies. On 29 May 1980, the CNOGEDC signed three contracts: one with the Japan National Oil Corporation for exploration and development in the Bohai Gulf; another with France's Société Nationale Elf Aquitaine, also for exploration and development in the Bohai; and a third with the Compagnie Française des Petroles (Total) of France for the Beibu Gulf area in the South China Sea. At the same time negotiations were conducted with the Atlantic Richfield Company (ARCO) and Santa Fe International of the United States for an exploration and development contract in a 9,000-square-kilometre area in the Ying Ge Hai Basin off the south coast of Hainan Island. After substantial delays, these negotiations finally bore fruit with the signing of a contract in September 1982.[6]

The years 1982 and 1983 saw a flurry of activity which put China's offshore oil development programme into high gear. First, in January 1982, the State Council promulgated the Regulations of the People's Republic of China on the Exploitation of Offshore Petroleum Resources in Co-operation with Foreign Enterprises (hereafter cited as the Petroleum Regulations) which provide the legal framework for exploration and development activities involving foreign entities.[7] Several weeks later, on 15 February 1982, the China National Offshore Oil Corporation (CNOOC) was created and was granted exclusive authority to negotiate and sign contracts with foreign oil companies.[8] On the following day, the CNOOC announced that 43 blocks totalling more than 150,000 square kilometres would be opened for competitive bidding.[9] Soon after, invitations were issued to 46 foreign companies that had participated in China's earlier seismic survey programme.[10] By April, 40 of these companies had responded positively to the invitation and had indicated an interest in submitting formal bids.[11] On 10 May these companies were invited by the CNOOC to Beijing to collect the 'bidding documents package', including a copy of China's 'Model Contract' which was intended to be the starting point for negotiations.[12] When the bidding deadline arrived on 17 August 1982, a total of 33 companies had submitted 102 formal bids to the CNOOC, thus indicating a desire to pursue detailed negotiations.[13] However, not until 10 May 1983 did the CNOOC sign the first exploration and development contract, with a consortium led by British Petroleum (BP) and including participants from Australia, Brazil, and Canada.[14] This contract was soon followed by others, including those signed by Exxon, Shell, Occidental, Texaco, and Chevron.[15]

The results of the exploration activity conducted under the contracts signed during 1980–3 have failed to meet initially optimistic expectations. After the expenditure of more than US$1.6 million and the drilling of more than seventy wells, only limited amounts of oil have been found.[16] The only bright spot has been a major gas discovery by ARCO in its Ying Ge Hai Basin block. However, development of this find will require significant investment at a time when the market price for gas remains low.[17]

Despite the disappointing results of the first round and the declining world price for crude oil, in late 1984 the CNOOC announced plans to offer additional offshore areas encompassing approximately 100,000 square kilometres in a second round of bidding.[18] The bidding was conducted in two stages. In the first stage, bids were called for a 13,300-square-kilometre area in the Ying Ge Hai Basin consisting of four blocks adjacent to the ARCO contract area.[19] In the second stage, twelve blocks totalling 50,000 square kilometres in the Pearl River mouth and six blocks with an area of 43,000 square kilometres in the southern Yellow Sea were offered.[20] By the end of 1985 more than twenty companies had submitted bids for blocks in the areas and several contracts had been signed.[21]

II. The Petroleum Regulations

The Petroleum Regulations provide the basic statutory foundation for China's policy to develop its offshore oil and gas resources in co-operation with foreign enterprises. Consisting of 31 articles, the law addresses five major topics: (a) the general principles under which China's co-operative offshore oil development programme is to be carried out; (b) the organization of the nation's oil bureaucracy; (c) the rights and obligations of the parties to petroleum contracts; (d) the conduct of petroleum operations, including exploration, development, and production activities; and (e) dispute settlement and enforcement measures.

A. General Principles

The first task accomplished by the Petroleum Regulations is the provision of a broad statement of purpose or legislative aims. Article 1 provides that the law has been formulated 'to permit foreign enterprises to participate in the co-operative exploitation of offshore petroleum resources' in order to 'develop the national economy' and 'expand international economic and technical co-operation'. In addition, the article states that the law is intended to safeguard China's 'national sovereignty and economic interests'.[22] At the outset, therefore, the Petroleum Regulations provide the necessary legal basis for China's negotiations with foreign oil companies and establish the basic principle that foreign participation in the nation's offshore oil development programme will be regulated so as to protect China's perceived economic and political interests.

Like China's other foreign investment legislation, the Petroleum Regulations provide that the activities, share of profits, and other 'legitimate rights and interests' of foreign enterprises making investments in China will be protected, 'in accordance with the law', by the Chinese government.[23] In return, foreign enterprises are required to comply with Chinese 'laws and decrees' as well as 'relevant stipulations of the State'.[24] In addition, the Petroleum Regulations require that all persons and enterprises engaged in oil exploration, production, and development activities in China be subject to 'inspection and supervision by the relevant competent authorities of the Chinese government'.[25]

Finally, the Petroleum Regulations also contain a statement of general principles relating to the ownership of China's petroleum resources and an assertion of legal jurisdiction over petroleum operations conducted within the nation's territory. The law provides that all oil and natural gas deposits located within China's internal and territorial waters and on its continental shelf, as well as deposits in other waters that are under China's control, are 'owned by' the People's Republic of China.[26] In addition, the law provides that China has jurisdiction over all buildings, structures, and vessels established or operating within such waters in order to serve the petroleum operations.[27] What the Petroleum Regulations fail to make clear, however, is the precise extent of such jurisdiction, a matter which is the subject of some dispute with China's neighbours.[28]

B. The Organization of China's Oil Bureaucracy

Article 4 of the Petroleum Regulations designates the Ministry of Petroleum Industry (MOPI) as the 'competent government authority in charge of the exploitation of offshore petroleum resources in co-operation with foreign enterprises'. The responsibilities and powers granted to the MOPI under the regulations are far-reaching. They include determining the forms of co-operation to be undertaken with foreign enterprises; demarcating concession areas within the zones designated by the state for co-operative development; developing plans for the co-operative exploitation of petroleum resources in accordance with the state's long-term economic programme; and formulating operational and management policies, as well as examining and approving 'the overall development programme' for offshore petroleum and gasfields.[29]

The Petroleum Regulations also provide for the creation of the CNOOC to handle the 'business' aspects of China's co-operative offshore oil development programme. Under the law, such tasks are to be 'unified under the full responsibility of the CNOOC'.[30] In addition, the regulations grant the CNOOC the power to call for bids, establish 'regional companies, specialized companies and overseas representative offices', and enter into contracts with foreign enterprises.[31] All contracts signed by the CNOOC in connection with the co-operative exploitation of China's oil and gas resources must be approved by the Foreign Investment Bureau of the Ministry of Foreign Economic Relations and Trade.[32]

Since the promulgation of the Petroleum Regulations, the organizational structure for offshore operations has become rather complex. At the apex of this structure, the CNOOC headquarters in Beijing has established twelve specialized departments dealing with foreign co-operation and contracts, foreign liaison matters, exploration and development, production operations, planning, personnel, finance, education, engineering, marketing, services, and general administration.[33] At the local level, the CNOOC has established four branch corporations.[34] The Bohai Oil

Corporation, based in Tanggu, will be responsible for petroleum operations in the Bohai Gulf, and the South Huang Hai Oil Corporation, headquartered in Shanghai, will take charge of operations in the South Yellow Sea concession areas. In the South China Sea region two branch corporations have been established, the Nanhai (West) Oil Corporation and Nanhai (East) Oil Corporation. The geographical boundary for the division of responsibility between the Nanhai (West) and Nanhai (East) Corporations will be the 113° 10′ line of longitude, which lies just to the west of Guangzhou.

With the focus of petroleum exploration and development activity now on the south, the CNOOC's operations there have grown in importance. The Nanhai (West) Corporation has established its headquarters and rear support base in Zhanjiang and is developing front bases in Wushi and Sanya on Hainan Island.[35] The Nanhai (East) branch, with its headquarters in Guangzhou, is developing front bases in the Shekou–Chiwan area and in Shantou.[36] In addition, the CNOOC has formally entered into a co-operative venture with Guangdong province in the form of the China-Nanhai Oil Joint Services Corporation (CNOJSC), which is intended to be the main service and supply organization for operations in both the western and eastern sectors of the South China Sea.[37] The CNOJSC itself is divided into a number of specialized subsidiaries, some of which are wholly owned by the CNOJSC and others of which are owned jointly with other Chinese organizations.

The CNOOC has also begun to move to establish at least a limited presence in oil and supply centres outside China proper. In January 1983, the CNOOC established a representative office in Hong Kong with the aim of co-ordinating oil-related activities of Hong Kong-based Chinese companies and foreign supply and service companies. Prior to this it was widely expected that the Chinese would attempt to exclude Hong Kong from any major back-up role in offshore oil development, particularly as the Petroleum Regulations require that service and supply bases must be located within the People's Republic.[38] Representative offices similar to the office set up in Hong Kong have been established by the CNOOC in foreign oil centres, including Houston and London.

C. *The Rights and Obligations of the Parties to Petroleum Contracts*

In addition to setting forth the basic principles governing, and the organizational framework for, China's co-operation with foreign enterprises, the Petroleum Regulations provide a general outline of the form such co-operation should take. Under Article 7 of the law, the terms of such co-operation are to be specified in the 'petroleum contract' entered into by the CNOOC and foreign oil companies. Unless otherwise provided by the MOPI or in the contract, the foreign contractor is required to undertake all exploration operations and must provide all exploration investment and bear all associated risks.[39] Once a 'commercial' oil- or gasfield is discovered, the field is to be developed by the CNOOC and the foreign contractor jointly, with both parties providing the necessary investment.[40] The law also provides that the foreign contractor bear responsibility for both 'development operations' and 'production operations', at least until such time as the CNOOC assumes responsibility for production operations pursuant to the terms of the contract.[41] Finally, the law states that foreign contractors shall be permitted to recover their investment and expenses and receive remuneration from the petroleum produced.[42] Petroleum received by foreign contractors may be exported, and sums attributable to investment recovery, profits, and 'other legitimate income' may be remitted abroad.[43]

The Petroleum Regulations also contain a number of provisions dealing with the operations of foreign contractors, subcontractors, and other foreign enterprises engaged in activities related to the development of offshore oil. For example, Article 11 requires that foreign contractors open a bank account in accordance with China's foreign exchange regulations. Article 9 requires enterprises engaged in petroleum operations, together with their employees, to pay taxes in accordance with Chinese law. Article 10 promises 'preferential' customs treatment for imported equipment and materials used in petroleum operations. And, finally, the law requires that both contractors and subcontractors establish a 'subsidiary or branch or representative office' in China at places to be determined through 'consultation' with the CNOOC.[44]

In the course of implementing the petroleum contract with the CNOOC, the Petroleum Regulations require that the foreign contractor assume a number of responsibilities. For example, the foreign contractor must employ 'appropriate and advanced' technology and managerial experience and must transfer such technology and experience to the Chinese side.[45] The contractor must also give priority to Chinese personnel when employing workers for the implementation of the contract and must 'keep the percentage of Chinese steadily rising' and 'train Chinese personnel in a planned way'.[46] Finally, the law also requires the foreign contractor to keep accurate and complete records and data regarding the petroleum operations and to 'submit regularly' such information together with technological, financial, accounting, and administrative reports to the CNOOC.[47]

D. Petroleum Operations

The fourth set of provisions contained in the Petroleum Regulations deals with matters pertaining to 'petroleum operations', defined as 'all exploration, development and production operations and other related activities carried out in the implementation of the petroleum contract'.[48] The provisions are essentially a group of requirements imposed on foreign operators, contractors, and subcontractors in connection with the conduct of such activities.

The first requirement set forth in the law pertains to operators, that is, the foreign oil companies that are responsible for undertaking petroleum operations pursuant to the petroleum contract. With the aim of maximizing potential recovery, Article 16 requires operators to formulate an 'overall development plan' for oil- and gasfields within their concession blocks. In addition, operators are required to carry out production operations—including extraction, processing, storage, transportation, lifting of crude oil, and so on—in accordance with the Petroleum Regulations and other 'relevant rules' promulgated by the MOPI.[49]

The Petroleum Regulations contain several provisions requiring that preference be given to Chinese entities or materials in the conduct of petroleum operations. For example, Article 18 provides that Chinese design corporations must be given priority by operators when they subcontract for overall designs and engineering designs required for implementation of the petroleum contract, provided that the terms offered by such Chinese corporations are competitive. Article 19 requires that operators give priority to Chinese manufacturers and engineering companies when concluding subcontracts for such facilities as platforms, buildings, and other structures, provided the Chinese companies are competitive in 'quality, price, terms of delivery and services'. Under Article 20, priority must also be given to Chinese equipment and materials, again provided that these are competitive. Finally, Article 21 requires that operators and subcontractors give priority to Chinese enterprises when concluding subcontracts and service contracts, such as contracts for geophysical prospecting, well-drilling, diving, aircraft, vessels, and bases. Again, the preference for Chinese enterprises is only required where such enterprises are competitive in price, efficiency, and service.

The Petroleum Regulations also address briefly the question of ownership of tangible and intangible property used or acquired by foreign contractors in the course of petroleum operations. The law provides that assets purchased or built by a foreign contractor in order to implement the petroleum contract shall become the property of the CNOOC after the foreign party has recovered its investment in accordance with the terms of the contract.[50] In addition, the law provides that the CNOOC shall be the owner of all 'data, records, samples, vouchers and other original information' connected with the petroleum operations and requires that the use, transfer, sale, or publication of such information shall be controlled in accordance with rules formulated by the MOPI.[51]

Another requirement imposed on foreign contractors by the Petroleum Regulations concerns the landing of petroleum. Article 25 provides that in general all petroleum produced within a contract area must be landed in Chinese territory and exported from designated points, although exceptions to this rule may be granted by the MOPI. In the event of war, or threat of war, or 'other emergency circumstances', the Petroleum Regulations empower the Chinese government to 'requisition by purchase or requisition for use' all or a part of the petroleum obtained or purchased by a foreign contractor.[52]

Finally, the Petroleum Regulations also require that foreign operators and subcontractors comply with Chinese environmental protection and safety laws and generally conduct their operations 'with reference to international practice'.[53]

E. Dispute Settlement and Enforcement

The Petroleum Regulations include two general provisions regarding the settlement of disputes between foreign and Chinese enterprises engaged in the co-operative exploitation of China's offshore oil reserves and the enforcement of the regulations. With respect to dispute settlement, Article 27 prescribes 'friendly consultations' as the first step in resolving conflicts. If a solution is unattainable, settlement may be attempted through mediation or arbitration in China, or through arbitration by 'another arbitration body agreed upon by both parties', which presumably includes third-country arbitration. With regard to enforcement, Article 28 of the law empowers the MOPI to handle violations of the Petroleum Regulations. The MOPI may issue warnings, make demands for remedial action, and even order a termination of operations. Economic losses in such cases are to be borne by the responsible parties. The law also provides that the MOPI may fine or bring a suit against parties who are responsible for 'serious violations' of the regulations.

III. The Model Contract

The Model Contract, which served as the starting point for the negotiation of China's concession contracts during the first round of bidding, is in many respects a lawyer's longhand version of the Petroleum Regulations. Consisting of thirty articles and four annexes spread over more than 129 pages, the Model Contract sets forth in detail the Chinese vision of the legal and business relationship between the CNOOC and the foreign oil companies which is outlined in the Petroleum Regulations. Reportedly developed after close study of petroleum contracts and arrangements in other countries, especially Indonesia and Norway,[54] the Model Contract calls for the establishment of a form of co-operation between the CNOOC and foreign oil companies which resembles something approaching a cross between a production-sharing arrangement and a co-operative or contractual joint venture. Although a number of revisions have reportedly been made to the Model Contract for use during the second round of bidding,[55] the basic structure of Chinese-foreign co-operation established by the original draft remains intact. The main features of this structure are described below.

A. The Basic Structure of Co-operation

The bulk of the Model Contract is concerned with the basic terms under which the CNOOC and the foreign contractor will co-operate in the development of offshore oil and gas resources within the blocks won by the foreign company in the bidding process. The contract divides the term of such co-operation into three periods—exploration, development, and production—which in total shall generally not exceed thirty years. Each of these periods carries with it different rights and responsibilities for the parties.

During the exploration period all responsibility is to be borne by the foreign contractor. It must provide all of the funds required and bears all risks associated with the exploration activities. The contract also requires that the foreign contractor fulfil a 'minimum exploration work programme', including completion of a minimum number of kilometres of seismic lines, and drilling and completion of a minimum number of metres of wildcat wells. In addition, the contractor must spend at least a fixed amount of funds as a 'minimum expenditure obligation' during the exploration period. The extent of the minimum work programme and expenditure pledged by contractors was one of the areas open to bidding by foreign oil companies and, presumably, was a major factor considered by the CNOOC in the award of contract areas.

The duration of the exploration period is dependent upon the size of the area awarded to the foreign contractor. Where the contract area is less than 2,000 square kilometres, the exploration period consists of a term of five years, divided into an initial phase of three years and a second phase of two years. In the case of a contract area of 2,000 square kilometres or more, the exploration period is fixed at seven years, divided into three phases of three years, two years, and two years.

Upon the completion of each phase of the exploration period the contractor is required to relinquish a certain portion of the contract area. For example, in the case of a contract area in excess of 2,000 square kilometres the foreign contractor must give up 25 per cent of the total area at the end of the third year of the exploration period. At the end of the fifth year the contractor must relinquish 25 per cent of the remaining contract area after deducting the area of oil- and gasfields that have been discovered and designated for development. Finally, at the end of the seventh year, the remaining contract area, excluding fields designated for development, must be relinquished. As a result of these requirements, the foreign contractor is forced to move quickly to assess which areas within its designated concession blocks are most promising, and thus warrant further exploration, and which should be given up.[56]

Upon the expiry of each phase prior to the last phase of the exploration period, the foreign contractor is given the option either of proceeding with exploration and entering the next phase or of terminating the contract. Therefore, if exploration operations have not been promising the foreign party may withdraw from the co-operation and sustain a loss equal to the total amount of exploration costs incurred to date. In addition, the contract provides for automatic termination upon the expiry of the full term of the exploration period if no commercial oil or gas reservoir has been discovered within the contract area during that time.

In the event that the contract is not terminated prior to or on the expiry of the exploration period, the operations move into the development phase. The period begins on the date of approval by the MOPI of the 'overall development plan', prepared by the foreign contractor or operator, which sets forth the plan for the development of oil- and gasfields discovered within the contract area and the time schedule for development.

In general, the costs required for the development operations are to be shared by the parties in proportion to their 'participating interests', fixed in the contract at 51 per cent for the CNOOC and 49 per cent for the foreign contractor. However, the CNOOC has the option of not participating in the development of any field or of participating at a level of less than 51 per cent. Such an option must be exercised by notice in writing to the foreign contractor within ninety days of the date of approval of the overall development plan. In the event that the CNOOC chooses not to participate in the development of a field or chooses to participate at a reduced level, the foreign contractor is required to provide all or the remaining part of the funds necessary for development of the field.

The production period of an oil- or gasfield begins on the 'date of commencement of commercial production' and may last for up to fifteen years. The 'date of commencement of commercial production' is defined in the contract to mean the date on which a cumulative total of not less than 100,000 metric tons of crude oil, in the case of an oilfield, or not less than 100,000,000 cubic metres of natural gas, in the case of a gasfield, has been extracted and delivered from the field in accordance with normal procedures.

The Model Contract sets forth a rather complex formula for the allocation of crude oil produced from a field during each calendar year of the production period. Under this formula, 17.5 per cent of the annual gross production is paid in kind to the Chinese authorities as a royalty and as payment of the Consolidated Industrial and Commercial Tax. Next, 50 per cent of the annual gross production is deemed 'cost recovery oil'. Finally, the remaining 32.5 per cent is designated as 'profit oil'.

Under the Model Contract, 'cost recovery oil' is first used to compensate the CNOOC and the foreign contractor for operating costs actually paid by them during the calendar year. Payment is made in kind after operating costs have been converted into an amount of crude oil in accordance with a pricing formula that is based on 'the prevailing price in arm's length transactions of similar quality crude oil on the main world markets'.

The remainder of the 'cost recovery oil', after payment of operating costs, is deemed by the contract to be 'investment recovery oil'. This amount is first used as payment to the foreign contractor for the reimbursement of exploration costs which have been incurred during the exploration period but which have not yet been fully recovered. Unrecovered exploration expenses in any calendar year are carried forward to succeeding years for recovery from the 'investment recovery oil' portion of annual gross production for such years. In the year during which exploration costs are recovered in full, the remainder of the 'investment recovery oil' for that year may be used as payment to the CNOOC and the foreign contractor for the recovery of development costs incurred but not yet fully recovered by them, together with 'deemed interest' on the amount of such costs calculated at the rate of 9 per cent. Payment to the parties is made in proportion to their respective participating interests in the oilfields where production is being allocated. Payment is made in kind, in accordance with the same price conversion formula that is used for payment of operating costs. Like unrecovered exploration costs, unrecovered development costs and 'deemed interest' thereon may be carried forward to succeeding calendar years until fully recovered. In the event that full recovery is not achieved by the date of expiry of a field's production period, unrecovered costs are deemed to be losses, borne by the parties in proportion to their respective participating interests. If full recovery is achieved prior to the date of expiry, however, any remaining 'investment recovery oil' is to be regarded as 'profit oil'.

The amount of annual gross production of crude oil designated as 'profit oil' is divided by the Model Contract into two components: 'share oil' and 'allocable profit oil'. The 'share oil' portion is paid only to the Chinese party and the remainder is divided between the CNOOC and the foreign contractor in proportion to their respective participating interests in the development costs attributable to the field. In general this will entail a split of 51 per cent for the CNOOC and 49 per cent for the foreign contractor, unless the CNOOC has opted not to participate in development or to participate at a lower percentage level, in which case the allocation will be in accordance with the parties' actual participation.

How much of the annual 'profit oil' is to be divided between the parties as 'allocable profit oil' is determined by multiplying the total amount of the 'profit oil' attributable to a field by an 'x factor' proposed by the foreign contractor as part of the competitive bidding process prior to the signing of the contract. The 'x factor' for each oilfield is applied on an incremental basis in accordance with eight tiers of annual gross production ranging from 500,000 metric tons or less in tier one to over 10,000,000 metric tons in tier eight. Based on this system, then, the amount of 'allocable profit oil' is calculated by applying the tier one 'x factor' to the amount of 'profit oil' equal to or less than 500,000 metric tons; the tier two 'x factor' to the amount from 500,000 to 1,000,000 metric tons; the tier three 'x factor' to the amount from 1,000,000 to 2,000,000 metric tons; and so on.

The Model Contract, echoing the Petroleum Regulations, provides that the foreign contractor is free to export from China and sell on foreign markets all crude oil received by it, whether as 'cost recovery oil', 'investment recovery oil', or 'allocable profit oil'. However, the contract also stipulates that the CNOOC reserves the right to regulate any such export sales by prohibiting transport by the foreign contractor to 'destinations which infringe on the political interest of the People's Republic of China'.

B. Management Organization

The Model Contract calls for the creation of a management organization by which the Chinese party is able to exercise firm control over both long-range budgeting and planning, and everyday operations. The heart of this management organization is the Joint Management Committee (JMC). Both the CNOOC and the foreign contractor have the right to appoint three to five representatives to the JMC. The chairman of the JMC is the chief representative designated by the CNOOC and the vice-chairman is the chief representative designated by the foreign party. JMC meetings must be held at least four times a year, once each calendar quarter, but they may also be called at any time by either party.

The JMC's duties and powers are far-reaching. They include reviewing the work programme and budget proposed by the foreign party; determining the commercial viability of each oil- and/or gasfield; reviewing the overall development programme and budget for each oil- and/or gasfield; approving certain expensive items for procurement and excess budget expenditures; determining 'the date of commencement of commercial operations' with respect to oil- and/or gasfields; and other matters. The contract requires that the decisions of the JMC should be made 'unanimously through consultation'. In the event that unanimity cannot be achieved, the contract merely states that 'the Parties may convene another meeting and shall attempt to find another solution based on the principle of mutual benefit'.

The Model Contract calls for the creation of several other organizations under the JMC. One of these is the secretariat, which serves as the administrative arm of the JMC. The others are the various 'expert groups' created to deal with specialized issues that arise in the course of the petroleum operations. Like the JMC itself, both the secretariat and the expert groups are composed of equal numbers of Chinese and foreign appointees.

Apart from the creation of a formal organizational structure consisting of the JMC, the secretariat, and the expert advisory groups, the Model Contract provides for Chinese penetration and control over management of the petroleum operations in other ways as well. The contract states, for example, that the CNOOC shall have the right to assign its own 'professional representatives' to 'all sectors' of the foreign contractor's administration, thereby creating a Chinese counterpart organization. Such Chinese personnel are to have access to all activities and information, and the foreign staff are required to discuss their work with them on a regular basis. All costs and expenses relating to such Chinese staff members are to be paid initially by the foreign contractor but may be recovered out of commercial production together with other expenses.

C. The Obligations of the Parties

The Model Contract imposes a number of specific obligations on the foreign operator and the CNOOC. In essence these require that the operator bear primary responsibility for carrying out the exploration, development, and production operations within the contract area and that the CNOOC provide assistance to the operator in the performance of these tasks.

In the course of carrying out the petroleum operations the operator is required to apply 'appropriate and advanced technology and business managerial experience' so that the operations are performed 'reasonably and economically according to sound international practice'; to prepare and, after approval, implement the budget and work programme; to assume responsibility for procurement and subcontracting; to prepare and, after approval, implement a personnel training programme; to develop an insurance programme; to issue cash call notices for financial contributions by the parties; to maintain accounting records in accordance with the accounting procedures stipulated in the contract; to make all preparations for JMC meetings; to inform all subcontractors and expatriate employees of their duty to abide by Chinese laws; and to report all aspects of its work to the JMC. In addition, the operator is required to grant the CNOOC access to all information, samples, and reports pertaining to the petroleum operations.

The CNOOC's main obligation under the Model Contract is to assist the contractor so as to enable him to carry out 'expeditiously and efficiently' the petroleum operations. Specifically, the CNOOC is to assist the contractor in obtaining necessary licences and approvals to open accounts with the Bank of China; in going through foreign exchange, visa, and customs formalities; in obtaining office space, supplies, transportation, and communications facilities; in obtaining permits to export samples and data for analysis or processing; and in contacting relevant Chinese departments as required. Expenses incurred by the CNOOC in providing such assistance are to be paid by the contractor.

The Model Contract contemplates that production operations within the contract areas are to be gradually assumed by the CNOOC. Prior to the recovery of development costs, transfer to the CNOOC of production operations is permissible only with the agreement of the contractor. However, the contract grants to the CNOOC a unilateral right to take over production operations 'at any time' after development costs have been recovered by the foreign contractor in full. In such an event, most of the obligations imposed by the Model Contract on the operator are transferred to the CNOOC.

D. Procurement

The Model Contract specifically provides that the procurement activities of the contractor shall be subject to the preference provisions set forth in the Petroleum Regulations. Therefore, the contractor is required to give priority to Chinese suppliers of goods and services provided they are 'competitive' with those provided by foreign suppliers.[57] In order to monitor the contractor's procurement activities and ensure that the preference provisions are being respected, the Model Contract provides that the CNOOC shall have the right to appoint its own representatives to work with the contractor's procurement staff. Such representatives shall inform the contractor of Chinese companies able to supply goods and services required for procurement and shall have the right to 'take part in' the bidding process, including the evaluation of bids and the award of contracts.

E. Personnel Training and Technology Transfer

In accordance with the Petroleum Regulations, the Model Contract requires that the contractor give priority to the employment of Chinese personnel in the petroleum operations and that it transfer technology and managerial experience to such personnel. The 'scope, approach and objective' of the contractor's programme for the training of Chinese personnel and the transfer of technology are to be determined by the parties during the negotiations and incorporated in an annex to the final contract prior to signing.

With respect to training, the Model Contract requires the contractor to develop a training programme proposal and submit it to the JMC for approval prior to the commencement of each of the exploration, development, and production periods. The programme is to include training for a wide range of Chinese personnel, including technical personnel, managers, economists, and lawyers. The expenses of the programme are to be paid by the contractor but may be charged as exploration costs, development costs, or operating costs, as the case may be. Upon the expiry of the training programme, the contractor is obliged to employ 'qualified' Chinese personnel. Candidates for positions are to be recommended by the CNOOC but may be tested by the contractor prior to employment.

F. Miscellaneous Provisions

In addition to the provisions described above, the Model Contract contains a number of miscellaneous articles worthy of note. For example, the contract reiterates language found in the Petroleum Regulations providing that the CNOOC shall be the owner of all data obtained in the course of the petroleum operations. Ownership of physical assets acquired with budgeted funds is to revert to the CNOOC after recovery in full by the contractor of the development costs. Assignment of the contractor's rights and obligations under the contract is permissible, provided that the CNOOC has consented to such assignment. By contrast, the foreign party's consent is not required if the CNOOC assigns its interest in the contract to a third party. In accordance with the Petroleum Regulations, the contract provides for 'consultations' between the parties as the primary dispute settlement medium. In the event that consultations fail, the dispute may be referred to arbitration in China or 'another arbitration party agreed' by the parties. Finally, the Model Contract provides that Chinese law shall be the governing law as regards matters relating to the validity, interpretation, and implementation of the contract.

IV. The Taxation of Offshore Oil Activities

Both the Petroleum Regulations and the Model Contract require that foreign companies engaged in oil- and gas-related activities in China pay taxes in accordance with Chinese law. The principal tax laws affecting the activities of foreign companies in China are (a) the Income Tax Law of the

People's Republic of China Concerning Foreign Enterprises (hereafter cited as the FEITL),[58] and (b) the Consolidated Industrial and Commercial Tax Regulations of the People's Republic of China (hereafter cited as the Consolidated Tax).[59]

A. The Foreign Enterprise Income Tax

The FEITL provides for an income tax of general application to the activities of foreign enterprises in China. The law states that income tax is to be levied on 'income derived from production, business and other sources by any foreign enterprise operating in the People's Republic of China'.[60] The broad scope of the law is confirmed by provisions contained in the implementing regulations for the FEITL (hereafter cited as the Implementing Regulations), issued by the Ministry of Finance.[61] These regulations provide that 'production' and 'business' are to be interpreted to include a wide range of profit-making activities, and 'income from other sources' is to include passive income such as dividends, rents, royalties, interest, and 'other income' as defined by the Ministry of Finance.[62]

The FEITL, together with the Implementing Regulations, establishes what are in effect three separate tax regimes. The first is a progressive tax on actual net income, the second is a gross receipts tax on passive income, and the third is what is commonly referred to as a tax on 'deemed profits'. In the following sections each of these tax regimes will be discussed in turn, focusing on their application in the context of offshore oil activities.

i. The Progressive Tax

The FEITL's progressive tax applies to enterprises that have 'establishments' in China. Under the Implementing Regulations, establishments are defined as 'organizations, places or business agents engaging in production or business operations which are established by foreign enterprises in China'. They include 'management organizations, branch organizations, representative organizations and factories, places where natural resources are being exploited and places where construction, installation, assembling, exploration and other projects are being undertaken'.[63] Given that foreign contractors are required by both the Petroleum Regulations and the Model Contract to set up branches in China in order to carry out the petroleum operations, it is clear that they will be deemed to maintain taxable establishments there.

Taxable income under the progressive tax is akin to the American notion of 'net income', that is, annual gross income minus allowable deductions. The rates provided for in the law range from 20 to 40 per cent.[64] In addition, the FEITL provides for a local income tax of 10 per cent on the same taxable income amount.[65]

Under the FEITL's Implementing Regulations, foreign companies engaged in co-operative activities with Chinese enterprises for the exploitation of China's offshore oil resources are deemed to receive income 'at the time they receive their share of crude oil'.[66] The law requires that the amount of such income be computed on the basis of 'a price which is adjusted periodically according to the international market price of crude oil of similar quality'.[67] As noted earlier, however, under the Model Contract a different standard is stipulated for computing the price of crude oil received by foreign parties. This standard involves reference to 'the long-term contract sales price of similar quality crude oil in the main world markets'. In an internal document issued by the Ministry of Finance in response to a request from the MOPI for clarification of the discrepancy between the two pricing formulae, the Ministry of Finance has implied that the Model Contract's pricing mechanism will be acceptable for tax purposes.[68]

The FEITL and the Implementing Regulations permit taxpayers to deduct a number of kinds of expenses when computing taxable income. Among the most important costs to foreign oil companies are interest expenses incurred on loans borrowed by their contracting entities in China from banks or affiliated companies during the production and development phases. Under the Implementing Regulations such expenses may be deducted if the local tax authorities have determined that the underlying interest rate on the loan is 'reasonable' and that the loan is a 'normal loan'.[69] Although Chinese tax officials have not yet stated what tests will be used to determine whether a loan is 'normal', they have indicated that an interest rate will be deemed 'reasonable' if it is based on the London Interbank Offered Rate (LIBOR) for US dollars, even where the loan itself is provided by an affiliate of the borrower.[70]

Another issue of concern to foreign oil companies is the deductibility of certain payments made by the China-based contracting entity to its head office. Although the law disallows a deduction for royalties paid to head offices,[71] 'administrative expenses' paid to the head office 'for services directly provided' by it may be deductible, provided such expenses are 'reasonable' and are supported by adequate documentation and a certified accountant's report and are approved by the local tax authorities.[72] Interestingly, the Model Contract takes a different approach to the issue of head office expenses for accounting purposes. Under the Model Contract's accounting procedure there is a limitation on the amount of head office overheads that may be charged to the joint interest account.[73] During the exploration phase, charges may not exceed a specific percentage of annual exploration costs; separate limitations are to be negotiated for the development and production phases. Although the issue remains unclear at present, it is likely that the tax authorities will take such limitations into account when determining whether the amount of head office expenses meets the 'reasonableness' test of the tax laws.

Generally speaking, the FEITL and the Implementing Regulations adhere to international tax practices with regard to the types of expenses that are disallowed as deductions.[74] However, the law's blanket provision that 'income tax payments and local tax payments' are not deductible expenses will cause problems for foreign contractors.[75] In normal practice, agreements with service subcontractors generally require that all payments be free of tax and that the contractor 'gross up' in the event that taxes are imposed. Whether such gross-up payments will be viewed as a part of the normal operating expenses of a contractor, and hence deductible, or as non-deductible tax payments, is a question that has yet to be finally resolved by Chinese tax officials.

One matter which has been resolved is the deductibility of pre-contract costs of foreign companies engaged in offshore oil exploration. Pursuant to rules issued in late 1985, costs incurred by foreign oil companies prior to the signing of petroleum contracts with the CNOOC are to be treated as exploration costs and amortized over a period of not less than one year beginning from the commencement of commercial production of the relevant oil- and/or gasfield.[76] Such costs include the cost of initial seismic surveys conducted in 1979 under agreements with the CNOGEDC; costs of processing the interpretation of seismic data; and costs related to the negotiation of the petroleum contract.

The FEITL's Implementing Regulations provide that the 'entire investment' of a foreign oil company during the development phase may be capitalized using the oil- or gasfield as the reference unit, and that allocable expenses may be recovered from commercial production of crude oil from the field.[77] In addition, 'reasonable exploration expenses' incurred within a contract area may also be capitalized and may be recovered from any oil- or gasfield within the contract area once it begins commercial production.[78] Fixed assets acquired by foreign oil companies for petroleum operations during and after the development phase may be depreciated on a composite basis over a period of not less than six years, and losses may be carried forward and amortized for a period not exceeding five years.[79]

A number of foreign oil companies either at present are or are likely to be involved in both onshore and offshore operations, or, if exclusively offshore, may operate in a number of different areas. Hence, an issue of concern to such companies is the extent to which their various operations may be consolidated for tax purposes. The Chinese have indicated that consolidation of onshore and offshore petroleum operations will not be permitted, although consolidation will be allowed to a limited extent for income and losses within different contract areas offshore.

According to Chinese tax officials, as a general rule a foreign oil company must calculate and pay income tax separately with respect to each contract area. If a company holds, and operates in, two contract areas, it may consolidate income and losses only if it 'terminates' operations in one of the areas.[80] Termination in this context is interpreted to mean abandonment of the area, not simply a temporary stoppage of operations. Therefore, only if a contract area is abandoned may losses and unamortized exploration and other expenses incurred in connection with such an area be applied or amortized against income derived from another contract area.

Finally, mention should be made of certain unresolved issues relating to accounting. Under the FEITL, foreign enterprises are required to submit their 'financial and accounting system' to local tax authorities 'for reference', but if the taxpayer's accounting methods conflict with provisions contained in the tax law the latter will govern.[81] Chinese tax authorities have yet to issue a clear statement regarding the acceptability for tax purposes of the accounting procedures mandated by the Model Contract. The issue is, of course, in no way an academic one, for important differences exist between the FEITL and the Model Contract with respect to accounting. One basic difference between the two relates to the accounting method employed by the taxpayer, the Model Contract requiring use of a 'cash basis' method and the FEITL Implementing Regulations calling for accounting on an 'accrual basis'.[82] Although the issue has been resolved by some foreign oil companies in the course of negotiations with the Chinese, reliance on the clear language of the tax law and the Model Contract would seem to require oil companies to maintain separate accounting systems for petroleum operations and tax payment.

ii. The Withholding Tax on Passive Income

The second tax regime created by the FEITL is set forth in Article 11 of the law. This article provides that foreign enterprises that do not have establishments in China shall pay income tax at a flat rate on income obtained from dividends, interest, royalties, rents, and other income 'the source of which is from China'. This tax on passive income is imposed on the gross amount of income received and is collected by means of withholding. For oil companies, the most important areas of application of the withholding tax will be interest payments made to foreign banks and affiliates as well as payments of royalties, rents, and other fees to either affiliated companies or unrelated third parties.

Under the FEITL, the withholding tax on passive income is imposed at a rate of 20 per cent.[83] However, rules issued in 1983 effectively amend the FEITL to provide for a reduction of the withholding tax to 10 per cent or a total exemption from the tax in certain circumstances. These rules are contained in the Provisional Regulations of the Ministry of Finance of the People's Republic of China Regarding the Reduction and Exemption of Income Tax Relating to Interest Earned by Foreign Businesses from China (hereafter cited as the Provisional Interest Tax Regulations) and the Provisional Regulations of the Ministry of Finance of the People's Republic of China Regarding the Reduction and Exemption of Income Tax on Fees for the Use of Proprietary Technology (hereafter cited as the Provisional Technology Tax Regulations).[84]

The Provisional Interest Tax Regulations were issued by the Ministry of Finance on 7 January 1983 but came into force on 1 January 1983. The rules do not apply to contracts that were signed and became effective before 1 January 1983. However, the parties to such contracts may take advantage of the concessions provided under the rules during any extension period of such contracts. Basically, the rules provide for three different kinds of tax concessions which are of interest to foreign oil companies: (a) a provisional reduction of the income tax on interest; (b) specific exemptions from the interest income tax; and (c) favourable treatment for income tax on leasing fees.

The interest income tax reduction provided for in the Provisional Interest Tax Regulations amounts to 50 per cent, which effectively reduces the withholding tax on interest income of foreign enterprises from 20 to

10 per cent. The tax reduction applies to interest earned by foreign companies from 'loans, advances and deferred payments' made pursuant to credit or trade contracts with Chinese companies signed between 1983 and 1985. In order to qualify for the reduction, the relevant contract need only be signed during this period; all payments of interest made during the period of the contract's effectiveness, not simply the period between 1 January 1983 and 31 December 1985, will be subject to the reduced withholding rate. In late 1985 tax officials indicated that the tax reduction period would be extended to the end of 1990, but no official document to this effect has been published to date.

The second type of tax concession provided under the regulations consists of five specific exemptions from income tax on interest. The exemptions provided for under the Provisional Interest Tax Regulations are in addition to those already specified in the FEITL and the Implementing Regulations.[85] The first exemption applies to interest income from loans made by foreign banks to China's state banks at an international interbank loan rate. According to Bank of China officials, this rate is intended to refer to a LIBOR, SIBOR, or HIBOR rate plus a slight margin. The same officials indicated that in general the guidelines that will be applied in determining 'permissible' margins are as follows: not more than 0.25 per cent for loans with a maturity of less than twelve months; not more than 0.375 per cent for loans with a maturity of less than twenty-four months; and not more than 0.5 per cent for loans with a maturity of more than twenty-four months. The second exemption applies to interest income from loans made by foreign banks to the CNOOC, provided the interest rate of such loans does not exceed the interest guidelines described above. The third exemption applies to interest on deferred payments by Chinese companies to foreign suppliers for the import of technology, equipment, and commodities financed by means of seller's credits provided by the foreign supplier's state bank. In order to qualify for the exemption, the rate of interest charged under the seller's credit cannot exceed the rate that would be charged under buyer's credits that would be provided to the Chinese side. The fourth exemption applies to interest earned by foreign banks and individuals on deposits placed with China's state banks, provided the rate of interest paid on such deposits is lower than the interest rate on deposits in the home country of such foreign banks or individuals. Finally, the fifth exemption applies to interest earned pursuant to compensation trade arrangements.

The Provisional Interest Tax Regulations also provide favourable treatment for income derived from 'leasing fees' which are defined as fees paid by Chinese companies for 'equipment and related articles' supplied by foreign leasing companies by means of the 'lease-trade method'. The regulations conceive of such fees as consisting of three elements: (a) the cost of equipment; (b) the basic interest charge or cost of funds; and (c) the lessor's 'special' or service charge. Under the regulations, taxable income derived from leasing fees consists only of elements (b) and (c), that is, the portion of the total amount of fees remaining after deducting the cost of equipment. Tax is levied on this amount at a reduced rate of 10 per cent.

However, if the contract and other supporting documentation can demonstrate that the rate of interest ('cost of funds' element) meets the criteria for exemption from tax applicable to seller's credits (described above), then the basic interest element may be exempt from tax and the amount remaining after the deduction of such interest (that is, the 'spread' or 'service charge' element) shall be subject to the reduced 10 per cent rate as described above. It should be noted that, as in the case of the interest income tax reduction, the reduced tax rate for income from leasing fees is to be applied on a 'provisional' basis and benefits only those contracts signed within the period between 1 January 1983 and 31 December 1985, now extended until the end of 1990. Moreover, it should be emphasized that the new provisions apply only to lease-sale type arrangements, not rents, the latter presumably still being subject to the 20 per cent withholding tax rate.

The major concessions provided under the Provisional Technology Tax Regulations[87] are tax reductions and exemptions with respect to income earned by foreign companies which take the form of 'fees for the use of proprietary technology'. Under Article 11 of the FEITL, foreign companies that do not have establishments in China are subject to a 20 per cent withholding tax on 'royalties' earned from China. The FEITL Regulations define 'royalties' in Article 27 to include 'income from all types of patents, proprietary technology, copyrights, and so on, provided for use in China'. It is unclear why the Provisional Technology Tax Regulations appear to have abandoned the concept of 'royalties' in favour of 'proprietary technology' fees, particularly as the latter term has never been defined. None the less, a close reading of the Provisional Technology Tax Regulations leads one to believe that 'proprietary technology' is an inclusive term, encompassing the items included in the FEITL Regulations' definition of 'royalties', as well as such items as fees for blueprints and documentation, technical service fees, and personnel training fees paid in connection with the transfer of technology. These latter items are specifically included within the scope of 'proprietary technology' pursuant to the Provisional Technology Tax Regulations.

The Provisional Technology Tax Regulations provide for a reduced withholding tax of 10 per cent on income from fees earned by foreign enterprises without China establishments in connection with the transfer of certain types of 'proprietary technology' to Chinese entities. The types of technology fees eligible for the tax reduction include those received in connection with the transfer of technology for 'China's key construction projects in exploring for energy . . .'. Moreover, a total tax exemption may be granted where 'the technology is advanced and the terms are preferential'. According to discussions with MOPI officials, the determination of whether a particular type of technology is 'advanced' will be based not on some abstract notion of international standards but on whether the particular technology, when compared with other available technology, best meets the needs of the Chinese party that will use it.[88] As to what criteria will be used to determine whether the terms of transfer are 'preferential', Chinese tax officials cited three factors; (a) the cost of the technology in comparison with that of the foreign supplier's competitors; (b) whether the foreign supplier/seller will provide free training to Chinese personnel for the initial period of use; and (c) whether the Chinese user will be permitted to continue to use the technology without the payment of an additional fee upon the expiry of the contract.[89]

In addition to the tax exemptions available for fees earned in respect of technology which falls within the five categories mentioned above and which meets the two requirements of being 'advanced' and transferred on 'preferential terms', the Provisional Technology Tax Regulations also provide for exemptions from the FEITL's withholding tax for certain types of income which do not arise in connection with technology transfer arrangements. The types of income eligible for the exemption are set forth in detail in the regulations and include certain kinds of service fees, technology instruction fees, technical assistance fees, and technical service fees.[90]

iii. The Deemed Profits Tax

Companies that provide services to the offshore oil industry on a subcontract basis are by nature extremely mobile and often work in different parts of a country for varying periods of time. As a result, calculating the taxable income of such subcontractors can be a difficult task. In order to facilitate tax administration, the Ministry of Finance has determined that foreign offshore oil subcontractors operating in China may pay tax in accordance with Article 24 of the FEITL's Implementing Regulations. This article provides that the profit rate and taxable income of foreign subcontractors shall be determined 'on the basis of the total income from the project', such deemed profit then being taxed in accordance with the FEITL's progressive rates. At present, the deemed profit margin fixed by the Ministry of Finance for offshore oil subcontractors is 10 per cent.[91]

According to a Ministry of Finance document issued in 1985,[92] the deemed profit system is not mandatory for all subcontractors; if the foreign company has set up an accounting system in China, can accurately document its income and expenses, and meets other requirements, it may apply to the local tax bureau to be taxed on an actual net profit basis. To date, however, as a practical matter most local tax bureaux—and foreign subcontractors—have preferred to be taxed on a deemed profit basis. If a foreign company has an establishment in China and is able to calculate net income and support its calculations with adequate documentation it may apply to the local tax authorities to pay tax on a net income basis.

B. The Consolidated Tax

Unlike the FEITL, which applies only to foreign enterprises, the Consolidated Tax is applicable to both foreign and Chinese entities engaged in business transactions in China.[93] The structure of the tax differs significantly from the FEITL tax regimes. Basically, the Consolidated Tax is a type of cascading turnover tax assessed on gross receipts arising from the sale or transfer of products. Tax liability arises at each level in the distribution system and the tax is paid by the seller or transferor. In the case of crude oil, for example, the tax would be paid by the producer upon production, by the refiner upon transfer of the refined product, and by the retailer upon sale to the consumer. The tax is also applicable to purchases of foreign goods. In such cases, however, the tax is imposed on the importer instead of the foreign exporter.

Items taxable under the Consolidated Tax are divided into two general categories: (a) industrial and agricultural products, and (b) commercial retailing, communications and transportation, and other service trades. Although the first category includes a list of more than 100 specific products, there is no list for petroleum or petroleum products as such. Rather, these items are classified under the last heading of 'other industrial products' and are taxed at a rate of 5 per cent. The second category contains a list of 'service trades' which includes most offshore oil subcontractor services. The tax rate applicable to such activities is 3 per cent.

C. Individual Income Tax

In addition to the Foreign Enterprise Income Tax and the Consolidated Tax, foreign companies engaged in offshore oil activities will also want to note the provisions contained in China's Individual Income Tax Law and the Implementing Regulations issued thereunder.[94] Under a Ministry of Finance ruling issued in 1983,[95] employees of foreign oil companies that have entered into contracts with the CNOOC and employees of foreign subcontractor service companies operating in China are not eligible to claim the benefits of the 'ninety-day tax exemption' rule. This rule, set forth in Article 5(1) of the Implementing Regulations, provides for an exemption from individual income tax for individuals who are resident in China for not more than ninety consecutive days in a tax year and are paid by employers outside China. As a result of this ruling, personnel engaged in most offshore oil activities will be subject to individual income tax on their wages and salaries earned during their actual periods of residence in China regardless of the duration of such residence. Under the Individual Income Tax Law, tax is assessed at progressive rates ranging from 5 to 45 per cent. A standard deduction of RMB800 is built into the tax schedule; no other deductions are allowed.

D. Tax Administration

Tax administration and enforcement matters relating to offshore oil are handled by a specially created government agency known as the Offshore Oil Taxation Bureau (OOTB). The background, organization, and responsibilities of the OOTB are discussed below.

On 12 June 1982 the Ministry of Finance submitted to the State Council a Petition Regarding the Establishment of the Offshore Oil Taxation Bureau (hereafter cited as the Petition). The Petition noted that business activities in connection with offshore oil development were marked by 'special characteristics' and that financial, accounting, and other matters were 'comparatively complex'. Therefore, the Petition proposed the establishment of a specialized bureau to handle tax matters related to offshore oil exploration and development activities, and went on to detail the scope of the duties of such a bureau, issues relating to organization and staffing, and other matters. Subsequently, on 7 August 1982 the State Council issued Document No. (82) *Guo han* 159 (hereafter cited as Document No. 159), addressed to the Ministry of Finance and the people's governments of Beijing, Shanghai and Tianjin municipalities, and Guangdong province.[96] Document No. 159 sanctioned the creation of the OOTB and specifically approved the proposals set forth in the Petition regarding the OOTB's functions, organizational structure, and staffing. The OOTB officially commenced its work in December 1982.

The Petition sets forth five main functions for the OOTB. These include:

(a) 'to thoroughly implement the state's tax laws', and specifically to exercise 'unified management' and 'unified taxation and collection' with respect to the various taxes imposed in connection with offshore oil activities;

(b) 'to research and draft supplementary regulations regarding offshore oil taxation, and to provide explanations of the relevant tax laws';

(c) 'to gather information, to grasp in a timely manner an understanding of the situation regarding the source of taxes and to make decisions regarding the calculation of taxes on the prices of oil and natural gas';

(d) 'to grasp the economic activities of taxpaying enterprises and individuals, and to solve problems regarding the handling of financial and accounting matters of taxable enterprises in a reasonable manner and in the light of international practice'; and

(e) 'to formulate measures regarding tax management, to strengthen the investigation and supervision of tax payment, to verify tax amounts and to organize in a timely manner work regarding the deposit of tax proceeds in the treasury'.

It should be noted that, despite its involvement in offshore oil activities, the OOTB is not related directly to MOPI. Rather, in terms of China's bureaucratic organization, it falls under the supervision of the General Taxation Bureau (GTB) of the Ministry of Finance. In fact, ties between the GTB and the OOTB are extremely close and most OOTB employees have been seconded from the GTB. The headquarters of the OOTB are based in Beijing. In addition, branches have been established in those areas where the CNOOC has established local operations, namely, Shanghai, Tianjin, Guangzhou, Zhanjiang, and Shenzhen.

According to the OOTB, in general its policies are formulated by the GTB in consultation with the MOPI. Branch organizations are 'guided by' the OOTB headquarters and are not permitted to act independently with respect to policy formulation and implementation. Finally, according to the OOTB, its decisions with respect to tax matters relating to offshore oil activities take precedence over those of municipal and provincial tax bureaux.

Rules regarding tax administration matters for foreign contractors who have entered into petroleum contracts with the CNOOC were issued by the OOTB in 1984.[97] The rules require all contractors, including both operators directly engaged in petroleum operations and non-operators, to register with the local OOTB office and file tax returns as required by law. Prior to the commencement of commercial production, the rules permit contractors to dispense with the filing of quarterly Foreign Enterprise Income Tax returns and require only that annual returns be filed. Annual returns are to be accompanied by the contract area's final accounts, various financial reports, and an audit report by a Chinese registered accountant.

Special rules pertaining to subcontractor service companies were also issued by the OOTB in 1985.[98] These rules require subcontractors to go through tax registration procedures with the local OOTB within thirty days of the commencement of operations. However, where the period of the contract is less than thirty days, tax registration is required before work commences. In order to strengthen the administration of tax, the rules require contractors for whom the services are being provided to report to the local OOTB within fifteen days of the signing of the contract and provide information regarding the nature of the project, its duration, cost, and other details. Regarding the payment of tax, the rules specify the requirements for obtaining tax treatment on an actual net profits basis as well as on a deemed profits basis. In addition, the rules contain provisions permitting subcontractors engaged in two or more projects at the same time to file and pay tax on a consolidated basis.

V. Registration, Customs, and Environmental Protection Rules

The Petroleum Regulations, the Model Contract, and China's tax laws provide the foundation of the regulatory regime for offshore oil exploration and development activity. In addition, a number of other laws have a bearing on the operations of foreign companies involved in offshore work. The most important of these include rules governing the registration of foreign contractors and subcontractors, special rules providing preferential customs treatment to companies engaged in offshore oil activities, and legislation concerning environmental protection.

A. Registration Regulations

Both the Petroleum Regulations and the Model Contract require foreign contractors and subcontractors to register with the appropriate Chinese authorities, but neither document specifies the procedures by which registration is to be accomplished. This task is fulfilled by a notice (hereafter cited as the Registration Notice) issued on 12 March 1983 by the State Administration for Industry and Commerce (SAIC) which came into effect on 1 April of the same year.[99]

According to the Registration Notice, all foreign contractors must apply to the headquarters of the SAIC in Beijing. The application process consists of filling in a form and submitting copies of the contract and the related Chinese approvals. Companies must also submit certificates pertaining to their legal status and creditworthiness, and information relating to service and supply subcontractors that they employ. Once the application has been approved by the SAIC the foreign contractor will be issued with a 'business licence'.

The Registration Notice provides that fees for the registration of foreign contractors are to be assessed in accordance with the standards set forth in regulations made public by the SAIC in March 1982 for the payment of registration fees by joint ventures.[100] On the basis of these standards, oil companies with a registered capital of RMB10 million will pay a fee equal to the sum of 0.1 per cent of the registered capital for the portion under RMB10 million and 0.05 per cent for the portion above that amount. According to the SAIC, no company will be required to pay registration fees in excess of RMB30,000 even if computation in accordance with the above formula yields a higher amount. Moreover, the rules themselves provide for 'preferential treatment' for oil companies during the exploration period when, under the terms of the Model Contract, they are to bear all financial risks. Registration fees during this period are fixed 'provisionally' at RMB2,000. Once commercial production begins, however, the foreign contractor must re-register with the SAIC and pay fees based on the standards described above.

The Registration Notice also requires all foreign subcontractors operating in China to register. The registration requirement applies not only to 'first-tier' subcontractors, that is, service and supply companies in a direct contractual relationship with the foreign contractor, but also to companies that have entered into contracts with subcontractors, that is, 'second-tier' and 'third-tier' subcontractors.[101] According to the SAIC, these companies are also subject to the registration requirement so long as their services are performed within China.

The Registration Notice provides that subcontractors ordinarily should go through registration procedures at local bureaux of the SAIC authorized to handle registration. However, if a subcontractor performs operations in several provinces or localities simultaneously, it should register with the central bureau in Beijing. According to the SAIC, the registration requirement applies no matter how long it takes a subcontractor to perform its job and registration must be effective before work can begin.[102] In addition, the registration will be valid only for a specific subcontract.[103] Therefore, if a subcontractor is engaged by foreign contractor X to perform a job with a duration of two weeks, it must register before commencing work, de-register upon the expiry of the subcontract, and re-register before beginning a new job with foreign contractor Y.

When applying for registration, the subcontractor must fill out an application form, signed by its chairman or president, describing the scope of operations of the project and attaching data relating to China-based employees during the contract period. In addition, applicants must submit copies of the subcontract together with a certificate of the local branch of the CNOOC at the place where the subcontract is being performed. Once approved, the applicant will be issued with a registration certificate.

Fees for subcontractor registration are calculated in accordance with a modified version of the system used for the calculation of fees for foreign contractors.[104] Under this system, 20 per cent of the total subcontract amount is to be taken as the base amount for fee collection purposes. If this base amount is the equivalent of RMB10 million or less, then the registration fee will be charged at the rate of 0.1 per cent. If the base amount is more than RMB10 million, the fee will be calculated at 0.1 per cent of the base amount for the portion under RMB10 million and at 0.05 per cent for the portion above that amount. The maximum fee for each single registration is RMB30,000.

B. Customs Provisions

To facilitate the conduct of the petroleum operations, the Chinese Customs authorities have issued a number of regulations and directives providing favourable customs treatment for foreign companies and their employees engaged in oil exploration and development activities. For example, under a 1981 regulation, foreign contractors and subcontractors may import machinery, equipment, and other 'production materials', without having first to obtain a formal import licence, provided such items have been confirmed by the Customs authorities as being 'within the scope of the project' concerned.[105] The same regulation also stipulates that 'foreign engineers and technical personnel' who come to China to engage in petroleum operations shall be granted the same favourable customs treatment as is extended to 'foreign experts' invited to work in China by the Chinese government. In general, the application of this standard will provide duty-free treatment for many personal items of daily use imported by or for such personnel.

Another important set of provisions are contained in regulations promulgated jointly by the General Administration of Customs and the Ministry of Finance on 1 April 1982.[106] These regulations provide for an exemption from export duties and the Consolidated Industrial and Commercial Tax for crude oil received by foreign contractors in accordance with the provisions set forth in the Model Contract and exported from China. In addition, the regulations exempt a wide range of imported items from import duties and the Consolidated Industrial and Commercial Tax, subject to 'verification and approval' by the Customs authorities. These include machinery, equipment, spare parts, and other materials used directly in exploration and development activities, as well as parts, components, and materials necessary for the manufacture of machinery and equipment in China for petroleum operations. In addition, the regulations exempt from taxation all 'machinery and other construction equipment' that is imported temporarily and guaranteed to be exported by the foreign party upon completion of the project for which it is being used.

Revised Customs regulations pertaining to offshore oil activities were implemented in 1984.[107] The regulations require that all foreign contractors and subcontractors register with the local Customs authorities before the import of equipment, materials, and personal effects. In addition, the rules strengthen Customs control over foreign exploration and service and supply vessels entering and leaving Chinese waters, and specify the procedures under which goods may be imported duty-free.

C. Environmental Protection

The Petroleum Regulations and the Model Contract both contain provisions requiring that petroleum operations be carried out in compliance with China's environmental protection laws. The most important of these laws as regards offshore oil activity is the Marine Environmental Protection Law of the People's Republic of China (hereafter cited as the MEPL).[108]

The MEPL is by its terms applicable to all enterprises and individuals engaged in exploration, development, production, and other activities within the maritime areas under the jurisdiction of China. In addition to imposing a general obligation on such enterprises and individuals to 'protect the marine environment' and to 'supervise and report' activities harmful to the environment, the MEPL contains in Chapter III a number of specific provisions relating to the prevention of pollution and damage to the marine environment due to oil exploration and development activities offshore. Among the most important of these provisions is one that requires enterprises engaged in offshore oil activities to prepare a written environmental impact study, including a report on measures to be taken to prevent pollution.[109] The report and study are to be submitted to the environmental protection department of the State Council for 'examination and ratification', which presumably must be obtained before operations can commence. The MEPL also requires the installation of 'appropriate anti-pollutant facilities and equipment' on vessels, platforms, and other structures operating offshore when exploring for or developing oilfields, and the taking of 'technical measures' to prevent blow-outs and oil leakage. In the event of a well blow-out, contractors are required to inform the relevant authorities, take interim measures to control the damage, and submit to an investigation by the maritime authorities. Enterprises and individuals found to be in violation of the law may be fined, or ordered to pay compensation, or may in serious cases be subject to criminal sanctions.[110]

VI. Conclusion

China's programme to develop its offshore oil resources in co-operation with foreign enterprises has necessitated the establishment of a regulatory regime that is in many ways distinct from that which has been put into place for other types of foreign investment activity. As the pace of activity off shore quickens a number of new laws are likely to be enacted.[111]

Among those reportedly now being considered are special labour management rules for personnel engaged in offshore work, safety regulations, and rules designed to implement the preference provisions of the Petroleum Regulations.

At the end of 1985 it appeared that China was poised to expand its co-operation with foreign companies in the exploration for oil and gas resources to include joint projects on shore. According to the MOPI, oil basins specified in the provisions will be opened for bidding by foreign companies in 1986.[112] Although legislation to govern these activities has not yet appeared, the Chinese government is expected to promulgate rules relating to onshore co-operation in the near future. It can be expected that these new laws, like the Model Contract and China's existing offshore oil legislation, will reflect China's determination to exercise firm control over oil exploration and development activities and to enhance her own capabilities to conduct future offshore oil operations independent of, but on a technological par with, the major foreign oil companies.

Notes

1. C. Brown, 'Tough Terms for Offshore Oil', *China Business Review*, July–August 1982, p. 34. See, also, S. Carlson, *China's Oil: Problems and Prospects* (Washington, DC, Georgetown University Center for Strategic and International Studies, 1979); Chen Senqiang, 'General Survey of Geological Structure and Prospects in Oil and Gas of the Continental Shelf in the Northern Part of the South China Sea', *Economic Reporter*, December 1981; and B. Knoll, 'China Oil: Looking Forward to a Better Future Offshore', in *China Energy Report* (Hong Kong, Energy Committee of the American Chamber of Commerce, 1982).

2. According to official Chinese statistics, onshore production reached a peak of 106.15 million tons in 1979 and has declined steadily since then. Production in 1980 was 105.95 million tons, decreasing to 101.22 million tons in 1981. See Knoll, p. 40, note 1 above. For background on China's offshore oil development policy see K. Fountain, 'The Development of China's Offshore Oil', in N. Ludlow (ed.), *China's Petroleum Organization and Manpower* (Washington, DC, The National Council for US–China Trade, 1980), pp. 63–76.

3. See 'China's Crude Oil Export Prospects, 1979–90', in Ludlow, p. 77, note 2 above.

4. For a discussion of China's geophysical survey programme and a legal analysis of the survey agreements, see M. Hoyt, 'Current Developments in Petroleum Exploration Offshore China', in *Energy Law 1979* (London, International Bar Association, 1979), topic I, paper 3.

5. For a synopsis of the terms of these contracts, see D. Jones, 'China's Offshore Oil Development: Japanese and French Contracts Offer Some Insights, Some Confusion', *China Business Review*, July–August 1980, pp. 51–6.

6. See *The New York Times*, 20 September 1982, p. 34.

7. The Petroleum Regulations were adopted by the State Council on 12 January 1982 and promulgated on 30 January 1982. An English-language translation of the law appears in F. Chu, M. Moser, and O. Nee (eds.), *Commercial, Business and Trade Laws: People's Republic of China* (Dobbs Ferry, Oceana Publications, Inc., 1982), Pt. 10.

8. *China Daily*, 17 March 1982, p. 1.

9. See F. Ching, 'China Opens Offshore Oil Bidding', *Asian Wall Street Journal*, 17 February 1982, p. 1; 'Bidding for Offshore Petroleum Exploitation',

Peking Review, 22 February 1982, p. 5; and 'China's Offshore Oil Now up for International Bidding', *Economic Report*, March 1982, pp. 8–10.

10. The invitations, or more accurately 'letters of notification of bidding', were issued in two groups at an interval of one month. Invitations issued on 16 February 1982 covered the Pearl River area and blocks in the northern part of the South Yellow Sea. Invitations sent on 16 March 1982 covered areas in the southern parts of the South Yellow Sea and the Beibu Gulf as well as the western part of the Ying Ge Hai Basin. See 'New Offshore Oil Corporation's Chief on Oil Exploitation Bidding in Interview with CEN', *China Economic News*, 22 February 1982, p. 2.

11. The deadlines for expressions of interest were 30 March 1982, for companies that had been issued invitations on 16 February, and 25 April 1982, for companies that had been invited to bid in the second phase on 16 March. Companies that expressed an interest in bidding were required to pay a fee of US$10,000–40,000, depending on the location and number of blocks. Upon payment of the fee, companies were issued with a 'Certificate of Qualified Bidder' by the CNOOC which certified that the holder was entitled to participate in the competitive bidding.

12. See '40 Foreign Oil Companies Receive Documents on Offshore Oil Bidding', *China Economic News*, 17 May 1982, p. 3.

13. According to the CNOOC, 25 of the 33 companies submitting bids organized themselves into 13 separate bidding groups and 8 companies bid independently. See '33 Foreign Oil Companies Forward Bid Proposals on Joint Exploitation of China's Offshore Petroleum Resources', *China Economic News*, 23 August 1982, p. 12.

The 33 foreign oil companies are: Agip (Overseas) Ltd. (Italy); Amoco Orient Petroleum Company (USA); Ampol Exploration Ltd. (Australia); Berkeley Exploration & Production Ltd. (UK); BP Petroleum Development Ltd. (UK); Broken Hill Proprietary, Ltd. (Australia); Chevron Orient Inc. (USA); Cities Service Orient Petroleum Co. (USA); Cluff Oil Ltd. (UK); CRS Ltd. (Australia); Esso Exploration Inc. (USA); Getty Oil International (Orient) Inc. (USA); Hispanica de Petroleos S.A. (Spain); Hunt Sedco International (USA); Indemnitsu Oil Development Co. Ltd. (Japan); Japan National Oil Corporation (Japan); Mobil Oil Corporation (USA); Natomas (Far East) Ltd. (USA); Occidental Eastern Inc. (USA); Pecten Orient Co. (USA); Pennzoil Far East Ltd. (USA); Petrobas International S.A. (Brazil); Petro-Canada Exploration Inc. (Canada); Phillips Petroleum International Corporation Asia (USA); Ranger Oil (Canada) Ltd. (Canada); Shell Exploration China Ltd. (UK); Société Nationale Elf-Aquitaine (France); Sun Orient Exploration Company (USA); Texaco Orient Petroleum Co. (USA); Texas Eastern Corporation (USA); Total Exploration (France); Tricentrol North Sea Ltd. (UK); and Union Oil Orient Ltd. (USA).

14. The consortium consists of five members with the following shareholdings; BP Petroleum Ltd. (45 per cent), Broken Hill Proprietary, Ltd. (20 per cent), Petrobas International S.A. (15 per cent), Ranger Oil (Canada) Ltd. (10 per cent), and Petro-Canada Exploration Inc. (10 per cent). BP will act as the operator for the consortium, which will explore and develop five contract blocks totalling 14,086 square kilometres in the Pearl River mouth and the South Yellow Sea. For further discussion, see 'CNOOC Says More Offshore Oil Contracts to Follow BP's Lead, Drilling in 2nd half of 1983', *China Economic News*, 23 May 1983, p. 1.

15. For a complete list of offshore exploration and development contracts signed between the CNOOC and foreign oil companies in 1979–83, see 'Offshore China Contracts 1979–1983', *Petroleum News*, January 1984, p. 16.

16. See 'Oil Search Bill off the Mainland Hits US$1.66', *South China Morning Post, Business News*, 2 October 1985, p. 1. For a summary of drilling results in the first round, see 'U.S. Oil Firms Express Caution on China Play', *Asian Wall Street Journal*, 31 May–1 June 1985, p. 1.

17. See N. Langston and M. Lee, 'Elephants' Graveyard', *Far Eastern Economic*

Review, 6 December 1984, p. 63; and N. Langston, 'A Fertile Formula', *Far Eastern Economic Review*, 6 December 1984, p. 64.

18. See 'China Opens Bidding for More Offshore Oil', *China Daily*, 22 November 1984, p. 1; 'Plans for New Offshore Oil Contracts Annual', *China Daily*, 31 August 1985, p. 1; and 'China Announces Terms for Oil Bidding', *Asian Wall Street Journal*, 31 January 1985, p. 3.

19. See Langston and Lee, p. 63, note 17 above.

20. See 'China Announces Terms for Oil Bidding', *Asian Wall Street Journal*, 31 January 1985, p. 3.

21. See '23 Oil Companies Submit Bid Proposals for Pearl River Mouth and South Yellow Sea', *China Economic News*, 8 July 1985, p. 1; 'Nine Groups Bid in Second Round Oil Exploration Competition', *China Market Intelligence*, July 1985, p. 6; and 'Petroleum Update', *China Market Intelligence*, December 1985, p. 4.

22. Petroleum Regulations, Art. 1, note 7 above.

23. Petroleum Regulations, Art. 3, note 7 above.

24. Petroleum Regulations, Art. 3, note 7 above.

25. Petroleum Regulations, Art. 3, note 7 above.

26. Petroleum Regulations, Art. 2, note 7 above.

27. Petroleum Regulations, Art. 2, note 7 above.

28. Conflicting jurisdictional claims over offshore resources exist between China, Japan, and Korea in the north, and between China and Vietnam in the south. Among others, Chinese and Vietnamese claims in the Beibu Gulf and Ying Ge Hai area to the south-west of Hainan Island could have a direct impact on petroleum operations in the South China Sea, particularly in light of the deterioration in relations between the two countries since the late 1970s. For general background on territorial disputes and their effect on offshore oil activities in Asia, see S. Harrison, *China, Oil and Asia: Conflict Ahead?* (New York, Columbia University Press, 1978).

29. Petroleum Regulations, Art. 4, note 7 above.

30. Petroleum Regulations, Art. 5, note 7 above.

31. Petroleum Regulations, Arts. 5 and 6, note 7 above.

32. Petroleum Regulations, Art. 6, note 7 above.

33. For an organization chart of the CNOOC's headquarters, see *China Market Intelligence*, March 1983.

34. See 'Four Regional Oil Corporations Set Up', *China Economic News*, 30 May 1983, p. 8; and 'China Sets Up Four Regional Oil Corporations', *Xinhua News Bulletin*, 17 May 1983, p. 21.

35. See 'How the Zhanjiang Oil Support Base Is Shaping Up', *Business China*, 16 June 1982, pp. 82–3; and 'Offshore Service Opportunities Tied to JVs with CNOOC', *Business China*, 13 April 1983, pp. 49–51.

36. See K. Woodward and R. Goodwin, 'Supplying Offshore Services', *China Business Review*, March–April 1982, pp. 17–18.

37. For a description of the CNOJSC and its subsidiaries, see 'China Nanhai Oil Service Corporation', *China Market Intelligence*, May 1983, p. 5; and D. Denny, 'The Quest for Control', *China Business Review*, May–June 1983, pp. 28–9.

38. Petroleum Regulations, Art. 17, note 7 above.

39. Petroleum Regulations, Art. 7, note 7 above.

40. Petroleum Regulations, Art. 7, note 7 above.

41. Petroleum Regulations, Art. 7, note 7 above.

42. Petroleum Regulations, Art. 7, note 7 above.

43. Petroleum Regulations, Art. 8, note 7 above.

44. Petroleum Regulations, Arts. 14 and 15, note 7 above.

45. Petroleum Regulations, Art. 12, note 7 above.

46. Petroleum Regulations, Art. 12, note 7 above.

47. Petroleum Regulations, Art. 13, note 7 above.

48. Petroleum Regulations, Art. 29(5), note 7 above.
49. Petroleum Regulations, Arts. 16 and 29(8), note 7 above.
50. Petroleum Regulations, Art. 22, note 7 above.
51. Petroleum Regulations, Art. 23, note 7 above.
52. Petroleum Regulations, Art. 26, note 7 above.
53. Petroleum Regulations, Art. 24, note 7 above.
54. The Norwegian state-owned oil company, Statoil, has played an important role in the formulation of China's offshore oil policies in general and in the drafting of the Model Contract in particular. See 'The Norwegian Experience and China's Oil Policy', *Petroleum News*, November 1980, pp. 39–43.
55. See 'Petroleum Update', *China Market Intelligence*, December 1985, p. 4.
56. Brown, p. 35, note 1 above.
57. Chinese-foreign joint ventures qualify as 'Chinese Suppliers' for the purpose of the preference provisions. See 'Offshore Service Opportunities Tied to JVs with CNOOC', pp. 49–51, note 35 above. On 1 July 1983 the CNOOC issued a circular which requires foreign oil companies to employ the services of Chinese companies and joint ventures in the fields of aviation, navigation, and radio control; positioning; communications; and supply vessels and bases. Other provisions in the circular attempt to strengthen the preference requirement for services outside these mandatory categories.
58. Adopted at the Fourth Session of the Fifth National People's Congress on 13 December 1981, and promulgated by an order of Ye Jianying, chairman of the Standing Committee of the National People's Congress, on 13 December 1981. The law came into effect on 1 January 1982. An English-language translation of the FEITL appears in Chu, Moser, and Nee, Pt. 13, note 7 above.
59. Adopted in draft form by the Standing Committee of the National People's Congress on 11 September 1958 and promulgated on 13 September 1958. The law came into effect on the date of promulgation. An English-language translation of the Consolidated Tax regulations appears in Chu, Moser, and Nee, Pt. 13, note 7 above.
60. FEITL, Art. 1, note 58 above.
61. Detailed Rules and Regulations for the Implementation of the Income Tax Law of the People's Republic of China Concerning Foreign Enterprises. The Implementing Regulations were approved by the State Council on 17 February 1982 and promulgated by the Ministry of Finance on 21 February 1982, but are retroactively effective to the effective date of the FEITL, 1 January 1982. For an English-language translation of the Implementing Regulations, see Chu, Moser, and Nee, Pt. 13, note 7 above.
62. Implementing Regulations, Art. 4, note 61 above.
63. Implementing Regulations, Art. 2, note 61 above.
64. FEITL, Art. 3, note 58 above.
65. FEITL, Art. 3, note 58 above.
66. Implementing Regulations, Art. 26, note 61 above.
67. Implementing Regulations, Art. 26, note 61 above.
68. Document of the Ministry of Finance No. (82) *Cai shui* 98, dated 20 March 1982, reads in part as follows: 'If the crude oil pricing method determined in a co-operative exploitation petroleum contract, after being examined by the relevant tax authorities, conforms to the principle of pricing method stipulated in Article 26 of the Tax Regulations, the corresponding pricing method in the petroleum contract will be allowed to compute the amount of income.'
69. Article 12 of the Implementing Regulations provides as follows: 'Interest paid by a foreign enterprise on loans may be listed as an expenditure at a reasonable interest rate when backed by documents certifying such loans and interest payments and after having been examined and verified by the local tax authorities as being normal loans.'
70. These remarks were made by Mr Liu Zhicheng, commissioner of taxation,

in a speech entitled 'Salient Features of the New Foreign Enterprises Income Tax Law', delivered at a seminar arranged by Price Waterhouse and held in Houston, Texas, on 30 June 1982.

71. Implementing Regulations, Art. 10(9), note 61 above.

72. Implementing Regulations, Art. 11, note 61 above.

73. See O. Nee, 'Taxation of the Offshore Oil and Gas Industry in China' (unpublished paper on file with the author).

74. Implementing Regulations, Art. 10, note 61 above.

75. Implementing Regulations, Art. 20(4), note 61 above.

76. The rules are contained in Document of the Ministry of Finance No. (85) *Cai shui* 204, issued by the Guangzhou Offshore Oil Tax Bureau on 12 December 1985.

77. Implementing Regulations, Art. 16, note 61 above.

78. Document of the Ministry of Finance No. (82) *Cai shui* 98, dated 20 March 1982, para 5.

79. Implementing Regulations, Art. 18, note 61 above; and FEITL, Art. 6, note 58 above.

80. Document of the Ministry of Finance No. (82) *Cai shui* 98, dated 20 March 1982, para. 4.

81. FEITL, Art. 9, note 58 above.

82. Implementing Regulations, Art. 38, note 61 above.

83. FEITL, Art. 11, note 58 above.

84. English-language translations of the Provisional Interest Tax Regulations and the Provisional Technology Tax Regulations are on file with the author.

85. See FEITL, Art. 11, note 58 above; and Implementing Regulations, Arts. 29, 30, and 31, note 61 above.

86. Personal communication to the author by Bank of China officials.

87. The Provisional Technology Tax Regulations were issued on 13 December 1982 and came into effect on 1 January 1983. Contracts signed prior to the effective date of the regulations are not eligible for the tax benefits provided therein, although the parties to such contracts may take advantage of the tax concessions during any extension period of the contract.

88. Personal communication to the author by MOPI officials.

89. Personal communication to the author by Ministry of Finance officials.

90. It is important to note that the exemption for these non-technology transfer fees relates only to the FEITL's withholding tax. Paragraph 11 of the Provisional Technology Tax Regulations makes it clear that in the event that the income recipient maintains an establishment in China, tax will be levied on income earned by such an establishment in accordance with the progressive tax set forth in Articles 3 and 4 of the FEITL. Therefore, if a foreign enterprise were deemed by Chinese tax authorities to have established a 'site' in China in connection with technology instruction or personnel training, instruction fees and training fees paid to the foreign enterprise would be taxable on an establishment, as opposed to a withholding, basis, thus denying the taxpayer the benefits of the exemption provisions.

91. See Ministry of Finance Document No. (82) *Cai shui* 103, dated 6 April 1982 (original Chinese version on file with the author).

92. See Document of the Ministry of Finance No. (85) *Cai shui* 45, dated 6 February 1985 (original Chinese version on file with the author).

93. For a detailed description of the Consolidated Tax see Chapter 2 of this volume.

94. The Individual Income Tax Law of the People's Republic of China (hereafter cited as the Individual Income Tax Law) was passed by the Third Session of the Fifth National People's Congress on 10 September 1980. The Detailed Rules and Regulations for the Implementation of the Individual Income Tax Law of the People's Republic of China (hereafter cited as the Implementing Regulations)

were approved by the State Council on 10 December 1980 and promulgated by the Ministry of Finance on 14 December 1980. For a detailed discussion of these laws, see Chapter 2 of this volume.

95. See Document of the Ministry of Finance No. (83) *Cai shui you zi* 330, issued in November 1983. The original Chinese text is in the possession of the author.

96. A copy of Document No. 159 is on file with the author.

97. See Document of the Ministry of Finance No. (84) *Cai shui you zheng zi* 11, issued on 28 July 1984 and transmitted by the OOTB. Original on file with the author.

98. See Document of the Ministry of Finance No. (85) *Cai shui* 45, dated 6 February 1985 and transmitted by the OOTB. Original on file with the author.

99. State Administration for Industry and Commerce Notice Concerning the Registration of Foreign Companies that Come to China to Engage in Co-operative Development and Contract Projects (original Chinese-language version on file with the author). For a discussion of the Registration Regulations, see M. Moser, 'China's Registration Rules for Foreign Oil Companies', *Asian Wall Street Journal*, 21 June 1983.

100. See Provisional Regulations on Standards for the Payment of Registration Fees by Joint Ventures Using Chinese and Foreign Investment, Art. 1. An English-language translation of the law appears in Chu, Moser, and Nee, Pt. 9, note 7 above.

101. This interpretation is contained in a document entitled Explanations Regarding the Notice Concerning the Registration of Foreign Companies that Come to China to Engage in Co-operative Development and Contract Projects, issued by the State Administration for Industry and Commerce on 4 May 1983 (hereafter cited as the Explanations). A copy of the original Chinese version of the Explanations is on the file with the author.

102. Explanations, para. 3, note 97 above.

103. Explanations, para. 3, note 97 above.

104. Explanations, para. 3, note 97 above.

105. See Provisional Measures of the Customs Authorities Concerning the Supervision and Control of Imports and Exports Required in the Co-operative Exploration and Development of Offshore Petroleum and Baggage and Articles of Engineers and Technical Personnel, issued by the General Administration of Customs of the People's Republic of China on 1 October 1981. An English-language translation of the law appears in Chu, Moser, and Nee, Pt. 10, note 7 above.

106. Regulations of the General Administration of Customs and the Ministry of Finance Concerning the Levy and Exemption of Customs Duties and the Consolidated Industrial and Commercial Tax on Imports and Exports for Chinese and Foreign Exploitation of Offshore Petroleum, approved by the State Council on 28 February 1982. For an English-language translation of these regulations, see Chu, Moser, and Nee, Pt. 10, note 7 above.

107. See Regulations of the Customs of the People's Republic of China Governing the Control over Inward- and Outward-bound Ocean-going Vessels of Foreign Registry for the Purpose of Chinese-Foreign Co-operative Exploitation of Offshore Petroleum and Personal Effects Belonging to Foreign Personnel Working in China, put into force on 1 June 1984.

108. The MEPL was adopted at the Twenty-fourth Session of the Standing Committee of the Fifth National People's Congress on 23 August 1982.

In addition to specific provisions contained in the MEPL, a number of other Chinese environmental protection laws will be of relevance to the operations of foreign contractors and subcontractors. For a general discussion of these laws, see J. Gresser, 'The Principle of Multiple Use in Chinese Environmental Law', in J. Cohen (ed.), *Legal Aspects of Doing Business in China 1983* (New York, Practising Law Institute, 1983), p. 104.

109. MEPL, Art. 17, note 103 above.

110. MEPL, Arts. 41, 42, 43, and 44, note 103 above.

111. Many of the new laws and regulations are likely to be issued by the MOPI pursuant to Article 30 of the Petroleum Regulations. This article grants the ministry the power to formulate 'detailed rules and regulations' for the implementation of the Petroleum Regulations.

112. See 'Petroleum Update', p. 4, note 21 above.

7. Representative Offices in China: The Legal Aspects of Registration and Control

CLARK T. RANDT, JR.

MUCH has changed since the stately clipper ships of the nineteenth century made their semi-annual journeys up the Pearl River to the foreign factories and trading houses in a restricted area of Guangzhou. Yet China's suspicion of, and consequent desire to control, the foreign commercial presence within her borders remains an important element of contemporary Chinese policy. The dilemma of how to build a strong modern China without sacrificing cultural identity or compromising internal security weighs as heavily on the nation's current leaders as it did on officials of the Qing dynasty. On the one hand, the presence of foreigners in China—bringing with them modern technology, know-how, managerial skills, and foreign exchange—is to be encouraged. On the other hand, the foreign presence is to be controlled and the activities of foreigners regulated so as to lessen the risk that they might interact with resident Chinese in a manner not in accordance with China's changing policies on this sensitive issue. As predicted in the first edition of this volume, the continued expansion of the foreign commercial presence in China has been met with increased supervision in the form of additional registration and reporting requirements.

At present the principal vehicle by which foreign companies are permitted to maintain a presence in China is the resident representative office (*changzhu daibiao jigou*). As of the end of 1985, 1,448 representative offices had been registered by foreign companies: 730 in Beijing, 240 in Guangzhou, and 202 in Shanghai, with the remainder spread over 23 other Chinese cities.[1] The registration and operational activities of these offices are governed by a number of regulations. The basic legislative framework is provided by a national statute promulgated in 1980, the Provisional Regulations of the State Council of the People's Republic of China Concerning the Control of Resident Representative Offices of Foreign Enterprises (hereafter cited as the Registration Regulations).[2] The Registration Regulations were subsequently supplemented by a Circular Concerning the Registration Procedures for Resident Offices of Foreign Enterprises by the General Administration for Industry and Commerce of the People's Republic of China (hereafter cited as the Circular), issued on 8 December 1981;[3] by the Measures of the State Administration of Industry and Commerce of the People's Republic of China Regarding the Control of Registration of Long-term Representative Offices of Foreign Enterprises (hereafter cited as the SAIC Measures), issued on 15 March 1983;[4]

and by various municipal announcements and notices which will be discussed later. In addition, Guangdong province and its special economic zones have each promulgated their own rules governing the establishment of representative offices, and separate regulations have been issued by the People's Bank of China concerning representative offices established by foreign banks and insurance companies.[5]

This chapter will provide a description and analysis of the legal aspects of the registration and control of foreign resident representative offices in China. The first part will discuss the registration requirement imposed on foreign companies maintaining a presence in China and the second part will describe the procedures to be followed when registering a representative office. The third part will describe various control aspects of the registration rules. Finally, the fourth part will examine the main features of the Guangdong registration rules and the regulations applicable to foreign financial institutions.

I. The Registration Requirement and the Benefits of Registration

The Registration Regulations do not make clear under what circumstances registration is mandatory or optional. Although the law does state that 'a foreign enterprise that has not obtained an approval and registered may not commence the business activities of a registered office',[6] the Chinese authorities have never provided any explicit guidance to foreign companies as to what types of activities or behaviour will be deemed to constitute 'the business activities of a resident office'. Moreover, the Registration Regulations themselves do not specify any penalties for failure to register. As a result, at the time the Registration Regulations came into effect in late 1980, many companies that were already operating in China through makeshift hotel-room offices ignored the new rules. According to Chinese press reports at the time, one month after the promulgation of the Registration Regulations less than one out of four foreign firms operating in China had obtained official approval to do so.[7]

Subsequently, efforts have been made by the Chinese authorities to clarify the scope of the registration requirement established by the Registration Regulations. In mid-1981, the General Administration for Industry and Commerce of the People's Republic of China issued an internal circular to Chinese organizations informing them that foreign companies operating in China that had not yet registered should not be permitted (a) to put up signs or nameplates before any hotel rooms or other space they may lease in China; (b) to refer to themselves as having an 'office' in China; (c) to use a seal identifying the company's 'office' in China; (d) to open accounts at banks in China; or (e) to 'engage in the business operations of resident offices'.[8] The implication of this circular was clear: a company may be deemed to be engaged in the 'business operations of a resident office' if it acts in the manner of such an office—by putting up signs, opening bank accounts, and so on—without being registered.

With the promulgation of the SAIC Measures in 1983, foreign enterprises acting in violation of the registration requirement became subject to sanctions for the first time. Under the SAIC Measures, foreign companies that 'engage without authorization in the business activities of a resident representative office' may be ordered to terminate their business activities in China and may be fined not more than RMB10,000.[9] As if to underscore the seriousness of the SAIC Measures with an example, a mere two weeks after their initial publication the China-Swiss Group Co. Ltd., in a much publicized case, was banned from China and subjected to the maximum fine for carrying out business operations without having registered.[10] In 1985, thirteen resident representative offices were charged with violations of Chinese law and eight were fined. Among the violations described were commencing business prior to registration and engaging in direct business activities, such as signing contracts with Chinese firms and hiring Chinese employees directly.[11]

Although the threat of sanctions provides an incentive to foreign companies formally to register their presence in China, a more powerful incentive is provided by the fact that registration can greatly facilitate the everyday operations of a company. Among the privileges extended to, and technically reserved for, registered representative offices and their representatives are the ability to enter into long-term office and room leases; to obtain long-term multiple-entry visas; to import office equipment and supplies; to import the personal effects of the resident representative duty-free, pursuant to the Regulations Concerning Import and Export of Articles by Resident Offices of Foreign Enterprises and Press, and their Staff in China, promulgated by the Customs General Administration with effect from 1 May 1984 (hereafter cited as the Resident Office Import Regulations);[12] to import an automobile or vessel for office use; to obtain a Chinese driving licence; to open bank accounts; to hire Chinese employees; to request visas for visitors to China; to rent telecommunications lines and equipment; and to display signs and use business cards identifying the company's presence in China. According to the Interim Regulations on Registration of Names of Industrial and Commercial Enterprises, once the company name is approved and registered by the local branch of the State Administration of Industry and Commerce (hereafter cited as the SAIC), it 'shall be protected by State laws and shall enjoy exclusive rights within the stipulated scope'.[13]

More recently, in the autumn of 1983, pursuant to announcements by municipal governments and notices from the municipal branches of the SAIC, registration also entitles the representatives and Chinese employees of foreign resident representative offices to identification cards and employee identification cards respectively.[14] These cards are in theory required by the representatives and Chinese employees of representative offices in order that they may hold meetings and discussions with Chinese organizations and carry on the work of a representative office.

II. Registration Procedures

The initial step in the registration of a resident representative office is to secure a formal approval document (*pizhunshu*) from the appropriate Chinese sponsor (*jiedai danwei*).[15] Without the support of such a Chinese sponsor the establishment of a representative office is impossible. Which Chinese units, then, are the appropriate sponsors for a given foreign company? Article 4 of the Registration Regulations provides that:

(a) traders, manufacturers, and shipping agents shall apply to the Ministry of Foreign Economic Relations and Trade (MOFERT);

(b) ocean shipping companies and ocean shipping agents shall apply to the Ministry of Communications;

(c) air transport companies shall apply to the Civil Aviation Administration of China; and

(d) others shall apply to the appropriate commission, ministry, or bureau 'in accordance with the nature of their work'.

Examples of this last category are oil companies, which are sponsored by the Ministry of Petroleum Industry; computer companies, which are sponsored by the Ministry of Electronics Industry; accounting companies, which are sponsored by the Ministry of Finance; and foreign tour operators, which are sponsored by the China National Tourism Administration. With respect to companies in the most common category above, those that are technically sponsored by MOFERT, in fact the initial application often is made directly to one of the many Chinese import-export corporations which then secures the approval document from MOFERT on behalf of the foreign company.

The statutory standard by which potential Chinese sponsor organizations determine whether a foreign company merits their support and approval is 'genuine need'.[16] To justify the issue of an approval document, the Chinese organization in practice must assess its own 'genuine need' for the representative office which has applied to it. Practice, in this respect, does not conform with the actual language of the Registration Regulations, which implies that it is the need of the foreign applicant, rather than that of any Chinese organization, which is determinative.[17] Justification of an approval tends to be based on historical business volume or, in the case of foreign companies whose names, products, or services are well known to the Chinese, on potential business volume.

To obtain the approval document, an application letter, signed by the chairman or the president of the company requesting registration and containing general information regarding the company, should be submitted to the prospective Chinese sponsor organization together with: (a) a copy of the applicant's official licence to conduct business in its home jurisdiction; (b) a letter of creditworthiness issued by the applicant's bank; (c) a completed Form of Application of Personnel and Content Amendment of the Representative Offices of Foreign Enterprises in triplicate, together with two photographs for each representative or staff member; and (d) a notarized authorization for each person appointed to the representative office.[18]

With respect to the first item noted above, the home-country business licence of the applicant, most companies registered to date have submitted the company's certificate of incorporation, business registration certificate, or certificate of good standing, as applicable, to fulfil this requirement. As a matter of practice, Chinese registration authorities will require that the copy of the document submitted be certified by an official of the foreign issuing authority as being true and correct.

The second requirement noted above is a letter from the applicant's bank attesting to the company's creditworthiness. Such a letter need not disclose any financial information about the company which is not already publicly available. A brief statement from the bank as to its relationship with the company and as to the company's record of meeting its financial obligations, together with the annual report of the company, have been sufficient to satisfy this requirement.

Copies of the Application of Personnel form may be obtained from the local SAIC office. Only basic information is required and, in the small square designated 'Résumé', a brief statement of the person's educational and professional qualifications will suffice. As to the certificate of authorization of each person appointed to the representative office, letters of appointment from the company's chairman or president are required.

Once a formal approval document is obtained, the foreign company has thirty days from the date of issue of the approval document to complete the registration procedures with the local branch of the SAIC.[19] The SAIC acts as China's companies' registry, among other responsibilities. Under the Registration Regulations foreign companies were required to effect registration with the SAIC's headquarters in Beijing.[20] However, both the more recent Circular and the SAIC Measures specifically authorize local SAIC branches to register a representative office of a foreign enterprise located in their jurisdiction.[21]

The final step in the registration process itself is the submission of the approval document within thirty days of its issue together with the registration fee of RMB600 to the local SAIC branch, and the completion of the form of Application for Establishment (Extension) of Representative Offices of Foreign Enterprises in triplicate, which forms are furnished at this stage of the process by the local SAIC branch. If the application is not filed within thirty days of the issue of the approval document, the approval document may be considered null and void and must be physically returned to the issuing unit.[22]

The information required in the application includes not only the representative office's name and location, number of representatives and foreign staff, and scope of business, but also the total value of the company's exports and imports to and from China for each of the past three years.

For the most part, the application is self-explanatory and straightforward, calling for responses that are short and to the point. This applies particularly to the section requiring a description of the representative office's scope of business. As will be discussed in Part III of this chapter, the SAIC Measures restrict the scope of a foreign representative office's activities to those which are 'not direct business operations'. Therefore, care should be exercised in determining and describing the activities of such an office. To avoid any possible implication that the company might be engaged in 'direct business operations', almost every representative office registered to date has used the characterization 'liaison' to describe its business scope.

The SAIC Measures now require annual renewals, but this procedure is merely routine.[23] Of more concern are notices first issued by the Beijing Municipal Bureau of Industry and Commerce in late 1983 (hereafter cited as the Extension Notice) requiring an 'extension' application every three years, which is procedurally a reregistration application.

As a result of a crescendo of complaints from Japanese companies regarding the visa requirements for their foreign staff, MOFERT's Bureau of Foreign Trade Administration reached an agreement with the Japanese, which was announced in early February 1983.[24] The policy, which applies to all foreign firms in China, entitles approved foreign staff members of representative offices to 'the same privileges as the official resident representatives with regard to their visas and other matters'.[25] It would appear, therefore, that a representative office may now obtain for its foreign staff members as many long-term visas as it can reasonably demonstrate that it needs. Deputy representatives are also commonly appointed if needed.

The local SAIC branch will, upon receipt, review all documentation submitted. Once it is satisfied that the application and supporting materials fulfil the statutory requirements, it will issue a registration certificate sealed with the stamp of the SAIC authority. Although the length of time needed by the SAIC to complete its review varies from locality to locality and from case to case, waiting periods of about one month are normal.

III. The Control Aspects of Registration

Chinese law provides for a high degree of continuing control over the activities of resident representative offices and their employees after registration has been completed. This control is exercised in a variety of ways, the most important of which are examined below.

A. Supplementary Registrations

Immediately after a representative office has received its registration certificate, the office and its personnel must comply with several additional registration formalities. First, the representative and his family members must register with the Public Security Bureau and obtain a foreigner's residence certificate (*waiguoren juliuzheng*) and a commercial domicile registration booklet (*hukou dengjibu*).[26] The Public Security Bureau will require that the representative present his resident representative identification card as well as his office approval certificate as conditions precedent to the issue of these documents. The representative must at all times carry his foreigner's residence certificate, which contains his photograph, the name of his company, and the length of his permitted stay in China. A circular of the Beijing Municipal People's Government issued on 20 April 1986 amends a 1983 provision on work certificates issued by the SAIC and requires that all Chinese employees be certified as supplied by the Foreign Enterprise Service Company (FESCO) and registered with the SAIC and the local Public Security Bureau.[27]

Secondly, the registered office and the resident representative are also required to register with the local tax authorities for the payment of enterprise income taxes and individual income taxes, respectively.[28] Both registrations are accomplished by filling in simple forms. Tax registration is strictly enforced. A supplementary regulation issued by the Ministry of Finance requires that tax registration be accomplished within thirty days of the date of 'commencement of operations'.[29] Failure to register on time exposes the company to a penalty of up to RMB5,000.[30] Recent unexpected and troubling developments with respect to the Chinese taxation of resident representative offices and their impact on registration will be considered briefly below.

A final supplementary requirement of the Registration Regulations is that the representative office shall open a foreign exchange account in its name with the Bank of China.[31]

B. Taxation

The taxation of resident representative offices in China is dealt with more extensively elsewhere in this volume. However, as recent developments in this area have created such unexpected problems and expense and impact directly on the choice of corporate vehicle used to register the representative office, a word regarding these developments is necessary here.

Formerly, it appeared self-evident that resident representative offices, limited as they are in theory if not always in practice by the SAIC to liaison and other non-profit activities, would not be subject to Chinese taxes. The Ministry of Finance disagreed. On 14 May 1985, the Ministry without warning promulgated the Interim Provisions for Collection of Industrial and Commercial Consolidated Tax and Business Income Tax from China-based Foreign Companies (hereafter cited as the Representative Office Tax Provisions) which provided that, as permanent establishments, such offices would be subject to both a foreign enterprise income tax of up to 50 per cent on net income[32] and a Consolidated Commercial and Industrial Tax levy of 5.05 per cent of gross revenues. Furthermore, the Representative Office Tax Provisions were made retroactive to 1 January 1985.[33]

Article 1 of the Representative Office Tax Provisions, however, contained what was generally considered to be a broad saving exemption from such taxes for resident representative offices engaged only in liaison and like services on behalf of their respective home offices 'provided that they do not receive proceeds for their operations or services as such'. In many cases, the relief provided by this exemption proved temporary. On

14 October 1985, the Beijing Municipal Tax Bureau disclosed that the 'home office' exemption is available only for services performed on behalf of the precise foreign legal entity appointing the representative office.[34] In other words, services on behalf of corporate affiliates are not generally exempted. Thus, the many multinationals which chose to appoint their representative office through a special-purpose China subsidiary, often incorporated in Hong Kong, in order to shield the parent company from possible future liability are now subject to taxation on their 'deemed commission' income. In the absence of satisfactory evidence to the contrary, Chinese tax officials have generally deemed there to be a commission of 3 to 5 per cent on gross sales revenues, half of which is allocated as income to the resident representative office.[35] If expenses cannot be satisfactorily substantiated, 10 per cent of this amount will be deemed taxable profit.[36] The resident representatives are subject to Chinese individual income tax.[37]

C. Annual Report, Updating, and Extension

Another method of control can be found in the annual report, registration renewal, updating, and extension requirements contained in the SAIC Measures, the Extension Notice, and Circular Number 27 of 7 March 1986 of the Beijing Municipal Bureau of the SAIC which requires annual reports by all resident representative offices on SAIC Registration Form Number 9 (hereafter cited as the Annual Reporting Regulation); the latter regulation appears to be the local manifestation of a nation-wide internal mandate issued by the SAIC. The stated purpose of the Annual Reporting Regulation is 'to provide for the supervision of representative offices... for the purpose of ensuring the protection of all rights and privileges of resident representative offices and their personnel and of safeguarding the conduct of their legitimate operations and activities'.[38] The form must be completed in Chinese and the chief resident representative will be held responsible for the truth and accuracy of the responses.[39] The reports are to be completed and received by the local SAIC office every year no later than 31 March.[40]

It is significant that the form itself requires details of the representatives and employees of the office, the types of services provided over the past year, signed contracts, service revenues, and Chinese taxes paid. A 'Trade Classification Code' will be assigned to the range of activities of the resident representative office pursuant to the National Economic Classification and Codification System of China.[41] This tends to confirm reports that selected registration and tax information is being computerized.

Foreign representative offices must renew their registrations annually by submitting an application for extension on a standard form together with an extension fee of RMB300.[42] In addition, the approval document from the Chinese sponsoring unit normally has a limited term of effectiveness and must also be extended, usually annually. Changes to the representative office's name, number and names of resident personnel, scope of business, or address, from those stipulated in the original registration application require the filing of an Application of Personnel and Content Amendment of the Representative Offices of Foreign Enterprises, together with RMB100.[43] Changes in personnel also require the submission of new photographs as well as letters of appointment.

The extension procedure described in the Extension Notice is tantamount to a three-year reregistration requirement, at which interval, apparently, the Chinese sponsor organization and the SAIC will reassess the 'genuine need' for the continuing presence of a particular resident representative office. An extension requires first that an extension approval certificate be procured from the applicant's Chinese sponsor unit. This certificate must then be presented to the relevant SAIC bureau, together with a completed standard extension application form and copies of the materials submitted to the Chinese sponsor unit to obtain the extension approval certificate.

D. Restrictions on the Scope of the Activity

One of the most important of the controls imposed on foreign enterprises in China relates to the statutory restriction on the permissible scope of activity of the representative office. As noted earlier, under the SAIC Measures representative offices are prohibited from engaging in 'direct business operations' (zhijie jingying huodong). Violations of this provision may be punished by fines of not more than RMB20,000 and the termination of business operations.

At present, the precise dimensions of the concept 'direct business operations' remain clouded. The SAIC Measures themselves contain no definition of the concept. According to conversations with SAIC representatives, production and sales activities will be seen to constitute 'direct business operations' while liaison activities will not. SAIC officials report that a 'resident representative office is an organization engaged in business-contact, service and non-direct-profit-making operations'.[44] Obviously, in the absence of a more specific categorization of the activities in which a representative office might engage, companies have little guidance as to the legality of their activities in China. From the perspective of the Chinese authorities, however, lack of clarity is viewed as an advantage as it broadens their scope of discretion and thus serves to facilitate supervision and control. The expanded annual reporting requirements reflect an intention to monitor more closely the activities of resident representative offices. For some companies, the restricted scope of activities permitted to representative offices makes this form of presence in China inapposite but, pending an overhaul of the registration system, there is often no viable alternative.

E. Customs Controls

Control over representative offices and their personnel is also exercised by the Chinese Customs authorities. Under Article 10 of the Registration Regulations and the Resident Office Import Regulations, registered representatives are required to file a declaration with Customs with respect to those items for office or personal use that they wish to import from abroad. In practice, this provision has been implemented by requiring the representative, after obtaining his foreigner's residence certificate, to submit to Customs two lists—one for the duty-free importation of personal goods, and one for office items—setting forth all the items that the office and the representative intend to import. Once the lists are approved by Customs, personal goods on the list may be imported without the payment of customs duties or related taxes in any number of shipments within the six-month period dating from the approval of the list. Listed office items may be imported at any time after the payment of customs duties and related taxes. If a representative wishes to amend the office list by adding additional items, he must go through separate application and approval procedures for such items. An application for the duty-free importation of personal items by each representative may only be made once.[45]

Finally, it should be noted that goods imported by representative offices and their registered personnel may not be privately sold or transferred in China without the prior permission of the relevant Customs office.[46] Direct sales may only be made to designated Chinese units such as the Friendship Stores for resale to foreign residents. Duties will be levied against items which were originally admitted duty free if they are later sold in China.[47]

F. The Employment of Staff

One of the most controversial of the control mechanisms instituted by the Chinese relates to the severe restrictions imposed on the freedom of representative offices to choose and employ staff. Under Article 11 of the Registration Regulations, a resident representative office is required to entrust 'local service units for foreigners or other units designated by the Chinese Government' with the hiring of work personnel. For registered offices in Beijing, this requirement was re-emphasized and underscored by Circular Number 64 of 20 April 1986 of the Beijing Municipal People's Government regarding the employment of Chinese nationals, and the Interim Staff Regulations[48] (hereafter collectively cited as the Employment Provisions). The stated purpose of these regulations is 'to improve and strengthen the provision of foreign-related services and employment'. The Employment Provisions require that all secretaries, drivers, and other office personnel, as well as household help employed by resident representatives, must be hired from authorized organizations providing services for foreign businesses. In Beijing such an organization is the Beijing Foreign Enterprises Service Corporation (FESCO). The Employment Provisions provide further for a system of employee registration and monitoring. Within ten days after the execution of a standard-form employment contract, the Chinese employee must be certified at the local SAIC branch by presenting the contract and his FESCO credentials. Following SAIC certification, the Chinese employee must register with the foreign section of the Public Security Bureau.[49]

Because of the wide variance in quality and the high cost of many FESCO staff, a large number of representative offices in Beijing and elsewhere in China have preferred to hire local expatriates such as foreign students and the spouses of diplomatic personnel to provide office assistance. In August 1983, the Beijing office of the SAIC moved to enforce the provisions mandating the use of FESCO staff, and issued a notice requiring all registered offices to submit to the SAIC a list of their personnel for approval.[50] Once approved, such personnel were issued with employee identification cards. According to announcements by the relevant municipal governments, no person is permitted to work in a representative office without having first obtained an employee identification card.[51]

According to Chinese sources, there exist a number of 'internal' (neibu) regulations supporting the SAIC's move to require all foreign representative offices to employ staff exclusively from FESCO. One such regulation reportedly requires that only foreigners who come from the home country of the registered foreign enterprise be permitted to work in its representative office in China, except for foreigners who were previously employed by the company outside China. Another regulation, reportedly issued by the Ministry of Foreign Affairs, prohibits family members of diplomatic personnel from working in the representative offices of foreign enterprises. Finally, Chinese officials have indicated that there exists an internal directive issued by the Ministry of Education prohibiting foreign students from working in China. To date, none of these prohibitions has been published and they have been enforced only haphazardly. The details concerning office personnel required in the annual report form discussed above will assist the Chinese authorities in monitoring and enforcing these provisions.

The Employment Provisions stipulate that violations will be dealt with, as appropriate, by the Public Security Bureau, the SAIC, and 'relevant government agencies', and that fines of up to RMB10,000 may be imposed.[52]

G. Supervision and Sanctions

Article 14 of the Registration Regulations requires representative offices and their registered personnel to abide by all relevant Chinese laws, regulations, and decrees. In addition to the Public Security Bureau and, in extreme cases, the newly constituted State Security Bureau, the Chinese Customs and tax authorities and the SAIC exercise supervision over the activities of representative offices and may penalize such offices and their personnel in the event of breaches of Chinese law or regulations. As noted earlier, for example, foreign enterprises that violate the prohibition on engaging in 'direct business operations' may be fined up to RMB20,000. The same Article provides for a fine of up to RMB5,000 for failure to effect changes to the office's registration certificate when such are required by changes in personnel or office location, or for other reasons.[53] Foreign business men should also be aware that China's Criminal Code, in effect since 1980, specifically applies to foreigners and contains prohibitions against dealing in state secrets. The concept of 'state secret' is extremely broad. Normal commercial intelligence may constitute state secrets, thereby exposing business men to grave criminal liability. Potential criminal liability in the event of an automobile accident is another source of concern.

IV. Variations from the National Registration Regime: Guangdong Province and Foreign Financial Institutions

The Registration Regulations and the SAIC Measures together provide the framework for the national registration regime applicable to foreign resident representative offices in China. Variations from this regime exist, however, in at least three special cases. The first relates to representative offices established generally in Guangdong province, the second concerns representative offices in the special economic zones of Guangdong province, and the third covers the special case of foreign financial institutions.

A. The Guangdong Rules

A little over six months after the promulgation of the national Registration Regulations, Guangdong province issued its own registration rules in a document consisting of 18 articles and entitled Provisional Measures of the People's Government of Guangdong Province for the Registration and Control of Resident Representative Offices of Foreign Enterprises and Overseas Chinese, Hong Kong and Macao Enterprises in Guangdong Province (hereafter cited as the Guangdong Rules).[54] The Guangdong Rules, by their terms, are 'based on the spirit' of the Registration Regulations but take into consideration the 'specific conditions' in Guangdong province.[55] In content, therefore, the rules parallel in most respects the provisions of the national registration regime but vest greater control in the provincial authorities.

One of the major differences between the Guangdong Rules and the Registration Regulations relates to the scope of the approval power of local authorities. The Guangdong Rules provide that Guangdong province may approve applications for the registration of representative offices by foreign enterprises without reference to the central authorities.[56] The provincial approval-granting authority under the Guangdong Rules is the Foreign Economic Affairs Committee of Guangdong Province.[57] In practice, however, airlines, shipping, and banking businesses must still be registered centrally.

In several key aspects the Guangdong Rules[58] anticipated developments in the national registration regime which were subsequently incorporated in the SAIC Measures. For example, the Guangdong Rules contain a clear prohibition against the commencement of business prior to the completion of registration formalities and limit the validity of the registration certificate to one year.[59] These provisions were not formally adopted nation-wide until the promulgation of the SAIC Measures two years later. In another example, Article 3 of the Guangdong Rules requires applicants to submit copies of their 'economic and trade agreements' to the approval-granting authority together with their other application documents. No similar requirement existed until the recent Extension Notice required that such information be included with an application for extension after an initial period of three years.

In 1982 alone, nine cases of non-registration were prosecuted administratively by the Guangdong provincial branch of the SAIC.[60] Most of the defendants were either Hong Kong or Macau compatriots, all of whom were reported to have ignored repeated warnings. Penalties in these cases included fines ranging from RMB300 to RMB3,000, coupled with the publication of the offenders' names and an account of their misdeeds.

B. The Guangdong Special Economic Zones

A separate framework has been set up for the establishment and registration of enterprises in the special economic zones of Guangdong province,[61] including, specifically, resident representative offices. Establishment and registration procedures in Shenzhen are further specifically governed by the Detailed Regulations for the Implementation of Registration and Administration of Enterprises in the Shenzhen Special Economic Zone of 18 January 1984. These provisions provide for a system substantially similar to that provided by the national regulations described above.

C. Foreign Financial Institutions

Foreign banks and insurance companies are subject to the national registration regime established by the Registration Regulations and the SAIC Measures. Supplementing this regime, however, is a separate set of regulations issued on 1 February 1983 by the People's Bank of China which, as China's central bank, is, through its Foreign Affairs Department, responsible for the activities of foreign financial institutions in China. These regulations are the Provisional Regulations for the Establishment of Representative Offices in China by Overseas Chinese and Foreign Financial Institutions (hereafter cited as the Financial Institutions Regulations).[62] Since 2 April 1985 foreign banks have also been permitted to establish branches in China's special economic zones but, as these are not representative offices, it is only necessary here to note the existence of such a provision.[63]

The basic purpose of the Financial Institutions Regulations, as stated in Article 1, is to exercise 'more effective control' over the activities of the representative offices of foreign banks and insurance companies. Therefore the Financial Institutions Regulations follow closely the general scheme established under the Registration Regulations and the SAIC Measures but impose additional obligations on banks and insurance companies and spell out more clearly the various limitations imposed on representative offices.

The Financial Institutions Regulations permit foreign banks and insurance companies to establish representative offices in Beijing and in the special economic zones; institutions with Beijing offices may establish 'subordinate' representative offices in 'other designated cities'.[64] Bank representative offices must bear names with the description 'representative office' or 'sub-representative office', and the representative offices of insurance companies are required to include the designation 'liaison office' in their names.[65]

Registration application procedures are in most respects identical to those required by the Registration Regulations. One significant difference, however, is found in the requirement that an 'authenticated power of attorney' be provided by the chairman or chief executive of the applicant in favour of the appointed representative.[66]

In contrast to the Registration Regulations and the SAIC Measures, the Financial Institutions Regulations provide a clear statement of the authorized scope of activity of registered representative offices. Article 8 provides that representative offices of banks and insurance companies must limit the scope of their activities to 'non-profit activities such as carrying on business negotiations, acting as liaison, and providing consultancy and other services. They shall not engage in any direct profit-making business activities.' While the Ministry of Finance has not to date subjected these particular representative offices to taxation under the Representative Office Tax Provision, which does not refer to banks or financial institutions, there are persistent rumours in Beijing's foreign banking circles that such a provision applicable to foreign financial institutions is under active consideration.

The Financial Institutions Regulations permit an approval term of three years rather than one, anticipating the effect of the Extension Notice.[67] Also, SAIC registration must still be renewed annually. The maximum number of representatives is fixed at four for a representative office in Beijing, three in the special economic zones, and two in other 'designated cities'.[68] However, the law specifically provides that there is no limit on the number of Chinese staff who may be employed from FESCO or equivalent organizations.[69] At least one foreign bank has nominated a FESCO employee to be its registered representative in Beijing.

Finally, it should be noted that the Financial Institutions Regulations provide the People's Bank of China with extensive powers to supervise the activities of the representative offices of foreign banks and insurance companies, and authorize the Bank to penalize such offices and their personnel in the event of breaches of the regulations.[70] Supervision is carried out by periodic unannounced visits and through various reporting requirements. In addition to the requirement that reports be made to the People's Bank of China when the office changes its address or any other item appearing on its original application for registration,[71] the representative office must provide an annual report to the People's Bank on or before 15 January giving a 'faithful account' of the office's work during the previous year.[72] Article 12 of the Financial Institutions Regulations also imposes a reporting requirement when the registered representative plans to be absent from China for a period longer than one month.[73] In such cases, the representative is required to designate another individual to assume his duties in his absence and to provide a written notice of such designation to the People's Bank of China.[74]

V. Conclusion

When China first initiated its open-door policy in the late 1970s, foreign companies wishing to establish a 'presence' in the People's Republic needed to do little more than rent a hotel room. Today, this situation has changed dramatically. As the number of foreign companies resident in China increases at a rate of more than 50 per cent each year,[75] Chinese measures to monitor, control, and tax the activities of these resident representative offices have similarly blossomed. In particular, the uncertainty regarding liability for Chinese taxes arising from such a permanent establishment in China is causing some companies to reconsider the costs and benefits of such offices and to proceed very cautiously in establishing such presences, helpful to all sides as these offices may be.

A recent well-publicized Chinese report of representative offices being fined for legal infractions concludes that: 'The Chinese industrial and commercial administration intends to step up efforts to make members of the foreign offices aware of and abide by Chinese law and conduct their business in a normal way.'[76]

Notes

1. 'Foreign Representative Offices Fined', *Beijing Review*, No. 16, 21 April 1986, p. 6.
2. Approved by the State Council and promulgated on 30 October 1980. An English translation of the Registration Regulations appears in F. Chu, M. Moser, and O. Nee (eds.), *Commercial, Business and Trade Laws: People's Republic of China* (Dobbs Ferry, Oceana Publications, Inc., 1982), Pt. 8, p. 3.
3. For an English translation of the Circular, see *Laws and Regulations of the People's Republic of China* (Hong Kong, Kingsway International Publications, 1982), Vol. 1, p. 158.
4. An English translation appears in *East Asian Executive Reports*, May 1983, p. 24.
5. These regulations are discussed in Part IV of this chapter.
6. Registration Regulations, Art. 2, note 2 above.
7. See *China Economic News*, 10 November 1980, p. 2.
8. See *China Economic News*, 1 June 1981, p. 2.
9. SAIC Measures, Art. 16, note 4 above.
10. 'Resident Office of China-Swiss Group Company Banned', *China Daily*, 1 April 1983, p. 1.
11. See note 1 above.
12. See *China Economic News*, 7 May 1984, p. 4.
13. See *China Economic News*, 15 July 1985, p. 4.
14. Beijing was the first municipality to establish this requirement by an Announcement of the Beijing Municipal People's Government published in the

Beijing Daily, 12 August 1983. By December 1983, Shanghai and Guangzhou also had such requirements. See the Interim Regulations on the Registration and Supervision of Staff Employed by Representative Offices of Foreign Enterprises in Beijing, issued by the Beijing Administration for Industry and Commerce and effective from 1 October 1986 (hereafter cited as the Interim Staff Regulations).

15. Registration Regulations, Art. 4, note 2 above; and SAIC Measures, Art. 7(1), note 4 above.

16. See Registration Regulations, Art. 2, note 2 above.

17. Registration Regulations, Art. 2, note 2 above.

18. Registration Regulations, Art. 3, note 2 above.

19. Registration Regulations, Art. 5, note 2 above.

20. Registration Regulations, Art. 5, note 2 above.

21. Circular, Section 1, note 3 above; and SAIC Measures, Arts. 4 and 6, note 4 above.

22. Registration Regulations, Art. 5, note 2 above.

23. SAIC Measures, Art. 11, note 4 above.

24. See 'Japanese Firms' Beijing Offices Increase Personnel', *China Economic News*, 7 February 1983, p. 7.

25. *China Economic News*, 7 February 1983, p. 7.

26. Registration Regulations, Art. 6, note 2 above.

27. See the Announcement referred to in note 14 as amended by the Beijing Municipal People's Government Circular No. 64, 20 April 1986.

28. Registration Regulations, Art. 9, note 2 above.

29. See Article 1 of the Provisional Regulations of the General Taxation Bureau of the Ministry of Finance of the People's Republic of China Concerning Tax Registration by Foreign Enterprises for the Commencement and Termination of Operations (hereafter cited as the Provisional Tax Registration Regulations) promulgated by the General Taxation Bureau of the Ministry of Finance on 5 April 1982.

30. Provisional Tax Registration Regulations, Art. 8, note 29 above.

31. Registration Regulations, Art. 8, note 2 above.

32. The Income Tax Law of the People's Republic of China Concerning Foreign Enterprises, passed by the Fourth Session of the Fifth National People's Congress on 13 December 1981.

33. The Interim Provisions for Collection of Industrial and Commercial Consolidated Tax and Business Income Tax from China-based Foreign Companies promulgated by the Ministry of Finance, 14 May 1985, Art. 7.

34. The Supplementary Provisions Concerning the Question of the Levy of Consolidated Industrial and Commercial Tax and Enterprise Income Tax on Resident Representative Offices of Foreign Enterprises promulgated by the Foreign Tax Sub-bureau of the Beijing Municipal Tax Bureau, Document No. 144, 14 October 1985.

35. Conversations with Chinese tax officials.

36. The Representative Office Tax Provisions, Art. 4, note 33 above, provides for a 15 per cent deemed profit rate but this has been revised downward to 10 per cent. See 'Tax Cut Heralds Better Conditions for Foreign Investors', *China Daily*, 9 October 1986, p. 1.

37. The Individual Income Tax Law of the People's Republic of China, passed by the Third Session of the Fifth National People's Congress on 10 September 1980.

38. The Annual Reporting Regulations, Instructions for Completing Form Number 9.

39. The Annual Reporting Regulations, paragraph 5, note 38 above.

40. The Annual Reporting Regulations, paragraph 5, note 38 above.

41. The Annual Reporting Regulations, paragraph 4, note 38 above.

42. SAIC Measures, Art. 11, note 4 above; and Circular, Section 5, note 3 above.

43. SAIC Measures, Art. 12, note 4 above; and Circular, Section 5, note 3 above.

44. See *China Economic News*, 10 November 1986, p. 5.

45. The Resident Office Import Regulations, Art. 3, note 12 above.

46. The Resident Office Import Regulations, Art. 7, note 12 above.

47. The Resident Office Import Regulations, Art. 7, note 12 above.

48. See note 14 above.

49. The Employment Provisions, Art. 4.

50. Notice of the Beijing Administration for Industry and Commerce (83), Industry and Commerce Reference No. 232, 11 August 1983. The Notice was distributed in Chinese to all registered representative offices of foreign companies in Beijing during August 1983.

51. See note 14 above.

52. The Employment Provisions, Art. 6, note 49 above.

53. SAIC Measures, Art. 15, note 4 above.

54. Approved by the People's Government of Guangdong Province, promulgated and effective on and as of 11 May 1981. An English translation of the Guangdong Rules appears in Chu, Moser, and Nee, Pt. 6, p. 11, note 2 above.

55. Guangdong Rules, Art. 1, note 54 above.

56. Guangdong Rules, Art. 2, note 54 above.

57. Guangdong Rules, Art. 2, note 54 above.

58. Guangdong Rules, Art. 2, note 54 above.

59. Guangdong Rules, Art. 13, note 54 above.

60. The author, discussion with the Guangdong SAIC.

61. The Provisional Regulations on the Registration of Enterprises in the Special Economic Zones of Guangdong Province, passed by the Thirteenth Session of the Standing Committee of the Fifth Guangdong Provisional People's Congress, 17 November 1981.

62. An English translation of the Financial Institutions Regulations appears in *East Asian Executive Reports*, May 1983, p. 26.

63. The Regulations Governing Foreign Banks and Joint Chinese-Foreign Banks in the Special Economic Zones of the People's Republic of China, passed by the State Council, 2 April 1985.

64. Financial Institutions Regulations, Art. 2, note 62 above.

65. Financial Institutions Regulations, Art. 3, note 62 above.

66. Financial Institutions Regulations, Art. 4(4), note 62 above.

67. Financial Institutions Regulations, Art. 7, note 62 above.

68. Financial Institutions Regulations, Art. 9, note 62 above.

69. Financial Institutions Regulations, Art. 10, note 62 above.

70. Financial Institutions Regulations, Arts. 14 and 17, note 62 above.

71. Financial Institutions Regulations, Art. 11, note 62 above.

72. Financial Institutions Regulations, Art. 15, note 62 above.

73. Financial Institutions Regulations, Art. 12, note 62 above.

74. Financial Institutions Regulations, Art. 12, note 62 above.

75. See note 1 above.

76. See note 1 above.

8. Contract Law in the People's Republic of China

PRESTON M. TORBERT

I. Introduction

Many aspects of China's economic policies since 1978 have attracted the attention of foreign firms interested in doing business with China, particularly the new laws and regulations concerning joint ventures, representative offices, taxation, and other features of foreign economic relations. Until recently, this legislation has affected mainly the newer and more complex transactions. While these transactions are significant because they define the limits of what can be done, they are not generally representative of the experience of most foreign firms in China, for whom the negotiation of their purchase or sales contract is the most important contact with China's new economic policy. Previously, China had no legislation concerning the formation, performance, and enforcement of contracts and still has not promulgated a complete Civil Code although the General Provisions of the Civil Code of the PRC were recently adopted.

On 21 March 1985, however, the Foreign Related Economic Contracts Law of the People's Republic of China (hereafter cited as the Foreign Contracts Law) was passed by the Standing Committee of the National People's Congress.[1] The Foreign Contracts Law applies to almost all contracts that foreign firms sign with Chinese entities—the most common type of contracts, purchase or sales contracts, as well as licensing and compensation trade contracts, and also the less common joint venture contracts. The discussion that follows deals with the Foreign Contracts Law and recent contract practice as a whole, but refers to the different types of contract where appropriate.

II. The Foreign Contracts Law

The Foreign Contracts Law is a breakthrough in China's legal development. It indicates that the Chinese authorities have decided to institutionalize through law the policy of opening China to greater foreign trade and investment. The Foreign Contracts Law is thus a result of this policy, but the law will also serve to promote it. In drafting the Foreign Contracts Law the Chinese authorities have resolved some contentious issues in a way designed to facilitate China's economic contacts with the rest of the world. For example, under the Foreign Contracts Law, foreign law can govern a contract between a Chinese party and a foreign party and certain contracts will enjoy 'grandfather clause' status that gives their terms priority over subsequent legislation. Under the Law, international practice can now be directly 'applied' to a contract, rather than simply be 'referred to'. The Foreign Contracts Law thus not only confirms certain contract principles already established in practice, but lays a foundation for further development in the direction of international practice.

The Foreign Contracts Law, as noted above, covers almost all types of contract between foreign firms and Chinese entities. This breadth of scope has two implications. First, the Foreign Contracts Law is an extremely important piece of legislation that foreign parties will want to take into consideration in conducting almost any type of business activity in China. Second, the Foreign Contracts Law, because it covers many diverse forms of contract, of necessity sets forth general principles only. More specific rules are to be found in legislation relating to particular types of contract, such as the Provisional Regulations on the Control of Technology Import Contracts, and will, in the future, be incorporated in the implementing regulations under the Foreign Contracts Law, which are to be promulgated by the State Council pursuant to Article 42 of the Law.

The Foreign Contracts Law became effective on 1 July 1985 and will apply to all contracts effective after that date. For contracts effective prior to that date, the parties may agree to apply its provisions. Amendments to contracts effective before 1 July 1985 would not be subject to the Foreign Contracts Law, but it is not clear whether the same is true for the extension of a contract effective before that date. In practice, if the contract to be extended is one which requires the Chinese governmental authorities to approve any extension, these authorities may decide whether the Foreign Contracts Law will apply by requiring (or not requiring) that the parties amend the contract to provide for the application of the Law.

The Foreign Contracts Law is not a long and complex statute. It consists of 43 articles divided into seven chapters. Of these seven chapters, the second, third, and fifth (that is, those relating to the formation of contracts; performance and liability for breach; amendment, cancellation, and termination of contracts) form the major part of the statute. The contents can be summarized as follows.

A. General Provisions

The Foreign Contracts Law applies to economic contracts[2] between enterprises or other economic organizations of the PRC and foreign enterprises, other economic organizations, or individuals, but not to international transport contracts. These contracts should be concluded in accordance with the principles of equality and mutual benefit and agreement through consultation, and should observe the laws of the PRC and not violate public policy. Parties to a contract may choose the applicable law to handle disputes as to the meaning of the contract, but where they have not done so, the law of the country with the closest connection with the contract will be applied. However, PRC law must be applied to certain contracts. In the absence of PRC law, international practice may be applied.

B. The Formation of Contracts

A contract is made when the parties have reached agreement on the terms in a written form and have signed it, but if the approval of the contract by Chinese authorities is required, the contract is effective only upon approval. Contracts that violate the laws of the PRC or public policy and contracts concluded through deception or coercion are invalid.

C. Performance of Contracts and Liability for Breach of Contracts

Parties to a contract should perform their contractual obligations. If one party does not perform its obligations, the other party has a right to claim compensation or take other reasonable remedial measures. The liability of the breaching party is equal to the damages suffered by the other party as a result, but will not exceed damages foreseeable at the time the contract was made. Liquidated damages may be provided for in a contract, but a court or arbitral body may reduce or increase them. A party is excused from its contractual responsibilities if it cannot perform due to *force majeure*.

D. Assignment of Contracts

The consent of the other party is required when an assignment is made. If the original contract required government approval, the assignment will also be subject to approval.

E. Amendment, Cancellation, and Termination of Contracts

Parties may by agreement amend a contract, but either party has the right to cancel the contract under certain circumstances. A contract is terminated by certain events, such as performance, mutual agreement, or the order of an arbitration body or court. Certain contractual rights and obligations survive the cancellation or termination of the contract.

F. Settlement of Disputes

Contractual disputes should be settled as far as possible through consultation and mediation by a third party, but the parties may submit a dispute to arbitration or, if the contract has no provisions for arbitration, to a court.

G. Supplementary Articles

The statute of limitations for bringing contractual disputes concerning the sale or purchase of goods to legal proceedings or arbitration is four years. Certain types of contract will take precedence over later legislation. Contracts effective before 1 July 1985 may apply the Foreign Contracts Law by agreement of the parties. Implementing regulations of the Law are to be promulgated by the State Council.

An understanding of the background to the Foreign Contracts Law begins with Article 55 of the Economic Contracts Law of the People's Republic of China passed by the National People's Congress on 13 December 1981 and effective from 1 July 1982 (hereafter cited as the Contracts Law). This article provides that a future statute concerning foreign economic trade contracts (that is, the Foreign Contracts Law) will be separately established 'in accordance with the principles of this law [the Contracts Law] and international practice'. In determining what constitutes international practice, draftsmen of the Foreign Contracts Law appear to have relied on the United Nations Convention on Contracts for the International Sale of Goods (hereafter cited as the United Nations Convention), completed on 11 April 1980.

The influence of these two documents on the Foreign Contracts Law is reflected in different ways. The Contracts Law forms the basis for the general provisions on contract law in the Foreign Contracts Law, while the United Nations Convention is the source for the provisions regarding the foreign aspects and international practice.

The influence of the Contracts Law on the Foreign Contracts Law can be seen first in the structure of the two laws. They both contain sections regarding the general principles of contracts, the formation and performance of contracts, liability for breach, the amendment and termination of contracts, and the settlement of disputes through mediation and arbitration. Further, the articles in these sections are in some cases quite similar. For example, the general principles that contracts made according to law are legally binding, are to be performed by the parties, and that neither party has the right to alter or cancel the contract unilaterally are expressed in both laws in almost identical language.[3] Provisions in the Foreign Contracts Law regarding the principles of equality and mutual benefit, that contracts should conform with the law, and that certain contracts are void also reflect the influence of the Contracts Law.[4] More specifically, the stipulations in the Foreign Contracts Law on the formation of contracts also reflect the influence of the Contracts Law. Both laws provide that a contract is made when both parties reach agreement and that a contract must be in writing.[5] Another example is the provisions in the Foreign Contracts Law regarding responsibility for breach of a contract. These generally resemble those in the Contracts Law, but differ in that they also treat the questions of suspension of performance, liquidated damages, and a limitation on liability. Finally, both laws have corresponding provisions regarding dispute resolution and the alteration or termination of a contract.

Notwithstanding the similarities, however, the Foreign Contracts Law differs from the Contracts Law in its purpose. The purpose of the Foreign Contracts Law is 'to safeguard the lawful rights and interests of the parties to *foreign* economic contracts and to promote the development of the *foreign* economic relations of China' (my italics). Accordingly, certain questions specific to international contracts are covered only in the Foreign Contracts Law. For example, unlike the Contracts Law, it contains provisions regarding choice of law and the effect of international treaties on contracts. In a similar manner, the Contracts Law contains provisions appropriate only to domestic contracts, such as that which stipulates that payment for contracts will be in the local currency, *renminbi*.

The most significant difference in the two laws, however, relates to the role of the government. The purpose of the Contracts Law is 'to protect the lawful rights and interests of the parties to economic contracts, to safeguard social and economic order, to improve economic results, *to guarantee the implementation of the state plans* and promote the progress of socialist modernization' (my italics). Since China is a planned economy, economic contracts between Chinese domestic enterprises play an important role in fulfilling the state economic plan. In this sense, the contracts are similar to administrative orders, rather than voluntary agreements entered into by the free will of the parties. The administrative role of economic contracts can be seen in many provisions of the Contracts Law. Economic contracts must, in accordance with Article 4 of the Contracts Law, be made not only in accordance with laws, but in conformity with the requirements of 'state policies and plans'. An economic contract in violation of government policy or plans is void, and the right to cancel an economic contract rests with the administrative authorities and the courts, not with the parties to the contract.[6] Further, the administrative departments in charge of the parties to the contract have the obligation to supervise and inspect the contracts. The People's Bank and other banks are also authorized to supervise the performance of economic contracts through credit control and settlement control.[7] Since foreign economic contracts involve a foreign party, these provisions concerning the administrative role of contracts are not appropriate, even though foreign-related transactions form part of the state foreign exchange and economic plans.

The influence of the United Nations Convention on the Foreign Contracts Law can be seen in the large number of similarities between the two documents. Both the United Nations Convention and the Foreign Contracts Law refer to international practice as a source of law.[8] The Foreign Contracts Law refers only to 'international practice' and does not define the term, but a Chinese official has quoted with authority the language in the United Nations Convention as indicative of what the Foreign Contracts Law means by this term—'a usage of which the parties knew or ought to have known and which in international trade is widely known to, and regularly observed by, parties to contracts of the type involved in the particular trade concerned'.[9] Similarly, both the United Nations Convention and the Foreign Contracts Law limit the damages obtainable for the breach of a contract to those foreseeable at the time of the formation of the contract.[10] The United Nations Convention provides that the limitation on damages is the loss which the breaching party foresaw or ought to have foreseen at the time of the conclusion of the contract in the light of the facts and matters of which he then knew or ought to have known as a possible consequence of the breach of contract. The Foreign

Contracts Law states that the limitation is the amount of damages which the breaching party should, when the contract was made, have foreseen could arise as a result of the breach of contract.

Further, both the United Nations Convention and the Foreign Contracts Law, in three consecutive articles, contain almost identical provisions.[11] These articles concern the obligation of the breaching party to mitigate damages, the payment of interest on payments in arrears, and the excuse for non-performance due to an event classified as a *force majeure*. The United Nations Convention defines *force majeure* as an impediment beyond the control of the party failing to perform which such party could not reasonably be expected to have taken into account at the time of the conclusion of the contract or to have avoided or overcome it or its consequences. The Foreign Contracts Law defines *force majeure* as 'events which the parties cannot foresee when the contract is made and whose occurrence and consequences the parties can neither avoid nor overcome'.[12]

While the Foreign Contracts Law shares certain similarities with the United Nations Convention, there are also certain fundamental differences. First, the Convention applies only to the sale of goods, while the Law applies to contracts of all types.[13] Second, the Law can be seen as a more general and less complex document than the Convention. The Convention treats in detail the role of offer and acceptance in the formation of contracts,[14] and the effect of delays or errors in the transmission of communications,[15] as well as containing detailed provisions on the obligations of a seller (for example, to deliver conforming goods free from third parties' claims)[16] and the obligations of the buyer (for example, payment of price).[17] Since the Law requires only a document in writing signed by both parties for the formation of the contract, it does not require detailed provisions concerning these matters such as those contained in the Convention.

The Foreign Contracts Law serves an important role in clarifying the legal basis for contracts between Chinese and foreign parties. But as noted above, the Law is a broad statute that leaves many questions unanswered. For example, the scope of application of the Law is not yet clear because there is no definition of 'enterprise' or 'economic organization'. The General Principles of the Civil Code of the PRC define a 'juristic person' and a 'corporation', but not an 'enterprise' or an 'economic organization'. These and other issues may be resolved in the future sections of the Civil Code or the implementing regulations to the Law. In the meantime, these and other questions may be handled by reference to past or current practice.

III. Standard-form Contracts

Any discussion of contract law in China must treat the standard-form contracts used by Chinese entities in the current practice of their economic relations with foreign parties.[18] In China's socialist economy, almost all transactions with foreign parties are conducted by state entities and therefore involve the interests of the state. In order to ensure that the state's interests are adequately protected, standard-form contracts are widely used. Now, as in the past, foreign parties doing business with socialist countries, including China, must generally sign such contracts for the most common transactions.

China's practice regarding standard-form contracts, however, has been influenced by changes in the country's foreign economic relations in the last ten years. Especially since 1979, under the leadership of Deng Xiaoping, China's economic policy has emphasized foreign trade and investment as a major element in China's modernization.[19] As a result, China's contacts with foreign companies have greatly increased. The monopoly of the former Ministry of Foreign Trade on almost all economic relations with foreign countries has been broken, and other ministries, provinces, and municipalities now have the authority to deal with foreign companies directly.[20] This decentralization of authority has had contradictory effects. In some respects it has resulted in more flexibility in the use of standard forms, since local enterprises may be more willing to negotiate amendments to them. However, it has also reinforced the use of standard forms. Because of the lack of lawyers or legal experts in China and the larger numbers of entities now involved in foreign trade, the use of standard-form contracts is an important means of protecting China's interests while allowing enterprises to engage in foreign economic relations without legal assistance.

Nevertheless, neither the standard forms used for the most common and simple transactions, nor those used for licensing agreements appear to have changed substantially in the last decade, although it is now easier to negotiate changes in certain provisions, such as arbitration. Nor are major changes in the agreements expected in the future, although such changes are possible because of the requirements of the Foreign Contracts Law, as noted above, or those of its future implementing regulations or other legislation.

At present, as in the past, the foreigner engaging in business activities in China will invariably meet the standard-form contracts in simple purchase and sales negotiations. In more complex transactions Chinese entities, sometimes those which have only recently engaged in foreign trade, tend to be more flexible. They may have a standard form, but they do not always insist that it be used for the particular transaction if the foreigner has his own standard form. This is most often the case in licensing, joint venture, co-operation, and compensation trade contracts. For example, the China National Offshore Oil Corporation (CNOOC) has reportedly drafted a model contract for offshore petroleum equity joint ventures which it offers to potential foreign joint venture partners. In early 1985, the Ministry of Foreign Economic Relations and Trade made public a Sample Contract for Joint Ventures Using Chinese and Foreign Investment and Sample Articles of Association for Joint Ventures Using Chinese and Foreign Investment.[21] In many cases the new entities engaging in foreign trade seem to have received copies of standard-form contracts from the older foreign trade corporations, such as the China National Technical Import Corporation (TECHIMPORT). However, in licensing, joint venture, compensation trade, and co-operation contracts the idiosyncrasies of a project are often sufficient to ensure that no standard form will be completely appropriate. In such cases, which are increasing with the growing complexity of China's economic relations with foreign countries, an appropriate contract is generally drawn up by the two parties together, at times based on a draft prepared by the foreign party.

The impact of the Foreign Contracts Law on the standard-form contracts used by Chinese entities in their economic relations with foreign parties will probably not be substantial. The standard-form contracts reflect in part international practice, and to a large degree comply with the obligatory provisions of the Law. In those cases where the Law allows the parties to a contract freedom to stipulate different provisions in the contract, the standard-form contract will reflect the Chinese side's determination of what the two parties should stipulate. Therefore, although the Foreign Contracts Law appears to allow more flexibility to foreign enterprises in the negotiation of their contracts with Chinese parties, this may not be so. For example, Article 5 of the Law states that the parties to a contract may choose the applicable law to deal with disputes. This allows the application of the law of the foreign party's country in the handling of a contract dispute. The standard-form contracts, however, generally do not provide for the choice of an applicable law, and Chinese negotiators will only very reluctantly agree to the application of foreign law to a contract. In practice, therefore, it is unlikely that many contracts calling for the application of foreign law will be signed.

IV. The Authority of the Contracting Party

The decentralization of foreign trade in China has raised significant questions for foreign companies signing contracts with Chinese enterprises. As noted above, in 1979 China abolished the monopoly of the former Ministry of Foreign Trade over China's economic contacts with foreign countries. The original eight Chinese foreign trade corporations[22] are no longer the only parties in China authorized to sign contracts with foreign companies. Now entities at the provincial, municipal, or even lower levels may conduct trade directly with a foreign firm.[23] In addition, many of the national ministries have their own foreign trade companies.[24] This decentralization has achieved its purpose of expediting foreign trade by giving the initiative to local or ministerial entities, but it has also presented foreigners with the problems of choosing among competing Chinese organizations and determining which Chinese entity is the most appropriate one with which to do business. An important part of the answer to such problems is whether the relevant Chinese entities are in fact authorized to engage in the contemplated transaction.

Previously, foreign firms could rely on tradition and experience in signing contracts with the eight foreign trade corporations, all of which were well known to foreign parties. Therefore, even though these foreign trade corporations might refuse to supply any documentation, such as their business licence, that indicated their authority to engage in foreign trade, foreign companies entered into contracts with them without great concern. But foreign firms have not been so willing to accept at face value the assertions of lawful authority made by the new corporations. On the one hand, this mistrust is due in part to an outdated belief that in China there can only be one organization authorized to deal with a particular product. If a foreign trade corporation still exists to handle a particular product, then some foreigners may suspect that any other organization claiming to deal with that product is not authorized to do so. On the other hand, this mistrust is also partly due to the fact that one Chinese organization may assert that it is the only organization in China authorized to deal with a particular product, thus contributing to the foreigner's misunderstanding.

The matter of the authority of the contracting party raises three principal issues that are not treated by the Foreign Contracts Law or other legislation available to foreigners.[25] Firstly, there is the question of whether the Chinese entity that has invited the foreign party to China for contract negotiations has the authority to discuss and sign contracts with foreign entities generally. Such authority would normally be contained in the articles of incorporation of the Chinese entity or in the business licence issued by the State Administration of Industry and Commerce. Some Chinese entities, such as the China International Trust and Investment Corporation and the Shanghai Investment and Trust Corporation, have published their articles of incorporation and are willing to provide them to foreign parties. Most Chinese organizations, however, will not provide such documentation when requested. One example of this reportedly occurred in May 1982 when a major foreign oil company negotiated with the CNOOC for concessions in the offshore petroleum sector. It seems that the company insisted that the CNOOC present some documentation other than the Regulations of the People's Republic of China on the Exploitation of Offshore Petroleum Resources in Co-operation with Foreign Enterprises to prove that it had the authority to sign the contract. The company reportedly suggested that the Ministry of Petroleum co-sign the contract. The CNOOC, however, refused and the contract was apparently signed by the CNOOC and the company without any additional written evidence by the CNOOC of its authority.

The second issue is the identity of any necessary approval authority. Here again the foreign party will probably not be able to obtain any document that clearly states the necessity of such approval and that lists the organizations that are entitled to grant it. This question is generally handled by making the contract's effectiveness subject to the approval of the appropriate 'Chinese governmental authorities'. Because the approval process is often considered an 'internal' matter by the Chinese entity, it may be unwilling to reveal which authorities must approve the contract and what standards will be applied in the approval process. Thus the specific Chinese organizations that will approve or disapprove the contract are not mentioned. It is common knowledge among foreign companies doing business with China that certain contracts must be approved by higher authorities, generally the particular ministry and, in certain cases, the Ministry of Foreign Economic Relations and Trade.[26] The foreign party, however, has no way of knowing whether a contract has in fact been referred to the authorities and whether it has been approved or disapproved. Presumably, any Chinese organization which misleads a foreign party as to the approval would be subject to disciplinary measures. But since the foreign party often either does not know which organization will approve or disapprove the contract, or does not wish to risk its goodwill with the Chinese party by approaching the approving organization directly, it is impossible to verify that the organization has approved or disapproved the contract. There is no known case of a Chinese organization misleading a foreigner in this respect. However, if a Chinese organization were to do so, it is doubtful whether the foreign party would ever come to hear of it. Thus, the secrecy often practised by Chinese organizations with regard to the approval process may cause foreign companies uneasiness, given their complete reliance on the Chinese party to the contract for information regarding the granting or refusal of approval by higher authorities. Some foreigners find consolation in the fact that the Chinese party often stands, in practice, in much the same position with regard to the foreign company's representations about export control approvals in its home country.

The third issue concerns the presence in licensing agreements of an intermediary. In such agreements, the entity signing the contract is an intermediary that negotiates the commercial terms on behalf of the Chinese factory that will implement the technology. The intermediary signing the contract generally does not present any evidence of its authority to act on behalf of the factory, or, if necessary, to make the factory observe the terms of the contract (particularly those relating to nondisclosure of the technology to third parties).[27] In most cases, the foreign party is not able to obtain documentary evidence indicating the relationship between the signatory of the contract and the factory and must rely on experience and appearances to reassure itself on these points.

The question of the authority of the contracting party is one which has occurred not only to foreign entities, but also to the Chinese themselves. In some cases Chinese enterprises have requested foreign entities to provide written evidence, such as a power of attorney, of the foreigners' authority to conduct negotiations and sign contracts; and certificates of the legal status of the signing parties are among the documents that may be required for approval of a technology transfer contract effective after 23 May 1985. Foreign contract negotiators should be aware, therefore, that if they do press the Chinese side for evidence of their authority, the Chinese may well request similar documentation from them.

In addition to requesting documentation from the Chinese party itself, foreign companies that desire confirmation of the authority of the Chinese party to conduct negotiations and execute foreign economic contracts may contact trade organizations, such as the National Council for US–China Trade in the United States, or the China Council for the Promotion of International Trade or China International Economic Consultants, Inc. in China, or the Chinese law firms recently established in China's major cities to handle foreign-related transactions, for assistance. Another possible alternative, the notarization of contracts, has not been used in the past but may be appropriate in some cases.[28]

V. The Enforcement of Contracts

A. The Enforceable Contract

Under American law a contract is generally considered to be an agreement between two parties that is enforceable in accordance with its terms.[29] Usually 'enforceable' is understood to mean enforcement directly through the courts. However, contracts signed with Chinese entities have not generally been enforceable directly through the courts, but through arbitration. Furthermore, disputes have generally been resolved by conciliation or friendly discussions prior to arbitration. In fact, there appear to be few, if any, non-maritime cases in which a Chinese party to a foreign trade contract has gone to arbitration outside China. The Foreign Contracts Law follows this practice, stating in Article 37 that the parties shall 'to the fullest extent possible' settle disputes through consultation or third-party mediation.

Given China's preference for conciliation and arbitration, it is notable that the Foreign Contracts Law does allow resort to court and that the Law on Civil Procedure of the People's Republic of China (hereafter cited as the Civil Procedure Law), promulgated for trial implementation on 8 March 1982, has a special chapter dealing with litigation involving foreigners. The Civil Procedure Law allows foreigners to bring contractual disputes to the economic chambers of the people's courts. Article 192 of the Law provides that disputes involving foreign economic relations, trade, transportation, and maritime matters can be referred to the Chinese courts. Both the Foreign Contracts Law and the Civil Procedure Law limit access to the courts in handling such disputes to cases where there is no written agreement between the parties providing for arbitration.[30] Since Chinese entities almost uniformly insist on an arbitration clause in the contracts they sign with foreign parties, resort to the economic courts by foreigners for enforcement of their contracts may not be generally available. Unless the penchant of China's contract negotiators for arbitration clauses declines, the bringing of foreign contractual disputes to court in China will continue to be rare.

It should be noted, however, that although an arbitration clause does generally preclude resort to court, this may not be so in all cases. In some jurisdictions preliminary protective measures, such as an injunction, are available through the courts to parties who have entered into an agreement containing an arbitration clause. For example, under Swedish law either party may apply to a court for protective measures before or during the arbitration proceedings.[31] It is unclear whether this would be permissible in China under the Civil Procedure Law if the relevant arbitration clause called for arbitration in Stockholm under the Stockholm Chamber of Commerce rules.[32] Some jurisdictions also allow a party to an arbitration agreement to sue in court to have an arbitration award overturned in certain circumstances.[33] In China, Article 193 of the Civil Procedure Law provides that such judicial review is not available for arbitration awards rendered by Chinese arbitration organizations.

While China's policy in favour of arbitration rather than litigation has been consistent over the last decade, the provisions in Chinese foreign trade contracts for arbitration have not remained the same. Previously, Chinese standard-form contracts provided for, and Chinese foreign trade entities generally insisted upon, arbitration in Beijing under the rules of the Foreign Trade Arbitration Commission of the China Council for the Promotion of International Trade.[34] Over the last decade Chinese entities have agreed to alter the standard-form contracts to provide for arbitration in third countries under the rules of foreign arbitral bodies. A review of arbitration clauses in a number of contracts between American and Chinese parties indicates that Sweden and Switzerland are popular sites for arbitration, that the local arbitration rules of the site of arbitration are often used, and that Chinese entities sometimes request the use of the Arbitration Rules of the United Nations Commission on International Trade Law (UNCITRAL). Chinese entities generally oppose a provision for arbitration under the International Chamber of Commerce rules because Taiwan is a member of the Chamber, while China is not.

B. The Retroactive Effect of Laws and Regulations

Another question related to the enforceability of a contract executed in China is the retroactive effect of subsequent laws and regulations. Since China is in the process of promulgating many new laws and regulations relating to foreign trade and investment, it is natural that subsequent legislation may affect the provisions of the contract. The general policy in this regard has been very favourable towards foreign parties. In the tax area in particular, where contracts provide for preferential tax treatment China has allowed such preference to continue to apply even in the face of subsequent legislation. One example of this is the Schindler joint venture contract (between the China Construction Machinery Corporation, Schindler Holding AG, and Jardine Schindler (Far East) Holdings, SA), dated 19 March 1980, that provided for a maximum tax rate of 31.5 per cent,[35] while the Joint Venture Income Tax Law promulgated subsequently provided for a maximum rate of 33 per cent.[36] Another example is a Ministry of Finance ruling of 29 March 1982 entitled 'Concerning the Problem of Taxation of Technology Transfer, Loans, Leasing and Other Contracts Approved Before the Promulgation of the Tax Law', which grants 'grandfather clause' status to clauses in agreements obligating the Chinese entity to take care of all taxes in China related to the transaction.[37] More recently, the Foreign Contracts Law seems not to apply to contracts effective before its effective date.[38] In addition, as noted above, the Foreign Contracts Law also grants 'grandfather clause' status to three types of contract (equity joint venture, co-operative venture, and co-operative natural resource exploration and development) if performed in China and approved by the government.[39]

The retroactive effect of subsequent laws has not proved to be a substantial problem in China, although each time new laws and regulations are promulgated that apply to transactions for which contracts have already been signed, the question arises of how the new provisions will affect existing contracts.

C. The Effect of Acts of Government on Contracts

Another aspect of enforceability is the impact of acts of government on executed contracts. On the Chinese side this question most often occurs in the context of changes in economic policy and the state economic plan. The first question is whether a contract that violates the state economic plan at the time of signing would be enforceable. With regard to transactions between Chinese domestic enterprises, the Contracts Law provides in Article 7(a) that such a contract would be void. The provision in the Foreign Contracts Law that contracts that violate Chinese law or public policy are void could be applied to such a contract to achieve the same result. The execution of a contract that would violate the state plan is, however, more a hypothetical than a practical problem. It is more likely that an executed contract could be affected by a subsequent change in the state economic policy or plan. (An example is the contract for the Baoshan Iron and Steel Complex discussed below.) In contracts between Chinese enterprises, the Contracts Law provides that in such cases the contract may be amended or terminated, but that such alteration or termination must be reported for prior approval to the relevant business department handing down the plan. The Contracts Law does not treat a revision or cancellation of the state plan as a case of *force majeure*. *Force majeure* is a separate ground permitting the amendment or termination of a contract.

Since the Foreign Contracts Law contains no provision excusing failure to perform a contract due to a revision or cancellation of the plan, it appears that such an event could be characterized as an event of *force majeure* under this statute. A revision or cancellation of the plan could presumably qualify as an event that the parties could not foresee when the contract was made and the occurrence and consequences of which the parties could neither avoid nor overcome. However, if the parties defined *force majeure* in their contract, as allowed under the Foreign Contracts Law, in such a way as to exclude a revision or cancellation of the plan, it is not clear how such an event would be treated under the Law. In foreign economic contracts Chinese organizations have generally not allowed acts of government, whether those of the foreign country or of China, to be regarded as instances of *force majeure* for the purposes of excusing contractual performance. This is true even though prior to the promulgation of the Contracts Law alterations in the state plan were considered for domestic purposes as incidents of *force majeure* excusing Chinese enterprises from fulfilling contractual obligations.[40] In addition, in at least one case a Chinese entity has reportedly not allowed foreign bidders to make their contractual obligations subject to the granting of an export licence by the United States government. However justifiable from the Chinese viewpoint, this demand put some American companies that were successful bidders at risk. If they were subsequently unable to obtain United States export licences for products to be supplied to China, they would be required to pay substantial sums under the mandatory performance bonds.

Perhaps the best known example of the difficulties caused by a change in the state plan is the Baoshan Iron and Steel Complex. This complex near Shanghai, originally designed as a state-of-the-art plant modelled on Nippon Steel's Oita complex, was part of China's ambitious development plans unveiled in 1978. The economic readjustment instituted shortly thereafter, however, caused changes in the state economic plan and criticism of the scale and cost of new construction projects, including the Baoshan Iron and Steel Complex. In contrast to the earlier Baoshan contracts, in this case the contracts had already come into force.[41] They did not contain any cancellation or penalty clauses. The Chinese entered into negotiations with the suppliers, primarily Japanese and German firms, and eventually agreed to pay them substantial amounts in compensation for their losses.[42]

While foreign companies dealing with China should be aware of the possibility that changes in the state economic plan may affect their contracts in China, Chinese entities are also aware of the danger that action by foreign governments may affect contracts that they sign with foreign companies. The United States government has, for example, imposed restrictions on the export of certain scarce materials, as in the case of ferrous scrap in 1973,[43] and has at times revoked export licences for exports to Communist countries, as in 1982 for exports to the Soviet Union of equipment related to a natural gas pipeline.[44]

The growing stability in China's economic planning and the loosening of restrictions on American export licensing procedures[45] may resolve some of the problems relating to the influence of subsequent government acts on contracts between Chinese and foreign parties. It is still unclear whether China under the Foreign Contracts Law will change its policy on how to deal with such government acts affecting executed contracts. The basis for China's past decision to compensate for the non-performance of contracts due to revision or cancellation of the plan may be that, since the Chinese foreign trade corporations are state owned, have been state subsidized, and their major contracts have been approved by the state, it is awkward for such corporations to rely on acts of the state for relief from their contractual obligations. This logic supports a result that may be appropriate when it is the Chinese party that is prevented from fulfilling the contract. The application of this same rule to cases of failure to perform by foreign corporations that are generally independent of the state is, however, open to question.

VI. The Interpretation of Contracts

The interpretation of contracts signed between foreign and Chinese enterprises is governed in large part by three factors: the Chinese view of contracts, the choice of governing law, and the choice of governing language.

Chinese parties have strongly held views about contracts and these views influence their interpretation of contracts. Article 3 of the Foreign Contracts Law expresses these views when it states that contracts should be concluded in accordance with the principles of 'equality and mutual benefit and agreement through consultation'. These beliefs are not so much legal as commercial concepts, which are familiar to foreigners who have conducted negotiations in China. The terms that Chinese parties often use in their contract discussions, such as 'long-term relationship', 'friendship', and 'equality and mutual benefit', reflect these beliefs. As these phrases indicate, the view of the Chinese is that contracts are not one-off transactions. They reflect the long-term friendly relationship between the parties. This relationship is a beneficial one to both parties and one of essential equality between the parties. Thus any disputes about a contract must be put into the perspective of the parties' desire for a long-term business relationship. The Chinese parties are willing, therefore, to make short-term concessions in the interests of long-term benefits. They expect the foreigner to do the same. For example, if a shipment of Chinese products does not conform with the terms of the agreement, and the foreign purchaser requests damages, the Chinese party will often try to negotiate a settlement by which discounts or 'friendly' prices will be offered on future orders.

In some cases a Chinese party's emphasis on a long-term friendly relationship has led it to overestimate the commitment of the foreign party. For example, a Chinese party to a contract, particularly one involving the import of technology, may look to the foreign supplier as the authoritative source for all information on the technology, including its implementation in China. The Chinese entity, thinking in terms of 'friendship' and a 'long-term relationship', may assume that under the contract the foreign party will do everything necessary to make the transfer of technology successful, regardless of the wording used in the contract. The foreign party is sometimes viewed, therefore, by the Chinese party, almost as a guarantor of the entire transaction. This is a point of which foreign suppliers should be aware and which they must handle with the greatest delicacy.

More familiar to lawyers are the problems of choice of law and choice of language. The standard-form contracts used by Chinese enterprises have not in the past included any choice of law clause or any other language in the contract which would allow a third party to determine what law should be used to govern the contract. This is still generally the practice, although governing law clauses are now beginning to appear in some contracts, such as one prepared by TECHIMPORT. Further, Article 5 of the Foreign Contracts Law provides that for equity joint ventures, co-operative venture contracts, and contracts for the co-operative exploitation and development of natural resources performed in China, the laws of China are to be applied.

The absence of a governing law provision in the standard-form contract does not mean that the Chinese party will allow reference to foreign law. On the contrary, the foreigner who demands a clause calling for foreign law as the governing law of the contract will probably be met with a demand by the Chinese party for the use of Chinese law. As a result, most contracts negotiated with China do not provide for any governing law. Where the contracts negotiated with Chinese entities have generally provided for the resolution of disputes in the last resort by arbitration in China, the application of Chinese law to govern the contract is probably inevitable. Since Chinese contracts signed with foreign entities now often contain arbitration clauses calling for arbitration in third countries, the lack of a governing law clause will result, under the Foreign Contracts Law, in the application of the law of the country having the closest connection with the contract.

If a contract without a choice of law clause were referred to arbitration in a third country, it seems likely that the arbitrators would apply the choice of law rules of the jurisdiction where the arbitration was being held. The result of such an application of the choice of law rules could differ according to the site of the arbitration. In Sweden, for example, the choice of law rules applied would be similar to the British 'closest connection' test.[46] Since, in many cases, the contracts are negotiated, signed, and largely performed in China, it seems that Chinese law would be applied to interpret the contract by application of the 'closest connection' choice of law rule. In fact, it has been suggested that the Chinese desire for the negotiation and signature of contracts in China is related to this rule. However, an increasing number of Chinese entities are now conducting contract negotiations and even signing contracts abroad. In such cases, the results under the choice of law rules turn on the particular facts of each situation.

In a few exceptional cases foreign parties have been able to have foreign law inserted in the contract as the governing law. The most notable example of this is in the lease contract between a foreign firm and the Civil Aeronautics Administration of China (CAAC) for a Boeing 747 SP aircraft. In that contract the CAAC reportedly not only agreed to the application of New York law to govern the contract, but also agreed to submit to the jurisdiction of the courts in New York for the purpose of the service of process, thus allowing resort to court, rather than arbitration, in the case of a dispute. In a few other cases the application of foreign law has been allowed, principally the law of the third country where arbitration proceedings are to be held. One question which arises in such cases is whether the foreign party should be content with a simple reference to the application of the law of the jurisdiction, or whether it should insist on the application of the substantive, rather than the procedural or choice of law, rules of the jurisdiction. Under the legal concept of *renvoi*, the mere reference to the law of the jurisdiction without further clarification could result in the application merely of the choice of law rules of the jurisdiction which, as noted above in the case of Sweden, could result in the application of Chinese substantive law to interpret the contract.

The question of the choice of language often does not arise until the very end of contract negotiations. In most cases where the Chinese side has prepared a standard-form contract for the basis of the negotiation, it is willing to accept the English version of the contract, on which the negotiations are based, as the only binding version. In such cases, the governing language of the contract is not a problem, since the Chinese side will sign the English version and will not insist that the Chinese translation be signed by the foreign party. In other cases, however, the Chinese entity will insist on equally valid Chinese and English texts of the contract even though its contract was the basis for negotiation. In still other cases, such as the standard-form sales or purchase contracts, there are interlinear Chinese translations of the contract. The use of the English language as the sole governing language of the contract is, in fact, one of the advantages of using the Chinese standard forms.

If the foreign party is fortunate enough to convince the Chinese side that the foreign party's draft contract be used as the basis of negotiations, then the question of the choice of language is invariably posed. In such cases, the Chinese side will negotiate from the contract prepared by the foreigner but will insist that a clause be inserted at the end of the contract indicating that both the English and the Chinese texts of the contract be equally valid and binding. Unfortunately, this problem often arises at the very end of negotiations when the foreign party is not prepared to have the two versions compared for accuracy. In many cases, the foreign party has little choice but to concede and sign both texts. But substantial discrepancies between the two versions can occur and may relate to important aspects of the foreign party's obligations, such as guarantees. The reasons for such inaccuracies are twofold. Firstly, the Chinese translators are often extremely busy when preparing the Chinese text of the contract and are unable to translate as carefully as they would like. Secondly, the translators and the Chinese negotiators may be unfamiliar with legal or commercial concepts used in international transactions, for in some cases no standardized translations for such terms exist in Chinese. Examples are the concept of disclaimer of a warranty of 'merchantability', and the per diem payments made to a licenser for the value of technical services. From a technical point of view, the foreign party might have an advantage in arbitration relating to a discrepancy in the language of the contract conducted in a third country where English, but not Chinese, was widely spoken. It is presumed that the arbitrators would give preference to the English text if they were able to read it and not to the Chinese text. Nevertheless, to avoid disputes regarding obligations in the contract, foreign parties should verify the Chinese text of the contract, if necessary, during the negotiations.

VII. Conclusion

In its economic relations with foreign parties China has experienced both continuity and change in contract practice. In the most common purchase and sale contracts, China continues to use and foreign parties continue to sign, without significant amendments, standard-form contracts prepared by the Chinese party. In the more interesting and complex licensing, compensation trade, and joint venture contracts, however, there is evidence of greater flexibility and creativity. This has been true in the past and will probably continue to be so in the future under the Foreign Contracts Law. The more complex contracts should become relatively more common and important if China's policy of encouraging foreign trade and investment continues with the same vigour that it has displayed in recent years. The Foreign Contracts Law has not forced substantial changes in these complex contracts (or in the simpler standard-form contracts), but it has institutionalized China's open policy and laid a foundation for the further approach of Chinese contract law towards international practice. It seems likely that foreign firms entering into contracts with Chinese entities will face many of the issues that they have faced in the past and will continue to try to resolve them by reference to the appropriate legislation and by negotiating appropriate provisions in their contracts.

Notes

1. The Foreign Economic Contracts Law of the People's Republic of China (hereafter cited as the Foreign Contracts Law). For evaluations of the Foreign Contracts Law see Charles J. Conroy, 'China's New Foreign Economic Contract Law', *International Financial Law Review*, May 1985, pp. 26–7; Jenkin S. F. Chan, 'Foreign Economic Contract Law: A Breakthrough', *East Asian Executive Reports*, April 1985, pp. 9 and 15–16; Jerome Alan Cohen, 'The New Foreign Contract Law', *The China Business Review*, July–August 1985, pp. 52–4; 'An Explanation of the (Draft) Foreign Economic Contracts Law of the PRC', *Zhongguo fazhi bao (China's Legal System Newspaper)*, 11 January 1985, p. 2; and Xu Donggen, 'The Special Characteristics and Principles of China's Foreign Economic Contracts Law', *Faxue (Jurisprudence)*, Vol. 6, 1985, pp. 31–3. See also Ren Jianxin and Zhuang Huichen, 'Several Questions of China's Foreign Economic and Trade Contract Legislation', *Zhongguo faxue (China's Jurisprudence)*, Vol. 1, 1984, pp. 113–20.

2. The Foreign Contracts Law, note 1 above, does not define the term 'economic contract'. The Economic Contracts Law of the People's Republic of China (hereafter cited as the Contracts Law) states in Art. 2 that 'an economic contract is an agreement between legal persons which specifies their mutual rights and obligations and which is for the purpose of realizing certain economic goals'. This definition is broad enough to apply not only to contracts between Chinese enterprises, but also to those between Chinese and foreign parties. It also raises the

question of what a 'legal person' is under Chinese and foreign law. Further, the implications of this definition for letters of intent and memoranda of understanding are unclear.

3. The Contracts Law, note 2 above, states in Art. 6 that 'an economic contract made in accordance with law is legally binding and the parties *must* perform *in all respects* the obligations stipulated in the contract and neither party shall alter or cancel the contract unilaterally' (emphasis added), while the Foreign Contracts Law, note 1 above, provides in Art. 16 that 'a contract made in accordance with law is legally binding. The parties *ought* to perform the obligations stipulated in the contract and neither party shall alter or cancel the contract unilaterally' (emphasis added). The reasons for the minor discrepancies in the language are not clear. It appears that the Foreign Contracts Law establishes an obligation of substantial performance, while the Contracts Law calls for the strict performance of contractual obligations.

4. See the Foreign Contracts Law, Arts. 3 (equality and mutual benefit), 16 (conformity with law), and 9 (voidness), note 1 above; and the Contracts Law, Arts. 5 (equality and mutual benefit), 6 (conformity with law), and 7 (voidness), note 2 above.

5. See the Contracts Law, Arts. 2 and 3, note 2 above, and the Foreign Contracts Law, Art. 7, note 1 above.

6. See the Contracts Law, Art. 7, note 2 above.

7. See the Contracts Law, Arts. 51 and 52, note 2 above.

8. See the United Nations Convention on Contracts for the International Sale of Goods, Art. 9(2), (hereafter cited as the United Nations Convention), *International Legal Materials*, 1980, p. 674; and the Foreign Contracts Law, Art. 5, note 1 above.

9. See Zhang Yuejiao, 'Law to Guarantee Reliability of Foreign Economic Contracts', *Intertrade*, July 1985, p. 66. Ms. Zhang is Deputy Division Chief, Department of Treaty and Law, Ministry of Foreign Economic Relations and Trade. See, also, 'The Foreign Economic Contracts Law Is a Law that Safeguards and Promotes the Development of Foreign Economic Relations', *Zhongguo fazhi bao*, 15 April 1985, p. 3, c. 5.

10. See the United Nations Convention, Art. 74, note 8 above, and the Foreign Contracts Law, Art. 19, note 1 above.

11. See the United Nations Convention, Arts. 77, 78, and 79, note 8 above, and the Foreign Contracts Law, Arts. 22, 23, and 24, note 1 above.

12. See the Foreign Contracts Law, Art. 24, note 1 above.

13. See the United Nations Convention, Arts. 1, 2, and 3, note 8 above, and the Foreign Contracts Law, Art. 2, note 1 above.

14. See the United Nations Convention, Arts. 14–19, note 8 above.

15. See the United Nations Convention, Arts. 20 and 21, note 8 above.

16. See the United Nations Convention, Arts. 30–42, note 8 above.

17. See the United Nations Convention, Arts. 53–60, note 8 above.

18. The basic provisions of these contracts since the 1970s have been described by several commentators: E. Theroux, *China's Standard Form Contracts and Related Legal Issues in US–China Trade* (Washington, DC, Special Report No. 13 of the National Council for US–China Trade, June 1973); Note, 'Legal Aspects of China's Foreign Trade Practices and Procedures', *Journal of International Law and Economics*, No. 12, 1977–8, p. 105; K. R. Shaney, 'Selected Legal Aspects of China's Conduct of Foreign Trade', *International Lawyer*, No. 11, 1977, p. 641; A. H. Smith, 'Standard Form Contracts in the International Trade of the People's Republic of China', *The International and Comparative Law Quarterly Review*, No. 21, 1972, p. 133; and Note, 'An Analysis of Chinese Contractual Policy and Practice', *Wayne Law Review*, No. 27, 1980–1, p. 1229. For examples of these contracts see also C. W. Chiu, *China Trade Agreement* (Hong Kong, Tai Dao Publishing Ltd., 1985).

19. See, generally, Chen Muhua, 'Prospects for China's Foreign Trade in 1983',

Beijing Review, No. 6, 1983, p. 14; and 'Interview: Wei Yuming', *Far Eastern Economic Review*, 25 December 1981, p. 46.

20. See, generally, V. K. Fung, 'China's Decentralization of Foreign Trade', *Asian Wall Street Journal*, 24 November 1982, p. 6; and Li Shude, 'General Review on China's Structural Reform of Foreign Trade System' (speech at a seminar organized by the Commission of the European Communities on the Reform of China's Foreign Trade System, Brussels, 7 and 8 July 1982). Mr Li is Director of the Third Department, Ministry of Foreign Economic Relations and Trade.

21. See *China Economic News*, Supplement, 1 April 1985, pp. 1–12. These sample contracts are reproduced as Appendices 3B and 3C to Chapter 3 in this volume.

22. The original eight Chinese foreign trade corporations are China National Chemicals Import and Export Corporation; China National Native Produce and Animal By-products Corporation; China National Light Industrial Products Import and Export Corporation; China National Textiles Import and Export Corporation; China National Cereals, Oils and Foodstuffs Import and Export Corporation; China National Machinery Import and Export Corporation; China National Metals and Minerals Import and Export Corporation; and China National Technical Import Corporation. The China National Chartering Corporation and the Chinese Foreign Trade Transportation Corporation are also sometimes considered to be foreign trade corporations. See Theroux, note 18 above.

23. Li Shude in his speech, note 20 above, said: 'Since 1980, special policies and flexible measures concerning foreign trade have been adopted in [the] Provinces of Guangdong and Fujian. These two provinces are entitled, under the guidance of unified foreign trade principles and planning, to manage on their own export of all the local products, with the exception of crude oil, refined oil, and some other products which are handled by the head offices.of relevant national import and export corporations. A certain percentage of the foreign currency earnings are kept by the provinces at [sic] their own disposal.

'To give full play to the advantages of the provinces and cities and to expand further China's foreign trade, Foreign Trade Corporations were set up in Beijing, Shanghai and Tianjin in 1980, and were given more power to manage import and export business. It was further decided earlier this year that the provinces, municipalities and autonomous regions, which are located along the sea coast and with necessary conditions, can manage in principle foreign trade business on the basis of independent accounting and bearing their own profits or losses.

'Independent management of foreign trade has also been approved to other provinces, municipalities and autonomous regions to various extent[s], with the power to negotiate directly with foreign companies.'

24. Examples of such trading companies are China Electronics Import and Export Corporation; China North Industries Corporation; China Atomic Energy Industry Corporation; China National Aerotechnology Import and Export Corporation; China State Shipbuilding Corporation; China Great Wall Industry Corporation; China Precision Machinery Import and Export Corporation; China Xinshidai Company; China Xiao Feng Company; China Metallurgical Import and Export Corporation; China Seeds Company; China Forest Seeds Import and Export Corporation; China Breeding Stock Import and Export Corporation; and China Oriental Scientific Instruments Import and Export Corporation.

25. An issue related to that of the authority of the contracting party is the authority of the person signing the contract. This issue does not arise often, but can involve three questions: firstly, how to know whether the Chinese person signing the contract is the person that he or she says that he or she is; secondly, how to know what position the person signing holds in the Chinese party to the contract; and, thirdly, how to know whether a person in such a position has the authority to sign the contract and bind the Chinese party. Where these issues

arise, the foreign party may take the same measures as noted below in the discussion of the authority of the contracting party to reassure itself.

26. The Procedures for Examination and Approval of Technology Import Contracts, effective from 18 September 1985, help to clarify, in Art. 3, the identity of the approval organization for technology transfer contracts. In most cases this is the Ministry of Foreign Economic Relations and Trade or its designees.

27. The Regulations of the PRC for the Administration of Technology Import Contracts, effective from 24 May 1985, address, but do not resolve, this problem. Art. 7 obligates only the 'licensee' (that is, the Chinese foreign trade corporation) to keep the confidential parts of the technology secret.

28. See the Provisional Regulations of the People's Republic of China on Notarization, promulgated by the State Council on 13 April 1982, and the major treatise on notarization, He Mingfu, *Gongzheng jiben zhishi* (*Basic Knowledge of Notarization*) (Beijing, The Masses Publishing Co., 1982).

29. According to the Restatement of Contracts, a contract is a promise or a set of promises for the breach of which the law gives a remedy, or the performance of which the law in some way recognizes as a duty. Restatement (Second) of Contracts (1979), §1. The Uniform Commercial Code, §1-201 (11), defines contracts as the total legal obligation which results from the parties' agreement as affected by the code and any other applicable rules of law.

30. See the Foreign Contracts Law, Art. 38, note 1 above, and the Law on Civil Procedure of the People's Republic of China (hereafter cited as the Civil Procedure Law), Art. 192.

31. See 'Provisional Security Measures' in Arbitration Institute of the Stockholm Chamber of Commerce, *An Introduction to International Arbitration in Sweden* (Stockholm, the Institute, 1981).

32. Art. 194 of the Civil Procedure Law, note 30 above, states that 'a PRC foreign arbitration organization' can apply to a people's court for such protective measures in certain circumstances, but it is unclear whether this applies only to arbitration proceedings in China or to those conducted abroad as well.

33. Different countries have varying practices with respect to judicial review. In England, under the Arbitration Act of 1979, parties to international contracts, other than those concerning maritime, insurance, or commodities matters, may foreclose judicial review by an exclusion agreement in the commercial contract. However, prior to the effective date of the Act, 1 August 1979, English courts could intervene extensively in arbitrations held in England and Wales. In Switzerland, in Zurich and Geneva, the judiciary may examine the merits of a dispute submitted to arbitration where one side believes the arbitrator committed an error. In the Netherlands, Sweden, and the United States, a *laissez-faire* approach is adopted, where error as such is not subject to review. France has an optional approach to arbitrator error, where parties may choose whether or not to prohibit appeal on the merits of the case (see W. W. Park, 'Judicial Supervision of Transnational Commercial Arbitration: The English Arbitration Act of 1979', *Harvard International Law Journal*, No. 21, 1980, p. 87).

34. Since 1980 the Foreign Trade Arbitration Commission has been renamed the Foreign Trade and Economic Arbitration Commission.

35. See the Agreement on the Establishment of a Joint Venture Elevator Company in the People's Republic of China, 1980, Art. 8(2).

36. The Income Tax Law of the People's Republic of China Concerning Joint Ventures Using Chinese and Foreign Investment, promulgated on 10 September 1980.

37. General Bureau of Taxation of the Ministry of Finance (ed.), *Zhongguo duiwai shuiwu shouce* (*Handbook of China's Foreign Taxation*) (Beijing, China Financial and Economic Publishing House, 1983), p. 37.

38. See the Foreign Contracts Law, Art. 41, note 1 above.

39. See the Foreign Contracts Law, Art. 40, note 1 above.

40. R. Pfeffer, *The Role of Contracts in China* (Cambridge, Mass., East Asian Research Center, 1970), pp. 54–5.

41. Y. Yamada, 'The Problems of China's Suspending Plant Import Contracts', *China Newsletter*, No. 22, July 1979, p. 16. For other cases see 'China: Contract Revisions', *Business International*, 27 July 1984, p. 240, and Amanda Bennett, 'China's Legal System Irks Westerners', *The Wall Street Journal*, 5 April 1984, p. 34.

42. 'Chinese Credibility on the Line Due to Baoshan Cancellation', *Business Asia*, 6 March 1981, p. 75.

43. 38 Fed. Reg. 17817 (3 July 1973).

44. 47 Fed. Reg. 141 (1982), to be codified in 15 CFR §§ 379, 385, and 399.

45. 48 Fed. Reg. 53064–71 (1983), to be codified in 15 CFR §§ 368–99; 50 Fed. Reg. 52908 (1985); 50 Fed. Reg. 37112–61 (1985); and 50 Fed. Reg. 52900–12 (1985).

46. See Stockholm Chamber of Commerce, *Arbitration in Sweden* (Stockholm, the Chamber, 1984), pp. 48–9.

9. Banking and Finance in the China Trade

FRANKLIN D. CHU

CHINA has greatly expanded its international commercial ties in recent years, but the amount of business it has concluded with foreign banks and financial institutions has remained small for a country with one-quarter of the world's population. This reflects a caution and restraint that is hardly surprising given China's traditional distaste for borrowing funds except on concessionary terms; inefficient bureaucratic structures; sensitivity to making mistakes; and lack of familiarity with many international financial practices.

China's fiscal restraint resulted in the accumulation of foreign exchange reserves in the early 1980s. In October 1984 the Central Committee of the Chinese Communist Party called for a significant increase in imports of needed technology, plant, and equipment, the construction of the infrastructure necessary to absorb much greater foreign investment, and the expansion of the rural economic reform programme to urban areas. The relaxation of economic controls, however, gave rise to dramatic spending, particularly on consumer and other manufactured goods, driving down reserves and turning a once consistent trade surplus into an expanding trade deficit. In 1983, 1982, and 1981, China had trade surpluses of US$3.86 billion, US$4.6 billion, and US$1.4 billion respectively.[1] By the end of April 1986, the annual trade balance stood US$4.4 billion in deficit.[2]

At the end of 1983 China had US$14.392 billion in foreign exchange reserves (more than the reserves of any developing country except Saudi Arabia), as well as 12.67 million troy ounces of gold, sufficient to cover imports for about eight months.[3] But at the end of the first quarter of 1986, foreign exchange reserves fell to US$10.34 billion, according to official sources, and significantly less according to unofficial sources. This situation indicates that the present tight controls over spending, which were imposed in the middle of 1985 when reserves were approximately US$10.85 billion, will continue in the short term. Gold reserves remained unchanged.[4]

China's foreign debt, however, has remained small. The Ministry of Finance reported that at the end of 1981 China had only US$4.7 billion in foreign debt, which approached US$6 billion in mid-1982 and decreased sharply to US$3.02 billion at the end of 1983.[5] After an increase in foreign borrowing of US$800 million over the first quarter of 1986, total foreign (commercial) debt still stood at approximately US$5.8 billion.[6]

Despite the swings in China's economic policies, foreign banks have continued their efforts to penetrate the China market. At the end of 1985, over 160 foreign bank branches or representative or sub-representative offices had been established in Beijing, Shanghai, Guangzhou, the Shenzhen special economic zone across the border from Hong Kong, and the Xiamen special economic zone in Fujian province. Although few of the banks involved have reaped significant profits, they seem committed to developing their long-term business relationships with China.[7]

China's financial institutions, Chinese business and financial practices, and Chinese laws and regulations applicable to banking transactions are in the process of evolution, which is likely to continue for the foreseeable future. This chapter focuses on banking and finance in the China trade from the late 1970s to the present. Four major areas will be discussed: (a) the organization of China's banking system, with an emphasis on those institutions engaged in international financial and investment activities; (b) the activities of foreign banks in China; (c) Chinese trade-financing practices in connection with letters of credit and export credits; and (d) China's foreign exchange control system and its impact on international business transactions.

I. The Organization of China's Banking System

China's banking system includes as major units the People's Bank of China, five specialized banks, the People's Insurance Company of China, the State General Administration of Exchange Control, and the China International Trust and Investment Corporation, all of which are to some extent under the direction of the State Council, the highest executive organ of government. Outside this core group the Ministry of Finance and the State Capital Construction Commission exercise certain supervisory and regulatory functions, and numerous trust and investment corporations have been authorized to engage in specified banking activities. In addition, the banking system has close links with twelve so-called 'sister' banks in Hong Kong and another in Macau and has two major affiliates in Hong Kong. China is also a member of several international financial organizations.

A. Domestically Oriented Units

i. The People's Bank of China
The People's Bank of China (hereafter referred to as the PBOC) is China's central bank and acts as a state administrative organ for the regulation of finance under the leadership of the State Council.[8] In the Chinese government hierarchy it enjoys ministry-level status.

The State Council has approved five primary roles for the PBOC: (a) to formulate national financial regulations and policies, to determine interest rates for *renminbi* deposits and loans and to implement such rates after State Council approval; (b) to print and issue currency and to regulate the circulation of currency in accordance with the plan approved by the State Council; (c) to co-ordinate and implement credit plans in a comprehensive manner, and to allocate credit funds in a unified manner; (d) to examine the establishment, termination, and consolidation of financial organs, to determine the division of operations and to co-ordinate and examine the business of financial organs, to administer financial markets, to examine and approve the establishment and winding-up of foreign financial institutions in China, and to supervise such foreign financial institutions according to law; and (e) to administer in a unified manner China's foreign exchange and bullion, to manage foreign exchange and gold reserves, to determine the exchange rates of the *renminbi* against foreign currencies, and to engage in related international activities on behalf of the government.[9] In addition to its banking activities, the PBOC oversees the activities of the People's Insurance Company of China.

In practice, certain of the PBOC's functions are carried out by other banking units under the PBOC's supervision. For example, the applications of foreign banks to establish representative offices or branches in China are usually screened and examined by the Bank of China and afterwards are sent to the PBOC for formal approval. The Bank of China also engages in the management and utilization of foreign exchange in both trade and non-trade areas.

On 17 September 1983, the State Council decided that the PBOC would thereafter restrict its functions to those of the country's central bank and not engage in the issue of credit funds to either enterprises or individuals. The PBOC, however, continues to exercise control over the specialized banks and other financial institutions, including the country's insurance companies, through economic measures supplemented by the necessary administrative measures. As part of the recent reorganization, the PBOC has set up a policy-making council, composed of the PBOC's president (who acts as the council chairman) and vice-presidents, several advisers and specialists, a vice-minister of the Ministry of Finance, a vice-minister of both the State Planning Commission and the State Economic Commission, the presidents of the specialized banks, and the general manager of the insurance company. If the council does not reach unanimous agreement on matters discussed, the chairman is authorized to adjudicate, while important issues are submitted to the State Council for decision.[10]

ii. The Industrial and Commercial Bank of China

The Industrial and Commercial Bank of China (hereafter referred to as the Industrial and Commercial Bank) was established on 1 January 1984 as a specialized bank to take over part of the PBOC's former activities with respect to the management of industrial and commercial credits and related payments. The primary tasks of the Industrial and Commercial Bank are handling the savings deposits of industrial and commercial enterprises; extending loans for working capital and technical transformation; managing payments; controlling the working capital of industrial and commercial enterprises; and handling savings deposits in cities and towns.[11]

iii. The Agricultural Bank of China

The Agricultural Bank of China (hereafter referred to as the Agricultural Bank) is directly subordinate to the State Council, but its supervisory management is entrusted by the State Council to the PBOC.[12] At times in its history the Agricultural Bank has operated as a department of the PBOC, but in 1979 it was reinstituted as an independent entity and assumed supervision over the rural offices of the PBOC.[13] The Agricultural Bank's principal tasks are examining, issuing, and utilizing state funds in support of agriculture and cash deposits for the purchase of agricultural products by the state; managing savings deposits and credit business for rural commune and production brigade enterprises, state-run agricultural enterprises and organizations, agricultural-industrial-commercial joint enterprises, and supply and marketing co-operatives; managing savings deposits and credit business for offices, people's organizations, schools, enterprises, and other units set up by the state in the countryside, as well as the settlement of accounting and cash control in the urban and rural areas; and supervising rural credit co-operatives.[14]

iv. The People's Construction Bank of China

The People's Construction Bank of China (hereafter referred to as the Construction Bank) is also directly subordinate to the State Council but its supervisory management is entrusted by the State Council to the Ministry of Finance and, to a lesser degree, to the PBOC and the State Capital Construction Commission.[15] The responsibilities of the Construction Bank include administering government appropriations and loans for capital construction; managing the deposits, loans, and final accounting of such units as construction and installation enterprises, geological prospecting units, and enterprises which supply and market goods and materials for capital construction; and controlling capital funds related to capital construction.[16]

v. The Ministry of Finance

The Ministry of Finance (hereafter referred to as the MOF) is an independent body reporting directly to the State Council and is in charge of fiscal management, the collection of most taxes, and the annual and long-term planning of the state budget. In the banking sector the MOF provides financial guidance to the Construction Bank and the Investment Bank of China.[17]

B. Internationally Oriented Units

i. The Bank of China

By far the most important Chinese entity involved in international banking and finance is the Bank of China (hereafter referred to as the BOC). According to its Articles of Association, which were approved by the State Council on 22 September 1980, the BOC is a state-owned socialist enterprise and is the foreign exchange bank of the People's Republic of China.[18] Supervisory management of the BOC is generally carried out by the PBOC on behalf of the State Council. Under this arrangement the

BOC will refer important business and administrative matters to the PBOC for resolution, although in some cases the BOC may also refer matters directly to the State Council for resolution. The day-to-day administration and business management of the BOC are conducted by the bank itself.[19]

The authorized activities of the BOC cover a broad range of international banking activities which include the international settlement of accounts, interbank deposits, and loans; handling international remittances, foreign currency deposits and loans, and deposits and loans in *renminbi* that are related to foreign exchange and have been approved by the PBOC; buying and selling foreign exchange and gold; organizing and participating in international lending syndicates; establishing banks and other financial institutions abroad; issuing foreign currency bonds and other securities that have been authorized by the state; and providing trust and advisory services and other banking services approved by the state.

The stated capital of the BOC as at 31 December 1985 was RMB3 billion, all appropriated by the government.[20] In addition, the MOF and the PBOC appropriate certain amounts of *renminbi* and foreign exchange as the BOC's working capital.[21] In 1985, the assets of the BOC were RMB260 billion and its net income was RMB1.843 billion, an increase of 30.07 per cent and 23.31 per cent respectively over 1984.[22]

The Board of Directors and Council of Supervisors of the BOC (whose members are appointed by the State Council) function as the bank's leading bodies and the President and the several Vice-Presidents act as chief executive officers.[23] The head office in Beijing is staffed by more than 500 personnel in the following departments: Administration and Secretariat, Personnel, General Co-ordination, International, Foreign Exchange and Funds, Credit, Accounting, and Research.[24] Each department is headed by its own general manager and deputy general managers.

The BOC has branches and sub-branches in the capitals of each province and autonomous region and in major cities, ports, and border areas where international business is concentrated. The BOC also has branches overseas in cities including London, New York, Singapore, Hong Kong, Sydney, Paris, and Luxemburg, and preparations to open a branch in Tokyo are under way.[25] In addition, it has over 1,000 correspondent banks in about 150 countries and regions.

One foreign legal expert has questioned whether the BOC is legally part of the Chinese state or whether it is a distinct legal person separate from the Chinese government.[26] The Chinese themselves appear to look upon the BOC as part of the Chinese government for some purposes and as an independent enterprise for others, although where the line is drawn is unclear. On the one hand, the Articles of Association of the BOC state that it is a state-owned socialist enterprise, which implies that it is an independent legal person that is responsible for its own assets and liabilities and can sue and be sued in its own name.[27] On the other hand, in an official notice describing the relationship between the PBOC and China's specialized banks, the State Council confirmed that the BOC is an 'economic unit at the general administrative level',[28] which implies that it is part of the Chinese government.

The legal status of the BOC is, of course, an important factor for foreign bankers in assessing credit risks and determining lending limits to single borrowers. The BOC itself has represented to both the United States Federal Deposit Insurance Corporation and the Export-Import Bank of the United States that its obligations are backed by the full faith and credit of the People's Republic of China.[29] While it is highly unlikely that the BOC would make such a representation if it had any doubts on the matter, there is at present no legislation passed by the National People's Congress that spells this out. According to press reports, the Japanese government in 1983 initially refused to accept a BOC guarantee in connection with the proposed issue of bonds by Fujian province in the Japanese market unless the State Council endorsed the BOC's guarantee.[30]

It is clear, however, that the obligations of many other state-owned enterprises are not backed by the full faith and credit of the Chinese government. Certain Chinese officials have expressed the opinion that if such other enterprises were to default on their obligations, the Chinese government would recognize only a moral obligation to assume payment.

The authority of the BOC's branches is another important consideration, as foreign banks frequently enter into transactions directly with branches of the BOC rather than with its head office. The scope of authority granted to the BOC's branches, however, is unclear and generally considered to be *neibu* (an internal matter not to be disclosed to foreigners). According to sketchy public information provided by the BOC with respect to its application to establish a New York branch, the prior approval of the BOC head office is necessary for 'certain major matters, including the annual budget of the New York branch, loans or syndicated loans to companies located outside the United States and loans to United States customers in excess of an approved limit, to be established'.[31] As is the case with foreign banks though, not all BOC branches exercise the same authority; foreign BOC branches appear to exercise greater authority than domestic branches. There are further differences among the domestic branches. For example, branches in the provinces of Guangdong and Fujian and the municipalities of Beijing, Shanghai, and Tianjin have independent authority to extend foreign currency loans in larger amounts than branches in other areas. In practice, foreign banks generally have assumed that the major BOC branches in Beijing, Shanghai, and Tianjin and in Guangdong and Fujian provinces would not enter into transactions with foreign banks unless they had the requisite authority, and foreign banks generally have not required evidence of head office approval unless the amount involved is substantial.

Apart from the issue of the authority of its branches, a question remains as to whether the BOC is responsible for its branches' liabilities. Under the general concepts of Western banking law, a bank is responsible for the liabilities of all its branches.[32] Unless certain exceptions or contractual provisions apply, refusal or inability by a branch to honour an obligation entitles a creditor to receive payment from the head office of the bank. There is currently no Chinese law or regulation that addresses this question with respect to Chinese banks or other entities. The issue has never arisen in an actual case involving the BOC. Should such a case arise, it would seem unlikely that the BOC would as a general matter disclaim responsibility for the liabilities of its branches, although other Chinese enterprises that do not have the same stature and international reputation as the BOC might have greater leeway to act otherwise.

In the last few years the BOC has significantly expanded its own international banking activities and the services that it offers to Chinese-foreign joint ventures and domestic entities involved in export trade. The most significant of these activities for foreign banks and companies are discussed below.

a. Participation in Syndicated Loans   The BOC participates, principally through its London branch, in Eurocurrency syndicated loans. Motivated by a desire to gain experience in international syndications and to take advantage of high interest rates in 1981 and 1982, as well as the necessity to recycle some of its increasing reserves, the BOC participated in at least fifteen Eurocurrency syndicated loans in 1982 alone.[33] Borrowers for these loans range from the Danish Export-Import Bank and the Ente Nationale Idrocaburi (the Italian national oil company), to the Veneer Hotel, a Singapore enterprise.[34]

The BOC has also been participating in syndicated loans for projects in China. In early 1983, the BOC agreed to participate in an international syndicate for a US$10,000,000 loan to the Xian Golden Flower Hotel Company, a Chinese-foreign joint co-operative enterprise.[35] By mid-1983, the BOC had gained sufficient experience to arrange as lead managers with its affiliate, CCIC Finance Ltd., a HK$700 million syndicated loan to Garden Hotel Holidays Ltd. to finance a hotel and office complex in Guangzhou.[36]

b. Loans to Foreign Companies for Projects in China   The BOC has also announced that it will provide loans to foreign companies involved in projects in China provided that the foreign company has a registered office in China and certain guarantees are obtained.[37] According to the BOC, from 1980 to the beginning of 1983 it made loans totalling US$50 million and RMB60 million to 54 Chinese-foreign joint ventures.[38] It is unclear what portion of these loans were made to the joint venture itself or to the Chinese partner as part of its equity contribution.

Both foreign companies and joint ventures operating in China may find it cheaper to borrow from the BOC than from foreign banks since the BOC, unlike foreign banks, is not subject to the withholding tax on China-source interest income. This does not mean, however, that the other terms of loan agreements that joint ventures sign with the BOC will be equally advantageous. Under current regulations, a joint venture must provide the BOC with a pledge of collateral security or a guarantee from a guarantor acceptable to the BOC.[39] The BOC has recently begun to consider accepting contractual mortgages over certain types of assets. But until Chinese laws and regulations relating to mortgages or other security arrangements are adopted, a parent company or bank guarantee generally would have to be provided, and this requirement lessens the appeal of a BOC loan. In addition, the regulations provide interest penalty payments ranging from 20 per cent to 50 per cent of the original interest rate, which are far in excess of the standard range of default interest rates set by foreign banks.

c. *Foreign Exchange and* Renminbi *Loans to Chinese and Other Entities* Of much greater magnitude are the foreign exchange and *renminbi* loans that the BOC provides to domestic entities engaged in foreign trade, communications, transportation, and energy development, and to small and medium-sized enterprises (particularly those manufacturing export products). From 1979 to June 1982, the BOC is reported to have approved foreign exchange loans totalling US$13.266 billion to domestic entities, of which US$10.256 billion was drawn down;[40] it is also reported that the BOC issued US$630 million of foreign exchange loans to Chinese small and medium-sized enterprises from January to November 1983. These included a US$2.94 billion loan to the Ministry of Communications to finance several hundred new ocean-going ships, a US$500 million loan to improve harbours, a loan to the Civil Aviation Administration of China to buy Boeing 747 aircraft, a US$2 billion low-interest buyer's credit for oil and coal production, and US$1.547 billion in loans to small and medium-sized enterprises.[41] The BOC's foreign exchange loans are made in US dollars, Japanese yen, Hong Kong dollars, British pounds, and French francs; in addition, the BOC drew up in 1984 Instructions on Foreign Exchange Loans, defining the categories of its foreign exchange loans available to borrowers, the application procedures, and the use of such loans.[42]

The BOC has also started to finance projects in China jointly with foreign banks. For example, the BOC, Shanghai branch, has jointly financed with Deutsche Bank AG the setting up of the Shanghai Shipyard Container Factory.[43]

The BOC's foreign exchange loans are sometimes used by Chinese borrowers to pay the down payment on imported plant and equipment, the remainder of the cost of which is financed by export credits provided by foreign banks. For example, this pattern was followed in a US$50 million note-purchase facility provided by a syndicate of foreign banks to the Yan Shan Petrochemical General Corporation and guaranteed by the Beijing Economic Development Corporation. It is worth noting that officials from the BOC's Beijing branch assisted the borrower in the negotiations with the foreign banks, a service the BOC is providing to an increasing number of Chinese borrowers. The BOC's participation in loan negotiations can be extremely helpful, particularly for obtaining the necessary government and foreign exchange approvals for the transaction.

d. *Direct Investment in Chinese Entities and Chinese-foreign Joint Ventures*   The BOC has also been making direct investments in projects in China. For example, the BOC has made two direct investments in the Shanghai Offshore Petroleum Engineering Corporation. The BOC, Shanghai branch, has also invested in the Shanghai-Pilkington Glass Co.,

Ltd. and the Shanghai Offshore Oil Engineering Joint Corporation, as well as other Chinese-foreign joint ventures. The BOC's general practice reportedly is to purchase a 10–25 per cent share in such joint ventures.[44]

e. International Trust and Consultancy Services   In 1980 the BOC began providing international trust and consultancy services, activities already engaged in by many other Chinese entities. The BOC's trust operations, which have little relation to the traditional trust services provided by foreign banks except for the receiving of inheritances from overseas Chinese, are primarily directed at raising and utilizing foreign capital for China's modernization programme in line with the state plan. By the end of 1981, the BOC and its branches had established 38 trust departments and companies involved in joint ventures, international leasing, transfers of surplus foreign exchange among Chinese units, compensation trade, processing and assembling arrangements, acting as business or purchase and sales agents, and supplying information on the credit standing of foreign companies.[45] In addition, by the beginning of 1984, the BOC had signed agreements on co-operation in trust and consultancy business with 42 foreign banks and companies. Generally, these are no more than short, one- to two-page agreements providing for co-operation between the parties and the cross-referral of clients. More recently the BOC has established the Bank of China Trust and Consultancy Company, which is a socialist state enterprise and an affiliate of the BOC, with a registered capital of RMB600 million.[46]

f. Activities in Hong Kong   Of the BOC's overseas operations, those in Hong Kong are by far the most extensive. In addition to its own branches in Hong Kong, the BOC controls twelve affiliated banks, known as 'sister' banks. In all, the BOC and its sister banks operate some 252 branches in Hong Kong.[47] Eight of these banks—Bank of Communications; Kwantung Provincial Bank Ltd.; Sin Hua Trust, Savings and Commercial Bank, Ltd.; Kincheng Banking Corporation; China and South Sea Bank Ltd.; China State Bank Ltd.; National Commercial Bank Ltd.; and Yien Yieh Commercial Bank Ltd.—are incorporated and have their head offices in China. The other four—Nanyang Commercial Bank; Hua Chiao Commercial Bank Ltd.; Chiyu Banking Corporation Ltd.; and Po Sang Bank Ltd.—are incorporated in Hong Kong. The Nanyang Commercial Bank has branches in the Shenzhen special economic zone and in San Francisco.[48] The Kwantung Provincial Bank Ltd. has a branch in Singapore. A thirteenth sister bank, Banco Nam Tung, is incorporated and operates in Macau.[49]

The BOC and its twelve sister banks in Hong Kong provide a full range of banking services, including their traditional trade-financing business, and are estimated to control about 20 per cent of the total bank deposits in Hong Kong.[50] In contrast to China's cautious approach in other international markets, the BOC and its sister banks aggressively expanded their loan portfolios between 1979 and 1981, with considerable exposure in Hong Kong's speculative property market. It is estimated that 40 per cent of the affiliated banks' HK$43 billion in loans at the end of 1981 had been granted to real estate developers.[51]

In the wake of the major downturn in Hong Kong's property market in 1982, the BOC and its affiliates apparently suffered serious losses, as did many foreign banks heavily involved in Hong Kong property loans. It seems that because of poor co-ordination between the BOC and its affiliates, the Chinese-controlled banks sometimes took a major share of a single syndicated loan to a property developer.

In the latter part of 1982, much more restrictive lending practices were adopted. Participation in any major loan or syndication by one of the sister banks must be approved by the group's business committee, which is composed of senior officials of the BOC and the chairmen of the twelve sister banks. Under the new policies, loans to local Hong Kong property developers and loans secured only by personal guarantees will be extremely difficult, if not impossible, to obtain.[52]

Aside from its sister banks, the BOC has two major affiliates which were established in Hong Kong in 1980. The first is CCIC Finance Ltd., a merchant bank formed by the BOC with the First National Bank of Chicago, the Industrial Bank of Japan, Ltd., and China Resources (Holdings) Co. Ltd., which has been China's major import-export agent in Hong Kong. The three banks each hold a 30 per cent interest and China Resources 10 per cent. In addition to developing its activities as a merchant bank, CCIC Finance Ltd. has concentrated on financing projects in accordance with China's economic policies in energy, communications, and light industry, and serving as a bridge for trade and finance between China and the United States and Japan.[53] Of particular note is the role of CCIC Finance Ltd. as financial consultant to both the China National Offshore Oil Corporation (CNOOC), which has overall responsibility for developing China's offshore petroleum resources, and China-Nanhai Oil Joint Services Corporation, a joint venture between the CNOOC and Guangdong province which has the responsibility for providing certain services for the exploration and development of petroleum resources in the South China Sea. CCIC Finance Ltd. has also reached agreements with more than 100 foreign banks for credit lines of several hundred million US dollars to be used for development financing in China, Hong Kong, and the Asia-Pacific region.[54]

Aside from CCIC Finance Ltd., the BOC has a 10 per cent interest in Kincheng-Tokyo Finance Company, a Hong Kong-incorporated finance company and merchant bank that was set up with Kincheng Banking Corporation (one of the sister banks) and the Bank of Tokyo. Kincheng-Tokyo Finance Company provides trade financing, investment advice, and assistance to joint ventures in China.[55]

ii. The Investment Bank of China

The Investment Bank of China (hereafter referred to as the Investment Bank) was established in December 1981 as a specialized bank for borrowing funds from international financial institutions, such as the World Bank, to lend to small and medium-sized Chinese enterprises, and to finance Chinese-foreign joint ventures.[56] As of early 1985, the Investment Bank had two loans from the World Bank totalling US$245 million, and had committed US$132 million to the financing of 96 technical upgrading projects.[57] The Investment Bank's funds have been limited to use in the renovation and transformation of existing small and medium-sized enterprises. It is significant that Investment Bank loans will be granted only after the approval of feasibility studies and that the Investment Bank will monitor the financed projects.

iii. The State General Administration of Exchange Control

The State General Administration of Exchange Control (hereafter referred to as the SGAEC) was established in early 1979 and is the administrative organ of China in charge of foreign exchange control. No financial institution other than the BOC may engage in foreign exchange business without the approval of the SGAEC.[58]

In theory the SGAEC reports directly to the State Council, but it is subordinate to the PBOC with respect to exchange-rate policy guidance and seems to function as an adjunct to the BOC. Indeed, the staff of the SGAEC are largely seconded from the BOC's foreign exchange departments and both the head office and branch offices of the SGAEC are housed in BOC offices.

The head office of the SGAEC has three departments. The first undertakes the planning of China's foreign exchange policies, the second drafts and implements China's exchange control regulations, and the third works with the BOC and the PBOC in setting China's foreign exchange rates.[59] The regulatory functions of the SGAEC are discussed below.

iv. The China International Trust and Investment Corporation and Other Special Organizations

The China International Trust and Investment Corporation (hereafter referred to as the CITIC) is a state-owned socialist enterprise established in 1979 under the direct leadership of the State Council.[60] Its Chairman is Rong Yiren, a Shanghainese who is perhaps China's best known former capitalist. In general, the CITIC functions both as a consulting firm and as a merchant bank, and its business operations have recently come under the control and supervision of the PBOC.[61]

According to its statutes, the CITIC is permitted to engage in the following activities: (a) to assist foreign companies and individuals, as well as Chinese entities, to negotiate and enter into joint venture and technological co-operation agreements and related contracts in China; (b) to accept funds from foreign companies and individuals and to raise funds abroad by issuing debentures or bonds for investment in China; (c) to provide consulting services to both foreign and Chinese entities on legal matters, taxation, foreign exchange control, labour wages, accounting, and auditing; (d) to act as the agent of foreign companies in business activities relating to advanced technology and equipment; and (e) to engage in joint ventures and to invest in projects inside and outside China.[62]

By the end of 1981, the CITIC had signed agreements with some forty foreign banks for credit facilities amounting to approximately US$1 billion. The CITIC has formed equity joint ventures with domestic entities such as the Yizhen Chemical Fibre Corporation, Ltd. and the China

Leasing Company Ltd. and, along with other Chinese entities, has established Chinese-foreign joint ventures such as the China Orient Leasing Company Ltd. with the Japanese Orient Leasing Company SA, and the Guang-Mei Foods Company Ltd. with Beatrice Foods. The CITIC has also invested some US$300 million in projects involving the production of chemical fibres, linen textiles, phosphate fertilizer, castings, and gelatine, as well as in non-ferrous-metal mines and shipping companies. In January 1982 the CITIC became the first Chinese entity to issue bonds abroad through a 10 billion yen private placement in Japan, and is considering tapping the Eurobond market.[63]

In early 1983 CITIC investment missions were sent to foreign countries to investigate equity investments in foreign companies operating in the resources field. The areas that reportedly most interest the Chinese include fertilizers, iron ore mines, and the aluminium and fisheries industries.[64]

Even more ambitiously, the CITIC launched itself as an international bank when it agreed in early 1986 to take over the Ka Wah Bank of Hong Kong. Primarily as a result of problem loans in Malaysia and Singapore, the Ka Wah Bank had suffered losses of over HK$500 million in 1985, an amount which exceeded its combined issued share capital and reserves. In the face of bankruptcy and liquidation for the bank, the CITIC stepped in with a cash injection of HK$350 million, and, under a complex capital reconstruction and write-down plan, took control of over 91 per cent of the troubled institution. Existing ordinary shares were written down to one-twentieth of their nominal value and consolidated into 18.2 million new ordinary shares, and then 200 million new ordinary shares and 150 million preference shares, convertible into additional ordinary shares, were issued in favour of the CITIC. The preference shares enable the CITIC to increase its ownership interest in the bank to over 95 per cent. The CITIC contributed the additional capital and guaranteed the collectibility of the loan portfolios of both the bank and its affiliate, Ka Wah International Merchant Finance Ltd., but in so doing took over an operating bank with trained personnel and a deposit base in Malaysia, Hong Kong, and Singapore.[65] It has been reported that, under the CITIC's control, the bank's two branches in New York and Los Angeles will be strengthened, in line with a change in focus for its investments and retail and wholesale business to the United States and Hong Kong, while operations in Singapore and Malaysia, major business areas for the bank in the past, will be reduced.[66]

The CITIC has the flexibility to offer a potential tax advantage to foreign lenders that many other Chinese borrowers are unable to provide. China's tax laws generally impose a 10–20 per cent withholding tax on interest earned by foreign enterprises that do not have an 'establishment' in China.[67] But the laws exempt from such withholding tax the interest income earned by foreign banks from loans to China's state banks and to trust and investment companies approved by the State Council to engage in foreign exchange business, where such loans carry an interest rate equal to the interbank offered rate.[68] The CITIC is one of the trust and investment companies approved by the State Council to engage in foreign exchange business within the scope permitted by the SGAEC.[69] To circumvent the withholding tax for loans destined for other Chinese borrowers, several foreign banks have enquired whether the CITIC would act as an on-lending vehicle. It appears, however, that the CITIC will only serve in this function in projects in which the CITIC itself will take an equity participation.

Regional trust and investment corporations have also been established to engage in many of the same activities as the CITIC. The most active of these corporations include the Beijing International Trust and Investment Corporation, the Shanghai Investment and Trust Corporation, the Tianjin International Trust and Investment Corporation, and the Guangdong International Trust and Investment Corporation.

C. China's Participation in International Financial Organizations

China's participation in international financial organizations revived in October 1979 when it borrowed US$15 million from the United Nations Development Programme. In mid-January 1980 China joined the United Nations International Fund for Agricultural Development.

By far the most significant development in this area came when China joined the International Monetary Fund (IMF) and the World Bank on 17 April and 15 May 1980, respectively. An extra seat on the IMF's executive board was created so that China could be represented without diminishing the number of seats of any other country.

China was also given a seat on the World Bank's Executive Board which was increased from 20 to 21 members to accommodate China. China and the World Bank have signed the following loan agreements providing for loans both from the World Bank's hard-loan source, the International Bank for Reconstruction and Development (IBRD), and from the World Bank's soft-loan source, the International Development Association (IDA): (a) US$200 million for instruments, computer equipment, and training at 26 key Chinese universities, consisting of a US$100 million hard loan and a US$100 million soft loan; (b) US$60 million for the control of waterlogging and soil salinity in three provinces in the North China plain, consisting entirely of a soft loan; (c) US$124 million for the expansion of three Chinese ports at Shanghai, Tianjin, and Huangpu; (d) US$75.4 million for agricultural education and research, consisting entirely of a soft loan; (e) US$80 million for building a land reclamation and grain production centre in the northernmost province of Heilongjiang, consisting of a US$45 million soft loan and a US$35 million hard loan; and (f) US$70 million for the Investment Bank, consisting of a US$40 million hard loan and a US$30 million soft loan.[70] Soft loans from the IDA generally carry only a 0.75 per cent annual service fee with a term of fifty years, while hard loans from the IBRD generally are for twenty years at market rates.

China also joined the Asian Development Bank (ADB) as its forty-seventh member in February 1986. In one stroke, it became the third largest subscriber in the ADB, behind only Japan and the United States, by taking 114,000 shares of stock, valued at US$1.3 billion.[71]

II. The Activities of Foreign Banks in China

A. The Registration of and Restrictions on Representative Offices

Until 1 February 1983 foreign banks were subject to the same general registration regulations as other foreign enterprises. On that date, however, the PBOC issued the Provisional Regulations for the Establishment of Representative Offices in China by Overseas Chinese and Foreign Financial Institutions (hereafter cited as the Registration Regulations).[72] As before, the application procedures for establishing a bank representative office under the Registration Regulations are simple. The applicant bank first fills out a short application form, which is obtainable from the PBOC and must be signed by the applicant's chairman or chief executive, and attaches copies of the following documents: the bank's charter or business licence; articles of association; by-laws; latest balance sheet and profit and loss statement; a list of the bank's directors; a power of attorney given to the chief representative that must be signed by the chairman or chief executive; and the curricula vitae of the chief representative and other representatives of the bank. The application is then submitted for approval directly to the PBOC or through a relevant financial institution, which for foreign banks is the BOC. Generally, approval will only be granted upon the favourable recommendation of the BOC.

After obtaining the approval certificate of the PBOC, the applicant bank goes through routine registration procedures with the local administrative bureau for industry and commerce and obtains a registration certificate. If there are no problems, the entire process can be completed in as little as two months, although some banks have waited considerably longer.

The Registration Regulations permit the establishment of representative offices in Beijing and/or any of China's special economic zones (SEZs), and subordinate representative offices in other designated cities like Shanghai and Guangzhou. Before a foreign bank may establish a subordinate representative office, however, it must first establish a representative office in Beijing.[73]

In assessing whether it will recommend approval for an application to establish a representative office in Beijing, the BOC apparently applies three criteria. The first, which rarely presents a problem, is whether the applicant bank's home country grants reciprocal rights to Chinese banks. The second reflects a desire to maintain a rough geographical balance in the numbers of banks from various countries. Although the optimum number of banks from any one country depends on the volume of its bilateral trade with China and the importance China attaches to their economic relations, it is clearly easier to obtain approval as the first bank from a particular country than as the fifth. The last criterion involves political considerations concerning the current state of relations between China and the applicant's home country.[74]

Article 8 of the Registration Regulations restricts representative offices to carrying out 'non-profit activities such as... business negotiations, acting as liaison, providing consultancy and other services'. Representative offices 'shall not engage in any direct profit-making activities'.[75] Furthermore, representative offices in an SEZ are limited to engaging in such non-profit activities within the confines of the SEZ.

The extent of the restrictions of Article 8 of the Registration Regulations has also been called into question by another set of regulations promulgated after the Registration Regulations but which came into force on 1 January 1983. Article 4 of the Provisional Regulations of the Ministry of Finance of the People's Republic of China Regarding the Reduction and Exemption of Income Tax Relating to Interest Earned by Foreign Businesses from China (hereafter cited as the Interest Income Tax Regulations) is intended to give foreign banks with representative offices in China preferential treatment with respect to China's withholding tax on interest income.[76] Under China's tax laws a foreign enterprise with an 'establishment' in China is subject to tax on net income at progressive rates from 20 per cent to 40 per cent of net taxable income and a local income tax equal to 10 per cent of the same taxable income.[77] A foreign enterprise without an establishment is generally subject to a 20 per cent withholding tax on the gross amount of passive income such as interest, although interest income earned with respect to loan agreements signed between 1983 and 1990 is subject to a reduced rate of 10 per cent.[78] One foreign banker has also reported that complete exemptions from the tax are available in special cases involving key development projects, such as energy-related projects or projects involving improvement of infrastructure and the transfer of technology. In addition, partial exemption can be effected through specially approved arrangements to apply the tax only to the margin collected by a lender over international interbank lending rates.[79]

Prior to the promulgation of the Interest Income Tax Regulations, local tax officials informed foreign bank representative offices that they would not be liable for any income tax because such representative offices engage only in liaison activities and earn no income. Under the Interest Income Tax Regulations, however, bank representative offices do constitute establishments and will be deemed to receive as taxable income 15 per cent of the amount of interest income earned in connection with the loan agreements that such offices sign with Chinese borrowers.[80] This appears to give banks with representative offices a definite tax advantage. For example, a bank making a loan of US$10,000,000 at an interest rate of 10 per cent will be liable for US$100,000 in withholding tax if the agreement is not signed by a representative office in China. But profit tax on the same loan concluded by a representative office in Beijing would amount to approximately US$46,500.[81] Moreover, if a representative office in the Shenzhen SEZ were to sign the same loan agreement it would only be subject to a profit tax of US$22,500, because of the lower rate of taxation in the SEZs. The crucial question, however, is whether the prohibition of Article 8 of the Registration Regulations against representative offices engaging in any direct profit-making business activities will preclude foreign banks from taking advantage of this favourable tax treatment on a regular basis. It has been thought that foreign banks' representative offices in China may sign loan agreements with Chinese enterprises if authorized to do so by their head offices.[82]

Assuming that representative offices are permitted to sign loan agreements, further questions arise regarding the breadth of Article 4 of the Interest Income Tax Regulations. For example, may a representative office sign a loan agreement on behalf of a syndicate, whose members do not all have representative offices in China, and be permitted to pass on the tax advantage to each syndicate member? Discussions with Chinese officials indicate that this is generally not permissible. The tax advantage apparently is intended only to benefit banks that have established representative offices in China.

B. Foreign Bank Branches

At the end of 1984, the scope of permissible activities of the four long-standing foreign bank branches in Shanghai was expanded to include the lending of foreign currency at unrestricted interest rates and the acceptance of deposits in foreign currency with interest payable at BOC rates. This liberalization was the precursor to the promulgation on 2 April 1985 of new Regulations Governing Foreign Banks and Joint Chinese-Foreign Banks in Special Economic Zones of the People's Republic of China (hereafter cited as the Foreign Bank Regulations),[83] which allow foreign banks to open new branches and to conduct basic retail banking business in the four SEZs.

The Foreign Bank Regulations permit Chinese-foreign joint venture banks to establish branches, and foreign banks to have their head offices or branches in the SEZs. Banking activities opened up, subject to the specific approval of the PBOC, include: (a) the granting of loans, in both local and foreign currencies; (b) the acceptance of remittances from foreign countries and the collection of foreign exchange; (c) the settlement of export and import transactions and outward and inward documentary bills; (d) the making of local and foreign currency investments and the issuance of foreign currency guarantees; (e) the buying and selling of stocks and securities; (f) the provision of trust, safe deposit box, credit investigation, and consultancy services; (g) the acceptance of foreign currency deposits by foreign enterprises and individuals; and (h) the handling of foreign currency deposits and loans in foreign countries.[84]

The requirements set forth in the Foreign Bank Regulations dilute somewhat their overall liberalizing effect. Other important commercial banking activities are not dealt with explicitly, leaving it unclear whether foreign banks may now engage in such activities or whether such activities remain prohibited. For example, stiff capitalization requirements will still effectively bar some foreign banks from entry—Chinese-foreign joint venture banks must have registered capital, in foreign exchange, of at least the equivalent of RMB80 million, and branches of foreign banks must have operating funds allocated from their head offices, again in foreign exchange, of at least the equivalent of RMB40 million.[85] Interest rates charged or offered by foreign or Chinese-foreign joint venture banks in respect of local or foreign currency deposits, loans, overdrafts, and bill discounts are controlled by the relevant local unit of the PBOC, with the resultant dampening effect on marketing and other competition.[86] The reserves required to be kept with the PBOC, interest free, against deposits in foreign bank branches in China are reported to be between 5 and 10 per cent of deposits.[87] By their silence, the Foreign Bank Regulations limit foreign bank branches to dealings with other foreign companies and joint ventures, leaving Chinese-controlled firms, which form the majority in even the SEZs, out of the picture, and thus frustrating still more foreign bankers.[88] In practice, foreign bank branches have been permitted to accept deposits only from foreigners and overseas Chinese, and *renminbi* deposits only when they have been acting as an agent of the Industrial and Commercial Bank. On the financing side, foreign bank branches may open letters of credit without restriction only for Chinese-foreign joint ventures and foreign companies. Chinese companies, including the major foreign trade corporations, have been required to obtain special approvals in order to open letters of credit through such branches.[89]

By late 1985, nine different banks had established branches in the SEZs, and additional branches are expected, especially in the Shenzhen SEZ. It is also said that the PBOC is considering allowing foreign bank branches to be established in other major cities. However, it would appear more likely that the current experiment in the SEZs will undergo substantial scrutiny before the scope of the new policy is broadened.

C. Banking Business with China

From 1978 to 1981 foreign banks concentrated their marketing efforts on extending loans to China. Such loans generally carried an interest rate of one-half of 1 per cent over the London interbank offered rate for periods of three or six months, although spreads of as low as three-eighths of 1 per cent were offered for short-term credits. Front-end fees were rarely obtained. In the period 1978–81, roughly US$10 billion in commercial credits was offered to China, but only about US$3 billion was actually drawn down.[90] In 1985, foreign borrowings were US$3.53 billion, with US$2.43 billion drawn down.[91]

A combination of conservative borrowing policies and high interest rates was in part responsible for the relatively small amounts utilized. Another significant impediment to the utilization of any type of foreign credit is that Chinese borrowers generally must not only demonstrate that the proposed project will produce sufficient foreign exchange to repay foreign debts but also justify the use of scarce domestic funds, materials, and facilities. China has a strong preference for low-interest or no-interest loans from foreign governments and international financial organizations and for subsidized government export credits.[92] Even with respect to loans at preferential interest rates, China has adhered to a conservative approach and has permitted availability periods to expire rather than borrow for hastily conceived projects.

In 1982 China literally stopped borrowing private commercial credits. Indeed, flush with the then growing trade surplus, China took the opportunity to prepay much of its existing commercial debt—to the disappointment of many foreign bankers. For example, in early 1982 the BOC prepaid after two years the entire sum—US$150 million—it had drawn down from the US$300 million syndicated loan led by the Union des Banques Arabes et Françaises.[93] The BOC has also refinanced at lower interest rates and for longer terms loans from foreign banks to other Chinese borrowers. This was the case for a US$35.2 million loan to the China International Travel Service, Nanjing branch, for the construction of the Jinling Hotel in Nanjing, that was arranged in 1980 by Wardley Ltd., a unit of The Hongkong and Shanghai Banking Corporation.[94]

The curtailment of lending to China in 1982 resulted also from the imposition of China's withholding tax on interest, which became effective on 1 January 1982. As a result, a significant portion of the loans made in 1982 were redirected to Hong Kong companies controlled by Chinese entities and to their Hong Kong branches.

More recently, it has been reported that China does plan substantial borrowings for the short-, middle-, and long-range requirements of the Seventh Five-Year Plan (1986–90), with estimates of the country's total level of borrowing during this five-year period running as high as US$40 billion.[95] Such borrowing is, however, expected to remain tightly controlled by the PBOC, and will still be significantly lower than the amount China will need for all of its planned or anticipated projects in the period.[96]

In the future, commercial banks are likely to concentrate their China-related lending efforts on participating in the provision of export credit facilities, the project financing of oil, gas, coal, phosphorus, non-ferrous metals, and certain rare metals, and in financing foreign parties and joint ventures in hotel and other projects.

As foreign banks have come to accept that the opportunities for direct lending to domestic Chinese borrowers are limited, they have gone back to promoting trade financing, traditionally the major source of their China profits. Typically, foreign banks open letters of credit for their customers to purchase Chinese imports and advise letters of credit for sales to China. Chinese practices in trade financing are discussed in detail below.

Foreign banks have also focused greater attention recently on equipment leasing, both direct to Chinese lessees and in conjunction with Chinese organizations such as the CITIC. Although virtually unknown in China prior to the 1980s, leasing arrangements made possible the importation of over US$500 million worth of equipment in 1984 alone. The surge in leasing has given foreign banks, some of which have gone so far as to form joint ventures with Chinese leasing companies, their first real opportunity to finance trade from within China,[97] and the leasing company vehicle has given some foreign banks a means to establish themselves in parts of China where branches are not yet permitted.[98]

III. Chinese Trade-financing Practices

China utilizes a variety of methods to settle foreign trade transactions, including barter trade, counter-purchase, compensation trade, cash settlement, buyer and supplier credits, private commercial credits, and official government credits. This section focuses on Chinese practices with respect to two methods not discussed elsewhere in this volume, namely letters of credit and government-subsidized export credits.

A. Letter-of-credit Financing of Exports and Imports

Traditionally, China's trade with foreign countries has been in the form of cash transactions paid through letters of credit. China is not a member of the International Chamber of Commerce (of which Taiwan is a member) and thus does not officially adhere to that body's Uniform Customs and Practice for Documentary Credits. Although the BOC and other Chinese entities generally follow these rules, in some instances they do not, and special Chinese practices have developed over the years to which foreign companies and banks should pay particular attention.[99]

i. The Export of Chinese Goods to Foreign Buyers
The general procedure for letters of credit used in connection with Chinese exports usually follows the sequence described below.

(a) The Chinese seller and the foreign buyer agree to the terms of the underlying contract, which generally provides for payment by an irrevocable and transferable letter of credit opened by the foreign buyer's bank and payable through sight drafts upon the presentation of documents. The letter of credit is usually opened soon after the contract is signed (particularly if the contract involves the manufacture of new products), since the Chinese party generally will not start production until the letter of credit is opened. Such a letter of credit remains valid for at least ten days following the shipment date. Generally, the opening bank must be a correspondent of the BOC; if it is not, the letter of credit must be advised through a correspondent bank, adding to the cost of the transaction.

(b) After the foreign buyer's bank opens the letter of credit, it instructs the advising bank located in China and specifies the documents to be presented. The advising bank is usually a domestic BOC branch, although in Shanghai the four foreign bank branches also perform this function. The BOC regulations require, however, that each foreign bank branch report, and supply a copy of, all incoming documentary credits and amendments thereto to the BOC, Shanghai branch. It is of crucial importance for the foreign buyer to understand that all charges incurred in China, including reimbursement and interest charges, are for the opener's account. A letter of credit that does not conform to this condition will be rejected by the advising bank.

Another problem that occasionally arises is determining whether a letter of credit has arrived at the BOC branch and whether it has been accepted by the Chinese seller. The BOC reportedly can be quite slow in responding to enquiries.

(c) Upon receipt of advice from the BOC, the Chinese seller will obtain the documents required under the letter of credit. Over the years Chinese suppliers have developed the types of documents generally acceptable in international commerce and in certain cases will even obtain special documents required by the opener (for example, documents in Spanish rather than English), although this will take more time. The following points, however, should be noted.

(i) Documents certified by a Chamber of Commerce or a consular office are generally unavailable.

(ii) Documents requiring notarization or other forms of legalization are difficult to obtain, although documents may be certified by the China Council for the Promotion of International Trade.

(iii) Unless the documentary credit specifically stipulates otherwise, the BOC and foreign bank branches are required to accept documents stamped with a Chinese seal rather than signed by hand, and to accept combined documents (for example, a combined invoice and certificate of origin). Separate documents, however, are generally obtainable.

It should also be noted that China almost always prefers to sell goods CIF. Specific restrictions in the letter of credit as to carrying vessels are generally not permitted (such as 'shipment should be made by a Conference Line vessel'), but general restrictions may be included (such as 'carrying vessel should not be more than 15 years old'). A typical insurance clause calls for an insurance policy covering the Ocean Marine Cargo Clauses All Risks (including Warehouse to Warehouse Clauses) and the War Risks Clauses (1/1/1976) of the People's Insurance Company of China. Supplementary risks such as strikes, riots and civil commotion, and rejection may also be covered.

(d) After obtaining all the necessary documents the Chinese seller will present them to the BOC branch or foreign bank branch. If the advising bank finds that the documents conform to the letter of credit, it will seek to effect payment from the issuing bank. In recent years most of the underlying sales contracts with Chinese entities have provided for payment in foreign exchange, a development that eliminates exchange risks for foreign buyers. The primary problem in effecting payment is one of timing. If the letter of credit is opened in Hong Kong, the BOC will grant a six-day 'grace' period after the negotiation of the sight drafts by the domestic BOC branch or the foreign branch for payment to be received from the issuing bank. The grace period is extended to twelve days if the letter of credit was issued outside Hong Kong. After this grace period interest will be charged to the issuing bank and hence to the foreign supplier.

Unless the underlying contract calls for telegraphic transfer (TT) reimbursement to the advising bank from the issuing bank, the BOC generally airmails the documents to the issuing bank and this can delay payment beyond the applicable grace period. Any delay in the payment will result in an interest charge to the foreign buyer who may have thought that he had already arranged for payment on time and in full to the Chinese seller.

ii. The Import of Foreign Goods by Chinese Buyers

The following procedures generally apply to letters of credit used in the importing of foreign goods.

(a) The underlying contracts always require that the BOC open all letters of credit. The BOC head office in Beijing usually issues such letters of credit although some domestic BOC branches will do so, particularly if the buyer is a local entity. Standard procedure calls for the BOC to issue an irrevocable letter of credit upon notification by the foreign seller that the shipment is ready. Such letters of credit almost always require that sight drafts be drawn on, and documents be presented to, a specified domestic BOC branch. In the past only foreign sellers with considerable bargaining power, such as grain suppliers, have been able to arrange for presentation of documents and payment outside China.

All charges incurred in China with respect to the letter of credit are always for the account of the beneficiary.

(b) After the letter of credit is opened, the foreign seller's bank, if it is a BOC correspondent bank, will advise the letter of credit. If it is not, a bank that is a correspondent will have to advise the letter of credit. BOC letters of credit, however, are not confirmed by foreign banks since the BOC considers that, given its position as a state-owned bank, a request for confirmation would be an affront. This poses a major problem for foreign suppliers since all negotiations will have to be with the BOC in China.

(c) China prefers to buy goods FOB so that Chinese shipping companies will transport the goods. To ensure this, BOC letters of credit generally require FOB shipments to have a 'certificate issued by the shipping agents that the vessel is chartered or booked by the China National Foreign Trade Transportation Corporation, Beijing or China National Chartering Corporation, Beijing (Charter-party Bills of Lading are acceptable)'. In the rare cases where foreign goods are sold CIF or C & F, BOC letters of credit contain as documentary requirements the 'Shipping Company's scheduled itinerary showing that the carrying vessel, prior to its arrival at destination, will not touch any port(s) of the Taiwan Area' and/or the letter of the foreign seller 'attesting that the nationality of the carrying vessel has been approved by the buyers'.

(d) Inherent risks for the foreign supplier arise after the foreign seller provides the documents to his bank for presentation to the BOC in China. Until the documents are negotiated, the foreign seller has neither possession of the goods or the documents nor payment. Several difficulties can be encountered. First, it is sometimes a problem to determine whether the documents have arrived at the BOC. Foreign bankers based in China can spend a considerable proportion of their time checking on the status of letters of credit. Before one foreign bank established a representative office in China, it even resorted to an interim arrangement with a foreign trading company based in Beijing to deliver documents to the BOC and to follow through until the BOC issued its payment instructions. Second, even after the BOC acknowledges receipt of the documents it will normally permit Chinese buyers to review the documents for compliance if they so request. This can frequently result in a one- or two-day delay and there have been reports that the BOC has in certain cases delayed payment until the goods have arrived and the Chinese buyer has inspected them to ensure that the underlying contract has been fulfilled. Finally, even after the documents have been found to be in order, payment instructions are usually sent by airmail, unless the underlying contract stipulates that the foreign seller's bank is entitled to receive TT reimbursement. Until it receives payment, the foreign supplier will in effect be extending interest-free credit to the Chinese buyer and, if there is any substantial delay, the loss of interest can wipe out slender profit margins.

At present there is no indication that the BOC will dramatically reform its letter-of-credit practices. The BOC is, of course, aware of these problems and in 1980 announced that it was considering measures to improve efficiency in examining letters of credit.[100]

B. Export Credit Financing

Broadly speaking, an export credit is extended to China whenever a Chinese buyer of foreign goods or services is allowed to defer payment for a period of time. There are two types of export credit. Under a supplier credit arrangement the exporter extends credit to the overseas buyer and is itself usually financed by its bank, whereas under a buyer credit a bank in the exporter's country provides financing direct to the overseas buyer, with the exporter receiving payment from the financing bank. Subsidized export credits arise when a government export credit agency in the exporter's country participates in the financing through an insurance programme and/or through a direct extension of credit so that preferential interest rates and the long-term repayment of principal can be extended to the overseas buyer.

Both supplier and buyer credits with and without the participation of a foreign government export credit agency have been offered to China. It can be expected, however, that China will primarily utilize subsidized buyer credits. In general, a buyer credit is considered a more appropriate mechanism for larger and more complex contracts of sale that require commissioning and other post-shipment responsibilities, whereas a supplier credit is considered more appropriate to finance contracts that involve little more than a straight supply of goods or equipment. Chinese buyers prefer the lower interest rates offered by subsidized export credits, a very large amount of which has not yet been utilized. To date many foreign governments, including those of France, Great Britain, Italy, Japan, Belgium, West Germany, Canada, Argentina, and the United States, have negotiated agreements with China which provide for a wide range of direct credits and subsidized commercial bank credits designed to stimulate Chinese purchases of foreign goods. The majority of credit lines negotiated thus far are tied to long-term government-to-government bilateral trade agreements. China is, however, under no obligation to draw down these lines of credit.

These government export credit programmes work in much the same manner with respect to China as they do in connection with other countries. The major difference, however, is the active participation of the BOC in all phases, from the approval of the export credit, to the drawdown of funds, to repayment. Government-subsidized buyer credits generally require complicated documentation. In China any single document tends to be simpler and shorter than those used in other countries, but because of the BOC's involvement the number of documents tends to be greater.

The overall framework for the utilization of government export buyer credits is set forth in credit agreements with the BOC, which acts as a conduit for on-lending to the ultimate borrower (either a Chinese entity or, in some cases, a Chinese-foreign joint venture or a co-operative enterprise). In contrast to the practice in other countries, such credit agreements are not concluded directly with Chinese borrowers. The foreign parties to such agreements are generally either a group of participating commercial banks from the relevant country (in the case of insurance-oriented export credit programmes—for example, those sponsored by Great Britain's ECGD, France's COFACE, and West Germany's HERMES), or the export credit agency itself (in the case of bank-oriented export credit programmes—for example, those offered by the Export-Import Bank of the United States or Eximbank of Japan).

Such credit agreements contain general provisions covering the maximum amount of credit offered; the availability period; utilization procedures and conditions to be fulfilled prior to utilization; the types of supply contracts and the percentage of the contract price eligible for financing; prepayment; taxes and related costs; events of default; and dispute settlement.[101] The repayment period, the interest rate, and the fees are generally set each time the BOC applies to utilize the funds under the credit agreement for particular supply contracts.

The underlying supply contract between the foreign supplier and the Chinese buyer must be approved by the BOC, the foreign government export credit agency, and commercial lenders, to ensure that it falls within the terms and conditions of the basic credit agreement. One of the principal difficulties with these supply contracts is that they are frequently negotiated between foreign suppliers and Chinese buyers without adequate attention to financing requirements.

On the basis of transactions with which this author has previously been involved, it is recommended that any foreign company, or its bank, contemplating export credit financing for a supply contract should involve the BOC in the contract negotiations when financing is discussed. It is preferable that officials from the BOC's head office should be involved since they, and not BOC branch officials, will be most familiar with the requirements of the available export credit facilities. In the case of Chinese-foreign joint ventures and co-operative enterprises, the BOC apparently decides on a case-by-case basis whether it will make export credit lines available and what procedures are to be followed. In the past, the BOC has required joint ventures to provide for the BOC's own internal planning purposes a pro forma breakdown of the amount and country of origin of each group of items to be procured abroad. This will be difficult to provide if the procurement is to be done through international bidding. Rather than complain about the difficulties of providing such a breakdown, it is better simply to provide it, on the understanding that it is subject to the results of the bidding.

Two additional agreements will generally be required where Chinese-foreign joint ventures and co-operative enterprises wish to utilize export credit financing. First, the joint venture or co-operative enterprise will be required to sign a loan agreement with the BOC for each supply contract to be financed through the on-lending of the funds that the BOC obtains pursuant to an export credit agreement. The BOC's practice for export credits utilized by domestic Chinese entities differs, but as to joint ventures, it has in the past charged a spread of approximately 1 per cent as a fee for its services. Second, the BOC requires a counter-guarantee from a foreign bank or syndicate of banks of the amount borrowed by the joint venture or co-operative enterprise. These requirements increase the complexity of documentation, the time for negotiation, and the cost of utilizing export credits.

A substantially different structure from that outlined above, which did not involve the BOC as a party, was used in the 1981 syndicated note-purchase facility provided to Yan Shan Petrochemical General Corporation to finance the purchase of plant and equipment of primarily Italian origin. In that transaction, the foreign banks purchased Yan Shan's negotiable promissory notes (which are guaranteed by the Beijing Economic Development Corporation) from the Italian supplier on a non-recourse basis. The foreign banks will hold the notes, which cover both principal and interest, until they mature, and in the interim will collect both fees and an interest make-up from the Italian government's Mediocredito Centrale. Furthermore, by purchasing the notes on a non-recourse basis from the Italian supplier and not obtaining a guarantee from an Italian government agency, the lenders were able to lower the cost of the financing and obtain a pure China risk with respect to the notes.

Whether the Yan Shan transaction will serve as a precedent for future transactions is unclear. A major obstacle is the great reluctance of Chinese buyers to issue negotiable promissory notes, the payment of which is not tied to the performance of the underlying supply contract.

IV. China's Exchange Control System and its Impact on International Transactions

Every trade, investment, and banking transaction with China must comply with China's foreign exchange control system. A variety of state plans, approval and licence procedures, rules, and regulations define the contours of this system, but its foundation is set forth in the Provisional Regulations of the People's Republic of China Governing Foreign Exchange Control (hereafter cited as the Foreign Exchange Regulations),[102] which came into effect on 1 March 1981. The Foreign Exchange Regulations implement 'a policy of centralized control and unified management of foreign exchange by the State' and designate the SGAEC and its branch offices as the administrative organ in charge of foreign exchange control. More detailed regulations have also been subsequently promulgated, including the Provisional Regulations on Violation of Exchange Control of the People's Republic of China (hereafter cited as the Foreign Exchange Violation Regulations), effective 5 April 1985,[103] and the Interim Banking Control Regulations of the People's Republic of China (hereafter cited as the Banking Control Regulations), effective 7 January 1986.[104]

The Foreign Exchange Violation Regulations make it an offence to 'engage in foreign exchange operations without prior SGAEC approval or on a scale beyond the limits set by the SGAEC';[105] they also specify as punishment the cessation of such unlawful operations plus the possible confiscation of unlawful foreign exchange earnings, a fine, or both.[106] The Banking Control Regulations specify the role of all banks and other financial institutions in a variety of areas, including foreign exchange,[107] and also define the PBOC as the 'central bank of the State' with responsibility for controlling foreign exchange.[108]

A. The Administration of Control

The SGAEC and its branch offices are granted specific approval authority over: (a) certain foreign exchange activities of Chinese domestic organizations; (b) the remittance out of China of foreign exchange by Chinese and certain foreign individuals; (c) the conversion into foreign currency of visa and certification fees received in *renminbi* by foreign diplomatic missions and consulates in China; and (d) the repatriation abroad by foreign partners in Chinese joint ventures of their portion of net profits and capital.

The SGAEC and its branch offices, however, do not exercise sole authority over foreign exchange activities. All foreign exchange retained by Chinese domestic organizations, non-trade foreign exchange and foreign exchange under compensatory trade received in advance for later payments, funds borrowed in convertible foreign currency, and other foreign exchange held with the approval of the SGAEC must be placed in foreign currency deposit accounts or foreign currency quota accounts opened with the BOC; this foreign exchange must be used within the scope prescribed by the BOC and is also subject to the supervision of the BOC. The BOC is granted specific authority to certify the remittance of foreign exchange retained by Chinese and certain foreign individuals residing in China and the foreign exchange required by foreign experts, staff members, and workers employed to work in Chinese domestic organizations. Chinese organizations are generally not permitted free use of retained foreign exchange. In practice, an organization is permitted to keep only a certain percentage of such foreign exchange in its foreign exchange account, with the percentage varying according to the industry or business of such organization.[109]

Certain foreign exchange activities are outside the authority of both the SGAEC and the BOC and must be approved by the State Council. For example, no Chinese domestic organization may issue securities with a foreign exchange value inside or outside China without the approval of the State Council. Furthermore, the State Council alone has authority to approve plans drawn up by provincial and local governments for loans to Chinese domestic organizations. It should also be noted that, as of the end of March 1986, the CITIC, 32 other international trust and investment corporations, and 19 financial institutions, including the BOC, the Investment Bank, and foreign bank branches in the SEZs and in Shanghai are authorized to engage in designated foreign exchange transactions, including the provision of loan guarantees.[110]

Foreign exchange transactions are generally made in accordance with China's foreign exchange plan. The Ministry of Foreign Economic Relations and Trade (hereafter referred to as MOFERT) prepares those parts of the plan which relate to foreign trade and external assistance and loans by China. The MOF prepares the foreign exchange budgets of other government departments. The SGAEC compiles that part of the plan which covers local and provincial non-trade transactions, receipts from overseas Chinese, and individual receipts. The SGAEC also co-ordinates the overall foreign exchange plan and, after it has been reviewed and reconciled with other plans by the State Planning Commission, submits it to the State Council for approval. After approval, the plan is sent back to the various subordinate organs for implementation under the supervision of the BOC.[111]

B. The Impact of Exchange Controls on International Transactions

The basic pattern of control is set forth in Article 4 of the Foreign Exchange Regulations:

All Chinese and foreign organizations and individuals residing in the People's Republic of China must, unless otherwise stipulated by law or decree or in these regulations, *sell* their foreign exchange proceeds to the Bank of China. Any foreign exchange required is to be sold to them by the Bank of China in accordance with the quota approved by the State or with relevant regulations.[112] [my italics]

As discussed below, Chinese-foreign joint ventures and foreign and overseas Chinese enterprises and individuals in China enjoy somewhat greater flexibility than that required by Article 4 in their foreign exchange dealings.

i. Trading Operations
Foreign trade is conducted in accordance with the annual foreign trade plan which is drawn up by MOFERT in conjunction with the State Planning Commission and approved by the State Council. Input for the plan is provided by all foreign trade corporations and foreign trade bureaux in the provinces, municipalities, and autonomous regions, which draw up lists of needed imports and of goods that are available for export.

In addition to complying with the annual foreign trade plan, all import and export transactions require a licence issued by MOFERT. The Foreign Exchange Regulations require banks handling import and export transactions to check the foreign exchange receipts and payments of domestic Chinese organizations against the import or export licence duly verified by the Customs or against the Customs declaration forms for imports or exports.[113] Part of the proceeds of some exports may be retained by domestic organizations in a foreign exchange deposit or foreign exchange quota account with the BOC, and such foreign exchange must be used within the scope prescribed therefor and be subject to the BOC's supervision. All other foreign receipts must be sold to the BOC unless specific approval is granted by the SGAEC. The BOC provides foreign exchange for imports, subject to the issuance of an import licence and the approval of the SGAEC.

In 1984 the BOC established an experimental trading system for foreign exchange in a few areas, including Beijing, Guangdong, Hefei, Shanghai, and Tianjin. National enterprises with large foreign exchange earnings, such as organizations exporting coal and oil, were permitted to sell such foreign exchange to other national enterprises which had quotas for spending foreign exchange, such as those importing large quantities of equipment. The BOC took a commission on such transactions, but did not participate on its own account, nor did it provide foreign exchange. It has since been decided that this trading system, rather than efficiently utilizing surplus foreign exchange, runs counter to policies governing foreign exchange allocations and market planning, and the system has therefore been dismantled.

ii. Loans to Chinese Organizations
In order that Chinese entities may borrow from foreign banks, such loans must be included in the annual plans for loans prepared by the departments under the State Council and the people's governments of provinces, municipalities, and autonomous regions. These plans must be submitted for examination to the SGAEC and the Foreign Investment Bureau within MOFERT, and must be approved by the BOC, the State Economic Commission, and the State Planning Commission.

The Foreign Exchange Regulations state that measures for examining and approving loans to Chinese organizations from foreign banks and companies shall be stipulated separately,[114] but such measures have yet to be promulgated. Although the existing Foreign Exchange Regulations make specific reference only to loans, it would be highly imprudent to conclude that contingent obligations like guarantees are not subject to the examination and approval of the appropriate authorities. One high-ranking BOC official has told this author that guarantees given by Chinese entities with respect to loans from both foreign and domestic sources would be subject to approval.[115]

It is important to understand that foreign exchange approval of a loan or a contract by the SGAEC or other relevant Chinese authorities does not mean that foreign exchange will definitely be made available to pay the obligation when due to the foreign bank or company. The only method of assuring payment in foreign exchange is to obtain a BOC guarantee.

iii. Chinese-Foreign Joint Ventures, Enterprises with Overseas Chinese
   Capital, and Enterprises with Foreign Capital
Rules for the Implementation of the Foreign Exchange Regulations have recently been published for enterprises with overseas Chinese capital, enterprises with foreign capital, and Chinese-foreign joint ventures (hereafter cited as the Foreign Exchange Implementation Rules).[116] These rules expand on the Foreign Exchange Regulations and in certain circumstances provide for preferential treatment for such enterprises, especially for foreign enterprises engaged in the co-operative exploitation of offshore petroleum resources in China.

As a general rule, joint ventures and enterprises with overseas Chinese or foreign capital should open both *renminbi* and foreign exchange deposit accounts in China with the BOC or any other bank approved by the SGAEC or its branch offices; payments and receipts in such accounts are subject to the supervision of the bank where such accounts have been established.[117] Such enterprises are also generally required to deposit all foreign exchange receipts in, and make all foreign exchange payments from, their accounts in banks in China.[118] However, according to MOFERT, joint ventures may open accounts with foreign banks, hold funds outside China, or make investments abroad, after approval by the SGAEC. They may even borrow from foreign banks after obtaining SGAEC approval, although the signed loan agreement must be kept on file with the SGAEC.[119]

Moreover, such enterprises must submit periodically to the SGAEC or its branch offices the following statements: (a) before 31 March of each year, its balance sheet as of 31 December of the previous year, its profit and loss statement, a statement of receipts and payments of foreign exchange for the previous calendar year, and the audit report by an auditor registered in China; and (b) before 1 December of each year, its budget of foreign exchange receipts and payments for the coming year.[120] The SGAEC and its branch offices are authorized to request such enterprises to provide information about their business activities involving foreign exchange and to inspect their foreign exchange income and expenditures.[121]

Preferential treatment is granted under the Foreign Exchange Implementation Rules to enterprises engaged in the co-operative exploitation of offshore petroleum resources in China. Such enterprises may deposit their solely borne exploration funds and co-operative production funds in banks in foreign countries, Hong Kong, or Macau that are agreed upon by their Chinese partners, and after approval has been granted by the SGAEC or its branch offices. Such enterprises shall submit to the SGAEC or its branch offices quarterly statements of payments into, and withdrawals from, such accounts outside China within thirty days after the end of each quarter.[122]

In order to carry out the petroleum operations specified in their contracts with Chinese enterprises, foreign oil companies may also pay directly outside China the wages, salaries, cost of procurements, labour costs, and service charges to foreign workers and staff members and to foreign subcontractors and suppliers, who shall remain obligated, however, to pay Chinese income tax on taxable income earned in China.[123] In addition, joint ventures and enterprises with overseas Chinese or foreign capital that are engaged in the co-operative exploitation of resources such as offshore petroleum and coal and other co-operative and joint ventures, whose costs are recovered and profits are taken in products in accordance with their contracts, may send such products out of China on the condition that taxes and other required payments are remitted back to China.[124]

Under the Foreign Exchange Regulations, all Chinese-foreign joint ventures and enterprises with overseas Chinese or foreign capital must use *renminbi* in the settlement of accounts with Chinese entities, enterprises, and individuals residing in China. But the Foreign Exchange Implementation Rules provide three exceptions to this general rule. Provided that the prior approval of the Chinese foreign trade authorities has been granted and the seller and buyer have reached agreement, such enterprises may use foreign currencies in the pricing and settlement of accounts for (a) sales of products to Chinese entities or enterprises engaged in foreign trade which would otherwise have to import such products, and (b) purchases, for the sake of production, of commodities exported or imported by Chinese entities engaged in foreign trade. In both cases, the prices of such products and commodities are to be commensurate with current world market prices. As a third exception, such enterprises may use foreign currencies in the payment for, and in the settlement of accounts related to, construction work performed by Chinese construction entities, provided that prior approval has been obtained from the SGAEC or its branch offices.[125]

One of the more onerous requirements of the Foreign Exchange Regulations and Foreign Exchange Implementation Rules is that joint ventures and enterprises with overseas Chinese or foreign capital must guarantee sufficient foreign exchange earnings to pay all their foreign exchange expenditures. This requirement appears to have been mitigated to some extent by the Implementing Act for the Law of the People's Republic of China on Joint Ventures Using Chinese and Foreign Investment (hereafter cited as the Joint Venture Implementation Regulations). Article 75 of the Joint Venture Implementation Regulations provides that, when a joint venture whose products are mainly sold on the domestic market in accordance with its approved feasibility study report and contract has an imbalance of foreign exchange income and expenses, the people's government of the relevant province, autonomous region, or municipality directly under the central government, or the department in charge under the State Council shall resolve the imbalance from their own foreign exchange reserves; and in cases where the imbalance cannot be so resolved, it shall be resolved after examination and approval by MOFERT together with the State Planning Commission.[126] However, no case in which Article 75 has been applied has ever been made public.

In January 1986, the State Council issued the State Council Regulations on Joint Ventures' Balance Between Foreign Exchange Revenue and Expenditure (hereafter cited as the Foreign Exchange Balancing Regulations), effective 1 February 1986, which provide mechanisms other than Article 75 for the remittance of foreign exchange profits.[127] The new mechanisms include an 'umbrella' type of corporate structure, allowing a foreign party involved in more than one joint venture to pool the foreign exchange reserves of its ventures to offset one venture's foreign exchange deficit with the surplus of another venture. Such an adjustment would require the consent of all partners to the various ventures.[128] The Foreign Exchange Balancing Regulations also allow foreign investors to invest *renminbi* earnings from one venture in other ventures which are capable of generating foreign exchange,[129] and permit joint ventures to be paid in foreign exchange by Chinese customers if the ventures' products are import substitutes or highly sophisticated goods produced with advanced technology.[130] The implementation of the Foreign Exchange Balancing Regulations is the responsibility of MOFERT, which has yet to publish detailed procedures, but the Regulations require the involvement of the government department which originally approved the underlying joint venture contract.[131]

The language of the Foreign Exchange Regulations and the Foreign Exchange Implementation Rules leaves several questions unanswered. For example, Article 4 of the Foreign Exchange Regulations prohibits the mortgage of foreign currency. Does this prohibition extend to commonly used security arrangements such as a pledge of foreign currency receivables? This question has not been generally addressed by the SGAEC, although in one transaction foreign lenders were permitted to obtain a pledge of rentals received in foreign exchange by a Chinese-foreign joint co-operative enterprise and deposited in its foreign exchange deposit account with the BOC.

Second, will a foreign investor that terminates its participation in a joint venture or other enterprise, whether because the term of co-operation has expired, heavy losses have been incurred, or a major dispute cannot be resolved, be permitted to remit in foreign exchange its share of the net book value of the joint venture or enterprise? Article 24 of the Foreign Exchange Regulations directs foreign investors to apply to the SGAEC or its branch offices for the transferring of foreign exchange capital abroad by debiting the foreign exchange deposit account of the joint venture or enterprise. But the word 'capital' may include only the capital originally invested and not retained earnings. Even if retained earnings may be remitted, this will be small comfort to the foreign investor if the foreign exchange deposit account does not contain an amount sufficient to cover the proposed outward remittance. Unless joint ventures and enterprises with overseas Chinese or foreign capital are permitted to purchase foreign exchange to cover their liabilities, or broadly come under the protection of Article 75 of the Joint Venture Implementation Regulations cited above, foreign investors may have to look to insurance coverage for foreign exchange convertibility.

A final problem for joint ventures and enterprises with overseas Chinese or foreign capital concerns the foreign exchange earnings of their foreign employees. Article 25 of the Foreign Exchange Regulations limits such personnel to remitting an amount not exceeding 50 per cent of their net wages and other legitimate earnings after tax. The limitation should not prove a problem for foreign oil companies engaged in the co-operative exploitation of offshore petroleum resources, since under the Foreign Exchange Implementation Rules they are permitted to pay directly outside China the wages and salaries of foreign workers and staff members. The Foreign Exchange Implementation Rules also ease, but to a lesser extent, this restriction for the personnel of other enterprises with foreign or overseas Chinese capital and of Chinese and foreign joint ventures. The personnel of such entities may remit amounts exceeding 50 per cent of their wages and legitimate earnings after tax deductions, if approved by the SGAEC or its branch offices, and as long as such excess amounts are debited to the foreign exchange deposit accounts of the employing enterprise.[132] A further relaxation is granted under Article 79 of the Joint Venture Implementation Regulations to foreign personnel working for joint ventures who, after the payment of Chinese individual income taxes, may apply to the BOC for permission to remit outside China all of the remaining foreign exchange, after the deduction of their living expenses in China.[133] There is no restriction on the remittance of earnings of the foreign resident representatives of foreign companies with representative offices in China.

iv. Transactions with the Special Economic Zones

Projects in China's SEZs are generally subject to more flexible regulations than those described above, which also provide for preferential treatment. Regulations in force for the SEZs in Guangdong province refer to the foreign exchange control measures of the special zones,[134] but these have yet to be promulgated.

V. Conclusion

Banking and financial transactions with China have become increasingly sophisticated in recent years. It can be expected that they will become somewhat easier to conclude in the future as China develops its legal system and gains more experience in international financial practices. The dollar volume of such transactions will also significantly increase in the long term, but in the short to medium term it would appear that China will concentrate on using the financial assistance of foreign governments and international financial organizations.

Notes

1. *South China Morning Post, Business News,* 31 January 1983, p. 8; and 'China's 1983 Imp-Export Volume Up 2.2% to US$40.14 Billion', *China Economic News,* 12 March 1983, pp. 4–5.

2. O. Sin, 'Slump in China's Forex Reserves', *South China Morning Post, Business Post,* 6 June 1986, p. 1.

3. 'China has "Mountain of Reserves"', *South China Morning Post, Business News,* 12 December 1983, p. 1; 'China's foreign exchange keeps upward trend', *China Daily,* 4 April 1984, p. 2; and 'China's Foreign Currency Reserves and Gold Total About $19 Billion', *Asian Wall Street Journal,* 5 April 1984, p. 3. Of China's foreign exchange funds, approximately US$4.5 billion is placed abroad in Eurodollar deposits, according to figures of the Bank for International Settlements. See 'China shy of commercial loans', *Hong Kong Standard,* 25 May 1983, Business News Section, p. 1.

4. Sin, p. 1, note 2 above.

5. F. Chu, 'Foreign Banks' Business Prospects in China', *International Financial Law Review,* June 1983, p. 35; 'Banks eager to give China credit, if. . .', *South China Morning Post,* 25 May 1983, p. 3; 'China has "Mountain of Reserves"', note 3 above; and 'China's Foreign Currency Reserves and Gold Total About $19 Billion', note 3 above.

6. Sin, p. 1, note 2 above.

7. A. LeBourgeois and S. Chung, 'Commercial Banks in China', *China Business Review,* January–February 1986, p. 26.

8. The role of the People's Bank of China is set forth in two Chinese-language documents, Notice of the State Council Approving the Transmitting the Request for Instruction by the People's Bank of China Concerning the Function of the People's Bank as the Central Bank and its Relationship with other Specialized Banks, and Request for Instruction by the People's Bank of China Concerning the Function of the People's Bank as the Central Bank and its Relationship with other Specialized Banks, which are published in *Zhonghua renmin gongheguo guowuyuan gongbao* (hereafter cited as the *State Council Gazette),* No. 13, 15 September 1982, p. 582.

9. *State Council Gazette,* p. 583, note 8 above.

10. 'China's Financial Organizations, Their Business and Mutual Relations', *China Economic News,* 5 March 1984, pp. 6–8; and 'China's Centralized Banking System Being Set Up, How System Works Explained by Official', *China Economic News,* 16 January 1984, pp. 4–5.

11. 'China's Financial Organizations, Their Business and Mutual Relations', p. 7, note 10 above.

12. P. Reynolds, *China's International Banking and Financial System* (New York, Praeger, 1982), p. 29.

13. Reynolds, p. 29, note 12 above.
14. 'China's Financial Organizations, Their Business and Mutual Relations', p. 7, note 10 above.
15. 'China's Financial Institutions', *China Business Review*, July–August 1980, p. 17; and 'China's Financial Organizations, Their Business and Mutual Relations', pp. 7–8, note 10 above.
16. 'China's Financial Organizations, Their Business and Mutual Relations', pp. 7–8, note 10 above.
17. 'China's Financial Organizations, Their Business and Mutual Relations', p. 8, note 10 above.
18. Articles of Association of the Bank of China, Art. 1. A translation appears in *Euromoney*, December 1980, pp. 109–10.
19. Application of Bank of China Dated 25 March 1981 to Establish A Federal Branch to the Comptroller of the Currency, p. 8 (hereafter cited as the NY Branch Application). On public file with the United States Comptroller of the Currency.
20. 'BOC's 1985 Total Assets Up 30%', *China Economic News*, 12 May 1986, p. 6.
21. NY Branch Application, p. 34, note 19 above.
22. 'BOC's 1985 Total Assets Up 30%', p. 6, note 20 above.
23. Articles of Association of the Bank of China, Chap. IV, note 18 above.
24. N. Ludlow and J. Stepanek, 'Inside the Bank of China', *China Business Review*, July–August 1980, p. 9.
25. 'BOC's 1985 Total Assets Up 30%', p. 6, note 20 above.
26. J. Cohen, 'The Bank of China Clears Up Its Legal Status', *Euromoney*, December 1980, p. 108.
27. Cohen, p. 108, note 26 above.
28. *State Council Gazette*, p. 583, note 8 above.
29. Application of Bank of China Dated 25 March 1981 to the United States Federal Deposit Insurance Corporation, Supplemental Information, p. 6 (on public file with the United States Federal Deposit Insurance Corporation); and Loan Agreement Dated 8 May 1981 Between the Bank of China and the Export-Import Bank of the United States, Art. 6.
30. V. Fung, 'Fujian Bonds Hit Roadblock in Japan, Fall Flat at Home', *Asian Wall Street Journal*, 28 April 1983, p. 1.
31. NY Branch Application, p. 20, note 19 above.
32. With respect to the United States see *Vishipco Line* v. *Chase Manhattan Bank*, N.A. 660 F.2d 854, p. 860 (2d Cir. 1981) cert. denied 103 S. Ct. 313 (1982); *United States* v. *First National City Bank*, 379 U.S. 378 (1965); *Sokoloff* v. *National City Bank of New York*, 130 Misc. 66, 224 N.Y.S. 102 (sup 1927), aff'd 223 App. Div. 754, 228 N.Y.S. 907 (1st Dept. 1928), aff'd 250 N.Y. 69, 164 N.E. 745 (1928); 1917 F.R.B. 198.
33. E. Lachica, 'China's Lending Expands as Reserves Balloon', *Asian Wall Street Journal*, 24 November 1982, p. 1.
34. Lachica, p. 1, note 33 above.
35. *Asian Wall Street Journal*, 13 January 1983, p. 3.
36. V. Fung, 'China to Extend its Biggest Loan Yet for Venture', *Asian Wall Street Journal*, 24–25 June 1983, p. 1.
37. F. Ching, 'China Considers Loans To Foreign Companies For Projects in China', *Asian Wall Street Journal*, 17 December 1982, p. 1.
38. *China Daily*, 13 March 1983, p. 2.
39. Provisional Measures for Providing Loans to Joint Ventures Using Chinese and Foreign Investment By the Bank of China, Art. 4(4). A translation of these measures appears in F. Chu, M. Moser, and O. Nee (eds.), *Commercial, Business and Trade Laws: People's Republic of China* (Dobbs Ferry, Oceana Publications, Inc., 1982), Pt. 9, pp. 21–5.
40. 'Growing BOC Credit Facilities Mirror Future PRC Foreign Exchange

Spending Patterns', *China Economic News*, 17 January 1983, p. 1; and 'BOC Extends US$630 Million Foreign Exchange Loans to Chinese Enterprises', *China Economic News*, 16 January 1984, p. 5.

41. 'Growing BOC Credit Facilities Mirror Future PRC Foreign Exchange Spending Patterns', p. 2, note 40 above.

42. 'Growing BOC Credit Facilities Mirror Future PRC Foreign Exchange Spending Patterns', p. 2, note 40 above. A translation of the Instructions of the Bank of China on Foreign Exchange Loans appears in *China Economic News*, 30 January 1984, pp. 3–4.

43. M.N. Shi, 'Briefing on the Business of the Bank of China, Shanghai Branch', speech given at the Celebration of the Second Anniversary of the Establishment of SITCO, Seminar, Session 10, 27 July 1983, p. 3.

44. Shi, p. 4, note 43 above; and 'BOC Shanghai Bank Invests in Joint Ventures', *China Economic News*, 2 January 1984, p. 4.

45. 'BOC's Fledgling International Trade and Consultancy Business Reviewed', *China Economic News*, 13 September 1982, p. 2.

46. 'BOC Signs Trust Consulting Agreements with 42 Overseas Banks, Companies', *China Economic News*, 2 January 1984, pp. 3–4; and 'Articles of Association of the Bank of China Trust and Consultancy Company', *China Economic News*, 2 January 1984, pp. 4–5.

47. J. Leung, 'China Bank Group Moves on Hong Kong', *Asian Wall Street Journal*, 20 May 1986, p. 1.

48. *South China Morning Post, Business News*, 31 January 1983, p. 1.

49. Reynolds, p. 58, note 12 above.

50. Leung, p. 1, note 47 above.

51. V. Fung, 'Peking Banks to Trim Property Loans in Colony', *Asian Wall Street Journal*, 11 November 1982, p. 1.

52. Fung, p. 1, note 51 above.

53. 'The First Sino-American-Japanese Finance Joint Venture Chalks Up Initial Success, Eyes Future Opportunities', *Economic Reporter*, June 1982, p. 20.

54. 'The First Sino-American-Japanese Finance Joint Venture', p. 20, note 53 above.

55. NY Branch Application, p. 7, note 19 above.

56. 'China Investment Bank Raises Funds for Selected Projects', *China Economic News*, 1 March 1982, p. 3.

57. X. Qin, 'World Bank Funds to Aid Technology', *China Daily*, 5 January 1985, p. 2.

58. Provisional Regulations of the People's Republic of China Governing Foreign Exchange Control (hereafter cited as the Foreign Exchange Regulations), Art. 3. A translation of these regulations appears in Chu, Moser, and Nee, Pt. 12, pp. 3–15, note 39 above.

59. Reynolds, pp. 32–3, note 12 above.

60. Statutes of China International Trust and Investment Corporation (hereafter cited as the Statutes), Art. 1. A translation of these statutes appears in China International Economic Consultants, Inc., and Economic Information & Consultancy Co. (eds.), *Guide to Investment in China* (Hong Kong, Economic Information & Agency, 1982) (hereafter cited as the *Investment Guide*), pp. 169–73.

61. 'China's Financial Organizations, Their Business and Mutual Relations', p. 8, note 10 above.

62. The Statutes, Arts. 6–11, note 60 above.

63. *Investment Guide*, pp. 168–9, note 60 above; and 'CITIC Official on Utilizing Foreign Capital in Economic Construction', *China Economic News*, 1 November 1982, p. 9.

64. M. Fenton-Jones, 'Chinese Mission Seeks Equity in Canadian Firms', *South China Morning Post, Business News*, 16 April 1983, p. 8.

65. 'CITIC Shakes Up Banking System in China', *Hong Kong Standard, Busi-*

ness Standard, 14 January 1986, p. 2; 'Ka Wah Provides Details of CITIC Take-over', *Asian Wall Street Journal*, 20 May 1986, p. 16.

66. P. Sham, 'CITIC Sweeps Board in New Look Ka Wah', *South China Morning Post, Business Post*, 24 June 1986, p. 1.

67. See The Income Tax Law of the People's Republic of China Concerning Foreign Enterprises, Art. 11 (which generally imposes a 20 per cent withholding tax), and Interim Provisions of the Ministry of Finance of the People's Republic of China Regarding the Reduction and Exemption of Income Tax Relating to Interest Earned by Foreign Businesses from China (hereafter cited as the Interest Income Tax Regulations), Art. 1 (which reduces the withholding tax to 10 per cent on interest obtained from loans, advances, and deferred payments under credit agreements signed between 1983 and 1985, a period subsequently extended to 1990—see note 78 below). A translation of the tax law appears in Chu, Moser, and Nee, Pt. 13, pp. 41–7, note 39 above; a translation of the interim provisions appears in *China Economic News*, 21 March 1983, pp. 1–2.

68. Interest Income Tax Regulations, Art. 2(1), note 67 above.

69. *China Economic News*, 1 November 1982, p. 10.

70. For reports of these loans, see, for example, 'World Bank Support for PRC Agriculture', *Business China*, 30 June 1982, p. 95; 'World Bank Loans US$60 Million for Agricultural Development in North China Plain', *China Economic News*, 12 July 1982, p. 1; 'World Bank to Loan China US$80 Million for China's Agricultural Development', *China Economic News*, 1 November 1982, p. 11; 'World Bank, China to Sign Loan Agreement For Agricultural Education and Research', *China Economic News*, 22 November 1982, p. 5; 'More World Bank Projects', *China Market Intelligence*, December 1982, p. 1; N. Ludlow, 'China and the World Bank', *China Business Review*, November–December 1982, p. 12; 'Equipment for China's 7 New Container Berths to be Financed by World Bank Loan', *China Economic News*, 31 January 1983, p. 6; and 'World Bank extends US$80M Loan for N.E. China Farm Project, Open Bids on Farm Equipment to be invited in May', *China Economic News*, 18 April 1983, p. 10.

71. 'China Becomes 47th Member of Asian Development Bank', *Wall Street Journal*, 12 March 1986, p. 38.

72. Provisional Regulations for the Establishment of Representative Offices in China by Overseas Chinese and Foreign Financial Institutions (hereafter cited as the Registration Regulations). A translation appears in *China Economic News*, 21 February 1983, pp. 1–3.

73. Registration Regulations, Art. 2, note 72 above.

74. Chu, note 5 above.

75. Registration Regulations, note 72 above.

76. Interest Income Tax Regulations, Art. 4, note 67 above.

77. The Income Tax Law of the People's Republic of China Concerning Foreign Enterprises, Arts. 1, 3, and 4, note 67 above.

78. The Income Tax Law of the People's Republic of China Concerning Foreign Enterprises, Art. 11, and Interest Income Tax Regulations, note 67 above; and 'China Extends Tax Holiday of Foreign Businessmen', *China Economic News*, 14 April 1986, p. 3.

79. O. Sin, 'How to Avoid Withholding Tax', *South China Morning Post, Business News*, 4 July 1985, p. 5.

80. Interest Income Tax Regulations, Art. 4, note 67 above.

81. F. Ching, 'China Softens Its Tax Regulations On Income By Foreign Companies', *Asian Wall Street Journal*, 14 March 1983, p. 1.

82. V. Fung, 'China Clarifies Rules on Foreign Banks', *Asian Wall Street Journal*, 29 June 1983, p. 1.

83. Regulations Governing Foreign Banks and Joint Chinese-Foreign Banks in Special Economic Zones of the People's Republic of China (hereafter cited as the Foreign Bank Regulations). A translation appears in *China Economic News*, 29 April 1985, pp. 2–4.

84. Foreign Bank Regulations, Art. 6, note 83 above.
85. Foreign Bank Regulations, Art. 7, note 83 above.
86. Foreign Bank Regulations, Art. 10, note 83 above.
87. 'China Opens Its Special Zones to Foreign Banks', *Hong Kong Standard, Business Standard,* 17 April 1985, p. 1.
88. 'Foreign Bankers Criticize China's New Banking Rules', *Asian Wall Street Journal,* 18 April 1985, p. 5.
89. LeBourgeois and Chung, p. 28, note 7 above.
90. Lachica, note 33 above; and Chu, note 5 above.
91. 'China Wild Card as ADB Plans its Credit Policies', *South China Morning Post, Business News,* 20 May 1986, p. 6.
92. M. Bu, 'China's Financial Relations with Foreign Countries', *Beijing Review,* 20 April 1983, p. 21; and Chu, note 5 above.
93. 'UBAF Loan's Surprise for Bank', *Business China,* 28 April 1983, p. 63.
94. V. Fung, 'China Bank Takes Over Foreign Loan for Hotel', *Asian Wall Street Journal,* 9 December 1982, p. 1.
95. LeBourgeois and Chung, p. 25, note 7 above.
96. O. Sin, '"Use More Credit" Call', *South China Morning Post, Business News,* 19 May 1986, p. 1.
97. J. Hsu, 'Financing Imports Through Leasing', *China Business Review,* January–February 1986, p. 29.
98. P. Sham, 'Beijing Plans to Plug Leasing Loopholes', *South China Morning Post, Business News,* 5 May 1986, p. 1.
99. The analysis of Chinese letter-of-credit practices is based on discussions with Chinese and foreign bankers and business men and an examination of the standard-form contracts used by Chinese trading corporations and the standard-form letters of credit issued by the BOC.
100. 'Bank of China Quickens Account Clearing Processes in Foreign Trade', *China Economic News,* 20 October 1980, p. 9.
101. See, for example, the Loan Agreement dated as of 8 May 1981 between the Bank of China and the Export-Import Bank of the United States; and the Credit Agreement dated as of 9 May 1979 among a group of French banks and the Bank of China to finance part of the contracts signed by French suppliers and corporations of the People's Republic of China for the delivery of French capital goods, industrial complexes, and services.
102. Foreign Exchange Regulations, note 58 above.
103. Provisional Regulations on Violation of Exchange Control of the People's Republic of China (hereafter cited as the Foreign Exchange Violation Regulations). A translation appears in *China Economic News,* 22 April 1985, pp. 1–3.
104. Interim Banking Control Regulations of the People's Republic of China (hereafter cited as the Banking Control Regulations). A translation appears in *China Daily,* 27 February 1986 and 1 March 1986.
105. Foreign Exchange Violation Regulations, Art. 6, note 103 above.
106. Foreign Exchange Violation Regulations, Art. 7, note 103 above.
107. Banking Control Regulations, Art. 2, note 104 above.
108. Banking Control Regulations, Art. 5, note 104 above.
109. LeBourgeois and Chung, p. 26, note 7 above.
110. *South China Morning Post, Business News,* 6 May 1986, p. 5.
111. International Monetary Fund, *Annual Report on Exchange Arrangements and Exchange Restrictions 1982,* p. 120.
112. Foreign Exchange Regulations, Art. 4, note 58 above.
113. Foreign Exchange Regulations, Art. 10, note 58 above.
114. Foreign Exchange Regulations, Art. 8, note 58 above.
115. See also text accompanying note 110 above.
116. Rules for the Implementation of Exchange Control Regulations Relating to Enterprises with Overseas Chinese Capital, Enterprises with Foreign Capital, and Chinese and Foreign Joint Ventures, which were approved by the State

Council on 19 July 1983 and promulgated by the SGAEC on 1 August 1983 (hereafter cited as the Foreign Exchange Implementation Rules). A translation appears in *China Daily*, August 1983, p. 2. Art. 2 of these rules defines: (a) 'enterprises with overseas Chinese capital' to mean 'corporations, enterprises or other economic entities registered in China with overseas Chinese capital or capital of compatriots in Hong Kong and Macao areas, and managed independently or jointly with Chinese enterprises'; (b) 'enterprises with foreign capital' to mean 'corporations, enterprises or other economic entities registered in China with foreign capital, and managed independently or jointly with Chinese enterprises'; and (c) 'Chinese and foreign joint ventures' to mean 'enterprises jointly established, owned and run in China by corporations, enterprises, other economic entities or individuals with overseas Chinese capital, capital of compatriots in Hong Kong and Macao areas or foreign capital and Chinese corporations, enterprises or other economic entities'.

117. Foreign Exchange Implementation Rules, Art. 4, note 116 above.

118. Foreign Exchange Implementation Rules, Art. 7, note 116 above.

119. *China Daily*, 8 April 1986, p. 4.

120. Foreign Exchange Implementation Rules, Art. 9, note 116 above.

121. Foreign Exchange Implementation Rules, Art. 9, note 116 above.

122. Foreign Exchange Implementation Rules, Arts. 6 and 7, note 116 above.

123. Foreign Exchange Implementation Rules, Art. 8, note 116 above.

124. Foreign Exchange Implementation Rules, Art. 14, note 116 above.

125. Foreign Exchange Implementation Rules, Art. 12, note 116 above.

126. A translation of the Implementing Act for the Law of the People's Republic of China on Joint Ventures Using Chinese and Foreign Investment (hereafter cited as the Joint Venture Implementation Regulations) is on file with the author.

127. State Council Regulations on Joint Ventures' Balance Between Foreign Exchange Revenue and Expenditure (hereafter cited as the Foreign Exchange Balancing Regulations). A translation appears in *China Economic News*, 3 February 1986.

128. Foreign Exchange Balancing Regulations, Art. 9, note 127 above.

129. Foreign Exchange Balancing Regulations, Art. 10, note 127 above.

130. Foreign Exchange Balancing Regulations, Art. 4, note 127 above.

131. Foreign Exchange Balancing Regulations, Art. 3, note 127 above.

132. Foreign Exchange Implementation Rules, Art. 15, note 116 above.

133. Joint Venture Implementation Regulations, Art. 79, note 126 above.

134. Regulations on Special Economic Zones in Guangdong Province, Art. 15. A translation of these regulations appears in Chu, Moser, and Nee, Pt. 14, pp. 3–11, note 39 above.

10. Selected Legal Aspects of Financing Transactions with the People's Republic of China

CHARLES J. CONROY AND MICHAEL J. MOSER

I. Introduction

The past five years have seen a rapid development of China's economy. While part of this economic development has been fuelled by direct foreign investment, a significant portion has been funded by foreign financial institutions, from both the private and the public sector. According to Chinese sources, from 1979 to 1985 Chinese borrowers signed loan and credit agreements with banks and other financial institutions abroad for more than US$20 billion.[1] Moreover, it is expected that both the pace and volume of China's borrowing will increase in the years ahead.

This chapter examines some of the more important legal issues related to the financing activities that foreign institutions conduct with China and addresses the issues of the most practical concern to foreign bankers dealing with China, including: which Chinese entities are authorized to borrow from foreign lenders; how a foreign bank ensures that the Chinese entity with which it is dealing is duly authorized to enter into the credit agreement; what security is available to foreign banks for foreign currency obligations owed by PRC entities; what form of documentation is typically utilized in credit agreements between Chinese borrowers and foreign institutions; whether the obligations of Chinese borrowers are enforceable. Each of these questions is discussed further below.

II. Chinese Entities and their Legal Characteristics

Prior to discussing specific legal problems which might arise in connection with the provision of credit facilities by foreign entities to Chinese entities, it is useful to distinguish among the various entities which might seek such services and consider the most important legal characteristics of each type of entity. In general, there are three types to be considered: (a) domestic Chinese entities, (b) Chinese entities that operate abroad, and (c) Chinese-foreign joint ventures.

A. Domestic Chinese Entities

There are various different kinds of domestic Chinese entities. Indeed, in 1984 it was reported that there were more than one million industrial, commercial, and service enterprises, contributing almost 80 per cent of all state revenues.[2] However, not all such entities possess the legal capacity to enter into commercial contracts with foreigners. In general, two requirements must be met before an entity will be deemed to possess foreign contractual capacity: (a) the entity must constitute a legal person (*fa ren*), and (b) the entity must possess foreign trade authority (*waimao quan*).

i. What is a legal person?

According to China's General Provisions of the Civil Code (cited hereafter as the Civil Code), an entity must possess the status of a legal person before it may assume civil responsibilities and undertake civil law acts in its own name.[3]

The basic attributes of a legal person are set forth in the Civil Code and are further elaborated upon in a civil law treatise published by the Institute of Civil Law of the Central Political-Legal Cadres' School.[4] These attributes may be summarized as follows.

(a) a legal person must have a definite organizational structure fixed by a corporate constitution or by regulations;
(b) a legal person must possess property or funds which it independently controls;
(c) a legal person must be able independently to assume property duties in civil matters and be responsible for its own profits and losses in its business operations and in the performance of its obligations;
(d) a legal person must be able to undertake civil law acts in its own name and sue and be sued in its own name; and
(e) a legal person must be approved as such by the state.

At present, in China, four different types of entities may qualify as legal persons. The first type is known as *shiye danwei*, or institutions. This category includes such entities as schools, hospitals, and similar organizations which generally are not engaged in business for profit.

The second type of legal person is the *guoying qiye*, or state-owned enterprise which includes a wide variety of entities, ranging from organizations like the China National Offshore Oil Corporation, major state production plants, and the national foreign trade corporations, to specialized local companies and enterprises established in the special economic zones.

The third type of legal person is the *jiti qiye*, or collective enterprise. The fundamental difference between this type of enterprise and a state-owned enterprise is that ownership is essentially in the hands of private shareholders, rather than the state. Collective enterprises established in the 1950s have evolved into a distinctive form which in many ways resemble state-owned enterprises. However, collective enterprises set up under regulations promulgated in 1983 are of a more private and capitalistic character. For instance, whereas older collectives are owned jointly and equally by all participants, most collectives established under the present regulations are owned by only some participants while other participants are employees of the collective. Many collectives today are generally small in scale and are formed in the light industrial and service sectors by urban youths waiting for jobs (*daiye qingnian*).

The fourth type of legal person is the *geti qiye*, or individual enterprise. These enterprises have been permitted only recently in China. They are privately owned by one individual or a single family and are generally found in the service sector.

It should be noted that governmental organs and agencies occupy a special position under Chinese law. Governmental organs are defined in China's Constitution as 'state administrative organs', as opposed to 'business units' or 'enterprises'.[5] Although China's Civil Code does provide that government agencies with 'independent funds' may obtain the status of a legal person,[6] current policies encouraging 'the separation of the enterprise from the state' (*zhengqi fenkai*) generally prohibit agencies and organs of the Chinese government from entering into commercial transactions with foreigners in their own name.

ii. Foreign Trade Authority

As mentioned above, not all Chinese entities which possess the status of a legal person have the capacity to enter into contractual relationships with foreigners. Before a civil obligation owed by a Chinese legal person to a foreigner will be deemed valid, the Chinese entity must also possess *waimao quan*, or foreign trade authority. In the absence of this authority, which is granted only by China's State Council and its entrusted organs, an entity which may be constituted as a legal person for Chinese domestic purposes will lack the requisite power to enter into legally binding contractual relations with foreigners. As a general rule of thumb, such authority is vested only in certain state-owned enterprises and collectives.

B. Foreign Companies Owned by Domestic Chinese Entities

In recent years, Chinese-owned entities have acquired an increasingly visible and active presence outside the People's Republic, particularly in Hong Kong. Apart from long-established entities such as the Bank of China's 'Seven Sister Banks', the China Merchants' Steam Navigation Co. Ltd., and China Resources Ltd., a number of local trading companies have been established directly by Chinese municipal or provincial governments or by domestic Chinese enterprises. Similar enterprises have been established outside Hong Kong in leading business centres in Europe, the United States, Japan, and Australia.

From a strictly legal perspective, Chinese-owned enterprises established abroad constitute independent entities separate from both their 'sending organizations' (*paichu jigou*) and the Chinese state. Most, in fact, are organized as limited liability companies under local law and the shareholders of record are often individuals rather than domestic Chinese entities. None the less, such companies enjoy close ties to domestic Chinese entities and are subject to restrictions imposed by their 'sending organizations'.

C. Chinese-foreign Joint Ventures

Chinese-foreign joint ventures are of two main types: equity joint ventures and contractual or 'co-operative' joint ventures. Equity joint ventures are established under Chinese law as 'limited liability companies'. As such, they constitute distinct legal persons and are responsible for their own profits and losses. By contrast, in the co-operative joint venture format, a distinct legal person may not be established and the foreign and Chinese parties may jointly engage in business activities while retaining their own separate legal identities.[7] For a more detailed discussion of joint ventures, see Chapter 3 of this volume.

III. Legal Issues Arising in Connection with Banking Transactions by Chinese Entities

Certain legal issues will typically arise in most PRC-related financial transactions. These problems are concerned primarily with the following matters: (a) corporate authority, (b) signing authority, (c) foreign exchange and other approvals, (d) authority to guarantee, (e) security, and (f) bankruptcy.

A. Corporate Authority

A fundamental requirement for the legality of any type of contractual relationship between a lender and a borrower is that the customer possess the requisite corporate authority for entering into the transaction. In the case of Chinese entities, special care must be taken to ensure that this requirement is fulfilled. This section discusses problems related to ascertaining the corporate authority of domestic Chinese entities and Chinese-foreign joint ventures.

i. Domestic Chinese Entities

Since the development of China's 'open-door' economic policies, many new business entities and organizations have emerged in China which purport to possess the authority to enter into contractual relations with foreigners. In many cases, the creation of these organizations has occurred in a haphazard fashion. In line with current Chinese policies, many entities which were previously designated as bureaux, sections, or other agencies of local and provincial governments have simply changed their names and now present themselves in commercial transactions as enterprises.

In most cases, newly established Chinese enterprises style themselves as 'companies' (gongsi). However, the legal implications and consequences of this designation are unclear, especially as China has not yet promulgated a national company law. Therefore it is crucial that care be taken to confirm the authority of Chinese entities by other means.

As discussed earlier in this chapter, a Chinese entity possesses authority to enter into a contractual relationship only when it is constituted as a legal person. In general, evidence showing that a Chinese entity enjoys the status of a legal person may be obtained in the form of a business licence (*yingye zhizhao*) issued by the Chinese authorities. Such licences include the name of the enterprise, its address, scope of business and registered capital, the names of the chief management officials of the enterprise, and the term of validity of the licence.

In accordance with regulations issued in 1982 and 1983, all Chinese state-owned enterprises are now required to apply for and obtain business licences before they may commence business operations.[8] The regulations require that registration be undertaken with the State Administration for Industry and Commerce upon the submission of an application for registration, an approval document issued by the enterprise's department-in-charge, and a credit-standing certificate.[9] Upon approval of the enterprise's application and issuance of a business licence, the enterprise attains the status of a legal person.[10] A similar registration requirement has been imposed on collective enterprises and individual enterprises.[11]

In light of the foregoing, it is now possible to ascertain the legal status of a Chinese entity by examining its business licence. In the past, it has been difficult for foreign parties to persuade Chinese entities to provide copies of the entity's licence on the theory that such documents are *neibu* (for internal use only). Today, however, such documents are relatively easy to obtain. For example, a number of licences relating to China's major industrial enterprises have been published in book form.[12] In addition, rules regarding foreign economic contracts in the Shenzhen SEZ require Chinese enterprises to provide a copy of their business licence to the foreign party upon execution of a commercial contract.[13]

Although the business licence may serve to confirm the status of a Chinese entity as a legal person, the holder of such a licence does not necessarily enjoy the authority to enter into contracts with foreign parties. As discussed earlier in this chapter, an additional requirement must be met, namely that the Chinese entity possess foreign trade authority (*waimao quan*).

A Chinese legal person obtains foreign trade authority pursuant to an authority granted by the State Council or the Ministry of Foreign Economic Relations and Trade (MOFERT) acting on behalf of the State Council. Evidence of such authority may be obtained in the form of a 'business certificate' (*yingye zhengshu*), issued by the State Administration for Industry and Commerce, which specifically states that the scope of business of the Chinese enterprise includes foreign trade transactions.

Generally, entities that have obtained a business certificate do not also hold a business licence. Rather, in such cases, the business certificate serves a dual function, as a licence and as evidence of foreign trade authority. It should be noted, however, that the issuance of business certificates is a relatively new practice. Therefore, some Chinese entities may hold both a business licence and a business certificate, while others hold only a business licence. In the latter case, separate confirmation of foreign trade authority must be obtained.

Chinese enterprises are normally unwilling to provide evidence of foreign trade authority in the form of documents of authorization from the State Council or MOFERT. Such documents are usually classified as internal and may not be provided to foreigners. Therefore, confirmation of foreign trade authority may in such circumstances only be obtained by securing a Chinese legal opinion.

In addition to obtaining copies of documents evidencing a Chinese entity's status as a legal person and confirming its possession of foreign trade authority, a foreign bank will also wish to obtain copies of the constitution, charter, or articles of association of the enterprise, as well as resolutions ratifying the transaction with the bank.

With respect to articles of association, no existing Chinese law requires that Chinese entities formulate a corporate constitution.[14] Rather, the practice of drafting such documents has emerged largely in response to the demands of foreigners. As a result, many Chinese entities do not have articles of association or similar documents. Those which do, however, on occasion have made copies available to foreigners and many are published in Chinese and overseas journals devoted to China trade matters.

Chinese corporate constitutions are generally quite short, dealing in broad terms with the scope of business, organizational structure, and constitution of the board of directors of the enterprise. Consequently, it is important that all such documents provided by a Chinese entity be accompanied by a legal opinion or confirmatory document from the enterprise's department-in-charge certifying that such articles have been approved by the relevant Chinese authorities.

A final matter relating to corporate authority pertains to resolutions passed by the governing body of a Chinese enterprise. In general, Chinese entities do not conduct meetings of boards of directors and pass resolutions regarding corporate matters in the same way as do American or European companies. However, upon request by foreign parties in the context of specific transactions, Chinese entities will provide corporate resolutions addressing particular matters.

ii. Joint Ventures
Chinese-foreign equity joint ventures are also Chinese legal persons and their activities are subject to Chinese law.[15] However, matters relating to the corporate authority of joint ventures are far clearer than those arising in connection with true domestic Chinese entities.

Under the regulations governing joint ventures,[16] a joint venture is required to obtain a business licence and to formulate articles of association setting forth the rules for governance of the joint venture company. In addition, the joint venture regulations provide that 'the Board of Directors is the highest authority of the joint venture' and empower the joint venture company to fix the limits of its corporate powers, subject to the approval of the Chinese approval-granting authorities.[17]

On the basis of these statutory provisions, it is a relatively simple matter to ascertain the contractual authority of equity joint ventures. Copies of the company's business licence may be easily obtained, and the company's articles of association, once certified as having been approved by the Chinese government, should specify clearly the authorized scope of the joint venture's activities. The participation of the foreign party in the company generally ensures that the venture's other corporate practices, such as the ratification of corporate actions, the passing of resolutions, and so on, are conducted in accordance with customary Western practices.

Where a co-operative joint venture is established as a legal person, its corporate authority may be ascertained in the same manner as that of an equity joint venture. Where no entity separate from the venture is formed, however, the borrowing may be entered into by the Chinese or foreign party directly, rather than by the venture as such.

B. Signing Authority

Another legal problem which a foreign bank will confront in transactions with Chinese entities relates to the authority to sign. In particular, the question will arise as to the extent to which a foreign bank will be entitled to rely on the signature of a representative of a Chinese entity as being binding on the entity itself.

It has become common in business transactions involving foreigners in China today for both the Chinese and the foreign parties to evidence their contractual undertakings by means of the signatures of their authorized representatives. On the other hand, in internal (*neibu*) dealings between Chinese entities signatures are rarely used. More typically, contracts, memoranda, and other documents issued by a Chinese entity will bear the organization's seal, thus evidencing the authenticity and binding effect of the document.

No published Chinese law draws a clear distinction between the legal effect of documents bearing authorized signatures and documents bearing a seal. Rather, the distinctions has arisen out of practice.

Because of the collective nature of the Chinese economic and political systems, authority for legal undertakings and acts is seen to stem from the unit (*danwei*) rather than from the individual. Therefore, it is commonly thought by many Chinese that such authority can only be properly evidenced by the unit's seal. Seals are carefully guarded by Chinese entities and detailed records of their use are maintained. Moreover, Chinese entities are required by law to register an impression of their seal with the Public Security Bureau before it may be used.

Ideally, contractual documents involving Chinese and foreign parties should be signed by an authorized signatory and bear the seal of the Chinese party. In certain cases, however, it may not be practical to require the use of a Chinese entity's seal, particularly as Chinese law prohibits Chinese entities from removing their seals from China. Therefore, where various documents are required to be executed abroad, a foreign bank may be forced to rely only on the signature of a representative of the Chinese party.

The signing authority of the Chinese representative should be evidenced by an explicit letter of authority from the Chinese unit which bears the unit's seal. If possible, the letter should normally be accompanied by a notarized certificate certifying the authenticity of both the seal and the representative's specimen signature.

C. *Foreign Exchange and Other Approvals*

A major issue which must be confronted by a foreign bank in providing banking services to Chinese entities relates to China's foreign exchange control regulations. The extent to which the operations of a Chinese entity will be subject to these rules depends on the nature of the entity.

i. Domestic Chinese Entities

Chinese regulations permit approved domestic Chinese entities to hold foreign exchange funds in their own name. The source of such funds may be either a periodic allocation made to the enterprise by the state or earnings from the enterprise's foreign trade transactions.

However, China's foreign exchange regulations impose strict controls on the management and disposition of foreign exchange held by Chinese entities.[18] For example, domestic organizations are required to place all foreign currency held by them in a deposit account opened with the Bank of China.[19] In addition, domestic Chinese entities are prohibited from depositing foreign currency abroad without the prior approval of the State General Administration of Exchange Control (the SGAEC).[20]

In an effort further to strengthen central control over the handling of foreign exchange held by Chinese entities, the State Council promulgated supplementary foreign exchange rules in 1985.[21] These regulations prohibit 'the retaining, spending or depositing abroad of foreign exchange' and the 'accepting of loans offered by banks or business enterprises in foreign countries or Hong Kong and Macau' by all domestic Chinese entities without prior approval from the SGAEC.[22] Chinese entities which violate these provisions may be subject to fines and, in serious cases, to criminal sanctions.[23]

In short, then, Chinese domestic entities will be required to obtain an approval from the relevant authorities of China before they may enter into a loan contract or engage in banking transactions in Hong Kong with a foreign bank. In general, such foreign exchange approvals are of two types. The first type of foreign exchange approval is essentially a blanket approval which authorizes the Chinese domestic entity to engage in foreign exchange business and be responsible for its own foreign exchange affairs. This type of approval is granted in extraordinary cases only. As at the end of April 1986, 57 banks and financial institutions, including the Bank of China and its branches and CITIC, have been granted this authority. In all other cases, a specific approval must be obtained from the

People's Bank of China and the SGAEC on a transaction-by-transaction basis.

According to a document issued by the State Council in October 1985, all borrowings by domestic Chinese entities from banks or financial institutions abroad are to be conducted under the overall management of the People's Republic of China.[24] The document requires that all borrowers should, in principle, have the ability to repay the loans with foreign exchange generated by themselves. Whereas entities holding a blanket foreign exchange approval from the People's Bank need only report their borrowings to the SGAEC 'for the record', other borrowers must submit an application for the borrowing to the SGAEC which will report it to the People's Bank for approval. The application process requires the submission of information about the lending bank; the amount, term, and interest rate of the loan; and supporting documents, including a feasibility study for the use of the loan proceeds and repayment arrangements.

ii. Chinese Companies Abroad

Companies established by domestic Chinese entities abroad are also subject to China's foreign exchange control regime. For example, the Foreign Exchange Regulations require that the foreign exchange of 'enterprises and establishments in foreign countries or in the Hong Kong and Macau regions must, except for that portion kept locally as working funds according to the plan approved by the state, be transferred back' to the Bank of China.[25] Moreover, the 1985 Penal Provisions make it illegal for Chinese organizations established abroad to retain or deposit abroad any foreign exchange which has been 'unlawfully acquired' by such organizations or which 'should have been repatriated in accordance with the government regulations of the People's Republic of China'.[26]

Given these provisions, it is possible that, without a specific approval from the SGAEC, the deposit, pledge, borrowing, or maintenance of foreign exchange funds with a foreign bank would constitute a violation of Chinese law. Consequently, it is important that a foreign bank in its dealings with foreign companies owned or controlled by Chinese domestic organizations require confirmation from the SGAEC that the banking transaction contemplated has been approved by the foreign exchange control authorities of China and would not constitute a violation of Chinese law. In the event that the foreign exchange authorities are unwilling to provide such confirmation, a foreign bank should at least require a certificate from the Chinese customer warranting that it possesses the requisite authority to deal with its foreign exchange and that the transaction to be entered into would not constitute a violation of Chinese law.

iii. Joint Ventures

As Chinese legal persons, equity joint ventures established in China are also subject to Chinese foreign exchange control rules. However, the rules applicable to Chinese-foreign joint ventures are significantly more lenient than those governing Chinese domestic organizations.

Under the foreign exchange rules applicable to joint ventures,[27] joint ventures are permitted to open foreign exchange deposit accounts abroad or in Hong Kong and Macau after first obtaining an approval from the SGAEC.[28] The regulations also permit joint ventures to borrow funds from abroad, requiring only that they report the borrowings later to the SGAEC 'for the record'.[29]

In general, the issuance of a SGAEC foreign exchange approval with respect to the foreign exchange dealings of a joint venture is a fairly simple matter. Moreover, such exchange permits, unlike many of those issued to domestic organizations, may be provided to foreigners for inspection.

D. Guarantees

Closely related to the issues of corporate approval and foreign exchange control is the problem of guarantees. Guarantees have long been the most common form of security provided in connection with banking transactions involving China. In the past, such guarantees have been provided primarily by the Bank of China. During the past two years, however, a number of new organizations have emerged in China purporting to possess the requisite authority to issue guarantees of foreign exchange indebtedness.

Alarmed by what was perceived to be the growing and unregulated issuance of guarantees by local organizations, the State Council issued an internal document in July 1984 spelling out rules for the provision of guarantees by Chinese entities. Although the text of this document has not been made public, it reportedly limits the authority to issue guarantees to the same organizations which have been granted a blanket authority to manage their own foreign exchange affairs. Organizations not on this list must obtain a specific approval from the SGAEC before a guarantee may be legally issued. It should be noted that the issuance of a SGAEC authority does not in and of itself evidence the guarantor's financial ability to pay nor does it imply that the guarantee would be 'backed up' financially by the SGAEC in the event of a default.

A further strengthening of the regulatory regime applicable to the issuance of guarantees was provided by the promulgation on 20 February 1987 of the Provisional Measures for the Control of the Provision of Foreign Exchange Guarantees by Organizations within China. These regulations restrict the issuance of guarantees to (a) financial institutions designated by law as authorized guarantors and (b) non-financial enterprises with the status of a legal person which have sources of foreign exchange income. The total amount of foreign exchange guarantee liabilities of financial institutions may not exceed twenty times the amount of their foreign exchange funds. Foreign exchange guarantee liabilities of non-financial enterprises may not exceed the amount of the foreign exchange funds possessed by them.

E. Security

One of the most difficult issues which any bank may expect to confront in engaging in banking transactions with Chinese entities relates to security.

In other jurisdictions, many banks require hypothecation, pledge of assets, and other forms of security from customers in connection with banking transactions. Although such requirements are likely to pose few problems for Chinese companies operating abroad and Chinese-foreign joint ventures, it may be difficult to obtain agreement from true domestic Chinese entities for such arrangements.

At present, China has no national law governing matters such as the pledge of a Chinese company's assets to entities abroad. Moreover, the concept behind such arrangements is inimical to the basic precepts underlying the role of state-owned enterprises in a socialist economy. As discussed earlier in this chapter, a fundamental characteristic of a legal person is that it enjoys the power independently to control property. It should be kept in mind, however, that the actual ownership of property held by a state-owned enterprise rests with the state. In Chinese legal terminology, such ownership is vested 'in the whole people'.

According to commentaries on Chinese civil law,[30] the property ownership right of state-owned enterprises is limited to a right to control and manage such property on behalf of the state. Moreover, such control and management powers must be exercised in accordance with the state plan and other directives of governmental authorities. Therefore any disposition of property entrusted to a state-owned enterprise which is in violation of state policy is, under Chinese law, null and void.

Given the above, the acquisition of a security interest in property owned by a Chinese state-owned enterprise is fraught with uncertainty. According to Chinese legal authorities, such arrangments may only be entered into upon approval, granted on a case-by-case basis, by 'the relevant authorities' of China. Therefore it is important that the validity of any such undertakings be confirmed by means of a Chinese legal opinion or a specific approval from the department in charge of the enterprise concerned.

While uncertainty does exist in this area, recent legal developments offer some guidance to foreign banks contemplating the creation of security interests in property located in China property. For example, Article 89 of the Civil Code recognizes the preferential right of a creditor in property furnished as security for a loan and Article 32 of the Enterprise Bankruptcy Law of the PRC, discussed further below, recognizes the preferential rights of a creditor in the property of a bankrupt enterprise furnished as security.

Of particular interest are the Regulations of the Shenzhen Special Economic Zone on the Administration of Mortgage Loans (cited hereafter as the Shenzhen Mortgage Regulations), which set forth detailed rules governing mortgage agreements between financial institutions and other entities within the SEZ. A mortgage agreement must be in writing.[31] The mortgage must be registered.[32] If real property is used to secure a loan, the mortgage must be registered with the Shenzhen Real Estate Administration Bureau. If the mortgaged property is damaged or destroyed due to the intentional act or negligence of the mortgagor, the mortgagor must provide a new security or guarantee within fifteen days. If the mortgagor fails to provide a new security or guarantee, the mortgagee may accelerate the repayment of the principal and interest.[33] The mortgagor may not rent, sell, transfer, or remortgage the property without the consent of the mortgagee.[34]

The Shenzhen Mortgage Regulations continue by providing that if the mortgagor fails to repay the interest and principal upon expiration of the loan agreement, the mortgagee may foreclose on the property.[35] The regulations provide specific procedures for foreclosing on mortgaged property. For example, if the mortgaged property is real estate, the foreclosure may be made only through public auction. The mortgagor must obtain an auctioning certificate from the Shenzhen Real Estate Administration Bureau. The auction must be undertaken by an auctioning agency designated by the Shenzhen People's Government. Proceeds from the auction will be used to repay the loan after deduction of foreclosure expenses and taxes. Failure to follow the foreclosure procedures will render the foreclosure ineffective.

As the Shenzhen Mortgage Regulations are quite new (having been promulgated only in February 1986) there is very little practical experience on which a foreign bank may rely to predict how they will be implemented. In evaluating the risks involved in taking a mortgage on property located in the Shenzhen SEZ, we believe that a foreign bank should consider the following factors.

(a) As mentioned above, the foreclosure procedures require the foreign bank to obtain an auctioning certificate from the Shenzhen Real Estate Administration Bureau and the auction to be conducted by an auctioning agency designated by the people's government. Clearly, a foreign bank will wish to ascertain whether the mortgaged property is owned directly or indirectly by a government agency or state enterprise. In cases where the property is owned by a government agency or state enterprise, one may question how effectively the government will enforce the foreclosure procedures when it is essentially foreclosing against itself.

(b) In addition, we presume that mortgaged property will typically be used to secure a loan by a foreign bank in foreign exchange (that is, US or Hong Kong dollars). Although the Shenzhen Mortgage Regulations set forth specific foreclosure procedures, there is no requirement that the auctioning agency sell the property for foreign exchange. Consequently, it is possible that the proceeds from the auction may be in *renminbi*, which presumably would not be satisfactory to the foreign bank.

(c) Furthermore, while the Shenzhen Mortgage Regulations require that, if the mortgaged property is damaged due to the intentional act or negligence of the mortgagor, the mortgagee may accelerate the loan and demand immediate repayment of interest and principal, they are silent on the mortgagor's obligation to maintain the property in good condition.

(d) The Shenzhen Mortgage Regulations provide that the foreclosure auction of a mortgaged property will be suspended if there is a dispute over the ownership of the property.[36] The regulations do not, however, state how such a dispute will be resolved, and it appears that the auction can be suspended indefinitely.

(e) The Shenzhen Mortgage Regulations do not provide, for example, that an unregistered mortgage is void or invalid, nor do they provide that a prior unregistered mortgage will be subordinated to a subsequently registered mortgage. On the contrary, they provide that if the mortgagor had not received the consent of the mortgagee before he remortgaged the property, the subsequent mortgage would be invalid.[37] Accordingly, if a foreign bank takes a mortgage on a property on which there is an unregistered prior mortgage, and if the mortgagor has not obtained the consent of the prior mortgagee, the prior mortgagee may be able to use this provision as a basis to challenge the foreign bank's right to foreclose on the property during the auctioning process.

Thus, by failing to define any adverse legal effect of not registering a mortgage, the Shenzhen Mortgage Regulations provide little enforcement incentive for mortgages to be registered and made public. If a property is mortgaged to a foreign bank but the bank fails to uncover a prior unregistered mortgage, the foreign bank may be surprised by the prior mortgagee's challenge when it later attempts to foreclose on the property. Moreover, if such a challenge is raised, it may suspend indefinitely the auctioning process, which is the only foreclosure method available under the Shenzhen Mortgage Regulations when the mortgaged property is real estate.

F. Bankruptcy

Another matter that deserves attention is the issue of bankruptcy. In this connection, two issues arise. First, in the event of the bankruptcy of a Chinese entity abroad which owes money to a foreign bank, what access would the foreign bank have to assets owned by the company in China? The second question is essentially the inverse of the first, namely, in the event of bankruptcy in China by a Chinese domestic enterprise which maintains assets or other property with a foreign bank abroad, what access would creditors of the bankrupt enterprise have to such assets?

The Enterprise Bankruptcy Law of the PRC (for trial implementation) (hereafter cited as the Bankruptcy Law) was adopted by the Standing Committee of the National People's Congress on 2 December 1986 after long debate. The Bankruptcy Law is scheduled to become effective, on a trial basis only, three months after the State-owned Enterprise Law of the PRC takes effect. It should be noted that the Bankruptcy Law as adopted applies only to Chinese state-owned enterprises, and not to joint ventures or wholly foreign-owned enterprises.[38]

Under the Bankruptcy Law, a debtor state-owned enterprise or any creditor of a state-owned enterprise may bring a bankruptcy action before a Chinese people's court in the event that the debtor has suffered serious losses and is unable generally to pay off its debts. Certain state-owned enterprises such as public utilities and enterprises which have an important bearing on the national economy will not be declared bankrupt if the government is providing them with financial assistance, and enterprises which have located a guarantee will not be declared bankrupt if such enterprises will pay off their debts within six months of the bankruptcy application. If the claim is upheld by the people's court after examination, the management of the bankrupted enterprise will be entrusted to a liquidation committee designated by the court.

The principal mandate of this committee is to establish a plan for liquidating the enterprise and distributing bankruptcy property. After liquidation, the proceeds from the sale of the bankrupt's assets are distributed on an equal basis to all creditors of the bankrupted enterprise, in proportion to each party's share of the bankrupt's outstanding debts. Certain bankruptcy expenses, such as expenses of litigation and other common expenses of creditors, are paid off on a priority basis. The Bankruptcy Law provides that creditors with rights secured by property which have arisen prior to the declaration of bankruptcy shall be accorded preferential rights. Unsecured creditors have no such preferential rights.

The Bankruptcy Law sheds little light on the effect of a bankruptcy with respect to assets held by the bankrupt enterprise outside China. The Bankruptcy Law provides that Chinese civil procedure regulations govern matters which remain unregulated under the Bankruptcy Law. The Chinese Civil Procedure Code does not apply to a Chinese enterprise outside China, and the Civil Code provides only that ownership rights to real property shall be governed by the law of the place where such property is situated. Thus, at least in the case of real property, it appears unlikely that domestic Chinese creditors of the bankrupted company would have access to assets of the bankrupt which are held by a foreign bank abroad.

It is also important to note the effect of Article 108 of the Civil Code which provides, in part, that if a debtor is temporarily incapable of repaying a debt, the debtor may, subject to permission from the creditor or a ruling from the people's court, repay the debt in instalments. An obvious issue of concern to foreign banks relates to whether the interest of the people's court would be the same as that of the foreign creditor.

IV. Form of Documentation

In the late 1970s and early 1980s, most foreign bankers recorded their credit relationships with PRC entities in documents which were generally abbreviated in form. (Some major credit agreements, such as those relating to the Great Wall Hotel in Beijing, were exceptions to this rule.)

From late 1982 and 1983 the form of documentation utilized in financing transactions in the PRC became more sophisticated. The present documentation closely resembles credit agreements utilized internationally and typically uses an English or Hong Kong law format. The lengthier versions of documents based on New York law are not commonly adopted in PRC transactions.

In practice this means that foreign financial institutions may anticipate loan agreements of approximately 30 to 50 pages supplemented by several annexes. The annexes would include such items as guarantees, assignments of ancillary contracts, and performance bonds. Most PRC credit agreements of any significance will contain many of the clauses generally found in international financing transactions, including sections on defined terms, conditions precedent, drawings and repayment, prepayment and cancellation, alternative interest rates, taxes, evidence of debt, representations and warranties, undertakings, events of default, set-off, amendment and waiver, and governing law and jurisdiction.

V. Leasing Transactions

While the subject of leasing transactions in China is difficult to summarize briefly, the following are some of the legal issues that financial institutions should consider when entering into PRC leasing transactions.

A. Documentation

Most of the leasing transactions that have occurred in the PRC to date involve the financing of aircraft. The form of documentation utilized in this area is generally similar to that used in most international aircraft finance transactions. Frequently Hong Kong or English law is the governing law, so that the documents used essentially follow the English law format.

Although it used to be said that China was unwilling to sign agreements which were more than two pages in length, this is clearly untrue today. In the aircraft finance area in particular, documentation is typically quite lengthy, and may exceed 100 pages. In other types of equipment leasing transactions in China, however, the documentation might be only 15 to 25 pages in length.

B. Definitions

In addition to the standard definitions found in international lease contracts, documents should also include specific references to the 'base rate interest', as this will be important later for determining the amount, if any, of the lease payment subject to withholding tax in China. Of course, references to the currency and guarantor should also be included, as should a definition of interest and principal.

C. Equipment, Purchase Contract, and Delivery

Again, the provisions on these issues in lease transactions in the PRC are similar to those found in standard international lease contracts. Nevertheless, it is obviously important from the lessor's perspective that these items be covered, in order that it may insulate itself from claims for defects in equipment or failure of delivery.

D. Guarantee

This is another critical part of most PRC lease transactions, as in any PRC financing transaction, in so far as many lenders look for guarantees to secure the payment of rentals. Sometimes these guarantees have 'trigger levels' for leases above certain monetary amounts. The area of guarantees is one of the most significant, especially since, as has been discussed elsewhere in this chapter, not every PRC entity has the legal capacity to issue foreign exchange guarantees.

E. Security Interests

In general, no formal registration procedure exists in China to register security interests in assets. However, as mentioned elsewhere in this chapter, foreign lessors should review the Shenzhen Mortgage Regulations because even though these regulations are in effect only in Shenzhen, they nevertheless have a national relevance.

The Interim Procedures for Bank Mortgage Loans, promulgated on 15 December 1984, are also important. In particular, paragraph 5C of the Procedures, while primarily a discussion of fixed assets, provides that if a borrower raises a mortgage on a factory building or house, the borrower should register the mortgage with the competent authorities 'to the effect that the buildings belong to the bank'. Of more relevance to our discussion regarding leasing is the final sentence, which provides that: 'Such liquid assets as large machines or equipment can also be mortgaged in this way.' This is one of the few places in China's laws where provision is made for the registration of the ownership of assets being used as security. It may serve as a precedent in other finance areas.

VI. Governing Law and the Enforcement of Legal Obligations

Depending on the specific provisions of a credit agreement, there may be circumstances in which a foreign bank may be obliged to seek the enforcement of a foreign court judgment in China. Alternatively, in certain types of transactions a foreign bank may be obliged to agree to arbitration or to seek recourse against a Chinese party in Chinese courts.

This section examines what recourse a foreign bank would have against Chinese entities in the event of a default on their legal commitments: (a) where the contract provides for dispute settlement by arbitration; (b) where the contract provides for recourse in Hong Kong courts; and (c) where a foreign bank seeks recourse in Chinese courts.[39]

A. Arbitration

Chinese contracts with foreign parties frequently provide for binding arbitration in a third country, often in Stockholm, Sweden, before the

Arbitration Institute of the Stockholm Chamber of Commerce, if the parties cannot resolve their differences within a certain period of time. While banks are generally averse to such clauses because they fear that the arbitration may result in a compromise, they often prefer the risks attached to arbitration to the risks attached to litigation. Thus, to the extent that such provisions can be obtained, many contracts will call for arbitration, and further provide that any arbitration award shall be final and binding, and shall be accepted by the parties as such.

If a foreign bank were to obtain an arbitration award, what recourse would it have if the Chinese party refused to honour the award? The People's Republic of China recently acceded to the United Nations Convention on the Recognition and Enforcement of Foreign Arbitral Awards of 1958 (the New York Convention or the Convention), and therefore is now under an international obligation to enforce arbitral awards against Chinese entities. In acceding to the New York Convention, China declared pursuant to Article 1 of the Convention that it would apply the terms of the Convention only to awards made in the territory of another contracting state and only as to commercial matters. In addition, if the Chinese entity has assets in a jurisdiction that also adheres to the New York Convention, the bank would be able to enforce its award to the extent of those assets in that jurisdiction as well.

If a Chinese party refuses to honour a foreign arbitral award, and if its assets are located exclusively, or almost exclusively, in China, it may be necessary for the recipient of the arbitral award to ask a Chinese court to enforce it. Despite China's recent accession to the New York Convention, the ability of a foreign recipient of a foreign arbitral award to use the courts of China for the enforcement of such an award still remains unclear.

Although Article 195 of the Chinese Civil Procedure Code[40] specifically provides that a party may apply to a people's court for the enforcement of an award by 'a foreign affairs arbitration organization of the PRC', the Code does not provide for the enforcement of an award by a non-Chinese arbitration organization. However, Article 204 does provide for the enforcement of a foreign court *judgment*. It states:

In dealing with a judgment or ruling which has already been determined and which a foreign court has entrusted a people's court of the PRC to execute, the people's court should examine the judgment or ruling on the basis of an international treaty signed or participated in by the PRC or in accordance with the principles of comity. It should issue a ruling to recognize the legal effect of such judgment or ruling and execute the same according to procedures if the court believes that such a judgment or ruling does not violate the basic principles of the laws of the PRC or China's national and social interests. Otherwise, the people's court should return it to the foreign court.

An arbitral award of, for instance, the Arbitration Institute of the Stockholm Chamber of Commerce can be confirmed, that is, converted into a 'judgment', by a Swedish court. However, so far as is known, Swedish courts will not request foreign courts to enforce Swedish judgments. That is, Swedish courts do not 'entrust' other courts to execute Swedish judgments in the way apparently contemplated by Article 204.

Perhaps most important is the fact that it is impossible to predict the outcome in a people's court of China if a foreign court were to 'entrust' a judgment to it. Article 204 authorizes the people's court to 'return' the judgment if it 'violate[s] the basic principles of the laws of China or China's national and social interests'. It is true that other jurisdictions have somewhat similar rules permitting a court to refuse to recognize a foreign judgment when recognition would be contrary to 'public policy'. However, in other jurisdictions, it is known that the 'public policy' exception to the enforcement of foreign judgments is narrowly applied. As the people's courts of China have not dealt with the issue, there is at present no assurance that they would narrowly interpret this part of Article 204, particularly if the court found that the underlying transaction was not properly authorized by the Chinese government or if a violation of Chinese law was involved. It should be noted that the New York Convention also provides that recognition and enforcement of an arbitral award may be refused if such recognition and enforcement would be contrary to the public policy of the country asked to recognize and enforce the award. It is impossible to predict how broadly Chinese courts may interpret that provision of the Convention.

Finally, it should be noted that a binding arbitration clause may not actually be binding under Chinese law. Article 192 of the Civil Procedure Code provides:

With respect to disputes arising from foreign economic, trade, transport and maritime affairs, if the parties have a written agreement to submit the dispute to a foreign affairs arbitration organization of the PRC for arbitration, they may not file a lawsuit in the people's courts. If there is no such written agreement, they may file a lawsuit in the people's courts.

Thus, as Article 192 is phrased, a Chinese party to a binding arbitration provision which provides for arbitration by an arbitral organization outside the People's Republic of China may ignore the provision and sue in a people's court instead. On occasion, Chinese officials have stated that Article 192 would not be literally applied by the people's courts, and that a Chinese party to a binding arbitration agreement providing for non-PRC arbitration would *not* be able to institute suit in a people's court in derogation of the provision. However, the issue has never come before a people's court.

B. Recourse in Hong Kong Courts

If the parties have not provided for binding arbitration, but the contract provides for a submission to the jurisdiction of the Hong Kong courts, the Chinese party may raise various defences in the proceedings. In the absence of an explicit waiver in the contract, one of these defences may be sovereign immunity.

In comparison to United States law,[41] the law on this subject which is applicable in Hong Kong is strikingly simple. The State Immunity Act 1978 (the SIA) of the United Kingdom occupies a place equivalent in Hong Kong law to that occupied by the Foreign Sovereign Immunities Act (FSIA) in United States law. The SIA was extended to Hong Kong in 1979.

Like the FSIA, the SIA preserves a presumption of immunity with respect to the governments of foreign states and their departments. However, a 'separate entity'—corresponding roughly to an 'agency' or 'instrumentality' in the FSIA's terms—is *not* entitled to a presumption of immunity. An entity is a 'separate entity' if it is 'distinct from the executive organs of the government of the State and capable of suing or being sued.'[42]

A separate entity will be immune from suit under the SIA only if 'the proceedings relate to anything done by it in the exercise of sovereign authority', *and* 'the circumstances are such that a State. . .would have been so immune'.[43] A state is not immune if the proceedings 'relate to a commercial transaction entered into by the State'.[44] The SIA specifically defines 'commercial transaction' to include:

any loan or other transaction for the provision of finance and any guarantee or indemnity in respect of any such transaction or of any other financial obligation. . .[45]

Therefore, neither a state nor a 'separate entity' belonging to a state will enjoy immunity from proceedings for payment of a debt in Hong Kong courts.

Besides the 'commercial transaction' exception to immunity from suit, a state will of course not be immune 'as respects proceedings in respect of which it has submitted to the jurisdiction of the courts of the United Kingdom [or Hong Kong]'.[46]

The SIA has separate rules regarding the execution of judgments. There may be occasions on which state property is sought in satisfaction of a judgment. If such property is 'for the time being in use or intended for use for commercial purposes', it is not immune, *regardless* of its relation to the claim on which the judgment is based.

Of course, if a judgment has been obtained against a 'separate entity' for failure to pay a loan, its property is not exempt whether used for 'commercial purposes' or not. However, the English courts are, if anything, more respectful of the distinctness of a 'separate entity' from the sovereign to which it belongs, and of its distinctness from other separate entities belonging to the same sovereign. Hence, it is quite unlikely that a judgment creditor would be able to enforce its judgment against an entity of the state other than the entity which actually borrowed the money.

There are separate rules for a state's 'central bank or other monetary authority'. They enjoy the same immunity from execution that a state enjoys, and, furthermore, 'property of a State's central bank or monetary authority shall not be regarded. . .as in use or intended for use for commercial purposes'.[47] Hence such property appears totally immune unless the creditor has obtained a waiver.

C. Recourse in the PRC Courts

In respect of most transactions with Chinese entities, the question of recourse ultimately devolves to questions of enforceability in the PRC courts. This is because most Chinese entities are not likely to have sufficient assets outside China to satisfy a judgment or arbitration award against them. However, there are no decided cases in the PRC on which to base an analysis of the likely result, regardless of whether the action is for enforcement, or is in the form of a suit commenced in Chinese courts in the first instance. Nevertheless, it is important to recall that in all such instances Chinese law will be applied to determine whether the transaction is in accordance with Chinese legal requirements. Therefore an action for enforcement of a foreign judgment, or a suit brought at first instance, could be denied on the argument that the Chinese party's actions exceeded its legal authority, or involved a violation of Chinese foreign exchange control laws, or were otherwise contrary to Chinese legal stipulations.

D. Waiver of Sovereign Immunity

As is well known, the issue of sovereign status is one of great historical interest to China. As a result of China's past experience with foreign countries, China is particularly sensitive to any request that it waive its immunity as a sovereign. Nevertheless, China recognizes its role as a responsible member of the international community and many PRC-related financing transactions will contain a waiver of immunity, even though abbreviated in form.

The waiver of immunity which a foreign financial institution may obtain from a PRC borrower will typically not exceed one or two paragraphs in length and usually takes the form of an acknowledgement by the PRC borrower that the execution and performance of the loan agreement is a commercial activity. The clause will frequently also 'expressly waive' any defence of sovereign immunity or any other defence based on the fact that the borrower may be a party or instrumentality of a state or government. Sovereign immunity will frequently be discussed in the context of the general subject of governing law and the jurisdiction for the enforcement of any arbitration order relating to the loan contract.

In summary, although the issue of sovereign immunity remains a sensitive one, most foreign financial institutions have succeeded in obtaining some form of waiver by PRC borrowers of any purported immunity. Of course, the foreign lender must ensure that a sufficient explanation is given to the PRC borrower describing why the waiver is customary in international finance transactions.

VII. Conclusion

This chapter has provided a brief overview of the main legal issues encountered in connection with financing activities between foreign financial institutions and entities in the People's Republic of China. While it is clear that numerous issues remain, particularly in the security, bankruptcy, and enforcement areas, foreign financial institutions should be encouraged by the significant progress China has made over the past five years in defining the legal relationship between foreign financial institutions and Chinese entities.

Notes

1. See 'How China Obtains International Commercial Loans', *China Market*, November 1986, pp. 7–9.
2. Decision of the Central Committee of the Communist Party of China on Reform of the Economic Structure, issued on 20 October 1984.
3. General Provisions of the Civil Code, adopted at the Fourth Session of the Sixth National People's Congress on 12 April 1986 and effective from 1 January 1987, Secs. 9 and 36.
4. See *Zhonghua renmin gongheguo minfa jiben wenti* (*Basic Problems in the Civil Law of the People's Republic of China*) (Beijing, Institute of Civil Laws of the Central Political-Legal Cadres' School, 1985), pp. 72–80.
5. See Constitution of the People's Republic of China, adopted on 21 April 1982, Art. 3.
6. Civil Code, Art. 50, note 3 above.
7. It should be noted, however, that the Chinese are now in the process of drafting a law governing co-operative joint ventures which reportedly will provide for the creation of legal persons along the lines of a partnership. In addition, Articles 30–5 of the Civil Code offer some information regarding partnerships between individuals.
8. See Regulations on the Registration and Administration of Industrial and Commercial Enterprises, promulgated by the State Council on 9 August 1982 (cited hereafter as the Enterprise Registration Regulations); Rules for the Implementation of the Regulations on the Registration and Administration of Industrial and Commercial Enterprises, promulgated by the State Administration for Industry and Commerce on 13 December 1982 (cited hereafter as the Enterprise Registration Implementing Rules); and the Provisional Regulations for State-owned Industrial Enterprises, promulgated by the State Council on 1 April 1983 (cited hereafter as the Enterprise Regulations).
9. See Enterprise Registration Regulations, Arts. 3 and 9, note 8 above; and Enterprise Registration Implementing Rules, Arts. 22 and 24, note 8 above.
10. See Enterprise Regulations, Art. 18, note 8 above.
11. See Policy Provisions of the State Council on Urban Non-Agricultural Individual Economy, promulgated on 7 July 1981, and Provisional Regulations of the State Council on Several Policy Questions Relating to Urban Collective Economy, promulgated on 14 April 1983.
12. See State Administration for Industry and Commerce (ed.), *Zhongguo qiye dengji nianlan* (*Annals of China's Enterprise Register*) (Hong Kong, China Look Publishing House, 1984).
13. See Provisional Regulations Regarding Foreign Economic Contracts of the Shenzhen Special Economic Zone, promulgated on 7 February 1984, Art. 9.
14. It should be noted, however, that since the promulgation of the Interim Banking Control Regulations on 7 January 1986, the People's Bank of China has begun to enforce a policy of requiring financing institutions to prepare articles of association for the approval of the People's Bank.
15. See Law of the People's Republic of China on Joint Ventures Using Chinese and Foreign Investment (cited hereafter as the Joint Venture Law), pro-

mulgated on 8 July 1979, Art. 2; and Implementing Act for the Law of the People's Republic of China on Joint Ventures Using Chinese and Foreign Investment (cited hereafter as the Joint Venture Law Implementing Act), promulgated on 20 September 1983, Art. 2.

16. See Joint Venture Law, Art. 3, note 15 above; and Joint Venture Law Implementing Act, Arts. 11 and 16, note 15 above.

17. Joint Venture Law Implementing Act, Arts. 16 and 33, note 15 above.

18. See the Provisional Regulations for Foreign Exchange Control of the People's Republic of China (cited hereafter as the Foreign Exchange Regulations), promulgated by the State Council on 18 December 1980.

19. Foreign Exchange Regulations, Art. 4, note 18 above.

20. Foreign Exchange Regulations, Art. 6, note 18 above.

21. See the Penal Provisions for Violation of Exchange Control (cited hereafter as the Penal Provisions), promulgated on 25 March 1985.

22. Penal Provisions, Arts. 4 and 6, note 21 above.

23. Penal Provisions, Arts. 3, 5, 7, and 10, note 21 above.

24. See 'How China Obtains International Commercial Loans', p. 8, note 1 above.

25. Foreign Exchange Regulations, Art. 8, note 18 above.

26. Penal Provisions, Art. 4, note 21 above.

27. See Rules for the Implementation of Exchange Control Relating to Enterprises with Overseas Chinese Capital, Enterprises with Foreign Capital and Chinese-Foreign Joint Ventures (cited hereafter as the Implementing Rules), promulgated by the SGAEC on 1 August 1983.

28. Implementing Rules, Art. 6, note 27 above.

29. Implementing Rules, Art. 17, note 27 above.

30. See *Basic Problems in the Civil Law of the People's Republic of China*, pp. 136–44, note 4 above.

31. See Regulations of the Shenzhen Special Economic Zone on the Administration of Mortgage Loans (cited hereafter as the Shenzhen Mortgage Regulations), promulgated in February 1986, Art. 11.

32. Shenzhen Mortgage Regulations, Art. 13, note 31 above.

33. Shenzhen Mortgage Regulations, Art. 17, note 31 above.

34. Shenzhen Mortgage Regulations, Art. 18, note 31 above.

35. Shenzhen Mortgage Regulations, Art. 22, note 31 above.

36. Shenzhen Mortgage Regulations, Art. 25, note 31 above.

37. Shenzhen Mortgage Regulations, Art. 18, note 31 above.

38. Enterprise Bankruptcy Law of the People's Republic of China (for trial implementation), *Renmin ribao* (overseas edition), 3 December 1986, p. 4. It is also interesting to note that local bankruptcy rules had been implemented earlier in some areas of China on a 'trial basis' and that in September 1986, a factory in Shenyang was the first enterprise in China to be found bankrupt.

39. The authors gratefully acknowledge the assistance of their colleague, B. Thomas Peele, in the preparation of this section.

40. The Civil Procedure Law of the People's Republic of China (cited hereafter as the Civil Procedure Code), adopted on 8 March 1982 for trial implementation.

41. For a discussion of United States law on this point, which is embodied in the Foreign Sovereign Immunities Act (FSIA), see B. T. Peele and E. Theroux, 'China and Sovereign Immunity', *China Law Reporter*, No. 2, 1983, p. 129.

42. SIA, § 14.

43. SIA, § 14(2).

44. SIA, § 3(1)(a).

45. SIA, § 3(3)(b).

46. SIA, § 2(1).

47. SIA, § 14(4).

11. Investing and Doing Business in China: The Environmental Implications

MITCHELL A. SILK

I. Introduction

A rise in foreign investment and domestic reforms in China have brought about a need for closer attention to the environmental aspects of investing and doing business in China. American investment alone has reached US$1 billion, with US$600 million invested in offshore oil exploration and exploitation and over US$150 million allocated to joint ventures involving machine-building, nuclear plants, coal-mining, chemicals, petroleum, motor vehicles, textiles, food, and the tourist industry.[1] Such ventures have a profound impact on China's environment. Furthermore, the post-Mao reform programme has led to heightened environmental awareness and realistic environmental decision-making.[2] The genesis of a theory of individualized property rights and their enforcement has led to the more efficient use of resources. The decontrol of prices has brought about a balance between market prices and scarcity values, and has thereby tended to discourage wasteful consumption. Administratively, the establishment of a State Bureau of Environmental Protection and the strengthening of related regulatory agencies both illustrate the greater importance attached to environmental betterment and, perhaps more significantly, allow for stronger enforcement. Indeed, there is a rising number of reports of stiff civil, administrative, and criminal penalties being meted out to both Chinese and foreign polluters.

This chapter will consider issues related to environmental protection that may confront the investor in China. Part II will trace the development of environmental law in China. Part III will examine the means by which post-Mao China is dealing with the regulation of the environment, focusing on the environmental laws and regulations which have a potential impact on investing and doing business in China. Specific attention will be paid to the Environmental Protection Law (for trial implementation) (1979), the Marine Environmental Protection Law (1983), and various regulations dealing with joint ventures. Part IV will analyse key liability issues arising in the enforcement of the environmental laws.

II. The Development of Environmental Law in China

Environmental protection is not a new problem in China. Scattered provisions bearing on the rational use of resources and environmental protection under Shang dynasty law,[3] and in the Qin,[4] Tang,[5] and Qing codes[6] are evidence of an early recognition of the evils of environmental degradation. After the fall of the Qing dynasty, the Nationalist government continued Imperial China's programme with a concerted effort to regulate the environment. This early effort laid the foundation for Taiwan's present environmental law framework.[7]

The People's Republic of China (PRC) first realized the potential threat that rapid modernization posed to the environment in the early 1950s. However, two factors served to constrain an early comprehensive approach to environmental protection. First, and most basic, much needed progress in reforms and modernization required a foundation. China thus had to give priority to economic development and political consolidation. Second, China, along with the rest of the world, lacked an adequate understanding of the issue of environmental protection. Indeed, the unsystematic nature of the regulations promulgated during this period are evidence of a failure to grasp the issue as a whole.[8]

The havoc of the Cultural Revolution impeded further efforts until the early 1970s. Then the PRC's official entrance into the United Nations,[9] as well as the severe state of environmental degradation,[10] pushed China into an intensified effort to manage the environment. In the international arena, China made a showing—albeit a politicized one—at the first United Nations Conference on the Human Environment. There it lobbied for the placing of the burden of pollution control on industrial states and argued that developing countries should have the right to exploit their own resources freely.[11] Domestically, in 1972, the State Council enunciated the 32-character basic policy, later to be codified as the guiding principles that were to be the driving force behind environmental protection.[12] In the following year the PRC's First National Environmental Protection Conference was convened.[13] This conference laid the groundwork for the establishment of an administrative organic structure (including the Office of Environmental Protection) and the drafting of numerous regulations on the protection and betterment of the environment.

The post-Mao reforms have ushered in a period of sophistication and fruition in China's efforts at environmental protection. Policy reports and the statements of high-ranking leaders reveal that environmental protection has gained the status of a policy priority even though it was not officially included in the Four Modernizations.[14] Furthermore, China has adopted a comprehensive approach in developing a corpus of legislation on environmental protection which specifies goals and individual rights, and provides for practical means for enforcement.[15] Provisions on environmental protection were included in the 1978 and 1982 Constitutions.[16] In 1979 China passed its first draft Environmental Protection Law[17] and Forestry Law.[18] These aside, China has since promulgated laws and regulations on, *inter alia*, the regulation of water pollution,[19] marine resources,[20] the preservation of land,[21] grasslands, fisheries,[22] water and soil conservation,[23] wildlife protection, and mineral resources.[24] Laws regulating air pollution, noise control, solid waste disposal, and toxic waste management are currently being drafted. Part III will examine the Chinese approach to the protection and betterment of the environment, and will focus on selected provisions of those environmental laws and regulations which bear on investing and doing business in China.

III. Environmental Protection in Post-Mao China

The rapid development of the Chinese laws governing environmental protection has brought to the fore yet another list of considerations and issues that affect investment decisions. This section will explore the evolving means by which China seeks to regulate and enhance the environment. These means include the enforcement of a hybrid form of property right which has come to be known as an 'environmental right'; direct government and/or Party regulation of pollution which may be both technology based and performance based, requiring payment for activities which generate pollution; and the subsidizing of private attempts at controlling pollution or otherwise bettering the environment.

A. The Enforcement of Environmental Rights

Prior to the advent of complex—and sometimes incomprehensible— statutory schemes in the West, the most basic approach to the control of the environment was through the maintenance of various property and tort actions. These actions were most commonly grounded in nuisance, trespass, and innocent-use theories. Specifically, courts often granted injunctions and/or damages to landowners injured by industrial pollution.[25] Recent legal and economic reforms have given rise to similar action under Chinese law. Actual practice in enforcing 'environmental rights'[26] in China reveals, on the one hand, growing environmental awareness, and yet, on the other hand, serious shortcomings in environmental administration and the maintenance of social order in China.

Four recent publicized pollution cases are illustrative of the trend. They share similar facts.[27] In each case, a controversy arose when a factory or industry, disregarding laws set in place, used simple, indigenous technology in production. This gave rise to serious pollution in one form or another. In the first case, the Linfei factory in Hubei province, operating in the late Mao period in an agricultural area, discharged large amounts of sulphur dioxide and noxious gases into the air and water. This caused agricultural production to drop by as much as 70 per cent in the surrounding area.[28] In China's most heralded pollution case, Wuhan's major coal-shipment pier offloaded coal on archaic conveyor belts that were not fitted with anti-pollution devices. The machines emitted clouds of black smoke, thereby endangering the health and welfare of 20,000 residents in the area.[29] In the third case, a cake and pastry factory in Beijing's Western district used archaic machinery that produced a deafening noise and shook so violently that the vibrations caused thermoses on table-tops in the adjoining area to bounce around. The incessant noise took its toll on neighbouring workers, who were unable to sleep.[30] In the last case, in Guilin, the manager of a restaurant located on the ground floor erected a 14-metre-high exhaust pipe, the mouth of which came right up to a fourth-floor resident's window. The pipe emitted large amounts of steam, smoke, dust, and carbon dioxide, causing the resident to pass out on numerous occasions.[31]

These circumstances gave rise to popular protest which took various forms. The residents staged rallies and lodged complaints with local government standing committees and administrative bureaux. They also sent letters to newspapers and pasted up *dazibao* (big-character posters). In all four cases, the complaints for the most part went unheeded. The degree to which remedial measures were pursued ranged from nil to informal negotiations.

This complacency led angered local citizens to take the matter into their own hands. Citizens living next to the Linfei factory sabotaged its power supply, thereby incapacitating it.[32] In the Wuhan port case, local residents damaged the port's electricity room and the unloading machines. Operations were halted for a week, causing a loss of 11,000 *yuan*.[33] Two young workers living in a house adjoining the Beijing cake and pastry factory shattered the factory's plate-glass window out of frustration. The glass fell into flour bins which had to be discarded.[34] Finally, residents living above the Guilin restaurant stopped up the exhaust pipe with cement and metal plates. This act forced the restaurant to shut down for over ten days and brought about a loss of over 4,200 *yuan*.[35] In all four cases, public security units detained the culprits. The accused's behaviour in each case was, prima facie, illegal under the applicable criminal laws or acts, and fulfilled the three basic criteria for actionable conduct under Chinese law: namely, the conduct endangered society, the act was intentional, and the act was proscribed by law.[36]

In all four cases, however, administrative or Party officials gleaned from the standing environmental protection laws an 'environmental right' which served to mitigate civil liability and criminal responsibility. Culprits already sentenced were released, exonerated, and awarded damages. Where the culprits were being held pending trial, they were simply let free. Furthermore, the factory management in each case was ordered to control the pollution, and prevent further degradation.

These cases serve the dual purpose of illustrating the genesis of environmental rights in China and underscoring problems in their administration and enforcement. On the one hand, the cases highlight the regime's growing concern with environmental protection. Ordinary citizens and even Party members who destroyed factory equipment in acts of desperation were eventually exonerated, while the polluters were criticized for failing to act in a socially responsible manner. On the other hand, however, the cases serve to reveal more troublesome administrative quirks both in regulating the environment and in maintaining social order as a necessary pre-condition to rapid modernization. The cases support the proposition that realizing gains in modernization within China's socialist economic system, and at the same time maintaining social order and regulating the environment, constitute yet another of China's great contradictions. On the one hand, the factories involved in the pursuit of higher productivity presumably acted at least with the tacit support, and possibly at the behest, of their parent ministries or bureaux. On the other hand, the public security apparatus was predisposed to protect state and collective property, and maintain social order without regard to mitigating circumstances. Caught between these opposing forces were the new environmental regulatory agencies. These agencies were largely powerless when it came to imposing their will on polluters, and had to rely on intervention from higher Party or government authorities.

In the light of the legal and administrative procedures followed, one is also led to question whether the implications of these cases serve to further environmental enforcement while maintaining social order. The protection of the culprits' 'environmental rights' was justified by the evolving doctrine of self-preservation or self-defence, which in effect allows individuals to take the law into their own hands in cases of dire danger when all legal remedies have been pursued to no avail, and when the action is proportionate to the danger.[37] However, in the light of dangerous precedents set in the cases above, the ends of invoking 'self-defence' to enforce 'environmental rights' deserve close scrutiny. It is indeed ironic that the Chinese have recognized—in contravention of their own legal principles —the right to violence. After all, the right to use force in self-defence is circumscribed and can only be used against individuals, and even then only in the face of imminent harm.[38]

Thus, whether the enforcement of 'environmental rights' will become a viable deterrent to pollution will depend in large part on the ability of China's legal and administrative system to react to the shortcomings mentioned above by adopting formal and concrete remedial measures. At the very least, the cases call for a clear delineation between unlawful acts of aggression and the legal use of force where environmental rights are concerned, and strengthened environmental and related regulatory agencies. The next section deals with some of the more formal and predictable controls used to limit pollution and regulate the environment.

B. Direct Regulation of the Environment

i. Regulating Pollution: The General Scheme
The Chinese have recently become more dependent on direct government and Party mechanisms to regulate the environment. These controls are generally either performance based or technology based. Technology-based controls require the installation of pollution-control devices at a specified level of technology which will ensure that discharges do not exceed prescribed levels. Performance-based controls, on the other hand, attempt to achieve or maintain the quality of the environment by setting standards for either (a) a specified ambient quality, or (b) the limit of discharges.

China has proceeded on both fronts. The first air- and water-quality standards appeared in 1962,[39] and were superseded by a second set of standards in 1973.[40] Technology-based regulations emerged in 1978.[41] The 1978 directive incorporated the 'three simultaneous points', which require the fitting of pollution-control devices and environmental assessment at the three stages of design, construction, and operation.

The 1979 Environmental Protection Law (for trial implementation) (hereafter cited as the EPL), and local regulations (such as the 1986 Provisional Regulations for Environmental Management in Foreign Economic Development Zones, hereafter cited as the 1986 Provisional Regulations) have codified both of these mechanisms, and have a built-in monitoring device in requiring submission and approval of an environmental impact assessment before design may begin.[42] All construction and production facilities, new or existing and under modification, must therefore first include in initial plans and then maintain 'effective' (*you xiao*) pollution-control measures.[43] Aside from the administrative drawbacks to the requirements, direct technology controls may represent an area of potentially substantial benefit to the foreign business man. For, in the light of foreign superiority in pollution-control technology, the potential for sales and investment in environmental-control and environmental-regulation technology, waste treatment, and instrument industries is great. In this regard, two major environmental-regulation and pollution-control technology exhibitions at which there was a strong foreign presence have taken place.[44] China is also negotiating and has concluded a number of major deals with foreign companies related to pollution control and solid waste management equipment.[45]

The EPL and the 1986 Provisional Regulations also embody performance-based controls in requiring that all discharges comply with set state or local standards.[46] Shortly after the EPL's promulgation, standards governing ambient air and water quality were issued.[47] The State Council Environmental Protection Leading Group and the Ministry of Urban and Rural Construction and Environmental Protection have since issued standards governing practically every aspect of the environment.[48] Thus, even if a specific law governing one type of pollution is lacking, polluters will still be held responsible under the relevant standards.

In practice, however, China's direct regulation system is not without its flaws. First, the entities responsible for enforcing performance-based controls lack sufficient means of monitoring compliance and have often been disregarded. With respect to quality standards, in contrast to the American system, for example, which monitors discharge quality through permits,[49] China still lacks a viable permit process.[50] Only recently were provisions governing permits included in the 1983 Marine Environmental Protection Law and the 1984 Water Pollution Prevention and Control Law (hereafter cited as the WPPCL).[51] As far as discharge standards are concerned, polluters have been known to argue that, in the words of one observer, 'Compliance [is] a matter of convenience rather than a legal obligation'.[52] A number of reasons support such defiance, for example, the unclear 'trial implementation' status of the EPL and other related laws and regulations, as well as weak administrative and judicial units. Second, in the absence of political support, technology-based controls have been widely disregarded. The media frequently report cases of shutdown orders and other administrative procedures remaining unenforced until high Party or government authorities intervene.[53]

ii. Regulating the Marine Environment[54]
The environmental rights and obligations of foreign investors in Chinese waters is of great practical significance in light of the magnitude of foreign interests in China's marine area. The major piece of legislation governing the marine environment is the 1983 Marine Environmental Protection Law (hereafter cited as the MEPL).

The MEPL is the culmination of China's efforts at regulating the marine environment. Prior to the MEPL, China promulgated numerous regulations bearing on the protection of aquatic resources and fishing waters, all of which included provisions on the marine environment.[55] On the international plane, China signed the 1982 United Nations Convention on the Law of the Sea (hereafter cited as the 1982 LOS Convention)[56] and in theory may be viewed as approving its provisions.[57] Article 194(1) of the 1982 LOS Convention provides that:

States shall take. . . all measures consistent with this Convention that are necessary to prevent, reduce and control pollution of the marine environment from any source, using for this purpose the best practicable means at their disposal and in accordance with their capabilities.

Of such measures and means, the Convention requires states to 'adopt laws and regulations to prevent, reduce, and control pollution of the marine environment from land-based sources' (Art. 207(1)), 'arising from or in connection with sea-bed activities subject to their jurisdiction' (Art. 208(1)), 'from activities in the area by dumping' (Art. 210(1)), 'from vessels' (Art. 211(1)), or 'from or through the atmosphere' (Art. 212(1)). Soon after signing the 1982 LOS Convention, China promulgated the MEPL.[58]

The MEPL deals with the effects on the marine ecology of coastal construction projects, offshore oil exploration and exploitation, pollutants from the land, damage by ships, and the dumping of wastes and toxic and thermal materials. This section will deal with the general regulatory scheme of the MEPL relevant to foreign investment, and analyse it in the light of international legislation and the general principles of the law of the sea.

a. Pollution from Vessels   The MEPL's substantive provisions on pollution from vessels are generally consistent with the relevant international legislation. Article 211 of the 1982 LOS Convention provides that:

States, acting through the competent international organization or general diplomatic conference, shall establish international rules and standards to prevent, reduce, and control pollution of the marine environment from vessels. . .

The International Maritime Organization (IMO, formerly IMCO) is the main international organization that deals with marine pollution. China has acceded to the IMO's two main treaties dealing with pollution from vessels,[59] namely, the 1969 International Convention on Civil Liability for Oil Pollution Damage (hereafter cited as the 1969 Brussels Convention),[60] and the International Convention for the Prevention of Pollution by Ships (hereafter cited as the MARPOL).[61]

The MEPL provisions on pollution from vessels incorporate into Chinese law, albeit broadly, selected provisions of these two conventions. The 1969 Brussels Convention deals mainly with the imposition and apportioning of liability upon the owners of ships spilling or discharging oil, and the provision of compensation. First, in terms of ensuring financial security, Article 28(2) of the MEPL[62] parallels Article VII(1) of the 1969 Brussels Convention.[63] Second, Article 43 of the MEPL, although not limited to pollution from vessels, which excuses liability in cases where marine pollution arises from an act of war, *force majeure*, or 'negligence or other wrongful acts on the part of the departments responsible for [lighthouses] or other navigational aides', resembles Article III(2) of the 1969 Brussels Convention.[64]

The MARPOL, along with its two Protocols, however, is concerned mainly with the elimination of marine pollution through prophylactic measures. This goal parallels the aim of China's environmental planners. Again, there is a striking similarity between Article 27 of the MEPL[65] and Regulation 4 of the MARPOL (73/78).[66]

The provisions of the MEPL and the two international conventions vary, however, in at least five regards. First, and most significant, the scope of the MEPL is far broader than that of the two conventions. Under Article 45 of the MEPL, the law applies to:

Pollution damage to the marine environment . . . through *any* direct or indirect introduction of substances or energy into the marine environment, which results in such deleterious effects as harm to marine living resources, hazards to human health, hindrance to fishing and other legitimate activities at sea, impairment of quality for use of sea water and degradation of the environmental quality [my italics].

The 1969 Brussels Convention, however, only regulates environmental damage attributable to oil. Second, and most troubling, is the issue of jurisdiction over foreign vessels. The language of the MEPL and China's stand on the extent of its jurisdiction in coastal waters manifest an expansive view of China's jurisdictional reach in the waters off its coast, namely, beyond its territorial sea and beyond a 200-mile limit.[67] Third, with regard to third-party liability, the right of recourse with regard to a third party only *partially* liable for damage is not as clear under Article 43 of the MEPL as the comparable provision under the 1969 Brussels Convention (Article III(2)(b)).[68] Fourth, the MEPL requires a mere fitting of anti-pollution devices, whereas the MARPOL requires inspection. Arguably, however, regardless of the difference in language, the goals of these two provisions coincide in that they both require all vessels of the specified weights to be equipped with anti-pollution devices of some sort. Last, the MEPL is not as specific as the MARPOL as to the exact anti-pollution devices required. This gap is filled in part by the Regulations of the People's Republic of China on the Prevention of Marine Pollution by Vessels (hereafter cited as the Vessel Regulations).[69] Article 15 of the Vessel Regulations requires the installation of many of the devices provided in the MARPOL's Regulation 4.

b. Pollution from Offshore Oil Exploration and Exploitation   Increased offshore testing and drilling activities have raised the potential for marine pollution from offshore oil exploration and exploitation.[70] The resulting pollution may take many forms.[71] Mobile and fixed platforms discharge, dispose of, and leak oil, waste, and other pollutants. Explosive blasts disrupt fishery resources. Worst of all, unanticipated oil spills, as illustrated by the spill off the coast of Santa Barbara in January 1969[72] and the Ekofisk incident of April 1977,[73] pose a threat to the marine environment. The MEPL, along with the Regulations of the People's Republic of China on Marine Environmental Protection from Oil Exploration and Exploitation (hereafter cited as the Oil Exploration Regulations),[74] contain provisions that govern each of these situations.

The MEPL and the Oil Exploration Regulations cover five general areas and adopt both performance- and technology-based controls. First, all operations must adhere to the relevant state standards and regulations when discharging pollutants into the water. Article 12 of the MEPL requires strict control of exploration and exploitation to prevent leakage. Articles 13 and 15 forbid the direct discharge of pollutants into the sea, and allow discharge only in accordance with state standards.[75] Article 14 prohibits the disposal of oily industrial wastes into the sea. Disposal of other wastes must not damage fishing grounds and waterways.

Second, all organizations engaged in offshore oil activities must submit an environmental impact statement.[76] The statement must include, *inter alia*: (a) the oilfield's name, geographic location, the probable types of pollutants to which it will give rise, and their quantity and method of discharge; (b) the condition of the natural marine environment and resources in the area surrounding the oilfield; (c) the environmental impact on waterways, scenery, and tourism in the surrounding area; and (d) the impact on the natural environment and resources, as well as comments on preventive measures, and the severe and unavoidable impact of oil development.[77]

Third, all enterprises must take measures to protect fishery resources when using explosives.[78] Explosives, which are commonly used in oil exploration, have serious adverse effects on the marine ecosystem. In the light of this, the MEPL bans explosive operations during the fishing or spawning seasons, or in spawning grounds. Operators must therefore take the relevant time and geographic circumstances into account when planning blasting.

Fourth, the MEPL embodies certain prophylactic measures aimed at controlling pollution from drilling activities. Article 16 requires that '[o]ffshore oil pipelines and oil storage installations shall always be kept in good condition fulfilling requirements against seepage, leakage, and corrosion . . . .'.

Last, measures must be taken to prevent and, in the case of actual occurrence, to handle blow-outs and oil spills.[79] Article 17 thus requires operators to have available 'appropriate anti-pollution facilities and equipment', and to take 'effective technical measures . . . to prevent blow-outs or oil spills'. In the case of a blow-out or oil spill, Article 17 also requires the organization to file a report immediately and to take effective measures to control and eliminate the pollution.

c. *Pollution from Ocean Dumping*   The unmonitored disposal into the sea of human, industrial, and hazardous wastes has created a serious marine environmental problem. The MEPL provisions on ocean dumping and the Regulations of the People's Republic of China on the Control of Marine Dumping (hereafter cited as the Dumping Regulations)[80] mark China's initial attempt at dealing with this critical problem.[81]

The MEPL places stringent restrictions on dumping in China's waters. Article 38 of the MEPL employs a permit process in requiring all entities to apply to the relevant state administrative department, in this case the State Bureau of Oceanography, for permission to engage in dumping activities. The application must contain, *inter alia*: (a) the location of the dumping; (b) the name, quantity, and form of substance being dumped; (c) the type and specifications of packing; and (d) the means of transport.[82] Second, Article 39 of the MEPL places loading, location, and time restrictions on all dumping activities, all of which will be set forth in the dumping permit.

Last, after the dumping is completed, Article 40 requires the submission of a detailed report of the operation. Reports should record transportation conditions, the actual time—from beginning to end—of the dumping, the actual location of the dumping, whether or not the packing stayed intact, and whether or not any waste leaked out.[83] Troubling, however, is the fact that neither the MEPL and the Dumping Regulations nor proposed legislation on the control of solid and hazardous wastes address the problem of the treatment or cleaning up of wastes dumped in the past.[84]

iii. The Preservation of Land and Natural Resources
China has placed a premium on the preservation of its land and natural resources. Constraints on space do not permit detailed analysis here of all the laws and regulations in this area. At the very least, when planning any ventures which have a potential impact on forests, fisheries, grasslands, or mineral resources, the investor should refer to the new laws and revisions in these areas, namely, the revised 1984 Forestry Law, the 1985 Grasslands Law, the 1986 Fisheries Law, and the 1986 Mineral Resources Law.[85]

China's interest in the rational use of land resources is manifested in the 1986 Land Management Law, which includes provisions on exclusive rights, land-use rights, land use and protection, the use of land in state construction, and the use of land in township and village construction.[86] China's concern with land management bears directly on the foreign investor in the areas of land valuation and the determination of land-use fees, which in the past have been computed for the most part unevenly, and sometimes even arbitrarily. The Land Management Law provides a basic framework for the calculation of land-use and reclamation fees; the foreign investor will, however, have to turn to emerging local standards and implementing regulations, and—assuming the enterprise qualifies— to Article 4 of the new State Council Regulations on the Encouragement of Foreign Investment in order to attempt to determine the fraction of the investment to be allotted for such fees. Local standards and regulations have already been promulgated in such places as Shenzhen, Xiamen, Tianjin, Dalian, and Ningbo.[87]

C. Economic Means of Pollution Control: Incentives and Disincentives

Economic means of controlling pollution may take one of two forms. First, the government may employ economic incentives to encourage the polluter to take appropriate control measures. These may take the form of direct subsidies or tax incentives for private attempts at controlling pollu- tion or otherwise bettering the environment. An alternative method is to use an economic deterrent, such as effluent fees, in requiring payment for activities which generate pollution. China has adopted both of these means.

i. Subsidies and Tax Incentives

There are two regulations which bear on direct government subsidization of, and tax incentives for, the installation of pollution-control devices. First, in 1977, the State Planning Commission, the State Capital Con- struction Commission, the Ministry of Finance, and the State Council Environmental Protection Leading Group issued a circular on the control and recycling of the industrial 'three wastes', which includes a provision granting tax benefits for the installation of industrial 'three-waste' control or recycling devices. Article 7 of the Circular Reproducing Some Regula- tions on Developing Industrial 'Three Waste' Multiple Use provides for the reduction or elimination of the tax liability of industrial enterprises that use 'three-waste' recycling technology. The amount of benefit is to be determined by the provincial, municipal, or autonomous region authorities.[88] However, the treatment of qualifying enterprises which have no tax liability in the year in question is not discussed.[89]

Second, a circular jointly issued by the Ministry of Finance and the State Council Environmental Protection Leading Group in 1979 grants subsidies, such as three- to five-year tax holidays, and allows the reten- tion of profits stemming from recycling.[90] While such subsidies are politi- cally and economically attractive, they also have their disadvantages. In terms of actual pollution control, the subsidies may not necessarily have a noticeable effect on the environment since they are normally funnelled into areas other than pollution control owing to output demands.[91] Furthermore, such subsidies are geared towards the adoption of specific technologies as opposed to socially beneficial behaviour.[92]

THE ENVIRONMENTAL IMPLICATIONS 413

ii. Disincentives: Effluent Fees

China has also implemented a system of making the polluter pay for certain discharges. The assessment of effluent fees was codified in the EPL,[93] and revenues deriving from these fees are to be used in environmental protection work. The fees are calculated according to the 1982 Provisional Measures for the Assessment of Effluent Fees.[94] In a related measure, polluters who, in good faith, clean up their activities are eligible for a rebate of up to 80 to 90 per cent of the fees assessed.[95]

IV. Enforcement of the Environmental Protection Laws: Practice and Procedure

A key to bettering the environment lies in the area of enforcement, for even the most complete and sound substantive provisions on environmental protection are meaningless without effective sanctions, implementation, and enforcement. Aside from the economic disincentives mentioned above, the environmental protection laws generally impose civil liability and criminal responsibility on those who breach the law. This section will deal with key environmental enforcement means and liability-related issues in the Chinese system, as highlighted by selected recent cases.

A. Criminal Responsibility

Of the extant legislation on environmental protection, the EPL,[96] the MEPL,[97] the WPPCL,[98] the Forestry Law,[99] and the Fisheries Law[100] all include provisions on criminal responsibility. Model cases reveal that the Chinese have not been bashful in meting out criminal responsibility for environmental infractions where the circumstances have warranted such action. In China's most publicized pollution case, the Suzhou Municipal Intermediate Court imposed a two-year prison sentence on a factory worker, Zhang Changlin, for the negligent discharge of 28 tons of a liquid chemical, cyanide, into a nearby river.[101] The factory suffered a loss of over 35,000 yuan, and the discharge killed over 130,000 fish, 10,000 clams, and other animals.[102] This sentence, the likelihood of bearing criminal responsibility for environmental infractions not actually included but analogous to provisions in the Criminal Law,[103] the fact that the Criminal Law is applicable to foreigners,[104] and the willingness of the Chinese to impose criminal responsibility on foreigners (especially where health and safety are at issue),[105] should be sufficient incentive for close environmental monitoring by foreign investors. It appears, however, that the foreign corporate manager or executive in question would have to participate actively in, or at the very least have specific knowledge of, the environmental infraction in order to be held criminally responsible in China, as opposed to the tendency in the United States of holding executives or management criminally responsible for plant violations or workplace negligence of which they were not necessarily but should reasonably have been aware.[106]

B. Civil Liability

An issue of far greater importance and less conjecture to the foreign entity doing business in China is that of civil liability for environmental infractions. The two environmental statutes most relevant to foreign activities in China both include provisions relating to civil liability. Article 32 of the EPL and Article 42 of the MEPL require polluters to pay damages for pollution of the environment. The measure of damages under the EPL will be based on the actual losses caused by the pollution, the costs incurred in eliminating the pollution, and the injured party's loss of any income.[107] Neither the EPL nor the MEPL specifies a ceiling on damages; however, at least with regard to the MEPL, a Chinese commentator has stated that China will adhere to the relevant provisions of any international convention to which it is a party.[108] Recourse under the MEPL would be to contest liability for the amount of damages pursuant to the Law of Civil Procedure of the People's Republic of China.

A recent pollution case involving a Hong Kong corporation, that was tried by the Shenzhen Intermediate People's Court and subsequently affirmed by the Supreme People's Court,[109] sheds light on the issue of civil liability for pollution in the context of a foreign investment in China's special economic zones. Kaida Enterprises, Ltd. (Hong Kong) built a wholly-owned foreign factory in the Shekou Industrial District in the early 1980s. The plastic-toy factory involved a total investment of US$16 million. Shortly after production began in 1982, the factory began to discharge large quantities of malodorous and toxic gases, and was operating at a noise level far in excess of state standards.

The local monitoring station attempted to persuade the factory on numerous occasions to control the situation. After the orders went unheeded the monitoring station brought an action in the Shenzhen Municipal Intermediate People's Court seeking an injunction and damages. Kaida pleaded that its agreement did not include any provisions on environmental control, and that it was not economically feasible to install pollution-control equipment. After careful investigation, from which it became evident that Kaida had in fact breached numerous environmental laws, the court ordered the company to take control measures by 31 October 1984, and pay a fine of HK$20,000 and court costs. This decision was subsequently affirmed by the Supreme People's Court.

The decision, the first of its kind and affirmed by no less a body than the Supreme People's Court, is instructive in a number of respects. First, the court made it clear that China's environmental laws are without question binding on foreigners operating in China—whether or not there are any contract provisions to that effect—and that foreign investors will most certainly be held responsible for failure to adopt pollution-control measures, and will be liable for damages arising from resulting pollution. This is consistent with the letter and spirit of various Chinese laws bearing on foreign business operations in China. For example, the 1985 Foreign Economic Contract Law, in the absence of relevant stipulations under Chinese law, employs international norms[110] and also requires that contracts dealing with the activities of certain ventures involving foreigners be carried out in spite of new legal provisions.[111] In fact, there have been reports that joint ventures involving foreign investment have been prompted to add additional pollution-control devices to facilities after the conclusion of negotiations, with the foreign party bearing the costs.[112] Second, the court emphasized that the principle of sovereignty embodies the right of a country to protect its environment, and thus grants the right to take pollution-control measures where nuisances arise within its jurisdiction. This reasoning echoes the most basic principle of international law, namely, that an independent state's sovereignty is inviolable.[113] Thus, in the light of this decision, the foreigner operating in China would be well advised either to determine actual environmental protection obligations and take pollution control into consideration in the initial investment calculation, or be prepared to pay later.

V. Conclusion

Environmental protection has been a concern in China since imperial times. China's recent efforts at reform and modernization have brought about a renewed and intensified interest in the area. In the post-Mao period, China has taken a comprehensive approach to the control and betterment of the environment. Environmental rights have emerged, and are zealously defended. Direct controls over all areas of the environment are now being implemented. Further, a host of economic means are now being used to control pollution. Recent cases indicate that foreigners also have a role in China's environmental drive, with non-conformers being subject to civil and criminal penalties. Certainly, though, active participation in the programme has its benefits for the foreign investor. Environmental planning in the early stages of a project will ensure fewer problems later, and may even be profitable given the incentives available. More obvious, however, is the tremendous potential available in aiding the Chinese in their drive for a better environment by providing much needed pollution-control and recycling technology.

Notes

1. See 'US Investment Up in China', *Beijing Review*, 25 November 1985, p. 30.
2. The major elements of these reforms include the introduction of a largely household-based agricultural contract-guarantee system instead of people's communes, a general decentralization of the market with market mechanisms taking the place of central procurement and distribution monopolies, and heightened foreign trade and investment. *The China Quarterly*, No. 100, 1984, is devoted to an analysis of the Chinese economic reforms. For background, see, generally, A. D. Barnett, *China's Economy in Global Perspective* (Washington, DC, Brook-

ings Institution, 1981); C.Y. Cheng, *China's Economic Development: Growth and Structural Changes* (Boulder, Colo., Westview Press, 1982); and J. Prybyla, *China's Economy: Problems and Policies* (Columbia, SC, University of South Carolina Press, 1981).

3. See Cai Shouqiu, 'On the Character of the Environmental Protection Law', *Faxue yanjiu (Studies in Law)*, No. 3, 1981, p. 15, citing the legalist philosopher Han Feizi (died 233 BC) on Yin dynasty (*circa* 1800–1200 BC) law.

4. The Qin dynasty lasted roughly from 221 BC to 206 BC. On environmental protection, the Qin Code included provisions forbidding the cutting of lumber in mountain forests in the spring; the blocking up of waterways; the burning of grass to be used as fertilizer unless in the summer; the picking of budding plants; the poaching of young animals, birds' eggs, and young birds; and the killing of fish and turtles with poison. Ma Xiangcong, 'Preliminary Discussion on the Law of Environmental Protection', *Faxue yanjiu*, No. 2, 1979, p. 40. Excavations conducted since 1975 in Hubei province have unearthed portions of the Qin Code. The first of its eighteen chapters, *Tian lu (Law on Land)*, contains numerous provisions on environmental management and protection. See Shuihudi Qin mu zhujian zhengli xiaozu, *Shuihudi Qin mu zhujian (Bamboo Writings from the Qin Tombs at Shuihudi)* (Beijing, Wenwu chubanshe, 1978), pp. 24–9.

5. The Tang dynasty lasted from 618 to 907 AD. In the 'Miscellaneous Articles' section of the Tang Code, there were provisions regulating, *inter alia*, the digging of pits (394), land use (including mountainsides and the shores of lakes) (405), and the burning of fields and wilderness lands during the wrong season (430). W. Johnson, *The T'ang Code* (Princeton, NJ, Princeton University Press, 1979), pp. 287–9.

6. The Qing dynasty lasted from 1644 to 1911. Numerous provisions in the Qing Code relate to environmental protection and conservation. See the relevant articles in 'Land and Tenements' (such as §§ 97 and 98), 'Miscellaneous Offences' (such as § 376), and 'Public Ways' (such as §§ 433 and 434), translated in G.T. Staunton, *Ta tsing leu lee (The Qing Code)* (Taipei, Ch'eng Wen Publishing Co., 1966 reprint), pp. 103–5, 411, and 471–3.

7. Taiwan's regulatory arsenal includes the Forestry Law (1932, last amended in 1972), the Water Conservation Law (1942, last amended in 1974), the Air Pollution Prevention and Control Act (1975, subsequently amended in 1982), the Water Pollution Prevention and Control Act (1974, subsequently amended in 1983), the Waste Materials Clean Up Law (1974, subsequently amended in 1980), and the Resource Control Law (1980). The Chinese texts are in Tau Baichuan and Wang Zeqian (eds.), *Liu fa quan shu (The Complete Six Codes)* (Taipei, San Min Book Co., 1983), pp. 1009–10, 1021–6, and 1456–65. The English texts of the air and water pollution amendments, as well as the Executive Order of 23 March 1981 by the Ministry of Communications Governing Marine Pollution, Jianfa (70), Zi No. 6250, are in Fa Jyh-pin, 'Legislation and Constitutional Interpretations of Human Rights in the Republic of China, 1982–83: An Overview', in H. Chiu (ed.), *Chinese Yearbook of International Law and Affairs*, Vol. 3 (Baltimore, Md., Occasional Papers/Reprints in Contemporary Asian Studies, 1983), pp. 87 and 93–7. For recent developments, see Qiu Congzhi, 'The Importance of Incorporating Environmental Protection Policy into the Law', *Lianhe bao (United Daily)*, 16 December 1985, p. 2.

8. During this early period, China promulgated the following regulations: Measures Governing Land Requisition for National Construction (1953), in *Zhongyang renmin zhengfu faling huibian (Collection of Laws and Decrees of the Central People's Government)* (Beijing, Falu chubanshe, 1955), Vol. 4, pp. 86–90 (hereafter cited as the FLHB); Provisional Measures on Highway Afforestation (1956), in *Zhonghua renmin gongheguo fagui huibian (Collection of Laws and Regulations of the People's Republic of China)* (Beijing, Falu chubanshe, 1956), Vol. 3, pp. 267–70 (hereafter cited as the FGHB); Provisional Programme for Water and Soil Conservation (1957), in FGHB, Vol. 6 (1958), pp. 433–8; Regula-

tions Governing the Safety of Drinking Water (1959), in FGHB, Vol. 10 (1960), pp. 410–16; and Regulations on Forest Protection (1963), in FGHB, Vol. 13 (1964), pp. 205–14.

9. Just before its twenty-sixth session, the United Nations General Assembly passed a resolution to admit the People's Republic of China. See United Nations General Assembly Resolution 2758 (XXVI), *UN Monthly Chronicle 8*, No. 10, November 1971, p. 61; and *UN Monthly Chronicle 8*, No. 11, December 1971, p. 26.

10. See, generally, Sen-dou Chang, 'Urban Environmental Quality in China: A Luxury or a Necessity?', in C. Pannell and C. Salter (eds.), *China Geographer*, No. 12, 1985, pp. 81–99; and V. Smil, *The Bad Earth: Environmental Degradation in China* (New York, M.E. Sharpe, 1985).

11. For coverage of China's participation in the 1972 Stockholm Conference, see J. Greenfield, *China and the Law of the Sea, Air, and Environment* (Germantown, Md., Sijthoff and Noordhoff, 1979), pp. 219–21; and J. Gresser, 'The Principle of Multiple Use in Chinese Environmental Law', in J. Cohen (ed.), *Legal Aspects of Doing Business in China* (New York, Practising Law Institute, 1983), p. 453. A summary of the Chinese position at the conference is given in *Beijing Review*, 23 June 1972, p. 9.

12. The policy espouses the following principles: comprehensive planning and rational resource allocation, multiple use and the conversion of harmful substances to beneficial uses, reliance on the masses and collective action, and protection of the environment and enrichment of the people's life. See Jiang Bikun and Guo Rui (eds.), *Huanjing baohu fa jianghua* (*Lectures on Environmental Protection Law*) (Zhangjiakou, Falu chubanshe, 1980), p. 30; Guo Jicai, Li Jiling, and Wang Zhenshao, 'The Four Modernizations and Enactments for Environmental Protection', *Faxue* (*Jurisprudence*), No. 8, 1982, p. 36; and Wen Boping, 'Notes on China's Environmental Protection Law', *Faxue yanjiu*, No. 1, 1980, pp. 21–5.

13. See sources cited in note 12.

14. Officials at the Third Plenum of the Eleventh Party Congress recognized that it was necessary to fit environmental protection into the scheme of socialist modernization since it would guarantee stable production rates, safeguard the masses' health, and quell environmental concerns. Furthermore, Vice-Premier Wan Li stated that economic development and environmental protection must proceed in tandem rather than the one before the other. See Cai, p. 15, note 3 above; Li Peng, 'Protecting the Environment Is a Major Task Facing China', *Renmin ribao* (*People's Daily*), 8 January 1984, p. 2; Ma Hong, 'Strive to Improve Our Country's Environmental Protection Work', *Huanjing baohu* (*Environmental Protection*), No. 2, pp. 4–6 and No. 3, pp. 2–5; Ma Xiangcong, 'A Study of the Legal System of Environmental Protection', *Zhongguo huanjing kexue* (*Environmental Sciences in China*), No. 1, 1981, p. 23; Song Qiping and Shao Boding, 'A Brief Talk on the Status and Fundamental Principles of Environmental Protection Law in China', *Zhongguo huanjing kexue*, No. 4, 1984, p. 45; and *Guangming ribao* (*Enlightenment Daily*), 1 January 1984, p. 1.

15. See Chen Lihu, 'Creating a Body of Local Environmental Civil Law', *Huanjing* (*Environment*), No. 5, 1984, pp. 28–32.

16. There are two articles regarding environmental protection in the 1978 Constitution. Article 6 provides that 'Mineral resources, waters and those forests, underdeveloped lands and other marine land resources owned by the state are the property of the whole people'. Article 11 provides that 'The state protects the environment and natural resources and prevents and eliminates pollution and other hazards to the public'. Chinese and English texts are in Fang Chun-ie, Zhang Xin, Chou Ling Ling, and Choy Mei-pik, *Zhonghua renmin gongheguo fagui xuanji* (*Laws and Regulations of the People's Republic of China*) (Hong Kong, Kingsway Publishers, 1982), Vol. 1, p. 1; and *Documents of the First Session of the Fifth National People's Congress of the People's Republic of China* (Beijing, Foreign Languages Press, 1978), pp. 125–72.

The 1982 Constitution, like that of 1978, also contains two provisions regarding environmental protection. Article 9 provides that 'Mineral resources, waters, forests, mountains, grassland, unreclaimed land, beaches, and other natural resources are owned by the state, that is, by the whole people, with the exception of the forests, mountains, grassland, unreclaimed land and beaches that are owned by collectives in accordance with the law... The state ensures the rational use of natural resources and protects rare animals and plants. The appropriation or damage of natural resources by any organization or individual by whatever means is prohibited'. Article 26 provides that 'The state protects and improves the living environment and the ecological environment, and prevents and remedies pollution and other public hazards... The state organizes and encourages afforestation and the protection of forests'. Texts in Foreign Languages Press, *The Constitution of the People's Republic in China* (Beijing, Foreign Languages Press, 1983); and *Renmin ribao*, 5 December 1982, p. 1.

17. The Chinese text of the Environmental Protection Law can be found in *Renmin ribao*, 17 September 1979, p. 2; Ministry of Urban and Rural Construction, Office of Environmental Protection, *Guojia huanjing baohu fagui wenjian huibian* (*Collection of Laws, Regulations, and Materials on State Environmental Protection*) (Beijing, Zhongguo huanjing kexue chubanshe, 1983), p. 38 (hereafter cited as the BFWH); and Chinese Academy of Environmental Science, *Zhonghua renmin gongheguo huanjing baohu yanjiu wenxian huibian* (*A Compilation of Research Materials on Environmental Protection in the People's Republic of China*) (Beijing, Falu chubanshe, 1983), p. 32 (hereafter cited as the HBYWX). The English text can be found in *Collection of Laws and Regulations of China Concerning Foreign and Economic Trade Relations* (Sydney, David Syme and Co., Ltd., 1983), Pt. XI, pp. 44–59; Gresser, pp. 45–54, note 11 above; Owen D. Nee, Jr. (ed.), *Commercial, Business and Trade Law: People's Republic of China* (New York, Oceana Publications, 1985), Vol. 2, Pt. 14, pp. 1–14; L. Ross and M. Silk, *Environmental Law and Policy in China* (Westport, Conn., Greenwood Press, 1986); Smil, pp. 231–8, note 10 above; and S. Swannack-Nunn, *Environmental Protection in the People's Republic of China* (Washington, DC, National Council for US–China Trade, 1979).

18. The Forestry Law was amended in 1984. The Chinese text is in *Renmin ribao*, 23 September 1984, and is translated in Ross and Silk, note 17 above.

19. The Water Pollution Prevention and Control Law (hereafter cited as the WPPCL). The Chinese text is in *Renmin ribao*, 13 May 1984, p. 3; *Xinhua yuebao* (*Wenxian ban* [Documents Edition]), No. 5, 1984, p. 63; *Zhonghua renmin gongheguo guowuyuan gongbao* (*Gazette of the State Council of the People's Republic of China*), No. 10, 1984, p. 307 (hereafter cited as *Guowuyuan gongbao*). The English text is in Nee, Pt. 14, pp. 43–60, note 17 above; and Ross and Silk, note 17 above.

20. The Twenty-fourth Session of the Standing Committee of the Fifth National People's Congress promulgated the Marine Environmental Protection Law (hereafter cited as the MEPL) on 23 August 1982. The MEPL came into effect on 1 March 1983. The Chinese and English texts are in *Collection of Laws and Regulations of China Concerning Foreign Economic and Trade Relations*, Pt. XI, p. 83, note 17 above. The Chinese text only is in *Renmin ribao*, 25 August 1982, p. 3, reprinted in *Falu*, No. 8, 1982, p. 68. The English text only is in Nee, Pt. 14, pp. 27–42, note 17 above; Ross and Silk, note 17 above; and *East Asian Executive Reports*, No. 5, 1983, p. 24.

Three sets of regulations have been promulgated under the MEPL. The first two are the Regulations of the People's Republic of China on the Prevention of Marine Pollution from Vessels and the Regulations of the People's Republic of China on Marine Environmental Protection from Oil Exploration and Exploitation. They were promulgated by the State Council on 12 December 1983. The Chinese texts are in *Guowuyuan gongbao*, No. 1, 1984, p. 6, note 19 above; and *Zhongguo fazhi bao* (*China Legal System Newspaper*), 13 January 1984, reprinted in *Xinhua yuebao* (*Wenxian ban*), No. 1, 1984, p. 75. The English texts are in Ross and Silk, note 17 above. For commentary, see E. Epstein, 'China's New Pollution Laws', *Petroleum News*, March 1984, p. 11; E. Epstein, 'Pollution Law Laid Down', *China Trade Report*, March 1984, pp. 4–5; 'Marine Environmental Regulations Promulgated', *Foreign Broadcast Information Service—China*, 11 January 1984, pp. K19–20 (hereafter cited as the FBIS—CHI); 'New Pollution Rules', *China Report*, March 1984, p. 75; and 'New Rules in Drive to Reduce Sea Pollution', *China Daily*, 13 January 1984, p. 1. The State Council more recently, on 6 March 1985, promulgated the Regulations of the People's Republic of China on the Control of Marine Dumping. The Chinese text is in *Guowuyuan gongbao*, No. 9, 1985, p. 222, note 19 above. The English text is in Ross and Silk, note 17 above.

21. The Standing Committee of the National People's Congress promulgated the Land Management Law on 25 June 1986. The Chinese text is in *Guowuyuan gongbao*, No. 17, 1986, pp. 531–9, note 19 above.

22. The Grasslands Law was adopted by the Eleventh Session of the Sixth National People's Congress Standing Committee on 18 June 1985. The Chinese and English texts are in *Renmin ribao*, 19 June 1985, p. 2; and Ross and Silk, note 17 above. See 'Earnestly Implement the Grasslands Law', *Renmin ribao*, 19 June 1985, p. 2.

The Fisheries Law was passed by the Fourteenth Session of the Sixth National People's Congress Standing Committee on 20 January 1986. The Chinese and English texts are in *Zhongguo fazhi bao*, 22 January 1986, p. 2; and Ross and Silk, note 17 above. See 'Apply the Law Promoting and Supervising the Fisheries', *Renmin ribao*, 22 January 1986, p. 2.

23. The State Council promulgated the Regulations on Water and Soil Conservation Work on 30 June 1982. The text is in BFWH, pp. 101–9, note 17 above, and is translated in Ross and Silk, note 17 above.

24. The PRC has issued a number of regulations on wildlife protection. See, for example, State Council Circular on the Stringent Preservation of Endangered Wildlife, in BFWH, pp. 214–16, note 17 above, translated in Ross and Silk, note 17 above.

The text of the Mineral Resources Law is in *Guowuyuan gongbao*, No. 8, 1986, pp. 195–201, note 19 above.

25. Normally, in order to maintain a nuisance action in this context, the plaintiff had to prove that societal benefits by far outweighed the cost of control. For examples of varying early theories in the United States, see *Parker v. American Woolen Co.*, 195 Mass. 591, 81 N.E. 468 (1907); *Suffolk Gold Mining & Milling Co. v. San Miguel Consolidated Mining & Milling Co.*, 9 Colo. App. 407, 48 P.2d 828 (1897); *Globe Aircraft Corp. v. Thompson*, 203 S.W.2d 865 (1947); *Martin v. Reynolds Metals Co.*, 221 Ore. 86, 342 P.2d 790, cert. denied, 362 U.S. 918 (1959); *Spur Industries v. Del E. Webb Development Co.*, 108 Ariz. 178, 494 P.2d 700 (1972); *Boomer v. Atlantic Cement Co.*, 26 N.Y.2d 219, 309 N.Y.S.2d 312, 257 N.E.2d 870 (1970); and *Georgia v. Tennessee Copper Co.*, 206 U.S. 230 (1907). See, also, W.L. Prosser, 'Private Action for Public Nuisance', *Virginia Law Review*, Vol. 52, 1966, p. 997; and J.C. Juergensmeyer, 'Control of Air Pollution Through Assertion of Private Rights', *Duke Law Journal*, Vol. 1967, 1967, p. 1126.

26. The concept of 'environmental rights' in China is dealt with in Cai Shouqiu, 'Preliminary Investigation into Environmental Rights', *Zhongguo shehui kexue* (*Social Sciences in China*), No. 3, pp. 29–39, translated in Ross and Silk, note 17 above.

27. This section is a summary of L. Ross and M. Silk, 'Post-Mao China and Environmental Protection: The Effects of Legal and Politico-Economic Reform', forthcoming in *UCLA Pacific Basin Law Journal*, 1986. The reader is referred to that article for more details on the cases, and the keen conclusions drawn by Professor Ross.

28. See Sun Xiangming, 'Was this A Counterrevolutionary Incident?', *Huanjing*, No. 1, 1984, pp. 24–5, translated in Ross and Silk, note 17 above.

29. See Jiang De and Qin Liwen, 'Chang Jiang Administrative Bureau Learns Lesson: Strong Emphasis on the Task of Environmental Protection Brings Preliminary Results', *Zhongguo fazhi bao*, 25 February 1983, p. 1, translated in Joint Publication Research Service, US Department of Commerce, *China Report (Science and Technology): China Addresses Environmental Issues*, 11 June 1984, pp. 142–3. See, also, Cheng Zhenkang, 'The Abuse of Rights and Self-Defence in Environmental Pollution Cases', *Zhongguo huanjing kexue*, No. 6, 1984, pp. 11–15. See translation and commentary in Ross and Silk, note 17 above.

30. See Ge Dalu, 'This Lawsuit Was Not Fair', *Huanjing*, No. 1, 1985, pp. 24–5.

31. The facts of this case are based on the notes of Professor Deng Jianxu, who personally investigated and tried the case. A copy of the facts is on file with the East Asian Legal Studies Program at the University of Maryland, School of Law.

32. See note 28 above.

33. See note 29 above.

34. See note 30 above.

35. See note 31 above.

36. See the Criminal Law of the People's Republic of China, Arts. 10 and 11 (hereafter cited as the Criminal Law). The English and Chinese texts are in J. A. Cohen, T. Gelatt, and Florence Li, *The Criminal Law and the Criminal Procedure Law of China* (Beijing, Foreign Languages Press, 1984). The culprits in the Linfei case were sentenced under Article 10 of the 1951 Act for the Punishment of Counterrevolution. The text is in J. Cohen, *The Criminal Process in the People's Republic of China* (Cambridge, Mass., Harvard University Press, 1968), pp. 299–302.

The three requirements to determine criminality under Chinese law are discussed in the following sources: Cao Zidian, 'Questions and Answers on China's Criminal Law', *Beijing Review*, 9 June 1980, pp. 19–20; Falu wenti bianxie zu, *Xingshi falu wenti* (*Questions and Answers on Criminal Law*) (Shanghai, Zhishi chubanshe, 1983); Tao Xijin, 'On Fundamental Problems of the Characterization of Crimes', *Faxue yanjiu*, No. 4, 1979, pp. 29–33; Feng Ertai, *et al.*, *Falu dawen sibai ti* (*Four Hundred Questions and Answers on the Law*) (Shanghai, Xuelin chubanshe, 1984), pp. 54 and 56–64; S.C. Leng and H. Chiu, *Criminal Justice in Post-Mao China* (Albany, NY, SUNY Press, 1985), p. 124; Zhang Shangzhuo, *Zhonghua renmin gongheguo xingfa gailun* (*The Essentials of the Criminal Law of the People's Republic of China*) (Beijing, Falu chubanshe, 1981), pp. 67–132; and Zhang Youyu and Wang Shuwen, *Faxue jiben zhishi jianghua* (*Lectures on Basic Knowledge in Law*) (Beijing, Falu chubanshe, 1979), pp. 94–101.

37. Article 17 of the Criminal Law, note 36 above, provides that 'Criminal responsibility is not to be borne for an act of legitimate defence that is undertaken to avert present unlawful infringement of the public interest or the rights of the person or other rights of the actor or of other people . . . Criminal responsibility shall be borne where legitimate defence exceeds the necessary limits and causes undue harm. However, consideration shall be given according to the circumstances to imposing a mitigated punishment or to granting exemption from punishment'. The principle of self-defence under Chinese law is similar to that in most other legal systems. Compare principles set forth in C. Jenks, *The Common Rights of Mankind* (London, Stevens, 1958), pp. 139–43 (establishing that all legal systems in the world recognize notions of self-defence) with, for Chinese criminal law, *Xingshi falu wenti*, pp. 8–10, note 36 above; Gao Minxuan, *Xingfa xue* (*The Study of Criminal Law*) (Beijing, Falu chubanshe, 1982), pp. 163–71; Zhang Shangzhuo, pp. 134–45, note 36 above; and, for tort theory under Chinese civil law, Dong Rou, *Minfa yuanze* (*The Principles of Civil Law*) (Beijing, Falu chubanshe, 1983), pp. 224–5.

38. The risk the Chinese take in setting such a precedent is a call for mob rule whenever there is an environmental infraction which is causing a health or safety hazard. The scope of this defence should thus be limited to very narrow circumstances. This is the case in the Japanese system. See J. Gresser, *Environmental Law in Japan* (Cambridge, Mass, MIT Press, 1981), pp. 48–50.

An analogous situation arises in the American system with regard to conditions at the place of work. Interestingly, the American system generally recognizes the right of the worker to refrain from working when confronted with unsafe working conditions, and even permits workers to engage in collective activity ('strikes') as a method of pressuring management into remedying the situation. Three federal statutory provisions bear on workers' rights with regard to health and safety matters. First, the Occupational Safety and Health Act of 1970, 29 U.S.C.A. §§ 651–678 (OSHA), provides a limited right to walk out of the job to avoid a health or safety hazard. The Supreme Court upheld a regulation promulgated under OSHA to this effect in *Whirlpool Corp.* v. *Marshall*, 445 U.S. 1 (1980). Second, the Supreme Court, in *Gateway Coal Co.* v. *United Mine Workers*, 414 U.S. 368 (1974), found a separate statutory right to a limited strike where a health and safety hazard existed. Third, sections 7 and 13 of the National Labour Relations Act (NLRA) provide workers generally with the right to strike under labour laws, 29 U.S.C. §§ 157, 163. NLRA health and safety strikes are, however, often restricted by general no-strike-clause provisions, but it appears that unorganized workers' rights may be superior. See *National Labor Relations Board* v. *Washington Aluminum Co.*, 370 U.S. 9 (1962). Note also that some states are developing exceptions to the traditional doctrine that employers may fire employees at will. This development may create additional rights. See, for example, *Adler* v. *American Standard Corp.*, 432 A.2d 434 (1981); and *Staggs* v. *Blue Cross of Maryland, Inc.*, 486 A.2d 798 (1985). But see Railway Labor Act, 45 U.S.C. §§ 151a, 152.

However, in contrast to the rulings in the case studies above, which appear to recognize worker violence as a legitimate method of pressuring management to ameliorate conditions in the place of work, the American system specifically rejects this principle. Thus, under the Norris–La Guardia Act, 29 U.S.C. §§ 101–15, and § 10 of the National Labor Relations Act, above, federal courts expressly granted the power to enjoin labour practice that involves violence, whereas the courts are otherwise prohibited from interfering with non-violent concerted activity. Furthermore, the American statutory scheme which generally prohibits courts from interfering with labour 'strikes' or other actions specifically grants courts the authority to enjoin labour practice. Norris–La Guardia Act, above.

The most noted incident of public protest over environmental conditions in the Soviet Union was the Lake Baikal affair. The outcome established that it is permissible within certain limits to question through public protest the environmental impact of a state project. But the dissent did not exceed the implicit limits of Party authority, let alone give rise to unlawful acts of aggression. It is likely that even if aggression was used, the culprits would have been dealt with through normal legal procedures without interference. For an account of the Lake Baikal affair, see T. Gustafson, *Reform in Soviet Politics—Lessons of Recent Policies on Land and Water* (London and New York, Oxford University Press, 1981), pp. 40–6.

39. See L. Ross, *Environmental Policy in China* (Berkeley, University of California Press, forthcoming), Chapter 4 on pollution control policy. The relevant standards are reproduced in Gresser, pp. 501–12, note 11 above; and Swannuck-Nunn, pp. 117–30, note 17 above.

40. The standards are reproduced in Gresser, pp. 519–26, note 11 above; and Swannack-Nunn, pp. 131–8, note 17 above.

41. See *Beijing Review*, 24 November 1978, p. 31.

42. See EPL, Art. 6, note 17 above. Environmental impact assessment re-

quisites are in Requirements for Environmental Impact Assessments for Large and Small-scale Construction Projects, in HBYWX, pp. 79–81, note 17 above, and are translated in Ross and Silk, note 17 above.

The Chinese text of the Provisional Regulations for Environmental Management in Foreign Economic Development Zones, promulgated on 15 March 1986, is in *Guowuyuan gongbao*, No. 12, 1986, pp. 426–7, note 19 above, and is translated in Ross and Silk, note 17 above.

43. See EPL, Art. 6, note 17 above; and State Planning Commission, *et al.*, Circular on the Strict Implementation of the 'Three Simultaneous Points' in Capital Construction and Technical Renovation Projects, in HBYWX, pp. 130–1, note 17 above. On the definition of 'effective' measures, see State Planning Commission, *et al.*, Procedures Governing Environmental Protection Control in Capital Construction, in HBYWX, pp. 76–9, note 17 above, translated in Ross and Silk, note 17 above.

44. CHINA ENVIRO 85 took place in Guangzhou from 7 to 12 March 1985, and EMETEX-ENPROTEX 85 was convened in Beijing from 18 to 25 September 1985. See M. Cohen, 'Chinese environmental protection: the business climate', *China Business & Trade*, 23 April 1985, p. 3.

45. See M. Cohen, note 44 above.

46. See EPL, Art. 6, note 17 above.

47. See Jiang and Guo, pp. 112–18, note 12 above.

48. There are at present standards related to, *inter alia*: the quality of the air, marine water, surface water, ground water, drinking water, and fisheries water; the regulation of urban and automobile noise; the discharge of pesticides, the industrial 'three wastes', pollution from vessels, and pollution related to oil exploration and exploitation; and discharges in the production of cane sugar and paper. For the texts of the major standards, see Ministry of Urban and Rural Construction and Environmental Protection, *Zhonghua renmin gongheguo guojia biaozhun—gongye wuranwu paifang biaozhun* (State Standards of the People's Republic of China—Emissions Standards for Pollutants from Industry), Series GB 3544-3553-83 (Beijing, Zhongguo biaozhun chubanshe, 1983).

49. See, for example, Federal Water Pollution Control Act, 33 U.S.C. § 1342.

50. See Shen Xin, 'On Implementing a [Pollution] Permit Process', *Zhongguo huanjing kexue*, No. 4, 1984, pp. 29–32.

51. See, most notably, MEPL, Art. 38., note 20 above, and WPPCL, Art. 14, note 19 above. For discussion of this procedure under the WPPCL, see Wen Boping, 'On the Water Pollution Prevention and Control Law', *Faxue yanjiu*, No. 5, 1984, pp. 74–8; and Wu Jingcheng, 'Prevent and Control Water Pollution, Protect the Aqueous Environment', *Chongqing huanjing baohu*, No. 2, 1985, pp. 47–51.

52. Ross, note 39 above, citing Chen Ren, 'How to Address Properly and Resolve Contradictions between Factories and the Masses', *Huanjing*, May 1984, p. 21.

53. See, for example, *Renmin ribao*, 31 May 1984, cited in Ross, note 39 above; *Renmin ribao*, 7 July 1985, p. 2; and Dong Dixun, 'Organize and Co-ordinate the Strength of All Sectors to Open a New Vista in Environmental Protection Work', *Huanjing guanli*, No. 1, 1984, p. 41.

54. This section is adapted from M. Silk, 'China's Marine Environmental Protection Law: The Dragon Creeping in Murky Waters', *Review of Socialist Law*, Vol. 11, 1985, pp. 249–73, revised and reprinted in *Occasional Papers/Reprints Series in Contemporary Asian Studies* (Baltimore, Md., University of Maryland School of Law, 1985), No. 6.

55. These include the State Council Order on Trawler Fishing in Forbidden Areas in the Bohai, Huanghai, and Donghai Seas, in HBYWX, pp. 295–6, note 17 above; the Regulations on Protecting the Breeding of Aquatic Resources, *Renmin ribao*, 29 March 1979; and the Provisional Regulation on Protecting the Breeding of Aquatic Resources, in HBYWX, pp. 89–97, note 17 above.

56. United Nations, *The Law of the Sea: United Nations Convention on the Law of the Sea with Index and Final Act of the Third United Nations Conference on the Law of the Sea* (New York, United Nations, UN Pub. Sales No. E.83.v.5, 1983).

57. At the very least, 'the fact that a state was willing to sign should give it "a certain provisional status as a reflection of the views of the signatories"'. R. Baxter, 'The Advantage of Stimulating the Growth of General International Law through Treaties', *Recueil des Cours*, Vol. 129, 1970–1, pp. 99–100, cited in H. Chiu, 'The 1982 United Nations Convention on the Law of the Sea and the Settlement of China's Maritime Boundary Dispute', in T. Buergenthal (ed.), *Contemporary Issues in International Law: Essays in Honor of Louis B. Sohn* (Arlington, Va., N.P. Engel Publishers, 1984), pp. 190–1 (hereafter cited as Chiu).

58. The MEPL embodies all relevant provisions of the 1982 UN Convention on the Law of the Sea except Article 212(1), which deals with marine pollution through the atmosphere. The Chinese contend that this is not a serious problem in China so that there is no need for such regulation. See Yang Jinsen, *Zhonghua renmin gongheguo haiyang huanjing baohu fa qianshuo* (*Talks on the Marine Environmental Protection Law of the People's Republic of China*) (Beijing, Falu chubanshe, 1983), p. 22.

59. See 'China Accedes to MARPOL', *China Report*, March 1984, p. 71; H. Chiu, *Agreements of the People's Republic of China—A Calendar of Events 1966–1980* (New York, Praeger Publishers, 1981), p. 219; E. Epstein, 'China's New Pollution Laws', p. 11, note 20 above; E. Epstein, 'A Legal Opinion', *China Trade Report*, July 1982, p. 13; and E. Epstein, 'Pollution Law Laid Down', pp. 4–5, note 20 above.

60. 26 U.S.T. 765, T.I.A.S. No. 8069, 1969 U.N.J.Y.B. 166.

61. IMCO 1973 Convention, modified by protocol in 1978 and 1983, 1973 U.N.J.Y.B. 81, 12 I.L.M. 1319, 1978 Protocol in 17 I.L.M. 546, and 1983 Protocol in D. Jackson (ed.), *World Shipping Laws* (Dobbs Ferry, NY, Oceana Publications, Inc., 1983), loose-leaf.

62. Article 28 of the MEPL provides that 'Any vessels carrying more than 2,000 tons of oil in bulk shall have a valid "Certificate of Insurance or other Financial Security in Respect of Civil Liability for Oil Pollution Damage", or a "Credit Certificate for Civil Liability Against Oil Pollution Damage", or hold other financial credit guarantees'.

63. Article VII(1) of the 1969 Brussels Convention provides that 'The owner of a ship registered in a contracting State and carrying more than 2,000 tons of oil in bulk in cargo shall be required to maintain insurance or other financial security . . . to cover his liability for pollution damage under this Convention'.

64. See A. Dicks, 'Some Problems of Maritime Law', in Cohen, pp. 366–7, note 11 above.

65. Article 27 of the MEPL provides that 'Any oil tanker of 150 tons gross tonnage and above or any other vessels of 400 gross tonnage and above shall be fitted with appropriate anti-pollution equipment and facilities . . . Any oil tanker less than 150 tons gross tonnage and any other vessel less then 400 tons gross tonnage shall be fitted with special containers for recovering residual and waste oil'.

66. Regulation 4 of MARPOL (73/78) provides that on surveys and inspections: '1) Every oil tanker of 150 tons gross tonnage and above shall be subject to the surveys specified below; a) This survey shall be as to ensure that the structure, equipment, systems, fittings, arrangements, and material . . . [and] c) equipment and associated pump and piping systems, including oil discharge monitoring and control systems, crude oil washing systems, oily-water separating equipment and oil filtering systems, fully comply with the applicable requirements of this annex and are in good working order.'

67. See Silk, pp. 254–6 and 259, note 54 above.

68. See Dicks, p. 367, note 64 above.

69. For texts and commentary, see note 20 above.

70. On offshore oil operations in the China Sea, see Y.J. Ma, *Legal Problems of Seabed Boundary Delimitation in the East China Sea* (Baltimore, Occasional Papers/Reprints Series in Contemporary Asian Studies, 1984); M. Moser, 'Offshore Oil Exploration and Development in China: The Current Regulatory Framework', in M. Moser (ed.), *Foreign Trade, Investment and the Law in the People's Republic of China* (Hong Kong, Oxford University Press, 1984, first edition), pp. 179–213; L.D. Rich, 'American Oil Interests in China', *Loyola of Los Angeles International and Comparative Law Journal*, Vol. 6, 1983, p. 119; and K. Woodard, 'The Drilling Begins', *China Business Review*, Vol. 10, 1983, p. 18.

71. See I.R. Manners, *North Sea Oil and Environmental Planning* (Austin, Tex., University of Texas Press, 1982), pp. 94–160.

72. See D.J. Walmsley, 'Oil Pollution Problems Arising Out of Exploitation of the Continental Shelf: The Santa Barbara Disaster', *San Diego Law Review*, Vol. 9, 1972, pp. 514–69; 'Huge Oil Slick Perils Pacific Area of Coast', *The New York Times*, 31 January 1969, p. 50; and 'Oil Slick Spreads, But Leak Slows', *The New York Times*, 1 February 1969, p. 32. On the issue of liability, see *Union Oil* v. *Oppen*, 501 F.2d 558 (1974).

73. This spill poured 28,000 tons of crude oil over an area of more than 300 square kilometres. See D.M. Johnston (ed.), *The Environmental Law of the Sea* (West Berlin, Erich Schmidt Verlag, 1981), p. 247.

74. For the text and commentary, see note 20 above.

75. For relevant standards, see note 48 above.

76. See MEPL, Art. 10, note 20 above.

77. See Oil Exploration Regulations, Art. 10; and Yang, *et al.*, p. 38, note 58 above.

78. See MEPL, Art. 11, note 20 above.

79. See Yang, *et al.*, pp. 41–2, note 58 above.

80. For texts and commentary, see note 20 above.

81. See Ouyang Xiu, 'The International Control of Marine Dumping', *Faxue yanjiu*, No. 4, 1984, pp. 90–5.

82. Yang, *et al.*, p. 60, note 58 above.

83. Yang, *et al.*, p. 61, note 58 above.

84. See discussion in Chen Lihu, 'On the Legal Regulation of Solid Wastes', *Faxue yanjiu*, No. 4, 1985, pp. 71–5; and Shi Qing, 'Management of Toxic Wastes', *Huanjing baohu*, No. 7, 1984, pp. 8–11, both translated in Ross and Silk, note 17 above.

85. See notes 18, 22, and 24 above.

86. For the text of the Land Management Law, see note 21 above.

87. The text of the State Council Regulations on the Encouragement of Foreign Investment is in *China Daily*, 14 October 1986. For local standards and regulations, see *China's Foreign Economic Legislation*, Vol. I (Beijing, Foreign Languages Press, 1984), pp. 233–9; *Wen wei po*, 6 December 1985, p. 8; 'A taxing problem', *China Trade Report*, April 1986, p. 12; 'Ground rules for land use', *China Trade Report*, January 1986, p. 12; *China Economic News*, 15 April 1985, pp. 1–2; *China Economic News*, 16 September 1985, pp. 7–9; and *China Economic News*, 20 January 1986, pp. 4–6.

88. The text is in BFWH, pp. 254–9, note 17 above. The original regulations were issued in 1973. Compare the approaches employed under these regulations with selected provisions of the United States Internal Revenue Code, for example, 26 U.S.C. §§ 169, 291, and 1363.

89. In the United States system tax credits are generally restricted to the amount of tax liability, and there is no refund for credit amounts above that. See relevant provisions of the Internal Revenue Code, for example, 26 U.S.C. § 46.

90. Ministry of Finance and State Council Environmental Protection Leading Group Circular Related to Procedures Governing the Retention of Profits from

Products Derived from Multiple Use of the 'Three Wastes' in Industrial and Mining Enterprises, 30 December 1979. The Chinese text is in BFWH, pp. 274-7, note 17 above, and HBYWX, pp. 127-8, note 17 above, and is translated in Ross and Silk, note 17 above.

91. See C.E. Ziegler, 'Economic Alternatives and Administrative Solutions in Soviet Environmental Protection', Policies Studies Journal, Vol. 11, 1982, pp. 175-87, cited in Ross, note 39 above.

92. See W.J. Baumol and W.E. Oates, Economics, Environmental Policy, and the Quality of Life (Englewood Cliffs, NJ, Prentice Hall, 1979), pp. 246-50, cited in Ross, note 39 above.

93. See EPL, Art. 18, note 17 above.

94. The text is in BFWH, pp. 278-83, note 17 above, and is translated in Nee, Pt. 14, pp. 15-25, note 17 above.

95. See Cao Fenglin, 'Grabbing the Bull's Nose in Environmental Management Work', Huanjing, January 1982, pp. 2-3, cited in Ross, note 39 above.

96. EPL, Art. 32, note 17 above.

97. MEPL, Art. 44, note 20 above.

98. WPPCL, Art. 43, note 19 above.

99. 1984 Forestry Law, Arts. 34-6, note 18 above.

100. Fisheries Law, Arts. 28 and 29, note 22 above.

101. Suzhou Trial of a Case Involving Heavy Responsibility for Serious Pollution of the Environment, Jiangsu Province, Suzhou Municipal Intermediate People's Court Opinion (79) Xingzi No. 26, on file with the author, and translated in Ross and Silk, note 17 above.

102. See Zhongguo baike nianjian, 1980 (China Encyclopaedic Yearbook, 1980), (Beijing, 1981), p. 277.

103. The Criminal Law, note 36 above, includes only three positive provisions on environmental offences: Article 128 (dealing with forestry protection), Article 129 (dealing with the protection of aquatic resources), and Article 130 (dealing with the protection of wildlife). The Criminal Law still retains, however, the principle of crime by analogy as embodied in Article 79 of the Criminal Law. Jurists cite numerous provisions of the Criminal Law which relate to the environment, such as: Articles 105, 106, and 115 (crimes endangering public security); Articles 128, 129, and 130 (sabotage against the socialist economic order); Article 156 (trespass); Articles 174 and 178 (disturbance of the administrative order of society); and Article 187 (misconduct in office). Jin Ruilin and Cheng Zhengkang, 'An Analysis of Crimes Relating to Environmental Damage', Zhongguo huanjing kexue, April 1981, pp. 71-6.

104. See Criminal Law, Arts. 3, 6, and 8, note 36 above.

105. See Lee Yee, 'Trial of a Salesman', Asian Wall Street Journal, 3 February 1986. The recent case of Richard O. Ondrick (an American business man sentenced to jail in China for causing a hotel fire that killed ten people in Harbin) is instructive. 'American Is Arrested in China', The New York Times, 28 June 1985, p. A2; J. Burns, 'Final Pleas Are Heard in Trial of American Businessman in China', The New York Times, 24 July 1985, p. A11; J. Burns, 'American on Trial Puts Chinese Justice to the Test', The New York Times, 7 August 1985, p. A2; 'China Jails 2 Workers for Role in Hotel Fire', The New York Times, 13 August 1985, p. 7; 'Hotel guest jailed for death blaze', China Daily, 14 August 1985, p. 3; FBIS—CHI, 14 August 1985, pp. B1 and B2, note 20 above; Renmin ribao, 13 August 1985, p. 1; and Renmin ribao, 14 August 1985, p. 1.

106. Recently three business executives were convicted of homicide for negligence in the place of work which resulted in the death of an employee. See Illinois v. Film Recovery Systems, Illinois Civil Nos. 83–11091 and 84–5064 (Cook County Circuit Court 1985). See also United States v. Park, 421 U.S. 658 (1975) (the defendant, president of a food chain, was held criminally responsible for health violations by the corporation).

107. He Ge, 'Legal Responsibility Issues in the Marine Environmental Protec-

FOREIGN TRADE, INVESTMENT, AND THE LAW

tion Law', *Zhongguo fazhi bao*, 18 March 1983, p. 3; and Ni Xin, 'Reparations Problems in Marine Environmental Pollution Accidents', *Huanjing guanli*, No. 1, 1985, pp. 35–6.

108. See He Ge, note 107 above.

109. For the lower court decision, see Qiu Guotang, 'Some Questions Involving Hong Kong Related Environmental Pollution Disputes', *Huanjing fa* (*Environmental Law*), No. 2, 1984, pp. 18–22. For the Supreme People's Court decision, see Decision on the Environmental Pollution Case between the Shenzhen Municipal Shekou District Environmental Monitoring Station and Kaida Enterprises, Ltd. (Hong Kong), reported in *Zhonghua renmin gongheguo zuigao renmin fayuan gongbao* (*Gazette of the Supreme People's Court of the People's Republic of China*), 20 September 1985, pp. 44–6, both translated in Ross and Silk, note 17 above.

110. See Foreign Economic Contract Law, Art. 5.

111. See Foreign Economic Contract Law, Art. 40.

112. This was the case with the Sino-American Food Products Company, a joint venture with Beatrice.

113. As defined by the *Island of Palmas Arbitration*, 'Sovereignty in the relations between states signifies independence. Independence in regard to a portion of the globe is the right to exercise therein, to the exclusion of any other state, the functions of a state'. *Island of Palmas Case (U.S. v. Neth.)*, 2 R. Int'l Arb. Awards 838 (1928).

12. Trade-mark Law in the People's Republic of China

JESSE T. H. CHANG AND CHARLES J. CONROY

I. Introduction

The concept of using trade marks in China to identify the source of manufacture is by no means new. Its history can be traced back to the early days of Chinese society. It is known that the pottery wares of a famous craftsman in the Northern Zhou dynasty (AD 556–80) carried a mark to distinguish his products from those of other craftsmen.[1] Today, objects of art with trade marks of manufacturers dating back to the Song dynasty (AD 960–1279) can be found on display at the Museum of Chinese History in Beijing.[2]

It was in 1904 that these early developments in the trade-mark area were formalized, when the government of the Qing dynasty promulgated China's first trade-mark law, the Trial Regulations for Trade-mark Registration (hereafter cited as the Trial Regulations). However, the Trial Regulations were not only drafted but also, in practice, administered by the foreigners who at that time controlled much of China's trade. Accordingly, it was not surprising that foreign trade marks received adequate protection under the provisions of the Trial Regulations. In fact, the Trial Regulations went so far as to provide that the settlement of trade-mark disputes was within the jurisdiction of the foreign consulates in China.

Two trade-mark laws were promulgated by the Nationalist regime during its period of administration. The first was the trade-mark law of 1923, which made few improvements to the Trial Regulations and continued to vest the authority for settling trade-mark disputes with the foreign consulates. The second was a revised trade-mark law, which was promulgated in 1931. Its provisions were, however, essentially adopted, without significant changes, from the trade-mark laws of other countries. The influence which foreign trade-mark practice asserted over the Chinese law is reflected nowhere more clearly than in the goods classification table used at that time, which was identical to the Japanese goods classification table.[3]

Shortly after the formal founding of the People's Republic of China (PRC), the PRC's first trade-mark law was released in 1950. Since that time, trade-mark legislation in China has undergone significant changes, with new laws being introduced in 1963 and 1983. These developments in China's trade-mark legislation, including China's present trade-mark law, are discussed in further detail below.

II. The Early Trade-mark Laws

A. The 1950 Provisional Regulations

The Provisional Regulations Governing Trade-mark Registration (hereafter cited as the 1950 Provisional Regulations) were promulgated by the Government Administration Council on 28 August 1950.[4]

Although the 1950 Provisional Regulations were quite brief and uncomplicated, they were nevertheless important as they introduced the concept of trade marks to socialist China. The 1950 Provisional Regulations recognized the monopolistic right of a party to use a trade mark; a right that seemed perilously close to capitalist principles. Indeed, Article 1 went so far as to provide that the 1950 Provisional Regulations 'are enacted for the protection of the rights of exclusive use of trade marks by industry and commerce in general'.

B. The 1963 Trade-mark Law

In April 1963, the State Council promulgated the Regulations of the People's Republic of China Governing the Control of Trade Marks (hereafter cited as the 1963 Trade-mark Regulations). Shortly thereafter, the Central Administration for Industry and Commerce (CAIC) promulgated the Detailed Implementing Rules of the 1963 Trade-mark Regulations (hereafter cited as the 1963 Implementing Rules).[5]

The most important aspect of the 1963 legislation was the recognition that the trade-mark law could be used as a means of controlling the quality of products. This concept of using trade marks as a means of quality control over goods has been cited by Chinese legal scholars as the rationale for adopting a trade-mark registration system in socialist China.[6] Thus, in contrast to the 1950 Provisional Regulations, which emphasized the connection between trade marks and exclusive use, the focus of the 1963 Trade-mark Law was on quality control.

The concern of the 1963 Trade-mark Law with quality control is evidenced by the definition of a trade mark as 'a distinctive sign representing the quality of the goods bearing it'.[7] The 1963 Trade-mark Law also stipulated that the authorities concerned should exercise supervision and control over the quality of the goods using trade marks.[8] In addition, it provided for mandatory registration of all trade marks used by any enterprise in China. Even if an enterprise did not display trade marks on its products, it had to indicate its name and address on the goods or packages in order to facilitate control by the CAIC.[9] The right of registration was granted to the first applicant.[10] No rights were accorded to first users as they are in most common-law jurisdictions.

Another important aspect of the 1963 Trade-mark Law was the omission of the requirement of 'prior use' or 'intention to use in the future'. This feature, together with the concern for quality control, has come to characterize Chinese trade-mark law.

Initially, foreign parties had only limited opportunities to register trade marks in China. Only those foreign parties with home registration and whose countries had reciprocal registration agreements with China were permitted to apply for registration.[11] The requirements of home registration and reciprocal registration agreements were subsequently waived in 1978, presumably to promote China's trade with foreign countries. Foreign applicants who met the registration requirements were obliged to use the Trade-mark Registration Agency of the China Council for the Promotion of International Trade (CCPIT) as their agent in filing the registration documents with the CAIC.[12]

III. The 1983 Trade-mark Law

A. Introduction

In order to attract more foreign investment to China, the People's Republic announced in 1978 its general intention to adopt an 'open-door' policy. As part of this effort, the Chinese leadership recognized the need to introduce more complete laws to govern and protect foreign investment in China. As discussed elsewhere in this volume, laws relating to joint ventures and taxation began to be promulgated for the first time in 1979. At the same time, it was clear that some of the existing laws, such as the 1963 Trade-mark Law, needed to be revised or replaced in order to accommodate the concerns of foreign businesses.

Accordingly, in 1983, two important pieces of trade-mark legislation were released to replace the 1963 Trade-mark Law. The first is the Trade-mark Law of the People's Republic of China (hereafter cited as the Trade-mark Law) which was passed on 23 August 1982 by the Twenty-fourth Meeting of the Standing Committee of the Fifth National People's Congress and which became effective on 1 March 1983. The second is the Detailed Implementing Rules of the Trade-mark Law of the People's Republic of China (hereafter cited as the Implementing Rules) which were promulgated and came into effect on 10 March 1983.[13]

At present, China's Trade-mark Law only provides for the registration and protection of marks for goods, and not for 'service marks' or the marks of service institutions such as banks.[14] Many countries, such as the United Kingdom, are now considering adopting a system for the registration of service marks. It is uncertain whether China will also move in this direction.

However, given the possibility of being able to register trade marks for brochures, advertisements, and other promotional materials on which trade names or service marks appear in classes 59 and 63 of the Chinese goods classification table, many foreign service establishments—such as hotels and banks—whose trade names are of vital importance to them have considered it necessary to seek protection by registering their names under those classes. Of course, the protection so obtained is limited to such or similar materials. But since neither service marks nor trade names are at present specifically protected in China by any law, the alternative protection under classes 59 and/or 63 is frequently adopted by many foreign parties as a short-term solution. In addition, foreign companies should note that it is now possible for them to seek protection of their trade names under the provisions of the Interim Regulations on Registration of Names of Industrial and Commercial Enterprises.[15]

As with the 1963 Trade-mark Law, the present Law contains no requirement of prior use or intention to use in the future, for the purpose of filing trade-mark applications. Prior use may, however, become important in order that priority between competing applications may be established.[16]

B. The Trade-mark Bureau

The Trade-mark Bureau, an agency consisting of about 250 personnel within the State Administration for Industry and Commerce (SAIC),[17] is responsible for trade-mark registration and control throughout China. Matters relating to the use or issue of trade marks are therefore within the jurisdiction of the Trade-mark Bureau. However, the task of actually enforcing the Trade-mark Law rests with the local departments of the Administration for Industry and Commerce (AIC).[18]

C. Quality Control

Like the 1963 Trade-mark Law, the present Law emphasizes the importance of the relationship between trade marks and quality control. Article 1 of the Trade-mark Law expressly states that the Law 'is specially enacted in order to strengthen trade mark control, to protect the right of exclusive use of trade marks, to impel producers to guarantee the quality of goods and uphold the reputation of trade marks, thereby safeguarding the interests of consumers . . .'. The interests of consumers are further advanced by a provision of the Trade-mark Law which states that trade-mark users must bear responsibility for the quality of the goods that bear their trade marks.[19]

It is interesting to note that the right of exclusive use is also clearly recognized by the new Law. The Law does this, in part, by defining a trade mark approved for registration by the Trade-mark Bureau as 'a registered trade mark [for which] the registrant of the trade mark enjoys the right of exclusive use of the trade mark and receives legal protection'.[20]

D. Other Provisions

Words and designs used for trade marks, or their composition, must be distinctive.[21] Goods displaying registered trade marks shall be marked with the Chinese words for 'Registered Trade-mark' (注册商标) or marked with the symbols ® or (注).[22] Although the Trade-mark Law specifies no penalty for failure to comply with this requirement, CCPIT trade-mark officials have expressed their support for the imposition in the near future of a penalty for non-compliance.[23]

The 1963 Trade-mark Law provided for compulsory trade-mark registration, whereas trade-mark registration is generally voluntary under the Trade-mark Law. However, the Trade-mark Law does not recognize common-law trade-mark rights derived from the use of unregistered marks.[24] Moreover, under Article 5 of the Trade-mark Law, certain goods may not be sold on the market unless and until they use registered trade marks.

For example, the Implementing Rules, in Article 4, impose such a requirement for the sale of pharmaceuticals.[25] Furthermore, a company which applies to register trade marks for pharmaceuticals must append to the application materials a document certifying approval of production issued by the relevant local health authorities.[26]

Where goods are sold in violation of Article 5 of the Trade-mark Law, the local departments of the AIC are empowered to prohibit the sale of the goods, confiscate unregistered trade-mark signs, and order an application for registration within a stated period.[27] These departments may also fine the infringing party up to RMB1,000.[28]

Tobacco products are covered by both the provisions contained in the Trade-mark Law and the Tobacco Monopoly Regulations of the People's Republic of China (hereafter cited as the Tobacco Monopoly Regulations), which require that cigarettes and cigars must have registered trade marks before they are sold on the market.[29] This requirement imposed by the Tobacco Monopoly Regulations is analogous to the quality control restriction imposed by the Trade-mark Law on pharmaceutical sales and appears to be directed towards the general protection of the consumer.

Consistent with the emphasis of Chinese trade-mark legislation on quality control, the SAIC issued a notice requiring that, with effect from 1 October 1985, goods with unregistered trade marks can only be sold on the market if the name and address of the enterprise selling the goods are indicated on both the goods and the package.[30] If it is not possible to indicate the seller's name and address on the goods, then the package must contain this information about the seller. According to the SAIC notice, this requirement stems from complaints lodged by consumers relating to many recent passing-off cases where the seller of goods using unregistered trade marks could not be traced.

E. Foreign Applicants

Foreign individuals or companies applying to register trade marks in China are subject to the Trade-mark Law. The promulgation of the Law is certainly a step forward, as foreign parties investing in or doing business with China can now rely upon a trade-mark registration system for their goods which is more consistent with common international trade-mark practice.

As in the past under the 1963 Trade-mark Law, foreign applicants are not allowed to file their applications directly with the Trade-mark Bureau, the agency actually responsible for consideration of trade-mark applications. Rather, they must appoint a Chinese entity to act as their agent for processing the application. Until the end of 1984, foreign applicants were obliged to appoint the Trade-mark Registration Agency of the

CCPIT as their agent to process their applications.[31] The CCPIT is a government organization with its headquarters in Beijing. Its Trade-mark Registration Agency (renamed the China Trade Mark Agency in 1984) in Beijing has a staff of about 30 personnel and previously was the only organization that was authorized to act in connection with trade-mark registrations for foreign parties in China. An affiliated organization, the China Patent Agent (HK) Ltd., was established in early 1984 in Hong Kong to serve foreign applicants.

For an agency fee of US$275 for each trade-mark application, the Chinese agent processes the application materials for submission to the Trade-mark Bureau. Foreign applicants are required to submit their application forms and materials in Chinese, or with Chinese translations.[32] If foreign applicants fail to provide the application materials in Chinese, the Chinese agent will perform any necessary translation services for an additional fee.

Foreign parties are also required to appoint the Chinese agent as their agent for 'handling other trade-mark matters'.[33] The precise type of assistance which falls within the category of 'other trade-mark matters' is not clear. However, in the past, CCPIT has been known to assist some American and Japanese multinational companies in settling amicably trade-mark disputes with Chinese entities.

F. Application Procedures

There is no official search system in China. For marks registered before the implementation of the Trade-mark Law, it is possible to search in the directory, *Quanguo zhuce shangbiao mingcheng huibian*,[34] which covers all registered trade marks for the fifty-year period up to July 1981. In addition, the Trade-mark Bureau publishes twice a month the *Shangbiao gonggao* (*Trade Mark Notices*), which is similar to the *Trade Marks Journal* in the United Kingdom. Trade marks that have been accepted are published in this journal. This publication is, however, printed only in Chinese. Foreign applicants who do not read Chinese or who do not have access to issues of the *Shangbiao gonggao* can request their Chinese agent to conduct a search.

In applying for the registration of a trade mark, applicants must complete and submit an application form indicating thereon the class and name of the product using the trade mark—in accordance with China's goods classification table.[35] The goods classification table at present in use has not changed significantly since 1963.[36]

A separate application must be made for each of the classes in which the applicant proposes to register a given trade mark.[37] In contrast to international practice, a separate application must be filed where the applicant wishes to use a registered trade mark on more than one product even though thay may be in the same class.[38] It is not necessary to have the application form notarized or legalized.

If it becomes necessary to change the words or design of a registered trade mark, the owner must make a new application for registration.[39]

Similarly, it is necessary to file an application for alteration where the name or address of the registrant changes.[40]

Foreign applicants, in addition to completing and submitting the trade-mark application form, must submit a power of attorney form.[41] The power of attorney form is required to be notarized, but whether legalization is necessary depends on the principle of reciprocity.[42] The requirement of legalization is generally waived for applicants from developed countries, such as the United States, West Germany, and Japan, most of which have reciprocal arrangements with China. The power of attorney form appoints the China Patent Agent (HK) Ltd. or the China Trade Mark Agency, as the case may be, to be the agent for the foreign applicant in processing the application.

The Chinese agent charges a fee of US$275 for each trade-mark application in each class. This fee includes the Trade-mark Bureau's application fee of RMB300. The registration fee is payable upon application and is not refundable if the mark is rejected. The total fee must be submitted together with the application form, power of attorney form, and the trade-mark specimens. The Trade-mark Bureau and the Chinese agent require ten and five specimens of the trade mark, respectively.[43] The time required to obtain a trade-mark registration is generally between one and two years from the date of the application.

G. Rejection

Certain elements are prohibited in both registered and unregistered trade marks, including the following: those that are the same as or similar to the state name, national flag, national emblem, military flag or medals of the PRC, or of other foreign countries; the commonly used name or design of the goods in question; words or designs directly expressing the quality, main raw materials, functions, use, weight, quantity, and other characteristics of the goods; those that exaggerate and are of a deceptive nature; and those that are harmful to the socialist morality or customs or have other 'bad influences'.[44]

Foreign applicants have generally found that the Trade-mark Bureau adopts a very broad interpretation of the criterion 'harmful to the customs of socialist morality or [having] other bad influences'. The Trade-mark Bureau is known to have rejected on this ground many registration applications of foreign trade marks which were registered in most other jurisdictions.

The Trade-mark Law, unlike the laws in most Western jurisdictions, does not expressly prohibit the use of geographical names. On the contrary, there are quite a number of registered marks in the PRC which are geographical names.[45] However, those marks may have been accepted by the Trade-mark Bureau because they have been widely used and have thus acquired a reputation within China. Foreign applicants should not assume that any geographical name will be accepted for registration.

The PRC Trade-mark Bureau also appears to adopt a flexible approach towards the registration of foreign surnames as trade marks. In contrast to the usual practice in most other jurisdictions, marks which are in the form of letters, initials, and numerals are accepted by the Trade-mark Bureau for registration without the imposition of any special conditions or disclaimers.

H. Examination and Re-examination

The Trade-mark Bureau is responsible for examining trade-mark applications. Once the Trade-mark Bureau is satisfied that the application conforms to the requirements of the Trade-mark Law, it grants preliminary approval and makes a public announcement of the preliminary approval.[46] However, an application for registration is rejected in cases where it does not conform to the relevant requirements of the Trade-mark Law, or where the trade mark is the same as or similar to one which is already registered, or which has received preliminary approval after examination.[47] In all such cases, the Trade-mark Bureau notifies the applicant in writing and makes no public announcement.[48]

If the applicant does not agree with the decision of the Trade-mark Bureau, he may apply for a re-examination within fifteen days of receiving the notification.[49] For this purpose, the applicant needs to submit a copy of the Application Form for Re-examination of Rejected Trade Marks to the Trade-mark Review Committee,[50] the body which is responsible for handling trade-mark-related disputes.[51] The applicant is notified in writing by the Committee of its decision, which is to be final and binding.[52]

Anyone who opposes the granting of the preliminary approval has three months from the date of the public announcement to 'raise objections' with the Trade-mark Bureau.[53] In raising objections, opponents must submit the Objections to Trade Marks Form to the Trade-mark Bureau.[54] The Trade-mark Bureau is to consider the facts and reasons stated by both the objector and the applicant and shall, after investigation and verification, render a decision.[55]

If a party does not agree with the decision of the Trade-mark Bureau, he may, within fifteen days of receiving notification, apply to the Trade-mark Review Committee for re-examination by submitting the Application Form for Re-examination of Objections to Trade Marks.[56] The Trade-mark Review Committee shall notify the parties in writing of its final ruling.[57] If there are no objections to the preliminary approval of the Trade-mark Bureau or if any objections are overruled by the Trade-mark Review Committee, the trade mark is to be registered.

Objections may also be raised to registered trade marks.[58] Within one year of the registration of a trade mark, an objection may be brought for a ruling by the Trade-mark Review Committee, provided that the same objection has not been raised and ruled upon during the period for objections to preliminary approvals. Opponents of trade marks which are already registered need to submit to the Trade-mark Review Committee an Application Form for a Ruling on Disputes Regarding Registered Trade Marks.[59]

I. Competing Applications

The Trade-mark Law adopts the 'first to apply' principle. The People's Republic acceded to the Paris Convention for the Protection of Industrial Property (hereafter cited as the Paris Convention) on 19 December 1984.[60] Hence, with the exception of applications claiming a right of priority under the Paris Convention,[61] where two or more applicants apply for the registration of the same or a similar trade mark on the same or a similar type of product, the Trade-mark Bureau grants preliminary approval after examination and makes a public announcement of such approval in respect of the trade mark which was applied for first.[62]

It is therefore important for applicants to comply with all the formal requirements of an application under the Trade-mark Law, as an application date may be lost or postponed where documents are subsequently returned by the Trade-mark Bureau because of non-compliance.

In cases where two applications are made on the same day, preliminary approval is granted after examination and a public announcement is made in respect of the trade mark which was used first.[63] Neither the Trade-mark Law nor the Implementing Rules provide any guidance on how the principle of use is to be interpreted by the Trade-mark Bureau. Nevertheless, Chinese trade-mark officials have unofficially stated that the principle of use is not restricted to use within China and includes use outside China. The proof required of such use is the date on which the product was first sold on the market, within or outside China.[64]

Where a registered trade mark has been revoked or cancelled, the Trade-mark Bureau is prohibited from approving, within one year of the date of such revocation or cancellation, any application for the registration of a trade mark which is the same as or similar to the cancelled trade mark.[65]

The 'first to apply' principle also overrides the concept of the source of goods. In other words, an applicant can be either the manufacturer, the selector, or the distributor of the goods bearing the trade mark. Under Chinese trade-mark law, priority is given to the person who applies first.

In practice, therefore, it is possible for a manufacturer's mark to be registered by a distributor, notwithstanding the fact that it is the manufacturer who affixes the mark to the goods and who is, strictly speaking, the 'source' of the goods. Accordingly, the manufacturer may not be able to rectify the registration by lodging a complaint that the public may be confused by the distributor's use of the mark.

J. Extensions

A registered trade mark is valid for ten years from the date of approval of registration, and not from the date of the filing of the application, as is the case in international practice.[66] An application for the extension of registration for an additional ten years can be made six months before or on the expiry of the basic ten-year term.[67] In cases where such an application is not made by the end of the ten-year validity period, the registered trade mark in question is no longer valid and is cancelled.[68]

K. Licensing and Assignment

In a significant improvement to the 1963 Trade-mark Law, the Trade-mark Law provides for the first time for the licensing of a registered trade mark in China.[69] Although the Trade-mark Law does not require the licenser or the licensee to obtain approval from the Trade-mark Bureau for licensing trade marks, it does provide that licensing agreements must be filed with the Trade-mark Bureau 'for the record'.[70]

Foreign licensers, such as foreign parties engaged in technology transfer agreements in China which include the licensing of the right to the use of registered trade marks in China, should note that trade-mark licensing agreements appear to be subject to the Regulations of the People's Republic of China for the Administration of Technology Import Contracts (hereafter cited as the Technology Import Regulations), which were promulgated by the State Council on 24 May 1985 and became effective on that date as well as the Procedures for Examination and Approval of Technology Import Contracts which were approved by the State Council on 26 August 1985 and published by the Ministry of Foreign Economic Relations and Trade (MOFERT) on 18 September 1985. The Technology Import Regulations provide that trade-mark licensing agreements require MOFERT's approval before they can become effective. In particular, foreign licensers should note the prohibition under Article 9 of the Technology Import Regulations against the imposition of restrictive provisions in licensing agreements.

Under the Trade-mark Law, licensers are obligated to 'supervise' the quality of the goods on which the licensees use their registered trade marks.[71] Licensees, in turn, are under an obligation to 'guarantee' the quality of the goods on which they use the registered trade marks.[72] As the Trade-mark Law does not specify the precise nature of the responsibility required from the licensing parties, the degree of supervision and the extent of the guarantee required remain to be clarified through experience.

In cases of assignment of registered trade marks, the assignor and the assignee must jointly file an application for the assignment with the Trade-mark Bureau.[73] The assignee must 'guarantee' the quality of the goods which use the relevant registered trade mark.[74] The Trade-mark Law does not specify whether this guarantee applies to goods produced by the previous owner of the trade mark, but Chinese authorities would be most likely to interpret the guarantee as applying to goods manufactured by the assignor. Such an interpretation could be based on the general guarantee provision imposed on trade-mark users under the Trade-mark Law.[75]

L. The Powers of the Trade-mark Bureau on Misconduct

In addition to handling complaints about misconduct made by third parties, the Trade-mark Bureau is empowered in some circumstances by the Trade-mark Law to order trade-mark registrants who breach the law either to correct their behaviour or to face the possibility of having their registered trade marks revoked by the Trade-mark Bureau.[76] These circumstances include changing the words or design of a trade mark, assigning a registered trade mark without following the stipulated procedures of the law, and the non-use of a trade mark for three consecutive years.[77]

The Trade-mark Law clearly disallows alterations of the registered mark which involve the addition of an extra word or an element to the design. However, according to the China Trade Mark Agency officials, it is permissible under the Trade-mark Law for a registrant of a black-and-white mark to use the same mark in colour. Such a change of colour is not regarded by Chinese trade-mark officials as an alteration to the registered black-and-white mark, and it would therefore not infringe the Trade-mark Law. Similarly, a trade-mark owner may register his mark in block letters and use the mark in stylized letters. This, again, without further amendments, would not be considered as an infringement of the Trade-mark Law.

A party which disagrees with the decision of the Trade-mark Bureau to revoke its registered trade mark may apply for re-examination of the decision by the Trade-mark Review Committee within fifteen days of receiving the Trade-mark Bureau's notification.[78] The Trade-mark Review Committee is obliged to render a final decision in writing to the applicant.[79]

In other situations where registrants violate the Trade-mark Law, such as when goods are 'manufactured in a rough and slipshod way, the inferior being passed off as good, deceiving consumers',[80] the relevant departments of the AIC are authorized 'to order rectification within a stated period and to circulate a notice on the matter or impose fines'.[81] In such cases, if the circumstances of the offence are minor, 'criticism education' is to be conducted and rectification demanded by the relevant local AIC departments.[82] However, where the circumstances are serious, 'self-criticism' is to be ordered and either a notice is to be circulated or a fine of up to RMB2,000 is to be imposed by the local department of the AIC.[83] The Trade-mark Bureau may also independently revoke the relevant registered trade mark.[84]

If a trade-mark owner, in using unregistered trade marks for the sale of certain goods, represents the mark as a registered trade mark or violates any of the provisions of the Trade-mark Law regarding the contents of the trade mark,[85] the local departments of the AIC are authorized to prohibit the sale of the goods in question, to stop any advertisement of the goods, to confiscate the trade-mark signs, and to order rectification within a stated period.[86] Such AIC departments may also, according to the seriousness of the circumstances, either circulate a notice on the matter or impose a fine of up to RMB2,000 on the violator.[87]

A party who is fined by the local AIC for misconduct under the Trade-mark Law may appeal in the people's courts within fifteen days of receiving notification of the fine.[88] However, if the fifteen-day period has elapsed and the infringing party has neither appealed nor taken remedial action, the local AIC department is to apply to the people's courts for compulsory execution of the fine.[89]

M. Infringement

The Trade-mark Law has filled a major gap in China's previous trade-mark legislation by providing a system of civil remedies for trade-mark infringement. Trade-mark infringement is defined broadly under the Trade-mark Law to include one of the following types of conduct:

(a) using a trade mark which is the same as or similar to a registered trade mark for the same or a similar product, without obtaining the licence of the registered trade-mark owner;

(b) the unauthorized manufacture or sale of another's registered trade-mark sign; or

(c) causing other damage to another's right of exclusive use of a registered trade mark.[90]

The Trade-mark Law provides an aggrieved registrant with a choice of remedies. Where his fundamental right of exclusive use of the registered trade mark has been infringed, he may bring a suit directly in the people's court,[91] or request the local AIC department to order the infringer to cease the infringing conduct immediately and to compensate him for his losses.[92] Where the circumstances of the infringement are serious, the local AIC department may also impose fines on the infringing party.[93]

However, aggrieved foreign parties cannot complain of infringement directly to the local AIC departments. Instead, foreign parties wishing to lodge infringement complaints must request that the Chinese agent handle the matter with the relevant departments of the local AIC. Moreover, if litigation in the people's courts is required, the Legal Counsel Office of the CCPIT is to be retained.[94] With the recent establishment of some Chinese law firms which are authorized by the Chinese Ministry of Justice to handle foreign investment-related legal matters in addition to local litigation, foreign companies now appear to have the option of utilizing the services of Chinese counsel other than the CCPIT Legal Counsel Office.

Under the Trade-mark Law and the Implementing Rules,[95] the local AIC departments entrusted with the investigation and disposition of a case involving the infringement of a registered trade mark may employ a variety of administrative weapons to deal with the infringing conduct. These include the sealing, confiscation, or destruction of counterfeit goods; the removal of trade marks from the products on which they appear; and the circulation of notices of criticism. In addition, where the circumstances are serious, a fine of up to RMB5,000 may also be imposed.

If the trade-mark owner remains unsatisfied with the result, he may, as discussed earlier, demand compensation for his losses. Since administrative sanctions may be imposed at the discretion of the relevant AIC departments entrusted with the handling of the matter, the registrant who decides to seek administrative relief may not agree with the amount of the fine imposed by the local AIC department. In that case, he may appeal before the people's court within fifteen days of receiving notification of the imposition of the fine.[96] The accused infringer, however, is also entitled to appeal to the people's court against the amount of the fine imposed. Where a suit has not been brought before the court by either the registrant or the accused party within the fifteen-day period and where the infringing conduct has not ceased and compensation has not been paid, the local AIC has the right to apply to the people's court for compulsory execution.[97]

In cases of counterfeiting another's registered trade mark (which includes the unauthorized manufacture or sale of another's registered trademark sign), the infringing party is liable to pay compensation to the registrant for his losses and faces the possibility of additional fines. Moreover, the criminal responsibility of the person(s) directly responsible for the infringement is to be 'investigated according to law by the judicial organs'.[98]

Under Chinese law, foreign parties whose marks have been infringed or whose goods have been counterfeited may institute legal proceedings in the people's court. However, as in Japan, litigation as a means for resolving disputes is discouraged in China. This is particularly the case with respect to disputes involving foreigners. Regardless of what is provided under the law, the commencement of a lawsuit in Chinese courts would be interpreted by the Chinese authorities as an 'unfriendly act', not simply *vis-à-vis* the infringing party but also the Chinese state. Therefore, the initiation of a lawsuit would perhaps be harmful to a foreign company's reputation and marketing prospects in China.

Another reason why pursuit of a legal remedy would be inadvisable for foreign companies is that the Chinese courts at the time of writing lack experience in handling trade-mark disputes. According to the Ministry of Justice, no case of trade-mark infringement involving foreigners has been brought before Chinese courts. A substantial element of uncertainty as to the outcome of such a case would therefore discourage a foreign company from resorting to bringing a lawsuit before the people's court.

As a result, most of the foreign companies who have been victims of counterfeits or other infringements have relied solely on administrative remedies. To date, experience indicates that administrative relief is generally only successful in containing, but not eliminating, trade-mark infringements.

On the other hand, as the Chinese government's concern about counterfeiting in the PRC has grown in recent years, local AIC officials have adopted a positive attitude towards efforts to eliminate illegal activities. The important role which the AIC and CCPIT officials have played in combating counterfeiting is to be commended. They have been particularly useful in locating trade-mark infringers, issuing 'freezing orders' against illegal activities, and in negotiating with offenders. On various occasions, the AIC department officials have seized and destroyed large quantities of counterfeit goods.

While administrative remedies may be preferable to legal proceedings as a means of eliminating counterfeiting in China, foreign trade-mark owners can expect to be confronted with a number of problems in working with Chinese administrative officials.

The most common difficulty which a foreign company faces relates to the question of the sufficiency of evidence of the alleged counterfeiting activity. Since the AIC and the Chinese administrative officials will act on behalf of foreign complainants only after they have been provided with sufficient evidence of the alleged infringement by the complainant himself, they will not conduct preliminary investigations of trade-mark violations without such evidence. However, given the linguistic, cultural, and political obstacles which foreign companies must conquer in their quest for information regarding the illegal activities, they invariably find the burden of providing the AIC officials with sufficient written materials difficult to discharge. Unless they can collect sufficient evidence of the counterfeiting activity, foreign companies can often be persuaded by AIC officials to drop their alleged cases of infringement. Some foreign concerns, in order to comply with the requirements of the AIC officials, appoint Hong Kong-based investigation firms to ascertain the source of the illegal activity. Unfortunately, after expending considerable time and incurring significant fees for professional assistance, the foreign companies are often disappointed to find that the reports of the Hong Kong-based agents are not accepted by the local AIC departments. Those reports, prepared by a non-PRC organization, are generally not sanctioned and are frequently viewed with suspicion by Chinese authorities.

Foreign companies which choose to pursue administrative remedies often find that potential conflicts between national and local interests complicate the resolution of trade-mark disputes. Although the national authorities may adopt an aggressive attitude in calling for the punishment of counterfeiting activity, local authorities may approach the issue with less enthusiasm. This is the case when sanctions prescribed by the Beijing authorities involve economic losses to local enterprises, and especially because the new 'contract' system implemented by the state makes state-owned enterprises responsible for their own profits and losses. Hence local authorities are frequently reluctant to sanction the wholesale destruction of counterfeit goods unless there has been sustained high-level pressure from Beijing, since the destruction of such goods means a loss of income to the locality. For similar reasons, it is often difficult to obtain monetary compensation from Chinese trade-mark infringers.

Finally, the style of work of Chinese administrative agencies also poses problems. For example, many documents and other communications between Chinese counsel retained by foreign companies and the AIC department officials are classified as *neibu* or 'internal' and, as such, their contents may not be revealed to foreigners. As a result, the foreign trade-mark owner must rely on the good faith of the Chinese authorities that they are acting in the best interests of the foreign party, as opposed to the interests of Chinese producers or sellers of counterfeit goods.

IV. Selecting a Trade Mark

The legal aspects of and the requirements for registering one's trade mark in China have been discussed above. However, it is also important to consider the practical aspects of choosing a trade mark for use in China. This subject is discussed in detail below and should assist foreign companies contemplating the registration of a mark in China.[99]

A. Chinese Language and Trade Marks

A foreign company which wishes to register a trade mark in Chinese must recognize some of the complexities of the Chinese language and its use in contemporary China. For example, there are eight dialects in China and numerous sub-dialects. These dialects can be so different that a person from Guangzhou (Canton) may not be able to understand a person from Beijing speaking the Beijing dialect. While the official national language for China is *putonghua* (Mandarin), for many Chinese people in Southeast Asia, *putonghua* is a second language. In Hong Kong, the Cantonese dialect prevails and even in neighbouring Guangdong province in China, the Cantonese dialect is frequently used. The existence of these various dialects means that even though the ideograph adopted for a trade mark may be recognized by people throughout China, the pronunciation of the character and of the resultant trade mark may be very different. For example, the character 好 meaning 'good' is pronounced quite differently in different dialects, as set forth below:

Dialect	Pronunciation
Cantonese	Hó
putonghua	Hǎo
Shanghainese	Hór
Hakka	Hōr
Chiu Chow	Hòr

The difference in pronunciation of one Chinese character can prove especially troublesome where a foreign company wants to use the same trade mark in several different Chinese-speaking jurisdictions, both within China and in overseas Chinese markets throughout South-east Asia. It is clearly essential to pay particular care and attention to the selection of the character and the determination of how it will be pronounced in the different jurisdictions.

B. Simplified Chinese Characters

It is also important for foreign companies to note that the ideographs used in China may differ from those used in other South-east Asian markets. In 1956, the PRC introduced a scheme of simplified characters in an attempt to facilitate the learning of Chinese by more Chinese people. This means that many of the traditional Chinese characters utilized before 1956 in China have now been simplified in format. However, even within China, not all traditional characters have been simplified. To complicate the matter further, territories outside China have not simplified the traditional Chinese characters. And, in general, overseas Chinese do not use or understand simplified Chinese characters. Foreign companies contemplating the use of the same Chinese-language trade mark in more than one jurisdiction should take note of this difference and ensure that the proper Chinese ideographs, whether traditional or simplified in format, are being used in the appropriate jurisdiction.

Examples of the differences between traditional and simplified characters can be seen from the following table:

Traditional	Simplified	Meaning
兒	儿	child
齒	齿	teeth
區	区	district
偉	伟	grand
東	东	east

C. Translating a Foreign Word Mark

There are two basic ways of translating a foreign word mark. One way is to use characters that represent the sound of the foreign word (the phonetic method). The other is to use characters that represent the meaning of the foreign word (the conceptual method). As a rough approximation, about half the foreign marks used in Hong Kong are translated phonetically, and half conceptually.

For example, the Chinese trade mark for APPLE computers is 蘋果, pronounced in Cantonese 'ping gwo' and in putonghua 'ping guo', and meaning 'apple'. The Chinese trade mark for JAGUAR cars in Hong Kong is 積架, pronounced in Cantonese 'jik gar' and in putonghua 'ji jia', meaning 'accumulate, frame'.

It would be possible to transliterate APPLE phonetically as 亞普 (ar-ple), meaning 'secondary, general' but this sounds unpleasant to a Cantonese speaker. It would be possible to translate JAGUAR as 豹 (pow), meaning 'leopard or jaguar', but instead the foreign nature of the original mark is preserved by opting for a roughly phonetic pronunciation. The phonetic transliteration sounds right in Cantonese, but rather strange in putonghua.

The choice of translation method is only available where there are Chinese characters conceptually equivalent to the foreign word. Many foreign marks (for example, KODAK, EXXON) have no conceptual equivalent, and can only be translated by the phonetic method.

Alternatively, a Chinese mark can be chosen which has absolutely no relationship with the original mark. Such a mark is not in any sense a translation of the original.

i. The Phonetic Method

Phonetic translation (or transliteration) can produce sounds that are reasonably close to the original English marks. However, the meanings of the characters used are entirely unrelated to the original mark or to the product.

Sometimes the characters that produce the closest phonetic equivalent have unacceptable or less desirable meanings and connotations. In such

cases the translation, while still based on the phonetic method, will abandon the characters that give the closest phonetic equivalent in favour of
alternative characters which, in addition to a rough phonetic equivalence,
also convey a more acceptable or desirable meaning. To take an example
from Hong Kong, the closest phonetic meaning of the brand name
HAAGEN-DAZS for ice-cream is 哈根達 (*har gun dat*), meaning 'laugh,
root, arrive'. However, the characters 喜見達 (*hay gin dat*), meaning
'happy to see it arrive', are used instead, because the conceptual association is better.

Where the goods concerned are manufactured in or imported from
Europe or the United States, the phonetic method of translation can suggest an 'imported product' quality. If the Chinese mark consists of several
characters which can provide little comprehensible meaning or an absurd
meaning, the Chinese consumer will immediately understand that the
Chinese mark must be a transliteration of a foreign trade mark. On the
other hand, a Chinese translation according to the conceptual meaning of
a foreign word mark may suggest to Chinese consumers that the product
is produced locally in Hong Kong or China.

ii. Problems with Phonetic Translation

In trying to select the most appropriate Chinese character for an English
word mark, it is important to take into account the following characteristics of the Chinese language, some of which were referred to above.

a. The Different Sounds of Characters in Different Dialects   In Hong
Kong, where English marks are rendered into Chinese characters by the
phonetic method, this will invariably be done according to the Cantonese
dialect because over 90 per cent of the Hong Kong population speaks
Cantonese as the mother tongue. If the mark is to be used in China, the
phonetic transliteration should be done in accordance with the *putonghua*
pronunciation. For example, the trade mark SUNKIST is translated
phonetically as 新奇士 (*sun kay si*), meaning 'new, wonder, scholar' in
Cantonese. In *putonghua*, these same characters would be pronounced as
'*xin qi shi*', but still retaining the meaning 'new, wonder, scholar', and
would yield different sounds again in other dialects.

b. Different Characters with the Same Pronunciation   Some words in
Chinese have exactly the same pronunciation and tone, but have different
meanings which are represented by different characters. This is similar
to certain groups of words in English such as 'two', 'too', and 'to'. For
example, all the following words are pronounced '*ga*' in the same tone
in Cantonese or '*jia*' in *putonghua*, but the meanings are completely
different:

Character	Meaning
家	family
加	add
嘉	good, excellent, fine
傢	furniture, tools

Despite the availability of multiple character options, a Chinese character may not be compatible with another Chinese character in tone or in meaning.

In Hong Kong the English mark KELLOGG'S for cereal products has the Chinese mark 家樂氏 (*ga lok si*), meaning 'family, happiness, clan'. If another Chinese character with the same pronunciation as 家 (*ga*) is substituted, such as 傢 (meaning 'furniture, tools'), the end-result will be incongruous in meaning—'furniture, happiness, clan'.

c. The Absence of Some English Sounds in Chinese   A Chinese character may have different variations of pronunciation with tones ranging from high to low. In most Chinese dialects, the tones of Chinese characters when spoken in succession may be different from those of the same characters when spoken in isolation. Furthermore, there are certain sounds in the English language which do not exist in the Chinese language. For example, there is no equivalent of the sounds '*sh*', '*ch*', '*th*', or '*cl*' in the Cantonese dialect. English words ending in '*s*', '*r*', or '*l*' equally cannot be phonetically transliterated into Cantonese. The usual solution in trying to overcome the incompatibility of the languages is to extend the English sounds or to make up some Chinese sounds similar to the English ones.

For example, in Hong Kong, BRANDS essence of chicken is transliterated as 白蘭氏 (*pak lan shi*, corresponding to the sounds '*br-an-ds*'), meaning 'white, orchard, clan'. The brand CLINIQUE for cosmetics is transliterated as 倩碧 (*sin pik*), meaning 'pretty jade'. The brand DUNHILL for cigarettes is 登喜路 (*dun hei lo*) meaning 'ascend, happiness, road'.

d. The Undesirable Connotations of Phonetically Translated Marks   A pronunciation in one dialect may evoke an entirely different and undesirable meaning to a person familiar with another dialect. For example, the mark CHILLO for water coolers could be transliterated in *putonghua* for use in China using the characters 七樓 (meaning 'seventh floor'). In *putonghua* these characters sound like '*chi lo*' (written *qi lou* in pinyin). In Hong Kong this sound has the colloquial meaning 'crazy guy' (黐佬). There is no problem when Hong Kong people see the characters 七樓, which are pronounced in Hong Kong as '*chut lo*'. But when a CHILLO salesman in Hong Kong uses the *putonghua* pronunciation to introduce himself, people smile. The problem can also arise in radio advertising and in television sound, which lack visual representation of the characters.

e. The Strange Meanings of Phonetic Translations   Sometimes, use of the phonetic method may produce a combination of Chinese characters with an absurd meaning. This absurdity can be accepted and overlooked in many situations where the English word mark is a proper name or surname.

For example in Hong Kong, McDONALD'S for hamburgers is transliterated as 麥當勞 (*mac don lo*) meaning 'wheat, when, labour'. It is important, however, not to view such an absurd literal meaning as being necessarily detrimental to the product. Once the Chinese mark becomes established through extensive use, people cease to think about the primary meaning of the characters. Instead of registering 'wheat, when, labour', they simply think of McDONALD'S.

To put this in proper perspective, consider the way in which country names are translated. 'America' is transliterated phonetically in Hong Kong and China as 美國 (*mei guo*), meaning 'beautiful country'. However, when people read these characters, they generally think only of the secondary meaning. In a way, this perception is similar to that of names like 'New York'. People seeing the name think of the place, and not of the literal meaning which suggests 'new' York replacing 'old' York.

iii. The Conceptual Method

a. Exact Word-for-word Equivalence   There are some foreign marks that have an exact conceptual correspondence with a Chinese character. We have already noted the example of APPLE for computers, which is translated as 蘋果, meaning 'apple'. The advantage of this translation is that 蘋果 means 'apple' in every Chinese dialect, although it is pronounced differently in different places.

b. The Lack of Word-for-word Equivalence   It is difficult to find a concise Chinese equivalent for every single English term or concept. During the process of finding a proper Chinese substitute, accuracy in meaning may be lost or distorted. Some English words can be translated conceptually into Chinese in several different ways. A good illustration is the English word 'beautiful' which can be represented by the Chinese characters 美, 艷, 秀, and 靚, without losing its general meaning. Yet each individual character represents a particular variant of the concept of 'beauty'.

Sometimes the conceptual method can produce an interesting play on words. The mark SMARTIES for sugar-coated chocolates is translated in Hong Kong as 聰明豆, meaning 'clever beans'. The mark EVEREADY for batteries is translated as 永備貓嘜, meaning 'perpetual ready cat brand', the reference to a cat being derived from the cat with nine lives which is used in EVEREADY advertising and labelling.

c. The Lack of a Conceptual Meaning   Some foreign marks have no conceptual meaning (for example, EXXON, KODAK) and cannot be translated conceptually. The corollary of this is that it is not possible to invent a completely meaningless word mark in Chinese. With a phonetic alphabet it is possible to invent words that can be pronounced but which are entirely meaningless. However, in Chinese, every character has an inherent meaning. In the PRC, KODAK is 柯达 (*ke da*), meaning 'stalk, arrive'.

d. Unfavourable Connotations   Any foreign company eyeing the huge Chinese-speaking market must take care, when using the conceptual method, to avoid any Chinese translation which has an unfavourable connotation. For example, the trade mark CANNON (with a cannon as a logo) for bed-covers and textile articles is translated in Hong Kong as 大炮嘜, meaning 'big cannon brand'. This is an exact literal translation. The problem is that the characters 大炮 have the strong connotation of 'telling a lie' in Cantonese. They may have even less desirable slang connotations in other regions.

iv. The Phonetic-conceptual Method

If translation is done by this method, the Chinese mark will become phonetically similar to the English mark while, at the same time, remaining descriptive of the function or benefits of the product. However, as discussed, foreign trade-mark owners must exercise care so as not to develop a Chinese mark which is laudatory or descriptive, and thereby precluded from registration.

D. Device Marks

In the past, many products had devices as trade marks to facilitate easy identification by consumers who were mostly illiterate. That is why there were many brands of ointments and medicines which had a tiger, an axe, or even a portrait of the producer or inventor on the goods. Modern device marks are more often in the nature of graphic designs or logos.

In China, device marks are very common, and abundant examples can be found in *Shangbiao gonggao*. The devices that appear most often include flowers, bridges, and scenery, but marks commonly used in China include tigers, swans, cocks, and the like. A high proportion of the packaged goods on sale in China's stores have device marks, as do the millions of bicycles which are sold under many different marks. When coupled with pinyin, which is the romanization of Chinese characters, such marks can assist communication with consumers who speak only dialect or minority languages.

Device marks are appropriate where goods are purchased by visual selection, or as part of an image-building exercise which is removed from the direct selling process. Device marks are less useful where the selling process involves aural or written communication. It can be difficult to use a device mark in a radio advertisement.

E. Maintaining Foreign Marks for Prestigious Products

If a foreign company wishes to sell goods which are commonplace items ordinarily purchased by the Chinese-speaking population, such as household products, it is advisable to establish and register a Chinese trade mark. The majority of Chinese people in Hong Kong and virtually all people in China associate staple products exclusively with their Chinese trade marks or nicknames.

If the goods in question are usually bought by the non-Chinese-speaking section of the population, the need for a registered Chinese trade mark is less pressing.

If the goods are high-quality and expensive products which cater for the demands of a more sophisticated segment of the market, the usual advertising policy is to associate these goods with a foreign name, on an international scale. The use of a Chinese name may only weaken the exclusiveness or the 'imported product' quality of these goods. Typical examples include LALIQUE, NINA RICCI, PACO RABANNE, FENDI, and TRUSSARDI. Even if a Chinese name for these products exists, most potential consumers would associate the product with its foreign name alone. For instance, not everyone would know to what products the mark 姬仙蒂啊 (read as '*gay sin tai or*') refers, but most Hong Kong consumers in the relevant economic bracket would understand that CHRISTIAN DIOR is a well-known mark for ladies fashion and cosmetic products.

Nevertheless, many international companies have registered or plan to register Chinese marks in China for their well-known products in order to strengthen their rights and to further protect their reputation.

F. Consequences of the Failure to Establish and Register a Chinese Trade Mark

i. Nicknames and 'Unofficial' Marks

Sometimes products sold only by reference to foreign trade marks acquire Chinese nicknames which are recognized throughout the local market, with the nicknames then becoming the 'trade marks' in Chinese-language advertising, and the badge of reference in Chinese-language invoicing, store displays, and conversation.

Many nicknames are derived from the device used on the products or from the shape of the goods. Thus TOBLERONE becomes 三角牌 ('triangle brand'), WRIGLEY becomes 白箭牌 ('white arrow brand'), CARNATION becomes 三花牌 ('three flowers brand'), QUAKER becomes 老人牌 ('old man brand'), and so on. None of these device translations is descriptive or laudatory of the product itself, and hence all are inherently suitable as candidates for registration.

The nickname is not always one with which the company would deliberately choose to be associated. For example, the mark POLO for clothing has a Chinese nickname which is based on the device of a mounted polo player, but which comes out as 三脚马, meaning 'three-legged horse'. There is a world of difference between the image of a deformed horse and the up-market sport of polo.

ii. Failure to Register

It is important to register distinctive nicknames as trade marks. The trade-mark-registration system within many large international companies is such that often only the Roman alphabet mark is registered, and the trade-mark department within the company does not even know that a Chinese nickname has been developed to a point where it is being used as a common-law trade mark. In such a situation an alert local competitor can register the nickname or a mark very similar to it as his own mark.

Even in Hong Kong, provided the competitor acts carefully, he may be able to benefit from the reputation of the nickname without actually infringing any common-law rights of the owner. Thus, over a period of time, the competitor may dilute or completely erode any value which the nickname may have developed as a once-exclusive mark. In China, where common-law rights are not recognized and prior use is of little or no relevance against a registered mark, registration is of paramount importance.

V. Conclusion

In tracing the history of Chinese trade-mark law since 1949, it is obvious that significant improvements have occurred. To begin with, the Trade-mark Law and China's recent accession to the Paris Convention have brought China's trade-mark system much closer to common international practice.

In addition, the Trade-mark Law's consideration of many areas of concern to foreign trade-mark owners which were not previously covered by the earlier trade-mark law demonstrates the advancement of trade-mark law in China. The most important examples of these changes are provisions in the 1983 Law relating to the licensing of the exclusive right to use registered trade marks and the offering of a range of civil remedies for infringements.

There have also been improvements with regard to the administration of the Law. For example, it is expected that the trade-mark registration process will continue to take between one and two years under the new Law, although the system has not yet been fully tested. This compares favourably with the length of time required for trade-mark registration in countries such as Italy and Australia.

Nevertheless, some areas of administration still require improvement. Many foreign applicants have urged the China Patent Agent (HK) Ltd. and the China Trade Mark Agency, in their roles as the sole agents for foreign applicants, to keep them more informed of the progress of their applications. Foreign applicants would also welcome any efforts which the Chinese agents may make in generally providing a better bridge of communication between foreign clients and the Trade-mark Bureau.

Notes

1. See Han Shaoyou, 'The Evolution of the Trade-mark Laws', *Jurisprudence* (Shanghai), October 1982, p. 37.
2. Han, p. 37, note 1 above.
3. For this and the preceding paragraph, see Han, p. 38, note 1 above.
4. The Government Administration Council was subsequently renamed the State Council.
5. The 1963 Trade-mark Regulations and the 1963 Implementing Rules will in this chapter be collectively referred to as the 1963 Trade-mark Law.
6. See, for example, Li Hongxiang, 'The Trade-mark Law with Chinese Characteristics', *China Finance and Trade Journal*, April 1983, p. 35.
7. 1963 Trade-mark Regulations, Art. 3.
8. 1963 Trade-mark Regulations, Art. 3.
9. 1963 Trade-mark Regulations, Art. 2.
10. 1963 Trade-mark Regulations, Art. 7.
11. 1963 Trade-mark Regulations, Art. 12.

12. 1963 Implementing Rules, Art. 15.

13. Unless otherwise specified in this chapter, a reference to the Trade-mark Law will include the Trade-mark Law as supplemented by the Implementing Rules.

14. Under the Trade-mark Law, foreign banks will be able to register their trade marks for tangible goods such as bank publications. Protection will, however, not be extended to banks' names and logos. See Timothy A. Gelatt and T. Y. Chan, 'China's New and Improved Trademark Law', *Asian Wall Street Journal*, 22 October 1982, p. 6.

15. The SAIC has pointed out that the business names regulations are very new and that it has limited experience in their implementation. Nevertheless, the authors suggest that on the basis of discussions with the SAIC in March 1986, some preliminary conclusions may be drawn as to the protection accorded to foreign companies' names under these regulations. Firstly, it appears that it is not necessary for a foreign enterprise to carry on business activities in China in order to register its name. However, it can only register the name which appears on its certificate of incorporation, and which must not be a Chinese name. Secondly, once a name is registered, the owner of that name enjoys exclusive rights to that name in China. Thirdly, a foreign enterprise may register a name containing the word '*Zhonghua*' or '*Zhongguo*' ('China') so long as the word is not at the beginning of the name. If 'China' appears at the beginning of the name, then the special approval of the SAIC is required.

16. See 'Competing Applications', p. 435 in this volume, for a more detailed discussion of prior use.

17. Previously, under the 1963 Trade-mark Regulations, the SAIC was known as the CAIC. The SAIC is under the direct supervision and jurisdiction of the State Council.

18. Trade-mark Law, Art. 6.

19. Trade-mark Law, Art. 6.

20. Trade-mark Law, Art. 3.

21. Trade-mark Law, Art. 7.

22. Trade-mark Law, Art. 7; and Implementing Rules, Art. 8.

23. This information is based on discussions held between the authors and CCPIT Trade-mark Registration Agency officials in Beijing in June 1983.

24. For details, see pp. 447–8 of this volume.

25. According to a circular issued jointly in July 1983 by the Ministry of Public Health, the State Pharmaceutical Administration, and the SAIC, the term 'pharmaceuticals' covers all pharmaceuticals, new patent drugs, traditional Chinese patent drugs, and medicinal liquors.

26. The July 1983 circular, see note 25 above, requires foreign enterprises to submit certificates approving production from their own governments.

27. Implementing Rules, Art. 22.

28. Implementing Rules, Art. 2. US$1.00 equals approximately RMB3.70 (November 1986).

29. See Article 16 of the Tobacco Monopoly Regulations. These regulations became effective on 1 November 1983.

30. Notice of the State Administration of Industry and Commerce Requiring that Goods Using Unregistered Trade Marks Must Clearly Indicate the Name and Address of the Enterprise, Doc. No. 119 *Gong shang* (85) issued on 15 July 1985.

31. Implementing Rules, Art. 29.

32. Implementing Rules, Art. 31.

33. Implementing Rules, Art. 29.

34. *Quanguo zhuce shangbiao mingchang huibian* (National Directory of Registered Trade Marks) (Beijing, State Administration of Industry and Commerce of the People's Republic of China, 1981).

35. Trade-mark Law, Art. 11.

36. For more details, see I. J. Kaufman, 'Trademark Protection in the People's

Republic of China', in Jerome A. Cohen (ed.), *Legal Aspects of Doing Business in China 1983* (New York, Practising Law Institute, 1983), p. 436.

37. Trade-mark Law, Art. 12.
38. Trade-mark Law, Art. 13.
39. Trade-mark Law, Art. 14.
40. Trade-mark Law, Art. 15; and Implementing Rules, Art. 7.
41. Implementing Rules, Art. 30.
42. Implementing Rules, Art. 31.
43. The specimens must be on glossy durable paper of a size not exceeding 10 centimetres by 10 centimetres. The specimens may be photocopies of the mark. However, if the mark is in colour, the specimens need also to be in colour, and an additional black-and-white ink draft of the mark is also required. The specimens must also be accompanied by an explanation of the meaning and derivation of the mark, unless the mark has no particular meaning—in which case no explanation is necessary. See Implementing Rules, Art. 3.
44. Trade-mark Law, Art. 8. It is interesting to note that one of the best-known beers in Beijing uses the registered trade mark Wuxing, meaning 'five star', which must come close to infringing the national emblem criterion. The five-star symbol is the national emblem of the People's Republic of China.
45. For example, 北京牌 or Beijing Brand, is registered as a mark for essential oils.
46. Trade-mark Law, Art. 16.
47. Trade-mark Law, Art. 17.
48. Foreign applicants receive only the CCPIT's written advice, which generally provides only the decision of the Trade-mark Bureau, and not any of the arguments which the CCPIT might have presented on behalf of the foreign applicant nor any of the counter-arguments which it might have received from the Trade-mark Bureau.
49. Trade-mark Law, Art. 21; and Implementing Rules, Art. 10. At meetings with the authors, CCPIT trade-mark officials have unofficially expressed their concern at the time limitation imposed on foreign applicants by the fifteen-day requirement. In their opinion, foreign applicants should be granted an extension beyond the fifteen-day period. See also C. L. Gholz, 'China's New Trade-mark Law', *China Law Reporter*, Vol. II, No. 2, Summer 1982, p. 106.
50. Implementing Rules, Art. 10.
51. Trade-mark Law, Art. 20.
52. Trade-mark Law, Art. 21.
53. Trade-mark Law, Art. 19.
54. Implementing Rules, Art. 11.
55. Trade-mark Law, Art. 22. It is not yet clear in practice whether the Trade-mark Bureau intends to notify the relevant parties of its decision in writing.
56. Trade-mark Law, Art. 22; and Implementing Rules, Art. 11.
57. Trade-mark Law, Art. 22.
58. Trade-mark Law, Art. 27.
59. Implementing Rules, Art. 12.
60. The Paris Convention provides for the protection of well-known marks. Under Article 6 of the Paris Convention, members undertake, ex officio if their legislation so permits, or at the request of an interested party, to refuse to or to cancel the registration, and to prohibit the use of a trade mark which constitutes a reproduction, an imitation, or a translation, liable to create confusion, with a mark considered by the competent authority of the country of registration or use to be well known in that country as being already the mark of a person entitled to the benefits of the Paris Convention and used for identical or similar goods. These provisions also apply when the essential part of the mark constitutes a reproduction of any such well-known mark or an imitation liable to create confusion therewith.
There is a potential conflict between this idea of the protection of well-known

marks under the Paris Convention and the 'first to apply' principle under the Trade-mark Law. At this stage, it is understood that if someone other than the proprietor applies for the registration of a well-known mark, the PRC will adhere to the principle of the Paris Convention. However, in the absence of a definition for well-known marks, the proprietor of a well-known mark may find that the PRC trade-mark officials may not recognize his mark, although it may be internationally accepted as being well known in China. In such circumstances, the 'first to apply' principle may prevail.

61. As in Hong Kong, any national of a country that is a member of the Paris Convention who files an application for the registration of a trade mark in any convention country, and subsequently files for the same mark in China within six months of the original filing, may claim the original filing date as the priority date. This rule became effective in China on 15 March 1985.

62. Trade-mark Law, Art. 18.

63. Trade-mark Law, Art. 18.

64. This information is based on meetings between the authors and CCPIT Trade-mark Registration Agency officials in May and June 1983.

65. Trade-mark Law, Art. 32.

66. Trade-mark Law, Art. 23.

67. Trade-mark Law, Art. 24.

68. Trade-mark Law, Art. 24.

69. Trade-mark Law, Art. 26.

70. Trade-mark Law, Art. 26.

71. Trade-mark Law, Art. 26.

72. Trade-mark Law, Art. 26.

73. Trade-mark Law, Art. 25.

74. Trade-mark Law, Art. 25.

75. Trade-mark Law, Art. 6.

76. Trade-mark Law, Art. 30.

77. Trade-mark Law, Art. 30.

78. Trade-mark Law, Art. 35; and Implementing Rules, Art. 28.

79. Trade-mark Law, Art. 35.

80. Trade-mark Law, Art. 34(3).

81. Trade-mark Law, Art. 34.

82. Implementing Rules, Art. 21(1).

83. Implementing Rules, Art. 21(2).

84. Implementing Rules, Art. 21(2).

85. Trade-mark Law, Art. 34(1) and (2).

86. Implementing Rules, Art. 23.

87. Implementing Rules, Art. 23.

88. Trade-mark Law, Art. 36; and Implementing Rules, Art. 25.

89. Trade-mark Law, Art. 36; and Implementing Rules, Art. 25.

90. Trade-mark Law, Art. 38.

91. The rules governing the conduct of civil lawsuits are contained in the Civil Procedure Law of the People's Republic of China, promulgated for trial implementation on 8 March 1982.

92. Trade-mark Law, Art. 39. The amount of compensation is stipulated by Art. 39 of the Trade-mark Law to be either the profits gained by the infringer or the losses suffered by the registrant during the period of infringement as a result of the infringing conduct.

93. Trade-mark Law, Art. 39. The local AIC departments appear to have discretion as to the amount of fines which may be imposed, as this is not specified in Art. 39 of the Trade-mark Law.

94. This information is based on the advice of the CCPIT Trade-mark Registration Agency given to the authors in August 1983.

95. Trade-mark Law, Art. 39; Implementing Rules, Art. 24.

96. Trade-mark Law, Art. 39; and Implementing Rules, Art. 25.

97. Trade-mark Law, Art. 39; and Implementing Rules, Art. 25.
98. Trade-mark Law, Art. 40.
99. See, generally, Xieneng, *Chinese Trade Marks* (Beijing, Xieneng, a division of the China Phone Book Company, Ltd., 1985), from which this section is adopted.

13. The Registration and Protection of Patents in China

MICHAEL J. MOSER AND DAVID Y.W. HO

I. Introduction

On 12 March 1984 the Patent Law of the People's Republic of China (cited hereafter as the Law) was passed by the Standing Committee of the National People's Congress.[1] Pursuant to Article 68 of the Law, the Implementing Regulations for the Patent Law (cited hereafter as the Regulations) were approved by the State Council and promulgated by the Patent Office on 19 January 1985.[2] Both the Law and the Regulations came into effect on 1 April 1985. More than five years in the making, this legislation provides the first significant statutory protection for inventions by foreigners since the founding of the People's Republic in 1949.[3] This chapter provides a description and brief analysis of the new Law and Regulations with special attention to their relevance to foreign businesses operating in China.

II. The Scope of the Law

The Law provides for three types of patentable subject-matter: inventions, utility models, and designs.[4]

Under the Regulations, an invention is defined as including 'any new technical solution relating to a product, a process or improvement thereof'[5] and a utility model is defined as 'any new technical solution relating to the shape, the structure, or their combination, of a product, which is fit for practical use'.[6] A utility model is at a lower level of inventiveness than an invention. A design is defined as 'any new design of the shape, pattern, colour, or their combination, of a product, which creates an aesthetic feeling and is fit for industrial application'.[7]

An applicant must apply for a patent in one of the three specified categories. Upon receipt of the application, the Chinese Patent Office will determine the appropriate categorization for the item on the basis of the description of the item in the patent application. If an application is determined to be wrongly characterized, the Patent Office will require that the application be resubmitted in the category deemed applicable. When reviewing applications for this purpose, the Patent Office will not take into account patent categorizations in other jurisdictions.

Under the Law, applicants must submit a separate application for each invention, utility model, or design.[8] If an application contains more than one patentable item, the Patent Office may request the applicant to divide his application into several applications. Alternatively, at any time before the publication of the application, the applicant may submit a request for the division of the application and divide it on his own initiative into several applications.[9]

Inventions and utility models are required to meet three criteria before patent rights may be granted. These criteria are: (a) novelty, (b) creativity, and (c) practicability.[10] Designs are only required to satisfy the condition of novelty to qualify for patent protection.[11] 'Novelty' is defined by the Law to mean that, before the date of the patent application, no similar invention or utility model has appeared in any publication inside or outside China or has been publicly used or made known to the general public inside China, and no application for a similar invention or utility model has been submitted by any other party to the Patent Office and been recorded in a patent application made public after the date of the application.[12] This concept of novelty is one of 'limited world novelty', essentially requiring no public disclosure anywhere and no public use inside China.

The notion of 'public disclosure', therefore, becomes quite critical. Inventions and creations are not patentable in China if they have already been published in a foreign magazine or patent gazette, regardless of how soon after such publication the patent application is filed in China, unless priority rights are granted. Publication in magazines or internal office memoranda which are not accessible to the public, however, does not amount to public disclosure, nor does publication within a unit or an enterprise for purposes of research or discussion. This follows the spirit of the Law which is to effectuate progress through the free flow and application of inventions and creations, and to promote the development of science and technology, while protecting legitimate patent rights.

Under the Law, novelty will not be lost where within six months prior to the submission of the application any of the following has occurred: (a) the invention or utility model has been exhibited for the first time in an international exhibition under the sponsorship of, or recognized by, the Chinese government; (b) the invention or utility model has been published for the first time at a specified academic conference or technical meeting organized by a department of the State Council or by a national academic or technological association; or (c) the contents of the invention or utility model have been revealed by third parties without the consent of the applicant.[13] In the first two situations, the applicant must make a declaration when filing the application and submit a certificate authorized by the relevant authority within two months before the filing to the effect that the invention or utility model has in fact been made public and stating the date of the publication.[14] In the third situation, the applicant must make a declaration when filing the application and the Patent Office may require the applicant to submit evidence.[15] These three events represent publication or public disclosure without loss of the required novelty.

The concept of 'public use' may also become important. Importation or sale of the invention, utility model, or design into China will constitute public use. If the invention, utility model, or design is a gift made subject to a condition of secrecy, however, the use of such a gift will not be considered to be public use.

The Law defines 'creativity' as meaning, with respect to inventions, that the invention possesses 'outstanding substantive characteristics' and 'represents obvious progress' and, with respect to utility models, that the utility model merely possesses 'substantive characteristics' and 'represents progress', in both cases as compared with technology already in existence before the date of the patent application.[16] 'Practicability' is defined to mean that the relevant invention or utility model can be used or manufactured and is capable of producing 'positive effects'.[17]

The Law requires that designs for which patent rights are applied should not be identical, nor bear a close resemblance, to designs that have already appeared in publications inside or outside China, or that have already been publicly used inside China before the date of the application.[18]

The Law further specifies a number of items with respect to which patent rights may not be granted. These include scientific discoveries; rules and methods of intellectual activity; methods of diagnosing and treating diseases; and substances obtained by means of nuclear transformation.[19] In addition, patent rights may not be obtained for foods, beverages, and seasonings; pharmaceuticals and other substances obtained through chemical processes; and varieties of animals and plants.[20] In these cases, however, the production methods relating to the products, if not the products themselves, are patentable.[21] If a patentee suspects by virtue of the production of an identical or substantially similar product that its patented process is being used by an unauthorized party, it may either ask the manufacturer of the identical product to furnish proof of the process used in the manufacture of its product and present a claim to the administrative authority for patent affairs to handle, or directly institute legal proceedings in a people's court.[22]

In addition to the specific exclusions from patentable subject-matter noted in the above paragraph, the Law prohibits the granting of patent rights to inventions and other creations that are illegal, that violate social ethics, or are injurious to the public interest.[23] Moreover, inventions and other creations that involve state security or the 'major interests of the state' and that need to be kept confidential shall be filed with the patent organization set up by the Science and Technology Department of the National Defence, and the Patent Office's decision shall be based on the recommendation of such patent organization.[24]

III. Procedures for Obtaining Patents

The Law permits foreign individuals, enterprises, and other organizations outside China to apply for patents in China in accordance with bilateral agreements signed between China and the applicant's home country, international agreements to which both China and the applicant's home country are signatories, or the principle of reciprocity.[25] China became a signatory to the Paris Convention for the Protection of Industrial Property on 14 November 1984, effective as of 19 March 1985. In addition, the Law also permits Chinese enterprises, foreign investment enterprises, and joint ventures using Chinese and foreign investment within China to apply for patents in China if the inventions and creations are accomplished by their personnel in the course of their duties, in the execution of work entrusted to them by their employers, or within one year from their resignation, retirement, or change of work.[26] However, if the inventions and creations are created outside the course of duty, the right to apply for patents belongs to the inventors or the designers who have made creative contributions to the substantive features of the inventions or designs, but not to personnel who are responsible only for organizational work or for offering facilities, or who take part in auxiliary functions.[27]

Under the Law, foreign applicants are not permitted to submit applications directly to the Patent Office but must entrust the agency designated by the State Council to handle applications and related matters on their behalf.[28] Such designated agencies include the Patent Agency of the China Council for the Promotion of International Trade (CCPIT), the China Patent Agent (Hong Kong) Limited, the Shanghai Patent Agency, and 'other patent agencies designated by the State Council'.[29]

The Patent Agent Regulations, which came into effect on 12 September 1985, provide for the establishment of patent agencies and the registration of patent agents.[30] A patent agency could be either a patent agency as designated by the State Council, or as approved by the appropriate government patent authority, or a law firm acting with the consent of the appropriate Chinese government patent authority. An applicant appointing a patent agency for filing a patent application with the Patent Office, or for dealing with other patent matters before the Patent Office, must submit a power of attorney specifying the scope of the patent agency's power.[31]

Foreigners resident in or having a business establishment in China have an option, if they wish, to apply for a patent through the local patent administration authorities in the same manner as a Chinese individual or entity, instead of working through CCPIT, the Shanghai Patent Agency, or any other designated patent agency.

The Law mandates a three-step procedure for obtaining patents. First, a formal application must be submitted to the Patent Office. The second step involves the examination of the application by the Patent Office and the issue of a decision either to reject or approve the application. The final step is the formal issue of letters patent with respect to the invention, utility model, or design for which patents are applied.

A. Application Procedures

Applicants for patents on inventions and utility models are required to submit to the Patent Office three documents: (a) a 'letter of request' (*qingqiu shu*) setting forth the name of the invention or utility model, the name of the inventor or designer, the name and address of the applicant, and other information; (b) a 'manual' (*shuoming shu*) consisting of an explanation of the invention or utility model, together with an 'abstract' (*zhaiyao*) of the main technical points; and (c) a 'letter asking for rights' (*quanli yaoqiu shu*) which is based on the manual and explains the scope within which patent protection is being requested.[32] Applications for patents on designs must include a letter of request together with a photograph or other representation of the design in question and must clearly state the product using the design and the classification to which it belongs.[33] Standard forms for the above-mentioned documents, as well as a classification schedule similar to that used for trade marks, have been developed by the Patent Office for use by applicants.

i. Application Documents
For inventions and utility models, five documents, in duplicate, must be included in the application.

The first is a letter of request setting out the following information:
(a) the name of the invention or utility model;
(b) the name of the inventor or creator;
(c) the name and address of the applicant;
(d) the nationality of the applicant;
(e) if the applicant is an enterprise or an organization, its name and the country in which the applicant has its principal business office;
(f) if the applicant has appointed a patent agency, the name and address of the patent agency and the name of the patent agent;
(g) if the applicant is an entity, the name of its representative;
(h) if the priority of an earlier application is claimed, the relevant matters should be indicated;
(i) the signature or seal of the applicant;
(j) a list of the documents constituting the application;
(k) a list of the documents appended to the application;
(l) if there is more than one applicant in the application and a patent agency has not been appointed, the first applicant named in the letter of request shall be considered as their common representative unless they agree otherwise;
(m) if an application for a patent for a design is filed, the request shall, when necessary, also contain a brief description of the design.[34]

The second document is a description which constitutes an exposition of the invention or utility model and generally contains:
(a) the title of the invention or utility model as appearing in the request;
(b) a specification of the technical field to which the invention or utility model relates;
(c) the prior art, as far as known to the applicant, which can be regarded as useful for the understanding, searching, and examination of the invention or utility model, and a citation of the documents reflecting such art;
(d) a description of the task which the invention or utility model is designed to fulfil;
(e) a disclosure of the invention or utility model in a manner sufficiently

clear and complete as to enable a person having ordinary skill in the art to carry it out;

(f) a statement of the merits or effective results of the invention or utility model as compared with the prior art;

(g) a brief description of the figures in the drawings, if any;

(h) a description in detail of the best model contemplated by the applicant for carrying out the invention or utility model, with reference to the drawings, if any.[35]

The description of the invention or utility model may contain chemical or mathematical formulae but not commercial advertising.

With regard to the drawings, the same sheet of drawings may contain several figures of the invention or utility model. The figures shall be numbered consecutively in Arabic numerals. The scale and the distinctiveness of the drawings shall be such that a reproduction with a linear reduction in size to two-thirds would still enable all details to be clearly distinguished. Moreover, the drawings shall not contain any other explanatory notes, except words which are indispensable.[36]

The third document required is an abstract, preferably in not more than 200 words, which indicates the technical field to which the invention or utility model pertains, the technical problems to be solved, and the essential features and uses of the invention or utility model; and which, if applicable, contains the chemical formula or the figure which best represents the invention or utility model.[37]

The fourth item of documentation comprises the claims.

(a) These must define clearly and concisely the matter for which protection is sought in terms of the technical features of the invention or utility model. If there are several claims, they shall be numbered consecutively in Arabic numerals.

The technical terminology used in the claims shall be consistent with that used in the descriptions. The claims may contain chemical or mathematical formulae, but not drawings. They shall not, except where absolutely necessary, contain such references to the descriptions or drawings as 'as described in part. . . of the description'.[38]

(b) The claims may be independent or dependent. An independent claim shall outline the essential technical contents and describe the indispensable technical features of an invention or utility model. A dependent claim relying on reference to one or more other claims shall refer only to the preceding claim or claims.[39]

An independent claim may take the following form: firstly, a preamble portion indicating the technical field to which the invention or utility model pertains and the technical features of the prior art which relate closely to the subject-matter of the invention or utility model; and secondly, a characterizing portion stating in a concise manner the technical features of the invention or utility model which, in combination with the features stated in the preamble portion, it is desired to protect.

Each invention or utility model shall have only one independent claim, which shall precede all the dependent claims relating to the same invention or utility model.[40]

A dependent claim may take the following form: firstly, a pre-amble portion indicating the serial numbers of the claims referred to (the reference to the serial number shall be placed at the beginning of the claims wherever possible); and secondly, a characterizing portion defining the above technical features by stating the additional technical features of the invention or utility model.[41]

In addition to the documents described above, foreign applicants must submit three original powers of attorney. If an application for a patent is filed by a foreign applicant who has no habitual residence or business office in China, the Patent Office may, if in doubt, require foreign applicants to submit a certificate concerning the nationality of the applicant; a certificate concerning the seat of the headquarters of a foreign enterprise; and a testimonial that the country to which the foreigner or foreign enterprise belongs recognizes that Chinese citizens and entities are entitled to patent rights and other related rights in that country.[42]

ii. Microbiological Processes or Products
If an application for a patent for an invention involves a microbiological process, microbiological products, or the use of a micro-organism which is not available to the public, the applicant is also required to fulfil the following obligations:
(a) deposit a sample of the micro-organism with a depository institution designated by the Patent Office on or before the filing date;
(b) describe in the application document relevant information on the characteristics of the micro-organism;
(c) indicate in the request the scientific (and Latin) name of the micro-organism, the name of the depository institution, the date on which the sample of the micro-organism was deposited, and the file number of the deposit, together with the deposit receipt from the depository institution.[43]

iii. Applications for Design Patents
To apply for patent rights for designs, an applicant must submit the following documents:
(a) a letter of request which must state the product using the design and the classification published by the Patent Office to which it belongs;
(b) one or more drawings or photographs of different angles of the design which must be of a size between 3 cm × 8 cm and 19 cm × 27 cm;
(c) for foreign applicants, three original powers of attorney.[44]

If an application for a patent for a design seeks protection of colour, a drawing or photograph of the design in black and white, with a statement endorsed in respect of the colours for which protection is sought, must be filed.[45] The Patent Office may require the applicant for a patent for a design to submit a sample or model of the product incorporating the design.[46]

Foreign applicants must indicate in the application the Chinese name of the inventor (designer) or applicant. If this information is not given, the Patent Agency will translate the name into Chinese as it deems fit.

iv. Language and Translation
All documents submitted according to the Law and the Regulations are required to be in Chinese.[47] If it is inconvenient for the foreign applicant to use Chinese, then English, German, French, or Japanese may be used instead and translated into Chinese. If any inconsistency arises between the Chinese and the foreign-language version, the Chinese version shall prevail.

Moreover, the Regulations specify that if the State has prescribed a standard scientific and technical term then this shall be used. Where no generally accepted translation in Chinese has been formulated for a foreign name or scientific or technical term, the name or term in the original language shall be indicated. The Patent Office may also require, within a specified time limit, Chinese translations of any certificate or certified document which is submitted in a foreign language.[48]

Translation can have an important impact on the extent of protection available upon the grant of a patent and on the question of patent infringement. Different countries use distinct approaches towards patent claiming. In the United States, the literal language of the claim controls the extent of the patent. In other countries, such as China, the exact extent of an invention is not explicitly claimed; but rather only the essence of the invention or creation, the inventive concept, is claimed. A claim originally phrased according to the literal approach may perhaps be distorted during the process of translation into Chinese because China uses the conceptual approach. This problem may be aggravated since the translated version will not normally be sent back to the applicant unless he specifically requests it. Such a request, however, may lead to a postponement of the filing date.

v. The 'Separate Application' Rule and its Exceptions
As noted previously, applicants are generally required to submit a separate application for each distinct invention or utility model.[49] An exception to this rule exists, however, in cases where one or more inventions or utility models are part of a single 'overall concept of invention'.[50] In such cases, a single application covering multiple inventions or utility models is permitted. Similarly, a separate application rule is also applied to designs for 'outward appearances', except that a single application may be submitted to cover multiple designs used for products of the same classification that are sold or used as one set.[51]

vi. Priority Rules
As a general rule, where two or more applicants file for patents on the same or similar inventions, utility models, or designs, the Patent Office is required to grant the patent right to the first applicant.[52] If two or more applicants file applications for identical inventions, utility models, or designs on the same day, upon notification by the Patent Office, they shall consult with each other to decide who shall file the application.[53] How-

ever, it is not clear who shall have the right to apply if they fail to reach an agreement. As a consequence of this 'race' provision in the notification by the Patent Office, the date of the application is of paramount importance. The rule of thumb established by the Law is that the date on which the Patent Office receives the application documents is deemed to be the date of application,[54] but exceptions to the basic rule are also provided. For example, where application documents are sent by post, the date of the postmark is taken as the date of application.[55] If the postmark is not readable, the actual date of receipt by the Patent Office shall be presumed to be the filing date unless the applicant can prove the actual date of mailing.[56]

The first day of any time limit shall not be counted. If a time limit is counted by the year or the month, it shall expire on the corresponding day of the last month or, if there is no corresponding day in that month, on the last day of that month. If a time limit expires on an official holiday, it shall be extended to the first working day after that official holiday.[57] Certain time limits prescribed in the Law and Regulations or by the Patent Office may be extended on the basis of *force majeure* or other justified reason. Time limits specified by the Patent Office may be extended on the basis of a justified reason upon application prior to the expiration of the time limit.[58]

The date of receiving any document sent by the Patent Office is deemed to be the eighth day from the date of mailing the document to any of the municipalities under the people's governments of the provinces or autonomous regions of China or the sixteenth day from the date of mailing the document to an addressee residing in any other place in China.[59] The Regulations have not, however, specified a presumed receiving date if the document is sent by the Patent Office to an addressee residing outside China.

Moreover, under the Law, which adopts the principle of *priority rights* which are provided for in the Paris Convention, a special priority right is granted in certain circumstances to foreign applicants. Where a foreign party submits an application in China for an invention or utility model within twelve months, or for an 'outward appearance' design within six months, of the date of the first application abroad for a patent with respect to the same invention, utility model, or design, the Patent Office may take the date of the applicant's foreign application to be the date of application in China.[60] The priority right is not automatic but must be requested by the applicant at the time of submission of the Chinese application documents.[61] When requesting the priority right, the applicant is required to submit a written declaration to the Patent Office containing relevant information pertaining to the foreign patent application.[62] Within three months of the date of the Chinese application, the applicant must also provide a certified copy of the foreign application documents to the Patent Office.[63] Failure to provide such materials constitutes sufficient grounds for denial of the priority right.[64] Submission of the declaration at a later date than the date of filing is permissible, but it must nevertheless be submitted within the period of validity of the priority (that is, twelve months for inventions and utility models). However, if such a submission is made, the original patent application must be withdrawn and a new filing date must be fixed.

It was previously unclear whether an applicant could receive a priority right predating 1 April 1985, the effective date of the Law. Subsequently, however, it was announced that the State Council had decided that a foreign patent applicant who submitted a patent application abroad for the first time after 1 October 1984 might enjoy a priority right on its Chinese patent application. That is, even though the Law and Regulations did not become effective until 1 April 1985, an application may be deemed to have been filed as early as 2 October 1984. Unfortunately for many potential foreign patent applicants, however, the converse also applies. This means that any invention or utility model for which an initial patent application was made outside China before 1 October 1984, while still good for filing in China if not yet disclosed (that is, pending the actual granting of a patent and its consequent publication in a patent gazette), cannot enjoy any rights of priority. If two or more priorities are claimed for a patent application, the priority period for the application shall be calculated from the earliest priority date.[65]

B. Examination and Approval Procedures

The Law prescribes different procedures for the examination and approval of patent applications for utility models and designs on the one hand, and patent applications for inventions on the other.

With respect to applications for patents on utility models and designs, the Law requires the Patent Office to conduct a preliminary examination of the application.[66] The contents of this examination are presumably limited to a review of the application documents to determine whether the application is prima facie in conformity with the requirements of the Law. If the Patent Office considers that the requirements have been met, it is required to announce the application and notify the applicants immediately.[67] No further substantive examination of the application is required.

Applications for patents on inventions are also subject to preliminary examination by the Patent Office. Applications considered to be in conformity with the requirements of the Law must be publicly announced within eighteen months of the date of the application.[68] Not later than three years from the date of the application, the applicant may request the Patent Office to conduct a substantive examination of the application.[69] If the applicant fails 'without legitimate reason' to request such an examination within the stipulated period, the application will be regarded as having been withdrawn, although the Patent Office may conduct a substantive examination of its own accord when it deems such to be necessary and notify the applicant accordingly.[70]

When requesting the substantive examination of a patent application, the applicant is required to submit reference materials relating to the invention.[71] If an application for a patent on the same invention has already been submitted abroad, the applicant must provide copies of the materials inspected by the foreign patent authorities, as well as any materials relating to the results of the examination.[72] Failure to provide such materials will be deemed to constitute a withdrawal of the application.[73] However, if the applicant cannot furnish such materials for a justified reason, he must make a statement to that effect and submit them when the materials are available.[74]

Upon completion of a substantive examination, the Patent Office is required either to approve and announce publicly the application or to notify the applicant that the application does not conform to the requirements set forth in the Law.[75] In the latter event, the Patent Office may request that the applicant submit its opinion regarding issues in connection with the application, or amend the application within a specified period of time.[76] If the applicant fails to make a response in the due time, or if the response fails to satisfy the Patent Office, the application will be rejected.[77]

The applicant for a patent for an invention may initiate amendments to the description and the claims within a period of fifteen months from the date of filing, or at the time when a request for substantive examination is made, or when a response is made with respect to an opposition.[78] The applicant for a patent for a utility model or a design may initiate amendments to the application within a period from the date of filing until the date of announcement of the application for patent or at the time when a response is made with respect to an opposition.[79] However, the amendment should not change the essential elements of the design. Unless the amendment is fairly insignificant, the amendment must be submitted in a prescribed form.[80]

An application for a patent will be rejected by the Patent Office in any of the following circumstances:

(a) if the application does not comply with the provisions of the Law, the definitions of invention, utility model, or design, or the requirements of novelty, creativity, practicability, or new design;

(b) if the application violates Chinese laws or social ethics, harms the public interest, or falls under a non-patentable item;

(c) if the foreign applicant has no right to apply for a patent on the grounds that the right to apply belongs to someone else, or because of the absence of agreements signed between his country and China, international treaties to which both countries are signatories, and the principle of reciprocity, or if a similar patent application has previously been submitted;

(d) if the application does not comply with the specified requirements of the description and abstract of the patent application or the application includes more than one invention, utility model, or design; or

(e) if the amendments to the application or the divisional applications go beyond the scope of disclosure contained in the initial description.[81]

After a patent application has been publicly announced, any person may file an opposition to the application with the Patent Office.[82] The opposition, together with the reasons, must be filed in duplicate within three months of the date of the announcement and copies of the opposition must be sent to the applicant.[83] An opposition to an application for a patent for an invention, a utility model, or a design may be filed on the basis of any of the statutory grounds for the rejection of patent applications.[84] In addition, an opposition to an application for a patent for an invention or a utility model may be filed if the application does not include a description or abstract which satisfies the relevant technical requirements; or if the amendments to the application or the divisional applications go beyond the scope of the disclosure contained in the initial description.[85]

An opposition to an application for a patent for a design may also be filed if the amendments to the application have changed the essential elements of the design.[86]

If the reasons for an opposition are not stated or do not fall within one of the above grounds for opposition, the Patent Office will reject it.[87] If the opposition does not conform to the prescribed requirements, the Patent Office shall notify the opponent to rectify it within the specified time limit. The opposition shall be deemed not to have been filed if it is not rectified within the time limit.[88]

The applicant is required to respond in writing to the opposition within three months of the date of receipt of the opposition.[89] Upon review of the opposition and response, the Patent Office will then decide either to reject or to concur with the opposition. If the opposition is upheld, the application will be rejected and the parties will be notified accordingly.[90]

The Law requires that the Patent Office establish a Patent Re-examination Board consisting of experienced technical and legal experts who are designated by the Patent Office to handle appeals in connection with patent applications.[91] The Director General of the Patent Office is also the Director of the Re-examination Board.[92] The applicant may appeal against a decision of the Patent Office to reject an application before the Patent Re-examination Board by filing, within three months of the date of notification of rejection, a request for re-examination, with reasons, together with the relevant supporting documents in duplicate.[93] The applicant may amend the part to which the decision of rejection of the application relates when he requests re-examination.[94]

If the request for re-examination does not comply with the prescribed form, the applicant shall rectify it within the time limit specified by the Patent Re-examination Board.[95] The request for re-examination shall be deemed to be withdrawn if the applicant fails to comply within the time limit.[96] The Patent Re-examination Board will also obtain the observations of the original examiner before making its decision.[87] After re-examination, if the request is found not in compliance with the Law, the applicant may submit his observations within the specified time limit.[98] The request for re-examination will be deemed to have been withdrawn if a response within the time limit is not made.[99] The applicant may withdraw his request for re-examination before the Patent Re-examination Board reaches its decision.[100]

In the event of disagreement over a decision of the Patent Re-examination Board, applicants for patents on inventions are permitted to bring a suit before the people's courts within three months of the date of notification of the Board's decision.[101] Re-examination Board decisions regarding requests for the re-examination of applications for patents on utility models and designs are final and may not be appealed against in the courts.[102]

The Regulations also provide for the impartiality of members of the Board. An examiner or a member of the Patent Re-examination Board shall, on his own initiative or upon the request of the applicant or any other interested party, be excluded from dealing with a patent application in the following circumstances:

(a) if he is a close relative of the applicant or the patent agent;
(b) if he has an interest in the application for a patent;
(c) if his relationship with the applicant or the patent agent may influence the impartial examination of the patent application.[103]

A member of the Patent Re-examination Board shall also be excluded from the re-examination if he has taken part in the original examination of the patent application.[104]

C. The Granting of Patent Rights

Once a patent application has been approved and publicly announced and any relevant objections and appeals have been disposed of, the Patent Office is required to grant exclusive patent rights to the applicant by issuing the letters patent and registering the patent in China.[105] Upon notification, the applicant shall pay a fee for a patent certificate within two months.[106] Failure to pay the fee within the time limit may result in the loss of the right to obtain the patent right.[107] Following registration, the patent holder has the right to use the patent and to mark patented products and the packaging of such products with their patent sign and number.[108] From the year the patent rights are granted, the patent holder will be obliged to pay annual fees to the Patent Office for the duration of the patent.[109]

The term for patent rights issued with respect to inventions is fifteen years; for patents on utility models and designs the term is five years.[110] In both cases, the term for patent rights is calculated from the date of the patent application. For patent holders enjoying rights of priority, the term is calculated from the date of the patent application in China. The holder of a utility model or a design patent may apply for extensions of three years prior to the expiry date[111] by presenting a request for renewal and a power of attorney and by paying the renewal fee.

The Law provides for several circumstances under which patent rights may be terminated or revoked prior to the expiry of the scheduled term. Termination may occur where the patent holder has failed to pay annual patent fees or where the patent right has been renounced by the holder in a written declaration.[112] Revocation may also occur where the Patent Re-examination Board determines that a patent has been granted in error.[113]

Under the Law, any unit or individual has the right to seek a declaration of the patent's invalidity from the Patent Re-examination Board if it believes that the granting of the patent was not in conformity with the Law.[114] A request for invalidation with reasons and the relevant documents is to be submitted to the Re-examination Board in duplicate.[115] A request for invalidation shall be rejected if no reason is specified in the request or the reasons specified do not comply with the circumstances required for a request for opposition.[116] The request for invalidation shall be rectified within the time limit fixed by the Re-examination Board.[117] The request shall be deemed to have been withdrawn if not rectified within the time limit.[118] The Re-examination Board will send copies of the request for invalidation and the relevant documents to the patent holder for observation.[119] If the patent holder does not respond within a specified time limit, he will be deemed to have no objection to make.[120]

Decisions of the Patent Re-examination Board regarding the revocation of patents on inventions may be appealed against in the people's courts,[121] but the Board's decisions regarding patents on utility models and designs are final.[122] Patent rights determined to be invalid are void *ab initio*.[123]

IV. The Assignment and Licensing of Patents

Under the Law, both rights to apply for patents and patent rights themselves may be assigned to third parties.[124] In the event of an assignment, the assignor and the assignee are required to conclude a contract in writing which is effective upon registration and announcement by the Patent Office.[125]

The Law also provides for the licensing of patents. The Law requires that before any entity or individual other than the patent holder may be permitted to 'use' a patent, that is, to manufacture patented products or to utilize patented processes, it must conclude a written licensing agreement with the patent holder and pay 'patent-use fees'. Such a licensing agreement does not, however, confer a right on the licensee to allow any other unit or individual to use the patent.[126] One exception to this rule pertains to patents held by Chinese state-owned enterprises. Under the Law, Chinese government authorities have the right to designate other units to use certain patents in their production activities in accordance with the State Economic Plan.[127] In such cases, patent-use fees are required to be paid to the patent-holding unit 'in accordance with state stipulations'.[128]

The second, and for foreign patent holders far more important, exception to the voluntary licensing rule lies in the provisions contained in the Law regarding compulsory licensing. The Law requires patent holders to use their patents in China or to license others to do so.[129] In cases where holders of patents on inventions and utility models have failed 'without legitimate reason' to use their patents by the end of the three-year period commencing from the date of the granting of the patents, the Patent Office may, upon application, grant compulsory licences to use the patents to units possessing the capability to do so.[130] Compulsory licensing may also occur where the use of a new patent which is technologically advanced is dependent on access to less sophisticated or older patented technology or inventions owned by another party. In such a case, the holder of the new patent may apply for the granting of a compulsory licence to use the older patent, and the holder of the older patent may request compulsory licensing of the new patent to it.[131]

When applying to the Patent Office for a compulsory licence to use a patent, the applicant is required to provide a request for a compulsory licence and supporting documents in duplicate to show that it was unable to conclude a voluntary licensing contract 'on reasonable terms' with the patent holder.[132] In the case of a compulsory licence which is due to a failure to use the patent without legitimate reason, the applicant must also furnish documents in duplicate to show that he is in a position to exploit the patent.[133] Upon receipt of the request for a compulsory licence, the Patent Office will request the patent holder to make his observations.[134] Failure to respond within the time limit will deem the patent holder to have no objection to the request for a compulsory licence.[135] If a compulsory licence is granted, the licensee does not enjoy an exclusive right to use the patent but shares the right with the original patent holder.[136] Moreover, the licensee is required to pay patent-use fees to the patent holder, the amount of which is to be agreed by the parties or, failing agreement, is to be determined by the Patent Office.[137] Decisions of the Patent Office regarding the granting of compulsory licences and patent-use fees may be appealed against in the people's courts.[138]

Any licence contract concluded between the patent holder and licensee must, within three months of the effective date of the licence contract, be submitted to the Patent Office for the record.[139] However, the consequences of failing to comply with the requirement for filing at the Patent Office are not clear.

V. The Protection of Patent Rights

The Law grants patent holders exclusive rights to use their patents. Under the Law, no unit or individual may, without the permission of the patent holder, manufacture, use, or sell for production or business purposes patented products, processes, or designs.[140] Conduct in violation of these provisions may constitute infringement of the patent holder's rights.

The standard to be applied in determining whether an infringement has occurred is whether the alleged infringing conduct has invaded the scope of protection of the patent right. In the case of patents on inventions and utility models, the scope of protection is the scope specified in the 'request for rights' submitted by the patent holder at the time of application.[141] The scope of protection for patents on designs is the patented product or the 'outward appearance' design patent as shown in pictures or photographs.[142]

In the event of an alleged infringement of patent rights, the patent holder or other interested party may either submit the case to the administrative authority for patent affairs set up by the relevant departments of the State Council and the people's governments of the provinces, autonomous regions, municipalities directly under the central government, open cities, and special economic zones or bring a suit before the people's courts.[143] Such proceedings must be initiated within two years of the date on which the patent holder or interested party learns of, or should have learned of, the alleged infringing conduct.[144] Where the case is submitted to the administrative authority for patent affairs, this body may order infringers to desist from any further infringing conduct and to compensate the patent holder for losses incurred due to the infringement.[145] Such orders may be appealed against by the alleged infringer in the people's courts within three months of the date of the order.[146]

In addition, if after the publication of an application for a patent for an invention, a utility model, or a design and before the grant of the patent right, any entity or individual has exploited the invention, utility model, or design without paying the appropriate fees, the patent holder may, after the grant of the patent right, request the administrative authority for patent affairs to require the entity or individual to pay the appropriate fees within the specified time limit, or he may institute direct legal proceedings in the people's court.[147] If any party disagrees with the administrative authority's decision, he may institute legal proceedings in the people's courts.[148]

The Law specifies five kinds of conduct which shall not be deemed to constitute infringement of patent rights.[149] The first pertains to cases where, after a patented product manufactured by or with the permission of the patent holder has been sold, the product is then used by or sold to a third party.[150] The second relates to cases where a patented product is used or sold by a party who did not know that the product was manufactured or sold without the permission of the patent holder.[151] The third exception applies to cases where products or processes of the same type as those which have been patented by another party had already been manufactured or used before the date of the patent application and where such manufacture or use is contained within the scope existing prior to the patent application.[152] The fourth exclusion pertains to the use of patents in the facilities and equipment of foreign aeroplanes and vessels that pass temporarily through China, provided that similar treatment is granted to Chinese means of transport in accordance with international treaties or the principle of reciprocity.[153] Finally, the fifth exclusion relates to patents used specially for scientific research and experiments.[154]

The Law provides for the enforcement of decisions regarding infringement in accordance with the compulsory execution provisions contained in the Law on Civil Procedure.[155] In addition, criminal penalties may be applied in serious cases of infringement.

VI. Other Matters

The Patent Office maintains a Patent Register which records the following matters: the grant of the patent right; the assignment of the patent

right; renewals of the term of the patent right; the cessation and invalidation of the patent right; the compulsory licence for the exploitation of the
patent; and changes in the name, nationality, and address of the patent
holder.[156]

The Patent Office publishes the Patent Gazette at regular intervals,
publishing or announcing the following information: bibliographic data
contained in the request of an application for a patent; abstracts of the
description of an invention or a utility model; requests for an examination
of the substance of an application for a patent for an invention and decisions made by the Patent Office to proceed on its own initiative to
examine the substance of an application for a patent for an invention; preliminary approvals after the examination of an application for a patent for
an invention and the announcement of the application for a patent for a
utility model or a design; rejections of applications for patents; decisions
concerning an opposition and any amendment made in an application for
a patent; the grant of patent rights; the cessation of patent rights; the
invalidation of patent rights; the assignment of patent rights; the grant of
compulsory licences for the exploitation of patents; the renewal of the
term of patents; the withdrawal of an application for a patent, including
any deemed to have been withdrawn and any abandoned; changes in the
name or address of the patentee; notifications to applicants whose address
is not known; and other related matters.[157]

The description, its drawings, and the claims of an application for a
patent for an invention or a utility model, and the drawings or photographs of an application for a patent for design shall be published in pamphlet form.[158]

The fees which shall be paid when an application for a patent is filed
with the Patent Office, or when other procedures go through the Patent
Office, are as follows:

(a) an application fee and an application maintenance fee;
(b) an examination fee, a re-examination fee, and an opposition fee;
(c) an annual fee;
(d) a handling fee for transacting other patent matters: a renewal fee for
    the patent for a utility model or a design, a fee for a change in the
    bibliographic data, a patent certificate fee, a fee for the proof of prior-
    ity, a fee for a request for invalidation, a fee for a request for a com-
    pulsory licence, and a fee for a request for an adjudication on the
    exploitation fee of a compulsory licence.[159]

The amounts of the fees listed above are to be prescribed by the Patent
Office separately.[160]

VII. Conclusion

China's new patent regime contains little that will come as a surprise to
foreign business men. The main features of the Law and the Regulations
closely follow the published reports of Patent Office officials on the draft
legislation.[161] Moreover, the Law and the Regulations conform in most

respects with internationally accepted patent practices and were clearly drafted with the Paris Convention for the Protection of Industrial Property in mind.

As was expected, the Chinese have chosen to exclude a number of items from patentability, including pharmaceutical and food products. In so doing, China has apparently decided to follow the lead of a growing number of developing countries which have denied patent protection to such products in order to encourage and protect local industrial capability in these areas. This view seems to be supported by the statement of Huang Kunyi, the Director of the Patent Office, who has written that the major justification for disallowing protection for the products themselves is that 'China's industrial and scientific level is comparatively backward'; he has indicated that the restriction may be reconsidered 'in view of actual conditions' at a later date.[162]

Although food and pharmaceutical products and the other items mentioned in the Law may not themselves be granted patent protection, the Law does provide for the patentability of the production processes of such products. Although these provisions to protect production processes are intended to alleviate the disappointment of foreign companies who had hoped to obtain full product patent protection under the new Law, the extent to which they will provide real protection to patent holders is unclear. The Law provides no obvious obstacle, for example, to the manufacture and sale by a Chinese unit of a pharmaceutical product similar to one marketed by a foreign producer whose production process is patented in China. So long as the Chinese producer's manufacturing process appears to be even slightly different from the patented process employed by the foreign manufacturer, it seems that no infringement will be deemed to have occurred.

The question of the patentability of computer programmes is not addressed directly in the Law. However, Chinese sources indicate that software will be treated as 'rules and methods of intellectual activity' and as such will not be eligible for the granting of patent rights.[163] In adopting this approach, China has followed the lead of a number of countries, including the United Kingdom.

A point of special significance to foreign business men which is raised by the new Law is how China's patent system will apply to existing inventions. Under the 'novelty' requirement imposed by the Law, the previous publication or use of an invention outside China will in most instances disqualify such inventions from patentability in China. Therefore, unless a foreign applicant is able to come within the scope of the 'priority right' provisions or otherwise avoid disqualification under the Law, attempts to register patents in China that have already been applied for or registered elsewhere will be unsuccessful. As a result, the main significance of the Law will be found in the protection afforded to future inventions and creations, rather than existing ones.

China's new Patent Law and Regulations are major contributions to the development of the nation's legal system. The legislation may be expected to provide significantly greater protection to foreign inventors and an additional incentive to investment and technology transfer in China.

Notes

1. The Patent Law of the People's Republic of China, passed on 12 March 1984 by the Fourth Meeting of the Standing Committee of the Sixth National People's Congress (hereafter cited as the Patent Law). All references to the Patent Law in this chapter are to an English translation on file with the authors.
2. The Implementing Regulations of the Patent Law of the People's Republic of China approved by the State Council and promulgated by the Patent Office of the People's Republic of China on 19 January 1985 (hereafter cited as the Patent Regulations). All references to the Patent Regulations in this chapter are to an English translation prepared by the Patent Office.
3. China provided limited protection to Chinese and foreign patents pursuant to the 1950 Provisional Regulations on the Protection of Inventions and Patent Rights, but this law was rescinded in 1963 and replaced by the Regulations on Rewards for Inventions, passed in the same year. The 1963 statute was repealed in 1978 and superseded by the Regulations of the People's Republic of China on Awards for Inventions, issued on 28 December 1978. Both the 1963 statute and the 1978 regulations rewarded inventors for their creations but vested ownership of all such inventions in the state.
4. Patent Law, Art. 2, note 1 above.
5. Patent Regulations, Rule 2, note 2 above.
6. Patent Regulations, Rule 2, note 2 above.
7. Patent Regulations, Rule 2, note 2 above.
8. Patent Law, Art. 31, note 1 above.
9. Patent Regulations, Rule 42, note 2 above.
10. Patent Law, Art. 22, note 1 above.
11. Patent Law, Art. 23, note 1 above.
12. Patent Law, Art. 22, note 1 above.
13. Patent Law, Art. 24, note 1 above.
14. Patent Regulations, Rule 31, note 2 above.
15. Patent Regulations, Rule 31, note 2 above.
16. Patent Law, Art. 22, note 1 above.
17. Patent Law, Art. 22, note 1 above.
18. Patent Law, Art. 23, note 1 above.
19. Patent Law, Art. 25, note 1 above.
20. Patent Law, Art. 25, note 1 above.
21. Patent Law, Art. 25, note 1 above.
22. Patent Law, Art. 60, note 1 above.
23. Patent Law, Art. 5, note 1 above.
24. Patent Law, Art. 4, note 1 above; Patent Regulations, Rule 8, note 2 above.
25. Patent Law, Art. 18, note 1 above.
26. Patent Law, Art. 6, note 1 above; Patent Regulations, Rule 10, note 2 above.
27. Patent Law, Art. 6, note 1 above; Patent Regulations, Rule 11, note 2 above.
28. Patent Law, Art. 19, note 1 above.
29. Patent Regulations, Rule 14, note 2 above.
30. Provisional Regulations Regarding Patent Agencies, approved by the State Council on 1 September 1985 and promulgated by the Patent Office of the People's Republic of China on 12 September 1985.
31. Patent Regulations, Rule 15, note 2 above.

32. Patent Law, Art. 26, note 1 above.
33. Patent Law, Art. 27, note 1 above.
34. Patent Law, Art. 26, note 1 above; Patent Regulations, Rule 17, note 2 above.
35. Patent Law, Art. 26, note 1 above; Patent Regulations, Rule 18, note 2 above.
36. Patent Regulations, Rule 19, note 2 above.
37. Patent Law, Art. 26, note 1 above; Patent Regulations, Rule 24, note 2 above.
38. Patent Regulations, Rule 20, note 2 above.
39. Patent Regulations, Rule 21, note 2 above.
40. Patent Regulations, Rule 22, note 2 above.
41. Patent Regulations, Rule 23, note 2 above.
42. Patent Regulations, Rule 34, note 2 above.
43. Patent Regulations, Rule 25, note 2 above.
44. Patent Law, Art. 27, note 1 above; Patent Regulations, Rule 27, note 2 above.
45. Patent Regulations, Rule 28, note 2 above.
46. Patent Regulations, Rule 29, note 2 above.
47. Patent Regulations, Rule 4, note 2 above.
48. Patent Regulations, Rule 4, note 2 above.
49. Patent Law, Art. 31, note 1 above.
50. Patent Law, Art. 31, note 1 above.
51. Patent Law, Art. 31, note 1 above.
52. Patent Law, Art. 9, note 1 above.
53. Patent Regulations, Rule 12, note 2 above.
54. Patent Law, Art. 28, note 1 above.
55. Patent Law, Art. 28, note 1 above.
56. Patent Regulations, Rule 5, note 2 above.
57. Patent Regulations, Rule 6, note 2 above.
58. Patent Regulations, Rule 7, note 2 above.
59. Patent Regulations, Rule 5, note 2 above.
60. Patent Law, Art. 29, note 1 above.
61. The priority right is available in accordance with the terms of bilateral agreements signed between China and the country of the applicant, investment treaties to which both China and the applicant's country are parties, or the principle of 'mutual recognition of priority rights'. Patent Law, Art. 29, note 1 above.
62. Patent Law, Art. 30, note 1 above.
63. Patent Law, Art. 30, note 1 above.
64. Patent Law, Art. 30, note 1 above.
65. Patent Regulations, Rule 33, note 2 above.
66. Patent Law, Art. 40, note 1 above.
67. Patent Law, Art. 40, note 1 above.
68. Patent Law, Art. 34, note 1 above.
69. Patent Law, Art. 35, note 1 above.
70. Patent Law, Art. 35, note 1 above.
71. Patent Law, Art. 36, note 1 above.
72. Patent Law, Art. 36, note 1 above.
73. Patent Law, Art. 36, note 1 above.
74. Patent Regulations, Rule 49, note 2 above.
75. Patent Law, Arts. 37 and 39, note 1 above.
76. Patent Law, Art. 37, note 1 above.
77. Patent Law, Arts. 37 and 38, note 1 above.
78. Patent Regulations, Rule 51, note 2 above.
79. Patent Regulations, Rule 52, note 2 above.
80. Patent Regulations, Rule 51, note 2 above.
81. Patent Regulations, Rule 53, note 2 above.

82. Patent Law, Art. 41, note 1 above.
83. Patent Law, Art. 41, note 1 above.
84. Patent Regulations, Rule 54, note 2 above.
85. Patent Regulations, Rule 54, note 2 above.
86. Patent Regulations, Rule 55, note 2 above.
87. Patent Regulations, Rule 57, note 2 above.
88. Patent Regulations, Rule 57, note 2 above.
89. Patent Law, Art. 41, note 1 above.
90. Patent Law, Art. 42, note 1 above.
91. Patent Law, Art. 43, note 1 above.
92. Patent Regulations, Rule 58, note 2 above.
93. Patent Regulations, Rule 59, note 2 above.
94. Patent Regulations, Rule 59, note 2 above.
95. Patent Regulations, Rule 60, note 2 above.
96. Patent Regulations, Rule 60, note 2 above.
97. Patent Regulations, Rule 61, note 2 above.
98. Patent Regulations, Rule 62, note 2 above.
99. Patent Regulations, Rule 62, note 2 above.
100. Patent Regulations, Rule 63, note 2 above.
101. Patent Law, Art. 43, note 1 above.
102. Patent Law, Art. 43, note 1 above.
103. Patent Regulations, Rule 38, note 2 above.
104. Patent Regulations, Rule 38, note 2 above.
105. Patent Law, Art. 44, note 1 above.
106. Patent Regulations, Rule 64, note 2 above.
107. Patent Regulations, Rule 64, note 2 above.
108. Patent Law, Arts. 11 and 15 , note 1 above.
109. Patent Law, Art. 46, note 1 above.
110. Patent Law, Art. 45, note 1 above.
111. Patent Law, Art. 45, note 1 above.
112. Patent Law, Art. 47, note 1 above.
113. Patent Law, Arts. 48 and 49 , note 1 above.
114. Patent Law, Arts. 48 and 49 , note 1 above.
115. Patent Regulations, Rule 65, note 2 above.
116. Patent Regulations, Rule 66, note 2 above.
117. Patent Regulations, Rule 66, note 2 above.
118. Patent Regulations, Rule 66, note 2 above.
119. Patent Regulations, Rule 67, note 2 above.
120. Patent Regulations, Rule 67, note 2 above.
121. Patent Law, Art. 49, note 1 above.
122. Patent Law, Art. 49, note 1 above.
123. Patent Law, Art. 49, note 1 above.
124. Patent Law, Art. 10, note 1 above.
125. Patent Law, Art. 10, note 1 above.
126. Patent Law, Art. 12, note 1 above.
127. Patent Law, Art. 14, note 1 above.
128. Patent Law, Art. 14, note 1 above.
129. Patent Law, Art. 51, note 1 above.
130. Patent Law, Art. 52, note 1 above.
131. Patent Law, Art. 53, note 1 above.
132. Patent Law, Art. 54, note 1 above; Patent Regulations, Rule 68, note 2 above.
133. Patent Regulations, Rule 68, note 2 above.
134. Patent Regulations, Rule 68, note 2 above.
135. Patent Regulations, Rule 68, note 2 above.
136. Patent Law, Art. 56, note 1 above.
137. Patent Law, Art. 57, note 1 above.

138. Patent Law, Art. 58, note 1 above.
139. Patent Regulations, Rule 13, note 2 above.
140. Patent Law, Art. 11, note 1 above.
141. Patent Law, Art. 59, note 1 above.
142. Patent Law, Art. 59, note 1 above.
143. Patent Law, Art. 60, note 1 above; Patent Regulations, Rule 76, note 2 above.
144. Patent Law, Art. 61, note 1 above.
145. Patent Law, Art. 60, note 1 above.
146. Patent Law, Art. 60, note 1 above.
147. Patent Regulations, Rule 77, note 2 above.
148. Patent Regulations, Rule 77, note 2 above.
149. Patent Law, Art. 62, note 1 above.
150. Patent Law, Art. 62(1), note 1 above.
151. Patent Law, Art. 62(2), note 1 above.
152. Patent Law, Art. 62(3), note 1 above.
153. Patent Law, Art. 62(4), note 1 above.
154. Patent Law, Art. 62(5), note 1 above.
155. See the Law on Civil Procedure of the People's Republic of China, promulgated for trial implementation on 8 March 1982, Arts. 171–84.
156. Patent Regulations, Rule 80, note 2 above.
157. Patent Regulations, Rule 81, note 2 above.
158. Patent Regulations, Rule 81, note 2 above.
159. Patent Regulations, Rule 82, note 2 above.
160. Patent Regulations, Rule 82, note 2 above.
161. See E. Theroux and T. Peele, 'China's Coming Patent Law', *East Asian Executive Reports*, April 1983, pp. 7–10; and C. Berney, 'China's Draft Patent Law', *China Business Review*, May–June 1981, p. 39.
162. See K.Y. Huang, 'China's Patent System Is Actively Being Established', *Guoji maoyi (International Trade)*, February 1984, p. 4.
163. See T. Gelatt and R. Sweetman, 'China's New Patent Law Needs Clarification', *Asian Wall Street Journal*, 2 April 1984.

14. United States Export Controls on Trading with China

JOHN F. MCKENZIE

I. Introduction

The United States Export Administration Act[1] and the Export Administration Regulations[2] impose controls on the export of United States origin commodities and technical data to achieve three basic purposes:

(a) to protect the national security of the United States by restricting the export of commodities and technical data with military applications to potentially hostile nations, or for use in a manner inconsistent with United States national security (for example, the proliferation of nuclear weapons);

(b) to further the foreign policy of the United States by restricting access to goods and technical data of United States origin as a means of bringing economic pressure to bear on countries that take actions which are inimical to United States foreign policy objectives (for example, support for international terrorism; the South African policy of apartheid); and

(c) to protect the domestic economy from the excessive drain of scarce materials or from the inflationary impact of foreign demand, by restricting the export of goods, particularly raw materials, which are deemed to be in short supply.

The Export Administration Act and the Regulations issued thereunder are a matter of key concern for United States firms, particularly high technology firms, that propose to trade with the People's Republic of China. In the past, the export to China of a large number of commodities and broad categories of technical data has been restricted or prohibited by the Export Administration Act and Regulations, and by the export licensing policies of the United States government agencies[3] that are charged with administering the Regulations. Indeed, prior to 1971, the United States maintained an almost complete trade embargo with respect to the People's Republic of China. There has been a dramatic relaxation of United States controls on exports to China, as the two nations have established diplomatic ties and important political, economic, and cultural relations. Recent amendments to the Export Administration Regulations and changes in United States export control policies have brought the controls on exports to China into substantial conformance with controls on exports to other friendly non-aligned nations. Significant differences in the level of export controls and the export licensing policies remain, however, and, as a result, United States firms that propose to export goods and/or technical data to the People's Republic of China must be cognizant of the effects of the United States export control programme, and of their responsibilities to comply with this programme.

For the purpose of export control, the Office of Export Administration of the United States Department of Commerce classifies the nations of the world into Country Groups, with each Country Group subject to a separate level of export control. (These Country Groups are listed in the Appendix to this chapter.) Immediately after the United States embargo on trade with China was lifted, China was classified in Country Group Y. Thus the export control requirements and policies for trade with China were virtually identical to those for trade with the Soviet Union and the Communist countries of Eastern Europe. In 1981, however, the Office of Export Administration began to liberalize controls on exports to China. At that time, China was moved into a new category, Country Group P, and on 29 December 1981, the Office of Export Administration announced a policy of approving export licence applications for the export to China of high technology commodities having technical levels approximately twice as high as those of commodities that would be authorized for export to the Soviet Union and Eastern Europe.[4]

In May 1983, the United States government announced its intention to further relax its restrictions on trade with the People's Republic of China, in order to permit the export of high technology electronic and telecommunications equipment to China, which had previously been restricted for national security purposes. On 23 November 1983, the Office of Export Administration of the Department of Commerce published amendments[5] to the Export Administration Regulations (cited hereafter as the 1983 Amended Regulations), which implement this policy of liberalization by reclassifying the People's Republic of China from Country Group P to Country Group V for export control purposes.[6] The effect of this reclassification is, in general, to make the export licensing requirements and policies for proposed exports to China conform to the licensing requirements and policies for proposed exports to Western Europe, Africa, the Middle East, and non-Communist Asia. The 1983 Amended Regulations, however, make a number of very significant exceptions to the general policy of bringing the export controls for China into conformance with the export controls for non-Communist countries. This chapter discusses the overall effects of the reclassification, as well as these important exceptions. Also described below are several policy changes that have been adopted since the 1983 Amended Regulations were issued, and very recent changes in COCOM review requirements, which may ameliorate what has been perceived as the greatest impediment to the export of United States high technology products to China.

II. The Reclassification of China from Country Group P to Country Group V

The export control programme embodied in the Export Administration Regulations is implemented by a licensing procedure administered by the Office of Export Administration of the Department of Commerce. Specific authorization, in the form of an individual validated export licence, is required for the export of any controlled commodity or technical data to any destination to which the controls are applicable.[7] As noted above, the classification of a country in a particular Country Group determines both the validated licensing requirements and the licensing policy for proposed exports to that country. Thus, for a number of commodities on the Commodity Control List, a validated export licence is required for exports to destinations in Country Groups Q, S, W, Y, and Z (and formerly Country Group P), but a validated licence is not required for exports to destinations in Country Groups T and V. By reclassifying the People's Republic of China from Country Group P to Country Group V, the validated licensing requirement was removed for the export of such commodities to China.[8]

The vast majority of commodities that are subject to export controls for national security reasons (generally, the items identified by the code letters 'A' and 'B' in the Commodity Control List) require a validated export licence for export to any destination except Canada. The Office of Export Administration's policy in granting or denying validated licence applications for such commodities, however, varies according to the Country Group. Validated export licence applications for proposed exports to destinations in Country Groups T and V of commodities which are controlled for national security purposes are generally reviewed on the basis of whether there is a significant risk that the commodities will be diverted from their stated destination to a country that is potentially hostile to the United States (that is, nations in Country Groups Q, S, W, Y, and Z). In contrast, validated licence applications for proposed exports of such commodities to destinations in Country Groups Q, S, W, and Y are reviewed on the basis of whether the commodities may make a significant contribution to the military potential of the country of destination.[9] Thus, the decision that the People's Republic of China should be reclassified from Country Group P to Country Group V produced a dramatic change in the standard of review for most validated licence applications for proposed exports to China. In most cases, the Office of Export Administration (and, if required, the Department of Defense) will consider whether there is a risk that the commodities will be re-exported to a potentially hostile nation (such as North Korea),[10] rather than whether the commodities will make a significant contribution to Chinese military potential.[11]

In implementing the new trade policy with China, the Office of Export Administration divided the commodities for which validated export licence applications are most frequently received into three lists, the 'green' list, the 'yellow' list, and the 'red' list. Items on the 'green' list, which are identified in various advisory notes to the Commodity Control List, are subject to the new standard of review and will generally be authorized for export to China.[12] Moreover, a Department of Defense review will generally not be required for export licence applications for proposed exports of 'green' list items to China. Validated licence applications to export items on the 'yellow' and 'red' lists, which involve higher levels of technology and which may be more directly adapted to military uses, will be reviewed by the Office of Export Administration and the Department of Defense under the more stringent standard of whether the commodities may make a significant contribution to Chinese military potential. Export licence applications for commodities on the 'red' list (which is classified) will generally be denied.

III. Major Differences in the Export Licensing Requirements for China and the Other Countries of Country Group V

As noted above, although the People's Republic of China has been reclassified from Country Group P to Country Group V, there remain a number of important differences between the controls on exports to China and the controls on exports to other countries in Country Group V. The most significant of these distinctions are the following.

A. The Use of the General Licence GLV

Part 371 of the Export Administration Regulations establishes a series of general export licences, which permit the export of United States origin commodities to some or all destinations without the necessity of a specific validated export licence. Among these general licences is the general licence GLV, which permits the export of controlled commodities in limited amounts (generally to the value of US$1,000 or less) to destinations in Country Groups T and V.[13] Although, before the 1983 Amended Regulations were issued, the regulatory provision governing the general licence GLV contemplated the use of that general licence for limited-value exports to China, in fact the value limit for exports of most commodities on the Commodity Control List to Country Group P (China) under the general licence GLV was zero.

This limitation on the availability of the general licence GLV has been retained, notwithstanding the reclassification of China for most export control purposes. With the inclusion of China in Country Group V, the 1983 Amended Regulations also make corresponding amendments to the provisions of the general licence GLV which limit the value of most commodities on the Commodity Control List, to provide that the GLV value limit for proposed exports to the People's Republic of China remains at zero.[14] This restriction is consistent with the policy of the Office of Export Administration, manifested at several points in the 1983 Amended Regulations, of continuing to examine each proposed export of controlled commodities and technology to China on a case-by-case basis.

B. The Use of the Distribution Licence Special Licensing Procedure

The necessity of obtaining an individual validated licence for each proposed export of a controlled commodity to any destination to which the controls are applicable (all destinations except Canada, in the case of 'A' and 'B' items) can be a time-consuming and expensive process. As a result, in order to facilitate multiple export transactions involving commodities for which a validated licence is required, Part 373 of the Export Administration Regulations creates a series of special licensing procedures which may be utilized, under certain specified conditions and in limited circumstances, in lieu of individual validated export licences. Of these special licensing procedures, the most important is the distribution licence. The distribution licence permits the exporter to make repeated exports over a period of two years (subject to renewal for an additional two years) of controlled commodities to approved consignees in specified destinations, pursuant to an international marketing programme.[15]

The distribution licensing procedure was previously available for exports of controlled commodities to approved consignees in Country Groups T and V only (thus excluding China, in Country Group P). The 1983 Amended Regulations retain this exclusion of China from the list of eligible countries under the distribution licence special licensing procedure.[16] This restriction is consistent with the policy of the Office of Export Administration, noted above, of generally examining proposed exports of controlled commodities to China on a case-by-case basis.

Although distribution licences are not available for the export of controlled commodities to China, in 1984 the Department of Commerce and the Department of Defense established an informal procedure for granting 'individual' validated export licences authorizing multiple shipments of relatively low-level computers and related peripherals for distribution in China. This informal procedure was formalized on 27 December 1985 by a new advisory note to the Commodity Control List entry governing electronic computers and peripherals.[17] Under this new procedure, it may be possible to obtain a multiple shipment export licence (or 'bulk' licence) to export large quantities of computers to China, provided that the machines (a) are limited to single 16-bit microprocessors or less; (b) have a processing data rate (PDR) of 15 megabits per second or less; (c) have a virtual storage capability of 1/2 megabyte or less. Such a bulk licence would probably limit the numbers of computers in the Chinese distributor's inventory at any one time, and would require that spare parts (at least advanced technology parts)[18] be provided to the Chinese distributor on a one-for-one replacement basis only. Finally, the United States exporter may be required to obtain from its Chinese distributor information regarding each end-user to whom a computer has been sold or delivered. The exporter would then make periodic reports of this information about end-users to the Department of Commerce.[19]

C. COCOM Approval

The United States participates in a programme of multinational export controls, along with Belgium, Canada, Denmark, France, West Germany, Greece, Italy, Japan, Luxemburg, the Netherlands, Norway, Portugal, Turkey, and the United Kingdom. This system of multinational controls is administered by an informal Coordinating Committee (COCOM) which reviews proposed exports of multilaterally controlled commodities (that is, commodities identified by the code letter 'A' on the Commodity Control List) to consignees in the Communist countries of Eastern Europe, the Soviet Union, and the People's Republic of China. Thus, even after the Office of Export Administration has determined to grant a validated licence for a proposed export of an 'A' item to one of these destinations, the licence application may have to be reviewed and approved by COCOM before the validated licence will be issued.[20]

Because the requirement of COCOM approval of validated licence applications for the export of certain controlled commodities to China is based upon an international (albeit informal) agreement, the 1983 Amended Regulations left the COCOM approval requirements for exports to China unchanged.[21] As a result of the continuing applicability of the COCOM approval requirements, validated licence applications for proposed exports of many 'A' items to China have taken considerably longer to process than those for such exports to other destinations in Country Group V. Indeed, since the 1983 Amended Regulations were issued, the COCOM review and approval process has been perceived as the principal impediment to expanded high technology trade between the United States and China. Two important recent developments may, however, ameliorate the problems arising out of the COCOM review and approval requirements.

In July 1984 the COCOM member nations, including the United States, agreed on a uniform control programme for the export of certain commodities, including computers, to the Soviet Union, Eastern Europe, and China. This COCOM agreement removed the controls on the export of certain products, including low-level eight-bit personal computers, to all destinations, including China. Moreover, the technical thresholds for which licence applications for proposed exports of more sophisticated products to the Soviet Union, Eastern Europe, or the People's Republic of China would have to be submitted to COCOM were revised significantly. In effect, the decision to licence or to reject proposed exports of these sophisticated commodities to China (or for that matter to the Soviet Union or Eastern Europe), which had formerly resided with COCOM, is now a matter at the discretion of the export control authorities of the exporting COCOM member nation (that is, in the case of the United States, the Office of Export Administration of the Department of Commerce). The COCOM agreement of July 1984 was implemented in the United States by two sets of amendments to the Export Administration Regulations, issued on 31 December 1984,[22] and 11 September 1985,[23] respectively.

One of the effects of the COCOM agreement of July 1984 has been to provide at least a partial solution to the problem of the impediment to expanded high technology trade between the United States and China posed by the COCOM review and approval process. However, considerable dissatisfaction with COCOM requirements and procedures as they apply to exports to China still exists. First, this process adds elements of delay and uncertainty to proposed transactions with China involving those commodities which remain subject to COCOM controls, and thus the COCOM process makes it more difficult for United States high technology firms to market their products in China. Second, there are at least suggestions that licence applications for proposed exports to China that do not raise significant national security concerns may be delayed in COCOM for essentially political purposes, as other COCOM nations seek to overcome United States resistance to licence applications for proposed exports to the Soviet Union. Finally, in view of the developing diplomatic and economic ties between the United States and China, the Chinese have objected to being treated in a manner similar to the Soviet Union for COCOM review purposes.

Apparently in response to these objections, in February 1985 the United States initiated negotiations with its COCOM partners, with the object of raising the technical levels of proposed exports requiring COCOM review for exports to China only. These negotiations culminated in an agreement in October 1985. The most important feature about this agreement is that, unlike that of July 1984, the COCOM review requirements for proposed exports of controlled commodities to China now differ dramatically from the review requirements for proposed exports of similar commodities to the Soviet Union or Eastern Europe. Thus, for a number of controlled commodities, the United States export control authorities may license exports to China without referral to COCOM, whereas proposed exports of similar or identical commodities to the Soviet Union or Eastern Europe would require COCOM review and approval. This agreement was implemented by amendments to the Export Administration Regulations which were issued on 27 December 1985.[24]

An important feature of these amendments is that, for the first time, they contemplate direct involvement by the Chinese government in the licensing process, in order to prevent the diversion of controlled United States origin commodities to an unauthorized destination. As noted above, under these amendments, licence applications to export 'A' items to China must now be supported by a PRC End-User Certificate, issued by the Technology Import and Export Department of the Chinese Ministry of Foreign Economic Relations and Trade.[25] By this document, the Chinese government formally assures the United States government that the goods in question will not be diverted or re-exported. Heretofore, the assurance against diversion or re-export has come solely from the Chinese customer (on Commerce Department form ITA-629P).

D. The Special Documentation Requirements for Computer Exports

Section 376.10 of the Export Administration Regulations established various special documentation requirements for validated licence applications for proposed exports of computers (ECCN 1565A) to any destination in Country Groups Q, W, and Y (and, formerly, Country Group P). Under Section 376.10, an applicant for a validated licence to export com-

puters to one of these destinations must submit (a) the computers' parameters on form ITA-6031P;[26] (b) documentation identifying the parties
to the transaction, the proposed location and end use of the computers,
and the technical justification for the end-user's need for the equipment;
(c) detailed information about the software to be supplied for use with the
computers; (d) appropriate assurances against diversion of the computers
from the stated destination and end use; and (e) the end-user's agreement
to visitation rights by representatives of the exporting firm to confirm
that the equipment has not been improperly diverted to an unauthorized
destination or use.[27] The 1983 Amended Regulations leave these special
documentation requirements for proposed computer exports to China
unchanged. Thus, notwithstanding the reclassification of China into
Country Group V, exporters that propose to export computers to China
are still required to submit form ITA-6031P and the other prescribed
documentation in conjunction with their validated export licence
applications,[28] whereas such documentation need not be submitted in
conjunction with licence applications for proposed computer exports to
other destinations in Country Group V.

E. The Special Documentation Requirements for Certain Machine Tool and Numerical Controls Exports

Section 376.11 of the Export Administration Regulations identifies additional information that must accompany any validated licence application
for a proposed export to any destination in Country Groups Q, W, and Y
(and formerly Country Group P), of the machine tools and numerical
controls which are identified in the Commodity Control List entry
ECCN 1091A.[29] This additional information is generally not required for
proposed exports of machine tools and numerical controls to destinations
in Country Group V, but with the inclusion of China in this group, Section 376.11 was modified by the 1983 Amended Regulations to retain the
special information requirements for proposed exports of those items to
China.[30]

F. Technical Data Export Controls

As noted above, the Export Administration Act and the Export Administration Regulations provide for the control of exports of not only commodities but also technical data.[31] In order to facilitate the international
exchange of technology, however, it has been possible, under Section
379.4 of the Export Administration Regulations, to export most technical
data, apart from those data having certain direct strategic applications,
to destinations in Country Groups T and V (except Afghanistan) under
general licence GTDR.[32] Thus, the exporter that proposes to export or
license its technology to an end-user in a country in Country Groups T
or V may generally make the export without a validated export licence,
although it may be necessary for the exporter to obtain a letter of assurance from the end-user that neither the technical data nor the direct product thereof will be re-exported to a controlled destination (the nations in

Country Groups Q, S, W, Y, Z, Afghanistan and, formerly, Country Group P).[33]

In contrast, a validated export licence has been required for almost all proposed exports of technical data to destinations in Country Groups Q, S, W, Y, and Z, as well as Afghanistan and, formerly, Country Group P. Section 379.4(b) of the Export Administration Regulations provides that general licence GTDR may not be utilized for technical data exports to destinations in Country Groups Q, W, or Y, or to Afghanistan,[34] except in two instances: the export of operating and maintenance technical data for commodities that have been licensed for export from the United States; and the export of limited types of sales and marketing technical data in support of an actual quotation, bid, or offer to sell commodities (apart from commodities identified by the code letter 'A' on the Commodity Control List).[35]

Thus, prior to 23 November 1983, a validated licence was required for virtually all transfers of proprietary technical data to China, except under the narrow conditions of general licence GTDR specified above. The 1983 Amended Regulations modified the broad restriction on the export of technical data to China under general licence GTDR, but did not bring the requirements for technical data exports to China into full conformance with the requirements for technical data exports to other destinations in Country Group V. Although general licence GTDR may now be used for some technical data exports to China, this general licence is not available for the export to China of any technical data related to any commodity that is controlled for national security, nuclear nonproliferation, or crime control reasons (essentially all commodities on the Commodity Control List identified by the code letters 'A' and 'B').[36] Thus, proposed technology transfer transactions to China should be carefully analysed for their export control implications. If a United States firm proposes to sell, license, or otherwise transfer to a Chinese entity information relating to the design, production, manufacture, utilization, or reconstruction of 'A' or 'B' commodities on the Commodity Control List, a validated export licence will be required for the transaction.

It should be emphasized that the concept of an 'export' of technical data is defined very broadly for export control purposes. Under Section 379.1(b) of the Export Administration Regulations, the concept of an export includes not only the physical shipment or transmission of technical data from the United States, but also the disclosure of technical data in the United States with the knowledge that the technical data will be transmitted abroad and the disclosure of United States origin technical data abroad.[37] This broad definition of the concept of an 'export' of technical data implies that United States export control considerations arise whenever a United States firm invites a Chinese trade delegation to visit a manufacturing facility in the United States, and whenever a United States firm dispatches a technician to China to provide some form of technical assistance or training. Thus, for example, if a United States firm invites a Chinese trade delegation to visit a manufacturing facility in the United States, and in the course of that plant visit, technical information relating to the design, production, operation, or use of 'A' or 'B' items on the Commodity Control List will be disclosed to the Chinese, a validated export licence will be required.[38] Correspondingly, if a United States firm dispatches a technician to a Chinese facility to provide technical assistance relating to an 'A' or 'B' commodity, a validated export licence will also be required.[39]

The applicability of the technical data provisions of the Export Administration Regulations to plant visits and foreign technical assistance services with respect to China is often overlooked, perhaps because similar technical data exports can generally be effected to other destinations in Country Group V under general licence GTDR. United States firms that are engaged in negotiations for technology transfers to China, which may involve such plant visits or on-site technical assistance services, should be particularly sensitive to this important difference between the technical data export control rules for China and the rules for other countries within Country Group V.

G. Exports of Computer Software

Under Section 379.1(a) of the Export Administration Regulations, computer software is specifically included within the definition of technical data for export control purposes,[40] and has, therefore, been subject to the controls applicable to technical data exports generally. As such, most computer software has been exportable to destinations in Country Groups T and V under general licence GTDR. In contrast, a validated export licence has been required for the export of virtually all unbundled computer software to Country Groups Q, W, Y, and S, as well as to Afghanistan and, formerly, Country Group P.

The reclassification of China from Country Group P to Country Group V did not eliminate the requirement of a validated licence for software exports to China. As noted above, under Section 379.4(i) of the Export Administration Regulations, a validated licence is required for the export to China of technical data relating to 'A' and 'B' items on the Commodity Control List.[41] Because software is related to an 'A' item (that is, electronic computers, ECCN 1565A), proposed exports of all computer software to China have remained subject to validated licensing requirements even after the 1983 Amended Regulations were issued.

On 26 April 1985 the Office of Export Administration issued new regulations governing the export of computer software (hereafter referred to as the Software Amendments).[42] As discussed in detail below, the Software Amendments eliminate the requirement of a validated licence for exports of many kinds of software to China. It should be emphasized, however, that important differences remain between the controls on the export of software to China and the controls on the export of software to other nations in Country Group V.

The Software Amendments set up a three-tiered hierarchy of controls on software exports. First, any applications software which is identified in Sections 379.4(c) and 379.4(d) of the Regulations,[43] or any software specifically identified in any Commodity Control List entry, requires a validated export licence for export to any destination except Canada.[44] Second, software identified in Supplement No. 3 to Part 379 of the Regulations requires a validated licence for export to Country Groups Q, S, W, Y, and Afghanistan, and to the People's Republic of China.[45] In contrast, such software may be exported to destinations in Country Groups T and V (except China) under general licence GTDR, although the United States exporter is required to obtain from its foreign consignee written assurance against the unauthorized re-export of the software or a direct product thereof to a controlled destination.[46] Finally, software that does not come within either of the first two levels of control may be exported to any destination (except Country Groups S and Z) including the People's Republic of China under general licence GTDR.[47] Thus, although most off-the-shelf personal computer software may now be exported to China under general licence GTDR, United States software firms that propose to sell or license their products in China should carefully review Supplement No. 3 to Part 379 before concluding that those products may be exported to China without validated export licences.

IV. Current Regulatory Developments

The preceding sections of this chapter have surveyed most recent and current developments concerning export controls and licensing for the People's Republic of China. However, special mention should be made of one important recent development concerning the processing of licence applications to export controlled commodities or technical data to China.

Although much of the delay in the processing of licence applications for proposed exports to China has been attributable to the COCOM review requirements, there have also been frequent complaints about processing delays within the Office of Export Administration. In response to these complaints, the Office of Export Administration established the 'China Team Center' in July 1985 for the specific purpose of expediting the processing of China export licence applications. This China Team Center is a self-contained unit within the Office of Export Administration, staffed by engineers, licensing officers, and licensing support personnel, which is intended to permit the processing of China licence applications in a single operation. In addition, steps have been taken to expedite the preparation of the required submissions for such China licence applications that must be submitted to COCOM. As a result, the backlog of China cases awaiting submission to COCOM has been virtually eliminated.[48]

V. Conclusion

The 1983 Amended Regulations, subsequent regulatory developments, and the new licensing policies adopted by the Office of Export Administration represent a major relaxation of United States trade policy with respect to China, and, as such, are opening up significant new export opportunities for United States firms, particularly in the high technology electronics area. Exporters that seek to pursue these new opportunities for trade with China should, however, be particularly sensitive to the differences between the export control requirements and policies with respect to China and the requirements and policies with respect to the United States' major Western trading partners. Exporters should also be aware of the fact that China remains a controlled country for COCOM purposes and that, therefore, applications for export licences to ship to China some products which incorporate very high technology remain subject to the delays and uncertainties that the COCOM review process implies.

Notes

1. The United States Export Administration Act (hereafter cited as the Export Administration Act). 50 USC App. §§ 2401ff. The Export Administration Act was most recently re-enacted and amended by the Export Administration Amendments Act of 1985, Pub. L. No. 99–64, 99 Stat. 120 (effective 12 July 1985).
2. The Export Administration Regulations, 15 CFR Parts 368–99.
3. The Office of Export Administration of the Department of Commerce, the Office of Export Control and the Office of Strategic Trade Policy of the Department of Defense, and, with respect to munitions exports, the Office of Munitions Control of the Department of State.
4. 46 Fed. Reg. 62836 (29 December 1981).
5. 48 Fed. Reg. 53064–71 (23 November 1983).
6. See 48 Fed. Reg. 53064, amending 15 CFR Part 370, Supp. No. 1.
7. The commodities that are subject to control are specified in the Commodity Control List, 15 CFR § 399.1, Supp. No. 1. This list is established by the Commerce Department, in conjunction with the Defense Department, under Section 5(c) of the Export Administration Act. The technical data controls are set forth in 15 CFR Part 379.
8. With the reclassification of China, Country Group P has been eliminated. See 48 Fed. Reg. 53064, amending 15 CFR § 370, Supp. No. 1.
9. See 15 CFR § 385.2(a)(1). The nations of Country Group Z are subject to an absolute embargo. See 15 CFR § 385.1.
10. See 48 Fed. Reg. 53067, adding 15 CFR § 385.4(g).
11. Under the Amended Regulations, validated licence applications for exports of controlled commodities to China may be approved even if the end-user is a military entity. Validated licence applications for proposed exports to China of commodities having direct military applications, such as items relating to nuclear weapons and delivery systems, electronic and anti-submarine warfare, intelligence gathering, power projection, and air superiority, will, however, generally be denied. See 48 Fed. Reg. 53067, amending 15 CFR § 385.4(c)(1).
12. It is anticipated that approximately 75 per cent of all validated licence applications for proposed exports of controlled commodities to China involve commodities on the 'green' list. Thus, for example, computers having a processing data rate of up to 155 Mbits/second are on the 'green' list. See 15 CFR § 399.1, Supp. No. 1, Export Control Commodity No. (ECCN) 1565A, Advisory Note 17, as amended by 50 Fed. Reg. 52900 and 52908 (27 December 1985). This should

cover virtually all 16-bit microcomputers and many medium-scale mainframe computers.

13. 15 CFR § 371.5. The Commodity Control List specifies a general licence GLV maximum value for each entry. This value limit is US$100, US$250, US$500, US$1,000, or US$2,000, depending upon the particular commodity. Certain commodities, however, which are controlled for nuclear non-proliferation reasons, have a general licence GLV value limit of zero for all destinations. See, generally, 15 CFR § 399.1, Supp. No. 1.

14. See 48 Fed. Reg. 53068–9, amending various entries in the Commodity Control List, 15 CFR § 399.1, Supp. No. 1.

15. 15 CFR § 373.3, as amended by 50 Fed. Reg. 21562–76 (24 May 1985).

16. 48 Fed. Reg. 53065, amending 15 CFR §§ 372.2(b)(3) and 373.3(a)(1)(ii).

17. 50 Fed. Reg. 52908 (22 December 1985), amending 15 CFR § 399.1, Supp. No. 1, ECCN 1565A, Advisory Note 20.

18. The concept of 'advanced technology parts' is defined in Advisory Note 7(c) to ECCN 1565A, as amended by 49 Fed. Reg. 50608 and 50614 (31 December 1984).

19. The requirement to report on end-users was established under the United States' obligations as a member of COCOM (discussed below). Previously, licence applications to export controlled commodities to China required Commerce Department form ITA-629 (a statement by the ultimate consignee and the purchaser) as a supporting document. The new Regulations issued on 27 December 1985 eliminate the requirement of the ITA-629 form for licence applications to export 'A' items to China. Instead, such licence applications must be accompanied by a PRC End-User Certificate, issued by the Technology Import and Export Department of the Chinese Ministry of Foreign Economic Relations and Trade. See 50 Fed. Reg. 52902 (27 December 1985), adding 15 CFR § 375.6. By this PRC End-User Certificate, the Chinese government assures the United States government that the goods covered by the export licence application are for use in China and will not be re-exported to a third country. See 50 Fed. Reg. 52902 (27 December 1985), adding CFR § 375.6. Thus, end-user reporting may be eliminated for computers exported under a bulk licence which is supported by a PRC End-User Certificate.

20. See, generally, 15 CFR § 370.13(1).

21. 48 Fed. Reg. 53064, amending 15 CFR §§ 370.11(c) and 370.13(1).

22. 49 Fed. Reg. 50608–32 (31 December 1984), amending 15 CFR § 399.1, Supp. No. 1, ECCN 1565A.

23. 50 Fed. Reg. 37112–61 (11 September 1985).

24. 50 Fed. Reg. 52900–12 (27 December 1985). These amendments add to or revise a number of advisory notes to the Commodity Control List, 15 CFR § 399.1, Supp. No. 1. Proposed exports to China of commodities that come within the technical parameters and specifications set forth in these advisory notes will generally not require COCOM review. Of particular interest may be Advisory Note 20 to ECCN 1565A (the computer entry on the Commodity Control List), which indicates that COCOM approval will not be required for bulk licences to make multiple exports of certain personal computers for distribution within China. See 50 Fed. Reg. 52908 (27 December 1985).

25. See 50 Fed. Reg. 52902, adding 15 CFR § 375.6(a).

26. Form ITA-6031P has recently been substantially revised, in order to bring it into conformance with the amendments to the Export Administration Regulations of 31 December 1984.

27. 15 CFR § 376.10. The foregoing is merely a summary of the special documentation requirements for computer exports to the controlled destinations. In fact, the section requires the exporter to provide a substantial amount of information in connection with a validated licence application to export computers to one of the destinations in question.

28. 48 Fed. Reg. 53066. Although Country Group P was eliminated by the

reclassification of China, Section 376.10 was correspondingly amended to provide specifically that the special documentation requirements remain applicable to proposed computer exports to the People's Republic of China.

29. 15 CFR § 376.11.

30. 48 Fed. Reg. 53066, amending 15 CFR § 376.11. The amendment was effected by simply deleting Country Group P and adding 'the People's Republic of China' to Section 376.11.

31. See 15 CFR Part 379. For export control purposes, 'technical data' is defined to include: 'information of any kind that can be used, or adapted for use, in the design, production, manufacture, utilization or reconstruction of articles or materials. The data may take a tangible form, such as a model, prototype, blueprint or an operating manual; or they may take an intangible form such as technical service.' (See 15 CFR § 379.1(a).)

32. See 15 CFR § 379.4. The types of technical data for which a validated licence is required for export to destinations in Country Groups T and V are specified in Sections 379.4(c) and 379.4(d) of the Export Administration Regulations. These technical data relate to the production and delivery of nuclear weapons, airborne navigation and guidance systems, civil aircraft, and various types of submersible watercraft.

33. The various written assurance requirements are set forth in Sections 379.4(f)(1), 379.4(f)(2), and 379.4(g) (relating to software) of the Regulations. Although Country Group P has been eliminated with the reclassification of China, the written assurance provisions of Section 379.4(f) retain the requirement that the consignee of technical data exported under general licence GTDR must provide written assurance that the technical data and its direct product will be diverted neither to the People's Republic of China nor to any other controlled destination. See 48 Fed. Reg. 53066, amending 15 CFR §§ 379.4(f) and 379.5(e).

34. A validated licence is required for virtually all exports of proprietary technical data (that is, technical data that are not in the public domain and are therefore not exportable under a general licence GTDA) to destinations in Country Groups S (Libya) or Z (Cuba, Kampuchea, North Korea, Vietnam). 15 CFR § 379.4(a). Validated licence applications to export technical data to any destination in Country Groups S and Z will be summarily denied. See 15 CFR § 385.1(a). See, also, 51 Fed. Reg. 2354 (16 January 1986), adding 15 CFR § 390.7 (Libyan Sanctions Regulations).

35. 15 CFR § 379.4(b), as amended by 50 Fed. Reg. 37112 and 37113–14 (11 September 1985).

36. 48 Fed. Reg. 53066, adding 15 CFR § 379.4(i).

37. 15 CFR § 379.1(b).

38. See 15 CFR § 379.1(b)(2)(i).

39. See 15 CFR § 379.1(b)(2)(iii).

40. 15 CFR § 379.1(a).

41. See 15 CFR § 379.4(i).

42. 50 Fed. Reg. 16469–79 (26 April 1985).

43. 15 CFR §§ 379.4(c) and 379.4(d). A validated licence is required for the export of Section 379.4(c) software (relating to sensitive nuclear activities) even to Canada.

44. The specific Commodity Control List entries which identify software for which a validated export licence is required for export to all destinations, except Canada, are ECCN 1091A (numerically controlled machine tools); ECCN 1354 (equipment for the manufacture of printed circuit boards); ECCN 1355 (equipment for the manufacture of electronic equipment); ECCN 1527A (cryptographic equipment); ECCN 1532A (precision linear and angular measuring systems); and ECCN 1567A (stored program controlled communications switching systems). See 15 CFR § 379.4(g).

45. See 15 CFR Part 379, Supp. No. 3, as amended by 50 Fed. Reg. 37112, 37115 (11 September 1985), and 50 Fed. Reg. 52902 (27 December 1985).

46. 15 CFR § 379.4(f)(1)(i)(a).
47. 15 CFR § 379.4(b)(3).
48. According to testimony given before the United States House Subcommittee on International Economic Policy on 10 October 1985.

Appendix. Export Control Country Groups

1. Canada		
2. Country Group T	Central and South America, Caribbean Islands, except Cuba	
3. Country Group V	Western Europe, Middle East (except Libya), Africa, non-Communist countries of the Asia/Pacific region, People's Republic of China (since 23 November 1983)	
4. Country Group P	People's Republic of China (before 23 November 1983)	
5. Country Group Q	Romania	
6. Country Group W	Poland, Hungary	
7. Country Group Y	USSR, Communist countries of Eastern Europe, Laos, Mongolia	
8. Country Group S	Libya	
9. Country Group Z	Cuba, Kampuchea, North Korea, Vietnam	

Source: Prepared from the Export Administration Regulations, 15 CFR, Part 370, Supp. No. 1.

15. The Application of United States Foreign Trade Laws to Imports from China

WINSTON K. ZEE

EVER since the normalization of relations between the People's Republic of China (PRC) and the United States, bilateral trade between the two countries has increased rapidly. Such increased trade has had the unfortunate effect of increasing legal disputes, many of which involve United States foreign trade laws. This chapter examines three United States foreign trade legislative measures—the antidumping law, the countervailing duty law, and the 'market disruption' provisions—and how they have been applied to imports from the PRC.

I. The Antidumping Law

A. What is Antidumping?

'Antidumping' is a remedy available to United States producers to protect them from certain types of import competition. The remedy is in the form of a special antidumping duty in addition to the normal customs duties imposed on imports.[1] For example, if the normal import duty on a particular type of merchandise is 5 per cent, and a United States producer brings a successful antidumping action against the importation of such merchandise, the imposition of a special antidumping duty of 20 per cent will result in the importers of such merchandise having to pay import duties of 25 per cent.

Before the special antidumping duty may be imposed on a particular product imported from the PRC, two facts must be established:
(a) that an industry in the United States is materially injured or is threatened with material injury by reason of the subject PRC imports;[2]
(b) that the subject PRC imports are sold in the United States at less than fair value.[3]

Unless both of these facts are established, the special antidumping duty will not be imposed on the PRC imports in question.

B. The United States Government Agencies Responsible for Antidumping Investigations

Each of the two issues above is separately investigated by a different agency of the United States Federal Government. The 'injury' issue is investigated by the United States International Trade Commission, and the 'less than fair value' issue is investigated by the United States Department of Commerce. These two agencies are completely independent of one another.

The United States International Trade Commission (USITC) is an independent federal agency, which is not part of the Executive Branch of the United States Federal Government. It is headed by six Commissioners who vote on all final decisions. The Commissioners are assisted in the investigations by a staff of 400 to 500 professionals, such as economists, accountants, industry specialists, and lawyers. An antidumping investigation is usually assigned to a team of three or four staff investigators, who prepare a written report for the Commissioners, stating the information gathered during the investigation. The Commissioners will make their final decision on the basis of this report, and the information and arguments submitted by the parties.

Unlike the USITC, the United States Department of Commerce (USDOC) is a part of the Executive Branch of the United States Federal Government. The less-than-fair-value (LTFV) issue in an antidumping investigation is handled by the International Trade Administration within the USDOC, and the main responsibility for supervising such investigations falls on the Deputy Assistant Secretary for Import Administration. Under this official are three offices: (a) investigation, (b) compliance, and (c) policy. The Office of Investigation has the largest number of personnel and is responsible for conducting the actual investigation of antidumping petitions. The Office of Compliance is responsible for determining periodically the applicable antidumping duties once 'dumping' is established. The Office of Policy is a relatively small office consisting of specialists such as economists and accountants who advise and assist the other two offices on special policy and technical questions.

C. Initiating an Antidumping Investigation

Although the statute permits the USDOC to start an antidumping investigation on its own initiative, an antidumping investigation normally commences upon the filing of a petition simultaneously with both the USITC and the USDOC.[4] An antidumping petition may be filed by only three types of entity:
(a) a United States producer, manufacturer, or wholesaler of a 'like product';
(b) a labour union of the workers of an industry engaged in the manufacture, production, or wholesale in the United States of a 'like product';
(c) a trade association a majority of whose members are engaged in the manufacture, production, or wholesale of a 'like product' in the United States.[5]

The key concept here is 'like product'; in order to have the standing to file an antidumping petition, the complainant must be engaged in the production, manufacture, or wholesale in the United States of a product which is 'like' the imports with respect to which the petition is filed.[6] For example, the Court of International Trade ruled in one case that a television picture tube was not a 'like product' when compared to a complete television set.[7] Consequently the United States producers of television picture tubes did not have the standing to file an antidumping petition with respect to imports of complete television sets, and their petition was rejected.

D. Injury to a United States Industry

As explained above, the USITC handles one of the two issues involved in an antidumping investigation, namely, whether a United States industry is materially injured, or is threatened with material injury, by reason of the subject imports. With respect to imports from the PRC, the injury issue involves two inquiries:

(a) whether the United States industry filing an antidumping petition against the PRC imports is suffering material injury or is threatened with material injury; and

(b) if the answer to the above question is affirmative, whether the material injury or threat thereof is caused by the subject PRC imports.

With respect to the first question, the USITC will look at data relating to the economic performance of the relevant United States industry, such as production, capacity utilization, employment, sales, inventory, profits, market share, and return on investment. The USITC will usually examine such data for the three-year period prior to the filing of the antidumping petition.[8]

With respect to the second question, the USITC will look at the import volume of the subject PRC imports, their increase during the three-year period prior to the filing of the antidumping petition, the United States market share of the subject PRC imports, the difference in price between the United States product and the PRC imports (in order to detect any price suppression or depression), and any information relating to sales lost as a result of United States customers switching from the United States product to the PRC imports.[9]

During the antidumping investigation, the USITC investigating staff will send out questionnaires to United States producers and importers to gather information relevant to the injury issue. It will also use the official import statistics compiled by the Bureau of Census of the USDOC. The USITC staff will prepare a written report to the Commissioners, based on these data as well as on information from other sources appropriate to the particular case. There will be a public hearing during which both the petitioner and the respondent will be permitted to testify and to present witnesses.[10] The parties will also be permitted to submit written information and arguments. The Commissioners will vote on the injury issue, taking into account the USITC staff report, the transcript of the public hearing, and the written submissions of the parties.

E. Sale at Less than Fair Value

Determining whether the subject PRC imports are sold at less than fair value (LTFV) involves a comparison of two prices: (a) the United States

Price (USP) and (b) the Foreign Market Value (FMV). If the USP is equal to or higher than the FMV, there is no sale at LTFV. If the USP is lower than the FMV, there is a sale at LTFV.[11]

The amount by which the FMV exceeds the USP is called the dumping margin and determines the size of the special antidumping duty. For example, if the FMV were 110 and the USP were 100, the dumping margin would be 10, and the special antidumping duty would be 10 per cent.

Calculating the USP and the FMV in an antidumping investigation involving imports from the PRC is a very complicated process. It cannot be understood without a preliminary explanation of an important concept in United States antidumping law, known as the 'state-controlled economy'.[12]

i. The State-controlled Economy
If the subject imports come from a market-economy country (such as Japan or Canada), the USP is the ex-factory price at which the product is sold for export to the United States, and the FMV is the ex-factory price of the same product sold in the home market of that exporting country. When the economy of the exporting country in question is state controlled, however, the United States Congress believes that the prices actually charged for the products of that country do not reflect their true market value and therefore cannot be relied upon in making the LTFV determination.

Neither the statute nor the regulations spell out the criteria for determining whether the economy of an exporting country is state controlled. In practice, however, only the economies of Communist countries have been held to be state controlled in the context of antidumping law.

In the case of imports from the PRC, there have been more than ten antidumping investigations. In some of these investigations, there were heated debates as to whether the PRC should be considered a state-controlled economy for purposes of antidumping. But the USDOC has consistently held that the PRC does have a state-controlled economy, and it is likely that the USDOC will in the near future continue to hold this opinion.

Since the PRC has been held to have a state-controlled economy, the prices actually charged for PRC products cannot be relied upon in determining whether the subject PRC imports are sold at LTFV. Rather, the LTFV determination must be made by referring to a surrogate economy.[13] The following discussion will describe how a surrogate economy for the PRC is selected, how the USP and the FMV are determined with reference to this surrogate economy, and what problems are posed by the surrogate economy method.

ii The Surrogate Economy
A surrogate economy must be a market economy. In selecting a surrogate economy for an antidumping investigation involving imports from the PRC, the USDOC will first look for a market economy which is at a stage of economic development comparable to that of the PRC (a 'comparable surrogate economy').[14] If a suitable comparable surrogate econ-

omy cannot be found, the USDOC will use a non-comparable market economy as the surrogate economy.

In determining whether the economy of a particular country is comparable to that of the PRC, the USDOC will use generally recognized economic criteria.[15] For example, in an internal memorandum, the Office of Policy of the USDOC stated:

[W]e examine the level of economic development by reference to the sectoral makeup of the economy... As economic development proceeds, labor force shifts from agriculture to the industrial sector, and from industry to services. We look at both labor force and value added data although we consider labor force data to be more accurate and reliable.[16]

To date, countries which have actually been used by the USDOC as comparable surrogate economies in antidumping investigations involving PRC imports include Paraguay, Thailand, Indonesia, and India, and countries which have been considered by the USDOC to be good candidates include Pakistan, Malaysia, and the Philippines.

iii. The United States Price
The USP is the ex-factory price at which a producer sells goods for export to the United States.[17] Goods exported from the PRC to the United States are typically sold by China's state-owned foreign trade corporations to United States importers on a CIF basis. Since an ex-factory price does not include freight or insurance, the USDOC, in calculating the USP, will deduct from the CIF price the following items:
(a) a discount or commission, if any;
(b) ocean freight, that is, the cost of transporting the goods from the PRC port to the United States port;
(c) inland freight, that is, the cost of transporting the goods from the PRC factory to the PRC port;
(d) an insurance premium.
The following example illustrates such a calculation.

	US$
Contract price (CIF San Francisco)	100.00
Less	
Discount (2 per cent)	2.00
Ocean freight	30.00
Inland freight	5.00
Insurance	0.50
USP (ex-factory price)	62.50

As explained above, the USDOC considers the PRC to have a state-controlled economy. Therefore, in calculating the USP from a CIF contract price, the USDOC would not deduct the freight and insurance costs actually paid by the PRC exporter, if such costs were paid to a PRC transportation or insurance company. Instead, the USDOC would use the freight and insurance rates of a surrogate economy.[18]

As for insurance costs, the use of a surrogate economy will usually not change the USP calculation significantly, because the insurance premium is normally a very small amount compared to the contract price. Ocean freight is similarly not an issue, because the freight rates of the China Ocean Shipping Company (the national shipping line of the PRC) are basically the same as those charged by non-PRC shipping lines for shipping goods from PRC ports to United States ports. The really significant issue is inland freight, and the best way to illustrate this problem is with an actual antidumping case.

In the case *Barium Chloride from the PRC*, one of the PRC barium chloride producers was located in Sichuan province.[19] The finished goods were transported from the factory to Chongqing, a river port along the Yangtze River, and from there by boat to Qingdao, a coastal port. At Qingdao, the goods were transferred to ocean-going vessels and shipped to the United States.

The issue was how much river-freight cost should be deducted from the contract price in calculating the USP. The USDOC in that case selected Thailand as the surrogate economy for the purpose of determining the FMV. The Chao Phraya River in Thailand, however, is less than one-fifteenth of the length of the Yangtze River and thus is clearly not an appropriate surrogate river for determining the river-freight cost. The PRC respondent gathered extensive data (including tariffs filed by United States barge companies with the United States Interstate Commerce Commission) to convince the USDOC to use instead the Mississippi River freight cost for a voyage of comparable distance. If the USDOC had in fact used the Mississippi River as the surrogate river, the resulting dumping margin would have been less than 5 per cent. Instead, the USDOC decided to use the Amazon River in Brazil as the surrogate river, resulting in a larger dumping margin of 14.5 per cent. Clearly the surrogate economy selected by the USDOC can significantly affect the outcome of an antidumping investigation involving imports from the PRC.

iv. The Foreign Market Value

As explained above, the USP is the ex-factory price at which a PRC producer sells goods for export to the United States, and goods are sold at LTFV when the USP is lower than the FMV. Accordingly, the FMV serves as the bench-mark of 'fair value'.

Since the USDOC has determined that the PRC has a state-controlled economy, the FMV in an antidumping investigation involving PRC imports is established in one of two ways:

(a) the FMV is the ex-factory price at which a producer in a comparable surrogate economy sells the same product in its home market, or, if its home market sales are too small (normally if less than 5 per cent of its export sales), the ex-factory price at which such a producer sells the same product for export;[20]

(b) if the USDOC cannot find a producer of the same product in a com-

parable surrogate economy or otherwise cannot use the method in
(a) above, it will use the 'constructed value' method to determine the
FMV.[21]

Both the surrogate producer method and the constructed value method
warrant further explanation.

v. The Surrogate Producer

Under the surrogate producer method, the USDOC will first identify
those countries which are at a stage of economic development comparable
to that of the PRC.[22] The USDOC will then contact the commercial section personnel of the United States embassies and consulates in these
countries. The commercial section personnel will subsequently contact
the relevant government agencies and industrial and commercial organizations (such as the Ministry of Industries, Chamber of Commerce, and
trade associations) to determine if any of these countries produces the
product in question. If so, the USDOC will seek the permission of the
host government to contact the producer for information. If permission is
granted, the USDOC will send a case officer to visit the prospective
surrogate producer.

If the surrogate producer is willing to co-operate, the USDOC case
officer will ask him to provide detailed information relating to his sales
during the investigation period, both in the home market and for the
export market. Such information will include prices, terms of sale, specifications, quantities, freight costs, discounts, and other information
necessary for calculating the surrogate producer's ex-factory price.
Adjustments to the surrogate producer's ex-factory price may be necessary to account for differences between the PRC producer's sales and
those of the surrogate producer. For example, such differences might
include the following:

(a) the specifications (for example, the size and quality) of the goods sold
by the surrogate producer could differ from those of the PRC exporter, and such differences might affect the costs (such as labour and
material inputs) of producing the goods;[23]

(b) the terms of sale of the surrogate producer could differ from those of
the PRC exporter, and such differences might affect the cost of sale
(for example, if the surrogate producer granted a ninety-day payment
term, whereas the PRC exporter required a letter of credit at sight,
the surrogate producer would incur interest and bad debt costs which
the PRC exporter would not incur).[24]

The surrogate producer's ex-factory price, after appropriate adjustments for the above-mentioned differences, will determine the FMV,
which will then be used by the USDOC to compare with the PRC exporter's USP to determine if there have been sales at LTFV.

vi. The Constructed Value

If the USDOC cannot find a producer of the same product in a comparable surrogate economy, or otherwise cannot use the surrogate producer
method, it will use the constructed value method to determine the
FMV.[25] This method involves the following two steps:

(a) a detailed examination of the production process employed by the PRC producer to identify all the 'inputs' used to produce the subject merchandise;

(b) a reconstruction of the production cost of the subject merchandise based on the value of such inputs in a comparable surrogate economy.[26]

The 'inputs' referred to in (a) above include the hours of labour required, the quantities of raw materials used, and the amount of energy consumed.[27] After the production cost of the subject merchandise is calculated in accordance with step (b) above, there will be added to it an appropriate percentage of factory overhead, 10 per cent general and administrative expenses, and 8 per cent profit.[28] The result of this calculation is called the 'constructed value' of the subject merchandise and is used by the USDOC as the FMV in its comparison with the USP.

The constructed value method can be illustrated by the following hypothetical example. Assume that an antidumping petition has been filed with respect to Chemical Y imported from the PRC and that the USDOC has decided to use the constructed value method to determine the FMV. At the request of the USDOC, the PRC producer of Chemical Y will furnish a detailed explanation of the processes it employs, as well as a list of the inputs it uses to produce Chemical Y. A typical input list might contain the elements shown in the following table.

Input	Amount of Input Actually Used by the PRC Producer to Produce One Metric Ton (t.) of Chemical Y
Raw materials	
Limestone	2.5 t.
Caustic soda	
(45 per cent solution)	0.9 t.
Soda ash	0.05 t.
Soft water	1.5 cu.m.
Energy	
Coal (5,000 kcal/kg)	0.5 t.
Electricity	45.0 kWh
Labour	
Supervisor	0.4 man-hours
Machine operators	10.5 man-hours
Machine maintenance	3.2 man-hours
General labour	1.8 man-hours

After receiving the above information from the PRC producer, the USDOC will send a case officer to the country which has been selected as the comparable surrogate economy to gather data on the value of these inputs in that country. The officer will also ascertain an appropriate percentage for factory overhead, based on the experience of local chemical producers with regard to the depreciation of plant and equipment and other indirect production costs. Based on these data, the USDOC will calculate the constructed value of Chemical Y as shown in the following table.

Input	Amount of Input Used by PRC Producer to Produce One Metric Ton (t.) of Chemical Y	Value of Input in the Surrogate Economy Selected by the USDOC (US$)	Value of Input for Producing One Metric Ton (t.) of Chemical Y (US$)
Limestone	2.50 t.	3.00/t.	7.50
Caustic soda (45 per cent solution)	0.90 t.	40.00/t.	36.00
Soda ash	0.05 t.	50.00/t.	2.50
Soft water	1.50 cu.m.	0.30/cu.m.	0.45
Coal (5,000 (kcal/kg)	0.50 t.	20.00/t.	10.00
Electricity	45.00 kWh	0.80/kWh	36.00
Supervisor	0.40 man-hours	2.00/man-hour	0.80
Machine operator	10.50 man-hours	1.40/man-hour	14.70
Machine maintenance	3.20 man-hours	1.70/man-hour	5.44
General labour	1.80 man-hours	0.75/man-hour	1.35
Subtotal			114.74
Factory overhead (15 per cent)			+ 17.21
Total production costs			131.95
General and administrative expenses (10 per cent)			+ 13.20
Total costs			145.15
Profit (8 per cent)			+ 11.61
Constructed value			156.76

In addition, the USDOC will send a case officer to visit the factory of the PRC producer to verify the 'inputs' information by examining the factory's original records.[29]

II. The Countervailing Duty Law

A. The Applicable Law

There are two United States countervailing duty statutes, both of which are currently enforced. The older statute was enacted in 1897 in substantially its present form.[30] During the Tokyo round of GATT negotiations in 1979, the United States became a signatory to the International Subsidies Code. Subsequently, Congress enacted as part of the Trade Agreements Act of 1979 the new countervailing duty statute, in order to bring United States domestic legislation into conformity with the new international agreement.[31]

Under the new statute, a countervailing duty will be imposed on a particular import if (a) the foreign producer or exporter of the merchandise receives a countervailable subsidy and (b) a United States industry is materially injured or is threatened with material injury by reason of the subsidized import.[32] In contrast, the old statute does not contain the 'injury' requirement, and a countervailing duty will be imposed if the foreign producer or exporter of the merchandise is found to receive a countervailable subsidy, regardless of whether the subsidized import has caused material injury or threat of material injury to a United States industry.[33]

The new countervailing duty statute is applicable when the imports in question come from a 'country under the Agreement', whereas imports from countries other than a 'country under the Agreement' are subject to the old statute. A 'country under the Agreement' is defined as a country which has signed the International Subsidies Code or which has entered into a bilateral agreement with the United States substantially equivalent to the International Subsidies Code.[34] The USDOC has determined that the PRC does not qualify as a 'country under the Agreement' and imports from the PRC are therefore subject to the old countervailing duty statute.[35] This means that a countervailing duty will be imposed on a particular PRC import as long as the PRC producer or exporter is found to receive a countervailable subsidy, and no consideration will be given as to whether a United States industry is materially injured or is threatened with material injury by reason of the subsidized PRC import.

B. What are Countervailable Subsidies?

Countervailable subsidies can be divided into two categories: (a) export subsidies, and (b) domestic subsidies.[36] Export subsidies are subsidies that are 'tied' to export performance. For example, a foreign producer may receive US$1.00 from the government for every 100 square feet of the merchandise he exports. Other examples of export subsidies include the following:

(a) currency retention schemes or any similar practices which involve a bonus on exports;

(b) internal transport and freight charges on export shipments, provided or mandated by governments, on terms more favourable than for domestic shipments;

(c) the delivery by governments or their agencies of imported or domestic products or services for use in the production of exported goods, on terms or conditions more favourable than for delivery of like or directly competitive products or services for use in the production of goods for domestic consumption, if (in the case of products) such terms or conditions are more favourable than those commercially available on world markets to its exporters;

(d) the full or partial exemption, remission, or deferral specifically related to exports, of direct taxes or social welfare charges paid or payable by industrial or commercial enterprises;

(e) the exemption or remission in respect of the production and distribution of exported products, of indirect taxes in excess of those levied in respect of the production and distribution of like products when sold for domestic consumption;

(f) the provision by governments (or special institutions controlled by governments) of export credit guarantee or insurance programmes, insurance or guarantee programmes against increases in the costs of exported products, or exchange risk programmes, at premium rates which are manifestly inadequate to cover the long-term operating costs and losses of the programmes.

Domestic subsidies are subsidies that are not tied to export performance. Examples of domestic subsidies include the following:

(a) an outright grant from the government to acquire machinery;

(b) a loan at below the market interest rate from the government or from a private bank under the order of the government;

(c) a loan guarantee provided by the government;

(d) a tax holiday or special tax breaks (for example, very favourable depreciation rules);

(e) purchase by the government of the foreign producer's stock at a price higher than its fair market value.

Under the United States countervailing duty law, all export subsidies are countervailable, whereas a domestic subsidy is countervailable only if it is conferred upon a specific region or industry of the exporting country.[37] For example, a domestic subsidy in the form of permitting accelerated depreciation for tax purposes is not countervailable if it is available to all industries, but accelerated depreciation available only to the steel industry is countervailable.

C. The History of Applying the Countervailing Duty Law to PRC Imports: the Textile Petition

On 12 September 1983, the United States textile industry filed a countervailing duty petition against various textile imports from China.[38] The textile petition represented the first attempt by a United States industry to apply the United States countervailing duty law to imports from a non-market-economy country. The subsidies alleged by the petitioner include (a) an 'internal settlement rate' which is different from the official exchange rate and which is used to convert foreign exchange for Chinese enterprises engaged in foreign trade, (b) preferential access to raw materials and transportation, (c) foreign exchange loans, and (d) preferential tax treatment.[39]

The textile petition raised a significant conceptual problem. The countervailing duty law presumes that the exporting country in question has a private free market for the factors of production, and that the producers in that country compete in that market for labour, raw materials, land, capital, and other inputs to produce the end-products for export. Subsidies conferred by a foreign government are considered unfair because they artificially lower the foreign producers' costs of production and give their exports a competitive edge which they would not have if they had to resort exclusively to the private free market for their factors of production. Accordingly, in order to determine the extent to which the foreign government's action may have unfairly skewed a foreign producer's cost of production (that is, the amount of the subsidy), the bench-mark would be what the producer's cost of production would have been had there been no government involvement. For example, in determining the amount of subsidy when a foreign government extends a low-interest loan to a producer, the USDOC has used as its yardstick the interest rate that the producer would have paid if it had borrowed the money from the private commercial lending market. The problem with applying the countervailing duty law to Chinese textile imports is that China does not have a market economy, and the USDOC is therefore required to speculate what the PRC producer's cost of production would have been had China had a market economy.

Applying the countervailing duty law to PRC imports is politically very sensitive. Unlike the antidumping law, which requires a determination of less-than-fair-value sales on a product-by-product basis, the countervailing duty law aims at government programmes and practices that may cover hundreds or thousands of products. For example, if the 'dual exchange rates' system alleged by the petitioner is found to confer countervailable subsidies, not only will countervailing duties be assessed on the textile products covered by the textile petition, but other petitioners may rely on this determination as a precedent for imposing countervailing duties on other non-textile products. The impact of such a result on the bilateral trade between China and the United States could be disastrous and an affirmative finding of countervailable subsidies could have ramifications that go far beyond the proceedings in question.

Conducting a countervailing duty investigation on PRC imports is also politically very sensitive. Although the respondent in the textile case was the PRC textile exporter, the real issue in that proceeding was whether certain government programmes and practices constitute countervailable subsidies. During an investigation such as this, the USDOC would send a questionnaire to the PRC respondent asking for details of those programmes and practices. This information may be available only from the PRC government, which may view such an investigation as infringing on its sovereign right to set economic policies within its own borders. If the PRC government refused to co-operate in the investigation and the

USDOC did not receive the requested information before the deadline, the USDOC would decide the case on the basis of the 'best available information', which normally means the information alleged in the petition. Because of the potential impact that an adverse finding in the textile case could have on bilateral relations between China and the United States, the Reagan Administration applied pressure 'behind the scenes' on the United States textile industry. Eventually, on 6 December 1983, when the USDOC was scheduled to issue its preliminary determination, the United States textile industry withdrew its petition and the investigation was therefore terminated.[40] As a result, it was unnecessary for the USDOC to decide the issues raised in that case.

D. The Subsequent Application of the Countervailing Duty Law to Non-Market-Economy Countries

In November 1983, several United States steel producers filed two countervailing duty petitions against carbon steel wire rod imported from Poland and Czechoslovakia. The USDOC issued its preliminary determination in February 1984, which ruled (a) that the United States countervailing duty law is applicable to imports from a non-market-economy country, but (b) that the government programmes alleged in the petitions did not constitute countervailable subsidies.[41]

One of the government programmes alleged in the petitions was a multiple exchange rates system. A similar system of multiple exchange rates was also alleged in the petition filed earlier against the PRC textile imports. Although the USDOC did not decide that issue in the textile case, its ruling that the multiple exchange rates system in Poland and Czechoslovakia did not constitute countervailable subsidies would serve as an important precedent if the same issue were raised again with respect to imports from China.[42]

On 7 May 1984, the USDOC issued its final determination in the Polish and Czechoslovakian carbon steel wire rod cases.[43] The USDOC overturned part of its preliminary determination and ruled that the United States countervailing duty law does not apply to imports from a non-market-economy country because, as a matter of law, subsidies cannot be found in countries with non-market economies.[44] On 31 May 1984, the USDOC dismissed two petitions filed under the United States countervailing law against potassium chloride imported from the Soviet Union and East Germany, relying on the final determination it issued in the countervailing duty case involving carbon steel wire rod imported from Poland.[45]

The United States petitioners in the carbon steel wire rod cases and the potassium chloride cases appealed against the USDOC final determinations to the United States Court of International Trade. On 30 July 1985, the Court reversed the decisions of the USDOC in those cases.[46] The Court held that the United States countervailing duty law is applicable to non-market-economy countries and concluded that the error of the USDOC was caused by 'the fundamental misconception that it takes distortion of a "market" to make a subsidy'.[47] In determining whether the government of a non-market-economy country has conferred counter-vailable subsidies, the Court offered the general guideline that the USDOC should 'detect patterns of regularity and investigate beneficial deviations from those patterns'.[48] The USDOC was directed to distin-guish between the normal operation of central government control and the exceptions that amount to favouritism towards the manufacture, pro-duction, or export of particular merchandise.[49]

It is unclear how the general guideline of the United States Court of International Trade will be applied in practice to determine subsidization by the government of a non-market-economy country. In the meantime, the USDOC has appealed from the Court's decision to the Court of Appeals for the Federal Circuit. Unless and until the lower court's de-cision is affirmed by the higher court, the USDOC will continue to take the position that the United States countervailing duty law is not appli-cable to imports from non-market-economy countries.

III. Market Disruption

Section 406 of the Trade Act of 1974 affords a United States industry an avenue for relief from competition from imports from Communist countries.[50] This section was enacted at the same time that the President was authorized to grant 'most favoured nation' treatment to Communist countries. The legislative history makes it clear that Congress feared that enterprises in centrally planned economies might be able to 'flood' the United States domestic market within a shorter time period than could occur under free market conditions.[51]

Section 406(a)(1) provides in pertinent parts as follows:

Upon the filing of a petition...the International Trade Commission...shall promptly make an investigation to determine, with respect to imports of an article which is the product of a Communist country, whether market disruption exists with respect to an article produced by a domestic industry.[52]

'Market disruption' is in turn defined in Section 406(e)(2) as follows:

Market disruption exists within a domestic industry whenever imports of an arti-cle, like or directly competitive with an article produced by such domestic indus-try, are increasing rapidly, either absolutely or relatively, so as to be a significant cause of material injury, or threat thereof, to such domestic industry.[53]

Thus, under Section 406, the USITC may make an affirmative deter-mination only if it finds that the following criteria have been met:
(a) the imports are from a Communist country;
(b) the imports are increasing rapidly;
(c) the domestic industry is materially injured, or threatened with mat-erial injury; and
(d) the increased imports are a significant cause of the material injury or threat thereof.

The Congressional debates which preceded the enactment of Section 406 indicate that Congress was concerned about protecting two separate and distinct interests. When the bill reached the Senate, the Senate Finance Committee amended it and stated in its report that not only domestic United States industries, but also non-Communist foreign suppliers would be permitted to petition for relief.[54] In the Conference Committee Report, however, the conferees made it clear that only domestic United States industries, and not foreign suppliers, were to be protected by the 'market disruption' provisions.[55]

In reaching its determination under Section 406, the USITC will consider factors very similar to those examined in making the injury determination in an antidumping proceeding. The USITC's investigative staff will send a questionnaire to both domestic producers and United States importers to gather information relevant to the competition in the United States markets. It will also request foreign exporters to supply information about the industry in the exporting country, such as production capacity, long-term export plans, and so on.

If the USITC makes a negative finding (that is, that there is no market disruption), the proceedings will be terminated.[56] If the USITC makes an affirmative determination (that is, that market disruption exists), it will recommend the type of import restriction that the President should impose in order to protect the domestic industry.[57] Such import restriction may take one of the following forms:
(a) increased import duty;
(b) quantitative restriction (import quota);
(c) a combination of the above.[58]

Under the statute, the President must decide whether imposing the import restriction recommended by the USITC is 'in the national economic interest of the United States'.[59] The President has delegated this task to the Trade Policy Staff Committee (TPSC), which is chaired by the United States Trade Representative and includes representatives from each department of the Executive Branch, such as Labor, Agriculture, State, and Commerce.

In determining whether the imposition of import restriction is in the national economic interest, the President is required to take into account a number of factors, including the following:
(a) the probable effectiveness of import relief as a means to promote the domestic industry's adjustment to becoming more competitive vis-à-vis the imports;
(b) the effect of the import relief on consumers; and
(c) the effect of import relief on the international economic interests of the United States.[60]

It is thus clear that in determining whether to impose the import restriction recommended by the USITC, the President is not limited to considering only the United States industry that filed the Section 406 petition. Rather, the President has to consider the broader interests of the country, and this makes the proceedings before the TPSC politically very sensitive.

For example, in 1982, the American Mushroom Institute filed a petition under Section 406, alleging that canned mushrooms from the PRC were causing 'market disruption' in the United States. On 21 September 1982, the USITC announced its decision.[61] Two of the four commissioners voted in the affirmative, while the other two ruled that market disruption did not exist.[62] As a result of the tied vote, the case went to the President for his final decision. In the proceedings before the TPSC, the American Mushroom Institute submitted in support of their position a letter signed by more than 200 Congressmen in the House of Representatives.

It happened that the PRC exporter of canned mushrooms in that case, the China National Cereals, Oils and Foodstuffs Import and Export Corporation (CEROILS), also handled grain purchases for China. In 1981, China was the largest purchaser of United States wheat and the fifth largest overall purchaser of grains from the United States. Accordingly, CEROILS was able to obtain the assistance of the trade associations of wheat, soyabean, and grain producers to lobby the TPSC in support of its position. In the end, the President determined that canned mushroom imports from China did not cause market disruption in the United States.

IV. Conclusion

This chapter discusses how three United States import legislative measures are applied to imports from China. It can be seen that the application of these three statutes creates a great deal of uncertainty. In the case of Section 406 of the Trade Act of 1974, the uncertainty is created by the political nature of the proceedings.

In the case of the antidumping law and the countervailing duty law, the uncertainty is created by the fact that the conceptual bases of these two statutes are simply inapplicable to a non-market economy such as that of China. The countervailing duty law was first enacted at the end of the nineteenth century, and the antidumping law in 1916. At that time, there was no significant socialist or non-market economy in the world. These laws were developed to remove artificial barriers to free trade between market economies. Later in the twentieth century, when socialist or non-market economies became a reality, the antidumping law and countervailing duty law were extended to apply to imports from such economies. Because these statutes were developed on the assumption that the United States would be trading with market economies, extending the application of these laws to imports from non-market economies unavoidably created a great deal of uncertainty.

A primary purpose of law is to give public notice of the criteria of lawful conduct, so that a person who does not want to violate the law will know in advance how to comply. The uncertainty created by the United States trade statutes not only defeats such a purpose, but also becomes an impediment to bilateral trade between China and the United States.

Notes

1. 19 United States Code Annotated (USCA) § 1673.
2. 19 USCA § 1673(2).
3. 19 USCA § 1673(1).
4. 19 USCA § 1673a.
5. 19 USCA § 1673a(b)(1) and § 1677(9).
6. 19 USCA § 1677(10).
7. *Zenith Radio Corporation, et. al. v. United States*, Slip Op. 83-82 (CIT 13/4/83).
8. 19 USCA § 1677(7)(C)(iii).
9. 19 USCA § 1677(7)(C)(i) and (ii).
10. 19 USCA § 1677c(a).
11. 19 USCA § 1673 (last clause).
12. 19 USCA § 1677b(c).
13. 19 CFR § 353.8(a).
14. 19 CFR § 353.8(b)(1).
15. 19 CFR § 353.8(b)(1).
16. The USDOC's internal memorandum from Messrs Christopher Parlin and Jeffrey Auspacher of the Office of Policy to Ms Melinda Carmen of the Office of Investigation, undated (Inv. No. A-570-004, Canned Mushrooms from the People's Republic of China), p. 1. (A copy of this memorandum can be found in the public file maintained by the USDOC for that proceeding.)
17. 19 CFR § 353.10.
18. The USDOC first adopted this policy in *Carbon Steel Wire Rod from Poland*, 49 Fed. Reg. 29434 (20 July 1984).
19. See the public file maintained by the USDOC for Investigation No. A-570-007.
20. 19 CFR § 353.8(a)(1).
21. 19 CFR § 353.8(a)(2).
22. 19 CFR § 353.8(b)(1).
23. 19 CFR § 353.16.
24. 19 CFR § 353.15.
25. 19 CFR § 353.8(a).
26. 19 CFR § 353.8.
27. 19 CFR § 353.8.
28. 19 CFR § 353.8.
29. 19 CFR § 353.51.
30. 19 USCA § 1303.
31. 19 USCA §§ 1671 *et seq.*
32. 19 USCA § 1671(a).
33. 19 USCA § 1303.
34. 19 USCA § 1671(b).
35. *Initiation of Countervailing Duty Investigations; Textiles, Apparel, and Related Products from the People's Republic of China*, 48 Fed. Reg. 46600 (13 October 1983).
36. 19 USCA § 1677(5).
37. 19 USCA § 1677(5)(B).
38. *Initiation of Countervailing Duty Investigations; Textiles, Apparel, and Related Products from the People's Republic of China*, 48 Fed. Reg. 46600 (13 October 1983).
39. *Initiation of Countervailing Duty Investigations; Textiles, Apparel, and Related Products from the People's Republic of China*, 48 Fed. Reg. 46600 (13 October 1983).
40. *Textiles, Apparel, and Related Products from the People's Republic of China; Termination of Countervailing Duty Investigations*, 48 Fed. Reg. 55492 (13 December 1983).

41. *Carbon Steel Wire Rod from Poland; Preliminary Negative Countervailing Duty Determination*, 49 Fed. Reg. 6768 (23 February 1984); *Carbon Steel Wire Rod from Czechoslovakia; Preliminary Negative Countervailing Duty Determination*, 49 Fed. Reg. 6773 (23 February 1984).

42. 49 Fed. Reg. 6770 and 6775.

43. *Carbon Steel Wire Rod from Czechoslovakia; Final Negative Countervailing Duty Determination*, 49 Fed. Reg. 19370 (7 May 1984); *Carbon Steel Wire Rod from Poland; Final Negative Countervailing Duty Determination*, 49 Fed. Reg. 19374 (7 May 1984).

44. *Carbon Steel Wire Rod from Czechoslovakia; Final Negative Countervailing Duty Determination*, 49 Fed. Reg. 19370 (7 May 1984); *Carbon Steel Wire Rod from Poland; Final Negative Countervailing Duty Determination*, 49 Fed. Reg. 19374 (7 May 1984).

45. *Potassium Chloride from the Soviet Union; Rescission of Initiation of Countervailing Duty Investigation and Dismissal of Petition*, 49 Fed. Reg. 23428 (6 June 1984); *Potassium Chloride from the German Democratic Republic; Rescission of Initiation of Countervailing Duty Investigation and Dismissal of Petition*, 49 Fed. Reg. 23428 (6 June 1984).

46. *Continental Steel Corp. et al. v. United States*, and *Amax Chemical, Inc. and Kerr-McGee Chemical Corp. v. United States*, Slip Op. 85-77 (CIT 30/7/85).

47. *Continental Steel Corp. et al. v. United States*, and *Amax Chemical, Inc. and Kerr-McGee Chemical Corp. v. United States*, Slip Op. 85-77 (CIT 30/7/85), p. 17.

48. *Continental Steel Corp. et al. v. United States*, and *Amax Chemical, Inc. and Kerr-McGee Chemical Corp. v. United States*, Slip Op. 85-77 (CIT 30/7/85), p. 17.

49. *Continental Steel Corp. et al. v. United States*, and *Amax Chemical, Inc. and Kerr-McGee Chemical Corp. v. United States*, Slip Op. 85-77 (CIT 30/7/85), p. 18.

50. 19 USCA § 2436.

51. S. Rep. No. 93-1298, 93rd Cong., 2nd Sess., p. 210 (1974).

52. 19 USCA § 2436(a)(1).

53. 19 USCA § 2436(e)(2).

54. S. Rep. No. 93-1298, 93rd Cong., 2nd Sess., p. 211 (1974).

55. H. Rep. No. 93-1644, 93rd Cong., 2nd Sess., p. 49 (1974).

56. 19 USCA § 2436(a)(3).

57. 19 USCA § 2436(a)(3).

58. 19 USCA § 2436(a)(3).

59. 19 USCA §§ 2436(b) and § 2252(a).

60. 19 USCA § 2252(c).

61. *Canned Mushrooms from the People's Republic of China*, USITC Inv. No. TA-406-9, USITC Pub. No. 1293(1982).

62. *Canned Mushrooms from the People's Republic of China*, USITC Inv. No. TA-406-9, USITC Pub. No. 1293(1982).

16. The Role of Arbitration in Economic Co-operation with China

JEROME ALAN COHEN

I. Introduction

China's policy of seeking to attract foreign investment and other forms of long-term economic co-operation with the international business community is still very new. For three decades after its founding in 1949, the People's Republic of China (PRC) engaged in the ordinary export and import of goods and conventional shipping activities. Only in 1979 did it begin to emphasize joint ventures, compensation trade arrangements of various types, assembly, processing, co-production, production sharing, leasing, service centres, wholly foreign-owned investments, and bank loans. These new forms of co-operation involve more intensive, extensive, and enduring collaboration with foreign business entities than China has previously experienced. They also require more detailed, complicated contracts than Chinese negotiators have been accustomed to, and the complexity of recording mutual understanding is enhanced by the need to agree upon both Chinese and foreign-language texts for each investment contract and associated legal documents as well as certain other types of contracts.

China's economic development and foreign trade policies are still in the process of evolution. So too is its legal system, which has only recently begun to develop the legislative and institutional infrastructure necessary to facilitate co-operation with private foreign commercial entities. Moreover, the world business environment will continue to be volatile and can be expected to have an increasing impact upon China, itself becoming ever more involved in the world economy. Even if foreign firms can convince Chinese negotiators that their contracts should seek to anticipate all foreseeable problems—an idea that is often resisted—many unanticipated contingencies are likely to occur.

Thus, even in the best of circumstances, disputes will inevitably arise in the interpretation and implementation of the new business contracts that China is concluding with foreign firms. How will these disputes be settled? If they can be disposed of fairly, promptly, and inexpensively, foreign confidence in China as a place to do business will grow, co-operation will expand, and this will have a correspondingly positive effect on China's modernization. If disputes cannot be handled in a mutually satisfactory manner, foreign interest in economic co-operation with China will diminish. China's reputation for settling disputes, like its reputation for paying its debts, will be a fundamental element of its standing in the international market-place.

II. Background

Unfortunately, although the Bank of China has an excellent record in paying its debts, China's record in settling trade and investment disputes is uneven. Since 1949 there have been a great many instances in which contract disputes with Chinese companies have been resolved in a friendly, equitable, and efficient manner generally consistent with the principle of 'equality and mutual benefit' that the Chinese never tire of invoking. Yet there have also been enough cases to the contrary to raise questions about the reliability of China's commitment to standard international dispute resolution processes. In 1958, when China broke off all trade relations with Japan as a result of a political dispute, Japanese firms thought it fruitless to pursue the arbitration remedies prescribed by their contracts with Chinese corporations. They decided instead to swallow their losses and await the opportunities for new profits that would come with the restoration of trade, which occurred in the early 1960s.[1]

During the worst days of the Great Proletarian Cultural Revolution in the late 1960s, when politics again interfered with trade, a number of foreign firms did seek to invoke the arbitration remedies provided by their contracts, but to no avail. In the best-known case, the Red Guards had prevented the Anglo-German firm, the Vickers-Zimmer Company, from completing the construction of a petrochemical plant in north-west China. When the foreign company then requested arbitration in Stockholm in accordance with the contract, China's response was twofold. It ignored the arbitration request and arrested two of the firm's employees as spies, sentencing one to deportation and the other to three years in prison.[2] It also announced that the Intermediate Court for Beijing had decided the civil dispute—without Vickers-Zimmer's participation—holding the foreign company liable for failure to fulfil its obligation under the contract and requiring it to pay precisely the amount of damages it claimed to have suffered, £650,000.[3]

The Vickers-Zimmer case was the worst blow that the Cultural Revolution inflicted on China's reputation for settling disputes. Yet even during the early 1970s European commercial attachés in Beijing regaled visitors with stories of how Chinese trade partners used one flimsy excuse after another to reject requests for arbitration of disputes. Letters would go unanswered. Personal visits would be deflected with promises to 'study the matter' or with entreaties to try a little harder to settle the problem by negotiation. Occasionally Chinese officials would bluntly state that 'a request for arbitration is an unfriendly act', making it plain that foreigners who wanted to continue to do business with China should resolve their problems informally, as other foreigners did.

Of course, during this era a great many disputes were settled to the satisfaction of both parties, through informal means, as are most disputes in the commerce of other countries. Business men and bureaucrats generally prefer to settle disputes through negotiation between the parties or third-party conciliation rather than through arbitration or court decision. This is as true in the China trade as in any other. Furthermore, if it is necessary to resort to some formal means of third-party decision-making to settle an international commercial dispute, Chinese representatives have so far shown a strong preference for arbitration rather than court adjudication. But what has been unique in the China trade has been the extreme reluctance of Chinese entities to seek or to countenance arbitration in the minority of cases in which more informal means of settlement fail to produce, within a reasonable period of time, an outcome acceptable to both parties.

This is not to say that China has lacked institutions for international commercial arbitration. In 1954 the Chinese government established, under the aegis of the China Council for the Promotion of International Trade (CCPIT), a 'non-governmental' organization that is actually part of the state apparatus and is modelled on the Soviet All-Union Chamber of Commerce, the Foreign Trade Arbitration Commission (FTAC).[4] In 1958 the government established a Maritime Arbitration Commission (MAC) under the CCPIT to handle the increasing number of maritime disputes that confronted China.[5] Although both of these institutions have been active, there has been little public evidence of their activity: they have disposed of most of the disputes brought to them without issuing an arbitration award, and, until recently, the awards made have not usually been publicized. Scholars have written learned discourses analysing the many decisions of the Soviet Union's international arbitration tribunals, but few similar materials allow comparable analysis of the work of their Chinese counterparts.[6]

However, the available information indicates that China's reluctance to arbitrate has not been limited to situations involving contracts that call for third-country arbitration or arbitration in the country of the defendant. This reluctance to arbitrate has also extended to contracts that provide for arbitration in China before the FTAC or the MAC. Very few of the cases handled by the two commissions during the late 1970s (approximately fifty per year) were disposed of by proceeding to an arbitration award; all the others were settled through conciliation.[7] Although during the 1980s the number of cases decided by arbitration in China has gradually increased, most disputes that are brought to arbitration continue to be settled by negotiation or conciliation. Moreover, as of mid-1986, in all of China only approximately 100 disputes were being processed by the commercial and maritime arbitration commissions.[8]

Occasionally China has sought to publicize the unique emphasis that its arbitration organs have placed upon conciliation. In October 1963, for example, the Chinese magazine, *Foreign Trade*, carried a lengthy description by the MAC of its successful role as conciliator in a dispute over the proper fee to be charged for Chinese salvage services for a Norwegian vessel that had run aground in Shanghai Harbour. That article took pains to point out the superiority of conciliation over arbitration in arriving at a mutually advantageous solution.[9]

Reference to the role of the judiciary may be useful as a final piece of background information on arbitration. Until very recently China's courts played virtually no part in the settlement of foreign trade disputes. The Vickers-Zimmer case mentioned previously was unusual in this respect as well as in others. Prior to the onset of the Cultural Revolution in 1966, the courts generally were not available to handle such disputes. After 1966 the judiciary was decimated by political turmoil and often served as the tool of 'ultra-leftist' forces hostile to foreign co-operation, as the Vickers-Zimmer judgment and other xenophobic judicial decisions demonstrated. The Chinese courts, which had never inspired foreign confidence, were not restored until the arrest of the ultra-leftist 'Gang of Four' following Chairman Mao's death in the autumn of 1976. And only since 1979, after the promulgation of an amended version of the law for the organization of people's courts, have the courts developed special economic tribunals that are available to decide disputes between Chinese and foreign parties as well as purely domestic matters. The Civil Procedure Code that was enacted on a provisional basis in 1982 has confirmed that Chinese courts are generally to be open to foreign nationals, enterprises, and organizations, although it prevents parties from instituting a suit if they have a written agreement to submit any disputes to a Chinese arbitration organization or if their dispute has already been arbitrated by such an organization.[10]

III. Arbitration

A. The Need to Reconcile International Agreements, Laws, and Regulations

China's new policy of welcoming a broad range of foreign economic co-operation has brought to the fore the entire question of dispute resolution, and of arbitration in particular. Foreign governments concerned with providing adequate dispute resolution facilities for their nationals engaged in the China trade have sought to negotiate assurances with China. The most elaborate provision thus far concluded is Article VIII of the Sino-American trade agreement of 7 July 1979, which states:

1. The Contracting Parties encourage the prompt and equitable settlement of any disputes arising from or in relation to contracts between their respective firms, companies and corporations, and trading organizations, through friendly consultations, conciliation or other mutually acceptable means.
2. If such disputes cannot be settled promptly by any one of the above-mentioned means, the parties to the dispute may have recourse to arbitration for settlement in accordance with provisions specified in their contracts or other agreements to submit to arbitration. Such arbitration may be conducted by an arbitration institution in the People's Republic of China, the United States of America, or a third country. The arbitration rules of procedure of the relevant arbitration institution are applicable and the arbitration rules of the United Nations Commission on International Trade Law recommended by the United Nations, or other international arbitration rules, may also be used where acceptable to the parties to the dispute and to the arbitration institution.

3. Each Contracting Party shall seek to ensure that arbitration awards are recognized and enforced by their competent authorities where enforcement is sought, in accordance with applicable laws and regulations.[11]

This leaves it to the parties to each contract to decide how to deal with arbitration. In agreements with certain other governments China has been more specific, stipulating that in commercial disputes between entities of the two countries any necessary arbitration shall take place in the country of the defendant.[12]

The question of the resolution of disputes between Chinese and foreigners has now been dealt with in a number of pieces of China's legislation. For example, Article 14 of the Law of the People's Republic of China on Joint Ventures Using Chinese and Foreign Investment (hereafter cited as the Joint Venture Law), promulgated on 8 July 1979, states:

Disputes arising between the parties to a joint venture that the board of directors cannot settle through consultation may be settled through conciliation or arbitration by a Chinese arbitration agency or through arbitration by another arbitration agency agreed upon by the parties to the venture.[13]

Again, it is up to the parties to the transaction to decide, if consultation (that is, direct negotiation) fails, whether to resort to conciliation prior to arbitration; they may also decide whether arbitration is to take place in China or abroad. The 1982 Regulations of the People's Republic of China on the Exploitation of Offshore Petroleum Resources in Co-operation with Foreign Enterprises (hereafter cited as the Petroleum Regulations) contain an almost identical provision.[14]

Article 37 of the Law of the People's Republic of China on Economic Contracts Involving Foreign Interests (hereafter cited as the Foreign Economic Contract Law), which came into effect on 1 July 1985, provides, in relation to all contracts between Chinese and foreign economic enterprises and bodies, that if consultation and mediation between the parties are unsuccessful the parties may submit the dispute between them to a Chinese arbitral body or another arbitral body for arbitration, in accordance with the arbitration provisions in the contract or a subsequent written arbitration agreement. If the parties did not include an arbitration clause in the contract and did not subsequently conclude an arbitration agreement, they are entitled to sue in the people's courts, pursuant to Article 38.[15]

These provisions, as well as the international treaties entered into by China, make it clear that arbitration, whether before a Chinese or a foreign arbitral body, is a permissible (and, in fact, a favoured) method of dispute resolution. The courts, of course, may become involved in the recognition and enforcement of arbitration awards, but Chinese arbitration specialists have long taken the position that China's courts do not entertain cases of foreign trade and maritime disputes when an arbitration agreement is in force. This position has been supported by the Civil Procedure Code (cited hereafter as the Code), as well as by Article 37 of the Foreign Economic Contract Law.

The language of the Code suggests, however, that the existence of a written agreement to submit disputes to a tribunal other than one convened by a foreign arbitration organization of the PRC, or actual arbitration by a non-Chinese tribunal, may not prevent the parties from filing suit in a Chinese court.[16] The provisions in the Code refer repeatedly to arbitration before an arbitral body of the PRC having responsibility for resolving disputes involving foreign nationals and do not refer to arbitration before a foreign arbitral body, although, even at the time the Code was drafted, it must have been known that many agreements providing for arbitration before a foreign arbitral body had been entered into.

Chinese judicial and trade officials, however, do not seem to believe that the Code should be interpreted in a literal fashion with respect to this question, precisely because to do so would yield an outrageous result that would strike a blow against China's foreign trade and investment contracts. The 1983 Implementing Act for the Joint Venture Law (hereafter cited as the Joint Venture Implementing Act) provides support for the view of these Chinese officials, precluding the parties to a joint venture contract from bringing suit in China if they have entered into a written arbitration agreement, without specifying that the agreement must call for arbitration by a Chinese organization.[17]

The position has been to some extent clarified by the enactment of the Foreign Economic Contract Law, which, as set out above, allows parties to institute suit in the absence of an agreement to arbitrate before a Chinese or other arbitral body. This suggests that such a party may not go to court in China if there is such an agreement, although Article 38 does not make this explicit. Similarly, the Article does not indicate what status the arbitration award of a foreign arbitral body, once made, has in China and whether its existence precludes a Chinese court from re-examining the merits of the dispute that was the subject of the award.

The provisions of the Code give rise to further questions. What is a 'foreign arbitration organization of the PRC'? For example, if the foreign and Chinese parties to a contract agree to arbitrate any disputes in China under the Arbitration Rules of the United Nations Commission on International Trade Law (UNCITRAL), will that arrangement meet the statutory standard?

Moreover, what does Article 193 mean by providing that 'When a case has been arbitrated by a foreign affairs arbitration organization of the PRC, the parties shall not be permitted to file a lawsuit in the people's courts'? When has a case 'been arbitrated'—at the moment when the dispute was submitted to the tribunal or only after an award has been rendered? This, too, is a practical problem of some significance. For example, if in the course of an arbitration hearing one party is dissatisfied with the proceedings and brings a lawsuit over the dispute, will a Chinese court refuse to entertain the suit because of Article 193 on the ground that the case 'has been arbitrated'?

Both the Civil Procedure Code and Article 38 of the Foreign Economic Contract Law suggest that, when deciding between forms of dispute resolution, the parties are always free to choose a judicial solution rather than arbitration. Yet foreign business men must take account of applicable international agreements and special Chinese legislation, which sometimes complicate the situation, particularly as the relationship between what appear to be conflicting legislative provisions is by no means clear.

There should be no problem under the Sino-American trade agreement, which authorizes the parties to settle their dispute 'through friendly consultations, conciliation or *other mutually acceptable means*' (my italics). Yet the Joint Venture Law and the Petroleum Regulations (both of which were promulgated before the Civil Procedure Code came into force) refer only to the possibility of arbitration. In China's first highly publicized manufacturing joint venture, the Schindler elevator transaction, which was approved in 1980, the contract originally provided for the settlement of disputes before the ordinary courts of the domicile of the defendant, but, upon review by the Foreign Investment Commission (now merged into the Ministry of Foreign Economic Relations and Trade, MOFERT), this provision was dropped in favour of an arbitration clause. With respect to joint ventures, the 1983 Joint Venture Implementing Act makes it clear that 'the parties may resolve their dispute through arbitration or *judicial means*' (my italics).[18] There has not yet been a clarification concerning the Petroleum Regulations, although Article 37 of the Foreign Economic Contract Law indicates that a judicial resolution must be possible. It should be noted that many judicial and trade officials still believe that the new economic tribunals of the courts should play a secondary role, enforcing arbitration awards but not displacing arbitration.

The option of bringing a lawsuit, however, is also provided for specifically in other legislation affecting foreign interests. The Regulations on Labour Management in Joint Ventures Using Chinese and Foreign Investment (hereafter cited as the Labour Regulations) provide that, if consultation between the parties fails to settle a joint venture labour dispute, any party to the venture may request arbitration by the provincial-level labour management department with jurisdiction over the venture, but, 'if one party does not accept the arbitration award, it may file a suit in the people's courts'.[19] Similarly, the 1981 Economic Contract Law gives the parties to a dispute the option of immediately initiating a lawsuit if consultation fails, instead of seeking mediation or arbitration by state contract administration authorities.[20] The 1983 Regulations on the Arbitration of Economic Contracts make it clear that this option is open even if one party to the contract seeks to institute arbitration.[21] If arbitration is selected and any party is not satisfied with the award, that party may file a lawsuit within fifteen days of receipt of the award. The economic contract legislation was designed to govern relations between domestic entities, including transactions between a Chinese-foreign joint venture and a Chinese enterprise. Neither the Labour Regulations nor the economic contract legislation make clear the nature of the lawsuit that may be brought by a party dissatisfied with an arbitration award. Whether the court is to conduct a *de novo* hearing or a more limited review of the merits of the case is not stated.

One possible method of dispute resolution that is not covered in legislation is that of permitting the parties to submit to the exclusive jurisdiction of a particular court system. It is therefore not possible to say, if a Chinese enterprise could be persuaded to agree to the exclusive jurisdiction of a foreign court, whether a Chinese court would refuse to entertain an action on the grounds that it did not have jurisdiction and whether a dispute could or could not be withdrawn from the Chinese courts on such a ground. This also relates to the general question of the basis on which a Chinese court will take jurisdiction over foreigners, a question to which the Code does not provide a satisfactory answer.

As China concludes new international agreements and promulgates special legislation regarding compensation trade, co-operative ventures, leasing, bank loans, and other forms of foreign economic co-operation, it will be necessary to take careful note of the extent to which these norms differ from the general framework established by the Civil Procedure Code and the Foreign Economic Contract Law.

B. Recent Developments Concerning Conciliation

Before discussing arbitration problems *per se*, we should touch upon some interesting developments with respect to conciliation, particularly the advent of joint conciliation of international economic disputes and the articulation in the Civil Procedure Code of what appears to be almost a compulsory conciliation procedure for litigated disputes.

Although China has necessarily begun to pay more attention to both arbitration and litigation than in the past, it continues to emphasize the desirability of settling disputes through conciliation. In recent years Chinese arbitration tribunals have continued their previous practice of making an award only when the dispute cannot be settled through conciliation. If either party insists on avoiding conciliation and going directly to arbitration, although this is not recommended, it is permissible unless it would violate a compulsory conciliation clause in the contract. Yet Chinese arbitration specialists make it plain that, ideally, consultation, conciliation, and arbitration are three successive stages, and their hope is that disputes can be settled at the first or second stage.

Similarly, the Civil Procedure Code provides that 'If a civil case that has been accepted by a people's court can be conciliated, the court should... conduct conciliation and urge the parties to understand each other's positions and reach an agreement.'[22] Although the Code further provides that 'If no agreement can be reached through conciliation, ...the people's court should conduct a trial and not prolong conciliation without resolving the issue',[23] so strong is the preference for informal settlement that the Code even authorizes further conciliation at the conclusion of the trial following the final arguments of the parties and prior to judgment,[24] and allows for conciliation during any appeal against the judgment.[25]

If read literally, the Joint Venture Law and the Petroleum Regulations suggest that, while arbitration of disputes may be conducted in China or abroad, conciliation may only be conducted by a Chinese arbitration institution. But in fact, as Chinese specialists have explained, conciliation under these laws may take place in any location and be conducted by non-Chinese as well as Chinese.

Moreover, in order to meet the concern for equality and mutual benefit, the CCPIT and the American Arbitration Association (AAA) began to experiment some years ago with joint conciliation for resolving disputes in Sino-American trade. Under this arrangement each organization appoints a conciliator, and the two co-operate in helping the parties to find a solution. Joint conciliation has already been successful in the trade area, and can be expected to operate in joint ventures and other forms of co-operation as well. The CCPIT subsequently decided to use joint conciliation to resolve problems arising under all Chinese commercial contracts, not merely those with American firms. It refers a dispute to a commission of two to six persons, composed of equal numbers from the CCPIT and an approved sponsoring organization from the country of the other party.[26] Alternatively, joint conciliation can simply take the form of the very informal *ad hoc* co-operation of two or more persons representing the respective parties. Chinese officials state that there have been many joint conciliations between European and Chinese companies in recent years.

Thus far, very few contracts have specifically referred to joint conciliation. The failure of contracts to provide for this new technique is not remarkable, however, in view of the fact that many contracts make no reference to conciliation in any form, despite its prominence in the China trade. Rather, they often give the impression that the parties will or should proceed directly from consultation between themselves to arbitration. Nevertheless, an increasing number of investment contracts contain a conciliation clause. Some joint venture contracts, for example, simply provide for the CCPIT's Foreign Economic and Trade Arbitration Commission (FETAC)—the former FTAC—to conciliate any dispute that the Board of Directors cannot settle. Another such contract authorizes conciliation by either the FETAC or an *ad hoc* panel composed of one conciliator appointed by each of the two parties and a third appointed by the first two conciliators. These contracts make it clear that arbitration is to occur only if conciliation fails.

It is highly unlikely that a foreign investor or trader would object to conciliation as a matter of principle. The experience of many countries demonstrates that conciliation can settle a large number of disputes and possesses distinct virtues. No one is eager to submit to arbitration or litigation. Yet, as the Civil Procedure Code recognizes,[27] an objection arises if conciliation drags on to the point of denying one or both of the parties a desired opportunity to conclude the dispute through a determination on the merits of the case. This is why some foreign firms have persuaded their Chinese counterparts to insert time limits into the dispute resolution clauses of their contracts, prescribing, for example, that if the conciliation process proves ineffective ninety days after it has been invoked, either party may initiate arbitration proceedings. Some parties

favour a clause that simply permits either party to resort to arbitration at
any time during conciliation.

C. The Site of Arbitration and the Designated Institution

As we have seen, both China's domestic legislation and its international
agreements authorize Chinese commercial entities to conclude contracts
that call for the arbitration of disputes abroad as well as at home. Yet
negotiations in many contexts have made it clear that China continues to
prefer that arbitration take place in China rather than abroad. Foreign
investors, however, have generally maintained the same attitudes as foreign firms that have exported major capital goods or have licensed technology to China—they tend to find arbitration in China an unacceptable
option in the present circumstances. Although they prefer arbitration in
their own country, they realize that this is likely to be unacceptable to the
Chinese. Some investors put forth such a suggestion in their earliest draft
contract, retreating to third-country arbitration as a second line of defence. Others simply start by proposing third-country arbitration.

When confronted with a foreign party's request for third-country
arbitration, the Chinese side frequently responds with one of two alternative proposals. According to one alternative, the Chinese party suggests
arbitration in the country where the defendant is domiciled. As previously mentioned, this principle appears in some of China's intergovernmental agreements, and has long been used in certain trade contracts. In
providing for arbitration or litigation of disputes arising under insurance
contracts for ocean marine or overland transportation, the People's Insurance Company of China prescribes that each shall take place where the
defendant is domiciled. And in insuring foreign investors against political
risks, the People's Insurance Company also provides for arbitration in the
defendant's domicile. A second Chinese alternative is to suggest that the
contract provide for arbitration in China unless the parties, at the time a
dispute occurs, agree upon arbitration elsewhere. For example, China's
Model Contract for Offshore Petroleum Co-operation with Foreign
Companies refers disputes to an arbitration body of China or to another
arbitration body agreed upon by the parties.

Potential foreign investors tend to reject both of these alternatives as
too similar in effect to a provision that calls for arbitration in China. They
believe that in most circumstances that concern them the Chinese party
would be the defendant, and thus in their view the formula that prescribes
arbitration in the defendant's domicile is tantamount to prescribing
arbitration in China. Moreover, they know from experience in other
jurisdictions that such a formula leads the parties to a dispute to manipu-
late their relationship in an effort to emerge as the defendant. The second
alternative is equally unacceptable for it simply offers a pious hope that, if
a dispute should occur, the Chinese party might agree to substitute third-
country arbitration for submission in China even though it refuses to
do so while the contract is being negotiated, when relations are still un-
marred by a dispute.

By and large, the result of this bargaining has thus far been that China accepts third-country arbitration in investment and loan contracts as well as in contracts for the purchase of capital goods and for the licensing of technology. In approving investment contracts, MOFERT seems to prefer Stockholm arbitration under the auspices of the Arbitration Institute of the Stockholm Chamber of Commerce to London, Geneva, or other possibilities. This has been true of many hotel and other service joint ventures and many manufacturing joint ventures, including the Schindler elevator transaction. The Schindler agreement originally provided that any party could invoke London arbitration if it did not wish to have the dispute decided in the ordinary courts of the defendant's domicile. After review by the Foreign Investment Commission, however, that provision was replaced by one that simply calls for Stockholm arbitration. Of course, the foreign investor in that transaction, the Jardine-Schindler Company, is a Hong Kong entity owned in part by Hong Kong British interests. Some loan agreements provide for Stockholm arbitration, but others do not. For example, there have been some semi-syndicated and bilateral foreign loan agreements in which the Bank of China has accepted the London Court of Arbitration for the arbitration of non-British loans, and the Zurich Chamber of Commerce for the arbitration of certain non-Swiss loans. Investment contracts that do not require the approval of the national government also constitute an occasional exception to the preference for Stockholm. For example, in at least one equity joint venture approved by Guangdong province, disputes are supposed to be arbitrated in London by three arbitrators pursuant to the UNCITRAL Rules.

What future policy will be is uncertain. If at the outset of every negotiation China is prepared to accept Stockholm or other third-country arbitration, the parties will be able to save a good deal of time and devote their energies to other questions. This does occur in some instances, and CCPIT arbitration specialists have stated that China generally agrees to Stockholm arbitration in foreign trade contracts. Yet one still encounters the odd negotiation in the provinces when Chinese representatives adamantly assert that China never accepts any third-country arbitration.

In view of the current close contacts between the CCPIT and the American Arbitration Association (AAA), it will be especially interesting to see whether MOFERT will accept arbitration in the United States under AAA auspices in a situation where one party to the venture is a Chinese entity and the foreign party is not American. China has already approved resort to the Court of Arbitration of the Zurich Chamber of Commerce in a contract that calls for an investment in China by a Swedish group.

The negotiations concerning China's offshore oil co-operation with foreign companies have yielded some interesting provisions regarding arbitration, although there is an inevitable time-lag, due to confidentiality restrictions, before such information becomes public. At least one early contract provided that, if the parties fail to resolve any dispute through friendly negotiations within ninety days of its occurrence, they may agree upon arbitration in China before the FETAC, but, if they do not agree upon the FETAC, then within thirty days of the expiration of the ninety-day period they may agree either to submit the matter to an international arbitration agency for resolution under its rules or to submit it for resolution by an *ad hoc* tribunal to be organized under a given set of international arbitration rules. If they fail to reach agreement on this choice, the Chinese party is required, within fifteen days of the end of the thirty-day period, to select an international arbitration organization from a list composed of the Arbitration Institute of the Stockholm Chamber of Commerce (for arbitration in Stockholm); the International Center for the Settlement of Investment Disputes (ICSID) with headquarters in Washington; and any other arbitration institution that the parties may agree to add to the list. Or, if the Chinese party prefers, it may decide not to choose any of the listed agencies and instead agree to arbitration under the UNCITRAL Arbitration Rules.

Perhaps the most interesting aspect of this imaginative and flexible compromise is China's willingness to list the ICSID as a potential agency for arbitration. The ICSID, which is part of the World Bank system, has been eager to have China adhere to the ICSID arrangements ever since China joined the World Bank. Although China has not yet decided to participate in the ICSID, the contractual provision described above is the most tangible evidence thus far available of its possible interest.

Nevertheless, at least some of the subsequent offshore oil contracts with foreign companies do not mention the ICSID and set forth a simpler formula than the earlier one. It provides that, if the parties fail to agree on FETAC arbitration, they shall form an *ad hoc* tribunal under the UNCITRAL Arbitration Rules, with each side selecting one member of the tribunal and the two thus selected in turn choosing the third member from the nationals of a country that maintains diplomatic relations with both China and the countries of the foreign oil companies involved.

Certainly there may be advantages to China in selecting a single foreign jurisdiction and arbitration institution for the settlement of most disputes outside China, especially at a time when China is still new to the actualities of international commercial arbitration. It would be difficult for the officials of any country in such a situation to become familiar with the variety of places and foreign arbitration organizations as well as the relevant legal environment in each jurisdiction. Concentrating on one place and one organization should simplify matters. China's general preference for Stockholm and the Arbitration Institute of the Stockholm Chamber of Commerce appears to be grounded in careful analysis based on continuing close contacts with officials of the Institute.

Yet other places, some of them much less distant from China than Stockholm and therefore, from the Chinese viewpoint, less expensive and more convenient as a forum, are beginning to vie for selection as a suitable site. For a time Tokyo seemed to be gaining favour in some quarters in China, not only because of geographic propinquity but also because of the belief that Japanese arbitrators might be more capable of understanding China's circumstances and attitudes toward law and contracts than would Europeans.

Hong Kong has more recently established itself as an arbitration centre for the Asian region and hopes to create conditions that will make it an attractive site for the settlement of China-related disputes. Hong Kong is geographically contiguous to China and relations between it and China are increasingly cordial. Hong Kong has strong linguistic, cultural, and economic bonds with China, and China has a great many government offices and companies operating there. Thus considerations of convenience would appear to favour Hong Kong arbitration. On the other hand, the CCPIT has established a branch of the FETAC in the Shenzhen Special Economic Zone of Guangdong province near Hong Kong, in order to facilitate on-the-spot resolution of disputes that arise from activities related to the zone. Initially, political sensitivity and competitive considerations appeared to lead Chinese arbitration experts to promote the Shenzhen organization while remaining unenthusiastic about Hong Kong as a forum for arbitration. However, now that China and the United Kingdom have reached accord on the restoration of China's sovereignty over Hong Kong in 1997, China seems willing to co-operate in promoting Hong Kong as an arbitral forum. Indeed, several Chinese-owned institutions, including the Bank of China, have made financial donations towards the establishment of the Hong Kong International Arbitration Centre. CCPIT officials have also begun to support the idea of arbitration in Hong Kong and to co-operate with the Centre. For example, the FETAC, responding to a request from the Centre, recently provided it with the names of ten Chinese experts who are available to serve as arbitrators under the auspices of the Centre.

If Hong Kong has indeed won the support of China as an arbitral forum, the interesting question now is whether Hong Kong will also be able to win the support of foreign parties, so that it may emerge as the leading arbitral forum in China business matters.

D. The Rules of Procedure

Under Chinese practice, the parties to a contract are free to choose the rules of procedure applicable to arbitration as well as the place of arbitration. More often than not, when a given institution is authorized to facilitate arbitration, Chinese contracts provide for the rules of procedure of that institution to apply. Although contracts that provide for arbitration in China generally state that it shall be conducted under the provisional rules of procedure of the relevant Chinese institution, in the Chinese view such a statement is not necessary. Chinese contract references to arbitration in the defendant's domicile do not usually mention anything about rules of procedure. Contract references to third-country arbitration frequently specify the rules to be used, normally those of the named organization. For example, one joint venture contract provides that:

In the event such conciliation cannot resolve the dispute, the matter shall be brought before the arbitration panel of the Stockholm Chamber of Commerce, Sweden, for arbitration, and shall proceed according to the arbitration regulations and procedure of that arbitration organization. The decision of the arbitration shall be final and will be binding on both parties.

Sometimes, however, the contract merely authorizes arbitration in Stockholm, adding only that the arbitration decision shall be final and binding on both parties.

Even while prescribing that the rules of a designated third-country institution shall be applied, Chinese contracts sometimes single out certain of those rules for emphasis or stipulate details that the rules contemplate will be agreed to by the parties or that modify the rules in some respects. For example, several Chinese-foreign loan agreements that authorize London arbitration, after stating that the rules of the London Court of Arbitration shall apply, go on to provide that the tribunal shall consist of three arbitrators, one selected by each of the two parties and the third by the London Court of Arbitration, and that the tribunal shall state in writing the reasons for its decision. Some such agreements spell out that the language of the proceedings shall be English. And it is not uncommon, as some of these loan agreements illustrate, for contracts to state that the rules to be applied are those of the relevant institution that are in effect on the date the contract is signed. This is usually inserted at the request of foreign parties who are concerned that the rules might subsequently be altered in unacceptable ways.

Consistent with its belief that the parties are free to choose the applicable rules of procedure, China is also willing, as the Sino-American trade agreement indicates, to substitute other international arbitration rules for those of the designated institution, if this is acceptable to the other parties and the designated institution. For example, China is happy to use the UNCITRAL Arbitration Rules under the administration of the Arbitration Institute of the Stockholm Chamber of Commerce, and, as the offshore oil contracts illustrate, some contracts call for an *ad hoc* tribunal to be constituted under the UNCITRAL Rules, sometimes designating the place of arbitration and at other times omitting any reference to the place.

Only the rules of the International Chamber of Commerce (ICC) remain unacceptable to Beijing. This is not because the ICC is *persona non grata* in Chinese eyes or because of any dissatisfaction with the rules themselves or the high costs of ICC arbitration, but because of Taiwan's continuing participation in the ICC. When this political question is resolved, the ICC rules should enjoy the same respect in Beijing's eyes as the UNCITRAL Rules and others. Both the Chinese and the foreign parties to the Schindler elevator joint venture contract were apparently unaware of this obstacle, for the contract originally provided, as an alternative to litigation in the defendant's domicile, for London arbitration in accordance with ICC rules. As should have been expected, upon review of the contract the Foreign Investment Commission disapproved this clause, and the parties had to remove not only the litigation option but also the reference to the ICC: they substituted arbitration under the Arbitration Institute of the Stockholm Chamber of Commerce.

For several years China has been considering whether to revise the rules of procedure of its own arbitration institutions. The State Council did approve a change of name for the Foreign Trade Arbitration Commission, which is now known as the Foreign Economic and Trade Arbitration Commission (FETAC). The new name is meant to symbolize the anticipated expansion of the Commission's work as it prepares to 'take cognizance of the disputes arising from the implementation of agreements and contracts in utilizing foreign funds, joint ventures, foreign technology, co-production by Chinese and foreign firms and compensation trade'.[28]

Although the language of the FETAC's rules, like its original name, is broad enough to encompass these transactions, some Chinese experts think it may be appropriate to change the rules to take account specifically of China's recent participation in such transactions. It is also reported that the Commission 'will be enlarged in proportion to the expansion of its business scope'.[29]

Whether significant changes will actually be made in the Commission's rules and practice remains unclear. One change that Chinese officials have considered would be to permit non-Chinese to serve as members of the arbitration tribunal to be constituted under the auspices of the FETAC. Because the rules have so far required all arbitrators to be chosen from among the members of the Commission, who are all Chinese, many foreign firms have preferred third-country arbitration in order to reduce the risk of confronting a potentially biased panel. Although both the FETAC and the MAC are said to be opposed to 'national egoism in making use of arbitration to favour the party of their own nationality',[30] foreigners would have more confidence in arbitration in China if membership in the tribunal were more broadly based. The FETAC took a first step towards that goal when it established its Shenzhen branch, which listed eight Hong Kong Chinese among its roster of fifteen available arbitrators. Whether the FETAC will now move to add foreigners to that roster remains to be seen.

Even if the rules of these institutions are not changed to allow foreign arbitrators, the contracting parties could provide for foreign representation on an arbitration tribunal, with the arbitration still being conducted in China, by inserting into their contract a clause that calls for UNCITRAL arbitration to take place in China.

E. The Enforcement of Awards

Although Chinese contracts usually state that the arbitration award shall be final and binding upon the parties, they often make no provision for enforcement. China has concluded a number of bilateral trade agreements and navigation treaties that, like the Sino-American trade agreement, obligate the participating governments to strive to ensure that arbitration awards are recognized and enforced by their competent authorities in accordance with applicable laws and regulations. Yet such provisions are general expressions that lack specific assurances and procedures. China hesitated for many years before deciding to join any of the international conventions for the enforcement of foreign arbitral awards, studying the implications of participating in such conventions. The 1982 enactment of China's first Civil Procedure Code was said by some Chinese officials to have been a necessary prerequisite to adherence to these multilateral conventions.

Finally, this situation changed with respect to many arbitral awards on 2 December 1986, when China agreed to adhere to the United Nations Convention on the Recognition and Enforcement of Foreign Arbitral Awards of 1958 (hereafter cited as the New York Convention). The New York Convention entered into force with respect to China ninety days after deposit of China's instrument of accession, which occurred on 22 January 1987. For awards involving commercial matters rendered in other contracting states the New York Convention now mandates enforcement by Chinese courts, with some exceptions to be discussed below. The legal framework for enforcing other awards will continue to be shaped by Chinese domestic law and practice.

There has been little experience with arbitration awards in the China trade. Although a large number of contracts with Chinese companies have provided for arbitration in Stockholm, as of 1 March 1987 no award had ever been made by a Stockholm panel relating to any such contract. Moreover, the number of FETAC awards each year, although increasing, is still very small. There is even less experience with respect to the enforcement of such awards. Knowledgeable Chinese officials have asserted that, since the founding of the People's Republic, there has not been a single case in which China's courts have decreed the enforcement of an award involving foreign interests. This is said to be because Chinese foreign trade and maritime entities are state-owned enterprises that recognize that a Chinese arbitration award has the force of law and must be executed by the parties within the time prescribed. Thus there has been no need to seek court enforcement. Even before the promulgation of the Civil Procedure Code, Chinese officials claimed that, should a Chinese enterprise fail to respect a Chinese award, the people's courts would accept a petition from the other party for enforcement.[31] Indeed, the governmental decisions establishing China's two principal arbitration commissions state that their awards are to be final, that 'neither party shall bring an appeal for revision before a court of law or any other organization', and that Chinese courts shall, upon the request of a party, enforce the award of these commissions in accordance with the law.[32]

Article 195 of the new Code confirms this arrangement. It provides that:

When one of the parties concerned fails to comply with an award made by a foreign arbitration organization of the PRC, the other party may request that the award be enforced in accordance with the provisions of this Code by the intermediate people's court in the place where the arbitration organization is located or where the property is located.

How the courts will carry out this mandate—for example, what the scope of their review of Chinese awards will be in an enforcement proceeding—is a matter of considerable interest to foreign companies.

Because the new forms of economic co-operation between China and the industrialized nations generally provide for arbitration outside China, the recognition and enforcement of foreign awards in China is a topic of even greater concern to foreigners. Responsible Chinese officials have long offered assurances that 'Chinese corporations and enterprises will, in fact, execute foreign arbitral awards so long as they are fair and not in violation of the Chinese laws and policies.'[33] In the event of the non-execution of awards, foreigners have been advised in the past by CCPIT officials not only to petititon the Chinese government department concerned but also to request the assistance of the CCPIT in persuading the Chinese party to carry out the award, or to seek enforcement through the people's courts.

In what circumstances can foreigners successfully seek enforcement of foreign awards through the Chinese courts?

Now that China's adherence to the New York Convention has become effective, foreign awards covered by the Convention, which will include the vast majority of awards, should be enforced upon presentation of the duly authenticated original award or duly certified copy thereof and the original agreement with respect to arbitration, in addition to a certified Chinese translation of both such documents. The Convention states that:

Each Contracting State shall recognize arbitral awards as binding and enforce them in accordance with the rules of procedure of the territory where the award is relied upon, under the conditions laid down in the following articles. There shall not be imposed substantially more onerous conditions or higher fees or charges on the recognition or enforcement of arbitral awards to which this Convention applies than are imposed on the recognition or enforcement of domestic arbitral awards.

Thus, under the New York Convention, the conditions on enforcing a foreign award should not be more onerous than those provided in Article 195 of the Civil Procedure Code.

When enforcement of an award is sought in court, however, the New York Convention does provide for certain defences, on the basis of which the request for enforcement may be refused. Most of these defences involve specific legal issues such as incapacity of the parties, invalidity of the agreement, lack of notice, lack of opportunity to present one's case, rendering of an award outside the scope of the arbitral agreement, invalidity of the arbitral authority or procedure in light of the parties' agreement or the law of the country in which the award was made, and lack of binding force of the award. Two other defences are more general. The Convention states that:

Recognition and enforcement of an arbitral award may also be refused if the competent authority in the country where recognition and enforcement is sought finds that:

(a) The subject matter of the difference is not capable of settlement by arbitration under the law of that country; or

(b) The recognition or enforcement of the award would be contrary to the public policy of that country.

Since the Chinese Civil Procedure Code provides for the enforcement by courts of arbitral awards with respect to disputes involving foreign nationals, and contemplates arbitration as a means of settling disputes arising from foreign economic relations, trade, transportation, or maritime affairs, sub-paragraph (a) should not present an obstacle to the enforcement of most arbitral awards. The real usefulness of the New York Convention for the enforcement of awards in China will depend in part on China's interpretation of sub-paragraph (b). The concept of public policy is notoriously flexible in China and occurs throughout Chinese law as an exception to various legal requirements. Only experience will indicate whether China's application of this concept to the enforcement of arbitral awards is in conformity with international practice.

For arbitral awards not covered by the Convention, the legal situation continues to be unclear. Even if the contract in question provides for enforcement of a foreign award 'by any court of competent jurisdiction' or 'in an ordinary court of law', such phrases do not make clear the prerequisites to judicial enforcement, and in any event cannot control the standards prescribed in the Civil Procedure Code for enforcement by Chinese courts. The Code appears to preclude direct judicial enforcement of a foreign award. Article 195, as mentioned above, only authorizes direct enforcement of an award made by 'a foreign arbitration organization of the PRC'. Article 195 is part of Chapter 20, entitled 'Arbitration', which is exclusively concerned with arbitration in China.

The possibility of enforcing a foreign arbitral award on the basis of Chinese law apart from the New York Convention must be considered in connection with Chapter 22, entitled 'Judicial Assistance'. This chapter is exclusively concerned with legal actions that Chinese courts and foreign courts may entrust each other to take on behalf of the other. Article 202, after establishing the general principle of mutual entrustment, authorizes a Chinese court to reject a case entrusted to the court 'if it violates the sovereignty and security of the PRC'. Article 204 provides that:

In dealing with a judgment or award that has already been confirmed and that a foreign court has entrusted a people's court of the PRC to enforce, the people's court shall examine the judgment or award on the basis of an international treaty concluded or participated in by the PRC or in accordance with the principles of reciprocity and shall determine to recognize the legal effect of such judgment or award and enforce the same according to procedures prescribed by this Code if the court believes that such a judgment or award does not violate the basic principles of the laws of the PRC or the interests of our country's state and society. Otherwise the matter shall be returned to the foreign court.

The structure appears to require that the enforcement of a foreign award not covered by the New York Convention be requested by a foreign court and suggests that the participation in that award by a foreign court (though not necessarily a court of the jurisdiction in which the award was made) is a prerequisite to enforcement in China.[34] Moreover, it is not known what kinds of awards will be deemed to violate the basic principles of Chinese law or the interests of the Chinese state and society, but plainly these criteria give great latitude to the courts. The courts, however, may interpret these standards along the lines of the 'public policy' exception applied by other countries in order to assure maximum international judicial co-operation.

If seeking initial confirmation by a foreign court seems too burdensome or if a foreign court will not request enforcement, perhaps the only alternative open to the party seeking satisfaction of the award would be to initiate a regular civil suit in China and to rely on the award as evidence in support of its claim.

In general, the Code stresses both international custom and reciprocity, and the ease with which foreign awards will be enforced in China even apart from the New York Convention will probably depend considerably on the treatment afforded to Chinese awards in the courts of foreign states.

F. Applicable Law

Until the enactment of the Foreign Economic Contract Law, which came into effect on 1 July 1985, it was not clear whether the parties had the autonomy to choose the law applicable to the contract between them. Article 5 of the Foreign Economic Contract Law, however, states:

The parties to a contract may choose the law to be applied to the handling of contract disputes. In cases where the parties have not chosen the applicable law, the law of the country with the closest relation to the contract is to be applied.

The law of the People's Republic of China is to be applied in the case of Chinese-foreign equity joint venture contracts, Chinese-foreign co-operative venture contracts, and contracts for the Chinese-foreign co-operative exploration and development of natural resources to be performed within the People's Republic of China.

On matters for which the law of the People's Republic of China has not yet made provision, international practice may be applied.

A provision similar to the first paragraph of Article 5 is found in Article 145 of the recent General Principles of Civil Law (hereafter cited as the Civil Law), which came into effect on 1 January 1987.[35]

While the scope of the expression 'the handling of contract disputes' in Article 5 is not explained, it appears that the intention of the draftsmen is to allow the parties the autonomy to choose the law to govern the contract except in the circumstances set out in the Foreign Economic Contract Law or other Chinese laws. The breadth of the principle is significantly limited in Article 5 itself, and potentially by Articles 4 and 9 of that law, as well as by Article 150 of the Civil Law. Article 4 of the Foreign Economic Contract Law provides that, in concluding contracts, the laws of China must be respected and no harm may be done to the social and public interest of China. Article 9 provides that contracts that violate the laws of the PRC or contravene the social or public interest are void. Article 150 of the Civil Law is in somewhat milder terms and provides that, in circumstances in which foreign law or international custom is applied, it shall not be applied so as to violate the common social interest of the PRC.

The relationship of Article 5 to Articles 4 and 9 of the Foreign Economic Contract Law is not clear. If Article 5 is interpreted so as to permit the parties to a contract to choose their own law, the provisions of the Foreign Economic Contract Law should, logically, cease to apply to that contract if the parties choose to be governed by foreign law. In practice, however, the principle of autonomy of choice of law is never unrestricted in any country. Wherever a contractual dispute is litigated or arbitrated, the forum will have its own conflicts rules regarding the proper law to be applied in relation to such matters as formal validity and the capacity of the parties. It will also be constrained by its own domestic laws in relation to the permissible subject-matter and the provisions of a contract. Most jurisdictions, in determining whether foreign law should be applied and to what extent, will not apply that law where the application would be contrary to the public policy of the forum. Similarly, the court of a forum may be constrained by its domestic law to apply a particular rule of that domestic law in relation to a contract, whether or not the contract is governed by foreign law.

In the context of China, this gives rise to two significant problems—the scope of the public policy exception, and the extent to which Chinese courts will consider that a contract is bound by Chinese law, even where the parties have decided that it is to be governed by foreign law. Both of these problems become relevant when a contract dispute is being heard in China (or possibly if the enforcement of an award or judgment is sought in China). If the parties have chosen foreign law to govern their disputes, as a practical matter it seems unlikely that, at present, a Chinese judicial or arbitral body will resolve these questions by simply ignoring the provisions of the Foreign Economic Contract Law and other Chinese laws. Chinese law will probably be applied to some extent (for example, in determining whether a contract that is required to be approved by the state has been formally concluded prior to the grant of that approval) regardless of the parties' choice, although there is as yet relatively little information on which to anticipate the approach that Chinese bodies will ultimately take or the conceptual basis that they will apply.

So long as transactions involve ordinary trade or even the sale of complex capital goods to China, the failure of contracts to specify the applicability of Chinese law does not seem to trouble Chinese negotiators, who are generally content if the contract is silent about the governing law. This is especially true if the contract calls for arbitration in China, for Chinese negotiators seem confident that Chinese arbitrators will apply private international law principles to any dispute that comes before them in a way that will assure due regard for the application of Chinese law.

It has been more difficult for Chinese officials to do without a Chinese governing law clause when negotiating with foreigners to build an office building, hotel, or manufacturing plant on Chinese soil, whether by means of an equity joint venture, a co-operative venture, or some other investment-type arrangement, and Article 5 of the Foreign Economic Contract Law, as well as Article 15 of the Joint Venture Implementing Act, now make it clear that in these circumstances a Chinese body may not recognize the validity of the choice of a foreign law. Given the history of foreign extraterritorial jurisdiction in China during the century that began with the Opium War of 1839–42, it is understandably important to the People's Republic, which came to power with a deep commitment to vindicating Chinese nationalism, that Chinese law apply to activities conducted in China.

From the point of view of the foreign business man, however, the Chinese legal system is still deficient in various respects in relation to contract disputes with foreigners. The promulgation of the Foreign Economic Contract Law, the Civil Law, and other laws aimed at regulating and protecting the economic interests of foreigners has created an atmosphere of somewhat greater certainty. Yet many other laws are needed, and the application of existing laws by Chinese administrative officials and business men is still uncertain, in comparison with countries with a complete and well-established legal structure. Moreover, China does not systematically publish its judicial and arbitral decisions, and in any event it will take decades before the Chinese courts and arbitration tribunals have authoritatively interpreted the many important provisions of the evolving legislative framework.

In non-investment contracts, if no choice of law is made, much depends on the domestic law rules to which the arbitrators consider themselves subject. In the absence of a clear choice of law, the tribunal will determine the proper law in the light of all the circumstances and its own conflicts rules. If the arbitral tribunal is Chinese, it is now clear that it should, subject to the provisions of Chinese law, decide which country's law has the closest connection to the contract. The way in which that determination will be made is not yet authoritatively known, though such factors as the origin of the parties and the places of negotiating, signing, and performing the contract are clearly relevant. Both the Foreign Economic Contract Law and the Civil Law state, however, that the tribunal should decide on the law of a particular country; the tribunal is not free to apply any principles it may think appropriate. Nevertheless, in both investment and non-investment contract disputes, if Chinese law is deemed to be applicable, the tribunal may resort to its understanding of 'international practice' to the extent that it determines that Chinese law lacks relevant provisions.

IV. Conclusion

In China, as in other socialist states based on Marxism-Leninism, international commercial arbitration is the creature of a government bureaucracy and the servant of a planned economy. Nevertheless, as part of its new policy of welcoming foreign investment, loans, and other forms of co-operation with business firms that generally are privately owned, the

People's Republic has taken several steps to improve the facilities for resolving the disputes that will inevitably arise in the course of these developing relationships.

Consistent with its traditional preference for conciliation rather than arbitration in those cases where the parties cannot resolve a dispute by themselves, China has adopted the innovation of joint conciliation as a means of expanding conciliation's acceptability and efficacy. And in line with its long-standing preference for arbitration rather than litigation in those cases where conciliation is unsuccessful, China, in order to make arbitration more attractive to foreign business men, has usually agreed to arbitrate in third countries under the procedural rules of the designated foreign institutions, even though China would prefer that arbitration take place in China or in the country of the defendant. Moreover, at least until China enacts a full set of commercial laws, it does not always insist that its non-investment contracts with foreign business partners prescribe Chinese law as the governing law but is often willing to leave the problem of applicable law to the arbitrators of any dispute. Finally, within certain limits, Chinese courts are now available to enforce arbitral awards, directly in the case of Chinese awards and foreign awards enforceable under the New York Convention and indirectly in other cases.

Such a reasonable and flexible system for dispute settlement can be expected to stimulate the economic transactions that China desires with the capitalist world. The challenge ahead will be to implement this system to the satisfaction of all concerned, while China's economic policy and legal system continue to evolve in ways that are sure to have an impact upon dispute resolution.

Notes

1. See Jerome Alan Cohen and Hungdah Chiu, *People's China and International Law* (Princeton, Princeton University Press, 1974), pp. 1088–94 and 1448.
2. Cohen and Chiu, pp. 656–68, note 1 above.
3. Cohen and Chiu, pp. 705–7, note 1 above.
4. English translations of the Decision of the Government Administration Council of the Central People's Government Concerning the Establishment of a Foreign Trade Arbitration Commission within the CCPIT (hereafter cited as the Decision Concerning FTAC) and the Provisional Rules of Procedure of the Foreign Trade Arbitration Commission of the CCPIT may be found in Gene T. Hsiao, *The Foreign Trade of China* (California, University of California Press, 1977), pp. 245 and 247, respectively.
5. English translations of the Decision of the State Council of the PRC Concerning the Establishment of a Maritime Arbitration Commission within the CCPIT (hereafter cited as the Decision Concerning MAC) and the Provisional Rules of Procedure of the Maritime Arbitration Commission of the CCPIT may be found in Hsiao, pp. 252 and 254, respectively, note 4 above.
6. In recent years Chinese arbitration experts have begun to disseminate substantial information about the actual handling of concrete arbitrations. See, for example, Tang Houzhi, 'Foreign Trade and Economic Arbitration in China', undated. Four cases discussed by Mr Tang, Deputy Chief, Division of Foreign Economic and Trade Arbitration, Legal Affairs Department of the CCPIT, are re-

produced in Walter Sterling Surrey and Stephen M. Soble, 'Recent Developments in Dispute Resolution in the People's Republic of China', in Jerome A. Cohen (ed.), *Legal Aspects of Doing Business in China* (New York, Practising Law Institute, 1983), pp. 402–9. See also Tang Houzhi, 'Arbitration—A Means Used by China to Settle Foreign Trade and Economic Disputes', transcript of a speech delivered in Beijing in February 1984. Eight cases handled by the FETAC are discussed.

7. Howard M. Holtzmann, 'Dispute Resolution Procedures in East-West Trade', *International Lawyer*, No. 13, 1979, p. 249.

8. These statistics were provided in an interview with CCPIT arbitration officials. In mid-1985 the MAC published an interesting pamphlet entitled 'Selection of Awards and Conciliation Statements' (Beijing, Publishing House of Law, 1985). The conciliation statements contained therein suggest that conciliation before the MAC often takes place after the MAC has heard the evidence and made a determination concerning the merits of the dispute but not the remedy. The same appears to be true in the CCPIT's handling of non-maritime disputes.

9. 'How the Case of the M/S *Varild* was Settled', in *Foreign Trade of the People's Republic of China* (Beijing), October 1963, p. 4; reproduced in Cohen and Chiu, pp. 1453–4, note 1 above.

10. See Arts. 186, 192, and 193 of the Civil Procedure Code. Note that Article 187 restricts foreign access to Chinese courts to the same extent as the foreigner's country restricts the access of Chinese persons or institutions to the courts of that country. For a discussion of these Code practices, see the text following note 15.

11. The English and Chinese texts of what is formally known as The Agreement on Trade Relations Between the United States of America and the People's Republic of China, dated 7 July 1979 and effective as of 1 January 1980, may be found, respectively, in Treaties and Other International Acts Series (TIAS), No. 9630, reproduced in *International Legal Materials*, No. 18, 1979, p. 1041, and *Chinese Yearbook of International Law* (Beijing, China Foreign Translation Publishing Company, 1982), pp. 428–32.

12. See, for example, 'The Protocol on the General Conditions for the Delivery of Goods Between the Foreign Trade Organizations of the People's Republic of China and the Union of Soviet Socialist Republics of 1950', and 'The Protocol on the General Conditions for the Delivery of Goods Between the Foreign Trade Organizations of the People's Republic of China and the People's Republic of Romania of 1961', English translations of which can be found in *Chinese Law and Government*, Vol. 5, 1972–3, pp. 14 and 109, respectively, as well as the Trade Agreement with Finland of 5 June 1953, and the Trade Agreement with the French Trade Delegation of 5 June 1953.

13. For an English translation of the Joint Venture Law, see *China's Foreign Economic Legislation* (Beijing, Foreign Language Press, 1982), Vol. 1, pp. 1–7.

14. See Art. 27 of the Regulations, which were promulgated by the State Council on 30 January 1982.

15. For an English translation of the Foreign Economic Contract Law, see Jerome Alan Cohen, 'The New Foreign Contract Law', *China Business Review*, July–August 1985, pp. 52 and 54–5.

16. Art. 192, para. 1, of the Civil Procedure Code provides that: 'In disputes arising out of foreign economic relations, trade, transportation or maritime affairs, if the parties have a written agreement to submit [such a dispute] to a foreign arbitration organization of the People's Republic of China for arbitration, then they may not institute proceedings in the people's courts; in the absence of such written agreement, proceedings may be instituted in the people's courts.'

17. Art. 111 of the Joint Venture Implementing Act, which was promulgated by the State Council on 20 September 1983.

18. Joint Venture Implementing Act, Art. 109, note 17 above.

19. See Art. 14 of the Labour Regulations, which were promulgated by the State Council on 26 July 1980.

20. See Economic Contract Law, Art. 48. For an English translation of the

Economic Contract Law, see *China Laws for Foreign Business*, 5–500 (Sydney, CCH Australia Ltd, 1985).

21. See Economic Contract Law, Art. 12, note 20 above. For an English translation of the Regulations on the Arbitration of Economic Contracts see *China Laws for Foreign Business*, 10–620, note 20 above.

22. Civil Procedure Code, Art. 97, note 16 above.

23. Civil Procedure Code, Art. 102, note 16 above.

24. Civil Procedure Code, Art. 111, note 16 above.

25. Civil Procedure Code, Art. 153, note 16 above.

26. Ren Jianxin, 'Some Legal Aspects of our Import of Technology and Utilization of Foreign Investment' (speech delivered in Hong Kong on 29 September 1980), translated and reprinted in *China Law Reporter*, Vol. 1, Fall 1980, pp. 85 and 99–100.

27. Civil Procedure Code, Art. 102, note 16 above.

28. From the State Council's Notice Concerning the Conversion of the Foreign Trade Arbitration Commission into the Foreign Economic and Trade Arbitration Commission, Beijing, 26 February 1980.

29. See note 28 above.

30. Ren Jianxin and Liu Shaoshan, 'Arbitration in China', translated and reprinted in Howard M. Holtzmann and Walter S. Surrey, eds., *Doing Business With China: Legal, Financial and Negotiating Aspects* (New York, Harcourt, Brace and Jovanovich, 1979), p. 222.

31. Ren Jianxin, 'The Establishment and Development of Foreign Trade, Economic and Marine Arbitration in China', speech reprinted in English, p. 7.

32. See Decision Concerning FTAC, Arts. 10 and 11, note 4 above, and Decision Concerning MAC, Arts. 10 and 11, note 5 above.

33. Ren and Liu, p. 228, note 30 above.

34. See Andrew K. N. Cheung, 'Enforcement of Foreign Arbitral Awards in the People's Republic of China', *American Journal of Comparative Law*, Vol. 34, 1986, pp. 295 and 311 for an illuminating and more detailed consideration of this question. This aspect of the law has also been criticized by Chinese commentators. See, for example, Dong Likun, 'On the Recognition and Enforcement of Foreign Court Judgments, *Zhongguo shehui kexue (China's Social Sciences)*, Vol. 2, 1985, pp. 209–23.

35. For a scholarly English translation of this major piece of legislation, see Whitmore Gray and Henry R. H. Zheng, *American Journal of Comparative Law*, Vol. 34, 1987, pp. 715–43.

17. On the Adjudicatory Jurisdiction of Chinese Courts over Foreign Investment Disputes

ZHENG ZHAOHUANG*

I. Introduction

It has long been the international practice for disputes over matters of trade and private investment to be settled by one of four methods: (a) friendly negotiation between the disputing parties; (b) conciliation or mediation by a third party; (c) submission of the dispute to arbitration; or (d) judicial settlement in a court which has competent jurisdiction. In conformity with this common practice, China resorts to the same approaches in resolving these kinds of dispute.

As the Chinese civil adjudication system of settling foreign economic disputes is still in an embryonic stage, the majority of such cases to date have been handled through arbitration or mediation by the Foreign Economic and Trade Arbitration Commission of the China Council for the Promotion of International Trade (CCPIT). This procedure is likely to continue for some time to come. Only a few cases of this kind have so far been decided by Chinese people's courts. But, with the adoption of the open-door policy and the acceleration of Chinese participation in the international economy, the CCPIT will be unable to take charge of all disputes involving foreign economic affairs and settle them to the satisfaction of the parties concerned. The convening in Beijing, in the spring of 1984, of the First Session of the National Working Conference on the Adjudication of Economic Lawsuits is a clear indication that the people's courts will soon play an increasingly important role in fulfilling the arduous task of resolving economic cases involving foreign nationals and enterprises.

This chapter attempts to provide a brief analysis of the general principles covering the judicial competence of the people's courts to deal with disputes which involve foreign economic affairs. These principles are prescribed in China's 1982 Civil Procedure Law for Trial Implementation (hereafter cited as the Civil Procedure Law or the said law).

---

*Responsibility for the views expressed in this chapter is entirely the author's, and these views have no official standing in whole or in part.

II. The Jurisdiction of Chinese Courts over Cases Involving Foreign Nationals or Enterprises

A. The Significance of the Delimitation of Jurisdiction

The term 'jurisdiction' employed in this chapter denotes the competent civil jurisdiction of the people's courts over lawsuits containing foreign elements. Since jurisdiction forms an integral part of state sovereignty, the delimitation of national jurisdiction has always been considered by all nations to be a matter of great significance.

Each nation's legal system is unique. Although the laws of some countries may have considerable similarities, they differ fundamentally in a number of areas. A case involving foreign nationals or enterprises, if dealt with by courts of different legal systems, will undoubtedly result in differing decisions that have an impact on the direct interest of the parties concerned.

As far as the parties to a dispute are concerned, each side generally prefers to address his plea to the court of his own country, and the governments concerned are more often than not disposed to put in their claims for jurisdiction over cases in which they have an interest. At the same time, they will do all in their power to deny other countries the right to claim jurisdiction over such cases. Some countries have even been known to enact laws with extraterritorial effect in order to intervene in the internal affairs of other sovereign states; hence, an increasingly bitter struggle for judicial control over cases involving foreign elements has arisen. All this underlines the importance of the delimitation of jurisdiction between nations.

B. Stipulations in the Civil Procedure Law on the Competence of Chinese Courts

In China, the competence of a local court is delimited by the jurisdictional region within which the court is located. To the two grounds in international law of territory and nationality is added registered permanent residence as the basis of competence of the people's courts over both Chinese and foreign civil law cases. Section Two of the Civil Procedure Law contains three kinds of jurisdiction, which are classified as general, specific, and exclusive, in accordance with the nature of the cause of action as well as the connecting factor that links the case with the local court of a specified area.

i. General Jurisdiction
In accordance with the principle, *actor forum rei sequitur* ('the plaintiff follows the forum of the defendant'), Article 20 of the Civil Procedure Law provides that a civil lawsuit comes under the jurisdiction of the people's court of the area where the defendant is registered as resident. If the area of the defendant's registered permanent residence differs from the area in which he resides, the lawsuit will come under the jurisdiction of the people's court in the area in which he resides. However, the author is

of the opinion that the application of this principle is more or less confined to lawsuits which are to be adjudicated in China, that is, to lawsuits in which the foreign defendant resides in China. If the defendant is a foreign corporation or a legal person, the case shall come under the jurisdiction of the people's court where its resident representative office in China is located.

In the case of an absent defendant, be it a natural or legal person, residing outside Chinese territory, the question arises as to whether the rule of 'the plaintiff follows the forum of the defendant' is applicable. Article 21 (2) of the said law provides that only in a case concerning the relationship of identity against a person residing abroad does the people's court of the area where the plaintiff resides in China have jurisdiction over the lawsuit. Such a provision gives the impression that in Chinese civil legislation there is only one exception to the rule. However, other provisions of the said law have reserved for the people's courts jurisdiction over cases concerning (a) contractual disputes concerning contracts signed or performed in China; (b) disputes over the infringement of rights where the infringement takes place in China; and (c) all lawsuits classified as coming under the exclusive jurisdiction of the Chinese people's courts. It follows that in most lawsuits brought against absent defendants residing abroad or beyond Chinese territorial jurisdiction, the people's courts of the areas where the plaintiffs reside in China shall have jurisdiction. Taking into consideration international customary practice, such provisions assure foreign investors or firms of full access to local courts on a par with Chinese nationals, so that their legitimate rights and interests can be protected.

ii. Specific Jurisdiction
The following five kinds of civil lawsuit fall within the area of specific jurisdiction under the Civil Procedure Law. First, a lawsuit caused by the infringement of rights comes under the jurisdiction of the people's court where the infringement takes place (Art. 22). Second, a lawsuit involving a contractual dispute comes under the jurisdiction of the people's court where the contract is being carried out or where the contract was signed (Art. 23). Third, a lawsuit concerning a maritime dispute arising from a demand for compensation for damages caused by the collision of ships or some other maritime accident falls under the jurisdiction of the people's court of the affected ship's initial destination, or of the place where the ship causing the accident is detained, or of the port where the ship causing the accident is registered (Art. 27). In a case involving a demand for compensation for rescue operations resulting from a disaster at sea, the lawsuit comes under the jurisdiction of the people's court of the place where the rescue originated, or of the rescued ship's initial destination (Art. 8). Fourth, a lawsuit arising from transport by air falls under the jurisdiction of the people's court of the place where the flight began or ended, or where the accident took place, or where the contract was signed (Art. 25). In the case of a lawsuit involving a demand for compensation for damages caused by an aviation accident, the people's court of the place where the

accident took place or where the aircraft initially landed, shall have jurisdiction (Art. 26). Finally, a lawsuit arising from railway, road, or water-borne transport falls under the jurisdiction of the people's court of the place where the administrative organ in charge of investigating the dispute is located (Art. 24).

iii. Exclusive Jurisdiction
There are certain specific civil law cases involving vital political and economic interests that every nation would like to reserve for the exclusive jurisdiction of its own courts. It follows that neither the jurisdiction nor the judgments of a foreign court concerning such cases will be recognized by Chinese people's courts. The following are the four kinds of lawsuit that are classified, under Article 30 of the said law, in the category of exclusive jurisdiction. First, a lawsuit over real estate comes under the jurisdiction of the people's court of the place where the real estate is located. Second, a lawsuit arising from port operations falls under the jurisdiction of the people's court of the place where the port is located. Third, a lawsuit arising from a registration dispute comes under the jurisdiction of the people's court of the place where the registration organization is located. Finally, a lawsuit concerning inheritance comes under the jurisdiction of the people's court of the place where the residence of the deceased legator is registered, or where the principal legacy is located.

iv. Submission to Jurisdiction by Agreement
In point of law, there should be a clear-cut distinction between the two terms 'submission to jurisdiction' and 'submission to arbitration'. The term 'submission to jurisdiction', in its legal sense, means to bring the case before a local court and not to submit it to an arbitration tribunal. Article 192 of the said law provides that in economic disputes arising between Chinese and foreign enterprises, a complainant who has submitted the dispute, by written agreement, to the appropriate Chinese arbitration organization is not entitled to bring the lawsuit before a people's court, while in economic disputes involving foreign enterprises outside China, the parties may, by written agreement, either submit the dispute to a Chinese arbitration organ or bring the case before the Chinese court which has jurisdiction over disputes involving foreign economic elements.

As regards economic disputes arising between Chinese and foreign enterprises, the law is silent on the question as to whether the disputing parties may, by agreement, submit the case to the forum of their own choice. In spite of this ambiguity, I believe that the customary rule of submission to jurisdiction by agreement has been accepted in principle by the Chinese people's courts, for it is explicitly set forth both in the 1958 Sino-Soviet Treaty of Commerce and Navigation and in a similar treaty that China concluded with the People's Republic of Mongolia in 1961.

In accordance with Article 8 of the Civil Procedure Law, there are two stages in the trial of a civil case by a people's court, the first being an initial hearing and the second being an appeal. The judgment or ruling on an appeal is final. For cases involving foreign interests, the intermediate courts will assume the function of the courts in an initial hearing and the higher courts the function of the courts in an appeal.

C. The Guiding Principles for Settlement

There are four guiding principles for the people's courts in handling such disputes. First, the principle of sovereignty safeguards China's sovereign right to exercise jurisdiction over cases involving foreign elements. Second, the principle of reciprocity defends the right of sovereign equality of states. Third, the principle of equal treatment of Chinese and foreign litigants ensures justice and equity to Chinese and foreigners alike. Finally, the principle of referring to international customary practice is intended to avoid conflict with the laws of other nations and to assimilate into China's legal system the common rules and regulations as required by trade and economic relations.

In brief, under the guidance of the above principles, China's policy in handling such cases aims not only at safeguarding her sovereign rights and national economic interests but also at protecting the legitimate rights and interests of foreign business men so as to inspire them with confidence in China's legal system.

D. The Scope and Extent of Competence of People's Courts over Foreign Economic Affairs Disputes

Under China's Organic Law of People's Courts, the economic sections or tribunals of the people's courts are empowered to handle disputes over foreign economic affairs. There are four types of such dispute:
(a) disputes arising in China involving economic, trade, transportation, and maritime affairs between Chinese and foreign enterprises;
(b) lawsuits filed with the people's courts involving disputes arising in China over economic, trade, transportation, and maritime affairs between foreign enterprises or organizations;
(c) lawsuits filed with the people's courts on the basis of written agreements for the settlement of disputes arising outside Chinese territory over economic, trade, transportation, and maritime affairs between foreign enterprises or organizations; and
(d) complaints lodged with the people's courts by foreign enterprises against the related Chinese administrative agencies concerning what the foreign enterprises regard as unjustifiable measures related to investment, tax, or labour problems.

These four kinds of dispute or lawsuit are all subject to the jurisdiction of the people's courts with the exception of those cases dealt with under Article 192 of the Civil Procedure Law, which provides that if, by agreement, the parties have submitted their dispute to arbitration, they may not bring the case before the people's courts.

As far as economic disputes arising in Hong Kong and Macau are concerned, there are in fact two kinds of lawsuit: one involving foreign nationals and enterprises, and the other concerning Chinese compatriots and their enterprises. The former is of genuine foreign concern, while the latter contains no foreign element at all. In principle, they should not be classified under the same category. However, in view of the present special status of Hong Kong and Macau, all the cases arising there involving Chinese compatriots and their enterprises as well as foreign nationals and enterprises shall be dealt with in accordance with the Special Stipulations Governing Civil Procedure Involving Foreign Nationals, as prescribed in the Civil Procedure Law.

Now that the Patent Law of the People's Republic of China has been promulgated, and exploitation of a patent registered by a foreign patentee without his authorization constitutes an infringement of the patent, the foreign patentee may institute legal proceedings in a people's court. According to Chinese law, all disputes arising from infringement of the patent rights of foreign patentees, as well as complaints lodged by foreign enterprises against the Chinese authorities, are to be dealt with by the people's courts. Even in cases of the breach of foreign investment contracts containing arbitration clauses, the parties concerned, after submitting their disputes to arbitration, still have to apply to the people's court for assistance in the execution of an arbitral award or in the adoption of measures for the preservation of the lawsuit. In sum, no disputes involving foreign elements can be completely resolved without the help of the people's courts. This demonstrates the importance of the adjudicatory jurisdiction of the people's courts over cases involving foreign entities.

E. The Legal Status of Foreign Investors under the Civil Procedure Law

The term 'legal status' or 'litigation rights' of foreign investors in China means that all foreign business men investing in China are entitled to free access to the people's courts to seek redress or protection of their rights. Under the guiding rule of national sovereignty, seven principles governing the legal status of foreign investors are prescribed in the Civil Procedure Law.

First, Article 185 sets out the principle of application of the Civil Procedure Law. As foreign investors engaging in litigation within Chinese territory are subject to the jurisdiction of the people's courts, any foreign investment disputes brought before a Chinese court should be settled in accordance with the Civil Procedure Law. This demand for respect of Chinese law demonstrates China's insistence on the principle of national sovereignty.

Second, Article 186 deals with the principle of equality between Chinese and foreign litigants. Foreign investors who file or respond to lawsuits in the people's courts enjoy the same litigation rights and obligations as Chinese citizens. On the basis of equality and mutual benefit, Chinese laws protect them against any discriminative restrictions imposed on their litigation rights.

Third, Article 187 lays down the principle of reciprocity. As litigation rights are granted to foreign investors on the basis of equality and mutual benefit, in the event that the courts of a foreign country impose restrictions on the litigation rights of Chinese citizens, enterprises, or organizations, the people's courts will follow the principle of reciprocity and will impose corresponding restrictions on the litigation rights of citizens and enterprises of that country, in order to safeguard China's sovereignty as well as to protect the rights and interests of Chinese citizens and enterprises abroad. China is fully justified in adopting such a policy, because only by this means can healthy relations between nations based on equality and mutual respect be established and the principle of non-discrimination and lack of restrictions for mutual benefit be implemented.

Fourth, Article 188 deals with the principle of judicial immunity. With respect to civil lawsuits brought against foreigners, foreign organizations, or international organizations enjoying judicial immunity, the people's courts will be guided by China's laws and the international treaties which China has signed or participates in. However, attention should be drawn to the fact that the stipulations in Article 188 only deal with diplomatic immunity and not with state immunity.

Fifth, Article 189 lays down the principle of the application of international treaties. China recognizes, as a sovereign state, the binding effect of all international treaties that she has signed or participates in, and will execute in good faith the obligations incurred by these treaties. However, according to Chinese practice, treaties automatically become operative as part of the law of the land without legislative implementation. When an international treaty which China has signed or participates in contains provisions different from those found in the Civil Procedure Law, the provisions of such a treaty will be applied, with the exception of those provisions with respect to which China has announced its intention to retain complete freedom to apply its own law.

Sixth, Article 190 specifies that the vernacular language is to be used in the people's courts when cases involving foreign investors are being tried. Translation will be provided on request for the foreign litigants, but the expenses must be borne by them. The essence of this principle lies in the fact that it upholds not only China's sovereignty but also the dignity of the people's courts in terms of their competent jurisdiction over cases involving foreign nationals or enterprises.

Finally, Article 191 states that lawyers of the People's Republic of China must be engaged to represent foreign litigants in the people's courts. Since lawyers constitute a component part of the legal system of a sovereign state, they should not practise outside the domain of their own country, for if they were to do so this would constitute interference in the internal judicial affairs of another state. Chinese law also stipulates that foreign lawyers may neither practise law nor set up law firms in China. Further, they cannot enter into partnership with any Chinese legal advisory office.

F. The Resolution of Disputes Involving Foreign Investment Enterprises

The term 'foreign investment enterprises' here denotes joint ventures using Chinese and foreign investment; Chinese and foreign co-operation agreements; and wholly owned foreign enterprises doing business in China. As the problem of the choice of jurisdiction may have a direct bearing upon the interests of the disputing parties, foreign investors have shown much concern over the matter. It is the opinion of this author that unless there is included in an investment contract an arbitration clause which pledges the parties concerned to use arbitration as a means of settling any present or future conflict, any dispute over foreign investment contracts arising in China should be subject to the jurisdiction of the Chinese people's courts. These courts are the only competent tribunals to handle such issues according to the principles of private international law as understood in China, for the following reasons.

First, according to the principle of territorial sovereignty, all persons (except those who enjoy diplomatic immunity) and objects within the territory of a sovereign state are under its 'dominion and sway' (in Oppenheim's words). This is a well-established rule of public international law, but it is also applicable to private international law where, in civil lawsuits, the local court of a state is entitled to assume jurisdiction over an alien or his property found within its territory on the basis of *lex loci*, that is, the law of the place where an act or event material to the case occurred.

Second, as a general rule, a state may claim jurisdiction over its nationals in any part of the world on the basis of the nationality principle. However, the civil legal status of an alien or of a foreign company in China is determined by the law of the state of his or its origin. Before Chinese law, all foreign business men and firms as well as joint ventures in China should abide by the law of the People's Republic of China and under no circumstances should they conduct their business activities outside the law. Here lies the line of distinction between the territorial principle and the nationality principle. In case of conflict, the former always prevails.

Finally, international law generally permits a state to reserve for its own courts exclusive jurisdiction over cases involving its vital economic interests, and to deny other states any claim of jurisdiction over such matters.

It is upon these three principles that China bases her claim of jurisdiction over the following foreign investment disputes.

First, in cases where disputes between Chinese and foreign investors arise, all foreign investors have concluded with the Chinese participants investment contracts for the conduct of their business operations in China. All of these contracts are concluded and are to be performed in China pursuant to Chinese laws and regulations governing foreign business activities within Chinese territory.

Given that investment disputes have taken and will inevitably take place in China, it follows that on the basis of the principle of territorial jurisdiction, any dispute arising between Chinese and foreign investors in the course of co-operation should be subject to the jurisdiction of the Chinese people's courts pursuant to the 1979 Law of the People's

Republic of China on Joint Ventures Using Chinese and Foreign Investment as well as the implementing regulations promulgated in 1983.

The second case arises where disputes occur between foreign investment enterprises and Chinese enterprises. As a rule, all foreign enterprises conduct their business activities in China in conformity with the contracts that they have signed with the Chinese enterprises concerned. Inasmuch as all joint ventures established in China as well as their Chinese counterpart enterprises are Chinese legal persons, such disputes have nothing to do with the extraterritoriality of the jurisdiction of a foreign country. On the basis of the principle of nationality, therefore, the Chinese courts have a perfect right to assume jurisdiction over these disputes pursuant to the Economic Contract Law as well as to other relevant laws and regulations enacted by the People's Republic of China. As far as foreign capital enterprises are concerned, any disputes arising in China with Chinese enterprises should also fall within the jurisdiction of the people's courts in accordance with the principle of territorial jurisdiction.

Thirdly, matters concerning the employment, recruitment, dismissal, and resignation of staff and workers in all joint ventures are all provided for in the labour contracts concluded between the enterprises and their staff and workers. Under the relevant laws and regulations, the validity or invalidity of these contracts must be determined in accordance with Chinese law, and is subject to the examination and approval of the Chinese authorities concerned. As these contracts were concluded and are to be performed in China, and one of the parties concerned is of Chinese nationality, and disputes arising from the execution of a labour contract fall indisputably within the competence of the people's courts according to the territorial as well as the nationality principle, and should be decided in accordance with the Regulations of the People's Republic of China on Labour Management in Joint Ventures Using Chinese and Foreign Investment, promulgated in 1980.

Finally, as explained above, the Civil Procedure Law has reserved to the people's courts exclusive jurisdiction over civil law issues involving China's vital economic interests, such as cases concerning real estate and the exploitation of offshore petroleum resources. Any lawsuits involving foreign investment enterprises that fall within this category come naturally under the exclusive jurisdiction of the people's courts, with the exception of those cases involving contracts containing arbitration clauses that bind the parties concerned in advance to submit all future disputes to arbitration pursuant to Article 27 of the Regulations on the Exploitation of Offshore Petroleum Resources in Co-operation with Foreign Enterprises, promulgated in 1982.

As regards the question of the choice of law applicable to such disputes, I believe that, with the exception of those contracts containing express choice-of-law clauses, the generally accepted rule in common law countries is the 'grouping of contacts theory', which applies the law of the place with the most significant contacts in the light of the total relationship. In other words, 'when the intention of the parties to a contract with regard to the law governing it is not expressed and cannot be inferred from the circumstances, the contract is governed by the system of law with which the transaction has its closest and most real connection' (J.H.C. Morris, *Conflict of Laws*, London, Stevens and Sons, 1980, second edition, p. 220).

The conclusion and performance of the above-mentioned contracts take place within China. The foreign parties to these contracts are required to register and conduct their business activities in China strictly in compliance with Chinese law. Their Chinese counterparts are of course Chinese legal persons. It stands to reason, therefore, that China unquestionably has the closest and most real connection with the transactions and that therefore Chinese law should be the applicable law for the settlement of investment disputes arising in China.

III. Problems Related to the Exercise of Jurisdiction

A. Service out of Jurisdiction (Art. 196)

In cases involving foreign nationals or firms, a people's court may deliver legal documents to a party residing outside Chinese territory by the methods stipulated in the Civil Procedure Law, as follows:

(a) It may deliver them through diplomatic channels, that is, through the Chinese embassy, consulate, or other diplomatic organs in the country where the party is present.

(b) In delivering the documents to a party of Chinese nationality, it may entrust delivery to the Chinese embassy or consulate in the country where the party is present, as is provided in Article 5 of the 1963 Vienna Convention on Consulate Relations to which China became a party in 1970.

(c) It may deliver the documents by mail if the law of the country where the party resides permits, and the delivery should be made in due observance of the law of the said country.

(d) If the country where the party resides has a judicial assistance agreement with the People's Republic of China, the people's court may entrust to a foreign court of that country the delivery of the documents on its behalf, or in other forms as prescribed in the agreement.

(e) It may deliver the documents through the litigant's agent *ad litem* (that is, through a Chinese lawyer).

(f) If it is unable to deliver the documents in any of the aforementioned ways, it may do so by means of the issue of a public notice. The documents are considered to be delivered six months from the date of the public notice. Another matter connected with service out of jurisdiction is the period of time allowed to a non-resident defendant to reply to the notification of a bill of complaint. The people's court should stamp the copy of the bill of complaint sent to the defendant as having been received, notifying him that he should forward his response within sixty days of receiving the copy. An extension of the deadline may be granted if the defendant so requests, but the extension may not exceed thirty days.

B. The Preservation of a Lawsuit or Interim Measures for Protection

In order to prevent any sale, transfer, or concealment of property, a people's court may, in the course of its proceedings in a legal action, issue an order to seal up, distrain, or freeze the property of a party to the lawsuit so that the execution of its final judgment may be ensured, and the legitimate interests of the party concerned may be protected. Measures for the preservation of a lawsuit are provided in Articles 92, 93, and 94 of the Civil Procedure Law. Special stipulations on the preservation of a lawsuit involving foreign nationals or enterprises have been provided in Part Five, Chapter 22, of the said law. In addition, the adoption of such measures is not confined to litigation in the people's courts, but is also applicable in cases submitted to arbitration, in which a party may file a request for a ruling on the preservation of the lawsuit against the other party.

Practically every foreign investment contract concluded in China contains an arbitration clause. According to the Civil Procedure Law, when a Chinese arbitration organization, at the instance of a party, deems it necessary, it may request a ruling of preservation from the intermediate people's court in the place where the property of the person against whom the action is directed is located, or in the place where the arbitration organization is located (Art. 194).

Under the Civil Procedure Law, specific measures for the preservation of a lawsuit in such cases are laid down, as follows. The people's court, at the request of either the plaintiff or the defendant, may issue a ruling on the preservation of the lawsuit. Upon the approval of such a request, the people's court should instruct the person against whom the application has been filed to provide security (mainly bank credit). If the party is willing to provide security, no measure against his property will be taken. However, if he refuses, the court should issue an order to distrain his property. Such property includes all that found within Chinese territory and is not limited to his property involved in the case, which may not be within Chinese territorial jurisdiction. The applicant should be responsible for any losses or expenses incurred as a result of any error made in the application. When the people's court finds that there is no longer any need for the distraint, it will issue an order to remove it, which will be carried out by the executor or the surveillance unit.

C. Judicial Assistance

The term 'judicial assistance' here means that, on the basis of the international agreements which the People's Republic of China has signed or participates in, a people's court and a foreign court may mandate each other to pursue certain litigious actions on each other's behalf. These actions comprise:

(a) the service of a process or the delivery of legal documents;
(b) the investigation and collection of evidence; and
(c) the recognition and enforcement of judicial judgments or arbitration awards.

As China has not yet signed or participated in any international agreement on judicial assistance, these litigious actions are conducted on the basis of the principle of reciprocity in accordance with the Civil Procedure Law.

Four restrictions on judicial assistance are set out in the Civil Procedure Law.

First, cases submitted by a foreign court will be rejected if they are incompatible with the sovereignty and security of the People's Republic of China. For example, a request by a foreign court for assistance in serving process upon top-level officials of the Chinese government in a lawsuit against the People's Republic of China, or a request by a foreign court for assistance in obtaining either evidence on cases which China has reserved for the exclusive jurisdiction of its own courts or evidence involving China's national defence secrets, will be rejected.

Second, if a case submitted by a foreign court is outside the jurisdiction of the Chinese people's court, the latter should return the case to the foreign court, giving its reasons for doing so.

Third, if a foreign judgment or ruling entrusted to a people's court for execution is incompatible with the basic principles of the People's Republic of China or China's national and social interests, the people's court should refuse to execute it and return it to the foreign court.

Fourth, as a token of mutual respect for national sovereignty, a Chinese version must be attached to any documents which a foreign court entrusts to a people's court for service or assistance in the execution of a judgment. Likewise a foreign-language version must be attached to any document which a people's court entrusts to a foreign court for service or assistance in the execution of a judgment.

Three conditions are laid down in the Civil Procedure Law concerning the procedure of recognition and enforcement of foreign judgments or arbitral awards.

First, as a friendly relationship between China and the entrusting country is predicated on the principle of reciprocity and mutual benefit, mutual assistance between the two countries is required. A people's court will recognize and enforce a foreign judgment or an arbitral award provided it is entrusted by the court of a country with which China has signed a treaty on judicial assistance.

Second, a judgment or award entrusted by a foreign court or arbitral organ must be final and conclusive and a request for assistance in any action must be specific and concrete, for a foreign court cannot ask a people's court to take charge on its behalf of the court-room proceedings of a lawsuit.

Third, a request for judicial assistance must be made by a foreign court. An application to a people's court for the enforcement of a foreign judgment filed directly by the parties concerned, or a request for judicial assistance made by a foreign organization other than a foreign court, will be rejected.

When entrusted with the execution of a foreign judgment or award, a people's court will issue a ruling recognizing the legal effect of such a judgment or award and will execute the same according to Chinese legal procedures, provided such a judgment or award does not violate the basic principles of the laws of the People's Republic of China.

A request from a people's court for judicial assistance from a foreign court is mainly based on the principle of reciprocity and mutual benefit as well as on international agreements on judicial assistance which the People's Republic of China has signed or participates in. According to the Civil Procedure Law, if an applicant files an application for the compulsory execution of a judgment passed by a people's court or a ruling made by an arbitration organization which has legal effect, and if the person against whom the application has been filed or his property is not in China, the people's court may request assistance in the execution of the judgment or award on its behalf from a foreign court. A people's court may mandate a foreign court to deliver legal documents, or to question on its behalf the party concerned or any witnesses to the lawsuit. The Chinese people's courts respect the sovereignty as well as the national interest of the country of the relevant court and always endeavour to ensure that, on the basis of the principle of reciprocity and international agreements, their adjudicatory power over such cases functions smoothly.

IV. Conclusion

In so far as its legal significance is concerned, judicial jurisdiction over foreign investment disputes is a matter not only of practical value but also of great complexity. It contains a maze of technicalities ranging from public and private international laws to domestic and foreign laws. Delimitation of national jurisdiction has an important bearing upon a nation's sovereignty. Nevertheless, to avoid jurisdictional conflicts with other nations, on no account should a nation assert its right of sovereignty beyond the limit of what is recognized as reasonable and justified by international law, lest it infringe the sovereignty of another state. I hazard the view that, in the course of drawing up the jurisdictional provisions of the Civil Procedure Law, such considerations were taken into account by the law-making authorities.

Since the beginning of China's open-door policy, a series of laws and regulations governing foreign economic relations have been promulgated and further relevant laws and regulations will be enacted in the near future. In addition to the protection of foreign investments provided for in the Chinese constitution, the people's courts adhere strictly to the principle of taking facts as the basis and the law as the criterion, so that justice can be served and the legitimate rights and interests of foreign investors can be protected. It is hoped that, with the steady progress in China's foreign economic legislation, new vistas for foreign investment in China will be opened up.

18. The Law of Foreign Sovereign Immunity in Relation to Trade with and Investment in China

THOMAS PEELE

I. Introduction

This chapter is intended to provide an overview of the law of foreign sovereign immunity as it bears on business relationships with Chinese entities. The law of foreign sovereign immunity has an important effect on commercial transactions with Chinese enterprises because state-owned enterprises, unlike private enterprises, are able in some circumstances to claim an immunity from suit or an immunity from execution of judgments against their property. Thus, a foreign party which takes a dispute to arbitration or litigation may find itself confronted at the outset of the proceeding with a contention from the Chinese party that the court or tribunal must, as a matter of law, dismiss the case because of the Chinese party's relation to the Chinese state. It is, of course, also important for Chinese enterprises to take into consideration the law of foreign sovereign immunity, particularly those Chinese enterprises which operate abroad, or whose operations may have significant effects abroad, since some of their activities may subject them to suit in other countries.

II. Background

The traditional doctrine of foreign sovereign immunity held that a sovereign state was entitled to an absolute immunity from suit in the courts of other states, and that the foreign state's property was absolutely immune from execution in satisfaction of a judgment. The doctrine has been understood to derive from the equality of states,[1] or from the principle of comity between states.[2] However, with the gradual erosion of 'domestic' sovereign immunity (so that suits against a state in the state's own courts came to be permitted in defined circumstances), the increasing interdependence of the world economy, and the rise of state trading corporations,[3] the doctrine of foreign sovereign immunity changed, as far as the courts of most Western nations were concerned, from an 'absolute' to a 'restrictive' doctrine. Under the 'restrictive' doctrine of sovereign immunity, a foreign state remains immune from suits in foreign countries when the suits are based on public acts (*acta jure imperii*), but is not immune from suits based on private acts (*acta jure gestionis*). In more modern terms, this distinction is sometimes characterized as one between sovereign and commercial acts, although the foreign sovereign immunity law of some states deprives foreign states of immunity from suit for certain non-commercial as well as commercial acts.[4]

Sir Robert Phillimore stated a common rationale for the denial of immunity to sovereigns for their commercial acts in 1873:

No principle of international law, and no decided case, and no dictum of jurists of which I am aware, has gone so far as to authorise a sovereign prince to assume the character of a trader, when it is for his benefit; and when he incurs an obligation to a private subject to throw off, if I may so speak, his disguise, and appear as a sovereign, claiming for his own benefit, and to the injury of a private person, for the first time, all the attributes of his character.[5]

The Belgian courts appear to have been the first to apply the restrictive doctrine of sovereign immunity to cases involving foreign governments. As early as 1857 the Court of Appeals in Brussels upheld a lower court decision awarding damages for injury relating to a contract for the sale of guano by an enterprise belonging to the government of Peru.[6] The doctrine was slow in gaining general acceptance, however; the United States adhered to the absolute doctrine until 1952,[7] and the United Kingdom accepted the absolute doctrine as late as 1976.[8] At present, the United Kingdom, the United States, Australia, Hong Kong, Singapore, Pakistan, South Africa, and Canada have enactments embodying the restrictive doctrine, and the restrictive doctrine has been applied by courts in Austria, Belgium, England, Egypt, France, West Germany, Greece, Hong Kong, Italy, Pakistan, the Philippines, and Yugoslavia.[9] The restrictive doctrine has been adopted in the European Convention on State Immunity and Additional Protocol of 1972,[10] the Inter-American Draft Convention on Jurisdictional Immunities of States,[11] and the Draft Convention on State Immunity of the International Law Association.[12]

Socialist states, however, do not regard commercial activity as nonsovereign, and they do not agree that foreign sovereigns should be denied immunity from suit based on their commercial activities. For instance, a Soviet commentator has stated that '[t]he economic activity or economic functions of a State, including so-called State trading or commercial activity, are no less important to any State, including States with a socialist economy, than its other functions. The State does not perform economic activities as a private individual, but precisely as a State, a sovereign bearer of public power.'[13] Thus, to Judge Phillimore, the socialist states would respond that they are not acting 'in disguise' when they enter into commercial transactions; the parties with whom they contract are aware that the party with which they are dealing is a sovereign, and, from the socialist viewpoint at least, enjoys the prerogatives of a sovereign.[14] Indeed, Soviet commentators have suggested that the doctrine of restrictive sovereign immunity is an instrument of domination by which more powerful states deny the sovereignty of less powerful states, thereby 'reducing sovereignty to relations of force'.[15]

Like the Soviet Union, the People's Republic of China also does not accept the restrictive doctrine of foreign sovereign immunity as applied to sovereign states. It maintains that, as a matter of international law, a sovereign state is entitled to absolute immunity from suit in the courts of other states. Chinese commentators have stated that '[a] state always acts in a sovereign capacity; it does not cease to be a sovereign state when engaged in commercial activities.'[16] Furthermore, 'the exercise of jurisdiction by some Western countries over the so-called nonsovereign acts of foreign states through their unilateral legislation and judicial practice constituted a violation of the principle of sovereign equality among states, was protested by the states concerned, and gave rise to issues of international responsibility.'[17]

Given these views, it is hardly surprising that, when a United States court in the state of Alabama entered a judgment by default against the People's Republic of China (PRC) in the amount of US$41.3 million in 1982, in a case brought for payment on Chinese Huguang Railway bonds issued in 1911 and sold by banks in France, Germany, England, and the United States,[18] the Chinese Minister of Foreign Affairs, Wu Xueqian, personally delivered an *aide-mémoire* to the United States Secretary of State, which stated (in part):

Sovereign immunity is an important principle of international law. It is based on the principle of sovereign equality of all states as confirmed by the Charter of the United Nations. As a sovereign state, China incontestably enjoys judicial immunity. It is in utter violation of the principle of international law of sovereign equality of all states and the UN Charter that a district court of the United States should exercise jurisdiction over a suit against a sovereign state as a defendant, make a judgement by default and even threaten to execute the judgement. The Chinese Government firmly rejects this practice of imposing US domestic law on China to the detriment of China's sovereignty and national dignity. Should the US side, in defiance of international law, execute the above-mentioned judgement and attach China's property in the United States, the Chinese Government reserves the right to take measures accordingly. . .

The Chinese Government hopes that the US Government will truly shoulder its responsibility, strictly act on the principles of international law, take effective steps to stop the aggravation of events and handle the case properly so that Sino–US relations and normal trade and economic exchanges may not be impaired.[19]

In a document subsequently submitted in that case by the United States, the Secretary of State stated that, during a visit to Beijing in February 1983, he met Deng Xiaoping, who 'vigorously stated his government's view that the PRC enjoys absolute immunity from the processes of United States or other foreign courts'.[20] Following that submission and a special appearance by the PRC, the district court that originally entered the default judgment dismissed the case in China's favour. The court determined that the rules of restrictive sovereign immunity codified in the United States law pursuant to which the judgment had been obtained, the Foreign Sovereign Immunities Act of 1976 (hereafter cited as the FSIA), could not be applied so as to permit suit on bonds issued in 1911, when absolute sovereign immunity was the rule.[21]

Thus, China's position on lawsuits against the People's Republic of China itself is quite clear. But it is less clear what position China will ultimately take with respect to foreign sovereign immunity for its state enterprises. The position taken on state enterprises is likely to be more important as far as foreign investment is concerned, since few investors will enter into contracts directly with the central government, government ministries, or provincial governments. Instead, they will deal with state-owned enterprises, which, although owned by the state, appear to be separate from it.

In the Soviet Union state enterprises that operate on the principle of 'economic accountability' (khozraschet) are legal persons.[22] As legal persons, they have the power to enter into contracts, and may sue or be sued in their own name in the courts of the Soviet Union.[23] These matters are established by statute. The newly promulgated General Provisions of the Civil Code of the People's Republic of China (hereafter referred to as the General Provisions) appear to adopt a similar scheme, and to provide for the registration of qualifying organizations as legal persons.[24] Furthermore, there is apparently no prohibition on suit against government organizations or offices in the people's courts of China, including ministries.[25]

The General Provisions make it clear that Chinese legal persons are subject to suit in the people's courts of China. Before the promulgation of the General Provisions, the question of whether foreigners would be permitted to bring suits in Chinese courts had arisen in *China National Technical Import Corporation* v. *United States*,[26] a United States case brought by China National Technical Import Corporation to recover damages for the loss of its property caused by the inadvertent surfacing of an American submarine under a Japanese freighter transporting the property. The United States court could not permit the suit to proceed against the United States until it had determined whether China would allow nationals of the United States to sue in the people's courts 'under similar circumstances'.[27] On the basis of Chinese laws,[28] an affidavit of an American law professor specializing in the study of Chinese law,[29] a legal opinion of the China Council for the Promotion of International Trade (hereafter referred to as the CCPIT),[30] and the acquiescence of the United States Department of Justice, the United States court concluded that such suits would be permitted in the people's courts in similar circumstances, and ordered that the United States lawsuit proceed.

There are indications that China does not regard suits in foreign courts against Chinese state commercial enterprises, based on their commercial activities, as being in violation of international law.[31] However, it remains important for foreign and Chinese enterprises to take into account the law of foreign sovereign immunity in states where a Chinese state enterprise might be sued in the event of a dispute, or where its property might be located if a judgment has been obtained. If the law of a particular state where such a lawsuit takes place provides a sovereign immunity defence to state enterprises such as those existing in China, it would be rash to assume that the enterprise would not attempt to avail itself of the defence.

Soviet practice in this respect may be instructive. Although it is possible to sue state enterprises in Soviet courts, these enterprises have claimed immunity when it was available as a defence in foreign courts. For instance, when suit was brought against the Soviet Novosti Press Agency in a United States court, a statement by the Soviet Ambassador, Dobrynin, that Novosti was an instrumentality of the USSR was submitted to the court. As a consequence of the court's finding that Novosti is an instrumentality of the USSR, Novosti was able to claim immunity in a suit for libel in a United States court.[32] In another United States court case,[33] the executor of the estate of an American tourist sued the Soviet agency Intourist, a legal person that presumably could have been sued in the Soviet Union. The defendant was found to 'qualif[y] for immunity as "an agency or instrumentality of a foreign state"'.[34] In a third case,[35] brought by an impresario for breach of a contract for performances by Russian artists in the United States and Great Britain, the defendants—Gosconcert, the Ministry of Culture, and the Union of Soviet Socialist Republics—moved for dismissal on grounds of immunity, and the motion was denied, because the court determined that suit was based on commercial activities.

In at least one United States court case, *Paterson, Zochonis (UK) Ltd.* v. *Compania United Arrow*,[36] a Chinese state enterprise has claimed immunity from suit. In that case plaintiffs who lost cargo originally shipped from Fuzhou and lost at sea sued China Ocean Shipping Company (hereafter referred to as COSCO) in a United States court for their losses. The court determined that COSCO is an agency or instrumentality of the People's Republic of China, and that, under United States jurisdictional rules regarding such entities, COSCO was immune from suit, and, consequently, dismissed the suit.[37]

In another United States court case,[38] a Chinese instrumentality, the China National Chemicals Import and Export Corporation, overcame the defence of foreign sovereign immunity raised by the Chilean government-owned defendants that it had sued for the loss of a cargo of bulk nitrates in a collision off Panama. There was no dispute that the Chilean defendants, as instrumentalities of a foreign state, would be entitled to immunity in the United States court unless the suit was found to be based upon a commercial activity.[39] The court found that the suit was based on a commercial activity, and denied the Chilean defendants' motion for dismissal of the case.[40]

Since trade with and investment in China is increasing, it can only be expected that the volume of such lawsuits will also increase, and that issues of foreign sovereign immunity will continue to arise in future cases.

III. Waivers of Sovereign Immunity

A. Explicit Waivers

Many companies dealing with Chinese organizations seek to deal with the problem of sovereign immunity straightforwardly, by including in their contracts with Chinese entities clauses irrevocably waiving sovereign immunity. Such provisions effectively withdraw the sovereign aspect from the transaction, so that the contract is the equivalent of one between two private parties, neither of whom is entitled to an immunity. For instance, a note-purchase agreement for Japanese yen notes to be issued by China International Trust and Investment Corporation (CITIC) included the following clause:

To the extent that CITIC has or may hereafter acquire any immunity, on the ground of sovereignty or otherwise, from legal proceedings or arbitration (whether in respect of service of process, obtaining of a judgment, attachment, execution of a judgment or otherwise) with respect to itself or its property or assets, CITIC hereby irrevocably waives such immunity from such legal proceedings or arbitration in respect of its obligations under this Agreement or the Notes (including the Conditions of the Notes) which may be instituted against it in any such court in Japan or tribunal in China or in any such arbitration.

The 'Conditions of Issue' for CITIC's 1985 Deutschmark issue included the following provision:

The Borrower [CITIC] hereby submits to the jurisdiction of the courts referred to in this subparagraph [Chinese people's courts and German courts] and hereby waives any right to claim lack of jurisdiction or immunity from suit, judgement, execution, attachment (whether after or before judgement), or other legal process in any of the countries in which proceedings may be taken for the enforcement of any rights of the bondholders.

Provisions waiving sovereign immunity in other contracts, such as joint venture contracts, are similar. For instance:

In any arbitration proceeding, any legal proceeding to enforce any award resulting from an arbitration proceeding and in any legal action between the Parties pursuant to or relating to this Contract, each Party expressly and irrevocably waives the defense of sovereign immunity and any other defense or exemption from suit, judgment or execution based on the fact or allegation that it is a subdivision, agency or instrumentality of, or represents, a government.

Waivers of immunity are generally respected by arbitral tribunals and by courts. Some states have statutes which make it clear that a waiver of immunity will be enforced. For instance, in United States courts, a foreign state that has given a waiver of immunity will not be immune from suit, even if the foreign state later withdraws its waiver (provided that the terms of the waiver do not permit it to make such a withdrawal).[41] Likewise, under the United Kingdom's State Immunity Act of 1978 (referred to hereafter as the SIA), a state is not immune 'as respects proceedings in respect of which it has submitted to the jurisdiction of the courts of the United Kingdom.'[42] The SIA further specifies which persons shall be deemed to have the authority to make such submissions on behalf of their states.[43]

B. Implicit Waivers

i. Arbitration Clauses

If the parties to a contract have not agreed to an explicit waiver of sovereign immunity, some other contract provision may be viewed as constituting an *implicit* waiver. The most commonly occurring such provision in contracts with Chinese entities is an arbitration clause. The SIA provides that a foreign state will not be immune 'as respects proceedings in the courts of the United Kingdom which relate to the arbitration', unless the arbitration agreement stipulates otherwise.[44]

United States law on the subject is more complicated. An arbitration provision calling for arbitration before the Foreign Economic and Trade Arbitration Commission (FETAC) of the CCPIT in Beijing is likely not to be regarded as an implicit waiver of immunity from suit in United States courts by the Chinese party.[45] Of course, many contracts with Chinese entities call for arbitration in a third country. Such agreements have properly not been viewed as implicit waivers of immunity from general judicial jurisdiction in United States courts.[46] As regards the jurisdiction of the United States courts in matters relating to the arbitration agreement, such as enforcement proceedings, it is possible that an award may not be enforceable in the United States if the arbitration clause provides that arbitration may take place in the territory of a state not a party to the United Nations Convention on Recognition and Enforcement of Foreign Arbitral Awards (familiarly known as 'the New York Convention').[47]

ii. Governing-law Clauses
A governing-law clause, which provides that 'the law of a particular country'[48] should govern a contract, may be regarded as an implicit waiver of sovereign immunity by United States courts, although this may be so only in the case of clauses providing that United States law is to be the governing law.[49] It has been argued that the choice of the law of a state which would not provide immunity to the state-owned party to the contract should be regarded as a waiver of immunity from jurisdiction.[50] To date, the argument does not appear to have been accepted by United States courts so far as the choice of a third country's law as governing law is concerned.[51] It seems even less likely that an argument of this nature would be accepted where the governing law is the law of the state to which the state-owned enterprise belongs, since it could be difficult to construe an insistence on one's home-state law as a waiver of any kind.[52] However, if this argument were accepted for contracts which provide that Chinese law is to be the governing law, Chinese enterprises entering into contracts with such a provision might not enjoy immunity in the United States courts, since they apparently enjoy no immunity in the people's courts of China.[53]

The United Kingdom law specifically provides that:

a provision in any agreement that it is to be governed by the law of the United Kingdom is not to be regarded as a submission [to jurisdiction].[54]

It should be noted, however, that the United Kingdom rule is more representative of the practice of other states than is the United States rule.[55]

IV. The Law of Foreign Sovereign Immunity

The law of foreign sovereign immunity varies from state to state, and the law to be applied in a particular forum is the law of that forum.[56] Thus it is important to be aware of the laws of sovereign immunity in states where a Chinese enterprise might be sued. The United States law of foreign sovereign immunity is outlined below, as illustrative of the principles of foreign sovereign immunity being applied by the courts of Western states today. Since many more foreign sovereign immunity decisions have been reported in the United States than in other jurisdictions, an examination of some of these cases will illustrate the kinds of issues that may arise during the course of a lawsuit against a foreign sovereign or state enterprise or proceedings to enforce a judgment obtained against a foreign sovereign or state enterprise. This section concludes with a brief examination of some other Western municipal enactments and judicial decisions regarding the law of foreign sovereign immunity.

A. United States Law

i. Parties that May Enjoy Immunity
The law governing sovereign immunity questions in the United States is the Foreign Sovereign Immunities Act of 1976 (the FSIA).[57] Under the FSIA, both a 'foreign state' and 'an agency or instrumentality of a foreign state' may be entitled to immunity in certain circumstances. If a Chinese entity qualifies neither as a foreign state nor as 'an agency or instrumentality of a foreign state', it will not be entitled to immunity from suit in United States courts or from execution. A political subdivision, such as a provincial government, is also considered to be a 'foreign state'. Parts of the foreign state, such as ministries, also qualify as a foreign state.[58]

'An agency or instrumentality of a foreign state' is an entity which (a) is a 'separate legal person', (b) is majority-owned by a foreign state or is an organ of a foreign state, and (c) is not incorporated in the United States or a third country. Examples of entities likely to qualify as agencies or instrumentalities of a foreign state include 'a state trading corporation, a mining enterprise, a transport organization such as a shipping line or an airline, a steel company, a central bank, an export association, a governmental procurement agency or a department or ministry which acts and is suable in its own name'.[59] The third criterion is not likely to present problems in application; it makes clear that, for instance, a United States-incorporated subsidiary of a Chinese enterprise cannot claim sovereign immunity. The second criterion, however, may be difficult to apply to enterprises in socialist states, and it also may be difficult to prove whether a particular enterprise constitutes a separate legal person or not.

The ownership/'organ' criterion presents difficulties because it is 'ill-suited to concepts which exist in socialist states'.[60] 'Organ' is not defined in the FSIA. The ownership criterion presumably would be satisfied for state-owned economic enterprises (*guoying qiye*). For instance, in *Yessenin-Volpin* v. *Novosti Press Agency*, a court concluded that the Soviet Novosti Press Agency satisfied the criterion, and in consequence was entitled to immunity in the lawsuit in question, 'whether one relies on the fact that more than 63% of the property over which Novosti exercises the rights of possession and use is actually "owned" by the state, or whether one looks to the essentially public nature of all organizations such as Novosti in the Soviet Union'.[61] However, in *Edlow Int'l Co.* v. *Nuklearna Elektrarna Krsko*,[62] a court denied instrumentality status to a Yugoslavian 'workers' organization'. The court stated that the '[p]laintiff's argument that NEK is an agency or instrumentality of [the Socialist Federal Republic of Yugoslavia] rests, at bottom, on the principle that all property under a socialist system such as Yugoslavia's is subject to the ultimate ownership and authority of the state; ... to accept plaintiff's argument on this point would be to characterize virtually every enterprise operated under a socialist system as an instrumentality of the state within the terms of the [FSIA].' Partly because the court regarded this as an absurd result, and because the Yugoslav government did not take a direct hand in the daily management of the organization, the court concluded that the workers' organization should not qualify as an agency or instrumentality of a foreign state. However, the definition of 'agency or instrumentality of a foreign state' does not make any reference to any degree of control or daily management by a central government, and would appear to compel the conclusion that the court resisted: that all state-owned enterprises qualify either as parts of the foreign state or as agencies or instrumentalities of the foreign state.[63]

The legislative history of the FSIA indicates that a 'separate legal person' ordinarily would be understood to be an organization with the power to sue and be sued, to contract in its own name and to hold property in its own name.[64] However, the FSIA does not specify under whose law one must be a 'separate legal person'.[65] While formerly it might have been very difficult to determine whether a particular entity was a 'separate legal person' under Chinese law, the promulgation and implementation of the General Provisions of the Civil Code of the People's Republic of China should make such determinations possible from now on.[66]

In so far as immunity from suit is concerned, it makes no difference whether an entity qualifies as a part or subdivision of the foreign state itself, or as an agency or instrumentality, because the rules governing immunity from suit for both categories of defendants are the same. The categorization of the entity, however, makes a very significant difference with respect to the rules on execution of judgments, which are discussed below.

ii. Exceptions to Immunity from Jurisdiction
Once it has been determined that an entity qualifies as a 'foreign state' or an 'agency or instrumentality of a foreign state', the next step is to determine whether or not the claim upon which the suit is based fits within one of the exceptions to immunity from suit. If the foreign state or

state instrumentality's activity fits within one of these exceptions, then it cannot claim immunity despite its sovereign status.

There are six exceptions to immunity:

(a) where the foreign state has given a waiver;
(b) where the action is based upon a 'commercial activity';
(c) where rights in property are taken in violation of international law;
(d) where rights in property in the United States acquired by succession or gift or rights in immovable property in the United States are in issue;
(e) damage actions for certain torts of the state or of its employees acting within the scope of their employment; and
(f) suits in admiralty brought to enforce maritime liens, where the maritime lien is based upon a commercial activity of the foreign state.[67]

a. The 'Commercial Activity' Exception   As has been discussed in Section III above, it will usually be possible to obtain a waiver of foreign sovereign immunity by contractual provision. When a waiver has not been obtained, it may nevertheless be possible to sue a foreign state or instrumentality under the 'commercial activity' exception, which denies immunity in suits

in which the action is *based* upon a *commercial activity* carried on in the United States by the foreign state; or upon an act performed in the United States in connection with a commercial activity of the foreign state elsewhere; or upon an act outside the territory of the United States in connection with a commercial activity of the foreign state elsewhere and that act causes a direct effect in the United States.[68]

It is necessary first to examine the definition of the term 'commercial activity' and the interpretation of this definition. The FSIA defines 'commercial activity' as follows:

A 'commercial activity' means either a regular course of commercial conduct or a particular commercial transaction or act. The commercial character of an activity shall be determined by reference to the nature of the course of conduct or particular transaction or act, rather than by reference to its purpose.

The 'nature of the activity' test is supposed to resolve some of the difficult questions of determining 'commerciality'. For instance, 'the fact that goods or services to be procured through a contract are to be used for public purposes is irrelevant; it is the essentially commercial nature of an activity or transaction that is critical. Thus, a contract by a foreign government to buy provisions or equipment for its armed forces or to construct a government building constitutes a commercial activity.'[69] 'Certainly, if an activity is customarily carried on for profit, its commercial nature could readily be assumed.'[70] 'If the activity is one in which a private person could engage, it is not entitled to immunity.'[71]

However, these interpretations of the 'nature of the activity' test are not necessarily easily applied, because a 'for profit' criterion appears to be a 'purpose of the activity' test, and may not apply readily in a socialist context.[72] Despite the difficulties in application, however, the legislative history of the FSIA shows that the United States Congress intended the courts to have 'a great deal of latitude in determining what is a "commercial activity" for purposes of [the FSIA]'.[73] Thus, the determination of what constitutes 'commercial' and 'non-commercial' activity is in a process of evolution, as precedents are being laid down which define the contours of 'commercial activity'. Since the FSIA has been in effect for only a decade, there is still much uncertainty as to the classification of particular activities.

The delegation to the United States courts by Congress of difficult problems of categorization may have had the result that the courts have on occasion apparently used their 'great deal of latitude' to refuse to hear certain cases (for example, cases which could embarrass the United States in its relations with foreign countries) by determining that the activity on which suits are based is non-commercial. Whether the activity upon which suit is based is determined to be 'commercial' will depend, of course, on how broadly or narrowly a court defines the activity in question. Activities involving the exploitation of natural resources in a foreign state appear to be regarded as particularly sensitive and may be characterized by the courts as 'non-commercial'. Thus, for instance, in *Matter of Sedco*,[74] a suit brought against the Mexican state-owned oil company, Pemex, based on the oil-well disaster in the Bay of Campeche, the court determined that 'short of actually selling these resources on the world market', Pemex's conduct with respect to the oil, such as exploratory drilling, was not 'commercial'. If, however, the court had looked to the 'fundamental unity of oil operations', and recognized that '[o]ne does not undertake the costly and risky business of exploration without the hope that it will be successful and lead to profitable exploitation',[75] the court might have characterized the activity on which the suit was based as 'commercial', and have permitted the lawsuit to proceed. In fact, the court later vacated its order, stating that it needed testimony in court on the issue before reaching a decision on immunity.

In *International Association of Machinists and Aerospace Engineers v. OPEC*,[76] suit was brought against OPEC for conspiracy to fix oil prices in violation of United States antitrust laws. The district court referred to United Nations resolutions on natural resources, stating:

In determining whether the activities of the OPEC members are governmental or commercial in nature, the Court can and should examine the standards recognized under international law. The United Nations, with the concurrence of the United States, has repeatedly recognized the principle that a sovereign state has the sole power to control its natural resources... The control over a nation's natural resources stems from the nature of sovereignty. By necessity and traditional recognition, each nation is its own master in respect to its physical attributes. The defendants' control over their oil resources is an especially sovereign function because oil, as their primary, if not sole, revenue-producing resource, is crucial to the welfare of their nations' peoples.

Having determined that the control of the resource was 'sovereign', the court concluded that the activity upon which suit was brought was not 'commercial'.[77]

Likewise, in *MOL* v. *People's Republic of Bangladesh*,[78] the court determined that Bangladesh was immune from suit on breach of a licensing agreement to permit a United States corporation to capture and export rhesus monkeys. The court held that '[t]his was not just a contract for trade of monkeys. It concerned Bangladesh's right to regulate imports and exports, a sovereign prerogative... It concerned Bangladesh's right to regulate its natural resources, also a uniquely sovereign function.'

Courts may also determine that certain suits are not based on 'commercial activity' if the contract on which suit is based contains 'terms which only a sovereign state could perform', such as relief from taxes. A federal district court so ruled in *Practical Concepts, Inc.* v. *Republic of Bolivia*,[79] holding that a breach of contract suit was barred by sovereign immunity because the Bolivian government agreed in the contract to relieve the plaintiff's staff from Bolivian taxes, provide for duty-free clearance of supplies and personal effects through customs, and permit the plaintiff's staff access to certain privileges reserved for diplomats, such as access to the United States Embassy commissary.[80] In *MOL* the court reasoned in a similar fashion, stating as an alternative basis for its decision the fact that '[a] private party could not have made such an agreement'. These decisions indicate a possibly problematical area for a number of contracts with Chinese entities, since such contracts sometimes recite that preferential treatment is being or will be granted, or that the special approval of the requisite high governmental organs of the People's Republic of China has been or will be obtained. If the benefits mentioned in a contract are generally available and the contract recites that such benefits exist, the mere recitation of the benefits should not prevent the contract's being characterized as 'commercial'.[81]

Even in circumstances where the FSIA itself and the FSIA's legislative history would seem to indicate rather clearly that a given activity is commercial, the courts still may decline to make such a characterization. For instance, the application of the 'nature of the activity' test would seem to compel the conclusion that a state's entering into a loan agreement must be a commercial activity: since an individual is capable of borrowing, a state, in borrowing, engages in a commercial activity.[82] Moreover, the legislative history of the FSIA indicates that loans would be regarded as 'commercial activities'.[83] Despite this, at least one court has expressed doubts as to whether all sovereign debt obligations should be classified as 'commercial'.[84] As a result, bills have been introduced in the United States Congress which would specify that all sovereign debts are to be regarded as commercial.[85] In the meantime, parties which do not agree to waivers of sovereign immunity or to arbitration in their loan agreements may wish to stipulate in the agreement that the loan is 'commercial in nature', in an effort to prevent a court from characterizing the loan as non-commercial.[86]

Another means by which a sovereign defendant may be able to avoid

suit in the United States in respect of its arguably commercial activities is
the 'act of state' doctrine. The *Sedco, OPEC, MOL, Bolivia*, and *Reclamantes* cases indicate that a number of activities which are arguably 'commercial' may not be considered as such by the courts, and that sovereign
defendants may be held immune from suit in respect of such activities in
the absence of a waiver or the availability of another exception under the
FSIA. The United States courts do not always employ a relatively narrow
construal of the term 'commercial': they have also declined to hear some
cases even where the 'commercial activity' exception apparently applies,
under the 'act of state' doctrine. The classic statement of the 'act of state'
doctrine was given in *Underhill* v. *Hernandez*[87] in 1897: 'Every sovereign
State is bound to respect the independence of every other sovereign State,
and the courts of one country will not sit in judgment on the acts of the
government of another done within its own territory. Redress of griev-
ances by reason of such acts must be obtained through the means open
to be availed of by sovereign powers as between themselves.' While the
theoretical underpinning of the act of state doctrine has been a subject of
much discussion,[88] there appears to be increased emphasis on the doctrine's usage in circumstances where United States legal action would be
insulting to implicated foreign states and would interfere with the efforts
of the political branches of the United States government.[89]

The leading post-FSIA example of the application of the act of state
doctrine in proceedings against sovereign defendants is the appeals court's
decision in the *OPEC* case.[90] The appeals court held that the suit was
barred by the act of state doctrine, different grounds from those offered
by the district court for its dismissal of the case. The appeals court stated
that '[t]he act of state doctrine is not diluted by the commercial activity
exception which limits the doctrine of sovereign immunity. While purely
commercial activity may not rise to the level of an act of state, certain
seemingly commercial activity will trigger act of state considerations.'[91]

In fact, Congress probably believed that the act of state doctrine would
not be applied in any case in which the commercial activity exception
applied, since the legislative history of the FSIA describes the act of state
doctrine as the doctrine under which 'United States Courts may refuse to
adjudicate the validity of purely public acts of foreign sovereigns, as distinguished from commercial acts, committed and effective within their
own territory'.[92]

The act of state doctrine has been used to bar the enforcement of an
arbitral award to which the New York Convention on the Recognition
and Enforcement of Foreign Arbitral Awards applies. In *Libyan American Oil Co.* v. *Socialist People's Libyan Arab Jamahirya*,[93] the court
denied enforcement of the LIAMCO Award on grounds of the act of
state doctrine. On appeal, the United States government filed a brief as
amicus curiae, criticizing the lower court's application of the act of state
doctrine.[94] Although the case was settled before decision of the appeal,
the court of appeals still ordered that the lower court decision be vacated,
at the request of the United States government; hence the vitality of this
usage of the act of state doctrine is highly questionable. Nevertheless, it

perhaps serves to illustrate the reluctance of some United States courts to render judgments against foreign sovereign defendants.[95]

A further aspect of the concept of 'commercial activity' is the requirement of affiliating contacts with the United States. In order that jurisdiction may be maintained under the commercial activity exception, the commercial activity must have certain minimum points of contact with the United States: a suit must be based on a commercial activity carried on in the United States, or on an act performed in the United States in connection with a commercial activity elsewhere; or an act performed outside the territory of the United States that causes a 'direct effect' in the United States.[96] For many of the potential disputes of foreign investors in China, the direct effect provision is likely to be the only available provision in the FSIA under which to bring suit in a United States court.

So far, the direct effect jurisdictional provision has been interpreted narrowly, possibly because of its potential for friction between governments, since it may require a United States court to rule on the validity of activity largely occurring within a sovereign foreign state's own territory, thus implicating the same concerns as are addressed under the act of state doctrine.[97]

Callejo v. *Bancomer*[98] is an example of the application of the direct effect provision to a situation which could arise in China. In that case the purchasers of certificates of deposit in a Mexican bank brought suit against the bank when the Mexican government promulgated exchange control regulations requiring that all deposits in Mexican banks, whether denominated in United States dollars or Mexican pesos, be repaid in pesos at rates of exchange well below market rates.[99] The district court which heard the case ruled that the activity on which suit was based was not a commercial activity.[100] The appeals court disagreed; it ruled that the activity sued upon was the breach of the bank's contractual obligation, not the promulgation of the regulations; therefore the activity was commercial. It further ruled that the breach had a direct effect in the United States. However, it then ruled that the case was barred by the act of state doctrine because the Mexican government's 'actions were clearly sovereign and not commercial in nature'.[101] Lawsuits involving similar actions of the Chinese government might well be treated in the same manner as *Callejo*.

The circumstances in which an injury suffered by an American corporation overseas would be regarded as causing a 'direct effect *in the United States*' (emphasis added) are uncertain.[102] In some cases based on the injury of individuals abroad, the courts have ruled that an injury incurred overseas, in an aircraft crash or other accident involving American tourists, does not cause a direct effect in the United States.[103]

b. Rights in Property Taken in Violation of International Law The FSIA's provision on 'rights in property taken in violation of international law' is designed to deal with expropriation claims.[104] It permits suits:

in which rights in property taken in violation of international law are in issue and that property or any property exchanged for such property is present in the

United States in connection with a commercial activity carried on in the United States by the foreign state; or that property or any property exchanged for such property is owned or operated by an agency or instrumentality of the foreign state and that agency or instrumentality is engaged in a commercial activity in the United States.

Kalamazoo Spice Extraction Co. v. *Provisional Military Government of Ethiopia*[105] illustrates the operation of this section of the FSIA. The Ethiopian government expropriated an American company's stock in an Ethiopian company. The Ethiopian company continued to ship goods to the American company for sale in the United States. When the American company failed to pay the accounts receivable due to the expropriated Ethiopian company, the Ethiopian company sued for payment, and the American company counterclaimed against the Ethiopian government for the expropriation of the American company's stock in the Ethiopian company. The district court initially dismissed the counterclaim by the American company, on act of state grounds. However, the appeals court reversed that ruling, on the grounds that a treaty between the United States and Ethiopia rendered the act of state doctrine inapplicable. On remand, the district court ruled that it had jurisdiction over the expropriation claim. Specifically, it ruled that the property in dispute (namely, the accounts receivable) was located in the United States and was owned by an instrumentality of the foreign state, and that the instrumentality was therefore engaged in commercial activity in the United States.

c. Property in the United States Acquired by Succession or Gift, and Rights in Real Property in the United States   Jurisdiction over foreign states exists in cases where 'rights in property in the United States acquired by succession or gift or rights in immovable property situated in the United States are in issue'.[106] This provision is unlikely to be of importance for trade with or investment in China, although it may of course grow in importance for Chinese organizations as they invest in the United States.

d. Certain Torts   The FSIA also permits suit against a foreign state:

in which money damages are sought against a foreign state for personal injury or death, or damage to or loss of property, occurring in the United States and caused by a tortious act or omission of that foreign state or of any official or employee of that foreign state while acting within the scope of his office or employment, except that this paragraph shall not apply to
(A) any claim based upon the exercise or performance or the failure to exercise or perform a discretionary function regardless of whether the discretion be abused, or
(B) any claim arising out of malicious prosecution, abuse of process, libel, slander, misrepresentation, deceit, or interference with contract rights.

Although this section of the FSIA was designed primarily to deal with the problem of traffic accidents caused by officials and employees of foreign states in the United States, it has already served as the jurisdictional basis for the suit brought against the Republic of Chile for the murder of

Orlando Letelier, the former Chilean ambassador to the United States.[107] Since the offending act or omission must have occurred in the United States in order for jurisdiction to be maintained pursuant to the tort exception to immunity, this section of the FSIA will be of significance chiefly in respect of the operations of Chinese organizations in the United States. If they operate through United States subsidiaries, of course, the partial immunity provided by subsection (B) will be of no avail, since United States-incorporated subsidiaries do not qualify as 'foreign states' under the FSIA.

e. Maritime Liens Based on Commercial Activity   This provision of the FSIA[108] permits suits to enforce maritime liens against vessels of a foreign state engaged in commercial activity. The claimant must serve the master of the ship and the foreign state itself.[109] No maritime arrest is permitted, except in accordance with a waiver given by the foreign state; if an arrest is made, the suit will be dismissed unless the plaintiff can show that it was unaware that the vessel belonged to a foreign state.[110] Although the maritime lien will be deemed to be an *in personam* claim, judgment may not exceed the value of the vessel or the cargo.[111]

iii. Attribution of Liability of Instrumentality to Central Government
or from One Instrumentality to Another
In most cases, an investor would be able to pursue an action only against the Chinese party which has caused the injury complained of, for example, against the Chinese party that entered into the contract if the suit is for breach of contract.[112] There may, however, be circumstances in which the legal separateness of agencies and instrumentalities from their parent states and from each other may be disregarded. Those circumstances are discussed below in the section on execution of judgments.

iv. Immunity from Execution
As with the rules governing immunity from jurisdiction, the property of a foreign state or an agency or instrumentality of a foreign state is immune unless an exception to immunity from execution set forth in the FSIA applies.[113] It is important to recognize that a foreign state's property may enjoy immunity from execution under the FSIA even when a judgment has been obtained against it pursuant to the FSIA. This was the result in *Letelier* v. *Republic of Chile*,[114] when the personal representatives and survivors of Letelier sought to execute the default judgment that they had obtained against Chile. A district court concluded that the Chilean national airline's assets in the United States would be subject to execution to satisfy the judgment against the Republic of Chile. A basis for the court's holding was that Congress could not have meant to create a right without a remedy for violation of the right.[115] However, the appeals court concluded just the opposite, that, in fact, the FSIA does not ensure that 'a party may execute on a judgment against a foreign state by attaching property, even if it may validly assert jurisdiction over that foreign state'.[116] Thus it is necessary to examine the FSIA's separate rules on execution of judgments to determine whether a judgment, once obtained, will be executable in the United States.

a. Property as to Which a Waiver Has Been Given   Property is not immune from execution if the foreign state has waived its immunity, either explicitly or implicitly.[117] Property used for a commercial activity in the United States is immune 'prior to the entry of judgment in any action brought in a court of the United States or of a State [of the United States]' unless the foreign state or instrumentality 'has explicitly waived its immunity from attachment prior to judgment'.[118] A waiver of immunity from 'legal proceedings including suit judgment and execution on grounds of sovereignty' has been held in one case to constitute a waiver of immunity from prejudgment attachment.[119] However, it would be advisable to provide for prejudgment attachment and the like explicitly in a waiver of immunity clause.

b. Property Used for Commercial Activities   Property of central governments and political subdivisions will be immune from execution unless the 'property is or was used for the commercial activity upon which the claim is based'.[120] The range of property upon which a judgment creditor will be able to execute will, of course, vary according to how broadly or narrowly a court defines 'the commercial activity upon which the claim is based'. This section of the FSIA is largely uninterpreted, and it remains to be seen how much property of a foreign state will become subject to execution in cases based on commercial activity.[121]

The FSIA is more liberal with respect to the property of agencies and instrumentalities of foreign states. If an agency or instrumentality is engaged in commercial activity in the United States, all of its property in the United States will be subject to execution to satisfy a judgment against the agency or instrumentality obtained under the FSIA's commercial activity, expropriation, or tort exceptions to immunity from suit, regardless of whether the property is or was used for the activity upon which the claim was based.[122]

c. Property Granted Absolute Immunity   Funds of a foreign central bank or monetary authority 'held for its own account' are immune unless an explicit waiver has been given. Funds are 'held for the central bank's own account' when they are 'used or held in connection with central banking activities, as distinguished from funds used solely to finance the commercial transactions of other entities or of foreign states'.[123] Property which is used or intended to be used in connection with a military activity, and which is of a military character or is under the control of a military authority or defence agency, is immune.[124]

d. The Separate Status of Instrumentalities from Each Other and from their Parent States   The legal separateness of instrumentalities from each other and from their parent foreign states is respected in most circumstances.[125] However, the 'presumption of independent status' of an agency or instrumentality can be overcome when the application of 'internationally recognized equitable principles' would require that the status be disregarded in order to 'avoid injustice'.[126] The United States Supreme Court held that the presumption had been overcome in *First National City Bank* v. *Banco para el Comercio Exterior de Cuba*.[127] In that case a claim was made by Banco para el Comercio Exterior de Cuba

(Bancec) on Citibank for payment of an irrevocable letter of credit in favour of Bancec. Because the Cuban government had nationalized Citibank's assets in Cuba, Citibank set off, against its liability on the letter of credit, part of Cuba's liability to it for the nationalization. Bancec argued that it was a separate entity from the Cuban government, that is, that it was an 'instrumentality', and that the Cuban government's liability to Citibank could not be set off against Citibank's liability to Bancec.

The Supreme Court agreed with Citibank's action. In 1961, the Cuban government had dissolved Bancec, transferred its assets to the Cuban Ministry of Foreign Trade, and then, after six days, transferred those assets to another instrumentality. Partly on the basis of the Cuban government's holding of those assets for six days, the Court concluded that '[g]iving effect to Bancec's separate juridical status..., even though it has long been dissolved, would permit the real beneficiary of such an action, the Republic of Cuba, to obtain relief in our courts that it could not obtain in its own right without waiving its sovereign immunity and answering for the seizure of Citibank's assets.'[128]

An attempt to overcome 'the presumption of independent status' failed in the Letelier case discussed above. The judgment creditors—Letelier's survivors—attempted to execute their judgment on the assets of the Chilean national airline. The appeals court found that the airline's participation in the tort was 'not the sort of "abuse" that overcomes the presumption of separateness established by Bancec'.[129]

Given the courts' respect for the separate status of state enterprises, it will be important also to consider how much property a state enterprise owns and whether it will be available for execution in the event of an arbitral award or court judgment against it. Again, the situation with respect to Soviet instrumentalities may provide some guidance in the absence of published Chinese laws affecting the subject: the liability of a Soviet state enterprise is limited under Soviet law mainly to the enterprise's pecuniary funds since all land belongs to the state,[130] and, by statute, capital assets such as buildings and equipment are not subject to execution.[131] State-owned shipping and fishing companies do not own their vessels, but instead have 'operational control' of them, with ownership remaining in the state; thus the Soviet Union takes the position that no attachment or execution may be had against those vessels when action is taken against one of the companies, because the vessels belong to the state itself and the state enjoys absolute sovereign immunity.[132]

The Constitution of the People's Republic of China specifies that all urban land is owned by the state, and all suburban or rural land is owned by the state or by rural collectives.[133] The General Provisions of the Civil Code of the People's Republic of China provide that corporations owned by the people 'shall undertake civil responsibility with the property given to it by the State for its operation and management', but do not specify what categories of property are included therein.[134] The formulation of the General Provisions appears to indicate that buildings and equipment of a state-owned corporation, as well as its pecuniary funds, would be subject to execution.

B. The Foreign Sovereign Immunity Laws of Some Other States

i. The United Kingdom: The State Immunity Act of 1978

The foreign sovereign immunities law of the United Kingdom is codified in the State Immunity Act of 1978 (referred to hereafter as the SIA), which has one great virtue that the FSIA lacks: (relative) simplicity. Under the SIA, the central government of the foreign state (referred to as the 'State') is entitled to immunity but, unlike the FSIA, a 'separate entity' owned by a state is not entitled to immunity unless it has acted in a sovereign capacity and the circumstances are such that the state would have been immune also.[135] If an Order in Council has been made by which a constituent territory of a federal state is granted the immunities of a state, the territory will receive the same treatment as the state itself. If no such Order in Council has been made, the territory will be treated like any 'separate entity'.

Like the FSIA, the SIA also denies immunity to a state in respect of its commercial activities: 'A State is not immune as respects proceedings relating to ... a commercial transaction entered into by the State.'[136] 'Commercial transactions' specifically include 'any contract for the supply of goods or services', 'any loan or other transaction for the provision of finance and any guarantee or indemnity in respect of any such transaction or of any other financial obligation', and 'any other transaction or activity (whether of a commercial, industrial, financial, professional or other similar character) into which a State enters or in which it engages otherwise than in the exercise of sovereign authority.'[137] A state also is not immune as respects 'an obligation of the State which by virtue of a contract (whether a commercial transaction or not) falls to be performed wholly or partly in the United Kingdom.'[138]

No execution may be had against a state, a constituent territory (when entitled to immunity), or a separate entity (when entitled to immunity) except in accordance with the exceptions stipulated in the SIA. Property 'which is for the time being in use or intended for use for commercial purposes' is subject to execution.[139] (This provision is broader than that provided in the FSIA for foreign states, because there execution is limited to property that is or was used for the commercial activity on which the claim is based.) However, the funds of a central bank or other monetary authority held for its own account are immune even if they are used or intended to be used for the purposes of commercial transactions, paralleling the FSIA.[140] Thus, in order to execute against central bank property, a waiver would be required. A separate entity's property is not immune from execution, except when it would have been immune from jurisdiction but for its having given a waiver; in that case the separate entity's property is entitled to the same immunity from execution as the property of the foreign state itself.[141]

The SIA has been extended to Hong Kong, and has been adopted with little change by Singapore,[142] Pakistan,[143] and South Africa.[144]

ii. Canada: The State Immunity Act of 1982

The Canadian State Immunity Act of 1982[145] (referred to hereafter as the

Canadian SIA) is similar to the SIA and the FSIA. Like those acts, it grants immunity from jurisdiction to foreign states, subject to certain exceptions. The exceptions may be somewhat broader—that is, they may deny immunity to foreign states in more instances—than the exceptions in the FSIA and SIA.[146]

- The Canadian SIA defines 'foreign states' to include the government of a foreign state, political subdivisions of foreign states, and 'agencies' of foreign states.[147] An 'agency of a foreign state' is 'any legal entity that is an organ of the foreign state but that is separate from the foreign state'.[148] The term 'organ' is undefined.

Following the FSIA, the Canadian SIA adopts a broad definition of 'commercial activity', leaving the task of interpretation to the courts. 'Commercial activity' is defined to mean 'any particular transaction, act or conduct or any regular course of conduct that by reason of its nature is of a commercial character'.[149] Immunity will also be denied where a foreign state has submitted to the jurisdiction of the court either before or after the commencement of proceedings.[150]

Following the United Kingdom's SIA, the Canadian SIA permits execution against property of a foreign state that is used or intended for a commercial activity, regardless of whether the commercial activity has any relation to the activity on which the suit was based.[151] Agencies of foreign states are not immune from execution at all, except with respect to property that is military in nature or is intended to be used in connection with a military activity.[152] Unlike the FSIA and SIA, the Canadian SIA permits execution against property of a foreign central bank held for its own account if used or intended for a commercial activity.[153]

iii. Australia: The Foreign States Immunity Act of 1985

The Foreign States Immunity Act of 1985 (referred to hereafter as the Australian FSIA) is based largely on the United Kingdom's SIA. There are, however, significant differences, reflecting the influence of the United States FSIA. A 'foreign state' includes provinces, self-governing territories, or other political subdivisions, and departments or organs of the executive government of states or political subdivisions.[154] The Australian FSIA employs the term 'separate entity of a foreign State', and grants the same immunity from jurisdiction to such an entity as is granted to a foreign state.[155] In this respect it follows the United States FSIA, and avoids the difficult question raised by the SIA's requirement that a 'separate entity' must have acted in 'the exercise of sovereign authority' in order to enjoy immunity.

Like the other acts, the Australian FSIA denies immunity in proceedings concerning commercial transactions. 'Commercial transaction' is defined to mean 'a commercial trading, business, professional or industrial or like transaction into which the foreign State has entered or a like activity in which the State has engaged'.[156] 'Commercial transactions' specifically include contracts for the supply of goods or services, loan agreements, and guarantees or indemnities in respect of financial obligations.[157] Bills of exchange, including promissory notes, are specifically excluded from the class of commercial transactions; instead, it is provided that a foreign state will not be immune from suit on a bill of exchange if it would not be immune from suit with respect to the underlying transaction or event.[158]

The Australian FSIA permits execution against the 'commercial property' of foreign states.[159] Following the SIA, the Australian FSIA denies any immunity to the property of a separate entity, except where the separate entity would have been immune but for a waiver of immunity from jurisdiction, in which case its property is subject to the execution immunity rules applicable to foreign states.[160] Like the Canadian SIA, the Australian FSIA does not confer a blanket immunity on the funds of a foreign central bank held for its own account; instead, funds in use for commercial purposes may be subject to execution.

C. Pleas of Immunity before Arbitral Tribunals

The rules discussed above apply to court proceedings, including court proceedings in respect of arbitration agreements and arbitration awards. But can a state enterprise, after having agreed to binding arbitration, successfully plead sovereign immunity before the arbitral tribunal? The short answer is that pleas of immunity from the arbitration proceedings have been uniformly rejected.[161] For example, in *Solel Boneh International Ltd. (Israel) and Water Resources Development International (Israel) v. Republic of Uganda and National Housing and Construction Corporation of Uganda* (ICC Case 2321), the arbitrator treated a plea of sovereign immunity as irrelevant as regards the arbitration proceedings:

I myself do not see the need for referring to any particular set of national law rules or the court practice of any particular country... Whichever the proper law of the contract may be, this has nothing to do with the defence of sovereign immunity. Sovereign immunity may operate as a bar to the exercise of jurisdiction or prevent enforcement measures but does not *per se* interfere with the legal relationship between the parties as defined in a contract or otherwise... It is... clear to me that the doctrine of sovereign immunity applies only in the relations between courts and other authorities on one side, and another state, its representatives or property on the other side. As arbitrator I am myself no representative or organ of any state. My authority as arbitrator rests upon an agreement between the parties to the dispute...

In *SPP (Middle East) Ltd., Hong Kong and Southern Pacific Properties Ltd. v. The Arab Republic of Egypt and the Egyptian General Company for Tourism and Hotels (EGOTH)*,[162] the Egyptian Tourism Organization and SPP agreed to a joint venture to develop a tourism complex in Egypt, and entered into an agreement which provided for ICC arbitration. The Egyptian Minister of Tourism signed the agreement which provided for arbitration, stating that he 'approved, agreed and ratified' it. The project was cancelled. The Egyptian government contended that the steps taken to cancel the project were measures of a legislative and executive character amounting to an 'act of state'. The arbitrators apparently treated the defence of 'act of state' as though it were a plea of sovereign immunity, and concluded:

The issue is whether submission to international arbitration by States and public entities should be regarded as an implicit waiver of immunity thus preventing concurrent application of other international or municipal rules granting sovereign immunity... It would indeed be frustrating to recognise full force and effect of general principles of international law aimed at protecting foreign investors and then admit that a state may, before an arbitral tribunal, rely upon domestic or international principles granting sovereign immunity as an excuse for acts amounting to contractual breaches.[163]

V. Conclusion

Only in the unfortunate event of an irreconcilable dispute will the rules of foreign sovereign immunity come into play. In most contractual and investment disputes, the dispute will go to arbitration, and, if an award is rendered against a Chinese party, foreign sovereign immunity rules are not likely to come into play, because the assets of most Chinese organizations are located in China, and the foreign party will seek enforcement of the award in the people's courts. In other cases, however, there may be actions in the courts of other states, particularly if more Chinese assets come to be located abroad in the future. Because the law of foreign sovereign immunity is still in a developmental phase, there will be a degree of uncertainty as to whether a judgment, or execution, can be obtained against a Chinese party in the courts of a particular state. Foreign and Chinese enterprises can, however, structure their transactions to remove at least some of the uncertainty, by, for instance, negotiating waiver clauses and the like.

Notes

1. See I. Brownlie, *Principles of Public International Law* (Oxford, Oxford University Press, 3rd edition, 1979), p. 323 (discussing foreign sovereign immunity as having its source in the principle of *par in parem non habet jurisdictionem*— 'equals do not have jurisdiction over equals'); G. Badr, *State Immunity: An Analytical and Prognostic View* (Dordrecht, Martinus Nijhoff, 1984), p. 89 (discussing the provenance of *par in parem non habet imperium*); H. Lauterpacht, 'The Problems of Jurisdictional Immunities of Foreign States', *British Year Book of International Law* (Oxford, Oxford University Press, 1951), Vol. 28, p. 220.

2. See *The Schooner Exchange* v. *M'Faddon*, 7 Cranch 116, 136, 3 L.Ed. 287 (1812); *Verlinden, B.V.* v. *Central Bank of Nigeria*, 461 U.S. 480 (1983); T. Giuttari, *The American Law of Sovereign Immunity* (New York, Praeger Publishers, 1970), pp. 27–43.

3. There are now a very large number of government-owned corporations, in both developing countries and advanced industrial countries. For instance, as of 1976 there were at least 21 corporations owned by the United States government that qualified as 'separate legal persons'. See Brief for Respondent, Appendix a1–a14, submitted in *First National City Bank* v. *Banco para el Comercio Exterior de*

Cuba, 462 U.S. 611 (1983). State enterprises are particularly prevalent in developing countries.

4. See M. Singer, 'Abandoning Restrictive Sovereign Immunity: An Analysis in Terms of Jurisdiction to Prescribe', *Harvard International Law Journal*, Vol. 26, 1985, pp. 2 and 17.

5. *The Charkieh*, L.R. 4A and E59ff. In 1824, Chief Justice John Marshall of the United States Supreme Court explained the principle of non-immunity for commercial acts as follows: '[W]hen a government becomes a partner in any trading company, it divests itself, so far as concerns the transactions of that company, of its sovereign character, and takes that of a private citizen... [I]t descends to a level with those with whom it associates itself, and takes the character which belongs to its associates, and to the business which is to be transacted.' *Bank of the United States* v. *Planter's Bank*, 22 U.S. (9 Wheat.) 904, 907 (1824).

6. *Pasicrisie*, 1857, II, 348.

7. The United States was one of the last Western nations to adopt the restrictive doctrine of sovereign immunity. It initially adopted the doctrine in 1952 in a letter from the Acting Legal Advisor of the State Department, Jack B. Tate, to the Acting Attorney General (hereafter referred to as the Tate Letter). The letter stated that ten countries supported the restrictive doctrine, while thirteen supported the absolute doctrine; that, 'with the possible exception of the United Kingdom little support has been found except on the part of the Soviet Union and its satellites for full acceptance of the absolute theory of sovereign immunity'; and that '[t]he Department [of State] has now reached the conclusion that [absolute] sovereign immunity should no longer be granted in certain types of cases'. Instead, 'it will hereafter be the Department [of State]'s policy to follow the restrictive theory of sovereign immunity in the consideration of requests of foreign governments for a grant of sovereign immunity.' The Tate Letter concludes that 'it will be the Department [of State]'s practice to inform you [the Department of Justice] of all requests by foreign governments for the grant of immunity from suit and of the Department [of State]'s action thereon.' Letter from Jack B. Tate, Acting Legal Advisor, Department of State, to Acting Attorney General Philip B. Perlman (19 May 1952), reprinted in *Department of State Bulletin*, Vol. 26, 23 June 1952, pp. 984–5. Under Tate Letter practice from 1952 until the effective date of the Foreign Sovereign Immunities Act of 1976, 28 U.S.C. § 1601 *et seq.* (hereafter cited as the FSIA) in 1977, the State Department made immunity determinations. One of the major changes made by the FSIA was to transfer the making of determinations from the Department of State to the judiciary. See H.R. Rep. 1487, 94th Cong., 2nd Sess., reprinted in *United States Code Congressional and Administrative News* (hereafter cited as *US Code Cong. & Ad. News*), 1976, p. 6607.

8. The United Kingdom's State Immunity Act of 1978 did not come into force until 22 November 1978. However, the restrictive doctrine may have been judicially adopted before the effective date of the Act, in *Trendtex Trading Corporation* v. *Central Bank of Nigeria* (1977). See W.T. John, 'Sovereign Risk and Immunity under English Law and Practice', *International Financial Law* (London, Euromoney Publications Ltd., 1980), p. 75.

9. The enactments are collected in *Materials on Jurisdictional Immunities of States and Their Property* (New York, United Nations Legislative Series, 1982), hereafter referred to as *Materials on Jurisdictional Immunities*, and in G. Badr, note 1 above. The United Kingdom's State Immunities Act of 1978 was extended to Hong Kong by the State Immunity (Overseas Territories) Order 1979. For cases applying the restrictive doctrine, see cases collected in *Alfred Dunhill of London, Inc.* v. *The Republic of Cuba*, 425 U.S 682, 702, n. 15 (1976).

10. 16 May 1972, Europ. T.S. 74, 1979, U.K.T.S. No. 74 (Cmd. 7742), reprinted in *International Legal Materials*, Vol. 11, 1972, p. 470.

11. 'Organization of American States, 21 January 1983', reprinted in *International Legal Materials*, Vol. 22, 1983, p. 292.

12. 'International Law Association, Report of the Sixtieth Conference (1982), Aug. 29–Sept. 4, 1982', reprinted in *International Legal Materials*, Vol. 22, 1983, p. 287.

13. Memorandum presented by Professor N. Ushakov, entitled 'Jurisdiction Immunities of States and Their Property', to the International Law Commission, 35th Sess., U.N. Doc. A/CN.4/371 (1983), p. 5. 'The state is always a single subject, but the expressions of its legal personality are manifold. If a state concludes a contract with or makes a loan to another state, it does not thereby lose its sovereignty, and continues to act as a sovereign in the economic field, as well as in the field of international scientific and cultural relations.' M.M. Boguslavsky, 'Foreign State Immunity: Soviet Doctrine and Practice', *Netherlands Year Book of International Law* (Dordrecht, Martinus Nijhoff, 1979), Vol. 10, p. 176.

14. '[T]he approach of many jurists to the "sovereign in the market place" is based on conceptions concerning the role of the state and the significance of state ownership which are inapplicable even to modern capitalist economies. It is this political aspect which makes it difficult for a restrictive principle: as it has been pointed out, economic activity of the state remains state activity.' I. Brownlie, pp. 332–3, note 1 above, quoted in Memorandum presented by Professor N. Ushakov, p. 7, note 13 above.

15. Memorandum of N. Ushakov, p. 3, note 13 above. See C. Osakwe, 'A Soviet Perspective on Foreign Sovereign Immunity: Law and Practice', *Virginia Journal of International Law*, Vol. 23, 1982, p. 14, n.4.

16. '*Fu zhu*', 'US Court Trial Violates International Law', *Beijing Review*, No. 11, 14 March 1983, p. 25.

17. '*Fu zhu*', note 16 above.

18. *Jackson* v. *People's Republic of China*, 550 F. Supp. 869 (N.D. Ala. 1982), vacated and dismissed, 596 F. Supp. 386, affirmed, 794 F. 2d 1490 (11th Cir. 1986), rehearing denied, 801 F. 2d 404 (11th Cir. 1986).

19. The full text of the *aide-mémoire* is reproduced in *International Legal Materials*, Vol. 22, 1983, p. 81 and in E. Theroux and T. Peele, 'China and Sovereign Immunity: The Huguang Railway Bonds Case', *China Law Reporter*, No. 2, 1983, p. 150.

20. Declaration of George P. Shultz, para. 6 (12 August 1983). The Statement of Interest of the United States which accompanied the Shultz declaration is reproduced in *International Legal Materials*, Vol. 22, 1983, p. 1077.

21. *Jackson* v. *People's Republic of China*, 596 F. Supp. 386 (N.D. Ala. 1984), affirmed, 794 F. 2d. 1490 (11th Cir. 1986). See 'Jackson v. The People's Republic of China', *American Journal of International Law*, Vol. 78, 1984, p. 675; 'Diplomacy Collides with U.S. Cases', *Legal Times*, 1 October 1984, p. 1; 'Defaulting of Foreign States and an Expansive Role for the Act of State Doctrine: Jackson v. People's Republic of China', *Whittier Law Review*, Vol. 6, 1984, p. 177.

The pendency of the Huguang Bonds Case may have impeded the entry of Chinese organizations into the United States bond market, because of apprehension that the plaintiffs in that case would seek to attach the proceeds of new bond offerings. See E. Morrison, 'Borrowing on World Bonds Markets', *China Business Review*, No. 13, 1986, pp. 20–1. Even though the Huguang Bonds were also issued in Germany, the China International Trust and Investment Corporation (CITIC) made two public offerings there, each of 150 million Deutschmarks, in June and September 1985. See E. Morrison, p. 20; 'China to Go Ahead with Bond Issue', *Hong Kong Standard*, 10 May 1985, p. 1. Post-war treaties signed by Germany may have removed impediments to bond issuances in Germany that remain in the United States as long as the Huguang Bonds Case, and other cases like it, such as *Carl Marks & Co.* v. *People's Republic of China*, 82 Civ. 8217 (S.D.N.Y. filed 10 December 1982), and *Carl Marks & Co.* v. *People's Republic of China*, 82 Civ. 8218 (S.D.N.Y. filed 10 December 1982), are pending.

22. O.S. Ioffe, '*Khozraschet*', in F. Feldbrugge, *Encyclopedia of Soviet Law*

(Dordrecht, Martinus Nijhoff Publishers, 1985), p. 414; G.C. Reghizzi, *'Khozraschet'*, in F. Feldbrugge, *Encyclopedia of Soviet Law* (Dordrecht, Martinus Nijhoff Publishers, 1973), p. 356.

23. A. Hastrich, 'Persons (including juristic persons)', in F. Feldbrugge (1985), p. 586, note 22 above. C. Osakwe, pp. 27–8, note 15 above.

24. See General Provisions of the Civil Code of the People's Republic of China, adopted on 12 April 1986 and effective on 1 January 1987, hereafter cited as the General Provisions, Arts. 36–53. See, also, *'Faren'* ('Legal Person'), *Faxue cidian* (*Legal Dictionary*) (Shanghai, Shanghai Lexicographical Publishing House, 1980), p. 454; *'Faren'* ('Legal Person'), *Zhongghuo da baike quanshu (faxue)* (*Great Encyclopaedia of China [Law Volume]*) (Beijing, Great Encyclopaedia of China Publishing House, 1984), p. 105.

25. See Civil Procedure Law of the People's Republic of China (for Trial Implementation), 8 March 1982, Art. 44 (hereafter cited as the Civil Procedure Code); 'Ministry refuses to appear in court', *China Daily*, 15 December 1984, p. 4.

26. Civ. No. 82-2205 (S.D.N.Y. filed 7 April 1982).

27. See 42 U.S.C. § 783.

28. Civil Procedure Code, Arts. 186 (foreigners have the same litigation rights as Chinese citizens), 187 (foreigners have same litigation rights as Chinese citizens provided that there is reciprocity in the foreigners' courts for suits by Chinese citizens), 192 (jurisdiction over foreign economic, trade, transport, and maritime affairs, except where there is an arbitration agreement), and 44 (jurisdiction over government organizations and offices), note 25 above; and the Constitution of the People's Republic of China, 1982, Art. 41 (remedy of Chinese citizens for losses through infringement of their civic rights by any state organ or functionary).

29. Affidavit of R. Randle Edwards, *China National Technical Import Corporation* v. *United States*, No. 82-9905 (S.D.N.Y. filed 7 April 1982).

30. Legal opinion of the China Council for the Promotion of International Trade, Ref. No. C1-C/82/8216A, *China National Technical Import Corporation* v. *United States*, No. 82-9905 (S.D.N.Y. filed 7 April 1982). See 'Unlocking China's Courts', *Business Week*, 3 May 1982, p. 76.

31. See Address of Ambassador Huang Jiahua to Sixth Committee of the Thirty-ninth Session of the United Nations General Assembly, para. 31 (1984) (U.N. Doc. A/C.6/39/SR.39); Address of Ambassador Huang Jiahua to Sixth Committee of the Forty-first Session of the United Nations General Assembly, 11 November 1986.

32. *Yessenin-Volpin* v. *Novosti Press Agency*, 443 F. Supp. 849 (S.D.N.Y. 1978). This decision has been criticized because '[t]he court essentially concluded that even though Novosti was a juridical person under Soviet law, it was entitled to invoke sovereign immunity because "Novosti fulfills all aspects of the definition of an 'agency or instrumentality of a foreign state'." . . . What the court failed to realize was that under Soviet law it is possible to be both a juridical person and an agency or instrumentality of the Soviet State, and that the grant of juridical status to an organization is conclusive of a waiver of that entity's jurisdictional immunity.' C. Osakwe, p. 31, n. 77, note 15 above. While this critique states that 'the court failed to realize ... that under Soviet law it is possible to be *both* a juridical person and an agency or instrumentality of the Soviet State' (emphasis added), in fact, under United States law an entity constitutes 'an agency or instrumentality of a foreign state' only *if* it is a juridical person. The critique further misconceives the nature of the court's inquiry under United States law, by treating Novosti's lack of immunity from suit in the Soviet Union as the criterion for determining whether it would be immune from suit in the courts of the United States. In fact, immunity determinations are made under United States law without regard to whether the defendants might or might not have been able to claim immunity if sued in their home state. See, generally, Section IVA below. As regards the notion of separate juridical status constituting a blanket waiver of juris-

dictional immunity from suit in Soviet *and* foreign courts, a Soviet commentator discussing Yessenin-Volpin apparently does not agree that Novosti's separate juridical status constitutes a waiver of immunity from suit in foreign courts: '[T]he court came to the conclusion that the Soviet organizations enjoyed immunity from judicial jurisdiction in accordance with the [U.S.] 1976 [Foreign Sovereign] Immunities Act. One cannot but agree with this conclusion.' M. Boguslavsky, p. 176, note 13 above. Moreover, in *Harris* v. *VAO Intourist*, 481 F. Supp. 1056, 1058–9 (E.D.N.Y. 1979), the court rejected a claim by plaintiffs that various statutes and treaties, 'though indicating a capacity of the defendants to sue or be sue at their option, do not reflect an intention to waive governmental immunity'.

'Enlightened as communist practice may seem at home, its aims and results abroad have been less than satisfactory. Initially, the Soviet trade monopolies sought to take full advantage of governmental immunities as recognized in international law and applied in Western courts.' S. Pisar, *Coexistence and Commerce: Guidelines for Transactions Between East and West* (New York, McGraw-Hill Book Co., 1970), p. 270. However, the seeming inconsistency between practice at home and abroad is not limited to the Soviet Union. For instance, even though the United States began to apply the restrictive theory of foreign sovereign immunity in United States courts in 1952, the Unites States government, when sued abroad, continued, at least during the early 1970s, to plead sovereign immunity in foreign courts in instances where, under United States practice, a foreign state would not have been granted immunity from suit in a United States court. *Policies and Practices of the United States of America with Respect to Litigation in Foreign Courts* (US Department of State, unpublished, n.d.). Since the 1970s, the United States government arguably has continued to claim immunity in some cases for which a foreign state would not be granted immunity if sued on the same claim in the United States. See, for example, Motion to Dismiss (29 December 1982), in *Garcia* v. *Philippine Area Exchange*, Civil Case No. 3378 (Court of the First Instance of Pampanga and Angeles City, Republic of the Philippines) (a wrongful discharge action of an employee of United States military post exchange); Memorandum of Fact and Law Submitted by the Defendant United States of America, Applicant, *Carrato* v. *United States*, No. 3597/82, Supreme Court of Ontario (17 December 1982) (action for unlawful trespass, entry, and seizure of goods located in Canada).

33. *Harris* v. *VAO Intourist*, 481 F. Supp. 1056 (E.D.N.Y. 1979).

34. 481 F. Supp. at 1057. Qualification as 'an agency or instrumentality of a foreign state' did not guarantee immunity from suit. It meant that the defendant's amenability to suit was to be determined pursuant to the applicable United States law on suits against foreign states and agencies and instrumentalities of foreign states. That law will not support jurisdiction over cases based on injury sustained in a foreign state arising from the commercial activities of an agency or instrumentality of a foreign state unless it causes a 'direct effect in the United States'. 28 U.S.C. § 1605(a)(2). The court determined that the negligent operation of a hotel in Moscow causing the death of an American did not cause a direct effect in the United States, and dismissed the case. 481 F. Supp. at 1062. It also dismissed the case as to the other defendants, the National Hotel of Moscow and VAO Intourist. See, also, *Frolova* v. *Union of Soviet Socialist Republics*, 761 F.2d 370 (7th Cir. 1985) (in which the Union of Soviet Socialist Republics was held immune from suit for tort not causing direct effect in the United States).

35. *United Euram Corporation* v. *USSR*, 461 F. Supp. 609 (S.D.N.Y. 1978).

36. 493 F. Supp. 621 (S.D.N.Y. 1980).

37. Technically, the suit was dismissed on the grounds of immunity, but this is due to the rather convoluted structure of the applicable United States law, the Foreign Sovereign Immunities Act of 1976, note 7 above. Under that law, if personal jurisdiction over the defendant—sufficient affiliating contacts of the defendant with the place where the suit is brought—does not exist, then, as a matter of

statutory definition, the defendant will be regarded as immune from suit. See 28 U.S.C. § 1605(a)(2); H. Smit, 'The Foreign Sovereign Immunities Act of 1976: A Plea for Drastic Surgery', *Proceedings of the American Society of International Law*, 1980, p. 51 (criticizing the 'deficient' structure of the Act). If the Act were written in a less convoluted manner, one might say that the case against COSCO was dismissed on grounds of lack of personal jurisdiction, not on grounds of immunity (which ordinarily would be an affirmative defence, to be addressed after personal jurisdiction had been found to exist).

38. *China National Chemical[s] Import and Export Corporation* v. *M/V Lago Hualaihue*, 504 F. Supp. 684 (D. Md. 1981). The defence of sovereign immunity of course does not come into play when a sovereign or sovereign-owned entity is the plaintiff (except as respects counterclaims). *China National Chemical Import and Export Corporation* appeared as a plaintiff also in *China National Chemicals Import and Export Corporation*. v. *Nitron International Corporation et al.*, Civil No. B-84-215 RCZ (28 March 1984). See 'Sinochem Sues US Trading Firm for Damages over Urea, DAP Sales', *Green Markets*, 16 April 1984, p. 1; 'China Sues Greenwich Firm for Fraud', *The Telegram* (Bridgeport, Conn.), 5 April 1984, p. 1. Chinese foreign trade corporations have appeared as respondents several times before United States government agencies administering the United States anti-dumping laws. See, for example, *Haarman and Reimer Corporation* v. *United States*, 1 CIT 127 (China National Native Produce and Animal By-products Import and Export Corporation appearing as defendant-intervenor in an appeal of negative preliminary determination of the Commerce Department in an anti-dumping investigation of menthol from China), later proceeding, 1 CIT 148, later proceeding, 1 CIT 207 (1981).

39. See 504 F. Supp. 688–90.

40. 504 F. Supp. 690.

41. 28 U.S.C. § 1605(a)(1). '[I]f the foreign state agrees to a waiver of sovereign immunity in a contract, that waiver may subsequently be withdrawn only in a manner consistent with the expression of the waiver in the contract. Some court decisions have allowed subsequent and unilateral rescissions of waivers by foreign states. But the better view, and the one followed in this section [§ 1605(a)(1)], is that a foreign state which has induced a private person into a contract by promising not to invoke its immunity cannot, when a dispute arises, go back on its promise and seek to revoke the waiver unilaterally.' H.R. Rep. No. 1497, 94th Cong., 2nd Sess. 7 (1976), reprinted in *US Code Cong. & Ad. News*, 1976, p. 6617, note 7 above.

42. The State Immunity Act of 1978 (referred to hereafter as the SIA), § 2(1).

43. 'The head of a State's diplomatic mission in the United Kingdom ... shall be deemed to have authority to submit on behalf of the State in respect of any proceedings; and any person who has entered into a contract on behalf of and with the authority of a State shall be deemed to have authority to submit on its behalf in respect of proceedings arising out of the contract.' SIA § 2(7), note 42 above.

44. SIA § 2(9), note 42 above.

45. 'With respect to implicit waivers, the courts have found such waivers in cases where a foreign state has agreed to arbitration *in another country* ...'. H.R. Rep. No. 1497, 94th Cong., 2nd Sess. 7 (1976), reprinted in *US Code Cong. & Ad. News*, 1976, p. 6617 (emphasis added), note 7 above. Compare *Maritime Int'l Nominees Establishment* v. *Republic of Guinea*, 693 F. 2d 1094, 1103 (D.C. Cir. 1982) (an agreement to ICSID arbitration does not constitute agreement to 'arbitration in another country'; the defendant Guinea held immune and the court lacked the jurisdiction to confirm the American Arbitration Association arbitration award).

The court in *Paterson, Zochonis (UK) Ltd.* v. *Compania United Arrow*, 493 F. Supp. 621 (S.D.N.Y. 1980) (mentioned in Section II above, see note 36 above) noted that the COSCO bills of lading issued to the plaintiffs provided for the resolution of all controversies in the People's Republic of China. The court went on to observe that the dispute resolution provision on the bills of lading would not be regarded as a waiver of immunity from the jurisdiction of United States courts, because such a provision would constitute an implicit waiver of sovereign immunity only if it provided for arbitration in a country other than China. 493 F. Supp. at 624, 624–5, n.8. However, it appears that the court's remark was inapposite, because the COSCO bills of lading did not provide for arbitration at all, as a telex from the China Council for the Promotion of International Trade (CCPIT) included as an appendix to the court's opinion makes clear. See 493 F. Supp. at 625–6. Apparently the court read a forum selection clause as if it were an arbitration clause.

46. See *Ohntrup* v. *Firearms Center Inc.*, 516 F. Supp. 1281, 1285 (E.D. Pa. 1981) (declining to find waiver where arbitration agreement did not specify arbitration in the United States); *Verlinden, B.V.* v. *Central Bank of Nigeria*, 488 F. Supp. 1284, affirmed on other grounds, 647 F.2d 320 (2nd Cir.), reversed on other grounds, 103 S. Ct. 1962 (1983) (same).

47. 330 United Nations Treaty Series p. 38, no. 4739 (1959), U.S.T.S. 2517, T.I.A.S. 6997. The United States government has disagreed with a federal district court which refused to enforce an award which might have been rendered in a state not party to the New York Convention. In its Brief for the United States as *amicus curiae* in *Libyan American Oil Co.* v. *Socialist People's Libyan Arab Jamahirya*, reprinted in *International Legal Materials*, Vol. 20, 1981, pp. 161 and 163, the United States government asserted that enforcement proceedings in the United States were foreseeable even though the parties had not agreed to a specific situs for arbitration, and even though Libya was not a party to the New York Convention; since such proceedings were foreseeable, the United States government argued, it was proper for the United States courts to maintain jurisdiction of the enforcement proceeding. The case eventually was settled, and the appeals court ordered the district court decision vacated.

In other cases, arbitration awards should be enforceable. In *Ipitrade International, S.A.* v. *Federal Republic of Nigeria*, 465 F. Supp. 824 (D.D.C. 1978), a French corporation entered into a contract for the sale of cement to the government of Nigeria. The contract provided for Swiss governing law and ICC arbitration. After the arbitration in Switzerland, Ipitrade applied for enforcement of the arbitral award in the United States under the New York Convention. The court held that immunity had been waived in respect of the enforcement proceedings.

A foreign arbitral award may be enforceable in China pursuant to the New York Convention, since the People's Republic of China is now a party to that Convention. An arbitral award may also be enforceable in accordance with the Civil Procedure Code of the People's Republic of China, note 25 above. However, while that Code specifically provides for the enforcement of Chinese arbitral awards, it is silent on the enforcement of foreign arbitral awards. Other provisions of the Code suggest that the people's courts may have broad discretion in deciding whether or not to enforce a foreign arbitral award. See Chapter 16, this volume.

48. H.R. Rep. 1487, 94th Cong., 2nd Sess., reprinted in *US Code Cong. & Ad. News*, 1976, p. 6617, note 7 above.

49. Compare *Resource Dynamics International* v. *General People's Committee*, 593 F. Supp. 572 (N.D. Ga. 1984) (immunity waived; parties agreed to Virginia law) and *Marlowe* v. *Argentine Naval Commission*, 604 F. Supp. 703 (D.D.C. 1985) (immunity waived; parties agreed to District of Columbia law) with *Verlinden, B.V.* v. *Central Bank of Nigeria*, 488 F. Supp. 1284, 1300–2, affirmed on other grounds, 647 F.2d 320, reversed on other grounds, 461 U.S. 480 (1983) (refusing to find implicit waiver where contract was governed by the law of a third country), and *Ohntrup* v. *Firearms Center, Inc.*, 516 F. Supp. 1281 (E.D. Pa. 1981) (same).

50. R.B. von Mehren, 'The Foreign Sovereign Immunities Act of 1976', *Col-*

umbia Journal of Transnational Law, Vol. 17, 1978, pp. 56–7; J. Stevenson, J. Browne, and L. Damrosch, *United States Law of Sovereign Immunity Relating to International Financial Transactions* (London, Euromoney Publications Ltd., 1983), p. 101.

51. *Verlinden, B.V.* v. *Central Bank of Nigeria*, 488 F. Supp. 1284, 1300–2, affirmed on other grounds, 647 F.2d 320, reversed on other grounds, 461 U.S. 480 (1983) (refusing to find implicit waiver where contract was governed by the law of a third country), and *Ohntrup* v. *Firearms Center, Inc.*, 516 F. Supp. 1281 (E.D. Pa. 1981) (same).

52. See *Harris* v. *VAO Intourist*, 481 F. Supp. 1056, 1058–9 (E.D.N.Y. 1979) (Soviet statutes and treaties 'indicating a capacity of the defendants to sue or be sued at their option, do not reflect an intention to waive governmental immunity' of Soviet instrumentalities).

53. See Section II above. It might be argued that *Chinese* rules of sovereign immunity should be applied in United States court actions based on contracts stipulating that Chinese law will be the governing law, regardless of whether the choice of law constitutes an implicit waiver under United States law. See J. Stevenson, J. Browne, and L. Damrosch, note 50 above (raising the possibility that the governing-law clause could cause non-United States rules of immunity to be applied). This would be an unusual argument, because the rules of foreign sovereign immunity are usually viewed as merely 'remedial' or 'procedural', not 'substantive', that is, as only creating jurisdictional rules for pre-existing substantive rights. See Plaintiffs' Opposition to Defendant's Motion for Relief from Judgment by Default and Motion to Dismiss 32–37 (14 October 1983), *Jackson* v. *People's Republic of China*, Civil Action No. 79-C-1272-E (N.D. Ala.). Under that view of the rules of foreign sovereign immunity, the immunity rules of the forum state should be applied. However, the United State Supreme Court held in *Verlinden, B.V.* v. *Central Bank of Nigeria* that 'every action against a foreign sovereign necessarily involves application of a body of *substantive* federal law' (emphasis added), that is, the federally enacted rules of foreign sovereign immunity. 461 U.S. 480, 497 (1983). See *Goar* v. *Compania Peruana de Vapores*, 688 F.2d 417 (5th Cir. 1982) (removal of immunity from foreign sovereigns creates rights and remedies that never before existed); *Arango* v. *Guzman Travel Advisors*, 761 F.2d 1527, 1535, n. 7 (11th Cir. 1985) (same). But see H.R. Rep. 1487, 94th Cong., 2nd Sess., reprinted in *US Code Cong. & Ad. News*, 1976, p. 6610 ('The bill is not intended to affect the substantive law of liability'), note 7 above. If the rules of foreign sovereign immunity are substantive, then arguably the *substantive* law specified in a contract (such as Chinese law), including the substantive immunity rules, should be applied. Nevertheless, it may be the public policy of the United States to apply its own foreign sovereign immunity rules regardless of a contract's governing-law provision, since the United States Foreign Sovereign Immunities Act provides that '[c]laims of foreign states to immunity should henceforth be decided by courts of the United States and of the States in conformity with the principles set forth in [the Foreign Sovereign Immunities Act of 1976]', and the legislative history also emphasizes the exclusivity of the immunity rules set forth in the FSIA. See H.R. Rep. 1487, 94th Cong., 2nd Sess., reprinted in *US Code Cong. & Ad. News*, 1976, p. 6610, note 7 above.

54. SIA § 2(2) (emphasis added), note 42 above.

55. 'Research has disclosed no United States case basing waiver of immunity on a choice of law clause in a private agreement.' H.M. Sklaver, 'Sovereign Immunity in the United States: An Analysis of S. 566', *International Law*, Vol. 8, 1974, p. 413. See Memorandum of Points and Authorities in Support of Defendant's Motion to Dismiss 5 (8 February 1985), *Marlowe* v. *Argentine Naval Commission* (D.D.C., Civil Action No. 84-1870).

56. Except, possibly, when a contract calls for the law of another state, such as China, to be the governing law. See note 53 above.

57. Pub. L. No. 94-583, 90 Stat. 2891, codified at 28 U.S.C. §§ 1330, 1332(a)(2), 1391(g), 1441(d), and 1602–1611.

58. See *Unidyne Corp.* v. *Aerolineas Argentinas*, 590 F. Supp. 398 (E.D. Va. 1984) (Argentine Naval Commission held to be part of a foreign state, not an 'agency or instrumentality of a foreign state'); *Marlowe* v. *Argentine Naval Commission*, 604 F. Supp. 703 (D.D.C. 1985) (same).

59. Thus, Chinese organizations such as the China National Chemicals Import and Export Corporation, China National Native Produce and Animal By-products Import and Export Corporation, China National Light Industrial Products Import and Export Corporation, China National Textiles Import and Export Corporation, China National Cereals, Oils and Foodstuffs Import and Export Corporation, China National Machinery Import and Export Corporation, China National Metals and Minerals Import and Export Corporation, China National Technical Import Corporation (state trading corporations), China Ocean Shipping Corporation (shipping), the Civil Aviation Administration of China (airline), and the People's Bank of China (central bank) apparently would qualify as agencies or instrumentalities that may be entitled to immunity.

60. *Yessenin-Volpin* v. *Novosti Press Agency*, 443 F. Supp. 849 (S.D.N.Y. 1978).

61. *Yessenin-Volpin* v. *Novosti Press Agency*, 443 F. Supp. at 854 (S.D.N.Y. 1978).

62. 441 F. Supp. 827 (D.D.C. 1977).

63. See J. Dellapenna, 'Suing Foreign Governments and Their Corporations: Sovereign Immunity (Part I)', *Commercial Law Journal*, Vol. 85, 1981, p. 171, for criticism of the Edlow decision ('when the corporation is created in a state where all means of production are subject to state ownership, the fact that the corporation has some degree of internal autonomy, but no private owners, should not change its treatment as a state instrumentality, leaving the restrictive theory to determine whether there is to be immunity'). In fact, the court in *Edlow* 'perhaps merely sought an easy way to resolve what otherwise might have been a difficult jurisdictional problem.' The difficult jurisdictional problem was whether one alien could sue another alien in a United States federal court under the FSIA, note 7 above. (The *Edlow* decision came before the United States Supreme Court resolved the question in *Verlinden, B.V.* v. *Central Bank of Nigeria*, 461 U.S. 480 (1983).) By ruling that the Yugoslav entity was not an agency or instrumentality of a foreign state, the court was able to find that it lacked both federal question jurisdiction and diversity jurisdiction (since the suit was between aliens), and accordingly dismissed the suit.

The 'control test' applied by the *Edlow* court had been used by the United States Supreme Court to determine whether a community action agency was an 'agent' of the United States government rather than an 'independent contractor' under the Federal Tort Claims Act. See *United States* v. *Orleans*, 425 U.S. 807 (1976) (community action agency not an agent). Community action agencies are indisputably not owned by the United States government, although they receive federal funding. See 425 U.S. p. 817. There is no indication in *Orleans* that it would be proper to apply a 'control test' to an agency owned by the government.

64. See H.R. Rep. No. 1497, 94th Cong., 2nd Sess. 7 (1976), reprinted in *US Code Cong. & Ad. News*, 1976, p. 6614, note 7 above; *First National City Bank* v. *Banco para el Comercio Exterior de Cuba*, 462 U.S. 611, 624 (1983) (the typical government instrumentality is 'established as a juridical entity, with the powers to hold and sell property and to sue and be sued'). In *Marlowe* v. *Argentine Naval Commission*, 604 F. Supp. 703, 705 (D.D.C. 1985), a federal district court held that the status of the Argentine Naval Commission was to be determined 'not by Argentine law, but by "principles . . . common to both international law and federal common law"', quoting *First National City Bank* v. *Banco para el Comercio Exterior de Cuba*, 462 U.S. 611, 623 (1983). However, *Banco para el Comercio Exterior de Cuba* does not stand for the proposition that a foreign entity's instrumentality status is to be determined by 'principles . . . common to both international law and federal common law', but for the very different proposition that the attribution of liability *among* separate entities of a foreign state (such as

the central government of the state and one of its instrumentalities) is to be determined by such principles. See 462 U.S. 622, n. 11 (1983).

65. Fed. R. Civ. P. 17(b) instructs federal courts to determine an individual's
capacity to sue or be sued by reference to the law of the individual's domicile; a
corporation's capacity by reference to the law under which the corporation is
organized; and, in all other cases, capacity is to be determined in accordance with
the law of the state in which the district court is located. Since one of the criteria
for determining separate legal person status is capacity to sue or be sued, the
determination of such status could depend in part on the application of the
choice-of-law rules set forth in Rule 17(b). However, the application of Rule
17(b) to non-United States entities for such determinations seems inappropriate.
The courts should look to the law of the state under which the foreign entity is
organized, whether it is a corporate entity or not.

66. See Section II above regarding the Chinese definition of 'legal person'
(faren).

67. 28 U.S.C. § 1605.

68. 28 U.S.C. § 1605(a)(1) and (2) (emphasis added).

69. H.R. Rep. No. 1497, 94th Cong., 2nd Sess. 7 (1976), reprinted in US Code
Cong. & Ad. News, 1976, p. 6615, note 7 above.

70. H.R. Rep. No. 1497, 94th Cong., 2nd Sess. 7 (1976), reprinted in US Code
Cong. & Ad. News, 1976, p. 6615, note 7 above.

71. Texas Trading v. Federal Republic of Nigeria, 647 F.2d 300, 309 (S.D.N.Y.
1982).

72. The 'nature of the activity' test may 'merely [postpone] the difficulty': 'To
what extent is it true to say that contracts made by the state for the purchase of
shoes for the army, or of a warship, or of munitions, or of foodstuff necessary for
the maintenance of the national economy, are not immune from the jurisdiction
for the reason that they are contracts and that an individual can make a contract?
For can it not be said that these particular contracts can be made by a state only,
and not by individuals? Individuals do not purchase shoes for their armies; they
do not buy warships for the use of the state; they are not, as such, responsible for
the management of the national economy.' H. Lauterpacht, pp. 220, 225, note 1
above. 'Start with "activity", proceed via "conduct" or "transaction" to "character", then refer to "nature", and then go back to "commercial", the term you
started out to define in the first place.' A.F. Lowenfeld, 'Litigating a Sovereign
Immunity Claim—the Haiti Case', New York University Law Review, Vol. 49,
1974, p. 435, n. 244. The 'for profit' interpretation of the 'nature of the activity'
test seems inappropriate as the key to the 'nature' of the activity, since it would
have a court determine the 'nature' of the activity by reference to its 'purpose',
that is, whether or not the activity is carried on for profit, even though 'nature' is
supposed to be determined without reference to 'purpose'. Furthermore, there
may well be significant problems in determining when a socialist enterprise has
carried on an activity primarily 'for profit' rather than to achieve some other
objective.

73. H.R. Rep. No. 1497, 94th Cong., 2nd Sess. 7 (1976), reprinted in US Code
Cong. & Ad. News, 1976, p. 6615, note 7 above.

74. 543 F. Supp. 561, 566 (S.D. Tex. 1982), vacated, 610 F. Supp. 306, re-
manded sub nom. Sedco, Inc. v. Petroleos Mexicanos Mexican Nat'l Oil Co.
(Pemex), 767 F.2d 1140 (5th Cir. 1985).

75. G. Delaume, 'Economic Development and Sovereign Immunity', American
Journal of International Law, Vol. 79, 1985, p. 328.

76. 477 F. Supp. 553 (C.D. Cal.), 649 F.2d 1354 (9th Cir.), cert. denied, 454
U.S. 1163 (1982).

77. The decision was subsequently affirmed, but on different grounds. See text
below.

78. 736 F.2d 1326 (9th Cir. 1984).

79. 613 F. Supp. 863, 869–70 (D.D.C. 1985).

80. The courts might take a more discriminating approach, and determine whether the particular cause of action is based on the 'commercial' portion of a contract, that is, the portion into which an individual was capable of entering, or the 'non-commercial' portion of the contract, that is, the portion that only a sovereign could agree to. Compare *Gibbons* v. *Udaras na Gaeltachta*, 549 F. Supp. 1094, 1110, n. 6 (S.D.N.Y. 1982) (suggesting that a contract might be regarded as 'mixed' as between 'commercial' and 'non-commercial').

81. See *Gibbons* v. *Udaras na Gaeltachta*, 549 F. Supp. 1094, 1110, n. 6 (S.D.N.Y. 1982) (if the defendant agency of the Republic of Ireland 'had been given de facto law-making power in order to offer prospective investors special tax incentives', action on the contract might be regarded as mixed commercial/non-commercial activity).

82. See von Mehren, p. 49, note 50 above.

83. 'Activities such as a foreign government's sale of a service or a product, its leasing of property, *its borrowing of money*, its employment or engagement of laborers, clerical staff or public relations or marketing agents, or its investment in a security of an American corporation, would be among those [activities] included within the definition' of 'commercial activity' (emphasis added). H.R. Rep. No. 1497, 94th Cong., 2nd Sess. 7 (1976), reprinted in *US Code Cong. & Ad. News*, 1976, p. 6615, note 7 above. The definition of 'a commercial activity carried on with the United States' is meant to include 'an indebtedness incurred by a foreign state which negotiates or executes a loan agreement in the United States, or which receives financing from a private or public lending institution located in the United States ...'. *US Code Cong. & Ad. News*, 1976, pp. 6615–16, note 7 above.

84. *Asociacion de Reclamantes* v. *United Mexican States*, 561 F. Supp. 1190, 1195–6, n. 10.

85. S. 1071 (99th Cong., 1st Sess.). It would add a new subsection (f) to 28 U.S.C. § 1605(a), which would provide that '[a] commercial activity includes any promise to pay made by a foreign state, any debt security issued by a foreign state, and any guarantee by a foreign state of a promise to pay made by another party.' The provisions of S. 1071 have been introduced in the United States House of Representatives as H.R. 3137 and H.R. 4592 (99th Cong., 2nd Sess.). See Arbitral Awards: Hearing Before the Subcommittee on Administrative Law and Governmental Relations of the Committee on the Judiciary of the House of Representatives on H.R. 3106, H.R. 4342, and H.R. 4592, 99th Cong., 2nd Sess. (1986).

86. Such a characterization would not bind a court faced with determining whether the activity on which suit was based was 'commercial', but may have some value. See G. Kahale, 'State Loan Transactions: Foreign Law Restrictions on Waivers of Immunity and Submissions to Jurisdiction', *Business Lawyer*, Vol. 37, 1982, pp. 1549 and 1566, n. 100; G. Delaume, p. 339, note 75 above.

87. 168 U.S. 250, 252 (1897).

88. See, for example, J. Dellapenna, 'Suing Foreign Governments and Their Corporations: Choice of Law (Part III)', *Commercial Law Journal*, Vol. 86, 1981, p. 438; J. Dellapenna, 'Suing Foreign Governments and Their Corporations: Choice of Law (Part IV)', *Commercial Law Journal*, Vol. 86, 1981, p. 486; 'Judicial Balancing of Foreign Policy Considerations: Comity and Errors Under the Act of State Doctrine', *Stanford Law Review*, Vol. 35, 1983, p.327.

89. See *International Association of Machinists and Aerospace Engineers* v. *OPEC*, 649 F.2d 1354 (9th Cir.), cert. denied, 454 U.S. 1163 (1982) (act of state doctrine should be applied where there is 'potential for interference with [US] foreign relations'). See, also, D. Rosenthal, 'Jurisdictional Conflicts Between Sovereign Nations', *International Lawyer*, Vol. 19, 1985, p. 498.

90. See Section IVA, subsection ii(a) above for a discussion of the case in the district court. See, also, D. Rosenthal, note 89 above.

91. *International Association of Machinists and Aerospace Workers* v. *OPEC*, 649 F.2d 1354, 1360 (9th Cir. 1981).

92. H.R. Rep. No. 1497, 94th Cong., 2nd Sess. 7 (1976), reprinted in *US Code*

Cong. & Ad. News, 1976, p. 6619, n.1, note 7 above. Bills have been introduced in the United States Congress to prohibit the application of the 'Federal act of state doctrine' 'with respect to any claim or counterclaim . . . based upon a breach of contract, nor shall such doctrine bar enforcement of an agreement to arbitrate or an arbitral award rendered against a foreign state'. S. 1071 § 3 (99th Cong., 1st Sess.), H.R. 3137 (99th Cong., 2nd Sess.) (amending 28 U.S.C. § 1606).

93. 482 F. Supp. 1175 (D.D.C. 1980).

94. Reprinted in *International Legal Materials*, Vol. 20, 1981, p. 161.

95. The act of state doctrine may result in the dismissal of a case between private parties when the decision would require the court to rule on the validity of an act of a foreign state taken within its own territory. See *Arango* v. *Guzman Travel Advisors*, 621 F.2d 1371, 1380 (5th Cir. 1980).

96. 28 U.S.C. § 1605(a)(2).

97. See 'Foreign Sovereign Immunity and Commercial Activity: A Conflicts Approach', *Columbia Law Review*, Vol. 83, 1983, p. 1445; 'Effects Jurisdiction Under the Foreign Sovereign Immunities Act and the Due Process Clause', *New York University Law Review*, Vol. 55, 1980, pp. 474–5, hereafter cited as 'Effects Jurisdiction'.

98. 764 F.2d 1101 (5th Cir. 1985).

99. 764 F.2d 1104 (5th Cir. 1985).

100. See 764 F.2d 1104.

101. 764 F.2d 1110, 1115.

102. See *Texas Trading and Milling Corporation* v. *Federal Republic of Nigeria*, 647 F.2d 300, 312, n.5 (2nd Cir. 1981), cert. denied, 454 U.S. 1148 (1982) (expressly leaving open the question of whether a company injured overseas suffers a direct effect in the United States); 'Effects Jurisdiction', p. 474, note 97 above (arguing for direct effect jurisdiction for financial losses).

103. See *Australian Government Aircraft Factories* v. *Lynne*, 743 F.2d 672 (9th Cir. 1984), cert. denied, 469 U.S. 1214 (1984) (injuries to the family of an American killed in a crash in Indonesia of a plane produced and leased by a division of the Australian state not a direct effect); *Upton* v. *Empire of Iran*, 459 F. Supp. 264 (D.D.C.), affirmed without opinion, 607 F.2d 494 (D.C. Cir. 1979) (effect on the family of an American killed in an Iranian airport terminal collapse not a direct effect); *Harris* v. *VAO Intourist*, 481 F. Supp. 1056 (E.D.N.Y. 1979) (injuries to the family of an American killed in a Moscow hotel fire not a direct effect).

104. 28 U.S.C. § 1605(a)(3).

105. 616 F. Supp. 660 (W.D. Mich. 1985).

106. 28 U.S.C. § 1605(a)(4).

107. 488 F. Supp. 665, later proceeding, 502 F. Supp. 259 (D.D.C. 1980).

108. 28 U.S.C. § 1605(b).

109. 28 U.S.C. § 1608.

110. 28 U.S.C. § 1605(b)(1). See *Jet Line Servs., Inc.* v. *M/V Marsa El Hariga*, 462 F. Supp. 1165 (D. Md. 1978).

111. 28 U.S.C. § 1605(b).

112. The FSIA is not intended to affect 'the attribution of responsibility between or among entities of a foreign state; for example, whether the proper entity of a foreign state has been sued, or whether an entity sued is liable in whole or in part for the claimed wrong'. H.R. Rep. No. 1497, 94th Cong., 2nd Sess. 7 (1976), reprinted in *US Code Cong. & Ad. News*, 1976, p. 6610, note 7 above.

113. 28 U.S.C. § 1609.

114. 748 F.2d 790 (2nd Cir.), cert. denied,—U.S.—, 105 S.Ct. 2656, 86 L. Ed. 2d 273 (1985).

115. The district court ordered execution against the airline's assets under a 'commercial activity' exception to immunity from execution even though the judgment had been obtained under the tort exception to immunity from jurisdiction. To reach this result, the district court reasoned that the arranging, facilitating

and carrying out of the assassination of Letelier constituted the 'commercial activity' 'on which the claim was based'.

116. 748 F.2d 798. The appeals court rejected the characterization of the events leading up to and including the assassination as 'commercial'. See note 115. The court also ruled that the district court had erred in ignoring the separate legal status of the national airline from the foreign state itself. See the subsection below on the separate legal status of instrumentalities from their parent states.

117. 28 U.S.C. § 1610(a)(1).

118. 28 U.S.C. § 1610(d).

119. *Libra Bank Ltd.* v. *Banco Nacional de Costa Rica*, 676 F.2d 47 (2nd Cir. 1982). See also *S & S Machinery Co.* v. *Masinexportimport*, 706 F.2d 411 (2nd Cir.), cert. denied, 464 U.S. 850 (1983). It has been held that a central bank is incapable of waiving its immunity from prejudgment attachment under the FSIA. *Banque Compafina* v. *Banco de Gautemala*, 583 F. Supp. 320 (S.D.N.Y. 1984).

120. 28 U.S.C. §§ 1610(b)(2), 1610(a)(2).

121. See M.C. Del Bianco, 'Execution and Attachment Under the Foreign Sovereign Immunities Act of 1976', *Yale Studies in World Public Order*, Vol. 5, 1978, p. 109.

122. 28 U.S.C. § 1610(b)(2).

123. H.R. Rep. No. 1497, 94th Cong., 2nd Sess. 7 (1976), reprinted in *US Code Cong. & Ad. News*, 1976, p. 6630, note 7 above.

124. 28 U.S.C. § 1611(b).

125. 'Section 1610(b) will not permit execution against the property of one agency or instrumentality engaged in a commercial activity in the United States in order to satisfy a judgment against another, unrelated agency or instrumentality... There are compelling reasons for this. If U.S. law did not respect the separate juridical identities of different agencies or instrumentalities, it might encourage foreign jurisdictions to disregard the juridical divisions between different U.S. corporations or between a U.S. corporation and its independent subsidiary.' H.R. Rep. No. 1497, 94th Cong., 2nd Sess. 7 (1976), reprinted in *US Code Cong. & Ad. News*, 1976, pp. 6628–9, note 7 above.

126. *First National City Bank* v. *Banco para el Comercio Exterior de Cuba*, 462 U.S. 611, 633 (1983).

127. 462 U.S. 611 (1983).

128. 462 U.S. at 632.

129. *Letelier* v. *Republic of Chile*, 748 F.2d 790 (2nd Cir.), cert. denied, 86 L. Ed. 2d 273, 105 S. Ct. 2656 (1985).

130. See A. Hastrich, p. 586, note 23 above.

131. See C. Osakwe, p. 32, note 15 above.

132. See M.M. Boguslavsky, pp. 172–3, note 13 above.

133. Constitution of the People's Republic of China, 1982, Arts. 9 and 10.

134. General Provisions of the Civil Code of the People's Republic of China, 1982, Art. 48, note 24 above.

135. SIA § 14(2), note 42 above.

136. SIA § 3(1)(a), note 42 above.

137. SIA § 3(3), note 42 above. SIA § 3 will not apply if the parties so agree in writing.

The act of state doctrine originated in England, and has recently been revived in *Buttes Gas & Oil Co.* v. *Hammer*, [1982] AC 888. Lord Wilberforce described it as a rule of non-justiciability respecting 'the transactions of foreign states'. In the dispute in question, he concluded that 'there are...no judicial or manageable standards by which to judge these issues, or to adopt another phrase..., the court would be in a judicial no-man's land...'. It is unclear how far the newly revived doctrine will be extended.

138. SIA § 3(1)(b), note 42 above.

139. SIA § 13(4), note 42 above.

580   FOREIGN TRADE, INVESTMENT AND THE LAW

140. SIA § 14(4), note 42 above.
141. SIA § 14(3), note 42 above.
142. State Immunity Act 1979, reprinted in *Materials on Jurisdictional Immunities*, note 9 above.
143. State Immunity Ordinance 1981, reprinted in *Materials on Jurisdictional Immunities*, note 9 above.
144. Foreign States Immunities Act 1981, reprinted in *Materials on Jurisdictional Immunities*, note 9 above.
145. Reprinted in *International Legal Materials*, Vol. 21, 1982, p. 798; *Materials on Jurisdictional Immunities*, note 9 above.
146. See 'The Canadian State Immunity Act', *Law and Policy in International Business*, Vol. 14, 1983, pp. 1197 and 1219.
147. Canadian SIA § 2.
148. Canadian SIA § 2.
149. Canadian SIA § 2.
150. Canadian SIA § 4.
151. Canadian SIA § 11(1).
152. Canadian SIA § 11(2).
153. Canadian SIA § 11(4).
154. Australian FSIA § 3(3)(a).
155. Australian FSIA § 22.
156. Australian FSIA § 11(3).
157. Australian FSIA § 11(3)(a), (b), (c).
158. Australian FSIA §§ 11(3), 19.
159. Australian FSIA § 32.
160. Australian FSIA § 35(2).
161. See J.G. Wetter, 'Pleas of Sovereign Immunity and Act of Sovereignty Before International Arbitral Tribunals', *Journal of International Arbitration*, Vol. 2, 1985, p. 7.
162. See *International Legal Materials*, Vol. 22, 1983, p. 752.
163. The arbitrators rendered an award against the Egyptian government. In French judicial proceedings in respect of the award in *SPP*, however, the arbitrators' award against the Egyptian government was annulled because the mere approval by the government of the contract containing an arbitration agreement did not constitute an agreement by the government to arbitrate. The result could be the same if, for instance, a foreign party attempted to compel China's Ministry of Foreign Economic Relations and Trade (MOFERT) to submit to arbitration on grounds that it had approved a particular contract containing an arbitration clause.

Appendix. Table of Legislation

Accounting (General)

Accounting Law of the People's Republic of China, 中华人民共和国会计法, promulgated on 21 January 1985 and effective from 1 May 1985.

Arbitration

Decision of the Government Administration Council of the Central People's Government Concerning the Establishment of a Foreign Trade Arbitration Commission within the CCPIT, 中央人民政府政务院关于在中国国际贸易促进委员会内设立对外贸易仲裁委员会的决定, adopted on 6 May 1954.

Provisional Rules of Procedure of the Foreign Trade Arbitration Commission of the CCPIT, 中国国际贸易促进委员会对外贸易仲裁委员会仲裁程序暂行规则, adopted on and effective from 31 March 1956.

Notice of the State Council Concerning the Conversion of the Foreign Trade Arbitration Commission into the Foreign Economic and Trade Arbitration Commission, 国务院关于将对外贸易仲裁委员会改称为对外经济贸易仲裁委员会的通知, issued on 26 February 1980.

Decision of the State Council of the People's Republic of China Concerning the Establishment of a Maritime Arbitration Commission within the CCPIT, 中华人民共和国国务院关于在中国国际贸易促进委员会内设立海事仲裁委员会的决定, adopted on 21 November 1958.

Provisional Rules of Procedure of the Maritime Arbitration Commission of the CCPIT, 中国国际贸易促进委员会海事仲裁委员会仲裁程序暂行规则, adopted on and effective from 8 January 1959.

Regulations of the People's Republic of China on the Arbitration of Economic Contracts, 中华人民共和国经济合同仲裁条例, promulgated on and effective from 22 August 1983.

Banking

See 'Finance'.

Bankruptcy

See 'State-owned Enterprises'.

Civil Law

Law on Civil Procedure of the People's Republic of China (for Trial Implementation), 中华人民共和国民事诉讼法(试行), promulgated on 8 March 1982 and effective from 1 October 1982.

General Principles of the Civil Law of the People's Republic of China, 中华人民共和国民法通则, promulgated on 12 April 1986 and effective from 1 January 1987.

Constitution

Constitution of the People's Republic of China, 中华人民共和国宪法, promulgated on and effective from 4 December 1982.

Contracts

Economic Contracts Law of the People's Republic of China, 中华人民共和国经济合同法, promulgated on 13 December 1981 and effective from 1 July 1982.

Foreign Economic Contracts Law of the People's Republic of China, 中华人民共和国涉外经济合同法, promulgated on 21 March 1985 and effective from 1 July 1985.

Regulations of the People's Republic of China on the Administration of Technology Import Contracts, 中华人民共和国技术引进合同管理条例, promulgated on and effective from 24 May 1985.

Procedures for Examination and Approval of Technology Import Contracts, 技术引进合同审批办法, promulgated on and effective from 18 September 1985.

Criminal Law

Criminal Law of the People's Republic of China, 中华人民共和国刑法, promulgated on 6 July 1979 and effective from 1 January 1980.

Criminal Procedure Law of the People's Republic of China, 中华人民共和国刑事诉讼法, promulgated on 7 July 1979 and effective from 1 January 1980.

Economic Policy

Policy Provisions of the State Council on Urban Non-Agricultural Individual Economy, 国务院关于城镇非农业个体经济若干政策性规定, promulgated on 7 July 1981.

Provisional Regulations of the State Council on Several Policy Questions

Relating to the Urban Collective Economy, 国务院关于城镇集体所有制经济若干政策问题的暂行规定 , promulgated on 14 April 1983.

Environmental Protection

Regulations on Protecting the Breeding of Aquatic Resources, 水产资源繁殖保护条例, promulgated on and effective from 10 February 1979.

Provisional Measures for the Assessment of Effluent Fees, 征收排污费暂行办法, issued on 5 February 1982 and effective from 1 July 1982.

Grasslands Law of the People's Republic of China, 中华人民共和国草原法, promulgated on 18 June 1985 and effective from 1 October 1985.

Fishery Law of the People's Republic of China, 中华人民共和国渔业法, promulgated on 20 January 1986 and effective from 1 July 1986.

Forestry Law of the People's Republic of China, 中华人民共和国森林法, promulgated on 20 September 1984 and effective from 1 January 1985.

Regulations Governing the Requisition of Land for State Construction, 国家建设征用土地条例, promulgated on and effective from 14 May 1982.

Marine Environmental Protection Law of the People's Republic of China, 中华人民共和国海洋环境保护法, promulgated on 23 August 1982 and effective from 1 March 1983.

Regulations of the People's Republic of China on Marine Environmental Protection from Oil Exploration and Exploitation, 中华人民共和国海洋石油勘探开发环境保护管理条例, promulgated on and effective from 29 December 1983.

Regulations of the People's Republic of China on the Prevention of Marine Pollution by Vessels, 中华人民共和国防止船舶污染海域管理条例, promulgated on and effective from 29 December 1983.

Regulations of the People's Republic of China on the Control of Marine Dumping, 中华人民共和国海洋倾废管理条例, promulgated on 6 March 1985 and effective from 1 April 1985.

Regulations on Water and Soil Conservation Work, 水土保持工作条例, promulgated on and effective from 30 June 1982.

Law of the People's Republic of China on the Prevention and Control of Water Pollution, 中华人民共和国水污染防治法, promulgated on 11 May 1984 and effective from 1 November 1984.

Finance

Notice of the State Council Approving the Transmission of the Request for Instruction by the People's Bank of China Concerning the Function of the People's Bank as the Central Bank and its Relationship with Other Specialized Banks, 国务院批转中国人民银行关于人

民银行的中央银行职能及其与专业银行的关系问题的请示的通知, issued on 14 July 1982.

Interim Banking Control Regulations of the People's Republic of China, 中华人民共和国银行管理暂行条例, promulgated on and effective from 7 January 1986.

Provisional Regulations for the Management of Financial, Trust and Investment Organizations, 金融信托投资机构管理暂行规定, promulgated on and effective from 26 April 1986.

Provisional Regulations of the People's Republic of China Governing Foreign Exchange Control, 中华人民共和国外汇管理暂行条例, promulgated on 18 December 1980 and effective from 1 March 1981.

Detailed Rules for the Implementation of Foreign Exchange Control Regulations Relating to Overseas Chinese Enterprises, Foreign Enterprises, and Chinese-Foreign Joint Ventures, 对侨资企业、外资企业、中外合资经营企业外汇管理施行细则, promulgated on and effective from 1 August 1983.

Penal Provisions for Violation of Exchange Control of the People's Republic of China, 中华人民共和国违反外汇管理处罚施行细则, promulgated on and effective from 5 April 1985.

Food Hygiene

Food Hygiene Law of the People's Republic of China (for Trial Implementation), 中华人民共和国食品卫生法(试行), adopted on 19 November 1982 and effective from 1 July 1983.

Measures of the People's Republic of China for the Hygiene Control of Foodstuffs for Export (for Trial Implementation), 中华人民共和国出口食品卫生管理办法(试行), promulgated on 20 July 1984 and effective from 1 January 1985.

Foreign Exchange Control

See 'Finance'.

Fourteen Coastal Port Cities (Economic and Technical Development Zones)

Measures of Dalian Economic and Technical Development Zone Governing Labour and Wages in Enterprises, 大连经济技术开发区企业劳动工资管理办法, promulgated on and effective from 15 October 1984.

Measures of Dalian Economic and Technical Development Zone on Land Use, 大连经济技术开发区土地使用管理办法, promulgated on and effective from 15 October 1984.

Measures of Dalian Economic and Technical Development Zone Governing Enterprise Registration, 大连经济技术开法区企业登记管理办法, promulgated on and effective from 15 October 1984.

Provisional Regulations of Guangzhou Economic and Technical Development Zone, 广州经济技术开发区暂行条例, promulgated on and effective from 9 April 1985.

Interim Regulations on Certain Questions Relating to Inland Associated Enterprises (Undertakings) in the Guangzhou Economic and Technical Development Zone, 广州经济技术开发区内联企业若干问题的暂行规定, promulgated on and effective from 9 April 1985.

Trial Measures of Guangzhou Economic and Technical Development Zone Governing Land Use, 广州经济技术开发区土地管理试行办法, promulgated on and effective from 9 April 1985.

Trial Measures of Guangzhou Economic and Technical Development Zone Governing Enterprise Registration and Administration, 广州经济技术开发区企业登记管理试行办法, promulgated on and effective from 9 April 1985.

Provisional Regulations for Import of Technology in Guangzhou Economic and Technical Development Zone, 广州经济技术开发区技术引进暂行规定, promulgated on and effective from 9 April 1985.

Provisional Regulations for the Economic and Technical Development Zone of Ningbo Municipality, 宁波市经济技术开发区暂行条例, adopted on 15 June 1985.

Implementing Measures of Ningbo Municipality Governing Land Use by Joint Ventures Using Chinese and Foreign Investment, 宁波市中外合资经营企业土地使用管理实施办法, adopted on 16 June 1985.

Regulations of Shanghai Municipality on Negotiations and Examination and Approval Procedures Relating to Establishment of Joint Ventures Using Chinese and Foreign Investment and Acceptance of Foreign Investment for Establishing Self-run Enterprises (for Trial Implementation), 上海市关于开办中外合资经营企业和接受外商投资开办自营企业的洽谈工作和审批程序规定(试行), promulgated on and effective from 1 July 1984.

Implementing Measures of Shanghai Municipality on Labour Management in Joint Ventures Using Chinese and Foreign Investment (for Trial Implementation), 上海市中外合资经营企业劳动管理实施办法(试行), promulgated on 8 October 1984 and effective from 1 November 1984.

Provisional Regulations of Shanghai Municipality on Supply and Distribution of Goods and Materials and the Control of Prices for Joint Ventures Using Chinese and Foreign Investment (for Trial Implementation), 上海市中外合资经营企业物资供销和物价管理规定, promulgated on 5 December 1984 and effective from 20 December 1984.

Regulations Governing Tianjin Economic and Technical Development Zone, 天津经济技术开发区管理条例, promulgated on and effective from 23 July 1985.

Regulations of Tianjin Economic and Technical Development Zone Governing Labour Management, 天津经济技术开发区劳动管理规定, promulgated on and effective from 25 July 1985.

Regulations of Tianjin Economic and Technical Development Zone Governing Land, 天津经济技术开发区土地管理规定, promulgated on and effective from 25 July 1985.

Regulations of Tianjin Economic and Technical Development Zone Governing Enterprise Registration, 天津经济技术开发区企业登记管理规定, promulgated on and effective from 23 July 1985.

Import/Export

Provisional Customs Law of the People's Republic of China, 中华人民共和国暂行海关法, promulgated on 8 April 1951 and effective from 1 May 1951.

Provisional Procedures of the Customs of the People's Republic of China for Levying Tonnage Dues on Vessels, 中华人民共和国海关船舶的吨税暂行办法, promulgated on and effective from 19 September 1952.

Procedures of the Customs of the People's Republic of China for the Supervision and Control of Small Vessels Coming from or Going to Hong Kong and Macau, 中华人民共和国海关对来自和开往香港、澳门小型船舶监管办法, promulgated on 7 July 1958 and effective from 1 September 1958.

Procedures of the Customs of the People's Republic of China for the Supervision and Control of Railway Trains Leaving and Entering Chinese Territory and the Cargo, Passenger Baggage, and Parcels Carried Thereon, 中华人民共和国海关对铁路进出国境列车和所载货物、行李、包裹监管办法, promulgated on 5 November 1958 and effective from 1 December 1958.

Procedures of the Customs of the People's Republic of China for the Supervision and Control of Vessels Engaged in International Navigation and the Cargo Carried Thereon, 中华人民共和国海关对国际船舶和所载货物监管办法, promulgated on 31 December 1958 and effective from 1 March 1959.

Trial Procedures of the Customs of the People's Republic of China for the Supervision and Control of Motor Vehicles Entering and Leaving Chinese Territory and the Cargo Carried Therein, 中华人民共和国海关对进出国境汽车及所载货物监管试行办法, issued on and effective from 29 August 1963.

Procedures of the Customs of the People's Republic of China for the Supervision of International Civil Aircraft, 中华人民共和国海关对国际民航机监管办法, promulgated on 10 September 1974 and effective from 1 October 1974.

Procedures of the Customs of the People's Republic of China for the Supervision and Control of Goods Imported for Exhibition, 中华人民共和国海关对进出口展览品监管办法, promulgated on and effective from 3 November 1975.

Regulations of the Customs of the People's Republic of China Governing the Import and Export of Articles by Foreign Diplomatic Missions in China and their Officers, 中华人民共和国海关关于各国驻华外交代表机关、外交官进出口物品的规定, effective from 1 January 1977.

Regulations of the Customs of the People's Republic of China Governing the Declaration of Articles Imported and Exported by Foreign Diplomatic Missions in China and their Officers, 中华人民共和国海关关于各国驻华外交代表机关、外交官进出口物品报关办法, effective from 1 January 1977.

Provisional Rules of the Customs of the People's Republic of China for the Supervision and Control of Articles in Baggage of Incoming and Outgoing Overseas Chinese and other Passengers, 中华人民共和国海关对进出国境华侨等旅客的行李物品监管暂行规定, promulgated on and effective from 5 April 1978.

Procedures of the People's Republic of China Concerning the Levy of Import Duty on Articles in Passengers' Baggage and Personal Postal Articles, 中华人民共和国关于入境旅客行李物品和个人邮递物品征收进口税办法, approved on 16 June 1978 and effective from 1 August 1978.

Regulations of the Customs of the People's Republic of China for Control over Baggage of Passengers Coming from or Going to Hong Kong and Macau, 中华人民共和国海关对来往香港或澳门的旅客行李物品的管理规定, effective from 1 July 1979.

Interim Procedures of the State Import-Export Commission and the Ministry of Foreign Trade of the People's Republic of China Concerning the System of Export Licensing, 中华人民共和国国家进出口管理委员会、对外贸易部关于出口许可制度的暂行办法, promulgated on 3 June 1980.

Provisional Procedures of the Customs of the People's Republic of China for the Supervision and Control of Bonded Cargo and Bonded Warehouses, 中华人民共和国海关对保税货物和保税仓库监管暂行办法, issued on 10 February 1981 and effective from 1 March 1981.

Provisional Measures of the Customs Concerning the Supervision and Control of Imports and Exports Required in the Co-operative Exploration and Development of Offshore Petroleum and Baggage and Articles of Engineers and Technical Personnel, 海关对合作勘探开发海上石油所需进出口物资及工程技术人员行李物品监管暂行办法, issued on and effective from 1 October 1981.

Regulations of the General Administration of Customs and the Ministry of Finance Concerning the Levy of and Exemption from Customs Duties and the Consolidated Industrial and Commercial Tax on Imports and Exports for Chinese-Foreign Co-operative Exploitation of Offshore Petroleum, 海关总署、则政部关于中外合作开采海洋石油进出口货物征免关税和工商统一税的规定, promulgated on 1 April 1982.

Regulations of the People's Republic of China on the Quarantine of Animal and Plant Imports and Exports, 中华人民共和国进出口动植物检疫条例, promulgated on and effective from 4 June 1982.

Regulations of the Customs of the People's Republic of China Governing the Supervision and Control over, and Duty Collection on, Inward and Outward Samples and Advertising Products, 中华人民共和国海关对进出口货样、广告品的监管征税办法, effective from 1 July 1982.

Rules of the Customs of the People's Republic of China Governing the Supervision and Control over Bonded Factories that Process Imported Materials, 中华人民共和国海关对进料加工保税工厂的管理规定, promulgated on 26 January 1983 and effective from 1 January 1984.

Rules of the Customs of the People's Republic of China Governing the Supervision and Control over Inward and Outward Containers and the Goods Contained Therein, 中华人民共和国海关对进出口集装箱和所装货物监管办法, promulgated on 31 August 1983 and effective from 1 January 1984.

Provisions of the Customs of the People's Republic of China for the Supervision of Luggage and Articles Carried into and out of China by Overseas Chinese who Return Home to Visit their Relatives, 中华人民共和国海关对回国探亲华侨进出口国境行李物品的管理规定, promulgated on 28 November 1983 and effective from 1 December 1983.

Provisional Regulations of the People's Republic of China on the System of Import Licensing, 中华人民共和国进口货物许可制度暂行条例, promulgated on and effective from 10 January 1984.

Detailed Implementing Rules to the Provisional Regulations of the People's Republic of China on the System of Import Licensing, 中华人民共和国进口货物许可制度暂行条例施行细则, promulgated on and effective from 15 May 1984.

Regulations of the People's Republic of China on the Inspection of Import and Export Commodities, 中华人民共和国进出口商品检验条例, promulgated on and effective from 28 January 1984.

Detailed Rules for the Implementation of the Regulations on the Inspection of Import and Export Commodities of the People's Republic of China, 中华人民共和国进出口商品检验条例实施细则, promulgated on and effective from 1 June 1984.

Regulations of the General Administration of Customs, the Ministry of Finance, and the Ministry of Foreign Economic Relations and Trade of the People's Republic of China Concerning the Supervision and Control over, and the Imposition of or Exemption from Tax on, Imports and Exports by Chinese-Foreign Co-operative Ventures, 中华人民共和国海关总署、财政部、对外经济贸易部关于中外合作经营企业进出口货物的监管和征免税规定, promulgated on 31 January 1984 and effective from 1 February 1984.

Regulations of the General Administration of Customs of the People's Republic of China and the Bank of China for Carrying Gold and Silver into or out of China, 中华人民共和国海关总署、中国人民银行对金银进出国境的管理办法, effective from 15 February 1984.

Regulations of the Customs of the People's Republic of China Concerning the Import and Export of Articles by Resident Offices of Foreign Enterprises and Press and their Staff in China, 中华人民共和国海关对外国企业、新闻等常驻机构和常驻人员进出口物品的管理规定, promulgated on 20 April 1984 and effective from 1 May 1984.

Regulations of the General Administration of Customs, the Ministry of Finance, and the Ministry of Foreign Economic Relations and Trade of the People's Republic of China Concerning the Supervision and Control over, and the Levy of and Exemption from Tax on, Imports and Exports of Chinese-Foreign Joint Ventures, 中华人民共和国海关总署、财政部、对外经济贸易部关于中外合资经营企业进出口货物的监管和征免税规定, promulgated on 30 April 1984 and effective from 1 May 1984.

Regulations of the Customs of the People's Republic of China Governing the Control over Inward- and Outward-bound Ocean-going Vessels of Foreign Registry and Goods for the Purpose of Chinese-Foreign Co-operative Exploitation of Offshore Petroleum and Personal Effects Belonging to Foreign Personnel Working in China, 中华人民共和国海关对中外合作开采海洋石油进出口外国籍船舶、货物和外国来华工作人员行李物品的管理办法, effective from 1 June 1984.

Measures for Inspection of Ships' Holds Carrying Cereals, Oils, Foodstuffs, and Frozen Products for Export, 出口粮油食品、冷冻品船舱检验办法, effective from 1 July 1984.

Regulations of the Customs of the People's Republic of China Governing Control over Inward- and Outward-bound Articles Brought in or Posted by Overseas Chinese Students and Students from Hong Kong and Macau Studying on China's Mainland, 中华人民共和国海关对回国和回内地学习的华侨、港澳学生携带和邮寄进出口物品的管理规定, promulgated on and effective from 20 August 1984.

Regulations of the Customs of the People's Republic of China Governing Supervision and Control over Inward- and Outward-bound Postal Articles,中华人民共和国海关对进出口邮递物品监管办法, promulgated on 25 September 1984 and effective from 1 October 1984.

Regulations of the Customs of the People's Republic of China Governing Supervision and Control over Personal Articles Sent to or from Hong Kong and Macau, 中华人民共和国海关对寄自或寄往香港、澳门的个人邮递物品监管办法, promulgated on 25 September 1984 and effective from 1 October 1984.

Regulations of the Customs of the People's Republic of China Governing Control over Outward-bound Cultural Relics Carried or Shipped by Passengers and Posted by Individuals, 中华人民共和国海关对旅客携运和个人邮寄文物出口的管理规定 , promulgated on and effective from 15 February 1985.

Regulations on Import and Export Duties of the People's Republic of China, 中华人民共和国进出口关税条例, promulgated on 7 March 1985 and effective from 10 March 1985.

Rules Governing Control over Inbound and Outbound Goods, Conveyances, Baggages and Postal Articles of the Special Economic Zones, 对进出经济特区的货物、运输工具、行李物品和邮递物品的管理规定, effective from 1 April 1986.

Industrial and Commercial Enterprises

Regulations on the Registration and Administration of Industrial and

Commercial Enterprises, 工商企业登记管理条例, promulgated on and effective from 9 August 1982.

Rules for the Implementation of the Regulations on the Registration and Administration of Industrial and Commercial Enterprises, 工商企业登记管理条例施行细则, promulgated on and effective from 13 December 1982.

Joint Ventures

Law of the People's Republic of China on Joint Ventures Using Chinese and Foreign Investment, 中华人民共和国中外合资经营企业法, promulgated on and effective from 8 July 1979.

Implementing Act for the Law of the People's Republic of China on Joint Ventures Using Chinese and Foreign Investment, 中华人民共和国中外合资经营企业法实施条例, promulgated on and effective from 20 September 1983.

Accounting System of the People's Republic of China for Joint Ventures Using Chinese and Foreign Investment, 中华人民共和国中外合资经营企业会计制度, promulgated on 4 March 1985 and effective from 1 July 1985.

Regulations of the State Council Concerning the Question of the Balance of the Foreign Exchange Receipts and Expenditures for Joint Ventures Using Chinese and Foreign Investment, 国务院关于中外合资经营企业外汇收支平衡问题的规定, promulgated on 15 January 1986 and effective from 1 February 1986.

Regulations on Labour Management in Joint Ventures Using Chinese and Foreign Investment, 中外合资经营企业劳动管理规定, promulgated on and effective from 26 July 1980.

Measures for the Implementation of the Regulations on Labour Management in Joint Ventures Using Chinese and Foreign Investment, 中外合资经营企业劳动管理规定实施办法, promulgated on and effective from 19 January 1984.

Provisional Regulations Concerning the Use of Land for Construction by Chinese-Foreign Joint Ventures, 关于中外合营企业建设用地的暂行规定, promulgated on 26 July 1980.

Provisional Measures for Providing Loans to Joint Ventures Using Chinese and Foreign Investment by the Bank of China, 中国银行办理中外合资经营企业贷款暂行办法, promulgated on 13 March 1981.

Measures for the Registration of Joint Ventures Using Chinese and Foreign Investment, 中外合资经营企业登记管理办法, promulgated on and effective from 26 July 1980.

Provisional Regulations of the General Administration for Industry and Commerce of the People's Republic of China on Standards for the Payment of Registration Fees by Joint Ventures Using Chinese and Foreign Investment, 中华人民共和国工商行政管理总局关于中外合资经营企业交纳登记费标准的暂行规定, issued in March 1982.

Notarization

Provisional Regulations of the People's Republic of China on Notarization, 中华人民共和国公证暂行条例, promulgated on and effective from 13 April 1982.

Offshore Petroleum Exploitation

Regulations of the People's Republic of China on the Exploitation of Offshore Petroleum Resources in Co-operation with Foreign Enterprises, 中华人民共和国对外合作开采海洋石油资源条例, promulgated on and effective from 30 January 1982.

Patents

Patent Law of the People's Republic of China, 中华人民共和国专利法, promulgated on 12 March 1984 and effective from 1 April 1985.
Implementing Regulations for the Patent Law of the People's Republic of China, 中华人民共和国专利法实施细则, promulgated on 19 January 1985 and effective from 1 April 1985.
Regulations Regarding Patent Agency, 专利代理暂行规定, promulgated on and effective from 12 September 1985.

Pharmaceuticals

Pharmaceutical Control Law of the People's Republic of China, 中华人民共和国药品管理法, promulgated on 20 September 1984 and effective from 1 July 1985.

Resident Representative Offices

Provisional Regulations of the State Council of the People's Republic of China Concerning the Control of Resident Representative Offices of Foreign Enterprises, 中华人民共和国国务院关于管理外国企业常驻代表机构的暂行规定, promulgated on and effective from 30 October 1980.
Announcement by the General Administration for Industry and Commerce of the People's Republic of China Concerning the Registration of Resident Representative Offices of Foreign Enterprises, 中华人民共和国工商行政管理总局关于外国企业常驻代表机构办理登记事项的通告, issued on 8 December 1980.
Measures of the State Administration for Industry and Commerce of the People's Republic of China Regarding the Control of Registration

of Resident Representative Offices of Foreign Enterprises, 中华
人民共和国工商行政管理局关于外国企业常驻代表机构的登记管理办法, pro-
mulgated on and effective from 15 March 1983.

Notice of the State Administration for Industry and Commerce of the
People's Republic of China Concerning the Registration of Foreign
Companies that Come to China to Engage in Co-operative Development and Contracted Projects, 中华人民共和国国家工商行政管理局关
于来我国合作开发和承包工程的外国公司注册登记问题的通知 , issued on
12 March 1983 and effective from 1 April 1983.

Explanations Regarding the Notice of the State Administration for Industry and Commerce of the People's Republic of China Concerning
the Registration of Foreign Companies that Come to China to Engage in Co-operative Development and Contracted Projects, 关于来
我国合作开发和承包工程的外国公司注册登记问题的通知的说明, issued on 4
May 1983.

Regulations of the People's Bank of China for the Establishment of
Resident Representative Offices in China by Overseas Chinese and
Foreign Financial Institutions, 中国人民银行关于侨资外资金融机构在
中国设立常驻代表机构的管理办法, issued on and effective from 1 February 1983.

Provisional Measures of the People's Government of Guangdong Province for the Registration and Control of Resident Representative
Offices of Foreign Enterprises and Overseas Chinese, Hong Kong,
and Macau Enterprises in Guangdong Province, 广东省人民政府关
于外国企业及华侨、港澳企业在广东内设立常驻代表机构登记管理暂行办法 ,
promulgated on and effective from 11 May 1986.

Special Economic Zones

Regulations Governing Foreign Banks and Joint Chinese-Foreign Banks
in the Special Economic Zones of the People's Republic of China,
中华人民共和国经济特区外资银行、中外合资银行管理条例,   promulgated
on and effective from 2 April 1985.

Regulations on the Special Economic Zones in Guangdong Province,
广东省经济特区条例, adopted on and effective from 26 August 1980.

Regulations Governing Accounting for Foreign Enterprises in the Special
Economic Zones of Guangdong Province, 广东省经济特区涉外企业会
计管理规定, promulgated on 14 February 1986 and effective from 1
March 1986.

Provisional Regulations of the Special Economic Zones of Guangdong
Province Governing Labour and Wages for Business Enterprises,
广东省经济特区企业劳动工资管理暂行规定, adopted on 17 November
1981 and effective from 1 January 1982.

Provisional Regulations of the Special Economic Zones in Guangdong
Province Governing the Entry and Exit of Personnel, 广东省经济特区
入境出境人员管理暂行规定, adopted on 17 November 1981 and effective from 1 January 1982.

Provisional Regulations of the Special Economic Zones of Guangdong Province Governing the Registration of Business Enterprises, 广东省经济特区企业登记管理暂行规定, adopted on 17 November 1981 and effective from 1 January 1982.

Provisional Measures of Shenzhen Municipality Governing Urban Construction, 深圳市城市建设管理暂行办法, effective from 1 July 1982.

Regulations of Shenzhen Special Economic Zone on Foreign Economic Contracts, 深圳经济特区涉外经济合同规定, promulgated on and effective from 7 February 1984.

Provisional Regulations Governing Land in Shenzhen Special Economic Zone, 深圳经济特区土地管理暂行规定, promulgated on 24 December 1981 and effective from 1 January 1982.

Measures of Shenzhen Special Economic Zone Concerning the Adjustment of Land-use Fees and Preferential Treatment for the Reduction of and Exemption from Land-use Fees, 深圳经济特区土地使用费调整及优惠减免办法, promulgated on 22 June 1984 and effective from 1 July 1984.

Implementing Measures of Shenzhen Special Economic Zone Governing Land-use Fees, 深圳经济特区土地使用费实施办法, promulgated on and effective from 22 November 1985.

Regulations of Shenzhen Special Economic Zone on the Control of Commercial Real Estate, 深圳经济特区商品房产管理规定, promulgated on and effective from 23 January 1984.

Interim Measures of Shenzhen Special Economic Zone on Mortgage Loans, 深圳经济特区抵押贷款管理规定, promulgated on and effective from 13 February 1986.

Regulations for the Control of Personnel Coming and Going Between the Shenzhen Special Economic Zone and Inland Areas, 深圳经济特区与内地之间人员往来管理规定, promulgated on 12 March 1986 and effective from 1 April 1986.

Detailed Implementing Rules of Shenzhen Special Economic Zone Governing the Registration of Business Enterprises, 深圳经济特区企业登记管理施行细则, promulgated on and effective from 9 February 1984.

Provisional Regulations of Shenzhen Special Economic Zone on the Introduction of Technology, 深圳经济特区技术引进暂行规定, promulgated on and effective from 8 February 1984.

Regulations of Xiamen Special Economic Zone on Economic Association with Inland Areas, 厦门经济特区与内地经济联合规定, promulgated on and effective from 24 February 1985.

Regulations of Xiamen Special Economic Zone on Labour Management, 厦门经济特区劳动管理规定, promulgated on and effective from 24 February 1985.

Regulations of Xiamen Special Economic Zone on Land Use, 厦门经济特区土地使用管理规定, promulgated on and effective from 24 February 1985.

Regulations of Xiamen Special Economic Zone on the Registration of Enterprises, 厦门经济特区企业登记管理规定, promulgated on and effective from 24 February 1985.

Regulations of Xiamen Special Economic Zone on the Import of Technology, 厦门经济特区技术引进规定, promulgated on and effective from 24 February 1985.

State-owned Enterprises

Enterprise Bankruptcy Law of the People's Republic of China (for Trial Implementation), 中华人民共和国企业破产法(试行), adopted on 2 December 1986 and effective from the date on which the Law on State-owned Industrial Enterprises will have been in effect for three months.

Interim Regulations on State-owned Enterprises, 国营企业暂行条例, promulgated on and effective from 1 April 1983.

Tax

Consolidated Industrial and Commercial Tax Regulations of the People's Republic of China (Draft), 中华人民共和国工商统一税条例(草案), promulgated for trial implementation on and effective from 13 September 1958.

Detailed Rules and Regulations for the Implementation of the Consolidated Industrial and Commercial Tax Regulations of the People's Republic of China (Draft), 中华人民共和国工商统一税条例施行细则(草案), promulgated for trial implementation on and effective from 13 September 1958.

Provisions of the Ministry of Finance Concerning the Levy of and Exemption from Consolidated Industrial and Commercial Tax on Import and Export Commodities, 财政部关于进出口货物征免工商统一税的规定, approved on 30 December 1980 and effective from 1 January 1981.

Notice of the Ministry of Finance Regarding the Adjustment of the Industrial and Commercial Tax Rates on Certain Products and the Expansion of Taxation Items, 财政部关于调整工商税若干产品税率和扩大征税项目的通知, issued on 10 June 1982 and effective from 1 July 1982.

[Document of the Ministry of Finance] Regarding the Question of the Levy of the Consolidated Industrial and Commercial Tax on Chinese-Foreign Joint Ventures, Co-operative Ventures, and Enterprises Wholly Owned by Foreign Investors, 关于对中外合资经营企业、合作生产经营企业和外商独资企业征收工商统一税问题, issued on 2 June 1983.

Provisional Regulations of the Ministry of Finance Regarding the Levy of the Consolidated Industrial and Commercial Tax and Enterprise Income Tax on Foreign Businesses Contracting for Project Work and Providing Labour Services, 财政部关于对外商承包工程作业和提供劳务服务征收工商统一税和企业所得税的暂行规定, issued on 5 July 1983.

Provisional Regulations of the State Council of the People's Republic of China Regarding the Reduction of and Exemption from Enterprise Income Tax and Consolidated Industrial and Commercial Tax in the Special Economic Zones and the Fourteen Coastal Port Cities, 中华人民共和国国务院关于经济特区和沿海十四个港口城市减征免征企业所得税和工商统一税的暂行规定, promulgated on 15 November 1984 and effective from the year 1984 (Enterprise Income Tax) and 1 December 1984 (Consolidated Industrial and Commercial Tax).

Provisional Regulations of the Ministry of Finance of the People's Republic of China on the Levy of Consolidated Industrial and Commercial Tax and Enterprise Income Tax on Resident Representative Offices of Foreign Enterprises, 中华人民共和国财政部对外国企业常驻代表机构征收工商统一税、企业所得税的暂行规定, promulgated on 14 May 1985 and effective from the year 1985.

Supplementary Provisions of the Foreign Tax Sub-bureau of the Beijing Municipal Tax Bureau Concerning the Levy of Consolidated Industrial and Commercial Tax and Enterprise Income Tax on Resident Representative Offices of Foreign Enterprises, 北京市税务局对外税务分局关于对外国企业常驻代表机构征收工商统一税、企业所得税问题的补充规定, promulgated on 14 October 1985.

Implementing (Trial) Measures of Guangzhou Economic and Technical Development Zone on Industrial and Commercial Tax, 广州经济技术开发区工商税收实施(试行)办法, promulgated on and effective from 9 April 1985.

Income Tax Law of the People's Republic of China Concerning Joint Ventures Using Chinese and Foreign Investment, 中华人民共和国中外合资经营企业所得税法, promulgated on and effective from 10 September 1980.

Detailed Rules and Regulations for the Implementation of the Income Tax Law of the People's Republic of China Concerning Joint Ventures Using Chinese and Foreign Investment, 中华人民共和国中外合资经营企业所得税法施行细则, promulgated on 14 December 1980 and effective from 10 Sepember 1980.

Decision of the Standing Committee of the National People's Congress Regarding Amendment of the 'Income Tax Law of the People's Republic of China Concerning Joint Ventures Using Chinese and Foreign Investment', 全国人民代表大会常务委员会关于修改《中华人民共和国中外合资经营企业所得税法》的决定, promulgated on and effective from 2 September 1983.

Notice of the Ministry of Finance Regarding the Earnest Implementation of the 'Decision of the Standing Committee of the National People's Congress Regarding Amendment of the "Income Tax Law Concerning Joint Ventures Using Chinese and Foreign Investment"', 财政部关于认真贯彻执行《全国人民代表大会常务委员会修改〈中外合资经营企业所得税法〉的决定》有关问题, issued on 12 October 1983.

Notice of the Ministry of Finance Regarding Several Questions on the Joint Venture Income Tax, 财政部关于中外合资经营企业所得税若干问题的通知, issued on 8 June 1981.

[Document of the Ministry of Finance] Regarding the Question of the Periods of Tax Reduction and Exemption for Newly Opened Joint Ventures, 关于新办合营企业的减免税期限问题, issued on 8 June 1981.

Explanation by the General Taxation Bureau of the Ministry of Finance Regarding the Scope of Fixed Assets, 财政部税务总局关于固定资产范围的解释, issued on 1 December 1981.

Notice of the State Council Regarding the Question of the Levy of Taxation on Chinese-Foreign Joint Venture and Co-operative Projects, 国务院关于对中外合资、合作项目征税问题的通知, issued on 21 September 1982.

Notice of the Ministry of Finance Regarding the Question of Calculating the Amount of Income Tax to Be Paid Quarterly in Advance by Joint Ventures, 财政部关于合营企业计算分季预缴的所得税额问题的通知, issued on 18 January 1984.

Income Tax Law of the People's Republic of China Concerning Foreign Enterprises, 中华人民共和国外国企业所得税法, promulgated on 13 December 1981 and effective from 1 January 1982.

Detailed Rules and Regulations for the Implementation of the Income Tax Law of the People's Republic of China Concerning Foreign Enterprises, 中华人民共和国外国企业所得税法施行细则, promulgated on 21 February 1982 and effective from 1 January 1982.

[Document of the Ministry of Finance] Regarding Questions Relating to Taxation of Such Contracts as Introduction of Technology Contracts, Loan Contracts, and Leasing Contracts Approved Before the Promulgation of the Tax Law [Concerning Foreign Enterprises], 关于税法公布前已批准的技术引进、借贷款、租赁等合同有关税收问题, issued on 29 March 1982.

[Document of the Ministry of Finance] Regarding the Question of Calculation of the Income of Enterprises Contracting for the Exploration and Development of Offshore Petroleum Resources, 关于承包勘探开发海洋石油资源企业的所得额计算问题, issued on 6 April 1982.

Provisional Regulations of the General Taxation Bureau of the Ministry of Finance Regarding Tax Registration of Foreign Enterprises for the Commencement and Termination of Operations, 财政部税务总局关于外国企业开业、停业税务登记暂行规定, promulgated on and effective from 15 April 1982.

[Document of the Ministry of Finance] Regarding the Question of the Levy of Income Tax on Revenue from Patent Rights and Proprietary Technology, 关于专利权、专有技术收入征收所得税问题, issued on 5 May 1982.

[Document of the Ministry of Finance] Regarding the Question of Listing Interest on Loans of a Foreign Enterprise as an Expense, 关于外国企业借款利息列支问题, issued on 7 May 1982.

[Document of the General Taxation Bureau of the Ministry of Finance] Regarding the Calculation and Levy of Income Tax on Fees for the Use of Proprietary Technology, 关于专有技术使用费计算征收所得税问题, issued on 14 October 1982.

Provisional Regulations of the Ministry of Finance Regarding the Reduction of and Exemption from Income Tax on Fees for the Use of Proprietary Technology, 财政部关于对专有技术使用费减征、免征所得税的暂行规定, issued on 13 December 1982 and effective from 1 January 1983.

Provisional Regulations of the Ministry of Finance Regarding the Reduction of and Exemption from Income Tax Relating to Interest Earned by Foreign Businesses from China, 中华人民共和国财政部关于外商从我国所得的利息有关减免所得税的暂行规定, promulgated on 7 January 1983 and effective from 1 January 1983.

Reply of the Ministry of Finance Regarding the Question of Exemption from Income Tax in Cases of the Use of Products to Repay the Price and Interest for Equipment and Fees for the Use of Proprietary Technology, 财政部关于用产品偿还设备价款、利息和专有技术使用费免征所得税问题的批复, issued on 9 March 1983.

Notice of the General Taxation Bureau of the Ministry of Finance Regarding the Question of the Levy of Tax on the Agency or Consignment Sale of Goods or the Establishment of Maintenance Service Centres and the Agency Sale of Spare Parts and Fittings by Chinese Corporations and Enterprises Entrusted by Foreign Businesses, 财政部税务总局关于外商委托我国公司企业代销、寄销商品或设立维修站代销零配件征税问题的通知, issued on 8 October 1983.

[Document of the General Taxation Bureau of the Ministry of Finance] Regarding the Levy of Income Taxation on the Interest Component of Lease Fees in Leasing Trade and on Loans to Investment and Trust Corporations, 关于租赁贸易的租赁费征收所得税问题, issued on 21 December 1983.

Notice of the Ministry of Finance Regarding the Permission for Provisional Exemption of Income Tax for Rental Payments Made for the Rental of Foreign Ships for Use in International Transport, 财政部关于租用外国船舶用于国际运输所支付的租金可暂免征所得税的通知, issued on 27 January 1984.

Notice [of the General Taxation Bureau of the Ministry of Finance] Concerning the Question of the Calculation and Levy of Tax on the Determined Amount of Income of Resident Representative Offices of Foreign Enterprises, 关于对外国企业常驻代表机构核定收入额计算征税问题的通知, issued on 19 September 1985.

Notice of the General Taxation Bureau of the Ministry of Finance Regarding Several Provisions Concerning Questions on the Levying of Income Tax on Chinese-Foreign Joint Ventures, Co-operative Production Ventures, and Wholly Foreign-Owned Enterprises, 财政部税务总局关于对中外合资经营、合作生产经营和外商独资经营企业有关征收所得税问题几项规定的通知, issued on 21 April 1986.

Individual Income Tax Law of the People's Republic of China, 中华人民共和国个人所得税法, promulgated on and effective from 10 September 1980.

Detailed Rules and Regulations for the Implementation of the Individual Income Tax Law of the People's Republic of China, 中华人

民共和国个人所得税法施行细则, promulgated on 14 December 1980 and effective from 10 September 1980.

Notice of the Ministry of Finance Regarding Questions of Individual Income Tax Payment by Foreign Personnel Working in China, 财政部关于外国来华工作人员交纳个人所得税问题的通知, issued on 24 October 1980.

[Document of the Ministry of Finance] Regarding the Question of Levy of and Exemption from Taxation on Wages and Salaries of Technical Personnel Sent to China to Work by Foreign Businesses in Order to Perform Contracts Signed before the Promulgation of the [Individual Income] Tax Law,关于外商为履行税法公布前签订的合同,派技术人员来华工作的工资、薪金所得征免税问题, issued on 20 November 1980.

Notice of the Ministry of Finance Regarding Several Questions of Individual Income Tax, 财政部关于个人所得税若干问题的通知, issued on 2 June 1981.

[Document of the General Taxation Bureau of the Ministry of Finance] on the Question of Levy of Taxation on the Income of Technical Personnel Sent to China by Foreign Companies to Provide Services, 对外国公司派技术人员来华提供服务的所得征税问题, issued on 8 June 1981.

[Document of the General Taxation Bureau of the Ministry of Finance] Regarding the Question of Levy of Taxation on Subsidies Earned by Foreign Taxpayers on Short Trips out of China, 关于外籍纳税人到中国境外短期出差所得津贴的征税问题, issued on 7 July 1981.

Supplementary Explanation II [by the General Taxation Bureau of the Ministry of Finance] to [Document of the Ministry of Finance] Regarding the Question of the Levy of and Exemption from Tax on the Lump Sum and Allowance Given by the Dispatching Unit to Foreigners Working in China, 对《关于外国来华人员由派出单位发给包干款项及津贴的征免税问题》的补充解释二, issued on 7 July 1981.

[Document of the General Taxation Bureau of the Ministry of Finance] Regarding the Question of Whether the American [......] May Deduct from his Income Alimony Payments to his Former Wife, 关于美籍 [......] 支付前妻的赡养费应否在所得中扣除的问题, issued on 12 December 1981.

Notice [of the Ministry of Finance] Regarding the Exemption from Reporting and Payment of Individual Income Tax for Income Earned Outside China by Personnel of Foreign Nationality Working in China, 关于在华工作的外籍人员从中国境外取得的所得免予申报缴纳个人所得税的通知, issued on 7 March 1983.

[Document of the General Taxation Bureau of the Ministry of Finance] Regarding the Question of Levy of Individual Income Tax on Subsidies Earned by Long-term Representatives of Foreign Businesses Travelling on Business within China, 关于对外商常驻代表在我国内出差取得的出差津贴征收个人所得税问题, issued on 12 May 1982.

Provisions of the General Taxation Bureau of the Ministry of Finance Regarding Various Policy and Operational Questions on Individual

Income Tax, 财政部税务总局关于个人所得税若干问题的规定, issued on 18 February 1986.

Supplementary Regulations of Shenzhen Special Economic Zone on the Question of Reduction of and Exemption from Taxes for Enterprises, 深圳经济特区企业减免税问题的补充规定, promulgated on 8 May 1986 and effective from 1 July 1986.

Provisional Urban Real Estate Tax, 城市房地产税暂行条例, promulgated on and effective from 8 August 1981.

Provisional Regulations of the People's Republic of China on Fees for the Use of Vehicles and Vessels, 中华人民共和国车船使用税暂行条例, promulgated on 15 September 1986 and effective from 1 October 1986.

Tobacco

Tobacco Monopoly Regulations, 烟草专卖条例, promulgated on 23 September 1983 and effective from 1 November 1983.

Trade-marks and Trade-names

Trade-mark Law of the People's Republic of China, 中华人民共和国商标法, promulgated on 23 August 1982 and effective from 1 March 1983.

Detailed Implementing Rules for the Trade-mark Law of the People's Republic of China, 中华人民共和国商标法实施细则, promulgated on and effective from 10 March 1983.

Notice of the State Administration for Industry and Commerce Requiring that Goods Using Unregistered Marks Must Clearly Indicate the Name or Address of the Enterprise, 国家工商行政管理局关于商品使用未注册商标时应当标明企业名称或地址的通知, issued on 15 July 1985.

Interim Regulations on Registration of Names of Industrial and Commercial Enterprises, 工商企业名称登记管理暂行规定, promulgated on and effective from 15 June 1985.

Wholly Foreign-owned Enterprises

Law of the People's Republic of China on Wholly Foreign-owned Enterprises, 中华人民共和国外资企业法, promulgated on and effective from 12 April 1986.

Index